Cherokee Reference Grammar

Cherokee Reference Grammar

Brad Montgomery-Anderson

University of Oklahoma Press : Norman

Published through the Recovering Languages and Literacies of the Americas initiative, supported by the Andrew W. Mellon Foundation

Library of Congress Cataloging-in-Publication Data
Montgomery-Anderson, Brad.
Cherokee reference grammar / Brad Montgomery-Anderson.
pages cm
Revised version of author's Ph.D. thesis
from the University of Kansas, ca. 2008.
Includes bibliographical references and index.
ISBN 978-0-8061-4342-2 (hardcover : alk. paper) —
ISBN 978-0-8061-4667-6 (pbk. : alk. paper)
1. Cherokee language—Grammar. I. Title.
PM782.M66 2015
497′.557—dc23
2014016573

This book is published as part of the Recovering Languages and Literacies of the Americas initiative. Recovering Languages and Literacies is generously supported by the Andrew W. Mellon Foundation.

The paper in this book meets the guidelines for permanence and durability of the Committee on Production Guidelines for Book Longevity of the Council on Library Resources, Inc. ♾

3 4 5 6 7 8 9 10

ᏕᎦᏥᏲᎯᏎᎸ ᎯᎠ ᎦᏬᏂᎯᏍᏗ ᎠᏆᏕᏣᏆᎥ ᎤᎪᏗ ᏗᎦᏄᏫᏍᏓᏁᏄ ᎾᏍᎩ ᎠᏂᏣᎳᎩ ᎠᏂᏴᏫ ᏧᏂᏁᏗ ᎦᏬᏂᎯᏍᏗ ᎤᎾᏁᏣᎳᏅᎡᎢ. ᎾᏍᎩ ᎾᏍᏉ ᎯᎠ ᏕᎦᏄᏫᏍᏓᏁᏄ ᏕᏥᏲᎯᏎ ᎠᏆᏓᎵᎢ Elizabeth ᎾᏍᎩ ᏂᏓᏓᏲᏍᎬᎾ ᎠᎩᎫᏍᏓᎥ ᎠᎴ ᎠᎩᎦᎵᏍᏓᏗᏍᏗᏍᎬ ᎾᏍᎩ ᎪᏪᎵᏍᎬ ᎯᎠ ᎦᏬᏂᎯᏍᏗ.

I dedicate this grammar to the efforts of the Cherokee People to pass on their language to a new generation. I also dedicate this work to my wife, Elizabeth, for her unfailing support and encouragement during the writing of this grammar.

Contents

Figures and Tables

Figures

Tables

Acknowledgments

This book would not have been possible without the incredible knowledge and guidance of my dissertation advisor, Dr. Akira Yamamoto. He first introduced me to the Cherokee community and gave me the invaluable opportunity to get involved with Cherokee Nation teacher training workshops in Tahlequah, Oklahoma. Once the writing of the grammar was underway, he provided detailed proofreading of several drafts of the manuscript. The other members of my committee have supplied much useful feedback during the revision process, and I would like to thank Dr. Anita Herzfeld, Dr. Lizette Peter, Dr. Clifton Pye, and Dr. Harold Torrence.

My decision to become a linguist came late in my college career. I would like to acknowledge Dr. David Rood at the University of Colorado for first encouraging my interest in linguistics. Dr. Terrence Kaufman, Dr. Roberto Zavala, and Dr. John Justeson provided me with wonderful fieldwork training during four summers in Mexico with the Project for the Documentation of the Languages of the Americas.

My dissertation has received important financial backing from the Phillips Fund of the American Philosophical Society. The Center for Latin American Studies at the University of Kansas (KU) supported my graduate career by providing a Foreign Language Areas Studies Fellowship as well as teaching opportunities. The KU Department of Linguistics also supported my studies through teaching opportunities and the Frances Ingemann Fellowship.

I am grateful to the Department of Languages and Literature at Northeastern State University (NSU) for allowing me course release time to prepare this book as well as the opportunity to teach Cherokee Grammar I and II. My students in these classes provided valuable feedback for earlier drafts of this work, especially Danielle Culp, Catherine Little, Carl Reynolds, Chris Smith, Ben Kester, Meda Nix,

Hayley Miller, Dianna Thompson, Jessica Bryan, Lisa O'Field, Cal Parmain, and Doug and Judy Cotter.

Both the College of Liberal Arts and the Cherokee Language Program at NSU have been very supportive through the generous provisions of travel funds to attend conferences and receive important feedback on this work. I appreciate the support and feedback of my colleagues in the Cherokee Language Program: Dr. Les Hannah, Harry Oosahwee, and Wyman Kirk.

This new version of my Ph.D. dissertation would not have been possible without the support of the Cherokee Nation Foundation and its director, Kimberlie Gilliland. It provided me with the funds, equipment, and speakers to record a large number of sample sentences for the Cherokee Electronic Dictionary (which are found throughout this grammar). Ed Jumper did a wonderful job of creating original Cherokee sentences and is responsible for the majority of the sentences in the online dictionary. I am grateful to Andrew Sikora for his technical expertise and the use of his recording studio as well as for many delightful hours of debate and discussion. *Dziękuję!*

The following individuals contributed many hours of work to help compile the database in the initial stages: many thanks to Denise Chaudoin, Charlene Drowning Bear, Robin Fritchey, Sherry Gammon, and Arlo Starr. I owe special thanks to Beth Bryson and Greg Trihus of the Summer Institute of Linguistics for setting up the Cherokee Online Dictionary.

I am deeply indebted to the Cherokee speakers I worked with for more than seven years. Benny Smith met with me a few hours a week for the first two years. I consider myself lucky to have had the opportunity to work with such master speakers as Rosa Carter, Marilyn Cochran, Anna Sixkiller, Ed Jumper, Harry Oosahwee, and Dennis Sixkiller. I owe special thanks to Anna Sixkiller for translating the dedication at the beginning of this work. The fieldwork done for this dissertation has been greatly facilitated by the Cultural Resource Center of the Cherokee Nation, in particular through support from its director, Dr. Gloria Sly. She allowed me the opportunity to get to know these speakers by inviting me to speak at numerous training conferences and workshops. Countless informal discussions with Harry Oosahwee and Wyman Kirk at the Cherokee Degree Program Office helped me to appreciate the intricacies of Cherokee grammar. Many wonderful hours of road-trip conversation with Akira and Kimiko Yamamoto, Lizette Peter, and Tracy Hirata-Edds gave me fresh ideas and insights.

Many thanks are due to Durbin Feeling for two reasons. First, the groundbreaking work on Cherokee in his 1975 dictionary and his grammar sketch with William Pulte have provided a wonderful foundation for the present work. He has also generously provided his time to record the audio tracks found on the accompanying CDs.

I am grateful to the reviewers who carefully read the manuscript of this work, including Greg Drowning Bear and Pamela Munro. Dr. Munro's assistance and advice have been especially invaluable in the creation of this work. *Chokmashki!* In addition to my committee members, I owe many thanks to the individuals who have proofread all or parts of this manuscript, including Eva Garroutte, Elizabeth Montgomery-Anderson, Kelly Harper Berkson, Wyman Kirk, Danielle Culp, Hayley Miller, and Christopher and Anita Mann. Danielle Culp carefully read the finished manuscript and provided many useful comments. I received invaluable technical support in the form of a surprise laptop as a gift from Shary and Dow Walker and Jan Montgomery. My friendships with Dave McKinney and Cristin Burke McKinney were a great help during the writing process.

I am deeply grateful to my parents, Bob and Jerene Anderson and Bruce and Irene Rose, who have helped and encouraged me through many years of college. Most of all, I would like to thank my wife, Elizabeth. She was willing to support my graduate career by starting a new life in Kansas. I thank her for her love and devotion during my studies.

Cherokee Reference Grammar

ONE

Introduction

The Cherokees are one of the largest groups of American Indians in the United States. The 2000 U.S. Census lists 390,902 ethnic Cherokees. Recent estimates claim 22,500 speakers of Cherokee, including approximately 14,000 speakers on the Oklahoma rolls as well as 8,500 in North Carolina. Two of the three federally recognized Cherokee tribes are located in Tahlequah, Oklahoma: the United Keetoowah Band of Cherokee Indians in Oklahoma and the Cherokee Nation. The Eastern Band of Cherokee Indians is located in the Qualla Boundary, North Carolina.

1.1. A Brief History of the Cherokees and Their Language

The Cherokee language is a member of the large and relatively well-known Iroquoian family. Linguists believe that the proto-Iroquoian ancestral language was spoken around the Great Lakes and split into the Northern and Southern Iroquoian branches approximately 3,500 years ago. Speakers of the Southern Iroquoian branch migrated southeast and settled in the Appalachians; the language of this group eventually became Cherokee. Members of the Northern branch, representing all of the Iroquoian languages but Cherokee, developed into communities that speak languages commonly known as Mohawk, Seneca, Cayuga, Oneida, Onondaga, and Tuscarora.

The name 'Cherokee' is an English pronunciation of the eastern dialect pronunciation *jaragi*, which is pronounced *jalagi* in the western dialect. According to the famed nineteenth-century ethnographer James Mooney, the English word 'Cherokee' is attested as early as 1708. Beliefs about the origin of the name *jalagi* vary, but it appears that the word itself may not be a native Cherokee word. Mooney states that the first evidence of this word appears in 1557 in its Portuguese version as *chalaque*; it later appears in 1699 in its French version as *cheraqui*. He suggests that the word might come from a Choctaw word meaning 'cave' that gained usage through the Mobilian Trade Jargon.

By the eighteenth century three recognized dialects of Cherokee existed. The Lower Dialect, also known as Underhill, is now extinct; it was originally spoken in northwestern South Carolina as well as in adjacent communities in Georgia. The Middle Dialect was originally spoken in western North Carolina and is now the dialect for the Qualla Boundary community in the same area. The third dialect, known as Overhill, Otali, or simply the Western Dialect, is now called Oklahoma Cherokee.

The Cherokees have the oldest and best-known Native American writing system in the United States. Sequoyah invented this writing system and first made it public in 1821. The Cherokees rapidly adopted the new system, resulting in widespread literacy as well as the creation of the first Indian newspaper in the country, the *Cherokee Phoenix*, which started publishing in 1828. A Cherokee scholar, David Brown, used the new writing system to produce a Cherokee translation from the original Greek of the New Testament in 1825. It has been estimated that literacy among the Cherokees in the early nineteenth century was as high as ninety percent. Writing became an important part of Cherokee culture; significantly, the more traditional the community, the higher the literacy rate tended to be. This writing system is fully explained in chapter 2 and is used throughout this work.

During the same decade in which Cherokee literacy was spreading, the tribe wrote a constitution in English and Cherokee based on the United States Constitution. In spite of these attempts to assimilate to Western standards of civilization, President Andrew Jackson was convinced that no Indians should occupy U.S. territory and pushed for the passage of the 1830 Indian Removal Act. This law called for the resettlement of the peoples then known as the Five Civilized Tribes (Cherokee, Choctaw, Chickasaw, Creek, and Seminole) to areas west of the Mississippi. Despite widespread opposition—the Supreme Court even ruled it unconstitutional—the president had his way. The state of Georgia had already enacted a series of stringent laws against the Cherokees, including nullifying their legislation, confiscating their property, and forbidding them from testifying in court. In 1835 federal authorities obtained the signatures of fewer than five hundred Cherokees—none of whom were elected tribal officials—on the New Echota Treaty that agreed to the tribe's removal.

The resulting forced resettlement of the Cherokees from the east, now known as the Trail of Tears, was one of the most infamous episodes in American history. It destroyed the unity of the Cherokee people. Some Cherokees managed to hide in the mountains of North Carolina until they were allowed to settle on land there in 1849. Some Cherokee families who had already moved to Arkansas in 1794 became known as the Western Cherokees or Old Settlers. The Cherokees who finally arrived in Indian Territory—now Oklahoma—consisted of the Old Settlers, the Treaty Party, and the Ross Party. This last group, led by Chief John Ross, was the largest and had opposed removal.

At a national convention in the new capital of Tahlequah, a constitution was written in order to unify the badly divided community. The Treaty of 1846 settled these conflicts through a compromise whereby the Ross Party accepted the New Echota Treaty and the Old Settlers and Treaty Party accepted the new constitution. Some Cherokees who had evaded removal remained behind in the mountains of eastern North Carolina; this community would grow and eventually gain federal recognition as the Eastern Band of Cherokee Indians (EBCI).

The brief period of calm and prosperity that followed removal was shattered by the Civil War. In the east as many as four companies of Cherokee soldiers fought for the Confederate cause. In the west two Cherokee regiments were raised and fought in several battles, the most important of which was Pea Ridge in northwestern Arkansas. Many Cherokees in Indian Territory also fought against the Confederacy, starting a period of internecine tribal warfare. After the surrender of the rest of the Confederate forces in April 1865, the Cherokee leader Stand Watie continued fighting until June and was the last Confederate general to lay down his arms.

In the meantime the United States forced the Cherokees to sign a new treaty in which they gave up lands in Kansas and allowed Plains Indians tribes to be relocated on tribal land. In 1898 the passage of the Curtis Act allowed for the breakup of tribal lands and apportioning of lands to individual tribal members. This new attack on tribal integrity occurred when what is now the western portion of Oklahoma was being organized into a territory and being settled during the famous Oklahoma Land Runs. In 1893 the federal government opened the Cherokee Outlet—land that had been set aside for relocating other tribes—in the largest Land Run in American history, involving over a hundred thousand settlers. The Indian Territory tribes made a last attempt at autonomy by asking Congress to admit them as the state of Sequoyah. Congress rejected this request and joined the Oklahoma Territory with the Indian Territory, which was admitted to the

Union as the state of Oklahoma in 1907. After the death of Chief W. C. Rogers in 1917, the federal government decreed that it would appoint all future Cherokee chiefs. As a result of this mandate the western Cherokees had no democratically elected representatives until the United Keetoowah Band of Cherokee Indians in Oklahoma was formed and recognized as a corporate entity by Congress in 1946. In the meantime the eastern Cherokees had managed to purchase land for their group and to create a constitution that went into effect in 1870.

Unlike the eastern group, the Cherokee Nation did not begin to elect its own chiefs again until 1971. The Cherokee Nation ratified a revised constitution in 1975, and the Bureau of Indian Affairs authorized the creation of Oklahoma Indian Courts in 1978. The Cherokee Nation gained recognition in 1985 with the election of Wilma Mankiller, the first woman in modern history to lead a major Native American tribe. During her ten years in office, the tribe grew from 55,000 to 156,000 tribal citizens. Today the Cherokee Nation is the second largest Indian tribe in the United States, with approximately 350,000 tribal citizens. The United Keetoowah Band, with its more restrictive membership criteria, has more than 14,000 citizens.

Compared to other Native Americans, the Cherokees have a large number of speakers of their traditional language. It has been suggested that the Cherokee **syllabary** has played a role in the maintenance of the language. Cherokee scholar Richard Allen (Cherokee Nation 2003:5) states: "It is our hypothesis that one of the principal means by which Cherokee as a language has survived both historically and contemporarily remains the strong association between the Cherokee language and its use in Cherokee spiritual life. It is clearly established that Cherokees use the syllabary to communicate with each other, to keep fastidious records and to retain 'sacred' knowledge." The strong spiritual and material resources of the Cherokees are indeed helping the tribes to take unprecedented measures to teach the language to a new generation of speakers. These efforts at language revitalization are discussed in the next section.

1.2. Cherokee Language Revitalization

In the last few decades all three tribes have shown a growing interest in the revitalization of Cherokee culture and language. For example, the Cherokee Nation Tribal Council passed laws in 1991 and 1995 establishing programs for the teaching and preservation of the language. Under the leadership of Principal Chief Mankiller, the council passed the Cherokee Nation Language and Cultural Preservation Act, which states:

> It shall be the policy of Cherokee Nation to take the leadership to maintain and preserve the Cherokee language as a living language. Such efforts shall include but not be limited to:
>
> A. Efforts to involve tribal members to the greatest extent possible in instruction in Cherokee language.
>
> B. Establishment of a permanent Cherokee Language Program within the Tribal Education Department subject to such funding limitations as may exist from year to year.
>
> C. Encourage the use of Cherokee language in both written and oral form to the fullest extent possible in public and business settings.
>
> D. Encourage creation and expansion of the number, kind, and amount of written materials in the Cherokee language and official encouragement for the development of materials on, by or through Cherokee Nation service programs. (Cherokee Nation 2003)

In addition to new language policies, a new language curriculum was created using the text *See, Say, Write Method of Teaching the Cherokee Language* (Vance and Feeling 2001). This curriculum was expanded and supplemented with audiotapes in 2000. The tribal council also approved the creation of the Cultural Resource Center (CRC) in 1995, a new agency that continues to play an important role in coordinating efforts to maintain the language and culture of the Cherokee Nation. This agency provides translation services, hosts Summer Youth Language and Culture Camps, and supports a weekly Cherokee radio show. CRC efforts have led to Cherokee signage in several locations in downtown Tahlequah as well as around Cherokee schools and administrative buildings.

In 2005 the United Keetoowah Band created a Department of Language, History, and Culture, whose website states that the first goal of this new agency is to "assure the use of Keetoowah Cherokee language in tribal activities and materials." The tribe has also created a Keetoowah Cherokee Youth Choir, which has provided an additional venue for the use and promotion of the language.

Recognition of the decline in the number of speakers has fueled a new commitment to reversing language shift. A Cherokee Nation survey in 2002 revealed that no one under forty spoke the language fluently and that less than 11 percent of Cherokee Nation citizens within the fourteen-county Cherokee Nation jurisdictional region used the language at home. Most significantly, the survey highlighted that children were no longer learning the language. In the United Keetoowah Band, up to 60 percent of the tribe still speaks the language.

The Eastern Band of Cherokee Indians conducted a language survey in 2005 and discovered that the band has 900 speakers, 72 percent of whom are over the age of fifty. According to the "Language Vitality and Endangerment" categorizations of language endangerment used by the United Nations Educational, Scientific and Cultural Organization (UNESCO), Cherokee is in the "Severely Endangered" category of languages because it is spoken only by the grandparental generation and upward and by a minority of the total population. Languages in this category will become extinct in three decades unless steps are taken to create a new generation of speakers.

To counter these language shift trends, the Cherokee Nation tribal council began a ten-year language preservation program for the period 2003 to 2012. This program developed a number of language preservation policies with the long-term goal that in fifty years 80 percent of all tribal members will be actively reengaged in the language and culture of the tribe. The Cherokee Nation is now taking significant steps to reverse language shift through systematic language planning. The most extensive of these efforts is the program to develop a new generation of fluent speakers in an early childhood immersion program.

This undertaking began in 2001 with one preschool class and has now grown to include kindergarten through sixth grade. Cherokee language instruction is now being offered in a wide variety of contexts throughout northeastern Oklahoma. Over three thousand students enroll in online classes every year. Community classes have enrollment of approximately five hundred students per year. The United Keetoowah Band offers ten community classes throughout northeastern Oklahoma and has been exploring the idea of language immersion for young children.

Both in North Carolina and in Oklahoma strong links exist between community revitalization efforts and the local university. Northeastern State University (NSU)—located in Tahlequah—established a Cherokee teacher certification program in 2005. This unique bachelor's in education degree is helping to create a new generation of Cherokee teachers for preschool through twelfth grade. The degree program consists of 124 credit hours, 40 of which must be Cherokee major courses such as Conversational Cherokee, Methods for Classroom Immersion, Cherokee Cultural Heritage, and Cherokee Grammar. Greg Drowning Bear was the first graduate of this program in 2008.

Western Carolina University (WCU) hosts an annual Language Revitalization Symposium that is supported by the Eastern Band and the Cherokee Nation. WCU's Cherokee Studies program teaches the language and has recently begun exchange programs with Cherokee language students in Oklahoma. This program recently received a $200,000 grant from the Cherokee Preservation Foundation for its language work and aims to expand opportunities to take college-credit Cherokee classes by offering online courses and classes in high school settings. The objective of the Eastern Band's Kituwah Preservation and Education Program has been the creation of an immersion school and master-apprentice training. The tribe's New Kituwah Academy (preschool to 5th grade) is now supplemented by a second school. Its website proclaims the long-term objective of reestablishing public functions, with the eventual goal of local bilingual media.

Thanks to recent collaborations between the Cherokee Nation Language Technology Program (consisting of Joseph Erb, Jeff Edwards, Durbin Feeling, and Roy Boney, Jr.) and companies such as Apple, Google, Facebook, and Microsoft, the Cherokee language is now automatically included as an available language on many electronic devices. Cherokee syllabary has been available on Apple's Macintosh Operating System since 2003, and Facebook and Google have added language support for Cherokee in the last two years. Windows 8 was released in 2012 with a complete Cherokee interface. Students at the Cherokee Nation Immersion School as well as the degree program at Northeastern State University have been encouraged to use this technology and to help create new domains and functions for the language.

The present grammar is intended to be a useful contribution to all of these continuing efforts to maintain and pass on the Cherokee language.

1.3. Development and Purpose of the Grammar

This work is a reference book and is not designed to teach conversational Cherokee. The main audience for this book will be scholars working on curriculum development or performing linguistic research. At the same time, the careful definition of all technical terms, the quantity of everyday examples, and the inclusion of audio CDs make this work a valuable aid to those individuals learning Cherokee as a second language. In particular I hope that the information gathered here will be the basis for future pedagogical works on the language; moreover, this overview of the language should make it clear that further linguistic research is warranted in many areas. The book is not meant to answer all questions about Cherokee grammar but to serve as a sourcebook for a new generation of Cherokee teaching, research, and curriculum development.

This grammar began in 2005 as my doctoral dissertation at the University of Kansas. During the first three years of dissertation research I worked primarily with Benny Smith in Lawrence, Kansas. While working on the dissertation I also spent three summers in Mexico preparing a database of the Chontal Mayan language. In 2007 (my last year of dissertation work) I was hired by Northeastern State University in Tahlequah, Oklahoma, the capital of the United Keetowah Band as well as the Cherokee Nation. Living in Tahlequah allowed me to concentrate more fully on work with native speakers. My primary consultants were Ed Jumper and Rosa Carter. I defended my dissertation and obtained the Ph.D. in the spring of 2008. Since that time my primary project has been expanding the computer database that I had begun to keep track of my dissertation data. The Cherokee Nation Foundation sponsored this work and provided me with technical equipment and speakers. The main speaker I worked with during the period after the spring of 2008 was Ed Jumper; I also did some work with Anna Sixkiller and Durbin Feeling. With the collaboration of the Summer Institute of Linguistics (SIL), the Cherokee Nation Foundation set up the Cherokee Electronic Dictionary to allow public access to this growing database. This dictionary (still very much a work-in-progress) is available at http://www.cherokeenationfoundation.org/dictionary/. Audio files for many of the sample sentences included in this grammar are posted on this website. All of my author royalties from this book will be donated to the Cherokee Nation Foundation to help continue its important work of improving educational opportunities for Cherokees.

I began reorganizing my dissertation in 2010 to prepare it for publication. The changes have been extensive: I put the more difficult material into a new part II, changed the writing system, and added a glossary. All glossary terms are in boldface when they first appear in a chapter. The current work benefits from improved analyses and explanations as a result of using it with my Cherokee Grammar classes. I have also added many new examples from the Cherokee Electronic Dictionary.

The focus of this work is on Oklahoma Cherokee, the language of the community with whom I have had the privilege of working. This book describes the speech of a specific group of people living in a specific geographic area. But my knowledge of Cherokee has been enhanced by the insights contained in descriptions of North Carolina Cherokee, especially those of King (1975) and Cook (1979). More detailed analyses of specific areas of Cherokee grammar will necessarily involve studies of the past and current styles of speech found in North Carolina. It is my hope that this grammar will support the language revitalization initiatives of all Cherokees, wherever they may be and whatever dialect of Cherokee they speak.

This work owes much to previous linguistic descriptions of Cherokee, especially Pulte and Feeling (1975), Scancarelli (1987), and the UCLA papers (Munro 1996c). Some of the pedagogical works have been useful for learning set phrases, in particular Holmes and Smith (1977). Geoffrey Lindsey's analyses of tone (1985, 1987) have been useful in determining what kind of **romanized writing** system to use and how to mark tone. In addition to these sources, a large part of this analysis rests on elicitation from native speakers in Oklahoma. The speakers represented thus far in the database are Benny Smith, Ed Jumper, Rosa Carter, Anna Sixkiller, Harry Oosahwee, Dennis Sixkiller, and Marilyn Cochran.

1.4. How to Use This Grammar

This grammar is written within the framework of descriptive linguistics; its primary audience is scholars involved in language revitalization initiatives. I have tried as much as possible to limit technical words and to explain their meaning when I do use them. Explanations and examples appear in the glossary in appendix C. Glossary terms appear in boldface the first time they occur in a given chapter. A section at the end of each chapter provides information on sources and additional reading suggestions as well as ideas for potential research topics. These sections are primarily intended for linguistic researchers and contain terms and concepts not explained in the glossary.

An immediately apparent feature of this grammar is the usage of the Cherokee syllabary throughout. At various times this writing system has been deemed unsuitable for linguistic purposes. While the syllabary does not express some crucial distinctions, it does often provide clues about the **underlying forms** of the words, which frequently change in complex ways when they are combined. More importantly, this writing system is the most famous and most recognizable identifier of the Cherokee people, their culture, and their language. This grammar is intended primarily as a tool in the effort to maintain the Cherokee language, so the syllabary is used whenever a natural **citation form** of a word is used. The syllabary spelling appears first, followed by **Roman characters** to represent the features that the syllabary ignores. A typical entry is seen below in example (1).

(1) ᎠᎦᏙᏍᏗ
aàktoósdi
a-agahthoósdi
3A-look.at:PRC
'He's looking at it.'

It should be noted that longer examples are broken into two or more sets of lines. The translation for the entire example is given at the end of the last set. Throughout this book, Cherokee words are broken down and presented in their

stem form. Many words, especially verbs, always appear with a **prefix.** When discussing Cherokee it is important to know what kind of "name" (citation form) to give verbs: a prefixed form recognizable to speakers or a more general form with the prefixes removed. One of the main goals of this grammar is to show the stems of words consistently by using the format exemplified in (1). Use of this format helps the language learner to understand the grammar and sound system by consistently labeling all the parts in each example.

This grammar is thus somewhat of a mix between a traditional linguistic grammar and a teaching grammar. It is organized as a traditional linguistic description, starting with a chapter on the sounds and writing system, followed by chapters dedicated to the different **parts of speech.** Syntax is presented in part II. This grammar is distinguished from other works on Cherokee by having a separate section on **pronominal prefixes** that appears before the discussion of the parts of speech (verbs, adjectives, adverbs, and nouns). These prefixes are typically discussed along with verbs; but they also appear on adjectives and nouns, so I have decided to discuss them in a separate section. In keeping with this organizational strategy, **prepronominal prefixes** (which appear mostly on verbs or words derived from verbs) are discussed in a separate chapter. The work is like a teaching grammar in that it presents the information in stages: the easier prefixes are found in part I, while the more complex ones are presented in part II. For example, the two basic sets of pronominal prefixes—the Set A and Set B prefixes—are presented in chapter 3, while the more difficult prefixes are presented in chapter 9. After this introduction, part I begins the description of the language itself with an explanation of Cherokee sounds and writing (chapter 2). Chapter 3 is dedicated to pronominal prefixes. Verbs are introduced in chapter 4, and chapter 5 discusses the more common prepronominal prefixes that can alter the meaning of the verb. Chapter 6 discusses nouns, the majority of which are derived from verbs. Chapter 7 focuses on modifiers, a term that encompasses **adjectives** and **adverbs.**

Part II begins with a discussion of the complex sound changes that take place in the language when different parts combine. In a traditional linguistic grammar this information would be at the beginning; I have chosen to present it after the reader has already been introduced to all the basic parts of the Cherokee verb as well as the basic building blocks of a sentence. Chapters 9 and 10, respectively, discuss the more complex pronominal and prepronominal prefixes introduced in chapters 3 and 5. Syntax is the main topic of chapter 11, and the remaining three chapters cover different types of **derivation** (the manner in which new words are created).

A useful feature of this grammar is the marking of **tones** and **vowel length.**

Such marking is not used in older linguistic works on Cherokee and only began with Feeling's dictionary (1975a). It is possible that many of the tones as well as vowel length are predictable. The rules underlying this predictability are not well understood, however; even if we had a systematic description of these rules, they would be too abstract and complex for the purposes of this grammar.

In keeping with the tradition of modern linguistic grammars, this work includes several texts presented in appendix A. Two of the texts are traditional stories involving a race between two animals; the third is a historical sketch of a search party traveling up the Arkansas River. In addition to these texts numerous phrases and sentences that appear throughout the grammar are a product of the most recent efforts toward language maintenance, including excerpts from articles in the *Cherokee Phoenix*. Most of the editions of this newspaper include several articles in both English and Cherokee. These translations are another service provided by the Cherokee Nation's Cultural Resource Center and are typically done by Anna Sixkiller, one of the consultants for my original dissertation. Excerpts from the *Cherokee New Testament* are also occasionally used, because this is the most widely available text written in the Cherokee syllabary. Words and phrases from a Cherokee broadcasting of a Lady Indians Sequoyah High School basketball championship game are also included. All examples are rewritten in the romanized writing system described in chapter 2; if the tone and vowel length are known from the source, they are represented as the authors represented them (this mainly applies to the examples taken from Feeling and Scancarelli). In other cases the example has been checked with a consultant to ensure accurate representation of tone and vowel length.

I hope that one of the more appealing features of this work will be the accompanying CDs containing various sentences and word lists. I did not have space to record everything, so I have selected items that are representative of important features of the language or are useful phrases to know. All of the examples are read by Durbin Feeling, author of the important and useful Cherokee-English dictionary (Feeling 1975a). A list of all the recordings is found in appendix B.

1.5. Sources and Additional Reading

The information in the historical background is based on Woodward (1963), Mooney (1995), and Conley (2005). Mooney (1995:15–16) is the chief source for possible origins of the name 'Cherokee'. Mankiller (1993) contains a good introduction to Cherokee history and culture that she weaves into her autobiography. The 2003 Cherokee Nation report as well as discussion with Cultural Resource personnel, particularly Gloria Sly, provided information on language revitalization efforts for the last two years. Eastern Band revitalization efforts are described in a recent report (Eastern Band of Cherokee Indians 2005), and the information on Keetoowah Band efforts is from their website. Issues related to Cherokee dictionary work are found in Munro (2002), Pulte and Feeling (2002), and Montgomery-Anderson (2008).

Linguists all agree that Cherokee is the sole representative of the Southern branch of the Iroquoian family of languages. Only a few articles, however, discuss the historical relationship. Lounsbury (1961) established the time depth of the split using glottochronology, and Hickerson, Turner, and Hickerson (1952) confirmed Lounsbury's grouping of the Iroquoian languages by applying tests of mutual intelligibility between the languages. Good overviews of the Iroquoian language family are found in Lounsbury (1978) and Charles (2010). Chafe (1964) discusses a possible relationship between the Iroquoian family and the Siouan family.

The first descriptions of Cherokee from the early 1800s have not survived (Scancarelli 1987:15). Perhaps the most significant loss is a grammar and dictionary by Samuel Worcester, the missionary who helped create the modern version of the syllabary and whose friendship with the Cherokees led to the seminal Supreme Court Case *Worcester vs. Georgia* in 1832. The earliest surviving descriptions of the Cherokee language are by John Pickering (1831) and Hans Conon von der Gabelentz (1852), both reprinted in Krueger (1993). A number of small sketches were published in the first half of the twentieth century (Hinkle 1935; Bender and Harris 1946), the most extensive being a series of three articles that appeared in the *International Journal of American Linguistics* (Reyburn 1953a, 1953b, 1954). The most significant recent works on Cherokee are two dissertation grammars of North Carolina Cherokee (King 1975; Cook 1979), a dissertation on grammatical relations and verb agreement (Scancarelli 1987), a dissertation on phonological variation in Western Cherokee (Foley 1980), a collection of UCLA linguistic articles devoted to Oklahoma Cherokee (Munro 1996c), and a Cherokee-English dictionary that includes a grammatical sketch (Pulte and Feeling 1975). This grammatical sketch is perhaps the most used among linguists and students. It was the result of collaboration between linguists William Pulte and Durbin Feeling; the latter is a native speaker and teaches language classes at NSU. Two chapter-length grammatical sketches (Scancarelli 2005; Walker 1975) and a number of individual linguistic articles have also been published. In addition to these linguistic resources, a number of "teach yourself" learning materials of varying size and quality are available. The largest and most used is Holmes and Smith's

Beginning Cherokee (1977). None of the pedagogical works approach the sound system and grammar of the language in a systematic or methodical way; they largely confine themselves to the presentation of vocabulary through drill and repetition. Grammatical structures are generally not explicitly explained. Holmes and Smith (1977) is an exception in that it attempts some overt explanation of structures and paradigms. This book is pedagogical in nature, and its main focus is on vocabulary presentation, drills, and explanations of culture.

Sociolinguistic issues and patterns of language use are discussed in Arrington (1971) and Berdan et al. (1982). Guyette (1975, 1981), Pulte (1979), and Brooks (1992) are studies of Cherokee as an endangered language. Berge (1998) addresses issues of language obsolescence and reacquisition. Frey (2013) describes language shift among the North Carolina Cherokees. A growing body of literature addresses the recent efforts toward language maintenance. Studies of Cherokee immersion experiences are found in Peter (2003, 2007), Oosahwee (2008), and Peter et al. (2008). Hirata-Edds et al. (2003) discuss training for the immersion teachers, and methods for assessing the success of these programs are explored in Hirata-Edds et al. (2003) and Peter and Hirata-Edds (2006). Hirata-Edds (2007) is an important study on the influence of the immersion experience on the students' first language (English). Montgomery-Anderson (2010, 2011, 2013) discusses issues related to NSU's Cherokee Language Program. Roy Boney provided me with a good summary of the many recent changes in technology that support online use of the Cherokee language.

Part I

TWO

Cherokee Sounds and How to Write Them

2.1. Inventory of Sounds

Cherokee has six **vowels** and twenty-three **consonants.** These sounds can be represented using the traditional **syllabary** or a system of **Roman characters** familiar to English speakers. All examples in this grammar are presented in both the Cherokee syllabary and a **romanized writing** system.

A syllabary is distinct from an **alphabet** in that it represents **syllables** instead of representing individual sounds. A Cherokee syllable is typically either a vowel or a consonant followed by a vowel. For example, each of the following syllables in the word 'Cherokee' is represented by two symbols in romanized writing but by only one symbol in the syllabary:

Ꮳ	Ꮃ	Ꭹ
ja	la	gi

To write this word in the **Roman alphabet** requires six symbols, but the syllabary needs only three symbols to represent the three syllables. This section describes Cherokee sounds using the Roman characters; the last section introduces the syllabary.

2.1.1. Consonants

Most of the following consonants are familiar to a speaker of English, both in the way they are pronounced and in the manner in which they are written.

(1) Consonant sounds Track 01

d	doosa	ᏙᏌ	'mosquito'
t	tohga	ᏙᎦ	'june bug'

g	giihli	ᎩᏟ	'dog'
k	kaáhwi	ᎧᏫ	'coffee'
dl	dlaameeha	ᏜᎺᎭ	'bat'
tl	tla	Ꮭ	'no'
gw	aàgwaduuli	ᎠᏆᏚᎵ	'I want it'
kw	kwana	ᏆᎾ	'peach'
j	jalagi	ᏣᎳᎩ	'Cherokee'
ch	chuhga	ᏧᎦ	'flea'
ts	jayeétsa	ᏣᏰᏣ	'laugh!'
l	loolo	ᎶᎶ	'locust'
hl	oohla	ᎣᏝ	'soap'
w	walóosi	ᏩᎶᏏ	'frog'
hw	goohweeli	ᎪᏪᎵ	'paper'
y	yijaduúlas	ᏱᏣᏚᎳᏍ	'would you like it?'
hy	hyadeehlohgwa	ᏯᏕᎶᏆ	'you can learn'
n	nohji	ᏃᏥ	'pine'
hn	hnadvv̀ga	ᎿᏛᎦ	'you did it'
h	hawiiya	ᎭᏫᏯ	'meat'
s	suúdali	ᏑᏓᎵ	'six'
m	meéli	ᎺᎵ	'Mary'
ʔ	hiʔa	ᎯᎠ	'this'

In comparison with other languages, Cherokee is unusual in its scarcity of sounds made with the lips: it has no /b/, /f/, or /v/ and very few words with the sound /m/. Several sounds in Cherokee are unusual to English speakers. One such sound is the **glottal stop.** This sound is similar to a catch in the throat and is heard in English in the middle of 'uh-oh' or in certain pronunciations of /t/ when it occurs in the middle of a word (e.g., 'kitten'). It is represented with the symbol ʔ. Typically a glottal stop separates two vowels, as seen in (2).

(2) words containing a glottal stop ❡ Track 02

ᏦᎢ	joʔi	'three'
ᎠᎩᎠ	aàgíʔa	'he's eating it'
ᎪᎢ	goʔi	'oil'
ᏔᎵ	taʔli	'two'

This sound contrasts with the sound /h/, as demonstrated in (3). These two sounds alternate in certain words (see chapter 8).

(3)

/ʔ/	ʔ	ᎪᎢ	goʔi	'oil'
/h/	h	ᎪᎯ	koòhi	'today'

The sound /hl/ is like /l/, but with the tongue closer to the roof of the mouth. The more restricted airflow results in a "slurpy l" sound. Some examples of this sound are found in (4).

(4) words containing /hl/ — Track 03

ᎯᏟᎰᎢ	hihlihóoʔi	'you sleep'
ᎦᎵᏉᎩ	gahlgwoógi	'seven'
ᎬᏟ	kvv́hli	'raccoon'
ᎩᏟ	giihli	'dog'

Perhaps the most difficult sound for English speakers is /tl/. This sound is a combination of /t/ with the above "slurpy l" sound.

(5) words containing or /tl/ — Track 04

Ꮭ	tla	'no'
ᎩᏟ	giitli	'strand of hair'
ᎠᏟ	aàtli	'she's running'
ᏓᎦᏟᎭ	daàktliíha	'he's shelling corn'

The sounds /n/, /w/, and /y/ (the sound at the start of English 'yes') have counterparts where the sound is pronounced together with an /h/sound known as **aspiration.** It is important to distinguish aspirated and unaspirated consonants, because the different sounds create distinct words. (6a–c) show several pairs of words where the difference in meaning hinges on the aspiration.

Track 05

(6a)	ᎬᎿ	gvvhna	'he is alive'
	ᎬᎾ	gv́vna	'turkey'
(6b)	ᎠᏁᎭ	aàneéha	'they live (there)'
	ᎠᏁᎭ	aàhneha	'he's giving it to him'
(6c)	ᎠᏰᎦ	aàhyéega	'she is taking it (by hand)'
	ᎠᏰᎦ	aàyéega	'she is waking up'

Examples of words containing the aspirated sounds /hn/, /hw/, and /hy/ are shown in (7)–(9).

(7) words containing /hw/ — Track 06

ᎪᏪᎵ	goohweeli	'paper'
ᎤᏩᏍᎦ	uùhwasga	'he's buying it'
ᏣᏩᎯ	jahwahi	'buy it!'

(8) words containing /hy/ — Track 07

ᏯᏖᎾ	hyahteéna	'board'

ᏯᏙᏟ	hyahtóóhli	'narrow'
ᏰᎦᎵ	hyehgahli	'quilt'

(9) words containing /hn/ — Track 08

ᎬᏅᎢ	gvvhnv́v́ʔi	'life'
ᏅᏅᏓᎩ	hnv́vhndági	'take it off'
ᏐᏁᎳ	sohneéla	'nine'

When /g/ and /d/ are at the beginning of a word or surrounded by vowels they are similar to English /g/ and /d/. When they are next to an /h/ they have the "hard" sound of English /k/ and /t/. This phenomenon is illustrated below in (10). The first two forms of the **verb** 'answer' have the sound /h/. In the third form the /h/ is no longer next to /n/ but is next to the /g/ of the *ga-* **prefix;** as a result, this prefix is pronounced as [*ka*]. This very regular and important process of aspiration is explained in depth in chapter 8.

(10) 'answer' with prefixes — Track 09

with *iijii-* prefix:	ᎢᏥᏁᎦ	iìjiihnéega	'you all are answering'
with *hi-* prefix:	ᎯᏁᎦ	hihnéega	'you're answering'
with *ga-* prefix:	ᎧᏁᎦ	kanéega	'he's answering'

The sound written as ⟨j⟩ is pronounced either as /j/ (the sound at the end of English 'page') or /dz/ (the sound at the end of English 'grounds'). The exact pronunciation varies from speaker to speaker.

(11) — Track 10

ᏦᎢ	joʔi	'three'
ᏣᎳᎩ	jalagi	'Cherokee'
ᏦᎯᏳᎭᏍ	joohiyuhas	'do you believe it?'
ᏣᏓᎦᏎᏍᏕᏍᏗ	jadaksesdéesdi	'take care of yourself!'
ᏥᎢᏓ	jiʔiída	'I just had it (in my hand)'
ᏣᏚᎵ	jaduuli	'you want it'
ᏣᏲᏏᎭ	jayóosiha	'you are hungry'

When /j/ combines with /h/ it is pronounced /ch/, as seen below in example (12). The process that causes these sounds to come together is discussed in chapter 8.

(12)

ᏣᏁᏍᏗ	ᏣᏚᎵ
chanesdi	jaduuli
ja-hnesdi	ja-aduuli
2B-speak:INF	2B-want:PRC

'You want to speak it.'

The sound /s/ may also be pronounced, depending on the speaker, as /sh/ (the initial sound of the English word 'sure'). In North Carolina /sh/ is much more common.

The sound /m/ only appears in a small set of native words; it is more commonly found in borrowed words and names from English. Some examples of words with /m/ are listed in (13).

(13) Track 11

ᎠᎹ	ama	'water'
ᎠᎹ	áama	'salt'
ᎤᎦᎹ	uúgáma	'soup'
ᎠᎹᏱ	amaayi	'near the water'
ᎠᎺᏉᎢ	améegwóóʔi	'ocean'
ᏔᎹᏟ	tamaahli	'tomato'
ᎧᎹᎹ	kamaama	'elephant', 'butterfly'
ᏓᎹᎦ	daamága	'horsefly'
ᎣᎦᎳᎰᎹ	oogalahoóma	'Oklahoma'
ᎺᎵ	meéli	'Mary'
ᎨᎻᎵ	keémíli	'camel'

2.1.2. Vowels

2.1.2.1. *Basic Vowels*

Cherokee has six vowels. Five of these—/a/, /e/, /i/, /o/, and /u/—are vowel sounds also found in English. The sixth vowel is represented in the romanized writing system as ⟨v⟩; it is like English "uh," but with a **nasal** sound.

(14) Cherokee Vowels Track 12

a	k<u>aá</u>hwi	'coffee'
e	s<u>eé</u>dı	'walnut'
i	<u>ii</u>sa	'flour'
o	<u>oo</u>síyo	'hello'
u	n<u>uú</u>na	'potato'
v	uun<u>vv́</u>di	'milk'

For many speakers a **word-final vowel** has a nasal sound.

2.1.2.2. *Length and Tone*

The difficult aspects of the Cherokee sound system for English speakers are **vowel length** and **tone.** Vowels are either long or short: a long vowel takes approximately twice as long to pronounce as its short counterpart. In this grammar's romanized writing system, length is represented by writing the vowel twice. Two examples of pairs of words distinguished by vowel length are shown in (15).

(15a) ᏥᎪᏩᏘᎭ jigoohwtíha 'I see it' — Track 13
ᏥᎪᏩᏘᎭ jiigoohwtíha 'I see him'

(15b) ᎠᎹ ama 'water'
ᎠᎹ áama 'salt'

In addition to length, vowels also are pronounced with distinct tones. Cherokee has six tones: **high, low, rising, falling, lowfall,** and **highfall.** The syllabary does not represent these tones. The two **level tones** remain at a constant pitch. These high and low tones can appear on all vowels, long or short. As seen in the two examples in (16), low tone does not receive any special marking; it is the most common tone and is therefore not indicated.

(16a) Short vowel, low tone — Track 14
ᏯᏂᏏ yansi 'buffalo'
ᎯᏓ hida 'lay it down (something long)!'
ᎣᏩᏌ owaása 'oneself'

(16b) Long vowel, low tone
ᎠᎬᎭᎵᎭ aàgvvhaliha 'he's slicing it'
ᎩᏟ giihli 'dog'
ᎣᏝ oohla 'soap'

An **acute accent** (an accent going upward from left to right) over a vowel indicates high tone on that vowel. (17a) shows three examples of short vowels with a high tone. The three examples in (17b) have long vowels with a high tone. If a high tone vowel is a long vowel, only the first letter has the accent.

(17a) Short vowel, high tone — Track 15
ᎯᏔᏲᎯᎭ hihtayoohíha 'you are asking for it'
ᎦᎷᎦ gáʔluhga 'he's arriving'
ᎣᏏᏲ oosíyo 'hello'

(17b) Long vowel, high tone
ᎬᎾ gv́vna 'turkey'
ᎢᏁᎦ iìnéega 'we are going'
ᎪᎦ kóoga 'crow'

The high and low tones are level tones (they stay at the same pitch throughout the pronunciation of the vowel). In addition to these two level tones Cherokee also has four **contour tones,** which change as they are being pronounced. These contour tones only occur on long vowels. To represent a rising tone, an acute accent is written on the second letter of the long vowel. Several examples of a rising tone are shown in (18).

(18) ᎦᏓ gaáda 'dirt','land' Track 16
ᏲᎾ yoóna 'bear'
ᏩᏥ waáji 'watch'
ᎩᎦ giíga 'blood'

Loan words from English often have a rising tone where the **stress** in the original English word falls, as shown in (19).

(19) ᏫᎵ wiíli 'Will' Track 17
ᎧᏫ kaáhwi 'coffee'
ᏩᏥ waáji 'watch'
ᏥᏌ jiísa 'Jesus'
ᎣᎦᎳᎰᎹ oogalahoóma 'Oklahoma'
ᎺᎵ meéli 'Mary'
ᎨᎻᎵ keémíli 'camel'
ᎹᎩ maági 'Maggie'

The least common tone in Cherokee is the falling tone. This tone is represented using an acute accent on the first letter and a **grave accent** (an accent going downward from left to right) on the second letter. Three examples are shown in (20); as a comparison, the fourth example does not have this tone

(20) ᏅᏬᏘ nvvwóòti 'medicine' Track 18
ᏥᏍᏉᏉ jiísgwóògwo 'robin'
ᎩᏳᎦ kiyúùga 'chipmunk'
ᎤᏄᏩ uùhnuwa 'he's wearing a coat'

In addition to these four tones, two more tones start at the same pitch as the level tones but then rise or fall out of the range of the level tones. The first of these, the highfall tone, is only found on the rightmost long vowel of the word. It is represented by an accent on both vowels. (21) shows four adjectives with the highfall tone.

(21) ᎡᏆ éégwa 'large' Track 19
ᎠᎩᎾ agíína 'young'
ᎦᎨᏓ gaagééda 'heavy'
ᎣᏍᏓ óósda 'good'

The highfall tone has an important role in Cherokee grammar that distinguishes it from the other tones. When a highfall appears on a verb, it changes the role of the verb in the sentence. For example, a highfall is sometimes used to indicate that the verb has been turned into a **noun** indicating a person or thing that performs the action of the verb. The tone change is indicated by the **abbreviation** AGT (**agentive**). An example of this change is shown in (22). In (22b) the highfall appears on the verb to indicate that it is now acting as a noun.

(22a) ᏕᎦᏕᏲᎲᏍᎪᎢ — Track 20
degadeèyoóhvsgóoʔi
dee-ji-adaa-eèhyoóhvsg-óoʔi
DST-1A-MDL-teach:INC-HAB
'I teach.'

(22b) ᏗᎦᏕᏲᎲᏍᎩ
digadeèyóóhvsgi
di-ji-adaa-eèhyoóhvsg-i
DST2-1A-MDL-teach:INC-AGT
'I'm a teacher.'

The use of the highfall to change the grammar of the word or sentence is explained in greater detail in chapter 11.

Another contour tone, the lowfall tone, starts as a low tone and falls lower. Like all contour tones, this tone only occurs on long vowels. As exemplified in (23), it is indicated by a grave accent on the second letter of the long vowel.

(23) — Track 21

ᏅᏯ	nvv̀ya	'rock'
ᏒᎩ	svv̀gi	'onion'
ᎫᎫ	guùgu	'tick'
ᎠᎩᏍᏗ	agiìsdi	'something to eat'

The grave accent is used to represent two different tones; in both cases it is only used on the second letter of a long vowel to indicate that the tone is lower than the preceding character in the long vowel. (24a) is an example of a lowfall tone, and (24b) is an example of the falling tone.

(24a) Lowfall:
ᏅᏯ nvv̀ya 'rock'

(24b) Falling:
ᏅᏬᏘ nvvwóòti 'medicine'

The eight possible length and tone combinations are represented in (25).

Cherokee vowels: length and tone Track 22

(25a)	e	short low	
	ᎨᎢ	ge̲ʔi	'downstream'
(25b)	ee	long low	
	ᎨᎵᎠ	ge̲e̲líʔa	'he thinks so'
(25c)	é	short high	
	ᏥᏲᏎᎭ	jiiyoòsé̲ha	'I'm saying to her'
(25d)	ée	long high	
	ᎨᎦ	gé̲e̲ga	'I'm going'
(25e)	eé	rising	
	ᎨᎻᎵ	ke̲é̲míli	'camel'
(25f)	éè	falling	
	ᎭᎵᏰᏑᏍᏛᏍᎦ	haliyé̲è̲suustv́sga	'you are putting a ring on'
(25g)	eè	lowfall	
	ᎮᎾ	he̲è̲na	'go!'
(25h)	éé	highfall	
	ᎪᎨᏱ	googé̲é̲yi	'spring'

Occasionally pairs of words differ only in tone. One such pair is shown below in (26).

(26a) ᏕᎾᏑᎴᏍᎪ
déenasuule̲e̲sgo
dee-iinii-asuuléesg-o
DST-1A.DL-wash.hands:INC-HAB
'We wash our hands.'

(26b) ᏕᎾᏑᎴᏍᎪ
déenasuulé̲e̲sgo
dee-iinii-asuuléesg-o
DST-1A.DL-take.off.pants:INC-HAB
'We take our pants off.'

Because the syllabary does not represent vowel length and tone, all Cherokee examples in this grammar are accompanied by a phonetic writing system. I refer to this type of writing as **extended phonetics.** In some cases it is useful to write in **simple phonetics,** a romanized form of representing Cherokee that does not indicate vowel length and tone. This kind of writing may be used in a beginning classroom setting; it is also useful for transcribing written materials where vowel length and tone are unknown. Simple phonetics represents the glottal stop with an apostrophe. All examples in the main body of this grammar are in extended phonetics; the sample sentences in the glossary are in simple phonetics.

2.2. Representing Sounds in the Syllabary

When Sequoyah developed the syllabary in the nineteenth century, the Cherokee people quickly achieved a high level of literacy through its use. The distinction between an alphabet and a syllabary is again demonstrated in (27), where each of the syllables is represented by at least two Roman characters but by only one symbol in the Cherokee syllabary:

(27) ᎩᏳᎦ kiyúùga 'chipmunk'

The eighty-five characters of the syllabary reflect combinations of a consonant and a vowel or just a vowel. The only exception is the character Ꮝ, which represents the sound /s/. The Cherokee syllabary is presented in table 2.1.

For the most part, the syllabary table is a straightforward cross-referencing of a vowel and a consonant. There are, however, a few complicating factors. As already mentioned, the sound /s/ has its own symbol, Ꮝ, and is in its own box in row 8. Note that many of the rows cross-reference two different consonant sounds. For example, row seven indicates the unaspirated sound /gw/ or the aspirated sound /kw/. Thus the symbol Ꭺ is an **aspiration-neutral syllabary character** and could represent /gwa/ or /kwa/; in like manner the symbol Ꭻ could represent /gwe/ or /kwe/; and so on.

Some of the rows, however, contain split cells, which indicate that a distinction is made for aspirated and unaspirated consonants. Thus in row 2 the symbol Ꭶ represents only /ga/ and Ꭷ represents only /ka/. The rest of the characters in this row do not make this distinction: they are aspiration-neutral characters. Ꭸ could represent either /ge/ or /ke/ and Ꭹ could represent either /gi/ or /ki/. Such differences indicate that Sequoyah felt that it was important to distinguish /ga/ and /ka/ but that /ge/ and /ke/ did not merit distinct representations. The sound /ga/ is in fact one of the most frequent sounds in Cherokee, as it represents a common **pronominal prefix.** Moreover, a large number of verbs have a present tense ending of /ga/. Its aspirated counterpart /ka/ is a less frequent but still common sound.

The sounds /y/, /l/, and /w/ have aspirated counterparts, yet none of these pairs are distinguished in the syllabary. In row 6, however, unaspirated Ꮎ /na/ is distinguished from aspirated Ꮏ /hna/. The third cell indicates a unique third

Table 2.1. Cherokee Syllabary

	a	e	i	o	u	v
1. —	Ꭰ	Ꭱ	Ꭲ	Ꭳ	Ꭴ	Ꭵ
2. g/k	Ꭶ Ꭷ	Ꭸ	Ꭹ	Ꭺ	Ꭻ	Ꭼ
3. h/hn	Ꭽ	Ꭾ	Ꭿ	Ꮀ	Ꮁ	Ꮂ
4. l/hl	Ꮃ	Ꮄ	Ꮅ	Ꮆ	Ꮇ	Ꮈ
5. m	Ꮉ	Ꮊ	Ꮋ	Ꮌ	Ꮍ	
6. n/hn	Ꮎ Ꮏ *	Ꮑ	Ꮒ	Ꮓ	Ꮔ	Ꮕ
7. gw/kw	Ꮖ	Ꮗ	Ꮘ	Ꮙ	Ꮚ	Ꮛ
8. s Ꮝ	Ꮜ	Ꮞ	Ꮟ	Ꮠ	Ꮡ	Ꮢ
9. d/t	Ꮣ Ꮤ	Ꮥ Ꮦ	Ꮧ Ꮨ	Ꮩ	Ꮪ	Ꮫ
10. dl/tl [hl]	Ꮬ Ꮭ	Ꮮ	Ꮯ	Ꮰ	Ꮱ	Ꮲ
11. j/ch/ts	Ꮳ	Ꮴ	Ꮵ	Ꮶ	Ꮷ	Ꮸ
12. w/hw	Ꮹ	Ꮺ	Ꮻ	Ꮼ	Ꮽ	Ꮾ
13. y/hy	Ꮿ	Ᏸ	Ᏹ	Ᏺ	Ᏻ	Ᏼ

distinction made for the sound /nah/. This character was written Ꮐ but has fallen out of usage in Oklahoma; the sound is now only represented with Ꮎ /na/.

A curious feature of the syllabary is the row representing the consonant /m/. As noted, only a handful of words in Cherokee use this sound. The sounds /ma/ and /me/ appear in the majority of these words; Ꮇ /mi/, Ꮌ /mo/, and Ꮍ/mu/ remain the most rarely seen of the syllabary characters. A number of names, most of which are of European origin, have the /m/ sound. The only gap in the table is for the syllable /mv/, which does not occur.

It has been noted that the syllabary does not precisely describe the sounds of Cherokee; it does not differentiate aspiration in most cases, for example, and never shows vowel length or tone. The romanized writing system is used to represent these crucial distinctions.

In addition to vowel length and tone, the syllabary does not represent the sound /h/ unless it occurs at the beginning of a syllable. This /h/ that is not reflected in the syllabary is known as **intrusive /h/**. Two examples are shown in (28).

(28)	Ꭶ<u>Ꮩ</u>Ꭶ	gaà<u>toh</u>ga	'tail'
	Ꭰ<u>Ꮩ</u>ᎩᏯᏍᎩ	a<u>toh</u>gíiyaàsgi	'candidate'

As already noted, many syllabary characters are aspiration-neutral. For example, the syllabary character Ꮩ in (28) is pronounced with the initial sound /t/; in (29) this same symbol is pronounced with an initial /d/.

(29)	Ꭶ<u>Ꮩ</u>	ga<u>do</u>	'what?'
	ᏓᏆ<u>Ꮩ</u>Ꭰ	daàgwa<u>dóo</u>ʔa	'my name is . . .'
	ᏗᏁᎵ<u>Ꮩ</u>Ꮧ	diinéehl<u>doh</u>di	'toy'

Thus the vowel represented by the syllabary character Ꮩ can be long or short and have different tones. Given the lack of such distinctions, a single syllabary sound can represent a large array of sounds. (30) is a list of the possible sounds that the single symbol Ꮩ can represent.

(30) Sound combinations represented by Ꮩ

doo	doò	toó	dóh
do	dóó	tóò	dóʔ
dó	to	toò	toh
dóo	too	tóó	toʔ
doó	tó	doh	tóh
dóò	tóo	doʔ	tóʔ

Because the syllabary does not usually reflect the difference in aspiration, occasionally two words have the same syllabary spelling but a different pronunciation. Two such pairs are shown in (31).

(31a) ᎯᏛᎦ hadvv̀ga 'you did it'
ᎯᏛᎦ hatvv̀ga 'you hung it up'

(31b) ᎪᎳ góóla 'winter'
ᎪᎳ koóla 'bone'

It should also be noted that the syllabary does not represent glottal stops, so occasionally two different words are written in an identical manner, as in (32).

(32) ᎠᏓ ada 'wood' Track 23
ᎠᏓ áʔda 'young animal'

As seen in (33), the sounds /j/, /ts/, and /ch/ are not distinguished in the syllabary.

(33) Ꮳ as symbol for /ja/, /tsa/, or /cha/ Track 24
Ꮥ<u>Ꮳ</u>ᏙᎠ dee<u>ja</u>dóoʔa 'your name is . . .'
ᏣᏰ<u>Ꮳ</u> jayeé<u>tsa</u> 'laugh!'
<u>Ꮳ</u>ᏁᎳ <u>cha</u>neéla 'eight'

A syllabary character that normally represents a consonant-vowel combination can also be used to represent a single consonant. In these cases the syllabary representation is said to have a **leftover vowel.** Two examples are shown in (34); in each case the underlined character has a leftover vowel.

(34) ᎠᏓ<u>Ꮕ</u>Ꮩ ada<u>hn</u>do 'heart'
<u>Ꮵ</u>ᎩᎵ <u>ts</u>gili 'ghost'

2.3. Stress

The **word-final vowel** in Cherokee words is usually unmarked for tone. This vowel carries the main stress of the word and generally has a high tone. Some words do have a higher tone on the final vowel if the **full form** of the word has a highfall on the next-to-last syllable and the final vowel is dropped. In such cases the final vowel is marked as the highfall and is clearly distinguishable from the default high tone that normally occurs at the end of words. In (35a) the first verb 'happen' has the final stress on the vowel /v/ after the full form is dropped off; the second verb in the sentence, 'be at', has been converted into a **subordinate verb** that indicates when the action of the main verb took place. This subordinate function is indicated by a special **suffix** with the highfall tone. The final syllable of the full form is dropped, but the remaining vowel /v/ has a higher tone than that of the main verb of the sentence. In this grammar an accent is also used on some vowels in a final position when an ending with a highfall tone of subordination has been shortened. In these cases the highfall (which underlyingly only appears on the rightmost long vowel; a final vowel is short) is still usually evident in the form of a higher tone. Another example is seen in (35b). In this example the suffix is shortened, but its tone is still evident as a higher tone on the remaining vowel.

(35a) ᎦᏙ ᎤᎵᏍᏔᏅ ᏓᏄᎪ ᏫᏤᏙᎸ
gado uùlstanv daahnuugó wijeédóòlv́
gado uu-alistan-v daahnuugó wi-ja-eédóòl-v́v́ʔi
what 3B-happen:CMP-EXP Vian TRN-2B-be.at:CMP-DVB
'What happened when you went to Vian?'

(35b) ᏛᏓᏁᏍᎨᎯᏌᏂ ᎤᏃᎴ ᎤᏲᏍᏔᏅ
dvvdahnesgehiísáhni uunoole uùyóostanv́
da-ii-iidii-ahnesgehiísáhn-i uunoole uu-yóo-stan-v́v́ʔi
CMF-ITR-1A.PL-build:CMP-CMF tornado 3B-break-CAU:CMP-DVB
'We will build the house again after the tornado destroyed it.'

The stress does not fall on the final vowel if there is a highfall tone elsewhere in the word. The highfall tone sounds like the rising tone with stress; this stress feature on the highfall makes it the most easily distinguishable tone. Moreover, the highfall tone is the only tone that expresses grammatical meaning. **Main verbs** never carry a highfall tone, but subordinate verbs and words that are the result of **derivation** almost always carry this tone. The example in (36a) is a verb; in (36b) the highfall helps to convey that the verb has been turned into a noun.

(36a) ᎦᏃᎭᎵᏙᎭ ganoohaliídóòha 'he is hunting' Track 25
(36b) ᎦᏃᎭᎵᏙᎯ ganoohaliidóóhi 'hunter'

This grammatical use of the highfall is further detailed in chapter 11.

2.4. Sources and Additional Reading

One of the most important contributions to understanding Cherokee sounds is a collection of UCLA papers (Munro 1996c). The description of Cherokee sounds provided in this grammar is based on descriptions in the UCLA papers and in Lindsey (1985, 1987) and does not deviate significantly from them. The romanized writing system in this grammar is my own creation but is mainly based on the orthography used in the UCLA papers.

Important unpublished descriptions of the tonal system are found in Lindsey (1985, 1987) and Johnson (2005). The linguistic works on Cherokee vary as to how tone and vowel length are marked. Of the four dissertations, two (King 1975 and Foley 1980) do not mark tone at all. Cook's dissertation (1979) only marks what he calls stress or high pitch. Scancarelli's dissertation on grammatical relations (1987) uses accents to mark tone; these diacritics correspond to the superscript numbers used by Feeling (1975a) and Pulte and Feeling (1975). Recent work on tone has been done by Uchihaṛa (2009, 2014).

Descriptions of the invention of the Cherokee syllabary are found in Mooney (1995), Cushman (2011), and Foreman (2012). Monteith (1984), Cushman (2011b), and Parins (2013) discuss syllabary literacy in the nineteenth century. Chafe and Kilpatrick (1963) discuss Cherokee spelling. Walker (1975) contains an exposition of the problems arising from using the syllabary to represent Cherokee and discusses Cherokee literacy and publications. Modern discussions of uses of the syllabary are found in Bender (2002a, 2002b, 2002c), Brooks (1996), and Cushman (2010, 2011a, 2011b, 2011c, 2012).

2.5. Directions for Further Research

Much research still remains to be done on Cherokee tone. Wright (1996) argues for a characterization of Cherokee as a language with lexically marked tone, as opposed to other linguists' view that the tone is a pitch accent system. Johnson (2005) describes Cherokee tone as a hybrid of a lexically marked system and a pitch accent system.

When a vowel is deleted in spoken Cherokee, the syllabary character used in writing often represents the underlying form. Certain underlying forms are less apparent than others, however, and in these cases literate speakers probably follow conventions as to which default character to use. More research could be done on these choices. For example, *gahngo* 'tongue' is often written with the syllabary character Ꮕ /nv/, but to my knowledge no form of this word shows what is the underlying vowel between /hn/ and /g/ (if any). If no underlying vowel exists, there is often a common conventional spelling with a leftover vowel. Spellings do differ, however, as shown in (37): the same noun, *gahngo,* is spelled in the New Testament with Ꮓ /no/ instead of Ꮕ /nv/.

(37) ᎠᎴ ᎦᏃᎪ ᎤᏒᏂᎴᎢ
ale gahngo uùsvvnílé?i
ale ga-hngo uu-asvvníl-é?i
and 3A-tongue 3B-touch:CMP-NXP
'. . . and he touched his tongue.' (*Cherokee New Testament,* Mark 7:33)

THREE

Pronominal Prefixes I

3.1. An Introduction to Parsing

The **verb** is the most important part of a Cherokee sentence and describes the main action or event of the sentence. All Cherokee verbs have a least two parts: the **stem** and the **pronominal prefix.** The stem is the verb itself; the pronominal prefix is the part indicating who or what is involved in what the verb is describing. Because all verbs (as well as many **nouns** and **adjectives**) have these prefixes, it is appropriate that we begin our discussion of Cherokee grammar by describing their use. These prefixes are like the English **pronouns** 'I' and 'you' with the important difference that they attach directly to the verb, thereby creating a single word. When these prefixes combine with verbs, they often undergo changes that can make them difficult to distinguish from the verb itself. For this reason most Cherokee sentences in this grammar appear in a **parsed** form, meaning that its individual parts are separated, shown in their basic form, and labeled. Parsed examples are shown in five lines, as in (1) below. In the first line the word is shown in the Cherokee **syllabary.** In this example the syllabary characters, read separately, represent the sounds /ha di ta s ga/. The line immediately below uses **Roman characters** to illustrate how this word is pronounced.

(1)	ᎭᏗᏔᏍᎦ	Cherokee Syllabary
	hadiitasga	Roman characters
	hi-adiitasga	Underlying forms (before changes occur)
	2A-drink:PRC	Gloss line
	'You're drinking it.'	English translation

The third line represents the individual parts of the word before they are combined. By comparing the second and third lines, we can see that the parts change when they come together. The verb 'drink' starts with the **vowel** /a/. In Cherokee two vowels cannot be next to each other, however, so one of the vowels disappears when the **Set A prefix** *hi-* ('you') attaches to the verb. In this case, it is the vowel /i/ that is at the end of the prefix *hi-*. This basic form of the prefix (before it loses its vowel) is known as the **underlying form.** The **hyphen** on the prefix indicates that it must attach to a stem; the hyphen on the stem indicates that it needs a prefix. The shortened form [*h*] is the **variant form;** these forms are written with **square brackets** (and never with hyphens) to distinguish them from the underlying forms. We know that *hi-* is the underlying form because when it combines with other verbs it does not change at all, as in (2).

(2) ᎯᏬᏂᎭ
hiwóoniha
hi-wóoniha
2A-talk:PRC
'You're talking.'

In both examples the fourth line, known as the **gloss line,** provides a one-word English translation (or **gloss**) for the stems as well as **abbreviations** for the **affixes (prefixes** and **suffixes)** and grammatical functions. These abbreviations are always written in small caps. For example, the abbreviation after the English gloss of the verb indicates that the verb is in its **Present Continuous** (PRC) form. This conveys the meaning that the action is happening right now. As we will see in chapter 4, most verbs appear in five forms. In addition, many different prefixes and suffixes may appear on the Cherokee verb. These are addressed below.

Two different sets of prefixes appear on verbs. The abbreviation 2A- indicates a **second person** ('you') **singular** Set A prefix. The use of Set A and **Set B** pronominal prefixes on verbs is the focus of this chapter.

3.2. Overview of Prefixes

In Cherokee all verbs must have exactly one pronominal prefix that indicates who or what is involved with the verb. If the verb is **intransitive,** this prefix refers to one **participant**—a **subject**. If the verb is **transitive,** the prefix refers to two participants—a subject and an **object.** Some adjectives and nouns also have these prefixes (see chapters 6 and 7). The three grammatical **persons** are **first person** (the speaker/s), second person (the person/s being spoken to), and **third person** (the person/s or thing/s being spoken about). When attached to a verb, these prefixes may also indicate whether the participant is the subject or object of that verb. If a verb has both a subject and an object, the subject is the participant more actively involved in the event described by the verb; the object is the participant affected by the event described by the verb. In (3) the pronominal prefix *ji-* indicates that the speaker is performing the action.

(3) ᏥᎦᏘᏯ jigaàtiíya 'I'm waiting for it'

In addition to indicating first, second, or third person, the pronominal prefixes express a **number** distinction of singular, nonsingular, dual, and plural. The **dual** form indicates that exactly two people are involved in the action, and the **plural** form that three or more are involved. These distinctions are exemplified in (4). In (4a) the prefix *hi-* indicates that only the person addressed is involved in the action. In (4b) the prefix *sdii-* indicates that two people ('you two') are involved in the action. The prefix *iijii-* in (4c) indicates that three or more ('you all') are involved. These examples are all with the Present Continuous verb stem of 'read'.

(4a)	ᎯᎪᎵᏰᎠ	higooliíyéʔa	'you are reading it'
(4b)	ᏍᏗᎪᎵᏰᎠ	sdiigooliíyéʔa	'you two are reading it'
(4c)	ᎢᏥᎪᎵᏰᎠ	iìjiigooliíyéʔa	'you all are reading it'

This dual number distinction only holds in first and second person; there is no special prefix that expresses the idea 'they two'. In (5) the third person **nonsingular** *anii-* indicates two or more women; the exact quantity is made clear by the numeral *jo'i*. The abbreviation 3A.NS should be read as "third person nonsingular Set A pronominal prefix."

(5)	Ꮎ	Ꮶ	ᎠᏂᎨᏯ	ᎠᏂᏌᎵᏗᎠ
	naʔ	joʔ	aniigeehy	aàniisaldiʔa
	naʔ	joʔ	anii-geehya	anii-saldiʔa
	that	three	3A.NS-woman	3A.NS-lift:PRC
	'Those three women are lifting it.'			

In addition to person and number, a third distinction is known as **inclusive/exclusive.** An exclusive pronominal prefix indicates that the person being addressed is specifically excluded from the action. An inclusive pronominal prefix includes the person being addressed. Thus the English word 'we' has four equivalents in Cherokee. These four meanings are exemplified in (6) and (7). The final example is shown in its parsed form in (7). The abbreviation 1A.PL.EX should be read as "first person plural exclusive Set A pronominal prefix."

(6a)	ᎣᏍᏗᏌᎵᏗᎠ	oòsdiisaldiʔ	'we two (not you) are lifting it'
(6b)	ᎢᏂᏌᎵᏗᎠ	iìniisaldiʔa	'you and I are lifting it'
(6c)	ᎢᏗᏌᎵᏗᎠ	iìdiisaldiʔa	'we all are lifting it'

(7) ᎣᏥᏌᎵᏗᎠ
oòjiisaldiʔa
oojii-saldiʔa
1A.PL.EX-lift:PRC
'We all (but not you) are lifting it.'

The third person pronominal prefixes do not have a gender distinction: depending on the context, the third person singular is 'he', 'she', or 'it'. As demonstrated in (8), singular and nonsingular do not indicate the gender of the persons involved.

(8a) ᎦᏟᎭ gahliha 'he/she/it is sleeping'
(8b) ᎠᏂᏟᎭ aàniihliha 'they are sleeping'

Table 3.1 shows the distinctions described above.

Table 3.1. Grammatical Person

Person Reference	*Singular*	*Dual (dl)*	*Plural (pl)*
First Person Inclusive	I	you and I	you, he/she/they, and I
First Person Exclusive (EX)		he/she and I	they and I
Second Person	you	you two	you all
Third Person	he/she	they	

Pronominal prefixes are used on all verbs and on some adjectives and nouns. In (9a) the pronominal prefix indicates the speaker, but in (9b) the same prefix indicates that the speaker is doing the action to a third person object ('it'). In (10) the first person Set A pronominal prefix *ji-* appears on an adjective and a noun, respectively. (This is discussed more fully in chapters 6 and 7; the discussion in this chapter focuses on verbs.)

(9a) ᏥᏬᏂᎭ jiwóoniha 'I am talking'
(9b) ᏥᎦᏘᏯ jigaàtiíya 'I am waiting for it'
(10a) ᏥᏌᎹᏗ jiʔsamáádi 'I am smart'
(10b) ᏥᏣᎳᎩ jijalagi 'I am Cherokee'

Combined local prefixes reference two grammatical persons. In (11a) the prefix *gvv-* expresses both a first person singular subject ('I') and a second person singular object ('you'). In (11b), the same prefix is used on a noun.

(11a)	ᎬᎦᏘᏯ	gvvgaàtiíya	'I am waiting for you'
(11b)	ᎬᏙᏓ	gvvdooda	'I am your father'

This chapter describes the Set A and Set B pronominal prefixes. The combined local prefixes and other sets are discussed in chapter 9.

3.3. Set A Pronominal Prefixes

3.3.1. Basic Paradigm

The basic Set A pronominal prefixes are shown in table 3.2. The third person singular form has an unpredictable variation between the forms *a-* and *ga-*. Verbs that take *ga-* instead of *a-* are known as ***ga-* verbs.** This phenomenon is further explained in the next section

Table 3.2. Set A Pronominal Prefixes

Person Reference	*Singular*	*Dual (dl)*	*Plural (pl)*
First Person Inclusive	ji-	iinii-	iidii-
First Person Exclusive (EX)		oosdii-	oojii-
Second Person	hi-	sdii-	iijii-
Third Person	a-, ga-	anii-	

3.3.2. Third Person *ga-* Pronominal Prefix

The Set A third person forms *a-* and *ga-* are exemplified in (12). The prefix *a-* in (12b) also appears as a long vowel on verbs. This rule of **pronominal lengthening** is explained in chapter 8.

(12a) ᎦᏬᏂᎭ
gawóoniha
ga-wóoniha
3A-talk:PRC
'He is talking.'

(12b) ᎠᏗᎠ
aàdiʔa
a-adiʔa

3A-say:PRC
'He is saying it.'

While it is not entirely predictable, the appearance of third person *ga-* instead of *a-* has certain general characteristics. One generalization can be made about its use: *ga-*appears on all Set A stems that start with the sounds /o/, /u/, or /v/. In (13) three verbs are listed with these initial vowels. When the *ga-* prefix appears before a vowel-initial stem, it loses its vowel and becomes [*g*]. Three examples of *ga-* verbs are seen in (13).

(13a) ᎬᏃᏌᏍᎦ
gvvnoosásga
ga-vvnoosásga
3A-sweep:PRC
'He is sweeping.'

(13b) ᎪᏘᏍᎦ
gootisga
ga-ootisga
3A-swell:PRC
'It is swelling.'

(13c) ᎫᏘᎭ
guutiha
ga-uutiha
3A-snow:PRC
'It is snowing.'

The shortened variant [*g*] may also appear before stems that begin with /a/ and /e/, but such stems may also appear with the *a-* prefix. An example of an /e/ initial verb is shown in (14).

(14) ᏌᏌ ᎨᏝ
saasa géehla
saasa ga-éehla
goose 3A-feed:PRC
'He is feeding the goose.'

The *ga-*/*a-* alternation only exists in the third person singular; in the nonsingular only the form *anii-* appears. A comparison of the singular and nonsingular forms is seen in (15).

(15a) ᎦᏬᏂᎭ
gawóoniha
ga-wóoniha
3A-speak:PRC
'She is talking.'

(15b) ᎠᏂᏬᏂᎭ
aàniiwóoniha
anii-wóoniha
3A.NS-speak:PRC
'They are talking.'

3.3.3. Set A Prefixes with Vowel-Initial Stems

As mentioned, two vowels cannot be next to each other in Cherokee. To avoid **vowel clash,** certain changes occur when prefixes attach to a vowel-initial stem. The most common change is the removal of the prefix's final vowel. (16a) shows that the prefix *hi-* undergoes **vowel removal** before the a-initial stem of 'walk'. This same vowel is also removed before the initial /v/ of the stem in (16b). In (16c) the prefix *ga-* appears as [g] before /e/. In each example below the removed vowel is underlined.

(16a) ᎭᎢ
háaʔi
hi̲-áaʔi
2A-walk:PRC
'You are walking.'

(16b) ᎲᏃᏌᏍᎩ
hvvnoosasgi
hi̲-vvnoosasgi
2A-sweep:IMM
'Sweep it!'

(16c) ᎨᎷᎲᏍᎪᎢ
geehluhvsgoʔi
ga̲-eehluhvsg-oʔi
3A-shout:INC-HAB
'He shouts.'

In (17) the first person plural Set A prefix precedes /a/, /e/, /o/, /u/, and /v/, respectively.

(17a) ᎢᏓᎢ
iìdáaʔi
iid_ii_-áaʔi
1A.PL-walk:PRC
'We all are walking.'

(17b) ᎢᏕᏡᏂᏍᎦ
iìdeehluuhv́sga
iid_ii_-eehluuhv́sga
1A.PL-scream:PRC
'We are screaming.'

(17c) ᎢᏙᏪᎵᏍᎪᎢ
iìdoohweelisgoʔi
iid_ii_-oohweeliisg-oʔi
1A.PL-write:INC-HAB
'We write.'

(17d) ᎣᏧᏓᎴᏍᎪ
oòjuudaléesgo
ooj_ii_-uudaléesg-o
1A.PL.EX-unplug:INC-HAB
'We unplug it.'

(17e) ᎢᏛᏓ
iìdvhda
iid_ii_-vhda
1A.PL-use:IMM
'Let's use it!'

This vowel removal rule holds for all of the nonsingular, dual, and plural forms. For the first person singular, however, the prefix *ji-* becomes [*g*] before a vowel. (18a) and (18b) show this change; (18c) shows the first person singular before a consonant.

(18a) ᎦᎢ
gáaʔi
ji-áaʔi
1A-walk:PRC
'I'm walking.'

(18b) ᎪᎩᏍᎦ
googiìsga
ji-oogisga
1A-smoke:PRC
'I'm smoking.'

(18c) ᏥᏬᏂᎭ
jiwóoniha
ji-wóoniha
1A-talk:PRC
'I'm talking.'

When the third person *a-* attaches to an /a/-initial stem, the vowel of the stem is removed. This removal is seen in (19a); it is necessary to use different prefixes on the verb stem, as in (19b), to determine that the stem starts with /a/.

(19a) ᎠᏗᏔᏍᎪ
aàdiitasgo
a-adiitasg-o
3A-drink:INC-HAB
'He drinks it.'

(19b) ᎭᏗᏔᏍᎪ
hadiitasgo
hi-adiitasg-o
2A-drink:INC-HAB
'You drink it.'

A few stems begin with /e/; these stems also cause the removal of the third person singular Set A prefix *a-*. Two examples are shown in (20).

(20a) ᎡᎦ
éega
a-éega
3A-go:PRC
'She's going.'

(20b) ᎡᏙᎰ
éedooho
a-éedooh-o
3A-be.at:INC-HAB
'She is there.'

If a verb is vowel-initial and takes third person *ga-*, the first and third person forms may be identical, because the first person form will also appear as [*g*]. An example is shown in (21).

(21a) JPoᏍA
gúuhlvsgo
ji-úuhlvsg-o
1A-cover:INC-HAB
'I cover it.'

(21b) JPoᏍA
gúuhlvsgo
ga-úuhlvsg-o
3A-cover:INC-HAB
'He covers it.'

In practice, such identical forms rarely occur due to changes in tone, as discussed in chapter 8.

3.3.4. Pronominal Prefixes with Animate Third Person Objects

The prefixes that have been discussed thus far can refer to a combination of a subject and a third person object that is not a human or an animal (i.e., an inanimate object). A special set of prefixes is used if the subject is first or second person and the object is third person and **animate.** These **animate object prefixes** are similar in form to the Set A prefixes that have already been discussed. The prefixes are displayed in table 3.3.

Table 3.3. Set A Pronominal Prefixes with Animate Third Person Objects

Person reference	*Singular*	*Dual (dl)*	*Plural (pl)*
First Person Inclusive	jii-	eenii-	eedii-
First Person Exclusive (EX)		oosdii-	oojii-
Second Person	hii-	eesdii-	eejii-

Two forms of the same verb that differ only in object **animacy** are shown in (22). The abbreviation 1A.AN should be read as "first person Set A prefix with animate third person object." The only difference between these two is that the pronominal prefix in the second example has a long vowel.

(22a) ᏥᎪᎵᏰᎠ
jigolíiyéʔa
ji-golíiyéʔa
1A-examine:PRC
'I am examining it.'

(22b) ᏥᎪᎵᏰᎠ
jiigolíiyéʔa
jii-golíiyéʔa
1A.AN-examine:PRC
'I am examining **him**.'

Vowel-initial stems with a first person subject and animate third person object have prefixes with rather different pronunciations. In (23a) the initial /u/ of the verb stem causes the first person pronominal prefix *ji-* to appear as [g], as discussed in the previous section. In (23b) the animate-object counterpart of this prefix is *jii-* This long vowel of the prefix is not removed; instead **consonant insertion** keeps the vowels of the prefix and the verb apart. In this case the consonant is /y/.

(23a) ᎫᏓᎴᎠ
guudaléeʔa
ji-uudaléeʔa
1A-unfasten:PRC
'I'm unfastening it.'

(23b) ᏥᏳᏓᎴᎠ
jiiyuudaléeʔa
jii-uudaleéʔa
1A.AN-unfasten:PRC
'I'm unfastening **him**.'

Because this animate/inanimate distinction occurs mostly with verbs, it is further illustrated in chapter 4.

3.4. Set B Pronominal Prefixes

3.4.1. Basic Paradigm

The Set B prefixes, like the Set A prefixes, distinguish inclusive/exclusive as well as dual number. These prefixes are presented in table 3.4. It should be noted that the Set B prefixes for the dual and plural second person are identical to the Set A prefixes.

Table 3.4. Set B Pronominal Prefixes

Person reference	*Singular*	*Dual (dl)*	*Plural (pl)*
First Person Inclusive	agi-	ginii-	iigii-
First Person Exclusive (EX)		ooginii-	oogii-
Second Person	ja-	sdii-	iijii-
Third Person	uu-	uunii-	

3.4.2. Set B Prefixes with Vowel-Initial Stems

As with the Set A prefixes, Set B prefixes often remove their end vowel to avoid vowel clash when attaching to stems beginning with a vowel. Two examples are shown in (24). The removed vowel is underlined in each case.

(24a) ᎢᎦᎦᏙᏍᏓ
iìgaktoósda
iigii-agahtoósda
1B.PL-look.at:PRC
'She's looking at us.'

(24b) ᏦᎯᏳᎭᏍ
joohiyuhas
ja-oohiyuha=s
2B-believe:PRC=Q
'Do you believe it?'

The prefixes *agi-* and *uu-* are exceptions to this pattern. The first person singular prefix *agi-* becomes [*agw*] before vowels. This variant is shown in (25). In (25a) the prefix appears in its basic form. In (25b) and (25c) the stems begin with /e/ and /o/, respectively.

(25a) ᎠᎩᏲᏏᎭ
aàgiyóosiha
agi-yóosiha
1B-be.hungry:PRC
'I am hungry.'

(25b) ᎠᏇᎯᏍᏓᏁᎭ
aàgwehisdaneha
agi-ehisdaneha
1B-hurt:PRC
'I ache.'

(25c) ᎠᏉᎯᏳᎭ
aàgwohiyuha
agi-ohiyuha
1B-believe:PRC
'I believe it.'

The second exception is the third person singular prefix *uu-*; this prefix appears as [*uuw*] before the vowels /e/, /o/, and /u/. (26) shows three examples of the third person prefix. The prefix appears in its basic form in (26a) and before /e/ and /u/ in the other two examples, respectively.

(26a) ᎤᏲᏏᎭ
uùyóosiha
uu-yóosiha
3B-be.hungry:PRC
'He is hungry.'

(26b) ᎤᏪᎷᎩᏍᎬ
uùweeluugiisgv
uu-eeluugiisg-v
3B-worry:INC-EXP
'He was worried.'

(26c) ᎤᏭᎯᎶᎡ
uùwuuhiilóoʔe
uu-uuhiilóoʔ-e
3B-wash:CMP-NXP
'He washed it.'

The combination of a stem-initial /v/ with the prefix *uu-* results in the unpredictable form [*uuwaa*], as shown in (27a). It is clear that this stem begins with the vowel /v/ when other prefixes attach to it, as seen in (27b) and (27c).

(27a) ᎤᏩᏃᏌᎲ
uùwaanoosahv
uu-vvnoosah-v

3B-sweep:CMP-EXP
'He swept it.'

(27b) ᏍᏛᏃᏌᎲᎢ
<u>sdvv</u>noosahvv̌ʔi
sdii-vvnoosah-vv̌ʔi
2B.DL-sweep:CMP-EXP
'You two swept it.'

(27c) ᎠᏋᏃᏌᎲ
<u>aàgwvv</u>noosahv
agi-vvnoosah-v
1B-sweep:CMP-EXP
'I swept it.'

If *uu-* appears before a stem that begins with /a/, the /a/is removed. Two examples are given in (28).

(28a) ᎤᏚᎵᎭ
uùduulíha
uu-<u>a</u>duulíha
3B-want:PRC
'He wants it.'

(28b) ᎤᏑᏰᏒᎢ
uùsuyesvv̌ʔi
uu-<u>a</u>suyes-vv̌ʔi
3B-choose:CMP-EXP
'He chose it.'

Some intransitive verbs (both Set A and Set B) have a meaning incompatible with first and second person and are only used in the third person. Two examples are given in (29).

Intransitive verbs with only third person reference

(29a) ᎤᎶᎩᎳ
uùlóògila
uu-lóògila
3B-cloudy:PRC
'It is cloudy.'

(29b) ᎠᎦᎵᎭ
aàgáaliha

a-gáaliha
3A-sunny:PRC
'It is sunny.'

3.5. /h/ Alternation

Certain prefixes cause the first /h/ of the stem to which they attach to be replaced with a **glottal stop** or a **lowfall tone;** this process is known as **/h/ alternation.** This alternation is very important in Cherokee and is explained at length in chapter 8. Two pairs of examples are presented below in (30) and (31); in the second example of each the prefix is an **/h/ alternator** (a prefix that triggers the alternation). In both pairs the presence of the Set A prefix *ji-* causes the /h/ to be replaced. In (30) the two words have an identical syllabary spelling but a slightly different pronunciation. In (31a), however, both the pronunciation and syllabary spelling are different: the presence of the *ji-* prefix causes the /h/ to be replaced by a glottal stop.

(30a) ᎪᏪᎵᎠ
goohweélíʔa
ga-oohweélíʔa
3A-write:PRC
'He's writing.'

(30b) ᎪᏪᎵᎠ
goò̱weélíʔa
ji-oo<u>h</u>weélíʔa
1A-write:PRC
'I'm writing.'

(31a) ᎫᎯᎶᎠ
guuhiilóoʔa
ga-uuhiilóoʔa
3A-wash:PRC
'He's washing it.'

(31b) ᎫᎢᎶᎠ
gu<u>ʔ</u>iilóoʔa
ga-uu<u>h</u>iilóoʔa
1A-wash:PRC
'I'm washing it.'

3.6. Sources and Additional Reading

The best sources on pronominal prefixes are Scancarelli (1987), Cook (1979), King (1975), and Pulte and Feeling (1975). Scancarelli (1987) thoroughly describes the interaction of the pronominal system and animacy; animacy and agreement are also discussed in Dukes (1996).

3.7. Directions for Further Research

The most comprehensive treatment of pronominal prefixes is found in Scancarelli (1987). Foley (1980) analyzes both simple and complex prefixes and proposes various phonological rules that derive the numerous surface forms from the underlying forms. He supports many of the underlying forms with comparisons from other Iroquoian languages. Further comparative work could yield more insights into the origins and functions of Cherokee pronominals.

Smythe (2003) has a novel reanalysis of the pronominal prefixes; she attempts to establish a clearer relationship between the pronominal prefixes and their arguments by accounting for situations where arguments have no overt information on the verb. She proposes that Cherokee is a pronominal argument language, using terminology from Jelinek (1984) and appealing to the characterization of Cherokee as a nonconfigurational language by Scancarelli (1987). Smythe (2003) uses these characterizations of Cherokee to argue for a zero third-person morpheme that is present for arguments lower on the Semantic Role Hierarchy proposed by Scancarelli. This analysis applies not only for intransitive and transitive verbs but for ditransitives as well. For ditransitive constructions Smythe points out that the patient is never indexed on the verb; instead she argues that this patient is indexed on the noun through noun incorporation. Additional investigations of this kind into Cherokee grammatical relations and their interaction with the language's syntax could make important contributions to theoretical linguistics.

FOUR

The Basic Verb

4.1. Pronominal Prefixes on Verbs

4.1.1. Overview

Cherokee **verbs** have more **inflection** than any other **part of speech.** Inflection occurs when the form of a word is altered to add grammatical information. Cherokee verbs inflect by adding **prefixes** and **suffixes** to different verb **stems.**

Verbs are the most important part of speech in Cherokee. In addition to being the central element of most sentences, they also serve as the base for creating many **nouns** and **adjectives.** They are distinguished from adjectives and nouns by distinct suffixes and **tone** patterns. In (1a) and (1b) the adjective and the noun take the **Set B third person pronominal prefix** but do not inflect for **tense, aspect,** or **mood.** In (1c), however, the verb appears in the **Completive stem** and has a **final suffix** indicating a completed action in the past. As with English, Cherokee verbs are the only part of speech that can express past, present, and future.

(1a) ᎤᏰᎸᏉᎢ
uuyeelvvháá?i
uu-yeelvvháá?i
3B-naked
'naked'

(1b) ᎤᎲᏬ
uuhnawo
uu-ahnawo
3B-shirt
'his shirt'

(1c) ᎤᏗᏔᎲᎢ
uùdiitahvv̋ʔi
uu-adiitah-vv̋ʔi
3B-drink:CMP-EXP
'He drank it.'

In **fast speech** the final suffix is often shortened by dropping the **final vowel.**

A verb stem is the base to which the pronominal prefixes and final suffixes attach. The stem, which is derived from more basic elements, can itself have more than one part. Verb stems may begin with any **consonant** or **vowel** except for /i/ and /m/. A few examples of consonant-initial stems are shown in (2). In this grammar the **citation form** is the **Present Continuous stem** without the pronominal prefix.

(2)	-giʔa	'eat (solid)'
	-gooliíyéʔa	'read', 'examine'
	-híha	'kill'
	-hwasga	'buy'
	-yóosiha	'be hungry'
	-ʔluhga	'arrive'

The first four verbs in the list above are **transitive** (they take objects), while the last two are **intransitive** (they do not take objects). In this grammar, (T) 'transitive' or (I) 'intransitive' notation appears after the translation of the verb when **transitivity** is not clear. The verb 'boil' can be used either transitively or intransitively in English; for example, 'the water is boiling' (a verb with only a **subject**, hence intransitive) versus 'we are boiling the water' (a verb with a subject and an object, hence transitive). In Cherokee verbs are either transitive or intransitive. In this instance the basic meaning of the verb 'boil' is transitive; a **parsed** example is seen in (3).

(3)	ᎭᎵᏟᏓᏍ	ᎠᎹ
	haliitldas	ama
	hi-aliitlda=s	ama
	2A-boil(T):IMM=Q	water
	'Did you boil the water?'	

The initial vowels of verb stems can be either **long** or **short** and bear different tones; an important exception is the **highfall tone** that only appears on nouns, adjectives, and **subordinate** verbs. Some examples of vowel-initial verbs are listed in (4).

(4) -adloohyíha 'cry'
-aduuliha 'want'
-éega 'go'
-eelíʔa 'think'
-oohla 'sit', 'remain'
-oohiyuha 'believe'
-uutéega 'pick up'
-uutiha 'snow'
-vvhwsda 'seem'
-vvhníha 'hit'

The stem is the most important part of the verb; it is the base to which the other parts are added. As noted, a Cherokee verb has at a minimum two parts: the pronominal prefix and the verb stem. An example of a **conjugated verb** is seen in (5).

(5) DSPᏍᏍ
aàgáaliha
a-gáaliha
3A-be.sunny:PRC
'It is sunny.'

All the information needed to create a correctly conjugated verb is illustrated for the **Set A verb** 'help' in (6). The appropriate prefixes and suffixes can be added to these five base forms to produce all the possible forms of the verb.

(6) -sdeelíha (A) 'help'
-sdeeliísg-/ -sdeéla/ -sdeelvvh-/ -sdehldi

The above citation form has five stems, which are listed in (7). Whether the verb takes **Set A** or **Set B prefixes** is unpredictable and thus is listed with the verb; the (A) after the citation form in (7) indicates that this is a Set A verb.

(7) The five stems of -sdeelíha (A) 'help'

1. Present Continuous:	-sdeelíha
2. Incompletive:	-sdeeliísg-
3. Immediate:	-sdeéla
4. Completive:	-sdeelvvh-
5. Infinitive:	-sdehldi

It is important to bear in mind that the last two stems undergo **prefix shift** and often have Set B rather than Set A prefixes; for this reason they are grouped together. The third person forms for the verb 'help' are displayed in (8). Note that stems 2 and 4 can take other final suffixes.

(8) The five stems of -sdeelíha (Set A) 'help':

The five stems of -sdeelíha (Set A) 'help':		Third person conjugation
1. Present Continuous:	aàsdeelíha	'he is helping'
2. Incompletive:	aàsdeeliísgvv́ʔi	'he was helping'
3. Immediate:	aàsdeéla	'he helped (just now)'
4. Completive:	uùsdeelvvhvv́ʔi	'he helped'
5. Infinitive:	uùsdehldi	'for him to help'

In addition to the pronominal prefixes, two of the five verb stems carry a final suffix. These stems are discussed later in this chapter. The **Incompletive** and Completive take several different suffixes. For example, the **experienced past** (EXP) is used on both stems to indicate that the speaker has personal knowledge of a past event because he or she witnessed it. These elements (the stem and the suffix) combine to create a complete picture of the verb's time frame. (9) has two examples of the experienced past suffix.

(9a) ᎤᏬᏂᏒᎢ
uùwóoniisvv́ʔi
uu-wóoniis-vv́ʔi
3B-speak:CMP-EXP
'He spoke.'

(9b) ᎦᏬᏂᏍᎬᎢ
gawóoniisgvv́ʔi
ga-wóoniisg-vv́ʔi
3A-speak:INC-EXP
'He was speaking.'

In (9a) the combination of a Completive stem and an experienced past final suffix expresses a completed event; in (9b) the combination of an Incompletive stem and an experienced past final suffix indicates an ongoing action in the past. When vowel-initial pronominal prefixes are used with main verbs, **pronominal lengthening** applies: the vowel is lengthened and a **lowfall tone** appears. This difference in the pronominal prefixes is seen in (10). In (10a) the prefix attaches to an adjective and the pronominal prefix appears in its basic form. In (10b) the attachment of the prefix to a verb triggers the pronominal lengthening. There is no difference in vowel length for the third person Set B prefix because it is already long. In (10c) the prefix is shown attached to a noun; in (10d) it is attached to a verb and has the lowfall tone. The difference between these prefixes in each pair is the lowfall. Pronominal lengthening is further illustrated in chapter 8.

(10a) ᎠᎩᏰᎸᎭᎢ
agiyeelvvháá?i
agi-yeelvvháá?i
1B-naked
'I am naked.'

(10b) ᎠᎩᏲᏏᎭ
aàgiyóosiha
agi-yóosiha
1B-be.hungry:PRC
'I am hungry.'

(10c) ᎤᎿᏬ
uuhnawo
uu-ahnawo
3B-shirt
'his shirt'

(10d) ᎤᏄᏩ
uùhnúùwa
uu-ahnúùwa
3B-wear.shirt:PRC
'He is wearing a shirt.'

A few verbs are **nonsingular verbs,** used only with nonsingular subjects. This feature is indicated by (NS) after the verb gloss. An example of a nonsingular verb is shown in the sentence in (11a). Its singular counterpart is shown in (11b).

(11a)

ᎠᏂᏍᎦᏯ	ᎠᏂᎾ	ᎠᏂᏧᏣᏃ	ᎠᏂᏙᎾ
aniisgay	aàníina	aniichúújahno	aàniidóòna
anii-sgaya	anii-na	anii-chúúja=hno	anii-dóòna
3A.NS-man	3A.NS-sit(NS):PRC	3A.NS-boy=CN	3A.NS-stand(NS):PRC

'The men are sitting and the boys are standing.'

(11b) ᎤᏬᏝ
uùwoóhla
uu-oóhla
3B-be.sitting:PRC
'He is sitting.'

4.1.2. Pronominal Prefixes on Intransitive Verbs

Intransitive verbs are verbs that have a subject but no object. Some sample intransitive verbs are listed in (12).

(12) Sample intransitive verbs

-kwalaagiíʔa	'snore'
-adloohyíha	'cry'
-ahnawéeʔa	'undress'
-hlvvsga	'be sleepy'
-ʔluhga	'arrive'
-noohiíli	'fly'
-hnaálúùga	'become angry'
-dóòga	'stand'

Many intransitive verbs normally take Set B prefixes. Many of these **Set B verbs** indicate the state that the **participant** is in or the emotion that the participant is experiencing. An example of a Set B intransitive verb is in (13); in this example the prefix *agi-* appears as [*aàk*]; this type of change is examined in chapter 8.

(13) ᎠᎩᏢᎦ
aàkdlv́vga
agi-hdlv́vga
1B-be.sick:PRC
'I'm sick.'

A sample list of Set B intransitives expressing states is given in (14).

(14) Sample intransitive Set B verbs expressing a state

-adiihlehga	'be hot'
-hnaála	'be angry'
-adanéegooyúha	'be wrinkled'
-adiisgáhla	'be in hiding'
-yóosiha	'be hungry'
-adoolihga	'be sorry'
-hnaálv́ha	'be angry'
-yvwéega	'be tired'

Verbs with the meaning 'get into a state of' also tend to use Set B prefixes. Some examples are given in (15).

(15) Intransitive Set B verbs with a change of state meaning

-adanilóosga	'get sick'
-adíwsga	'heal', 'recover'
-aluudesdíiha	'get dizzy'
-hnaálv́v̀ga	'get angry'
-dlv́sdiína	'get sick'
-hyvsdéesdiiha	'get drunk'
-gaanawoosga	'get warm'

Many intransitive verbs that indicate an involuntary action or physical or emotional state are Set B verbs. Some sample verbs are listed in (16).

(16) Intransitive Set B verbs indicating typically involuntary action

-loodeesdi	'trip'
-eesdáaneeha	'ache'
-hnáàsvvhíhi	'slip', 'slide'
-eeluhga	'scream'
-haloósdîiha	'yawn'

4.1.3. Pronominal Prefixes on Transitive Verbs

Transitive verbs are verbs that have a subject and an object. The subject is generally more in control of the action, while the object is generally undergoing the action. It is difficult for beginners to know when to use which pronominal prefix, but it helps to keep in mind the grammatical distinction between **local persons** and **nonlocal persons.** Local persons are **first person** and **second person** (the speaker and the person being spoken to: the two people "locally" present for the conversation), while nonlocal is **third person** (the person[s] being spoken about, who is not necessarily "locally" present for the conversation). The possible combinations of local/nonlocal and subject/object are expressed using Set A and Set B prefixes as well as **combined prefixes. Object focus prefixes** are used when the subject is unknown or put in the background. The combined and object focus prefixes are discussed in chapter 9.

In the Present Continuous, Incompletive, and Immediate stems, a Set A prefix is almost always used if the subject is a local person and the object a third person. The Set A prefixes introduced in chapter 3 are presented again in table 4.1.

Table 4.1. Set A Pronominal Prefixes with Local/Nonlocal Distinctions

	Person Reference	*Singular*	*Dual (dl)*	*Plural (pl)*
Local	First Person Inclusive	ji-*	iinii-	iidii-
	First Person Exclusive (EX)		oosdii-	oojii-
	Second Person	hi-	sdii-	iijii-
Nonlocal	Third Person	a-, ga-	anii-	

An example of a verb with a Set A prefix is shown in (17). This verb is transitive, so the action is understood as happening to an **implied object** 'it'.

(17) ᎯᏔᏖᏲᎭ
hinúuteeyóha
hi-núuteeyóha
2A-twist(T):PRC
'You are twisting it.'

A few transitive Set B verbs use Set B prefixes to refer to combinations of local person subjects with third person objects. For these verbs the kinds of participants involved make a difference. Many transitive verbs involve a subject that is performing the action and an object undergoing the action. It is noteworthy that many of the Set B verbs that are transitive do not have a subject that is actively performing the action (known as an **agent**) but a subject that is experiencing or undergoing something (known as an **undergoer**). A conjugated example of one such Set B transitive verb is shown in (18). Some Set B transitive verbs are listed in (19).

(18) ᎠᎩᎸᏉᏗ
aàgilv̋kwdi
agi-lv̋kwdi
1B-like:PRC
'I like it.'

(19) Transitive Set B verbs

-ahnta	'feel', 'know'
-aníʔwa	'wear'
-htadeegi	'crave'
-sgwaanagoósga	'be curious about'

-htvvgáàsda 'listen to'
-hwsv́vga 'smell'
-oohiyúha 'believe'

Only a few transitive verbs that have agent subjects (subjects that are deliberating performing the action) are Set B verbs. (20) lists these verbs.

(20) Transitive Set B verbs with agent subjects
-níiʔa 'hold in one's hand'
-yoosga 'release'
-hwisga 'buy'
-adéega 'throw'
-hyoha 'look for'
-gaseesdi 'watch for'

Set A prefixes do not appear on Completive stems with an experienced past (EXP) suffix. An example of a Set A verb in the Completive past is shown in (21). In this example the prefix can refer either to the subject or to the object.

(21) DᎩᎪᏙT
aàgigoohv́v́ʔi
agi-gooh-v́v́ʔi
1B-see:CMP-EXP
'I saw it.'
'It saw me.'

Transitive verbs with both a local person subject and a third person **animate** object, however, use **animate object prefixes** even with these stems, as shown in (22).

(22) ᎩᏟᏍ ᏥᏩᏎ
giihlis hiiwase
giihli=s hii-hwas-e
dog=Q 2A.AN-buy:CMP-NXP
'Did you buy the dog?'

As stated earlier, the choice of a Set A or Set B pronominal prefix is unpredictable and must simply be learned with each verb. Verbs that can use the Set A prefixes in the Present Continuous, Incompletive, and Immediate stems are called Set A verbs. It is important to note, however, that Set B prefixes can be used for all verbs, particularly with some uses of the Completive and **Infinitive** stems, as shown in (23a) and (23c). In (23b) the Set A animate object prefix appears. In (23d) and (23e) the Present Continuous stem and the Incompletive stem, respectively, use the Set A prefix.

(23a) DYᏅᎦᎸᏉᎢ
aàginvvgalvvhvv̋ʔi
agi-nvvgalvvh-vv̋ʔi
1B-clean:CMP-EXP
'I cleaned it.'

(23b) ᏥᏅᎦᎸᏉᎢ
jiinvvgalvvhvv̋ʔi
jii-nvvgalvvh-vv̋ʔi
1A.AN-clean:CMP-EXP
'I cleaned him.'

(23c) DYᏅᎦᎸᏗ ᎠᏆᏚᎵ
aginvvgahldi aàgwaduuli
agi-nvvgahldi agi-aduuli
1B-clean:INF 1B-want:PRC
'I want to clean it.'

(23d) ᏥᏅᎦᎵᎭ
jinvvgalíha
ji-nvvgalíha
1A-clean:PRC
'I am cleaning it.'

(23e) ᏥᏅᎦᎵᏍᎪ
jinvvgaliisgo
ji-nvvgaliisg-o
1A-clean:INC-HAB
'I clean it.'

While these descriptions are meant to provide a brief overview, the interaction of stems and pronominal prefixes is discussed in greater depth in the individual sections on stems.

To summarize the terminology thus far, Set A verbs are verbs that take Set A prefixes in the Present Continuous, Incompletive, or Immediate stems. Set B verbs almost always take the Set B prefixes, the sole exception being the small set of transitive Set B verbs that may take the animate object prefixes.

It is clear that Cherokee treats local and nonlocal persons in different ways.

The Set A prefixes can refer to the subject of an intransitive verb or the combination of a local person (first or second person) subject and a nonlocal (third person) inanimate object of a transitive verb. Both are shown in (24).

(24a) ᏥᏰᎦ
jiyéega
ji-yéega
1A-wake:PRC
'I am waking up.'

(24b) ᏥᏅᎦᎵᎠ
jinvvgalíʔa
ji-nvvgalíʔa
1A-clean:PRC
'I am cleaning **it**.'

With both the Set A and Set B prefixes, the unexpressed third person object (or implied object) is understood to be singular and inanimate. If the object is nonsingular and inanimate, the **prepronominal prefix** *dee-* is added to the verb. As the name suggests, prepronominal prefixes come before the pronominal. They are the subject of chapters 5 and 9. For the current discussion of the minimal verb, it is only necessary to mention the most common prepronominal prefix, *dee-*. This prefix is known as the **distributive,** and one of its functions is to indicate nonsingular, **dual,** or **plural** objects. (25) is an example of a verb both with and without this prefix. **Vowel clash** with the vowel of the distributive causes the removal of the pronominal prefix vowel in (25b). A Set B verb with this prefix is shown in (25c).

(25a) ᎢᏥᏫᏍᎦ
iijiihwisga
iijii-hwisga
2A.PL-plant:PRC
'You are planting it.'

(25b) ᏕᏥᏫᏍᎦ
déejiihwisga
dee-iijii-hwisga
DST-2A.PL-plant:PRC
'You are planting them.'

(25c) ᏕᏣᏕᎦ
deejadéega

dee-ja-adéega
DST-2B-throw:PRC
'You are throwing them.'

In other environments it is the vowel of the prepronominal prefix that is removed. Examples of this **vowel removal** before a stem-initial /a/, /o/, and /u/ are shown in (26).

(26a) ᏓᏗᏔᏍᎪᎢ
daàdiitasgóoʔi
dee-a-adiitasg-óoʔi
DST-3A-drink:INC-HAB
'She drinks them.'

(26b) ᏙᏍᏗᎪᏩᏘᏍᎪᎢ
doòsdiigoohwtiísgóoʔi
dee-oosdii-goohwtiísg-óoʔi
DST-1A.DL.EX-see:INC-HAB
'We two see them.'

(26c) ᏚᏍᏆᎵᏐᏅ
duùsgwáàlsohnv
dee-uu-sgwáàls-ohn-v
DST-3B-break(T):CMP-TRM:CMP-EXP
'He broke them.'

An animate object prefix is used if the subject is local and the object is third person animate. These forms have been discussed in the previous chapter and are repeated below in table 4.2. If the third person object is animate and nonsingular, an **animate nonsingular** prepronominal prefix is used. This prefix is discussed in chapter 5.

Table 4.2. Set A Pronominal Prefixes with Animate Singular Third Person Object

Person reference	*Singular*	*Dual (dl)*	*Plural (pl)*
First Person Inclusive	jii-	eenii-	eedii-
First Person Exclusive (EX)		oosdii-	oojii-
Second Person	hii-	eesdii-	eejii-
Third Person	a-, ga-	anii-	

Several differences from the Set A prefixes are apparent. The first and second singular forms display a lengthened vowel. The inanimate and animate object forms are contrasted in (27). These words are written the same in the syllabary.

(27a) ᏥᏄᏖᏲᎭ
jinúuteeyóha
ji-núuteeyóha
1A-twist:PRC
'I am twisting it.' (Feeling 1975a:112)

(27b) ᏥᏄᏖᏲᎭ
jiinúuteeyóha
jii-núuteeyóha
1A.AN-twist:PRC
'I am twisting him.' (Feeling 1975a:112)

In the case of a vowel-initial stem, a /y/ is inserted. As a result of this **consonant insertion,** the stem with an animate object prefix can appear quite distinct from its inanimate object counterpart. An example is shown in (28).

(28a) ᎦᏬᎠ
gawóoʔa
ji-awóoʔa
1A-bathe(T):PRC
'I am bathing it.'

(28b) ᏥᏯᏬᎠ
jiiyawóoʔa
jii-awóoʔa
1A.AN-bathe(T):PRC
'I am bathing him/her.'

The nonsingular **inclusive** prefixes all start with the element [*ee*]. Like their Set A counterparts, these prefixes lose their final vowel when attached to a vowel-initial stem. All of these forms trigger **/h/ alternation** (if an /h/ is present in the stem, it will be deleted). Examples of these forms are shown in (29). In (29a) and (29c) the /h/ that is deleted is underlined. /h/ alternation is discussed in chapter 8.

(29a) Ꮎ ᎠᎨᎯ ᎡᏃᏟᎦ
na ageéhya eènooliìga

na ageéhya eenii-oolih̲ga
the woman 1A.DL.AN-recognize:PRC
'We recognize the woman.'

(29b) Ꮎ ᎤᏛᏐᏅ ᎡᏗᏲᎵᎦ
na uutvsoohnv́v́ eèdiiyooliga
na uu-atvsoohnv́v́ eedii-yooliga
the 3B-old.man 1A.PL.AN-greet:IMM
'We greeted the old man.'

(29c) Ꮎ ᎤᏲᏏᏍᎩ ᎠᏍᎦᏯ ᎡᏍᏕᎶᎦ
na uuyoosíísgi asgaya eèsdeeloòga
na uu-yoosiisg-i a-sgaya eesdii-eeh̲loòga
the 3B-be.hungry:INC-AGT 3A-man 2A.DL.AN-feed:IMM
'You two fed the hungry man.'

(29d) Ꮎ ᏍᏕᏱᏓ ᎡᏥᏅᏁᎸ
na sdeeyída eèjiinv́vneelv
na sdeeyída eejii-nv́vneel-v
the rope 2A.PL.AN-give(flexible):CMP-EXP
'You all gave him the rope.'

The exclusive animate object prefixes *oosdii-* and *oojii-* are identical in form to their Set A counterparts used with inanimate objects, as shown in (30a) and (30b).

(30a) ᎦᎶᏪ ᎣᏥᏕᎸ
galoowe oòjiideelv
galoowe oojii-deel-v
gun 1A.PL.EX.AN-give(long):CMP-EXP
'We gave him a gun.'

(30b) ᎣᏍᏓᏬᎠ
oòsdawóoʔa
oosdii-awóoʔa
1A.DL.EX.AN-bathe(T):PRC
'We two are bathing him.'

The animate object prefixes all trigger /h/ alternation; this is sometimes the main property that distinguishes them from their Set A counterparts. These distinctions are further exemplified in chapter 9.

It should be noted that transitive verbs can distinguish between an animate and inanimate object only in the case of a local person subject. In the examples in (31) both subject and object are third person, with no animacy distinction for the object.

(31a) DhAPβD
aàniigooliíyéʔa
anii-gooliíyéʔa
3A.NS-examine:PRC
'They are examining him/her/it.'

(31b) DAPβD
aàgooliíyéʔa
a-gooliíyéʔa
3A-examine:PRC
'He/she/it is examining him/her/it.'

(31c) APA
goohlgo
ga-oolihg-o
3A-understand:INC-HAB
'He/she/it understands him/her/it.'

4.2. Verb Stems

Cherokee uses different stems to express grammatical information about tense, aspect, and mood. Tense refers to the time frame relative to the moment of speaking and indicates whether an action is happening in the past, present, or future. Aspect refers to the manner in which the action is performed: whether it is completed, habitual, or in progress. Mood indicates the speaker's attitude toward the event described by the verb; this concept includes ability and obligation as well as the speaker's degree of certainty about an event.

The three concepts of tense, aspect, and mood are interconnected in Cherokee; no single element expresses only one of these concepts. For example, the Present Continuous stem indicates an action or state that is taking place at the moment the speaker is describing it. This stem contains both tense and aspect information: the tense is Present, and the aspect is Continuous. The Incompletive stem indicates that the action, whether it be past, present, or future time, is **habitual** (when used with the habitual suffix) or is ongoing and not completed (when used with either of the past suffixes or the **progressive future** suffix). The Immediate stem either indicates an action that took place in the immediate past or is used to give a command.

The Set A verbs use Set A prefixes for the first three stems. In the last two stems the basic (non-animate object) Set A prefixes are not used because of prefix shift. The Completive stem indicates actions that take place in the past as well as the future. The Infinitive stem is used, among other functions, to indicate ability or obligation; it also serves as the base for forming many **derived nouns.** When used to express past events, the Completive stem takes Set B prefixes. The Infinitive stem also uses Set B prefixes for most functions.

Most verbs have these five stems. An example of the verb 'arrive' is shown in (32). Note that the first three example sentences have Set A prefixes; the last two are in the Completive and Infinitive and have Set B prefixes. The first four are complete sentences, while the Infinitive in (32e) needs to accompany another verb to form a complete sentence.

The five stems of -ʔluhga ('arrive')

(32a) -ʔluhga — Present Continuous Stem
ᎢᏂᎷᎦ
iǹiiʔluhga
iinii-ʔluhga
1A.DL-arrive:PRC
'You and I are arriving.'

(32b) -ʔluhg- — Incompletive Stem
ᎢᏂᎷᎪᎢ
iǹiiʔluhgóoʔi
iinii-ʔluhg-óoʔi
1A.DL-arrive:INC-HAB
'You and I arrive.'

(32c) -ʔluhgi — Immediate Stem
ᎢᏂᎷᎩ
iǹiiluhgi
iinii-ʔluhgi
1A.DL-arrive:IMM
'You and I (just) arrived.'

(32d) -ʔluhj- — Completive Stem
ᎩᏂᎷᏨᎢ

giniiʔluhjvv́ʔi
ginii-ʔluhj-vv́ʔi
1B.DL-arrive:CMP-EXP
'You and I arrived.'

(32e) -ʔluhisdi Infinitive Stem
ᏱᏂᏢᎯᏍᏗ
giniiʔluhisdi
ginii-ʔluhisdi
1B.DL-arrive:INF
'. . . you and I to arrive.'

4.2.1. Present Continuous (PRC) Verb Stem

The Present Continuous stem indicates that an action or state is happening at the time of speaking. These stems end in an /a/ or /i/ that is often dropped in **fast speech.** The Present Continuous stem does not take final suffixes. Three examples of this stem are given in (33); the first two verbs are actions, while the third is a state.

Examples of Present Continuous stems

(33a) ᎡᏗᎦᏘᏯ
eèdigaàtiíya
eedii-gahtiíya
1A.PL.AN-wait.for:PRC
'We're waiting for her.'

(33b) ᎭᏟ
hatli
hi-atihtli
2A-run:PRC
'You are running.'

(33c) ᎤᏴᏜ
uùhyvvdla
uu-hyvvdla
3B-be.cold:PRC
'It's cold.'

In this grammar the Present Continuous stem without its pronominal prefix is treated as the citation form of the verb (the "name" of the verb).

4.2.2. Incompletive (INC) Verb Stem

The Incompletive stem indicates that the action is not completed. Unlike the Present Continuous stem, four different final suffixes can attach to the Incompletive. In (34a) the habitual (HAB) suffix and the Incompletive stem together denote an ongoing activity in the **general present** (something that happens generally, but not necessarily right now). The experienced past (EXP) suffix combines with the Incompletive stem in (34b) to indicate an ongoing activity in the past of which the speaker has personal knowledge. The example in (34c) has the same tense and aspect frame as (34b), but the **nonexperienced past** (NXP) suffix indicates that the speaker has not directly witnessed the event and is stating what has been reported by others. In (34d) the **progressive future** (PFT) suffix denotes an activity that is ongoing in the future through the active effort of the participant.

Incompletive stem of 'speak' with different final suffixes

(34a) DhᏫhᏍAT
aàniiwóoniisgóoʔi
anii-wóoniisg-óoʔi
3A.NS-talk:INC-HAB
'They talk (maybe not right now, but typically or habitually).'

(34b) DhᏫhᏍET
aàniiwóoniisgv́v́ʔi
anii-wóoniisg-v́v́ʔi
3A.NS-talk:INC-EXP
'They were talking (I saw them).'

(34c) DhᏫhᏍᎨT
aàniiwóoniisgéeʔi
anii-wóoniisg-éeʔi
3A.NS-talk:INC-NXP
'They were talking (somebody told me).'

(34d) DhᏫhᏍᎨᏍᏗ
aàniiwóoniisgéesdi
anii-wóoniisg-éesdi

3A.NS-talk:INC-PFT
'They will be talking.'

4.2.3. Immediate (IMM) Verb Stem

The **Immediate** stem presents an action that took place in the recent past; it can also be used as a command to express an action that should be done in the near future. When used with the **irrealis** prepronominal prefix, it expresses an action that could take place in the near future. Four examples of the immediate past use are shown in (35a) through (35d). This irrealis prefix is used to indicate hypothetical or unreal events, as explained in chapter 5.

(35a) ᏥᏲᎵᎦ
jiiyooliga
jii-ooliga
1A.AN-greet:IMM
'I (just now) greeted him.'

(35b) ᎩᎳᏩᏳᏍᏗ ᎣᏣᎴᎾ
kilawayúúsd oòjaleéna
kilawayúúsdi oojii-aleéna
moment.ago 1A.PL.EX-start(I):IMM
'We just started.'

(35c) ᎦᏙ ᎠᏅᏛᎦ
gado aàndvvga
gado anii-advvga
what 3A.NS-do:IMM
'What did they do?'

(35d) ᎦᎵᏅ
gahlvv́na
ga-hlvv́na
3A-sleep:IMM
'He just went to sleep.'

The Immediate is also used to form commands. These two different uses are contrasted in (36).

(36a) ᎦᎪ ᎠᏫᎦ
gaago aàhvv̀ga

gaago a-hvv̀ga
who 3A-set.down:IMM
'Who set it down?'

(36b) ᎯᎲᎦ
hihvv̀ga
hi-hvv̀ga
2A-set.down:IMM
'Set it down!'

Six examples of Immediate commands are shown below in (37); (37a) contains two commands.

(37a) ᎭᎵᏍᏇᏚᎩ ᏥᎪᎵᏯ
halsgweetuhgi jigooliíya
hi-alisgweetuhgi ji-gooliíya
2A-take.hat.off:IMM 1A-examine:IMM
'Take your hat off. Let me look at it.' (Feeling 1975a:43)

(37b) ᎧᏫ ᏍᎩᏁᎲᏏ Track 26
kaáhwi sgineehvsi
kaáhwi sgi-neehvsi
coffee 2/1-give(liquid):IMM
'Give me the coffee!'

(37c) ᎯᏍᏚᎲᎦ ᎦᎶᎯᏍᏗᎢ Track 27
hisduùhvv̀ga galoohisdííʔi
hi-sduùhvv̀ga galoohisdííʔi
2A-close:IMM door
'Close the door!'

(37d) ᎢᎾᎵᎢᏓ ᎭᏰᎵᏍᏗ
iìnaaliʔiída hayeelsdi
iinii-aaliʔiída hayeelsdi
1A.DL-exchange:IMM knife
'Let's trade knives.' (Feeling 1975a:40)

(37e) ᏣᎳᎩ ᎬᏗ ᏂᏫ Track 28
jalagi gv́hdi hniwi
jalagi gv́hdi ni-hi-wi
Cherokee with NI-2A-say:IMM
'Say it in Cherokee!'

The Immediate is also used to refer to events that will happen or could happen as well as to the ability to perform an action. For all of these meanings, the Immediate is used with the irrealis prepronominal prefix *yi-*. Two examples are shown in (38). The first example indicates a possible future event; the second expresses the ability to do something.

(38a) ᏱᎾᏛᎦ ᎠᏗ
yinaadvvg aàdi
yi-ni-a-advvga a-adi
IRR-NI-3A-do:IMM 3A-say:PRC
'He will do it, he says.'

(38b) ᎡᎵᏊ ᏔᎵ ᎢᏯᏔᏬᏍᏔᏅ ᏱᎨᏓ ᎠᎹᏱ ᎭᏫᏂ
eelíígwu taʔli iyátahwoòstanv yigeéda amaáyi hawííni
eelíígwu taʔli iyátahwoòstanv yi-ji-eéda amaáyi hawííni
possible two minute IRR-1A-be.at:IMM in.water under
'I can stay under water for two minutes.' (Feeling 1975a:129)

The irrealis prefix is discussed in chapter 5.

The Immediate is the third stem listed in the five stems of the verb. It is one of the three verb stems that do not take a final suffix; the other two are the Present Continuous and the Infinitive. Frequently the Immediate stem looks like a shortened form of the Present Continuous stem, as in (39b), or differs from that stem only in the tone and/or the final vowel, as in (39a) and (39c).

Comparison of immediate and present continuous stems

(39a) ᎦᏬᏂᎭ gawoòniíha 'he talked'
ᎦᏬᏂᎭ gawóoniha 'he is talking'

(39b) ᎠᏗᏔ adiíta 'he drank it'
ᎠᏗᏔᏍᎦ adiitásga 'he is drinking it'

(39c) ᎦᏅᎩ ganvv̀gi 'he fell'
ᎦᏅᎦ ganv́vga 'he is falling'

The Immediate stem takes two distinct forms of the distributive (DST) prefix. If a past or future meaning is intended, the form *dee-* is used as in (40a), while the **secondary form** *di-* (DST2) is used when the Immediate has a command meaning, as in (40b). In both examples the distributive indicates a nonsingular object.

(40a) ᎩᎳᏭ ᏕᎯᎪᎵᏯ
kilawu deehígooliíya
kila=wu dee-hi-gooliíya
just.now=DT DST-2A-examine:IMM
'You just examined them.'

(40b) ᏗᏍᏗᎪᎵᏯ
disdiigooliíya
di-sdii-gooliíya
DST2-2A.DL-examine:IMM
'Examine them!'

4.2.4. Completive (CMP) Verb Stem

The fourth stem, the Completive, indicates a past or future completed action. Like the Incompletive, it can be used with the experienced past, nonexperienced past, and progressive future suffixes. In (41a) it appears with the experienced past (EXP) final suffix to express that the action is completed and took place in the past. Its use with the nonexperienced past (NXP) suffix, as in (41b), indicates the same time and aspect frame, but with the added information that the speaker obtained this information from some other party. Finally, in (41c) the progressive future (PFT) suffix expresses that the action will be completed at some time in the future.

The Completive stem of -wóoniha 'talk' with three final suffixes

(41a) ᎤᏂᏬᏂᏒᎢ
uùniiwóonisvv́ʔi
uunii-wóonis-vv́ʔi
3B.NS-talk:CMP-EXP
'They talked.'

(41b) ᎤᏂᏬᏂᏎᎢ
uùniiwóoniséeʔi
uunii-wóonis-éeʔi
3B.NS-talk:CMP-NXP
'They talked (somebody told me so).'

(41c) ᎤᏂᏬᏂᏎᏍᏗ
uùniiwóoniséesdi
uunii-wóonis-éesdi

3B.NS-talk:CMP-PFT
'They will have talked.'

It is important to remember that what is a Set A prefix in other stems shifts to a Set B prefix in the Completive past. For example, the verb 'drink' is a transitive Set A verb; its designation as Set A means that it takes the Set A prefix in the Present Continuous, Incompletive, and Immediate; however; in the Completive past and some Infinitive uses it undergoes prefix shift. These five forms are compared in (42).

Five stems of -adiitásga ('drink')

(42a) ᎭᏗᏔᏍᎦ
hadiitásga
hi-adiitásga
2A-drink:PRC
'You are drinking it.'

(42b) ᎭᏗᏔᏍᎪᎢ
hadiítasgóoʔi
hi-adiitasg-óoʔi
2A-drink:INC-HAB
'You drink it.'

(42c) ᎭᏗᏔ
hadiíta
hi-adiíta
2A-drink:IMM
'You (just) drank it.'

(42d) ᏣᏗᏔᎥᎢ
ja-adiitah-vv́ʔi
ja-adiitah-vv́ʔi
2B-drink:CMP-EXP
'You drank it.'

(42e) ᏣᏗᏔᏍᏗ ᏣᏚᎵ
jadiitasdi jaduuli
ja-adiitasdi ja-aduuli
2B-drink:INF 2B-want:PRC
'You want to drink it.'

When it is used with both the **completive future** prefix *da-* and suffix *-i* (both known by the abbreviation CMF), the Completive stem indicates that something will occur. An example is shown in (43).

(43) ᏓᏣᎪᏂᏲᏥ
dajagoohniíyóòji
da-ja-goohniíyóòj-i
CMF-2B-be.late:CMP-CMF
'You'll be late.' (Feeling 1975a:165)

The combination of the Completive stem and the **future command** suffix *-vvʔi* creates a command, as shown in (44).

(44)	ᎠᏕᎳᏧᏢᎢ	ᎢᏁᏒᎢ
	adeélajuhlv́v́ʔi	iìneesvvʔi
	adeélajuhlv́v́ʔi	iinii-ees-vvʔi
	California	1A.DL-go:CMP-FCM
	'Let's go to California.'	

4.2.5. Infinitive (INF) Verb Stem

The Infinitive has many different uses; for most of these functions it appears with another verb rather than alone. One of the most common uses of this stem is the **Infinitive complement** function: to serve as an object to another verb. As with the Completive past, Set A verbs appear with Set B prefixes for this function. This use is exemplified below in (45). This type of Infinitive has a less common **long form** that may appear when the Infinitive is at the end of the sentence, as in (45c). The short form of the Infinitive ends in [*di*], while the long form ends in [*díiʔi*].

(45a)	ᎤᏍᏚᎢᏍᏗ	ᎤᏚᎵ	ᎧᏁᏌᎢ
	uùsduʔiisdi	uùduuli	kaneèsáʔi
	uu-sduʔiisdi	uu-aduuli	kaneèsáʔi
	3B-open:INF	3B-want:PRC	box
	'He wants to open the box.'		

(45b)	ᏧᏃᎩᏍᏗ	ᎤᎸᏉᏗ
	juuhnoogiìsdi	uùlv́v́kwdi
	di-uu-hnoogiìsdi	uu-lv́v́kwdi
	DST2-3B-sing:INF	3B-like:PRC
	'He likes to sing.'	

(45c)	ᎠᏁᎵᏗ	ᎤᏓᎨᏒ	ᎤᏲᎱᏎᏗᎢ
	aànehldi	uudagesv	uuyoohuúsehdííʔi
	a-anehldi	uudagesv	uu-yoohuúsehdííʔi
	3A-try:PRC	weight	3B-lose:INF

'He is trying to lose weight.'

The **adjectival Infinitive** describes a function, purpose, or other quality of a noun. When the prefix for this function is third person, a Set A verb uses a Set A prefix. This Infinitive can complement a subject in a verbless sentence, as in (46a), as well as modify a noun as an **attributive adjective,** as in (46b). These functions are further described in chapter 11. As shown in (46c), these Infinitives can appear in the long form.

(46a)	ᏥᏳᎪᏗ	ᏗᏍᏗᏗᏍᏗ	ᏧᏯᏖᎾ
	jiiyúúkdi	diisdiidiisdi	juuyahtééna
	jiiyúúkdi	di-a-sdiidiisdi	juuyahtééna
	straight	DST2-3A-lay.down(long):INF	board

'You must put the boards down straight.'
('The boards are to be put down straight.')

(46b)	ᎤᏲᏢ	ᏎᎵ	ᎣᏍᏓ	ᏗᎪᏪᎵ	ᎠᎪᎵᏰᏗ
	uuyóóhlv	seéli	óósda	digoohweèli	agooliíyéèdi
	uu-yóóhlv	seéli	a-óósda	digoohweèli	a-gooliíyéèdi
	3B-poor	Sarah	3A-good	book	3A-read:INF

'*Poor Sarah* is a good book to read.'

(46c)	ᎬᎾ	ᎨᏯᏔᎯ	ᏍᏓᏱ	ᎦᏂᏴᏗᎢ
	gv́v́na	gééhyatahi	sdááyi	ganihydííʔi
	gv́v́na	ga-ééhyatahi	sdááyi	ga-nihydííʔi
	turkey	3A wild	hard	3A-catch:INF

'A wild turkey is hard to catch.'

The **adverbial Infinitive** is used with the meaning 'in order to'. This construction is described in chapter 11, and an example is shown in (47). Note that the pronominal prefix on 'earn' undergoes **/gw/ reduction;** this phenomenon is described in chapter 8.

(47)	ᎠᏕᎳ	ᎠᏩᏓᏠᎯᏍᏗ	ᏓᎩᎸᏩᏍᏓᏁ
	<u>adeéla</u>	<u>awadadlohísdi</u>	daàgilv́v́hwsdaane
	adeéla	agi-adadlohísdi	dee-agi-lv́v́hwsdaane

money 1B-earn:INF DST-1B-work:PRC
'I'm working to earn money.'

Another use of the Infinitive is to express obligation or ability. This function is accompanied by a **modal tone** change, indicated by the abbreviation \MOD after the stem. Three examples are shown in (48).

(48a)	Ꮎ	ᎠᏓᏍᏓᏯᏙᏗ	ᏧᎯᎶᏍᏗ
	na	adáásdahydohdi	juuhiilóósdi
	na	adáásdahydohdi	ja-uuhiiloòsdi
	the	pot	2B-wash:INF\MOD

'You have to wash that pot.'

(48b)	ᎤᎯᎸᏍᏗ	ᏄᎵᏍᏔᏅ	ᏗᏂᏲᏟ	ᎤᎾᏦᏙᏗ
	uuhiilv́v́sdi	nuùlstanv	diiniiyóóhli	úúnajododi
	uu-hiilvvsdi	ni-uu-alstan-v	di-anii-yóóhli	úúnajododi
	3B-drive:INF\MOD	NI-3B-occur:CMP-EXP	DST2-3A.NS-child	bus

'He had to drive the children's school bus.'

(48c)	ᎦᎵᏦᏕ	ᎦᎶᏁᏙᏗ	ᎠᎩᏒᎲᏍᏗ
	gahljoóde	galóónedohdi	áksvhvsdi
	gahljoóde	ga-loonedohdi	agi-svhvsdi
	house	3A-paint:INF\INS	1B-use.up:INF\MOD

'I have to use up the house paint.'

Finally, the Infinitive is also used to create certain nouns. These nouns most commonly appear with a third person prefix. Noun **derivation** is described in chapter 12; three examples are shown in (49). In (49a) the derivation undergoes an **instrumental tone** (\INS) change to create an **instrumental noun** used for performing the action of the verb. The last two examples are **place nouns** and indicate where an activity occurs. As seen in (49c), these place nouns can appear in the optional long form. An instrumental noun is also shown above in (48c).

(49a) ᎦᏬᏂᎯᏍᏗ
gawooníìhisdi
ga-wooniihisdi
3A-speak:INF\INS
'language'

(49b) ᏧᏂᏒᏍᏗ
juuniisvvsdi

di-uunii-svvsdi
DST2-3B.NS-go.to.bed:INF
'hotel'

(49c) ᏧᏂᏆᎾᏲᏍᏗᎢ
juuniikwanayosdííʔi
di-uunii-kwanayosdííʔi
DST2-3B.NS-play.cards:INF
'casino'

4.3. Final Suffixes

The Incompletive and Completive stems can take a number of final suffixes. These suffixes, in combination with the stems, provide information about the time of the action (tense) as well as whether or not the action has been completed (aspect).

4.3.1. Habitual (HAB) Final Suffix

The habitual suffix attaches to the Incompletive stem; these two elements combine to convey an action or event that occurs habitually in the general present. The **final vowel** of the suffix frequently is dropped in fast speech. Two examples are shown in (50).

(50a) ᎠᏕᏝᏆᏍᎪ
aàdehlgwaasgo
a-adehlgwaasg-o
3A-learn:INC-HAB
'He learns.'

(50b)	ᏕᏠᎬᎢ	ᏓᏩᏕᏙᏍᎪᎢ
	deehlgv̋v̋ʔi	daàwaktoosgóoʔi
	dee-hlgv̋v̋ʔi	dee-agi-agahtoosg-óoʔi
	DST-tree	DST-1B-look.at:INC-HAB
	'I look at the trees.'	

The combination of the Incompletive and habitual can also express a general statement; an example is the verb 'die' in (51).

(51)	ᎠᏓᏅᏙ	ᏳᎴᏫᏍᏔᎾ	ᎠᏲᎱᏍᎪ	ᏴᏫ
	adahndo	yuuléého̱wistana	aàyoohuusgo	yvvw

a-adahndo yi-uu-aleehwistan-a a-yoohuusg-o yvvwi
3A-heart IRR-3B-stop(I):CMP-CVB 3A-die(human):INC-HAB human
'When the heart stops, a person dies.' (Feeling 1975a:5)

Note that English verbs conveying states have a less precise time frame. This is not the case in Cherokee, as seen in (52). In this example this state is occurring only in the moment of speaking.

(52) ᎠᎵᎯᎵᎦ
aàliheélîiga
a-aliheélîiga
3A-be.happy:PRC
'He's happy.'

4.3.2. Experienced Past (EXP) Final Suffix

The experienced past indicates that the speaker has firsthand knowledge of an event that took place in the past. It attaches to the Completive and Incompletive stems, as shown in (53). As with the habitual, this suffix more commonly appears in the short form seen in (53b).

(53a) ᎬᏃᏌᏍᎬᎢ
gvvnoosasgvv́ʔi
ji-vvnoosasg-vv́ʔi
1A-sweep:INC-EXP
'I was sweeping.'

(53b) ᎤᎦᏙᏍᏓᏅ
uùktoósdanv
uu-agahtoósdan-v
3B-look.at:CMP-EXP
'He looked at it.'

This suffix is also used for events that the speaker may not have personally witnessed but knows for certain took place. Two examples are shown in (54). It should be noted that longer examples such as (54b) are broken into two or more sets of lines, with the translation given at the end of the final set.

(54a) ᏏᏉᏯ ᎤᏬᏢᏅ ᏣᎳᎩ ᏱᏗᎦᏪᏍᏗ
sigwooya uùwotlvvvhnv jalagi yidigawéésdi
sigwooya uu-otlvvvhn-v jalagi yi-di-ga-weesdi

Sequoyah 3B-make:CMP-EXP Cherokee NI2-DST2-3A-say:INF\INS
'Sequoyah invented the Cherokee syllabary.'

(54b) ᎤᏂᏴᏙᏝ ᎠᎴ ᎤᏂᎦᎾᏩ
uuniihyv́v́dla ale uuniigáanawa
uunii-hyv́v́dla ale uunii-gáanawa
3B.NS-north and 3B.NS-south

ᏚᎾᏟᏲ ᏓᏂᏩ
duùnahlilv daahnawa
dee-uunii-ahlil-v daahnawa
DST-3B.NS-fight:CMP-EXP war
'The North and South fought the Civil War.'

4.3.3. Nonexperienced Past (NXP) Final Suffix

The nonexperienced past suffix (NXP) *-eeʔi* indicates an action in the past that the speaker has not witnessed, either because the speaker was physically absent or because the event has not actually taken place. (55a) is an example of the experienced past; the first person pronominal prefix and the lack of negation (the event actually did take place) make this suffix necessary. The verb in (55b), however, could take either suffix; in this case the use of the nonexperienced past is an indication that the speaker was told about the event by someone else. It is more common to see this suffix in the short form shown in (55b).

(55a) ᎠᏆᎰᏑᎸᎢ
aàgwuuhiilóoʔv
ayi-uuhiilóoʔ-v
1B-wash(T):CMP-EXP
'I washed it.'

(55b) ᎤᏬᏑᎸᎡ
uùwuuhiilóoʔe
uu-uhiilóoʔ-e
3B-wash(T):CMP-NXP
'He washed it.'

As shown in (56), the nonexperienced past suffix attaches to both the Incompletive and Completive stems.

Nonexperienced past suffix on Incompletive and Completive stems

(56a) ᎠᏂᏰᎨᎢ
aàniiyéegéeʔi
anii-yéeg-éeʔi
3A.NS-wake(I):INC-NXP
'They were waking up.'

(56b) ᎤᏂᏰᏤᎢ
uùniiyéejéeʔi
uunii-yéej-éeʔi
3B.NS-wake(I):CMP-NXP
'They woke up.'

Because this final suffix implies that the speaker was not present for the event described, it is frequently used to ask a question about a past event, as seen in (57).

(57a)

ᎯᎳᏳ	ᏣᎷᏤ
hilayu	jáʔluhje
hilayu	ja-ʔluhj-e
when	2B-arrive:CMP-NXP

'When did you arrive?'

(57b)

ᎭᏢ	ᏣᎩᏎ	Ꮎ	ᎤᎵᏑᏫᏓ	ᎠᏓᏴᎳᏛᏍᎩ
haadlv	jagíise	na	uulsúúhwida	adayv́v́latvsgi
haadlv	ja-gíis-e	na	uu-alsúúhwida	adayv́v́latvsgi
where	2B-get:CMP-NXP	the	3B-color	television

'Where did you get the color television?'

4.3.4. Progressive Future (PFT) Final Suffix

The suffix *-éesdi* indicates an event that will take place in the future; it attaches to the Completive and Incompletive stems. Two examples are shown in (58). In (58b) the progressive future attaches to a Completive stem.

(58a) ᏚᏂᏲᏏᏍᎨᏍᏗ
duùniiyóosisgéesdi
dee-uunii-yóosisg-éesdi
DST-3B.NS-be.hungry:INC-PFT
'They will be hungry.'

(58b) RᏓᏑᏰᏎᏍᏗ
eèdasuuyéeséesdi
eedii-asuuyées-éesdi
1A.PL.AN-choose:CMP-PFT
'We will have chosen him.'

This suffix is also used for forming commands. Two examples are shown in (59).

(59a) ᏣᏛᏓᏍᏕᏍᏗ Track 29
tstvdasdéesdi
ja-htvdasd-éesdi
2B-listen:INC-PFT
'Listen!'

(59b) ᏣᏓᎦᏎᏍᏕᏍᏗ
jadaksesdéesdi
ja-adaad-agasesd-éesdi
2B-RFL-be.careful:INC-PFT
'Take care of yourself!'

4.3.5. Future Command (FCM) Final Suffix

This suffix attaches to the Completive stem and generally expresses a command for an action that will occur further in the future than an action with the Immediate command or progressive future suffix command. This suffix also expresses a command that is more polite than a command using the Immediate stem. Two examples are shown in (60).

(60a) ᎢᎮᏙᎸᎢ
iihéedóòlvvʔi
ii-hi-eédóòl-vvʔi
ITR-2A-be.at-FCM
'You come again.'

(60b) ᏙᎾᏓᎪᎲᎢ Track 30
doonadaagoohvvʔi
dee-ii-iinii-adaad-gooh-vvʔi
DST-ITR-1A.DL-RFL-see:CMP-FCM
'Let's see each other again!'

This suffix is distinct from the experienced past suffix in that it always has a long vowel with a **low tone;** moreover, this suffix more frequently appears in its **full form** than does the experienced past suffix.

4.3.6. Completive Future (CMF) Final Suffix

The completive future suffix is used with either the completive future prefix, as in (61a), or the ***ni-* prefix** (not very common), as in (61b), to express a future time frame. In both cases the Completive stem of the verb is used.

(61a) ᏓᎩᏂᏯᎵ
daginiihyali
da-ginii-hyal-i
CMF-1B.DL-search.for:CMP-CMF
'You and I will search for it.'

(61b) Ꮭ Ꮣ ᏂᎦᏛᏁᎵ
tlale nigadv́vneeli
tla=le ni-ji-adv́vneel-i
NEG=OS NI-1A-do:CMP-CMF
'I'm not going to do it.'

If another suffix follows *-i*, an /s/ appears. As seen in (62), this construction can be used to express a future event in a past tense framework.

(62) ᏓᎦᏬᏂᏍᏋᎢ
dagawóòniisíisvv́ʔi
da-ga-wóoniis-i-vv́ʔi
CMF-3A-speak:CMP-CMF-EXP
'He was going to speak.'

4.4. Classificatory Verbs

The **classificatory verbs** have distinctive forms depending on the physical properties of the object. Cherokee has five categories of classificatory verbs indicating solid, liquid, living, long, and flexible items. The five categories, with example objects, are illustrated in (63) with the verb 'have'.

The five 'have' verbs

(63a) ᎦᎶᏇ ᎠᏋᏯ
galoògwe aàgwvv́ya
galoògwe agi-vv́ya
gun 1B-have(long):PRC
'I have a gun.'

(63b) ᏐᏈᎵ ᎠᎩᎧᎭ
soógwíli aàgikáha
soógwíli agi-káha
horse 1B-have(living):PRC
'I have a horse.'

(63c) ᎤᎦᎹ ᎠᎩᏁᎭ
uúgáma aàginéha
uúgáma agi-néha
soup 1B-have(liquid):PRC
'I have soup.'

(63d) ᎠᏑᎶ ᎠᎩᎾᎠ
aàsuulo aàginá?a
aàsuulo agi-ná?a
pants 1B-have(flexible):PRC
'I have pants.'

(63e) ᎧᎵᏎᏥ ᎠᎩᎭ
kalseéji aàgiha
kalseéji agi-ha
candy 1B-have(solid):PRC
'I have candy.'

The solid category is also the default category; if an object doesn't fit anywhere else, it goes in this category. For example, as seen in (64), a question where the speaker does not know the physical properties of the object would use the solid-specification verb.

(64) ᎦᏙ ᎤᏍᏗ ᎤᎭ Track 31
gado uúsdi uúha
gado uúsdi uu-ha
what thing 3B-have(solid):PRC
'What does he have?'

By comparing the set in (65) with the set above in (64) it becomes apparent that an element */ka/* is part of the verbs with living objects, while an element */neh/* is part of the verbs with liquid objects.

The classificatory verbs (with stems) of 'give' (Feeling 1975a)

(65) 'give (long)'
-déeha/-déeh-/-diìsi/-déel-/-déhdi
'give (living)'
-akaaneha/-akaaneeh-/-akaàsi/-akaaneel-/-akaanéhdi
'give (liquid)'
-neehneha/-nehneéh-/-neehvvsi/-neehneél-/-neehnéhdi
'give (flexible)'
-nv́vneha/-nv́vneeh-/-nvv̀si/-nv́vneel-/-nvvhéhdi
'give (solid)'
-hneha/-hneéh-/-hvsi/-hneél-/-hnéhdi

Cherokee has about forty classificatory verbs. Many of them have to do with handling, manipulating, or carrying something. Because the exact element that specifies the object's features is often no longer distinguishable, the verbs must simply be learned as separate vocabulary items. Occasionally a classification is extended to include objects that do not possess the defining property of that category. The word 'email' in (66) is treated as flexible because the compound is based on 'letter' (an object that is typically flexible).

(66)	ᎠᎾᎦᎵᏍᎩ	ᎪᏇᎵ	ᏫᏥᏅᎥᏍᎦ
	anaàgaliísgi	goohweeli	wijínv́ʔvsga
	a-naàgaliísg-i	goohweeli	wi-ji-nv́ʔvsga
	3A-lightning:INC-AGT	letter	TRN-1A-send(flexible):PRC
	'I am sending an email.'		

4.5. Existence and Location Verbs

As in many languages, the verb 'be' is irregular in Cherokee. Often it is not needed at all in simple phrases that link a person or thing with a property or characteristic. Such a meaning is conveyed by attaching the appropriate pronominal prefix to an adjective or noun. (67) shows three examples of this type of construction with nouns; (68) shows two examples with adjectives.

Nouns with pronominal prefixes

(67a) ᎯᏣᎳᎩ
hijalagi
hi-jalagi
2A-Cherokee
'You are Cherokee.'

(67b) ᏥᎦᎾᎦᏘ
jigáʔnakti
ji-gáʔnakti
1A-doctor
'I am a doctor.'

(67c) ᏔᎵᏁ ᎣᏍᏓᏓᏝᏅᏝ ᎼᏏ
taliine oosdadaatlahnv́v́tl moosi
talii-ine oosdii-adaad-tlahnv́v́tla moosi
two-ORD 1A.DL.EX-RFL-brother Mose
'Mose is my cousin.'

Adjectives with pronominal prefixes

(68a) ᎢᎦᏔᎾ
íígatana
iigii-ắtana
1B.PL-big
'All of us are big.'

(68b) ᏥᎦᏳᎳ ᎠᎴ ᎠᏩᎵᏦᎯᏓ
jigayúúl ale awaljóóhida
ji-gayúúla ale agi-aljóóhida
1A-old and 1B-fat
'I am old and fat.'

Many expressions in English that consist of the verb 'be' and an adjective are verbs in Cherokee. Adjectives and other modifiers are described in detail in chapter 7.

These examples are verbless sentences. Because verbs are the only part of speech that can fully indicate tense and aspect, verbless sentences are assumed to refer to a present time frame. In order to indicate other tense and aspect information it is necessary to use a **helping verb** to carry this information. In (69a) the adjective refers to the general present, while in (69b) the verb 'be' appears to express the past.

(69a)	ᎣᏍᏓ	óósda	'good', 'it is good'
(69b)	ᎣᏍᏓ ᎨᏒᎢ	óósda geèsvv́ʔi	'it was good'

The root of the verb 'be' is *-g-*, which is only used in the third person. This is the only verb that appears without a pronominal prefix (it is possible that the /g/ that always appears is a **frozen prefix**). Its stems are listed in (70).

The forms of 'be'

(70)	Present continuous	-gi
	Incompletive	-geès-
	Immediate	-ga
	Completive	-geèh-

(71) shows two examples of the Incompletive stem of 'be' with the progressive future suffix; (72) shows two examples of this stem with the experienced past suffix.

(71a)	ᎣᏍᏓ ᎨᏎᏍᏗ	óósda geèséesdi	'it will be good'
(71b)	ᎠᏧᏣ ᎨᏎᏍᏗ	achúúja geèséesdi	'it will be a boy'
(72a)	ᎣᏍᏓ ᎨᏒᎢ	óósda geèsvv́ʔi	'it was good'
(72b)	ᎠᏧᏣ ᎨᏒᎢ	achúúja geèsvv́ʔi	'it was a boy'

An example of this verb in the Incompletive stem is provided in (73).

(73)	ᎨᏌᎵᏂ	ᎠᏟᏍᏗ	ᎤᏏᏩ	ᎨᏒᎢ
	geesaálíini	adliìsdi	úúsihwa	geèsvv́ʔi
	geesaálíini	adliìsdi	uu-x̋x̋sihwa	geès-vv́ʔi
	gas	tank	3B-empty	be:INC-EXP
	'The gas tank was empty.'			

Because verbless sentences are understood as being in the present, the Present Continuous form of 'be' is not necessary in many sentences. It is frequently used, however, to make statements more emphatic. Three examples are shown in (74).

(74a)	ᎦᏰᏉᏂ	ᏅᎩᏁ	
	gayeegwoóni	nvhgiine	
	gayeegwoóni	nvhgi-iine	
	July	four-ORD	
	ᎠᎹᏰᏟ	ᎤᏕᏘᏱᏍᎬ	ᎢᎩ
	amáyéehli	uudeetiyiísgv	iigi

ama+ayééhli uu-adeetiyiísgv ii-gi
water+center 3B-birthday ITR-be:PRC
'The Fourth of July is America's birthday.'

(74b) ᏓᎪᎲᏂᎢ ᎤᏍᏗᏊ ᎦᏚᎲ ᎢᎩ
dagoohvv́níiʔi uusdíigwu gaduuhv iigi
dagoohvv́níiʔi uu-asdíi=gwu gaduuhv ii-gi
Proctor 3B-small=DT town ITR-be:PRC
'Proctor is just a small town.'

(74c) ᏣᏥ ᎬᏂᏓ ᎠᏂᎩᏚᏩᎩ ᎤᎬᏫᏳᎯ ᎢᎩ
jaáji gvvhnida aniigiduuhwaagi uugvvwiyuuhi iigi
jaáji gvvhnida anii-giduuhwaagi uu-gvvwiyuuhi ii-gi
George Wickliffe 3A.NS-Keetoowah 3B-chief ITR-be:PRC
'George Wickliffe is chief of the Keetoowah.'

As stated above, it is possible to have a complete and correct Cherokee sentence with no verb whatsoever. Such verbless sentences are understood to describe a present event or a general state of affairs. Five more examples are shown in (75).

(75a) ᎯᎠᎾᏍ ᏚᏳᎪᏛᎢ Track 32
hiʔanas duuyuukdv́ʔi
hiʔa=na=s duuyuukdv́ʔi
this=FC=Q correct
'Is this correct?'

(75b) ᎦᏙᎤᏍᏗ ᎪᎯᎢᎦ
gadoʔúúsdi koohiʔiíga
gadoʔúúsdi koohiʔiíga
what today
'What day is today?'

(75c) ᎣᏳ ᎣᏍᏓ ᏗᏕᏠᏆᏍᏗᎢ Track 33
ooyu óósda diideehlgwaasdíiʔi
ooyu óósda di-a-adeehlgwaasdíiʔi
OU good DST2-3A-learn:INF
'OU is a good school.'

(75d) ᏌᎶᎵ ᎦᏙᎩ ᎤᏂᏳᏆᏗᏍᎩ ᏅᏬᏘ
saloóli gaàtohgi uuniihyúgwadiisgi nvv́wóòti
saloóli gaàtohgi uuniihyúgwadiisgi nvv́wóòti

squirrel tail toothache medicine
'Squirrel tail is toothache medicine.'

(75e) ᎠᎦᏓᏢᏓ ᎣᏍᏓ ᎠᏑᏴᏗ ᎧᏫᎢ
akdadlv́v́da óósda asuuyv́v́di kahwííʔi
akdadlv́v́da óósda a-asuuyvvdi kahwi-ʔi
cream good 3A-mix.in:INF\TOP coffee-LOC
'Cream is good to mix in your coffee.'

As shown in (76), the progressive future suffix is used with the Incompletive stem to form a 'be' command.

(76) ᎤᏔᎾᏯ ᏱᎦᏬᏂᎭ ᎡᏝᏪ ᎨᏎᏍᏗ
uutanaaya yigawooniíha eehlawe geèséesdi
uu-atanaaya yi-ga-wooniíha eehlawe geès-éesdi
3B-elder IRR-3A-talk:PRC\SUB quiet be:INC-PFT
'When an elder is talking, be quiet.'

There is no Infinitive stem of 'be'. What is often translated as 'be' is the Infinitive stem of the verb 'become'. An example of this verb is shown in (77).

(77) ᏐᏁᎵᏁᎢᏍ ᏱᏣᎵᏍᏙᏗ ᏣᏚᎵᎭ
sohnelinééʔis yijalsdohdi jaduuliha
sohnela-iinééʔi=s yi-ja-alisdohdi ja-aduuliha
nine-ORD=Q IRR-2B-become:INF 2B-want:PRC
'Do you want to be the ninth?' (Feeling 1975a:154)

Many location expressions in English that use the verb 'be' take a verb with a more specific meaning in Cherokee. In (78a) the cat 'sits' on the table, while in (78b) the book 'lies' on the table. In (78c) and (78d) the object is the same, but the difference is in elevation.

(78a) ᎦᏍᎩᎸ ᎤᏬᏝ ᏪᏌ
gaasgilv uùwoohla weésa
gaasgilo-v uu-oohla weésa
table-LOC 3B-be.sitting:PRC cat
'The cat is on the table.'

(78b) ᏗᎪᏪᎳ ᎦᏍᎩᎸ ᏕᎦᎾ
digoohweela gaasgilv deegána
digoohweela gaasgilo-v dee-ga-na
book table-LOC DST-3A-be.lying:PRC
'The book is on the table.'

(78c) ᏍᏆᏞᏍᏗ ᎠᎭ ᎠᏰᏍᏓᎥ
sgwaàhléésdi aàha aayeésdaʔv
sgwaàhléésdi a-ha aayeésdaʔv
ball 3A-be.on.ground:PRC carpet
'The ball is on the carpet.' (Koops 2008b:2)

(78d) ᏍᏆᏞᏍᏗ ᎠᏝᎭ ᎦᏍᎩᎸ
sgwaàhléésdi aàhlaha gaasgilv
sgwaàhléésdi a-hlaha gaasgilo-v
ball 3A-be.elevated:PRC table-LOC
'The ball is on the table.' (Koops 2008b:2)

General location is often expressed using a distinct verb meaning 'be at', as in (79).

(79) ᎭᏢ ᎠᏁᏙ
haadlv aàneèdo
haadlv anii-eèdóoh-o
where 3A.NS-be.at:INC-HAB
'Where are they?'

The verb *-yaʔa* indicates being in an enclosed space large enough to walk around in, while *-jaʔa* indicates being in a more constricted space. These two verbs are exemplified in (80).

(80a) Ꮩ ᎤᏍᏗ ᎧᏅᏑᎸ ᎠᏯᎢ
do úúsd kanvsulv aàyáʔi
do úúsdi kanvsulv a-yáʔi
what thing room 3A-be.in:PRC
'What room is he in?'

(80b) ᏪᏌ ᎧᏁᏌᎢ ᎤᏣᎠ
weésa kaneèsáʔi uùjáʔa
weésa kaneèsáʔi uu-ajáʔa
cat box 3B-be.inside:PRC
'The cat is inside the box.' (Feeling 1975a:170)

4.6. Verb Functions

4.6.1. Describing Past Events

Past events are described with the Incompletive, Immediate, or Completive stems. The Incompletive is used for ongoing events in the past, as in (81a), while the Completive is used for completed actions in the past, as in (81b). The Immediate, as shown in (81c), indicates that an event has just occurred.

(81a) ᏕᎧᏃᎩᏍᏛᎢ
deekánoogíisgvv̂ʔi
dee-ga-hnoogíisg-vv̂ʔi
DST-3A-sing:INC-EXP
'He was singing.'

(81b) ᏚᏃᎩᏒᎢ
duùhnoogíisvv̂ʔi
dee-uu-hnoogíis-vv̂ʔi
DST-3B-sing:CMP-EXP
'He sang.'

(81c) ᏕᎧᏃᎩ
deekanóogi
dee-ga-hnóogi
DST-3A-sing:IMM
'He sang (just now).'

Both the Completive and Incompletive can use the nonexperienced past suffix to indicate that the past event was not personally witnessed, as in (82a). This suffix is also found with negated forms, as in (82c), and questions, as in (82b).

(82a)

ᎠᎴ	ᎦᏃᎪ	ᎤᏒᏂᎴᎢ
ale	gahngo	uùsvvnílé̂ʔi
ale	ga-hngo	uu-asvvníl-é̂ʔi
and	3A-tongue	3B-touch:CMP-NXP

'. . . and he touched his tongue.' (*Cherokee New Testament,* Mark 7:33)

(82b)

ᎦᏙ	ᎤᏍᏗ	ᏨᏂᎴᎢ
gado	úúsdi	jvvhnílé̂ʔi
gado	úúsdi	ja-vvhníl-é̂ʔi
what	thing	2B-hit:CMP-NXP

'What did you hit?'

(82c) Ꮭ ᏯᏉᏢᏤᎢ
tla yaàgwohljéeʔi
tla yi-agi-olihj-éʔi
NEG IRR-1B-understand:CMP-NXP
'I didn't understand.'

4.6.2. Describing Present Events

The Present Continuous stem describes events that are happening at that moment. Two examples are shown in (83); in (83b) the action that is happening is commented on by the verb 'say', which is also in the Present Continuous.

(83a) ᎦᏅᏓᏗᎠ
ganvv̀dadíʔa
ji-anvhdadíʔa
1A-remember:PRC
'I am remembering it.'

(83b) ᏧᏴᏢ ᎦᏯᎴᏂ ᎫᏘᎭ ᎠᎾᏗᎭ
juúhyv́vdlv́ gayaléeni guutiiha aànadiiha
juúhyv́vdlv́ gayaléeni ga-uutiiha anii-adiiha
North Carolina 3A-snow:PRC 3A.NS-say:PRC
'They are saying it's snowing in North Carolina.'

To describe habitual events in the general present or events that are generally true, the Incompletive stem is used with the habitual suffix *-ooʔi*. Two examples are shown in (84).

(84a) ᏧᏅᎩᎶᏍᏗ ᎢᎦ ᏕᎦᎩᎶᏍᎪᎢ
juuhngiilóóɔdi iiga déckgiilóoɜgóoʔi
juuhngiilóósdi iiga dee-ga-vhgiilóosg-óoʔi
Friday day DST-3A-wash(flexible):INC-HAB
'She does her laundry on Fridays.' (Feeling 1975a:137)

(84b) ᏆᎻᏏ ᎠᎩᏩᏍᎪ ᎤᏅᏗ
gwaámsi aàkiwasgo uunvv́d
gwaámsi agi-hwasg-o uunvv́di
Braum's 1B-buy:INC-HAB milk
'I buy milk at Braum's.'

For verbs whose meaning describes an ongoing state rather than an action, either the Incompletive, as in (85a), or the Present Continuous, as in (85b), may be used.

(85a) ᏍᏘᏍᏓ ᎢᎨᏐ ᏲᏓᏟ ᏓᏄᎪᎢ
sgwíísda iigeeso yoodaàtli daahnúugóóʔi
sgwíísda ii-gees-o yoodaàtli daahnúuga-ʔi
lot ITR-be:INC-HAB mistletoe Vian
'There's lots of mistletoe in Vian.'

(85b) ᏙᏧᏩ ᏚᏙᎠ
toòjuúhwa duùdooʔa
toòjuúhwa dee-uu-adooʔa
redbird DST-3B-be.named:PRC

ᏌᏊ ᎦᏘᏲ ᎤᎾᎵᏍᎩᏍᏗ
saàgwu gaátíiyo uunalsgiìsdi
saàgwu gaátíiyo uunii-alisgiìsdi
one stompground 3B.NS-dance:INF
'Redbird is the name of one stomp ground.'

4.6.3. Describing Future Events

The Completive stem, used with the completive future prefix *da-* and the completive future suffix *-i,* creates the meaning 'going to' or 'will'. Two examples are shown in (86).

(86a) ᏣᎳᎩ ᎤᏴᏢ ᎦᏯᎴᏂ ᎪᎨᏱ ᏫᏓᎨᏙᎵ
jalagi uúhyv́vdlv́ gayaleeni googééyi widageédóòli
jalagi uúhyv́vdlv́ gayaleeni googééyi wi-da-ji-eédóòl-i
Cherokee North Carolina spring TRN-CMF-1A-be.at:CMP-CMF
'I'm going to Cherokee, North Carolina, in the spring.'

(86b) ᏛᎦᏂᏍ ᎮᎵᎠ
dvvgaahnanis heelíʔa
da-a-gaahnan-i=s hi-eelíʔa
CMF-3A-rain:CMP-CMF=Q 2A-think:PRC
'Do you think it will rain?'

The combination of the Incompletive stem with the progressive future suffix *-éesdi* creates the meaning 'will be VERBing'. Two examples are shown in (87).

(87a) ᏏᏅᏓ ᎢᏴᏓᎵ ᏗᎦᏚᎴᏂ ᎦᏈᏱᏍᎨᏍᏗ
siinv́v́da iyv́vdááli diiktuuléeni gagwiyiísgéesdi
siinv́v́da iyv́vdááli diiktuuléeni ji-akwiyiísg-éesdi
every.month often car 1A-pay:INC-PFT
'I will be paying for the car every month.'

(87b) ᏔᎵᏁ ᎢᎦ ᏙᎩᏂᏢᏫᏍᏓᏁᎮᏍᏗ
taliine iiga doòginiilvvhwisdaàneehéesdi
tali-iine iiga dee-ooginii-lvvhwisdaàneeh-éesdi
two-ORD day DST-1B.DL.EX-work:INC-PFT
'Tuesday we will be working.'

The combination of the Completive stem with the *-éesdi* suffix as shown in (88) is another way to create a future meaning for some speakers.

(88) ᎠᏂᏩᏘᎮᏍᏗ
aàniihwatiihéesdi
anii-hwatiih-éesdi
3A.NS-find:CMP-PFT
'They will find it.' (Scancarelli 2005:369)

The completive future prefix and suffix are used to create a future meaning in a past time frame. The suffix appears as [*is*] followed by a suffix indicating the past, as in (89).

(89) ᎦᎶᏇ ᎡᏂᏕᎵᏒᎢ
galogwe eeniidéeliisvv́ʔi
galogwe eenii-déel-i-vv́ʔi
gun 1A.DL.AN-give(long):CMP-CMF-EXP
'We were going to give him that gun.'

4.6.4. Describing Hypothetical Events

The **irrealis** prefix *yi-* attaches to any of the five stems to indicate potential or hypothetical events. In (90a) and (90b) the verb does not refer to a specific event that has occurred, while in (90c) the irrealis prefix is used to indicate what might have happened but did not.

(90a) ᎱᏓᎴᏒᎢ ᎠᏍᏆᏂᎪᏗᏍᎩ ᏯᎾᎦᎵᎭ
huudaléesvvʔi asgwangoodíisgi yanáágalíha
hi-uudalées-vvʔi a-sgwangoodiisg-i yi-a-naagalíha

2A-unplug:CMP-FCM 3A-store:INC-AGT IRR-3A-lightning:PRC\SUB
'Unplug the computer if there's lightning.'

(90b) ᏱᏚᏯᏪᏣ ᏱᎦᏅᎩᏊ
yiduuyawéėj yigánv́vgigwu
yi-dee-uu-yawéej-a yi-ga-nv́vgi=gwu
IRR-DST-3B-be.tired:CMP-CVB IRR-3A-fall:IMM=DT
'When he gets tired, he'll just fall.' (The Turtle and the Rabbit, line 56)

(90c) ᎣᏍᏓ ᏱᏓᏂᏃᎩᏍᎨ ᏯᏆᎵᏍᎩᏎ
óósda yidaniihnoogiisgé yagwalsgíise
óósda yi-dee-anii-hnoogiisg-e yi-agi-alsgíis-e
good IRR-DST-3A.NS-sing:INC-NXP\SUB IRR-1B-dance:CMP-NXP
'If they had sung well, I would have danced.'

In (90c) both verbs have the irrealis prefix, but the verb in the **subordinate clause** receives a special tone that marks it as a **subordinate verb.** These hypothetical event constructions are discussed in greater detail in chapter 11.

4.6.5. Asking Questions

'Yes/no' questions are formed by adding a suffix-like element known as a **postfix** to the verb. Postfixes are distinguished from final suffixes by their ability to attach to any word; instead of a **hyphen** they are separated from their base by an **equals sign.** The most common question postfix is =*s*; two examples are shown in (91).

(91a) ᎦᎵᏦᏕ ᏣᏩᏎᏍ
gahljoóde jahwases
gahljoóde ja-hwas-e=s
house 2B-buy:CMP-NXP=Q
'Did you buy the house?'

(91b) ᎯᎦᏘᏰᏍ
hiigaàtiíyes
hii-gahtiíy-e=s
2A.AN-wait:CMP-NXP=Q
'Did you wait for her?'

The **conducive question** (CQ) postfix in (92) is used when a 'yes' answer is expected.

(92) ᏩᎶᏏᏧ ᏘᏩᏛᎯ
waloósíju tiihwahtvv́hi
waloósi=ju da-hii-hwahtvv́h-i
frog=CQ CMF-2A.AN-find:CMP-CMF
'Are you going to find the frog?'

4.6.6. Expressing Ability

The most common way to express ability is by using the Immediate form of the verb with the irrealis prefix *yi-*. An example is shown in (93). This construction is often accompanied by the word *eelíígwu* 'it is possible'.

(94) ᎡᎵᏊᏍ ᏱᏍᏕᎳ
eelíígwus hyiisdeela
eelíígwu=s yi-hii-sdeela
possible=Q IRR-2A.AN-help:IMM
'Can you help him?'

A less common means of expressing ability is with the Infinitive with a **high-fall tone** (indicated by \MOD) and the *gaa-* prefix. This construction is further discussed in chapter 10; an example is shown in (94).

(94) ᎬᏩᎾᏓᏬᏍᏗ ᏱᎩ ᏯᏓᏬᏣ
gvvwandawóósdi yígi hyadawoója
gaa-uunii-adaa-woosdi yi-gi yi-hi-adaa-awoója
GA-3B.NS-MDL-bathe(T):INF\MOD IRR-be\SUB IRR-2A-MDL-bathe(T):IMM
'If they can swim, so can you!'

The verb *-gahtaha* 'know how to' is used to express the ability to do something based on knowledge or training, as in (95).

(95) ᏗᎦᏓᏲᏍᏗ ᏧᎾᏁᎶᏗ ᎠᏂᎦᏔᎭ
digadayoosdi juunaneéhldi aàniiktaha
di-gadayoosdi di-uunii-aneéhldi anii-gahtaha
DST2-marble DST2-3B.NS-play:INF 3A.NS-know.how:PRC
'They know how to play marbles.'

The irrealis prefix *yi-* is used before the *gaa-* prefix on an Immediate stem to express inability, as in (96a). *Gaa-* also appears on the Infinitive, as in (96b); in this example a helping verb appears in order to indicate the lack of ability.

(96a) Ꮭ ᏱᎦᎦᏊᏯ
hla yigaagagwiiya
hla yi-gaa-ji-akwiiya
NEG IRR-GA-1A-pay:IMM
'I can't pay it.'

(96b) ᏚᏳᎪᏛ ᎬᎩᏃᎮᏗ ᏂᎨᏒᎾ
duuyuukdv gvkinoohehdi nigeesv́v́na
duuyuukdv ga-agi-hnoohehdi ni-gees-v́v́na
truth GA-1B-tell:INF NI-be:INC-NDV

ᏱᎩ ᎦᏥᏍᎪᏍᎪ
yigi gajiìsgóosgo
yi-gi ji-ajiìsgóosg-o
IRR-be:PRC 1A-lie:INC-HAB
'If I can't tell the truth, I lie.'

To express the inability to do something the verb 'fail' may also be used along with the Infinitive form of the verb, as in (97).

(97a) ᎤᏄᎸᎲᏍᎦ ᏭᏗᏅᏗ
uùnuulv́vhvsga wuudiínv́v̀d
uu-nuulv́vhvsga wi-uu-adiínv́v̀di
3B-fail:PRC TRN-3B-throw:INF
'She can't throw it in.'

(97b) ᎠᎩᏅᎸᎲᏍᎪ ᏣᎳᎩ ᎠᎩᏬᏂᎯᏍᏗᎢ 🔊 Track 34
aàginvv́lv́v̀hvsgo jalagi agiwooniíhísdííʔi
agi-nvv́lv́v̀hvsg-o jalagi agi-wooniíhísdííʔi
1B-fail:INC-HAB Cherokee 1B-speak:INF
'I can't speak Cherokee.'

4.6.7. Expressing Obligation

The **obligation Infinitive** is used with a highfall tone (indicated by \MOD) to express the need or obligation to perform an action. Three examples are shown in (98). In (98c) the tone appears on a short vowel and is a **shortened highfall tone.**

(98a) ᏗᏍᏛᏗᏰᏗ ᏗᏖᎵᏙ
disdvvdííyéèdi diiteliido
di-sdii-vvdiíyéèdi di-ateliido

DST2-2B.DL-wash:INF\MOD DST2-dish
'You two have to wash dishes.'

(98b) ᏧᏪᏥᎨ ᏗᎩᏩᏍᏗ
juwééjike díígihwasdi
di-uu-ééji=ke di-agi-hwasdi
DST2-3B-egg=OQ DST2-1B-buy:INF\MOD
'Do I need to buy eggs?'

(98c) ᎠᏆᏴᏗ ᎠᏚᏓᎸᏙ
ákwihydi aduudalvv̀do
a-kwihydi aduudalvv̀do
3A-pay:INF\MOD bond
'One has to pay a bond'

As seen above, the modal tone (MOD) change that expresses obligation appears on the rightmost long vowel of the Infinitive stem. For a few verbs this puts the tone on the pronominal prefix, as in (99a). For comparison, the **nominal clause** use of this same verb stem is given in (99b).

(99a) ᎤᎾᎵᏍᏓᏴᏗ
úúnalsdayhdi
uunii-ali-sdayhdi
3B.NS-MDL-provide.meal:INF\MOD
'They have to eat.'

(99b) ᎤᎾᎵᏍᏓᏴᏗ ᎤᎾᏚᎵ
uunalsdahydi uùnduuli
uunii-ali-sdahydi uunii-aduuli
3B.NS-MDL-provide.meal.INF 3B.NS-want.PRC
'They want to eat.'

A helping verb such as 'be' or 'become' is used to express obligation or necessity in the past or future, as in (100).

(100) ᏑᎾᎴᏛ ᏦᏪᎶᏗ ᎨᏎᏍᏗ
sunáaléédv joohweélóódi geèséesdi
sunáaléé=dv ja-oohweélóòdi geès-éesdi
tomorrow=EM 2B-work:INF\MOD be:INC-PFT
'You will have to write it tomorrow.'

The negated form of the verb 'be' appears as a helping verb with the obligation Infinitive to express the idea that one doesn't have to do something, as in (101).

(101) Ꮭ ᏗᏍᏛᏗᏰᏗ ᏱᎩ ᏗᏖᎵᏙ
tla disdvvdiíyéèdi yigi diiteliido
tla di-sdii-vvdiíyéèdi yi-gi di-ateliido
NEG DST2-2B.DL-wash:INF\MOD IRR-be:IMM DST2-dish
'You don't have to wash the dishes.'

4.6.8. Giving Commands

One of the ways to give commands is with the Immediate stem. Three examples are shown in (102). These commands can be first person and third person as well, as in (102b) and (102c).

(102a) ᎦᏘᏲ ᎤᎾᎵᏍᎩᏍᏗ ᎭᎵᏍᎩ
gaátíiyo uunalsgiìsdi halsgi
gaátíiyo uunii-alisgiìsdi hi-alsgi
stompground 3B.NS-dance:INF 2A-dance:IMM
'Dance at the stomp dance.'

(102b) ᏥᎪᎵᏯ
jigooliíya
ji-gooliíya
1A-look.at:IMM
'Let me look at it.'

(102c) ᏩᏂᏍᏆᏓ
waàniisgwada
wi-anii-sgwada
TRN-3A.NS-finish:IMM
'Let them finish!'

Another common way of forming commands is with the Completive stem and the future command suffix, as in (103).

(103a) ᎠᏕᎳᏧᏢᎢ ᎢᏁᏒᎢ
adeélajuuhlv́v́ʔi iìneesvvʔi
adeéla+di-uu-hl-v́v́ʔi iinii-ees-vvʔi
money+DST2-3B-have:CMP-DVB 1A.DL-go:CMP-FCM
'Let's go to California.'

(103b) ᏱᏂᏤᏨᎢ
hihneejvvʔi
hi-hneej-vvʔi
2A-answer:CMP-FCM
'Answer it.'

A third way of forming commands is with the Incompletive stem and the progressive future suffix *-éesdi,* as in (104).

(104a) ᏦᏱᏳᏑᏎᏍᏗ
joohiyúuséesdi
ja-oohiyúus-éesdi
2B-have.faith:INC-PFT
'Have faith.' (Feeling 1975a:184)

(104b) Ꭰ Ᏸ ᏍᎩᎦᏙᏍᏕᏍᏗ
aya sgiktoósdéesdi
aya sgi-gahtoósd-éesdi
1PRO 2/1-look.at:INC-PFT
'Look at me!'

There are several ways to form negative commands. All start with the **negative command** (NEG.COM) adverb *tleesdi.* One of the ways in which Set A verbs form negative commands is with the Completive stem and the completive future suffix *-i,* as in (105a); another is with the future command suffix, as in (105b). In both constructions the prepronominal c**ommand** prefix *jii-* also appears.

(105a) ᏞᏍᏗ ᏥᏥᏰᎢᏍᏔᏂ ᎤᏍᏗᎢ
hleèsdi jiihiiyéeʔistáni uusdííʔi
hleèsdi jii-hii-yéeʔistán-i uu-asdííʔi
NEG.COM COM-2A.AN-wake:CMP-CMF 3B-baby
'Don't wake the baby.' (Feeling 1975a:63)

(105b) ᏞᏍᏗ ᏥᏙᏥᏍᏚᎢᏒᎢ ᏗᏍᏆᏂᎪᏗᏍᎩ
hleèsdi jiidoojiisduʔììsvvʔi diisgwangoodíísgi
hleèsdi jii-dee-iijii-sduʔììs-vvʔi di-a-sgwangoodiísg-i
NEG.COM COM-DST-2A.PL-turn.on:CMP-FCM DST2-3A-store:INC-AGT
'Don't turn on your computers.'

Verbs also form negative commands with a Set B prefix and the Completive stem. For these constructions the future command suffix (FCM) appears; moreover, the prepronominal prefix is not used. Two examples are shown in (106).

(106a) ᏝᏍᏗ ᏫᏤᏅᏒᎢ
hleèsdi wijeenv́vsvvʔi
hleèsdi wi-ja-eenv́vs-vvʔi
NEG.COM TRN-2B-go:CMP-FCM
'Don't go there.'

(106b) ᏝᏍᏗ ᏣᏗᏔᎲᎢ Ꮎ ᏅᏬᏘ ᎠᏓᎯᎯ
hleesdi jadiitahvvʔi na nvv́wóòti adááhihi
hleesdi ja-adiitah-vvʔi na nvv́wóòti adááhihi
NEG.COM 2B-drink:CMP-FCM the medicine killer
'Don't drink that rubbing alcohol.' (Feeling 1975a:149)

Negative commands with Set B may also be formed with the *-éesdi* suffix attached to an Incompletive stem. In this construction the prepronominal prefix *yi-* appears. The examples in (107) show the contrast between an affirmative and a negative command; each uses a different stem, and the irrealis prepronominal prefix appears on the negative one.

(107a) ᏝᏍᏗ ᏱᏤᎵᎯᏍᎨᏍᏗ ᎭᎵᎮᎵᎩ
hleèsdi yijeeliíhîisgéesdi haliiheeliìgi
hleèsdi yi-ja-eeliíhîisg-éesdi hi-aliiheeliìgi
NEG.COM IRR-2B-worry:INC-PFT 2A-be.happy:IMM
'Don't worry, be happy.'

(107b) ᏝᏍᏗ ᏱᏗᏣᎵᎪᏎᏍᏗ ᏗᏣᎦᎴᎾ
hleèsdi yidiijaliigooséesdi diijagáláleena
hleèsdi yi-di-iijii-aliigoos-éesdi di-iijii-agáláleena
NEG.COM IRR-DST2-2B.PL-be.together:INC-PFT DST2-2A.PL-separate:IMM
'Don't stay together, separate.'

4.7. Sources and Additional Reading

Most works on Cherokee treat the final vowel of the Present Continuous and the Immediate stems as final suffixes. Because the final vowel of this stem is unpredictable, I have chosen to treat this vowel as part of the stem itself. Scancarelli (1987:314) and Cook (1979:95) refer to the Immediate stem as the punctual. King (1975:72) calls it the imperative and states that it conveys "an immediate point in time, either future or past." Scancarelli (1987:314) speculates that these stems "are probably historical perfectives. Punctuals view telic events as single wholes, and stative verbs generally do not have punctual stems." Foley (1980) applies a generative model to try to discover the abstract lexical forms that underlie that bewildering array of possible verb forms. He makes frequent comparisons to the other members of the Iroquoian family to justify some of the underlying forms. In the current work I have avoided overly abstract forms and have adopted the concept of principal parts as a more practical tool for teaching the grammar of the language.

Several authors have identified verbs of motion as taking *-i* rather than *-a* in the Present Continuous and have thus labeled it motion (Cook 1979:127). However, some nonmotion verbs in the Present Continuous take this ending (e.g., *-agahtosdi* 'look at' and *-lvkwdi* 'like') and some verbs of motion do not take this ending (the most obvious example being the verb *-ega* 'go'). While historically this suffix may have denoted motion, I have chosen to treat the final vowel as part of the Present Continuous stem itself because its appearance as /a/ or /i/ is unpredictable. Cook notes that the future construction is formed from the toward prefix (discussed in chapter 10) and what he calls the motion suffix (Cook 1979:127): "The ta- future can thus be analyzed as an idiom literally as 'I am coming to . . .' parallel to English 'I am going to . . .'"

As far as final suffixes are concerned, King (1975:82) calls the experienced past the definitive. Cook (1979:128) and Scancarelli (1987:xi) refer to it as the assertive. Pulte and Feeling (1975:290) call it the past, but Pulte (1985:543–44) later suggests the terms 'experienced' and 'nonexperienced' that I use in this work. He points out that the nonexperienced past refers to all past actions or states not perceived by one of the senses. King (1975:83) calls the nonexperienced past the quotative and states that it "is used to report events of which the speaker has no personal knowledge. It serves to indicate that the information was given to the speaker by a third party."

King (1975:82) calls the progressive future the intentive; Pulte and Feeling (1975) refer to it as the future. Scancarelli (2005:369) uses "expectational" and states that it "is used to express future tense and certain imperatives." King (1975:83) states that "this suffix is used to express an intention either as affirmative or negative statement." He refers to the commands formed from this suffix as emphatic imperatives.

Blankenship (1996) provides an overview of the classificatory verb system, including discussions of the kinds of stems formed and the semantic properties of the verbs that participate in this construction. King (1978) examines the forty classificatory verbs of Cherokee and isolates previously productive morphemes for the different categories.

The classic work on aspect is Comrie (1977); I have taken the terms Present Continuous, Incompletive, and Completive from his definitions.

4.8. Directions for Further Research

Pulte and Feeling (1975) list two instances where the Completive stem has a habitual suffix attached to it. These are shown in (108). Both have other features as well; the example in (108a) is negative, while the example in (108b) has a *ni-* prepronominal prefix and a highfall tone. Pulte and Feeling (1975:291) have an example identical to (108a) except that it has the expected Incompletive stem, which they translate as 'He doesn't speak habitually.'

(108a) Ꮭ ᏳᏬᏂᏍᏗ
hla yuúwóòniisóoʔi
hla yi-uu-wóoniis-óʔi
NEG IRR-3B-speak:CMP-HAB
'He never speaks.' (Pulte and Feeling 1975:291)

(108b) ᏄᏬᏂᏍᏗ
nuúwóòniisóóʔi
ni-uu-wóonis-óʔi
NI-3B-talk:CMP-HAB\SUB
'He had already spoken (prior to some other event).' (Pulte and Feeling 1975:291)

In my own research I have not encountered many other speakers who use this construction. Dialect surveys as well as research into archival materials can shed light on the use and distribution of such less commonly encountered constructions.

Corpus studies of Cherokee speech are needed to describe the contexts in which the different command forms are used and to help shed light on the distinct uses of the progressive future and the completive future. Although a relatively large amount of work has been done on the verb, there is little detailed discussion of the semantics and pragmatics of tense, aspect, and mood.

Koops (2008a, 2008b) has done useful studies related to the concept of location and the different types of verbs that are used to convey this kind of information. This is an area that could be further explored.

FIVE

Prepronominal Prefixes I

5.1. Overview of Prepronominal Prefixes

The basic verb structures presented in the previous chapter can be added to in two ways. The first is to add **prepronominal prefixes** that specify such features as **nonsingular objects,** location, and negation, among others. Second, **derivational suffixes** can be added to the verb stem itself to alter its meaning. Most of the discussion in this chapter pertains to verbs. Many **nouns** and **adjectives,** however, also bear some of the prefixes described in this chapter; if the noun or adjective is derived from a verb, then it must bear the same prefixes as the verb from which it derives. Nouns and adjectives are discussed in chapters 6 and 7.

The prepronominal prefixes occur before the pronominal prefix and convey more specific ideas about the verb. Each prefix has a number of **variant forms** depending on what comes before or after it, and some prefixes cause tone changes in the verb. For example, the **distributive** prefix *dee-* expresses more than one object or action and can add a **high tone** to the following **syllable,** as seen in (1).

(1) ᏕᎯᎪᏩᏗᎭ
deehígoohwtíha
dee-hi-goohwtíha
DST-2A-see:PRC
'You see them.'

Several of the prepronominal prefixes have two different basic forms depending on what kind of stem is present. The form that occurs less often—the **secondary form**—includes '2' in its **abbreviation.** For example, the form of the distributive prefix that occurs most commonly is *dee-*; this form has the abbreviation DST. The secondary form *di-* occurs with the **Infinitive** stem, derived nouns and adjectives, and the command form of the **Immediate;** this form has the abbreviation DST2. Both of these basic forms have variant forms that have undergone predictable changes according to their environment.

Twelve different prepronominal prefixes can occur. Sometimes several occur at the same time, but it is rare to find more than three prepronominal prefixes together. This chapter introduces prepronominal prefixes by describing six specific prefixes: *wi-*, *yi-*, *dee-*, *jii-*, *da-*, and *gaa-*.

5.1.1. Translocative (TRN) Prepronominal Prefix

The **translocative** *wi-* indicates a motion away from the speaker as well as an action that is taking place at a distance from the speaker. Three examples are shown in (2).

(2a) ᎠᏅᎦᎵᏍᎩ ᎪᏪᎵ ᏫᏣᏅᏁᏍ
anaàgaliísgi goohweeli wijanv́vnes
a-naàgaliísg-i goohweeli wi-ja-nv́vn-e=s
3A-lightning:INC-AGT letter TRN-2B-send(flexible):CMP-NXP=Q
'Did you send an email?'

(2b) ᏫᎦᎸᎦ
wigahlvv̀ga
wi-ga-hlvv̀ga
TRN-3A-put.in.container:IMM
'She put it in.'

(2c) ᏫᏥᎪᎵᏯ
wiìjiigooliíya
wi-iijii-gooliíya
TRN-2A.PL-examine:IMM
'You guys go and examine this.'

The prefix has the variant form [*w*] before vowels, as in (3).

(3a) ᎤᏔᎴᏒ ᏩᏴᎭ ᏌᎶᎳ
uùtaleesv waàyvv́ha saloóla
uùtaleesv wi-a-yvv́ha saloóla
hole TRN-3A-enter:IMM squirrel
'A squirrel just entered his hole.'

(3b) ᏩᏩᏕᎦ
waàwadéega
wi-agi-adéega
TRN-1B-throw:PRC
'I'm throwing it there.'

A few verbs always take this prefix. The verb 'send' requires it, because this action assumes a place at some distance from the speaker. The basic form of the translocative often adds a high tone to the following pronominal prefix. Because the pronominal prefix in (4) is a long vowel, this results in a falling tone.

(4) ᎺᎵ ᏫᏥᏅᏁᎭ
meéli wijîînvv̀neha
meéli wi-jii-nvhn-eha
Mary TRN-1A.AN-send:CMP-APL:PRC
'I'm sending it to Mary.'

For some verbs the prefix is simply part of the verb even if the idea of an actual place is absent, as in (5).

(5) ᏫᏗᏢᎾ
wiìdiitlvv́na
wi-iidii-tlvv́na
TRN-1A.PL-sleep:IMM
'Let's go to sleep!'

An /h/ immediately after the prefix causes the vowel of *wi-* to delete, resulting in the combination [*hw*]. This common process of **vowel deletion** is further explained in chapter 8. Two examples are shown in (6). In some pronunciations, as in (6a), the aspiration may not be realized.

(6a) ᏫᎩ Track 35
(h)wigi
wi-hi-igi
TRN-2A-get:IMM
'Get it!'

(6b) ᏪᎾ
hweèna
wi-hi-eèna
TRN-2A-go:IMM
'Go!'

The *wi-* prefix also serves the function of indicating an event that takes place before another event, as in (7). This construction is explained in greater detail in chapter 11.

(7a) ᏫᏥᎪᎠ ᎠᏆᏅᏔᏛᎢ
wijiigóóʔa aàgwahntadvv́ʔi
wi-jii-gooh-a agi-ahntad-vv́ʔi
TRN-1A.AN-see:CMP-CVB 1B-think:CMP-EXP
'As soon as I saw him I thought of it.'

(7b) ᏄᎳ ᏄᎾᏗᏅᏓᏊ ᎦᎵᏦᏕ ᏫᏂᎷᏨᎢ
núúla nuundiinv́v́dagwu gahljoóde wiiniiʔluhjvvʔi
núúla ni-uu-nadiinvv-da=gwu gahljoóde wi-iinii-ʔluhj-vvʔi
hurry NI-3B-sell-PCP=DT house TRN-1A.DL-arrive:CMP-FCM
'Hurry! Let's get there before he sells the house.' (Feeling 1975a:104)

The translocative also appears on adjectives to create a **superlative** meaning, as in (8); this usage is further discussed in chapter 7.

(8) ᏩᏃᏍᏓᏴᎢ
wanoosdayv́v́ʔi
wi-anii-oosday-v́v́ʔi
TRN-3A.NS-sharp-DVB
'They are the sharpest.'

5.1.2. Irrealis (IRR) Prepronominal Prefix

The **irrealis** prefix *yi-* references an action that has not occurred and/or might occur. One of the most important functions of this prefix is negation. When performing this function it is always accompanied by the **negation adverb** *tla,* commonly pronounced *hla* in Oklahoma. In (9a) *yi-* appears in its **full form** before a consonant; in (9b) it shortens to [y] before a vowel.

(9a) Ꮭ ᏱᎪᎵᎦ
tla yigooliìga
tla yi-ji-oolihga
NEG IRR-1A-understand:PRC
'I don't understand it.'

(9b) Ꮭ ᏯᏆᏅᏔ
tla yawahnt
tla yi-agi-anvhta

NEG IRR-1B-know:PRC
'I don't know.'

Note that it is not necessary for *tla* immediately to precede the *yi-*; an example is shown in (10).

(10) Ꮭ ᎣᏍᏓ ᏯᎩᏰᎸ
hla óósd yagiyeelv
hla óósda yi-agi-yeelv
NEG good IRR-1B-feel:PRC
'I don't feel good about that.'

Certain combinations of pronominal prefixes with prepronominal prefixes are indistinguishable when written in the syllabary but can be distinguished in their pronunciation. For example, the combination of the irrealis and the pronominal prefix *iijii-* in (11b) leads to the loss of the prepronominal prefix vowel, resulting in a distinct pronunciation from the prepronominal prefix in (11a).

(11a) ᏱᏣᏚᎵᎭ Track 36
yijaduulííha
yi-ja-aduulíiha
IRR-2B-want:PRC\SUB
'if you want it'

(11b) ᏱᏣᏚᎵᎭ
yiìjaduulííha
yi-iijii-aduulíiha
IRR-2B.PL-want:PRC\SUB
'if you all want it'

When the irrealis is used without *tla* it creates a conditional meaning that can be translated as 'if' or 'when(ever)' or to express a contrary-to-fact or hypothetical situation. Two examples are shown in (12).

(12a) ᎠᏓᏯᏍᎨᏍᎪ ᏳᏰᏣ
aàdaahyáàsgeesgo yuuyééja
a-adaa-hyáàsgeesg-o yi-uu-yéej-a
3A-MDL-stretch:INC-HAB IRR-3B-wake:CMP-CVB
'He stretches when he wakes up.'

(12b) ᏯᎩᏬᏂᏌ ᎠᎩᎾᎸᎪ
yagiwóoniís aàkinaálv́v̀go
yi-agi-wóoniis-a agi-hnaálv́v̀g-o

IRR-1B-talk:CMP-CVB   1B-get.angry:INC-HAB
'Whenever he talks to me I get angry.'

For these constructions a highfall tone appears on the rightmost long vowel to indicate that the verb is modifying the main part of the sentence. In these examples the verb also ends with a special **converb** (CVB) suffix. This complex construction is further explained in chapter 11.

Yi- attached to the Immediate stem also expresses possibility and can be translated as 'can' or 'will', typically used for something that can take place in the near future. Two examples are shown in (13).

(13a)
ᎲᎴᏊ   ᏱᏣᎴᎾ
hvleegwu   yiijaleéna
hvleegwu   yi-iijii-aleéna
immediately   IRR-2A.PL-start:IMM
'Immediately you can all start.'

(13b)
ᎦᎵᏉᎩᏃ   ᏕᎧᎾᏢᏛ   ᏱᏕᎾᎵᎪᎾ
gahlgwoógíhnóo   deekánahltv   yidéenalgoóna
gahlgwoógi=hnóo   dee-kanahltv   yi-dee-iinii-algoóna
seven=CN   DST-hill   IRR-DST-1A.DL-arrive.first:IMM
'We will see who gets to the seven hills first.' (The Wolf and the Crawdad, line 8)

As demonstrated in (14), this prefix also conveys the ability to perform an action.

(14)
ᏣᏂ   ᎢᎦ   ᎤᏓᏝᏂᎩᏓ
jaáni   íiga   uudahlaníigid
jaáni   íi-ga   uu-adahlaníigida
John   ITR-be:PRC   3B-strong

ᏰᎵᏊ   ᏐᏈᎵ   ᏱᎫᏔᎩ
yeeliíw   soógwíl   yiguutagi
yi-eeliígwu   soógwíli   yi-ga-uutagi
IRR-can   horse   IRR-3A-pick.up:IMM
'John is so strong he can pick up a horse.'

The irrealis is sometimes used to form a conditional meaning, as in (15).

(15)
ᏱᏣᏚᎳᏍ   ᏣᎳᎩ   ᏗᏣᏕᏠᏆᏍᏗ
yiijaduulas   jalagi   diijadeehlohgwaasdi

yi-iijii-aduula=s jalagi di-iijii-adeehlohgwaasdi
IRR-2B.PL-want:IMM=Q Cherokee DST2-2B.PL-learn:INF
'Would you all like to learn Cherokee?'

5.1.3. Distributive (DST) Prepronominal Prefix

This is the most common prepronominal prefix. Its two basic meanings are to indicate the presence of a nonsingular object or the distribution and/or multiplication of an action. The two forms are known as DST and DST2. Which form is used depends on the type of stem to which it attaches. The examples in (16) demonstrate that the *dee-* form (DST) is used on the verb, while the secondary form *di-* (DST2) is used on the noun.

(16a) ᏗᎿᏬ ᏚᎧᏲᏛ
diihnawo duùkayoodv
di-a-ahnawo dee-uu-kayood-v
DST2-3A-clothing DST-3B-dry:CMP-EXP
'He dried the clothes.'

(16b) ᏚᏍᏆᎵᏐᏅ ᏂᎦᏓ ᏗᎬᏃᏌᏍᏗ
duùsgwáàlsohnv nigáád digvvnoosásdi
dee-uu-sgwáàls-ohn-v nigááda di-ga-vvnoosásdi
DST-3B-break:CMP-TRM:CMP-EXP all DST2-3A-sweep:INF
'He completely broke all the brooms.'

The basic form *dee-* appears on verbs before **consonants,** as seen in (17a). In this example the full form of the prefix causes a high tone to appear on the following vowel. In (17b) and (17c) the vowel of the distributive prefix is removed before another vowel.

(17a) ᏕᎭᏑᎴᎭᏍ
deehásuuleéhas
dee-hi-asuuleéha=s
DST-2A-wash.hands:PRC=Q
'Are you washing your hands?'

(17b) ᏃᏊᏛ ᏥᏓᏑᎳ
noógwúdvv jidasuúla
noógwu=dvv ji-dee-a-asuúla
now=EM REL-DST-3A-wash.hands:IMM
'He just washed his hands.'

(17c) ᏚᎾᏑᎴ
duùnasuúle
dee-uunii-asuúl-e
DST-3B.NS-wash.hands:CMP-NXP
'They washed their hands.'

The initial vowel /i/ of pronominal prefixes undergoes **vowel removal** when it follows a distributive, while the distributive prefix receives a high tone. Two examples are shown in (18).

(18a) ᏂᎪᎸ ᏕᎾᏑᎴᏍᎪ
nigoólv déenasuúléesgo
nigoólv dee-iinii-asuúléesg-o
always DST-1A.DL-wash.hands:INC-HAB
'You and I always wash our hands.'

(18b) ᎠᏕᎳᏍ ᏕᏥᏝ
adeélas déejiihla
adeéla=s dee-iijii-hla
money=Q DST-2A.PL-have:PRC
'Do you all have some money (in your pockets)?'

The *di-* form of the distributive (DST2) appears on nouns, adjectives, Immediate commands, verbs with the irrealis prefix, and Infinitive stems. The sentence in (19a) contains both forms; the *dee-* form appears on the verb and the *di-* form on the noun. The noun 'eyeglasses' always has this prefix. In (19b) the presence of the irrealis prefix triggers the *di-* form on the verb.

(19a) ᏗᏣᎦᏘᏅᏘᏗᏍ ᏕᏣᏚᎦ
dijaktinv́v́tdis deejaduuga
di-ja-aktinv́v́tdi=s dee-ja-aduuga
DST2-2B-eye.glasses=Q DST-2B-throw:IMM
'Did you throw your glasses away?'

(19b) ᏝᏃ ᏍᏓᏱ ᏱᏗᏣᎸᏫᏍᏓᏁᎰ
tlahnóo sdááyi yidijalv́hwsdaàneeho
tla=hnóo sdááyi yi-di-ja-lv́hwsdaàneeh-o
NEG=CN hard IRR-DST2-2B-work:INC-HAB
'You don't work very hard.'

Like *dee-*, this *di-* prefix has variant forms triggered by adjacent sounds. In (20a) it causes the removal of the pronominal prefix vowel. As a result of this removal the vowel of the prepronominal prefix is lengthened, giving it the form [*dii*]. The vowel of *di-* also lengthens before /i/, as seen in (20b). When *di-* appears before the vowels /e/, /o/, or /u/ it becomes [*j*], as in (20c). In (20d) the /a/ of the pronominal prefix is removed and the distributive vowel is lengthened.

(20a) ᏗᏑᏢᏗ
diisuhldi
di-a-asuhldi
DST2-3A-wash.hands:INF
'sink'

(20b) ᏂᎦᏓ ᏗᏣᏑᎳ
nigááda diìjasuùla
nigááda di-iijii-asuùla
all DST2-2A.PL-wash.hands:IMM
'Everybody wash your hands!'

(20c) ᏧᏑᏢᏗ ᎤᏚᎵ
juusuhldi uùduuli
di-uu-asuhldi uu-aduuli
DST2-3B-wash.hands:INF 3B-want:PRC
'She wants to wash her hands.'

(20d) ᏗᎩᏅᎦᏝᏗ ᎠᏆᏚᎵ
diiginvvgahldi aàgwaduuli
di-agi-nvvgahldi agi-aduuli
DST2-1B-clean:INF 1B-want:PRC
'I want to clean them.'

The DST2 form *di-* combines with the second person singular Set A pronominal prefix *hi-* to form the single syllable [*ti*]. This change is demonstrated in (21a). In (21b) and (21c) the vowel of the pronominal prefix is removed before a vowel-initial stem; as a result, the combination is [*ta*] in (21b) and [*to*] in (21c). In (21a) and (21b) the **aspirated syllabary characters** distinguish the aspirated syllables as Ꮨ and Ꮤ, respectively, while in (21c) the character Ꮩ could be either [*do*] or [*to*].

(21a) <u>Ꮨ</u>ᏃᎨᏂ
<u>ti</u>hnoogééni
<u>di-hi</u>-hnoogééni
DST2-2A-arm
'your arms'

(21b) ᏔᏟᏂᏆᎥᎦ
tahlniigwaʔvv̀ga
di-hi-alihniigwaʔvv̀ga
DST2-2A-kneel:IMM
'Kneel!

(21c) ᏙᏪᏝᎠ
toohweelaʔa
di-hi-oohweelaʔa
DST2-2A-write:IMM
'Write them!'

Some verbs always have the distributive prefix; in these cases the prefix is treated as part of the word. This type of prepronominal prefix that is an inseparable part of the verb is called a **frozen prefix.** While there are some patterns as to which verbs take *dee-*, it is generally unpredictable and must simply be learned as part of the verb. One pattern is for *dee-* to appear with verbs that indicate ongoing or repeated events or states. For example, the verbs in (22) all carry the distributive.

(22)
-asehíha 'count'
-yawéega 'be tired'
-hnogíiʔa 'sing'
-adeehlgwaʔa 'learn'
-adloohyíha 'cry'
-aneeloóhv́sga 'play'
-vhgiilóoʔa 'wash (something flexible)'
-adooʔa 'be called'

Many **intransitive** verbs take *dee-* if the subject is nonsingular. Two examples are shown in (23). The second example has the **iterative** (ITR) prefix; this and other prepronominal prefixes not discussed in this chapter are described in chapter 10.

(23a) ᏙᎩᏲᏏᎭ
doògiiyóosiha
dee-oogii-yóosiha
DST-1B.PL.EX-be.hungry:PRC
'We are hungry.'

(23b) ᏙᎾᏓᏍᏕᎸᎲᎢ
doonadasdeelvhvvʔi

dee-ii-iinii-adaad-sdeelvh-vvʔi
DST-ITR-1A.DL-RFL-help:CMP-FCM
'Let's help each other again!'

Sometimes the addition of a distributive prefix will create a different word with a slightly different meaning. Three pairs of words differentiated by *di-* are shown in (24)–(26).

(24a)	ᎠᎦᏘᏯ	aktiya	'guard' (from the verb 'wait')
(24b)	ᏗᎦᏘᏯ	diiktiya	'waiter', 'pastor'
(25a)	ᎠᏓᏬᏍᎩ	adawóósgi	'swimmer' (from the verb 'swim')
(25b)	ᏗᏓᏬᏍᎩ	diidawóósgi	'Baptist'
(26a)	ᎠᏐᏅᏍᏙᏗ	asonsdohdi	'button' (from the verb 'press down')
(26b)	ᏗᏐᏅᏍᏙᏗ	diisonsdohdi	'keyboard'

The mandatory use of prepronominal prefixes varies from speaker to speaker. Feeling (1975a) lists the verb 'iron' under the letter ⟨d⟩, indicating that this verb in his dialect of Cherokee always has a distributive. Some speakers, however, can use it without the prepronominal prefix, as in (27).

(27)	ᎠᎿᏬ	ᏥᏍᎩᏁᏅ	ᏥᏖᏍᎦ
	ahnawo	jisginéehnv̋	jiìteesga
	a-ahnawo	ji-sgi-néehn-v̋	ji-hteesga
	3A-shirt	REL-2/1-give:CMP-DVB	1A-iron:PRC

'I am ironing the shirt you gave me.'

5.1.4. Command (COM) Prepronominal Prefix

The **command** prefix *jii-* appears with negative commands in certain contexts. It does not co-occur with the irrealis prefix *yi-*. It can be used with Immediate stem commands as well as Completive stem commands. As shown in (28c), the presence of the *jii-* prefix changes the following distributive (DST) prefix from *dee-* to [*doo*].

(28a)	ᎴᏍᏗ	ᏥᏫᎦᏕᏏ
	hleesdi	jiiwiìgadeesi
	hleesdi	jii-wi-iigii-adeesi
	NEG.COM	COM-TRN-1B.PL-throw:IMM

'Let's not throw it away!'

(28b)	ᏞᏍᏗ	ᏥᎦᎯᏕᎸ	Ꮎ	ᎦᎶᏇ
	hleesdi	jiigaahiidéelv	na	galoògwe
	hleesdi	jii-gaa-hii-déel-v	na	galoògwe
	NEG.COM	COM-ANS-2A.AN-give(long):CMP-FCM	that	gun
	'Don't give them that gun!'			

(28c)	ᏞᏍᏗ	ᏥᏙᎭᏓᎴᏴᏔᏂ
	tleesdi	jiidoohadaaleehytani
	tleesdi	jii-dee-hi-adaad-leeyvhtan-i
	NEG.COM	COM-DST-2A-burn:CMP-CMF
	'Don't burn yourself!'	

The *jii-* prefix is also used for commands where an action is to be repeated. This prefix also changes the quality of the following vowel by lengthening it and raising its tone. Because the word *hleesdi* is not present, these commands would not be interpreted as negative commands. Five examples are shown in (29).

(29a)	ᏏᏊ	ᏥᏂᎯᏫ	Track 37
	siígwu	jiiniíhiwi	
	siígwu	jii-ni-hi-wi	
	again	COM-NI-2A-say:IMM	
	'Say it again!'		

(29b)	ᏏᏊ	ᏥᎭᏗᏔ	Track 38
	siígwu	jiihádiita	
	siígwu	jii-hi-adiita	
	again	COM-2A-drink:IMM	
	'Drink it again!'		

(29c) ᏥᏫᎮᎾ
jiiwiiheèna
jii-wi-hi-eèna
COM-TRN-2A-go:IMM
'Go back!'

(29d) ᏥᏓᎴᎾ
jiidaleèna
jii-iidii-aleèna
COM-1A.PL-begin:IMM
'Let's begin again.'

(29e) ᏥᏂᏣᏛᎦ
jiiniijadvv̀ga
jii-ni-iijii-advv̀ga
COM-NI-2A.PL-do:IMM
'You all do it again!'

5.1.5. Completive Future (CMF) Prepronominal Prefix

The **completive future prefix** *da-* attaches to a Completive stem along with the completive future suffix *-i*. Both prefix and suffix have the abbreviation CMF. (30) shows three examples of this construction. In (30b) vowel deletion is triggered by the *hi-* pronominal prefix that follows the completive future prefix; the resulting syllable is [*ti*]. The *da-* future construction indicates that an event will happen in the near future and is translated as 'will' or 'going to'.

(30a) ᏓᎦᏬᏂᏏ
dagawóoniisi
da-ga-wóoniis-i
CMF-3A-talk:CMP-CMF
'She is going to talk.'

(30b) ᏂᎯ ᏘᏩᏛᎯ
nihi tihwahdvvhi
nihi da-hi-hwahdvvh-i
2PRO CMF-2A-find:CMP-CMF
'You will find it.'

(30c) ᏓᎬᏔᏂᏌᏂ
dagvv̀taniisáhnı
da-ji-vhtan-iisáhn-i
CMF-1A-use:PRF-DPL:PRF-CMF
'I'm going to use it again.'

It is important to note that, unlike the past tense use of the Completive stem, Set A prefixes can appear with the future use of the Completive. The completive future prefix undergoes changes that have not been seen on the previously discussed prefixes. The combination of /a/ and /a/ produces [*vv*]; thus the completive future prefix combines with the third person Set A prefix *a-* to produce [*dvv*]. Three examples are shown in (31).

(31a) ᏛᏴᏖᏏ
dvvhyvhtéesi
da-a-ahyvhtées-i
CMF-3A-kick:CMP-CMF
'He will kick it.'

(31b) ᏛᏗᏔᎯ
dvvdiitahi
da-a-adiitah-i
CMF-3A-drink:CMP-CMF
'He will drink it.'

(31c) Ꮭ ᏒᎩ ᏱᏛᎩᏩᏏ
hla svvg yidvvkiwasi
hla svvgi yi-da-agi-hwas-i
NEG onion IRR-CMF-1B-plant:CMP-CMF
'I'm not going to plant onions.'

When future *da-* combines with /i/, the /i/ undergoes vowel removal, as seen in (32), but the vowel of the prepronominal prefix is lengthened and lowered.

(32a) ᏓᎩᎷᏤᎵ
daàgiiluhcheéli
da-iigii-luhj-eél-i
CMF-1B.PL-arrive:CMP-APL:CMP-CMF
'He will come up to us.'

(32b) ᏓᏗᏌᏔᏓᏂ
daàdiisaldaani
da-iidii-saldaan-i
CMF-1A.PL-lift:CMP-CMF
'We will lift it.'

When *da-* combines with any other vowel, a /y/ is inserted, as shown in (33).

(33a) ᏓᏳ̈ᏯᎵ
dayuùhyali
da-uu-hyal-i
CMF-3B-look.for:CMP-CMF
'He will look for it.'

(33b) ᏓᏲᎬᎨᏍᏏ
dayoògvvkewsi
da-oogii-vkews-i
CMF-1O.PL.EX-forget:CMP-CMF
'We will be forgotten.'

The completive future is distinct in use from the progressive future. *-éesdi* only refers to a time that is later than the present moment, but it does attach to either a Completive or Incompletive stem and is therefore capable of expressing aspectual nuances. To express a future time frame in the past, however, the completive future prefix and suffix must be used. In (34) the future suffix is itself followed by a final suffix; in this case /s/ is inserted before the final suffix.

(34) ᏙᏓᏥᎶᏁᎢᏒ
doodajiloónéʔisv
dee-da-ji-loónéʔ-is̲-v
DST-CMF-1A-oil:CMP-CMF-EXP
'I was going to oil it.' (Feeling 1975a:101)

5.1.6. Animate Nonsingular (ANS) Prepronominal Prefix

For some speakers the **animate nonsingular** prepronominal prefix *gaa-* is used to reference third person nonsingular animate objects; other speakers use the distributive prefix *dee-*. The prefix *gaa-* is an older usage, but in Oklahoma Cherokee it is becoming common to use the distributive prefix to refer to both animate and inanimate nonsingular objects. Some speakers use *gaa-* and *dee-* interchangeably for animate nonsingular objects. Two examples with the animate nonsingular *gaa-* are shown in (35). In (35c) the *dee-* appears to reference the nonsingular animate object.

(35a)	ᎦᎯᎪᏩᏘᏧ	Ꮎ	ᎩᏟ
	gaahiigoohwahtíju	na	giihli
	gaa-hii-goohwahti=ju	na	giihli
	ANS-2A.AN-see:PRC=CQ	that	dog
	'Do you see those dogs?'		

(35b) ᎦᏥᏯᏙᎵᎦ
gaajiiyadooliiga
gaa-jii-adooliiga

ANS-1A.AN-pity:PRC
'I pity them.'

(35c) ᏓᏘᏂᏙᎲ ᏓᏔᏩ ᎠᏁᏙ
daàtihniídóòhe daahnaw aneedóó
dee-a-ahtihn-iídóòh-e daahnawa anii-eedooh-i
DST-3A-lead:INC-AMB:INC-NXP war 3A.NS-be.at:INC-AGT
'He was leading a war party' (The Search Party, line 6)

5.2. Sources and Additional Reading

The term 'prepronominal prefix' is used to describe other Iroquoian languages. The groundwork for the modern study of Iroquoian languages was done by Lounsbury (1953) in his study of Oneida verb morphology. Both Cook (1979:54) and King (1975:44) use the label 'distributive' for the *dee-* prefix, while Pulte and Feeling (1975:247) refer to it as plural object. In the literature *yi-* has been labeled counterfactual, conditional, and simply negative, while King (1975:61) describes it as "conditional or negative." I use 'irrealis' to encompass all of these functions. Cook (1979:55) and King (1975:62) both use the label 'translocative' for the *wi-* prefix.

5.3. Directions for Further Research

Some speakers do not allow the completive future *da-* to co-occur with the prepronominal prefixes *yi-*, *wi-*, or *ni-*, but other speakers find such constructions acceptable. Also, it is unclear whether the ordering of prepronominal prefixes is fixed or whether there is some dialectal variation.

Walker (1975: 205) points out that *da-* seems to indicate a near-future action that has a degree of certainty as to its occurrence. This meaning seems to make it semantically incompatible with these other prepronominal prefixes.

As previously noted, what Feeling (1975a) lists as a frozen distributive prefix apparently can be left off in some contexts. The mandatory use of prepronominal prefixes varies from speaker to speaker; future studies could clarify the types of variation that do occur and to what extent they are based in dialect differences.

It is clear that the semantics and pragmatics of movement and location are in need of in-depth study. Koops (2008a) explores the idea of a contrast in visibility between the translocative and the toward (TOW). Two of his examples are shown in (36).

(36a) ᏩᏓᏬ
wádawo
wi-a-adaa-awo
TRN-3A-MDL-bathe(T):PRC
'She's swimming (e.g., down at the creek, not here).' (Koops 2008a:2)

(36b) ᏗᏓᏬ
diidawo
di-a-adaa-awo
TOW-3A-MDL-bathe(T):PRC
'She's swimming (over there, in sight, as when pointing).' (Koops 2008a:2)

Taken together, these facts serve to highlight the complexity of prepronominal prefixes in Cherokee and indicate that many areas still bear investigation.

SIX

Nouns

6.1. Functions of Nouns

The four major **parts of speech** in Cherokee are **nouns, verbs, adverbs,** and **adjectives.** Nouns are distinguished from the other three classes by several criteria. First, nouns have distinct functions in a sentence. In the examples below, a noun is acting as a **subject** (1a), a **secondary object** (1b), a **primary object** (1c), and a location (1d). In (1e) the noun is a **direct addressee.**

(1a) ᎠᎩᏍᏗ ᎠᎪᏍᎦ
agiísdi aàgoosga
a-giísdi a-goosga
3a-eat:INF 3A-rot:PRC
'The food is turning rotten.'

(1b) ᏦᎳ ᏥᏥᏁᎸᎢ
joola jijiìneélv́vʔi
joola ji-jii-hneél-v́vʔi
tobacco REL-1A.AN-give:CMP-EXP
'I gave him tobacco.'

(1c) ᎠᏍᎦᏯ ᏕᏥᏯᎧᏁ ᎩᏟ
asgaya deejíiyaàkáàne giihli
a-sgaya dee-jii-aàkáàne giihli
3A-man DST-1A.AN-give(living):PRC dog
'I'm giving the man dogs.' (Scancarelli 1987:69)

(1d) ᏓᎵᏆ ᏩᏪᏙᎸ ᏞᎦ
dalígwa waàwedoolv tléėga

dalígwa wi-agi-edool-v tlééga
Tahlequah TRN-1B-be.at:CMP-EXP while
'I was walking around Tahlequah a short while.'

(1e) ᎯᏆᎵᏏ ᏘᎨᏫ
higwalisi tikewi
hi-gwalisi di-hi-kewi
2A-pharisee DST2-2A-blind
'Blind Pharisee!' (*Cherokee New Testament,* Matthew 23:26)

In (2) the noun 'Cherokee' is the object of the **postposition** 'with'. The functions of such **postpositional phrases** are discussed in chapter 7.

(2) ᎦᏙ ᎠᏗ ᏣᎳᎩ ᎬᏗ Track 39
gado ad jalagi gv́hdi
gado a-adi jalagi gv́hdi
what 3A-say:PRC Cherokee with
'How does one say it in Cherokee?'

Nouns can also serve as a **subject complement** in a verbless sentence. In Cherokee the verb 'be' is not necessary in a sentence expressing 'NOUN is NOUN.' For example, in (3a) the noun 'sibling' is the subject (what the **clause** is about), while the noun 'doctor' is the subject complement (what is said about the subject). Similarly, in (3b) 'Tahlequah' is the subject; the subject complement identifies it as 'the capital of the Cherokee Nation'.

(3a) ᎤᏂᏙ ᎠᎦᎾᎦᏘ
uuniido agaʔnakt
uunii-do a-gaʔnakti
3B.NS-sibling 3A-doctor
'Their sister is a doctor.'

(3b) ᏓᎵᏆ ᏣᎳᎩ ᎠᏰᏟ ᎤᏙᎵᏒ
dalígwa jalagi ayééhli uudoohlvsv́
dalígwa jalagi ayééhli uudoohlvsv́
Tahlequah Cherokee center place
'Tahlequah is the capital of the Cherokee Nation.' (Feeling 1975a:73)

As seen in chapter 4, only verbs are normally inflected for **tense, aspect, mood,** and **modality.** When sentences like those in (3) above refer to the past or future, a **helping verb** is needed to bear the **final suffixes** that indicate the time frame. This distinction is shown in (4).

(4a) ᎠᏓᏫ ᎠᎦᎾᎦᏘ
aádawi agaʔnakti
aádawi a-gaʔnakti
Adam 3A-doctor
'Adam is a doctor.'

(4b) ᎠᏓᏫ ᎠᎦᎾᎦᏘ ᎨᏒᎢ
aádawi agaʔnakti geèsvv́ʔi
aádawi a-gaʔnakti geès-vv́ʔi
Adam 3A-doctor be:INC-EXP
'Adam was a doctor.'

(4c) ᎠᏓᏫ ᎠᎦᎾᎦᏘ ᎨᏎᏍᏗ
aádawi agaʔnakti geèséesdi
aádawi a-gaʔnakti geès-éesdi
Adam 3A-doctor be:INC-PFT
'Adam will be a doctor.'

In addition to this inability to indicate tense and aspect, most nouns have several other features that distinguish them from verbs. Verbs with **pronominal prefixes** undergo **pronominal lengthening,** adding a **lowfall tone** on the **third person singular** and **nonsingular** forms. In (5a), for example, the pronominal prefix becomes **long** and has the lowfall; the **vowel** in the prefix on the noun 'swimmer' in (5b), however, remains **short.**

(5a) ᎠᏓᏬᏍᎪᎢ Track 40
aàdawóosgóoʔi
a-adaa-awóosg-óoʔi
3A-MDL-bathe:INC-HAB
'She swims.'

(5b) ᎠᏓᏬᏍᎩ
adawóósgi
a-adaa-awóosg-i
3A-MDL-bathe:INC-AGT
'She's a swimmer.'

The *dee-* form of the **distributive prefix** generally only appears on verbs; the majority of nouns (and all adjectives) use the **secondary form** *di-* (DST2). When *di-*appears before a short /a/, the /a/ is removed. A trace of the removed vowel remains, however, in the lengthened form [*dii*]. An example of this is shown in

(6); in (6a) the singular form of the noun appears with the *a-* pronominal prefix, while in (6b) only the lengthened-vowel **variant** of the distributive appears.

(6a) ᎠᏗᏔᏍᏗ — Track 41
adiítasdi
a-adiitasdi
3A-drink:INF\INS
'a drink'

(6b) ᏗᏗᏔᏍᏗ
diidiítasdi
di-a-adiitasdi
DST2-3A-drink:INF\INS
'drinks'

The combination of *di-* with a following /i/ is as shown in (7).

(7) ᏗᏗᏃᎩᏍᎩ
diìdiihnoogíísgi
di-iidii-hnoogiísg-i
DST2-1A.PL-sing:INC-AGT
'We are singers.'

When *di-* occurs before vowels other than /a/ and /i/, it has the variant [*j*]. Again, this use of DST2 does not generally appear on verbs; the sole exceptions are the command forms of the **Immediate** and some uses of the **Infinitive.** In (8) four examples of this [*j*] variant are demonstrated for the vowels /e/, /o/, /u/, and /v/, respectively.

(8a) ᏤᏁᏲᎲᏍᎩ
jeeneèyóóhvsgi
di-eenii-eehyoóhvsg-i
DST2-1A.DL.AN-teach:INC-AGT
'We're his teachers.'

(8b) ᏦᏍᏓᏓᎸᎢ
joosdadaalv̋ʔi
di-oosdii-adaad-lv̋ʔi
DST2-1A.DL.EX-RFL-sister
'She and I are sisters.'

(8c) ᏧᏂᏒᏍᏗ
juuniisvvsdi

di-uunii-svvsdi
DST2-3B.NS-go.to.bed:INF
'hotel'

(8d) ᏨᏆᏟᎶᏍᏔᏅᎢ
jvvgwahliiloòstanv́v́ʔi
di-vgi-ahliiloòstan-v́v́ʔi
DST2-1O-photograph:CMP-DVB
'pictures of me'

The *di-* form of the distributive combines with second person *hi-* (*hii-* as an **animate object prefix**) to create the single syllable [*ti*]. The reasons for this change are explained in chapter 8. An example is shown in (9).

(9) ᏘᏰᏲᎲᏍᎩ
tiiyeèyóóhvsgi
di-hii-eehyoóhvsg-i
DST2-2A.AN-teach:INC-AGT
'You're his teacher.'

Noun inflection depends on whether the noun is a **root noun** or a **derived noun.** Derived nouns are created from another part of speech, typically a verb. Root nouns are simple nouns that were not created from something else. The class of root nouns is rather small; the majority of nouns are verbs that have been made into nouns.

Root nouns typically include common animals, relationship terms, and basic cultural items. Many of these root nouns have two **syllables.** A representative list is shown in (10). This list does not include the nouns for people or relationship terms; these nouns are always inflected and are discussed in their own sections.

Two syllable root nouns Track 42

(10)	ᎠᏓ	ada	'wood'
	ᎠᎵ	aali	'sweat'
	ᎠᏂ	aʔni	'strawberry'
	ᏓᎩᏏ	daksi	'turtle'
	ᏜᏯᎦ	dlahyga	'blue jay'
	ᏙᏌ	doosa	'mosquito'
	ᏗᎵ	dili	'skunk'
	ᎩᏟ	giihli	'dog'
	ᎩᎦ	giíga	'blood'
	ᎪᎢ	goʔi	'grease'

ᎫᏇ	guhgwe	'quail'
ᎫᎫ	guugu	'bottle'
ᏦᎳ	joóla	'tobacco'
ᏃᏥ	nohji	'pine'
ᎣᏝ	oohla	'soap'
ᏌᏌ	saasa	'goose'
ᏎᎷ	seélu	'corn'
ᏘᎾ	tina	'head lice'
ᏪᏌ	weésa	'cat'
ᏲᎾ	yoóna	'bear'

Many root nouns also have three syllables. A sample list of these nouns is provided in (11).

Three-syllable root nouns

(11)	ᏥᏍᏛᎾ	jíisdvvna	'crawdad'
	ᎠᏕᎳ	adeéla	'money'
	ᎠᎪᏓ	agoóda	'prairie'
	ᎠᏣᏗ	ajáʔdi	'fish'
	ᏔᎳᏚ	taláadu	'tree frog'
	ᎠᏥᎾ	ajina	'cedar'
	ᏓᎹᎦ	daamága	'horsefly'
	ᏓᏬᎵ	dawóoli	'mushroom'
	ᎡᎶᎯ	eloohi	'earth'
	ᎦᏢᏦᏕ	gahljoóde	'house'
	ᎦᏅᏃ	ganvvno	'road'
	ᎩᏔᏯ	gitaaya	'cherry'
	ᎢᎾᏓ	iinada	'snake'
	ᏥᏔᎦ	jitaága	'chicken'
	ᎩᏳᎦ	kiyúùga	'chipmunk'
	ᏔᎷᏣ	taluúja	'basket'
	ᎤᎦᎹ	uugama	'soup'

All root nouns in their **underlying** form are at least two syllables long and end in a vowel. This vowel is often /a/ or /i/; a few end in other vowels. Most of these root nouns—except for people, clothing, and body parts—do not normally inflect for **person** or **number** and cannot be directly possessed.

Derived nouns are generally verbs that have been turned into nouns, although it is possible to derive nouns from adjectives as well as from other nouns. Some examples of derived nouns are shown in (12). The first word is the derived noun; the word below it is the third person conjugated form of the verb from which it derives. Derived nouns always have a **Set A** or **Set B** pronominal prefix and may also have the distributive prepronominal prefix *dee-*. (12a) and (13a) are the names of objects involved in the action of the verb and are derived from the Infinitive stem of the verb. (14a) is a noun indicating a person who performs an action and is based on the **Incompletive** stem of the verb. In (15a) the noun is an object that is a result of the action of the verb and is based on the **Completive** stem.

(12a) ᎠᎩᏍᏗ
agiìsdi
a-giìsdi
3A-eat:INF
'food'

(12b) ᎠᎩᎠ
aàgiʔa
a-giʔa
3A-eat:PRC
'He eats it.'

(13a) ᎠᏓᏅᏖᏗ
adahntehdi
a-adahntehdi
3A-know:INF
'thought', 'mind'

(13b) ᎠᏓᏅᏖᎭ
aàdahntéha
a-adahntéha
3A-know:PRC
'He is thinking.'

(14a) ᏗᏕᏠᏆᏍᎩ
diideéhlohgwaàsgi
di-a-adeéhlohgwáàsg-i
DST2-3A-learn:INC-AGT
'student'

(14b) ᎠᏕᏠᏆᏍᎪᎢ
aàdeéhlohgwáàsgóoʔi

a-adeéhlohgwáàsg-óo?i
3A-learn:INC-HAB
'She learns it.'

(15a) ᎠᏁᏟᏔᏅᎢ
ahnéhltanv́v́?i
a-ahnéhltan-v́v́?i
3A-translate:CMP-DVB
'translation'

(15b) ᎤᏁᏟᏔᏅᎢ
uùhnéhltanvv́?i
uu-ahnéhltan-vv́?i
3B-translate:CMP-EXP
'She translated it.'

The process for deriving nouns is discussed in chapter 12.

As with verbs, nouns typically lose their **final vowel** in **fast speech.** A few examples are shown in (16). Note that the **syllabary** spelling preserves this final vowel.

(16a)	ᎠᏕᎳ	adeéla	→	adeél	'money'
(16b)	ᎠᎹ	ama	→	am	'water'
(16c)	ᎩᏟ	giihli	→	giihl	'dog'

If the final syllable starts with /h/, the entire syllable is dropped, as in (17).

(17) ᎠᎨᏯ agééhya → agéé 'girl'

6.2. Root Noun Pronominal Inflection

Many nouns have a pronominal prefix as well as a distributive prepronominal prefix. Pronominal prefixes can have a **reference, possession,** or **participant function.** A pronominal prefix with a reference function indicates the person as well as the number of the noun itself. A pronominal prefix with a possession function indicates something with some relationship with the noun (typically a possessor of the noun) but does not indicate the person and number of the noun itself. In (18a) the first person Set A pronominal prefix has a reference function and indicates that the person and number of the noun is first person singular. In (18b) the prefix has a possession function.

(18a) ᏥᏍᎦᏯ
jisgaya
ji-sgaya
1A-man
'I'm a man.'

(18b) ᎦᎵᏍᏇᏚᏬ
galiisgweètuwo
ji-alisgweètuwo
1A-hat
'my hat'

In (19) the derived noun 'school' indicates a location. The pronominal prefix is first person plural, but the noun 'school' itself is third person. The prefix translates as 'our school', but the literal meaning is 'place where we learn.' In this situation the pronominal prefix has a participant function, expressing a participant of the verb from which the noun is derived.

(19) ᏦᎦᏕᏝᏆᏍᏗᏍ ᏖᏙᎵ
joogadeehlgwasdis teédóòli
di-oogii-adeehlgwasdi=s da-hi-eédóòl-i
DST2-1B.PL.EX-learn:INF=Q CMF-2A-be.at:CMP-CMF
'Are you coming to our school?'

Noun inflection in Cherokee is complex and depends on several factors, including whether the noun is human or **animate.** These factors are considered in the following section.

6.2.1. Root Nouns without Pronominal Prefixes

6.2.1.1. *Nonhuman Root Nouns*

Most nonhuman root nouns do not normally inflect for person or number. Nouns that refer to people, body parts, or clothing, however, do inflect and are discussed in a later section. In some special instances the normally uninflected nouns do take inflection. Labeling them as uninflected is justified, however, because that is their usual state; moreover, the true inflected nouns are always marked for person and number.

Root nouns in Cherokee are less complex than the verbs; many remain unchanged most of the time. For example, to indicate number, nonhuman root nouns do not change from their singular counterpart. The verb indicates whether the noun is singular or nonsingular. (20a) is an example of the noun *giihli* referring to a single dog. In (20b) the noun remains the same; only the *gaa-* prefix on the verb indicates that the object is nonsingular.

(20a) ᎯᎪᏩᏘᏧ Ꮎ ᎩᏟ
hiigoòwahtíju naʔ giihli
hii-goohwahti=ju naʔ giihli
2A.AN-see:PRC=CQ that dog
'Do you see that dog?'

(20b) ᎦᎯᎪᏩᏘᏧ Ꮎ ᎩᏟ
<u>gaa</u>hiigoòwahtíju naʔ giihli
gaa-hii-goohwahti=ju naʔ giihli
<u>ANS</u>-2A.AN-see:PRC=CQ that dog
'Do you see those dogs?'

Another example is shown in (21), where the speaker indicates the animate object is more than one with distributive *dee-*.

(21a) ᏌᏌ ᎨᏝ
saasa géehla
saasa ga-éehla
goose 3A-feed:PRC
'He's feeding the goose.'

(21b) ᏌᏌ ᏕᎨᏝ
saasa <u>dee</u>géehla
saasa dee-ga-éehla
goose DST-3A-feed:PRC
'He's feeding the geese.'

Nonhuman root nouns normally have no inflection and in this way are distinct from human nouns. Human root nouns, as will be seen, always have a pronominal prefix with a reference function. Compare the two examples in (22). In (22a) the noun could be singular or nonsingular; the noun in (22b), however, can only refer to a single man.

(22a) ᏥᏍᏚ
jiisdu
'rabbit', 'rabbits'

(22b) ᎠᏍᎦᏯ
asgaya
a-sgaya
3A-man
'man'

In certain special contexts, it is possible for these noninflected nouns to receive inflection in order to emphasize person or number. For example, in (23) the normally uninflected nouns bear the third person nonsingular prefix.

(23a) ᎾᎾ ᎦᏙ ᎤᏍᏗ ᎠᏂᏥᏍᏚ
naana gado úúsd aniijiisdu
na=na gado úúsdi anii-jiisdu
that=FC what thing 3A.NS-rabbit
'What are those?' 'Those are rabbits.'

(23b) ᎠᏂᏩᎶᏏ Ꮎ ᏓᎩᏏ ᎤᎾᎩᎳ
aaniiwalóosi na daksi uùhnkiʔla
anii-walóosi na daksi uunii-ahkiʔla
3A.NS-frog that turtle 3B.NS-be.sitting.on:PRC
'The frogs are sitting on the turtle.'

(23c) ᏧᎾᏔᎾ ᎠᏂᏐᏈᎵ
júúnatana aniisoógwíli
di-uunii-ắtana anii-soógwíli
DST2-3B.NS-big 3A.NS-horse
'The horses are big.'

In (24a) the nonsingular pronominal prefix emphasizes that more than one dog is present; the more typical way of saying this is shown in (24b). In both examples its nonsingular number is clear because of the prefix on the adjective.

(24a) ᎠᏂᎩᏟ ᎠᏁᏯᏔᎯ
aniigiihli anééytahi
anii-giihli anii-ééytahi
3A.NS-dog 3A.NS-wild
'wild dogs'

(24b) ᎩᏟ ᎠᏁᏯᏔᎯ
giihli anééytahi
giihli anii-ééytahi

dog 3A.NS-wild
'wild dogs'

Animal root nouns referring to people can be nonsingular. This occurs when the animal represents a clan, as in (25a), or a sports team, as in (25b).

(25a) ᏣᏥᏍ ᎠᏂᏩᏯ
jajis aniiwahya
ja-ji=s anii-wahya
2B-mother=Q 3A.NS-wolf
'Is your mother wolf clan?'

(25b) ᏓᎵᏆ ᎠᏂᎵᏓᏥ
dalígwa aniihlvvdaji
dalígwa anii-hlvvdaji
Tahlequah 3A.NS-tiger
ᏓᏃᏎᎰ ᎠᎾᎳᏍᎦᎵᏍᎩ
daànoóséèho anlaàsgalíísgi
dee-anii-oóséèh-o anii-alaàsgaliisg-i
DST-3A.NS-call:INC-HAB 3A.NS-play.ball:INC-AGT
'Tahlequah calls their athletes Tigers.'

Many of the nonhuman root nouns are common animals. A sample list of these nouns is shown in (26).

(26)	ᏓᎩᏏ	daksi	'turtle(s)'
	ᏜᏯᎧ	dlaayka	'blue jay(s)'
	ᏙᏏ	doosi	'mosquito(s)'
	ᏗᎵ	dili	'skunk(s)'
	ᎩᏟ	giihli	'dog(s)'
	ᎠᏣᏗ	ajáʔdi	'fish'
	ᎠᎭᏫ	ahawi	'deer'
	ᏥᏍᏛᎾ	jíisdvvna	'crawdad(s)'
	ᏓᎿᎪ	daahnúugo	'gar(s)'
	ᏌᏌ	saasa	'goose', 'geese'
	ᎢᎾᏓ	iinada	'snake(s)'
	ᏥᏔᎦ	jitaága	'chicken(s)'
	ᏔᎳᏚ	taláadu	'tree frog(s)'
	ᎫᏇ	guhgwe	'quail(s)'
	ᏪᏌ	weésa	'cat(s)'

	ᏲᎾ	yoóna	'bear(s)'
	ᏩᎭᏱ	wahayi	'wolf,' 'wolves'

Some important trees and plants are also root nouns. A sample list of these nouns is given in (27).

(27)	ᏦᎳ	joóla	'tobacco'
	ᏃᏥ	nohji	'pine(s)'
	ᎠᏥᎾ	ajina	'cedar(s)'
	ᏎᎷ	seélu	'corn'
	ᎧᎶᏪᏗ	kalooweédi	'locust tree(s)'
	ᎠᏂ	aʔni	'strawberry(s)'
	ᏓᏬᎵ	dawóoli	'mushroom(s)'
	ᏔᎹᏟ	tamaahli	'tomato', 'tomatoes'

Many root nouns are concrete items that are common in everyday life. A sample list of these is given in (28).

(28)	ᎦᏅᏍᏓ	gansda	'stick(s)'
	ᎦᏅᏃᏩ	ganvvnoowa	'pipe(s)'
	ᎫᎴ	guule	'acorn(s)'
	ᏦᎳᏂ	joólani	'window(s)'
	ᎪᎳ	koóla	'bone(s)'
	ᏃᏈᏏ	nokwsi	'star(s)'
	ᏅᏓ	nvvda	'sun', 'moon'
	ᏅᏃᎯ	nvvnoóhi	'road(s)'
	ᏅᏯ	nvv̀ya	'rock(s)'
	ᎣᏏ	óosi	'stove(s)'
	ᏒᏙᏂ	svvdooni	'barrel(s)'
	ᎥᏓᎵ	vvdali	'pond(s)'
	ᎠᏥᎸ	ajiíla	'fire(s)'
	ᎠᏍᏗ	asti	'string(s)'
	ᎠᎹ	ama	'water'
	ᎡᎶᎯ	eloohi	'earth'
	ᎦᎵᏦᏕ	gahljoóde	'house(s)'
	ᏔᎷᏣ	taluúja	'basket(s)'
	ᎤᎦᎹ	uugama	'soup'
	ᎠᎹ	áama	'salt'
	ᎠᏓ	ada	'wood'
	ᎠᎵ	ali	'sweat'

DSW	adeéla	'money'
DAᏓ	agoóda	'prairie'
ᏳᎦ	giíga	'blood'
ᎪᎢ	goʔi	'grease'
ᎫᎫ	guugu	'bottle(s)'
ᎣᏝ	oohla	'soap'
ᏩᏥ	waáji	'watch(es)'
ᏩᎦ	wahga	'cow(s)'

Nonhuman root nouns indicate possession by attaching a Set B prefix to the **possession pronoun** (POS.PRO) *-ajeéliíʔi* (typically shortened to *-ajeéli*). This pattern is exemplified in (29).

(29)	ᎩᏝ ᎠᏆᏤᎵ	giihli agwajeéli	'my dog'
	ᎩᏝ ᏣᏤᎵ	giihli jajeéli	'your dog'

Two examples of this construction are shown in (30). Note that in (30b) the possession pronoun follows the possessor.

(30a) ᏐᏈᎵ ᎠᏆᏤᎵ
soógwíl agwajeéli
soógwíli agi-ajeéli
horse 1B-POS.PRO
'my horse' (Feeling 1975a:17)

(30b) ᎤᏙᏓ ᎤᏤᎵ ᏓᏆᎴᎳ
uudooda uujeéli dagwaléela
uu-dooda uu-ajeéli dagwaléela
3B-father 3B-POS.PRO car
'his father's car' (Feeling 1975a:20)

6.2.2. Root Nouns with Pronominal Prefixes

6.2.2.1. *Human Root Nouns*

Human root nouns usually have a Set A prefix. The dictionary form of these nouns includes the third person Set A prefix. For example, the root for 'man' is *-sgaya,* but a Cherokee speaker always gives the word with its default third person Set A prefix as *asgaya.* This prefix has a reference function rather than a possession function. The three singular forms are shown in (31).

(31a) ᏥᏍᎦᏯ jisgaya 'I'm a man.'
(31b) ᎯᏍᎦᏯ hisgaya 'You're a man.'
(31c) ᎠᏍᎦᏯ asgaya 'man', 'He's a man.'

Many human root nouns refer to people according to general categories of gender, age, and ethnicity. A list of the gender and age-related terms is given in (32). On all these forms the third person Set A pronominal prefix is a short vowel, because pronominal lengthening does not typically apply to nouns.

(32)	ᎠᏍᎦᏯ	asgaya	'man'	Track 43
	ᎠᎨᏯ	ageéhya	'woman'	
	ᎠᏫᎾ	awíína	'young man'	
	ᎠᏔᏄᏣ	atanúúja	'teenage girl'	
	ᎠᏧᏣ	achúúja	'boy'	
	ᎠᎨᏳᏣ	ageehyúúja	'girl'	
	ᎠᎦᏴᎵᎨ	agayvv́lige	'old woman'	

Human nouns also refer to people according to their ethnic or national group. A list of some examples is given in (33).

(33)	ᎠᏴᏫᏯ	ayvvwiiya	'Indian'
	ᎠᏣᎳᎩ	ajalagi	'Cherokee person'
	ᎠᏣᏗ	ajahdi	'Choctaw person'
	ᎠᏆᏌᏏ	akwsaasi	'Osage person'
	ᎠᏥᎦᏌ	ajiigasa	'Chickasaw person'
	ᎠᏎᎻᏃᎵ	aseminoli	'Seminole person'
	ᎠᎫᏏ	aguúsi	'Creek person'
	ᎠᏌᏩᏄᎩ	asaawanuúgi	'Shawnee person'
	ᎠᏳᏥ	ayuuji	'Euchee person'
	ᎠᎾᏥ	anaaji	'Natchez person'
	ᎠᏛᏥ	advvji	'German person'
	ᎠᏍᏆᏂ	asgwááni	'Mexican person'
	ᎠᎦᎸᏥ	agalvvji	'French person'

Three examples of human nouns in the third person nonsingular are given in (34).

(34a) ᎠᏂᏧᏣ
aniichúúja
anii-chúúja

3A.NS-boy
'boys'

(34b) ᎠᏂᎨᎯ aniigeéhya 'women'
(34c) ᎠᏂᏍᎦᎯ aniisgaya 'men'

Many of these human root nouns can also be used as nouns referring to languages; in such cases the Set A prefix can be left off, as in (35), although some speakers leave it on.

(35)	ᎯᏬᏂᏍᎪᏍ	ᎫᏏ
	hiwóoniisgos	guúsi
	hi-wóoniisg-o=s	guúsi
	2A-speak:INC-HAB=Q	Creek
	'Do you speak Creek?'	

As shown in (36), pronominal prefixes can also be used on direct addressee nouns.

(36)	ᎢᏍᏗᏧᏣ	ᎡᏍᏗᏴᎭ
	iisdiijúúja	eesdiiyv́vha
	iisdii-júúja	ee-sdii-yv́vha
	2A.DL-boy	TOC-2A.DL-enter:IMM
	'You two boys come inside.'	

This pattern of directly attaching Set A prefixes to nouns indicating group names is a regular process and is used with new words in the language. (37) gives a sample of two borrowed names in their singular and nonsingular forms from the *Cherokee New Testament*. The prefixes are absent in the singular but do appear in the nonsingular forms.

(37a)	ᏆᎵᏏ	gwaálisi	'Pharisee'
	ᎠᏂᏆᎵᏏ	aniigwaálisi	'Pharisees'
(37b)	ᏧᏏ	juúsi	'Jew'
	ᎠᏂᏧᏏ	aniijuúsi	'Jews'

The nouns listed above refer to people according to basic categories of age, gender, or ethnic group. All of these nouns appear to be root nouns, not derived from another word. The majority of people nouns refer to more specific categories such as occupation, position, or some other characteristic. Such nouns are almost always derived from verbs. In the example in (38), the noun 'teacher' comes from the verb 'teach'; this verb contains a **frozen** distributive prefix. This prefix appears as *dee-* (DST) on most verbs, but appears as *di-* (DST2) on nouns. This prefix must also appear on the derived noun.

(38) ᏗᏕᏲᏅᏍᎩ
diideehyóóhvsgi
di-a-adaa-eehyoóhvsg-i
DST2-3A-MDL-teach:INC-AGT
'teacher'

These derived human nouns and how to form them are discussed in chapter 12.

A small set of animal terms also take this type of inflection. Some of these are listed in (39).

(39a)	ᎠᏨᏯ	achvvya	'male animal'
	ᎠᏂᏨᏯ	aniichvvya	'male animals'
(39b)	ᎠᏓ	áʔda	'young animal'
	ᎠᏂᏓ	aníída	'young animals'
(39c)	ᎠᎩᎾ	agíína	'young animal'
	ᎠᏂᎩᎾ	aniigíína	'young animals'
(39d)	ᎠᎩᏏ	agiísi	'female animal'
	ᎠᏂᎩᏏ	aniigiísi	'female animals'

These terms could simply be exceptions or derived words with roots whose meanings are no longer known.

6.2.2.2. *Body Parts*

Body parts, clothing, and relationship terms are the only other nonderived nouns that regularly carry pronominal prefixes. Unlike human root nouns, body parts and clothing use the pronominal prefixes with a possession function rather than a reference function. A comparison of these three classes in (40) demonstrates that only the human nouns have prefixes with a reference function; the other two have prefixes with a possession function.

(40a)	ᎯᏍᎦᏯ	hisgaya	'you are a man'	but not: 'your man'
(40b)	ᎯᎴᏂ	hiʔlééni	'your ear'	but not: 'you are an ear'
(40c)	ᎭᎿᏬ	hahnawo	'your shirt'	but not: 'you are a shirt'

Most body parts can have a pronominal prefix to indicate possession; in fact, many body parts must always be possessed. These body parts are understood always to belong to someone, indicated by either a Set A or Set B prefix. For example, in (41a) the noun bears a Set B prefix, while in (41b) the Set A prefix occurs.

(41a) DᏉᏰᏂ
agwoyééni
agi-oyééni
1B-hand
'my hand'

(41b) ᏥᏍᎪᎵ
jiìskóól
ji-skóólii
1A-head
'my head'

Some body parts are **Set A nouns** and take Set A prefixes; others are **Set B nouns** and take Set B prefixes. As with verbs, this choice is unpredictable and is simply learned as part of the information about the noun. A list of the more common body parts is given in (42) for Set A and in (43) for Set B. They are presented in their root form. Additional information is presented in parentheses; for example, many nouns take the third person *ga-* or appear with a frozen distributive prefix. These examples are written without the prefix and are thus not actual words; for this reason they are not written in the syllabary.

Set A body parts

(42)	-ʔléėni	'ear'	(*ga-*)
	-hyvvsóóli	'nose'	(*ga-*)
	-hndóhgv́v́ʔi	'tooth'	(*ga-*)
	-nvvwóóʔi	'shoulder'	(*ga-*)
	-nvv̀sgééni	'leg'	(*ga-*)
	-teèsgééni	'backbone'	(*ga-*)
	-áagalo	'thigh'	(*ga-*)
	-aagwali	'butt'	(*ga-*)
	-gvtegééna	'forehead'	
	-hóóli	'mouth'	
	-yelv́v́li	'body'	
	-ʔgwali	'cheek'	
	-hngóóʔi	'tongue'	(*ga-*)
	-hnoogééni	'arm'	(*ga-*)

-yeesaʔdv́v́ʔi	'finger'	(*ga-*)
-hndóhgv́v́ʔi	'tooth'	(*ga-*)
-nvvwóóʔi	'shoulder'	(*ga-*)
-nv̀vsgééni	'leg'	(*ga-*)
-hyvjééni	'throat'	
-kasgééni	'hip'	
-gahtóóli	'eye'	
-skóóli	'head'	

Set B body parts

(43)

-oòyééni	'hand'
-asuhgahlv́v́ʔi	'fingernail'
-neegalv́v́ʔi	'skin'
-ahanéegalv	'lip'
-akátv	'face'
-alahstéena	'foot'
-adaahndo	'heart'
-adiiyvvdi	'navel'
-yuukálv	'chin'
-stigv	'hair'
-giihli	'hair (animal hair)'
-eéla	'liver'
-aksééni	'butt'

All countable body part terms can be inflected for number. For most of the body parts this prefix is the expected distributive (DST2) *di-* form that appears on nouns. Two examples with 'leg' are shown in (44).

(44a) ᏗᎦᏅᏍᎨᏂ
diganv̀vsgééni
di-ga-nv̀vsgééni
DST2-3A-leg
'his legs'

(44b) ᏗᏂᏅᏍᎨᏂ
diiniinv̀vsgééni
di-anii-nv̀vsgééni
DST2-3A.NS-leg
'their legs'

Many of the body part terms have a slightly different way of indicating the nonsingular. These body parts are distinguished by their *-v́v́ʔi* suffix. This derivation is unusual in that the distributive prefix is *dee-* rather than the *di-* used on most nouns; this **verbal noun** derivation is discussed further in chapter 12. Several nonsingular forms of these body part terms are listed in (45). In (45a) and (45c) the distributive has the variant form [*d*] before a vowel; if the *di*-form were used, it would appear as [*j*] before a vowel.

(45a) ᏚᏬᏁᎦᏞᎢ
duùhanéegaʔlv́v́ʔi
dee-uu-hanéegaʔlv́v́ʔi
DST-3B-lip
'her lips'

(45b) ᏕᎯᏙᎬᎢ
deehídoogv́v́ʔi
dee-hi-doogv́v́ʔi
DST-2A-tooth
'your teeth'

(45c) ᏚᏫᏢᎢ
duùhwídlv́v́ʔi
dee-uu-hwídlv́v́ʔi
DST-3B-wrist
'his wrists'

All body parts, with the exception of blood, bones, and internal organs, have pronominal prefixes. Some body parts have alternate forms to show that they are not possessed. Although a few general patterns exist, it is not possible to predict which term uses which pattern. If the body part in question is not possessed, this prefix has no semantic value and is merely part of the word. The distinction between possessed and nonpossessed is therefore indicated in one of three ways. The first way is when the body part has one set of prefixes when possessed and a third person singular **dummy prefix** from the opposite set when not possessed. This pattern is exemplified in (46).

(46)	ᎤᏄᎳᏥ	uunulaji	'her rib'
	ᎦᏄᎳᏥ	ganulaji	'rib'

A second pattern is for the pronominal prefixes to remain the same but with a slight change in the word itself. Two examples of this pattern are given in (47).

(47) ᎠᎦᏙᎵ <u>a</u>któóli 'his eye' ᎠᎦᏔ <u>a</u>kta 'eye'
ᎦᏅᎪᎢ <u>gaà</u>hngóóʔi 'her tongue' ᎦᏅᎦ <u>gaà</u>hnga 'tongue'

A third pattern is a combination of the first two strategies and involves both a change in the shape of the word and a prefix from the opposite set. This pattern is demonstrated in (48).

(48) ᎤᏁᎦᎸᎢ <u>uu</u>neegalv́v́ʔi 'his skin' ᎦᏁᎦ <u>ga</u>neega 'skin'
ᎠᏍᎪᎵ <u>a</u>skóóli 'her head' ᎤᏍᎧ <u>uu</u>ska 'head'

Some Set B body parts can use the **impersonal Set B prefix** *oo-* when not possessed. This alternation is seen in (49). This prefix is further discussed in chapter 9.

(49) ᎤᏁᎸᏒᎢ <u>uù</u>hneelv́vsv́v́ʔi 'his scar' ᎣᏁᎸᏒᎢ <u>oò</u>hneelv́vsv́v́ʔi 'scar'

A few body-related terms are not normally possessed; in other words, in their **citation form** they have no pronominal prefix. Two of these are listed in (50).

(50) ᎩᎦ giíga 'blood'
ᎪᎳ koóla 'bone'

It is possible for these items to enter a possessive relationship in certain contexts. The example in (51) is from the *Cherokee New Testament*; not only is 'blood' possessed, but so is the normally uninflected word for 'flesh'.

(51) ᎠᎩᏫᏯ ᎠᎩᏍᎩ ᎠᎴ ᎠᎩᎩᎬ ᎠᏗᏔᏍᎩ
agiwiiya agiisgi ale agigiigv adiitasgi
agi-wiiya a-giisg-i ale agi-giigv a-adiitasg-i
1B-flesh 3A-eat:INC-AGT and 1B-blood 3A-drink:INC-AGT
'one who eats my flesh and drinks my blood' (*Cherokee New Testament*, John 6:54)

6.2.2.3. *Clothing*

Basic clothing terms are not always possessed, but they bear a pronominal prefix when possessed. They also display the nonsingular pattern typical for nouns, with the *di-* distributive prefix. Three examples with 'shirt' appear in (52). In (52b) the vowel of the prefix is lengthened after it causes the removal of the adjoining pronominal prefix vowel. In (52c) the *di-* prefix appears in its expected [*j*] variant form before vowels other than /a/ and /i/.

(52a) ᎠᏤ ᎠᏆᏂᏬ
aje agwahnawo

aje agi-ahnawo
new 1B-shirt
'my new shirt'

(52b) ᏗᏆᎭᏃᏬ
diigwahnawo
di-agi-ahnawo
DST2-1B-shirt
'my clothes'

(52c) ᏣᏂ ᏧᎭᏃᏬ
jaáni juuhnawo
jaáni di-uu-ahnawo
John DST2-3B-shirt
'John's clothes'

Unlike body part terms, individual clothing terms only indicate possession with Set B prefixes. A sample set of the more common terms in their basic forms is given in (53).

Clothing terms

(53)	-ahnawo	'shirt', 'clothing'
	-ahyvtli	'tie'
	-asuulo	'pants'
	-asano	'dress'
	-aliyo	'sock'
	-adleèsido	'apron'
	-alsgweètuwo	'hat'
	-aliyeèsuulo	'glove'
	-alaàsuúlo	'shoe'
	-adadlosdi	'belt'
	-aliyeèsuústawo	'ring'
	-aasaléérni	'coat' (*ga-*)

A few more examples of possessed forms are shown in (54).

(54a) ᏦᎦᏌᏃ
joogaàsano
di-oogii-aàsano
DST2-1B.PL.EX-dress
'our dresses'

(54b) ᏗᏣᎵᏰᏑᎶ
dijaliyeesuulo
di-ja-aliyeesuulo
DST2-2B-glove
'your gloves'

(54c) ᏧᎾᎵᏍᏇᏚᏬ
juunalsgweètuwo
di-uunii-alisgweètuwo
DST2-3B.NS-hat
'their hats'

For items that are considered inherently nonsingular, the distributive always appears. (55) shows three possessed examples with 'glasses'; the fourth example is not possessed but has a Set A dummy prefix that appears as a lengthened vowel on the distributive.

(55a) ᏗᏩᎦᏘᏅᏗ
diiwaktinv́v́di
di-agi-agahtinv́v́di
DST2-1B-glasses
'my glasses'

(55b) ᏗᏣᎦᏘᏅᏗ
dijaktinv́v́di
di-ja-agahtinv́v́di
DST2-2B-glasses
'your glasses'

(55c) ᏧᎦᏘᏅᏗ
juuktinv́v́di
di-uu-agahtinv́v́di
DST2-3B-glasses
'his glasses'

(55d) ᏧᎦᏘᏅᏗ
diiktinv́v́di
di-a-agahtinv́v́di
DST2-3A-glasses
'glasses'

A few clothing terms take the third person dummy prefix *ga-* when not possessed. An example is 'coat', shown below in a nonpossessed construction in (56a) and in possessed constructions in (56b) and (56c).

(56a) ᎦᎠᏌᎴᏂ
gaasalééni
ga-aasalééni
3A-coat
'coat'

(56b) ᎠᏆᏌᎴᏂ
agwaasalééni
agi-aasalééni
1B-coat
'my coat'

(56c) ᎤᏌᎴᏂ
uusalééni
uu-aasalééni
3B-coat
'his coat'

6.2.2.4. *Relationship Nouns*

Relationship nouns refer to humans and typically indicate a family member but can also refer to nonfamily members such as friends and neighbors. Such nouns typically have a prefix with both a reference and a possession function. Because a relationship implies two or more participants, pronominal prefixes on relationship terms in most cases reference two or more people. If the person referred to by the relationship noun is a **local person** and the possessor is third person, then a Set A **animate object** prefix is used. This pattern is exemplified in (57) for the noun 'mother'.

(57a) ᏥᏥ
jiiji
jii-ji
1A.AN-mother
'I am his mother.'

(57b) ᎯᏥ
hiiji

hii-ji
2A.AN-mother
'You are his mother.'

If the reference function is third person, then Set B prefixes are used, as seen in (58).

(58a) DᎩᏥ
agiji
agi-ji
1B-mother
'she is my mother', 'my mother'

(58b)	GᏥ	jaji	'she is your mother', 'your mother'
(58c)	ᎤᏥ	uuji	'she is her mother', 'her mother'
(58d)	ᎤᏂᏥ	uuniiji	'she is their mother', 'their mother'

If both persons are local a **combined local prefix** is used, as seen in (59). These prefixes, which are discussed in chapter 9, are used to refer to a local person subject and a local person object.

(59a) ᏍᎩᏥ
sgiji
sgi-ji
2/1-mother
'You are my mother.'

(59b) ᏋᏙᏓ
gvvdooda
gvv-dooda
1/2-father
'I am your father.'

A list of some relationship nouns is given in (60).

Relationship nouns

(60)	-dooda	'father'
	-ji	'mother'
	-adaatiínáʔa	'offspring'
	-duuda	'grandfather (maternal)'
	-líisi	'grandmother (maternal)', 'grandchild'

-niísi	'grandparent (paternal)'
-duji	'uncle'
-tlogi	'aunt'
-do	'sibling (opposite gender)'
-nv́v́tla	'brother'
-luugi	'sister of a woman'
-alííʔi	'friend'
-alííkdi	'boyfriend', 'girlfriend'
-hyééhi	'husband'
-daliiʔi	'wife'
-eéji ageehúúja	'daughter'
-eéji achúúja	'son'

Some of these relationship nouns have a special **family pronominal prefix** *ee-* that is used to address someone directly. This prefix is only used on family relationship terms; its abbreviation is 1B.FAM. Two examples are given in (61).

(61a) ᎡᏙᏓ eedooda 'father!'
(61b) ᎡᏥ eeji 'mother!'

In modern Cherokee this prefix is replacing the first person Set B pronominal prefix *agi-* and can now be used to talk about the person and not just to address him or her. For example, the phrase 'my mother' occurs four times in Feeling (1975a); in all four cases the family pronominal prefix is used, even though it is clear in each case from the context that 'my mother' is not being spoken to. One example from the dictionary is shown in (62).

(62) ᏂᎪᎯᎸ ᏗᏰᎦᏟ ᏕᎦᏰᏫᏍᎪ ᎡᏥ
nigoóhíilv diihyehgahli deegáayewsgo eeji
nigoóhíilv di-a-hyehgahli dee-ga-x́xyewsg-o ee-ji
always DST2-3A-quilt DST-3A-sew:INC-HAB 1B.FAM-mother
'My mother is always sewing quilts.' (Feeling 1975a:131)

Some other terms that indicate a relationship other than a biological one also follow the relationship pattern of possession. The word 'friend' usually has a non-singular, dual, or plural pronominal prefix because the relationship is considered mutual. Three examples with 'friend' are shown in (63).

(63a) ᎣᎩᎾᎵᎢ
oogina lííʔi
ooginii-alííʔi

1B.DL.EX-friend
'my friend'

(63b) ᏍᏓᎵᎢ sdalííʔi 'your friend'
(63c) ᎤᏃᎵᎢ uunalííʔi 'his friend'

It is possible to use a singular form of 'friend' if nonsingular number is implied for one part but not the other, as in (64). In these examples nonsingular number is expressed by the *di-* form of the distributive. In (64a) *di-* appears as the variant form [*j*] before a vowel.

(64a) ᏧᎵᎢ
juulííʔi
di-uu-alííʔi
DST2-3B-friend
'his friends'

(64b) ᏗᏣᎵᎢ
dijalííʔi
di-ja-alííʔi
DST2-2B-friend
'your friends'

(64c) ᏗᏆᎵᎢ
diigwalííʔi
di-agi-alííʔi
DST2-1B-friend
'my friends'

Terms for siblings follow a similar pattern but with an added layer of complexity. The nouns for 'brother' and 'sister' are both **reciprocal relationship nouns.** If both siblings are local persons, the **reflexive** (RFL) prefix *-adaad-* is used; some speakers often also use a distributive prepronominal prefix. In (65a) the distributive prefix appears as [*j*] before the vowel /o/. The reflexive is discussed in chapter 9.

(65a) ᏦᏍᏓᏓᏅᏟ
joosdadaanv́v́tl
di-oosdii-adaad-nv́v́tla
DST2-1A.DL.EX-RFL-brother.of.man
'my brother'

(65b) ᏗᏂᏓᏅᏟ
diindaanv́v́tl
di-anii-adaad-nv́v́tla
DST2-3A.NS-RFL-brother.of.man
'his brother'

In the third person, the reciprocal form is interchangeable with a form similar to that described in the beginning of this section for 'mother' and 'father'. This form uses the Set B prefix. Compare (65b) above with its nonreciprocal counterpart in (66) below. Besides lacking both the distributive and the reflexive prefixes, it also does not have the highfall tone.

(66) ᎤᏅᏟ
uuhnvvhli
uu-hnvvhli
3B-brother
'his brother'

These sibling terms change depending on the gender of the person who is considered the possessor. Instead of a two-way system (as in English 'brother' and 'sister') Cherokee has a three-way distinction. The noun *-do* indicates a sibling of the opposite gender (67a), while 'brother of a man' (67b) and 'sister of a woman' (67c) have distinct terms. The more generic term *-do* treats the relationship asymmetrically, without a reflexive prefix or a distributive prefix. The reciprocal relationship nouns, however, have both of these prefixes.

(67a) ᏣᏙ
jado
ja-do
2B-sibling.of.opposite.gender
'your sister (of a man)', 'your brother (of a woman)'

(67b) ᏗᏍᏓᏓᎵᎢ
disdadaalv́v́ʔi
di-sdii-adaad-lv́v́ʔi
DST2-2B.DL-RFL-sister (of a woman)
'your sister (of a woman)'

(67c) ᏗᏍᏓᏓᏅᏟ
disdadaanv́v́tla
di-sdii-adaad-nv́v́tla

DST2-2B.DL-RFL-brother (of man)
'your brother (of a man)'

These special reciprocal terms, despite the dual pronominal prefix and the distributive prepronominal prefix, are still treated as singular nouns for purposes of verb inflection. In (68a) the lack of a prepronominal prefix on the verb makes it clear that the speaker only sees one brother. In (68b) a plural form appears; the speaker in this case indicated that the distributive could appear on the noun without a change in meaning.

(68a)	ᏗᏍᏓᏓᎸᏉᎢ	ᏫᏥᎪᎥᎢ
	disdadaalv́v́ʔi	wijiigoʔvv́ʔi
	di-sdii-adaad-lv́v́ʔi	wi-jii-gooh-vv́ʔi
	DST2-2B.DL-RFL-sister (of woman)	TRN-1A.AN-see:CMP-EXP
	'I saw your sister there.'	

(68b)	ᎢᏣᏓᎸᏉᎢ	ᏕᏥᎪᎥᎢ
	iijadaalv́v́ʔi	deejiigoʔvv́ʔi
	iijii-adaad-lv́v́ʔi	dee-jii-gooh-vv́ʔi
	2B.PL-RFL-sister (of woman)	DST-1A.AN-see:CMP-EXP
	'I saw your sisters.'	

Cherokee does not have specific terms for 'niece' and 'nephew'. These relationships are expressed by referring to the aunt or uncle, as illustrated in (69).

(69a)	Ꮎ	ᎠᏂᏔᏞ	ᎠᏂᏧᏣ	ᎦᏥᏚᏥ
	naʔ	aniitaʔli	aniichúúja	gaajiiduuji
	naʔ	anii-taʔli	anii-chúúja	gaa-jii-duuji
	that	3A.NS-two	3A.NS-boy	ANS-1A.AN-uncle
	'I am uncle to those two boys.'			

(69b)	ᎭᏢ	ᎠᏩᏓᏚᏥᎢ
	haadlv	awadaaduujiiʔv́v́ʔi
	haadlv	agi-adaad-duujiiʔv́v́ʔi
	where	1B-RFL-uncle
	'Where is my niece/nephew?'	

If the second party in the relationship is not mentioned, the reflexive prefix (RFL) appears. This prefix typically only appears on verbs; an exception is this special usage on relationship terms. Two examples are shown in (70). The word for 'uncle' is different from the word above due to dialect difference.

(70a) ᎠᏩᏓᏧᏥᎠ
awadaaduujiiʔa
agi-adaad-duujiiʔa
1B-RFL-uncle
'I am an uncle.'

(70b) ᎠᏩᏓᏢᎩᏴᎢ
awadaahlogiiyv́v́ʔi
agi-adaad-hlogiiyv́v́ʔi
1B-RFL-aunt
'I am an aunt.'

Several examples with 'child' are presented in (71). A first or second person possessing a third person takes the Set B prefix as in (71a); but the third person non-singular is used if both possessor and child are third person singular, as in (71b).

(71a) ᎠᏇᏥ
agweéji
agi-eéji
1B-child
'my child'

(71b) ᎤᏪᏥ
uweéji
uu-eéji
3B-child
'his child'

(71c) ᏗᏇᏥ
diigweéji
di-agi-eéji
DST2-1B-child
'my children'

(71d) ᏧᏁᏥ
juuneéji
di-uunii-eéji
DST2-3B.NS-child
'their children'

6.2.2.5. *Irregular Root Nouns*

A few nonhuman nouns do not appear to be derived but do have prefixes with a reference function. A list of some of these nouns is given in (72). The nouns are shown with their nonsingular forms to indicate that the initial /a/ or /u/ is indeed a pronominal prefix.

(72a)	ᎤᎦᏐᏣᏁᏓ	uuksoòjanééda	'goat'
	ᎤᎾᎦᏐᏣᏁᏓ	uunaksoòjanééda	'goats'
(72b)	ᎤᏦᎾᏘ	uujoonati	'rattlesnake'
	ᎤᏂᏦᎾᏘ	uuniijoonati	'rattlesnakes'
(72c)	ᎤᎩᏔ	uukta	'seed'
	ᎤᏂᎩᏔ	uuniikta	'seeds'
(72d)	ᎤᏥᏯ	uujiiya	'worm'
	ᎤᏂᏥᏯ	uuniijiiya	'worms'
(72e)	ᎤᏃᏕᎾ	uunoòdééna	'sheep'
	ᎤᏂᏃᏕᎾ	uuniinoòdééna	'sheep (NS)'
(72f)	ᎠᎪᎳ	agoola	'perch'
	ᎠᏂᎪᎳ	aniigoola	'perch (NS)'
(72g)	ᎠᏣᏗ	ajaʔdi	'fish'
	ᎠᏂᏣᏗ	aniijaʔdi	'fish (NS)'
(72h)	ᎤᏃᎦ	uunohga	'bass'
	ᎤᏂᏃᎦ	uuniinohga	'bass (NS)'
(72i)	ᎠᏥᏍᎬᏂᎨᎢ	ajisgvnigééʔi	'carp'
	ᎠᏂᏥᏍᎬᏂᎨᎢ	aniijisgvnigééʔi	'carp (NS)'
(72j)	ᎤᎦᏑᏘ	uuksúuti	'diamondback rattler'
	ᎤᎾᎦᏑᏘ	uunaksúuti	'diamondback rattlers'

Because there are so few of these nouns it seems likely that they are old derivations that have become shortened and/or that the root from which they originally derived has fallen out of use.

6.3. Pronouns

Pronouns stand in place of more specific **noun phrases.** They can serve in the same roles as nouns but cannot be modified by an adjective or a **demonstrative.**

6.3.1. Personal Pronouns

There are only two **personal pronouns** in Cherokee. Their basic meaning is singular, but in the proper context they can also refer to nonsingular persons. These pronouns are typically used for emphasis or to answer a question. Two examples are given in (73).

(73a)	ᎠᏴ	ᏥᎦ
	ahyv	géega
	ahyv	ji-éega
	1PRO	1A-go:PRC
	'I am going.'	

(73b)	ᏂᎯᏅ	ᏣᏯᏄᎵᏧ
	nihinv	jayanúúliju
	nihi=nv	ja-yanúúli=ju
	2PRO=FC	2B-fast=CQ
	'Are you fast?'	

These pronouns are also used as single-word answers to questions. Three examples are shown in (74). Depending on the context, this first person pronoun can be translated in three different ways in English.

(74a)	ᎦᎪ	ᎤᏤᎵ	ᎯᎠ	ᎩᏟ	ᎠᏯ
	gáago	uujeéli	hiʔa	giihli	aya
	gáago	uu-ajeéli	hiʔa	giihli	aya
	who	3B-POS.PRO	this	dog	1PRO
	'Whose dog is this?' 'Mine.'				

(74b)	ᎦᎪ	ᎤᎵᏍᎦᏟᏤ	ᎯᎠ	ᎩᏟ	ᎠᏯ
	gáago	uùlsgahlje	hiʔa	giihli	aya
	gáago	uu-ali-sgahlj-e	hiʔa	giihli	aya
	who	3B-MDL-bite:CMP-NXP	this	dog	1PRO
	'Who did the dog bite?' 'Me.'				

(74c)	ᎦᎪ	ᎤᏢᎦ	ᎠᏯ
	gáago	uùdlv́vga	aya
	gáago	uu-hdlv́vga	aya
	who	3B-be.sick:PRC	1PRO
	'Who is sick?' 'I am.'		

As evidenced by these examples, these pronouns differ from their English counterparts in that they only specify grammatical person; the specific context makes it clear whether the pronoun refers to a subject, an object, or a possessor. The first and second person pronouns are usually understood as singular but in the proper context can be used to refer to dual or plural persons. Two examples are shown in (75). In (75a) the **postfix** *=hnoo* 'and' is attached to the first person pronoun.

(75a)

Ꮶ	ᏱᏣᏂ	ᎨᏎ
joʔ	yiijani	geèse
joʔ	yi-iijii-ani	geès-e
three	IRR-2A.PL-exist.there:PRC	be:INC-NXP
ᎠᏯᏃ	ᎣᏍᏗᏔᎵᏭ	ᏥᎨᏒᎢ
ayahnoo	oosdiitaʔliwu	jigeèsvv́ʔi
aya=hnoo	oosdii-taʔli=wu	ji-geès-vv́ʔi
1PRO=CN	1A.DL.EX-two=DT	REL-be:INC-EXP

'There were three of you and only two of us.'

(75b)

ᎠᏯ	ᎢᎩᏲᎱᎯᏍᏗ	ᎤᎬᏫᏳᏎ
aya	iìgiiyoohúúhisd	uùgvvwiíyúse
aya	iigii-yoohuuhisdi	uùgvvwiíyúse
1PRO	1B.PL-die:INF\MOD	instead
ᏏᏃ	ᏥᏌ	ᎦᎶᏁᏓ
siihno	jiísa	galoonééda
siihno	jiísa	ga-looneé-da
than	Jesus	3A-anoint-PCP

'It should have been our death instead of Jesus Christ's.'

6.3.2. Interrogative Pronouns

Interrogative pronouns are used to ask the identity of a subject or an object. The pronoun *gaago* or *googo* (depending on the speaker's dialect) is used to ask the identity of a person. Three examples are given in (76).

(76a)

ᎪᎪ	ᎯᎪᏩᏔ	ᏗᎦᏚᎲ
góogo	hiigoòwaht	digaadúuhv
góogo	hii-gohwahta	di-gaadúuhv
who	2A.AN-see:IMM	TOW-town

'Who did you see in town?'

(76b)

ᎪᎪ	ᏣᎦᏘᏰ
góogo	jaktiíye
góogo	ja-gahtiíy-e
who	2B-wait:INC-NXP

'Who was waiting on you?'

(76c) ᎦᎪ ᎯᏩᏛᎯᏓᏍᏗ ᏣᏚᎵ
gaago hiìwahtvvhiídáàsdi jaduuli
gaago hii-hwahtvvhiídáàsdi ja-aduuli
who 2A.AN-visit:INF 2B-want:PRC
'Who do you want to visit?' (Feeling 1975a:27)

The pronoun *gado* is used as the question word 'what?' Two examples are given in (77); in (77b) the pronoun is shortened to *do*.

(77a) ᎦᏙ ᎯᎪᏩᏘ
gado higoohwti
gado hi-goohwti
what 2A-see:PRC
'What do you see?'

(77b) Ꮩ ᎠᏛᏁ
do aàdv́vne
do a-adv́vne
what 3A-do:PRC
'What is he doing?'

If the question focuses on the identity of the subject or object, the interrogative pronoun appears with *úúsdi*. (78) shows four examples of this pronoun.

(78a) ᎦᏙᏍᎩ ᏄᏍᏗ ᎠᏯᎢ ᎧᏁᏌᎢ
gadosgin úúsd aàyáʔi kaneèsáʔi
gado=sgini úúsdi a-yáʔi kaneèsáʔi
what=CS thing 3A-be.inside:PRC box
'What kind of thing is in the box?'

(78b) ᎦᏙ ᎤᏍᏗ ᏕᏣᏙᎢ
gado úúsdi deejadooʔi
gado úúsdi dee-ja-adaa-ooʔi
what thing DST-2B-MDL-name:PRC
'What is your name?'

(78c) Ꮩ ᎤᏍᏗ ᏓᏤᏝ
do úúsdi daàjeéhla
do úúsdi daàjeéhla
what thing better
'Which is better?'

(78d) ᎦᏙ ᎤᏍᏗ ᎦᏘᎦ Track 44
gado úúsdi gaatihga
gado úúsdi ga-xxtihga
what thing 3B-mean:PRC
'What does this mean?'

6.3.3. Indefinite Pronouns

Indefinite pronouns are used to refer to a person, place, or thing when a more specific identity is unknown or irrelevant. A list of indefinite pronouns is given in (79).

(79)	ᎩᎶ	kilo	'somebody'
	ᏐᎢ	so?i	'other'
	ᏂᎦᏓ	nigááda	'all'
	ᎪᎱᏍᏗ	gohúúsdi	'something'
	ᎥᏍᎩ	vsgi	'it', 'that'

The pronoun *kilo* is used when the identity of a human noun has not been previously mentioned. The verb conjugation treats this indefinite pronoun as third person singular. In (80b) *kilo* refers to a subject: it translates as 'nobody' when the **negation adverb** *tla* is placed before it. In (80c) this same indefinite pronoun refers to an object; in (80d) it refers to the possessor of another noun.

(80a) ᎩᎶ ᎤᏩᏎ
kilo uùhwase
kilo uu-hwas-e
someone 3B-buy:CMP-NXP
'Someone has bought it.'

(80b) Ꮭ ᎩᎶ ᏳᎩᎶᎡ
tla kilo yuhgiilo?e
tla kilo yi-uu-hgiilo?-e
NEG someone IRR-3B-wash:CMP-NXP
'Nobody washed it.'

(80c) Ꮭ ᎩᎶ ᏱᏥᎪᏩᏔ
tla kilo yijiigoòwahta
tla kilo yi-jii-gohwahta

NEG	someone	IRR-1A.AN-see:IMM	

'I didn't see anybody.'

(80d)	ᏄᏓᎴ	ᎩᎶ	ᎤᏑᎶ	ᎤᏑᎳᏅᎢ
	nuúdale	kilo	uusuulo	uùsuuláànvv́ʔi
	ni-uúdale	kilo	uu-asuulo	uu-áasuuláàn-vv́ʔi
	NI-different	someone	3B-pants	3B-put.on.pants:CMP-EXP

'He put on someone else's pants.' (Feeling 1975a:55)

If the unknown subject or object is inanimate, the indefinite pronoun *gohúúsdi* or its shortened form *gúúsdi* is used. The two are used interchangeably by speakers.

(81a)	ᎩᏝ	ᎪᎯᏍᏗ	ᏓᏍᎪᏂᎭ
	giihla	gohúúsd	daàsgooníha
	giihla	gohúúsdi	dee-a-sgooníha
	dog	something	DST-3A-howl:PRC

'The dog is howling at something.'

(81b)	ᎪᎯᏍᏗ	ᎤᏂᏫᏑᏗ	ᎤᎾᏚᎵ
	gohúúsd	uuniihwisuudi	uùnduuli
	gohúúsdi	uunii-hwisuudi	uunii-aduuli
	something	3B.NS-plant:INF	3B.NS-want:PRC

'They want to plant something.'

(81c)	Ꮭ	ᎩᎶ	ᎪᏍᏗ	ᏳᏅᏙ	ᎠᎭᏂ
	tla	kilo	góósd	yuuhnto	ahani
	tla	kilo	góósdi	yi-uu-anvht-o	ahani
	NEG	somebody	something	IRR-3B-know:INC-HAB	here

'No one here ever knows anything.'

The forms *vsgi* and *vsgina* are used for known objects, as shown in (82).

(82a)	Ꮭ	ᎥᏍᎩ	ᏱᎩ
	hla	vsgi	yigi
	hla	vsgi	yi-gi
	NEG	that	IRR-be:IMM

'That's not it.' (Feeling 1975a:130)

(82b)	ᎥᏍᎩᎾ	ᎠᎪᏩᏘᎭ
	vv̀sgina	aàgoohwtíha
	vv̀sgi=na	a-goohwtíha

that=FC 3A-see:PRC
'He sees that one.' (Pulte and Feeling 1975:325)

Some indefinite pronouns can be modified by an **adjectival clause,** a type of clause that modifies a noun. This type of clause is discussed in chapter 11. An example is given in (83).

(83) ᏂᎦᏓ ᏂᏍᎩᏯᏛᏁᎸ ᎦᎵᎡᎵᎪ
nigáád <u>niisgiiyadv̌vneélv̌</u> galiiʔeélîigo
nigááda ni-iisgii-adv̌vn-eél-v ji-aliiheélîig-o
all NI-2/1.PL-do:CMP-APL:CMP-EXP\SUB 1A-be.appreciative:INC-HAB
'I appreciate everything <u>you have done for us.</u>'

6.3.4. Indefinite Relative Pronouns

Indefinite relative pronouns are always followed by an adjectival clause; the combination of these two elements creates a **nominal.** These constructions are described in chapter 11; two examples are shown in (84) with *nuusdv* and *iiyúúsdi.* In each example the pronoun and its following adjectival clause are underlined. The underlined segments in both examples are nominals because they are acting as the object of another verb.

(84a) ᎤᏅᏔᏍ ᎢᏳᏍᏗ ᎨᏒ ᏣᏓᏅᏍᎦ
uùhntas <u>iiyúúsdi</u> <u>geèsv́</u> <u>jadanv́v́sga</u>
uu-anvhta=s iiyúúsdi geès-v́ ji-a-adanvv́sga
3B-know:PRC=Q what be:INC-DVB REL-3A-order:PRC\SUB
'Does he know <u>what he's ordering?</u>'

(84b) ᏄᏍᏛ ᎠᎦᏛᏛᏅ ᎠᏉᎵᏨ
<u>nuusdv́v́</u> <u>aktvv́dv́vhnv́</u> aàgwoohljv
nuusdv́v́ agi-ahtvv́dv́vhn-v́ agi-oolihj-v
what 1B-ask:CMP-DVB 1B-understand:CMP-EXP
'I understood <u>what he asked me.</u>'

6.3.5. Emphatic Pronoun (EMP.PRO)

The **emphatic pronoun** *-vvsa* always appears with a Set B pronominal prefix. It often accompanies a verb with a **reflexive** or **reciprocal** meaning. Two examples are shown in (85); in (85a) the combination of the prefix *uu-* with the initial /v/ of the pronoun results in the form [*uwa*].

(85a)	ᎤᏓᏛᏂᎸᎢ	ᎤᏩᏌ
	uùdaadvvhnílv́vʔi	uwaása
	uu-adaad-vvhníl-vv́ʔi	uu-vv́sa
	3B-RFL-hit:CMP-EXP	3B-EMP.PRO
	'He hit himself.'	

(85b)	ᎣᎦᏓᏙᎵᏨ	ᎣᎬᏌ
	oògadaadoohljv	oogvv́sa
	oogii-adaad-oolihj-v	oogii-vv́sa
	1B.PL.EX-RFL-recognize:CMP-EXP	1B.PL.EX-EMP.PRO
	'We recognized each other.'	

As demonstrated in (86), this pronoun also has a nonreflexive meaning and serves to emphasize the verb's subject.

(86)	ᎠᏗᏔᏍᏗ	ᏱᏣᏚᎵ	ᏨᏌ	ᏣᏟᏍᏙᏗ
	adiítasdi	yijaduuli	jvv́sa	jadliisdohdi
	a-adiítasdi	yi-ja-aduuli	ja-vv́sa	ja-dliisdohdi
	3A-drink:INF	IRR-2B-want:PRC	2B-EMP.PRO	2B-pour:INF
	'If you want something to drink you pour it yourself.'			

6.3.6. Possession Pronoun (POS.PRO)

As discussed earlier in this chapter, some nouns are able to indicate possession through a pronominal prefix. Nouns that are unable to take such a prefix express possession with the possession pronoun *-ajeélííʔi;* this pronoun bears a pronominal prefix to indicate the possessor of the noun that it accompanies. Two examples are given in (87).

(87a)	ᎩᎶ	ᏧᏤᎵ	ᏕᎯᎦᏘᏅᏛᏍᎦ
	kilo	juujeéli	deehaktinvvtv́sga
	kilo	di-uu-ajeéli	dee-hi-agahtinvvtv́sga
	someone	DST2-3B-POS.PRO	DST-2A-put.on.glasses:PRC
	'You are putting on someone's glasses.'		

(87b)	ᎤᏙᏓ	ᎤᏤᎵ	ᏓᏆᎴᎳ	ᎠᎯᎴᎭ
	uudooda	uujeéli	dagwaléela	aàhileha
	uu-dooda	uu-ajeéli	dagwaléela	a-hileha

3B-father 3B-POS.PRO car 3A-drive:PRC
'He's driving his dad's car.' (Feeling 1975a:20)

6.4. Modifying the Noun Phrase

A noun phrase may consist of just a noun but often includes other elements that modify it, such as adjectives, demonstratives, and postpositional phrases. In (88) the first noun phrase consists of the adjective 'old' and the noun 'ways'. The second noun phrase consists of the demonstrative *na* followed by 'stomp ground dance religion'; the two words preceding the noun translated as 'religion' (literally 'that which they have allegiance to') act as modifiers to that noun. The third noun phrase is the adjective 'sacred' modifying the noun 'fire'.

(88) ᎠᏉᎯᏳᏃ ᎤᏪᏘ ᏧᏂᎶᏒᎢ
aàgwoohiyúhno uuwééti juuniiloosv̋v̋ʔi
agi-oohiyú=hno uu-ééti di-uunii-loos-v̋v̋ʔi
1B-believe:PRC=CN 3B-old DST2-3B.NS-pass:CMP-DVB

ᎠᏉᎯᏳ Ꮎ ᎦᏘᏲ ᎠᎾᎵᏍᎩᏍᎬ
aàgwohiyu na gaátíiyo analsgiisgv́
agi-oohiyu na gaátíiyo anii-alisgiisg-v́
1B-believe:PRC that stomp ground 3A.NS-dance:INC-DVB

ᏚᎾᏁᎲᏙᏛ ᎠᎴ ᎦᎸᏉᏗ ᎠᏥᎳ
duunanehldohdv́ ale galv̋v̋kwdi ajiíla
dee-uunii-anehldohd-v́ ale galv̋v̋kwdi ajiíla
DST-3B.NS-have.allegiance.to:CMP-DVB and sacred fire
'I believe in old ways. I believe in traditional stomp dance religion and the traditional sacred fire.' (*Cherokee Phoenix*, February 2005)

These different ways of modifying the noun phrase are explained in chapter 7. Noun phrases may contain inside them another noun phrase that acts as the possessor of the main noun. Three examples are shown in (89); in (89a) the noun phrase 'John' is giving more information about 'son'. In (89b) the noun phrase 'brother' is modifying the main noun phrase 'friend'.

(89a) ᏣᏂ ᎤᏪᏥ ᎤᏔᏲᎵ
jaáni uweéji uùtayoohlv
jaáni uu-eéji uu-ahtayoohl-v
John 3B-offspring 3B-ask:CMP-EXP
'John's son asked for it.'

(89b) ᏦᏣᏓᏅᏝ ᎤᎾᎵᎪ ᎯᎦᏗᏯ
joojadaanv́v́tl uunaaliigóó hiigaàtiíy
di-oojii-adaad-nv́v́tla uunii-aaliigóó hii-gahtiíya
DST2-1A.PL.EX.AN-RFL-brother 3B.NS-friend 2A.AN-wait:PRC
'You are waiting for my brother's friend.'

In (90) the possessive noun phrase in each example consists of the possession pronoun with a Set B pronominal prefix indicating the possessor.

(90a) ᏣᏂ ᎤᏤᎵ ᎤᏍᏗ
jaáni uujeéli uusdi
jaáni uu-ajeéli uusdi
John 3B-POS.PRO baby
'John's baby.'

(90b) ᏏᏉᏲ ᎤᎾᏤᎵ
sigwoóyó uunajeéli
sigwoóya-ʔi uunii-ajeéli
Sequoyah-LOC 3B.NS-POS.PRO
'It belongs to the Sequoyah team.'

(90c) ᎭᏢ ᎠᏆᏤᎴ ᎤᏩᏥ
haadlv awajeele uuwaáji
haadlv agi-ajeele uuwaáji
where 1B-POS.PRO watch
'Where is my watch?'

Unlike adjectives, **participles** (adjectives and nouns derived from verbs) frequently follow the noun they modify, as in (91).

(91) ᏓᏆᎴᎳ ᎦᏃᏍᎩᏓ ᎬᏍᎦᎸᏍᎦ
dagwaléela ganoosgíida gvvsgahlv́sga
dagwaléela ga-noosgii-da ga-vvsgahlv́sga
car 3A-steal-PCP 3A-hide:PRC
'He is hiding a stolen car.' (Feeling 1975a: 128)

6.5. Sources and Additional Reading

This discussion of nouns has benefited from the descriptions of Pulte and Feeling (1975) as well as Cook (1979) and King (1975). Williams (1996) discusses Cherokee possession and the status of *-ajeéli* and explores how Cherokee uses lexical items as well as morphosyntax to express possession. He shows how alienably possessed nouns can express possession by affixing pronominal markers to *-ajeéli.*

6.6. Directions for Further Research

Work on archived Cherokee material is necessary to recover the older meanings of many nouns as well as words that are simply no longer used. Holmes and Smith (1977:160) state: "The Cherokee language used to contain a larger variety of relationship terms, such as special words for grandparents, aunts and uncles on the mother's or father's side, and for older or younger brothers. These have dropped out of use." Future investigation into these and similar topics will enhance our understanding of nouns in Cherokee.

SEVEN

Modifiers

The four main **parts of speech** in Cherokee are **verbs, nouns, adjectives,** and **adverbs.** Adjectives are descriptive words that are able to modify a noun as part of a **noun phrase** or as the **subject complement** of a **clause.** Numerals and **demonstratives** are similar to adjectives in that they help to modify the noun; they are distinct from adjectives in their **inflection.** Adverbs are words that modify the other three parts of speech (verbs, adjectives, and other adverbs) as well as entire clauses and sentences. Unlike the other three parts of speech, adverbs are never found as **predicates** and always modify another word or phrase. **Postfixes** are optional elements that attach to the end of a word.

7.1. Adjectives

Adjectives are descriptive words. As a subject complement, the adjective bears the main meaning of the clause by describing the **subject** of the clause. An **attributive adjective** describes a noun as part of a noun phrase. Most adjectives act like verbs in that they appear with **pronominal prefixes** that indicate the grammatical distinctions of **person** and **number;** unlike verbs, they do not indicate **tense, aspect, mood,** or **modality.** Attributive adjectives generally come immediately before the noun they are modifying. Two examples are given in (1). In both cases the attributive adjectives (as well as other parts of the sentence) are shortened.

(1a) ᎦᏢᏦᎯᏓ ᎠᎨᏯᏧ
gahljóóhid ageehyúúj
ga-ahljóóhida a-geehyúúja
3A-fat 3A-girl
'fat girl'

(1b) Ꮎ ᎤᏁᎫᏥᏓ ᏪᏌ ᏗᎪᏍᏓᏯ ᏚᏩᏯᏑᎦᏢ
na uuneégújida weésa digoósday duùwáayasuhgahlv
na uu-neégújida weésa di-ga-oósdayi dee-uu-áayasuhgahlv
that 3B-mean cat DST2-3A-sharp DST-3B-claw
'That mean cat has sharp claws.'

A **predicate adjective** is the predicate of a verbless clause and describes the subject of the clause. An example is shown in (2).

(2) ᎤᏬᏘᏓ ᎤᏥᏍᏆᎸᏛᎢ
uwóótida uùtsgwalvvtv́v́ʔi
uu-ooti-da uu-tsgwalvvtv́v́ʔi
3B-swell-PCP 3B-ankle
'His ankle is swollen.' (Feeling 1975a:185)

Like many nouns and all verbs, adjectives can take **Set A** or **Set B pronominal prefixes.** Adjectives in Cherokee can be distinguished from verbs and nouns by their lack of tense and aspect inflection as well as their role in the sentence. An important difference between verbs and adjectives is the **tone** pattern. While verbs only have a **highfall tone** in **subordinate** constructions, almost all adjectives bear this tone. Because the highfall tone is nearly always associated with **derived** forms rather than root forms, this feature suggests that most adjectives historically derive from some other part of speech. A few adjectives are listed in (3); for each adjective it is necessary to state whether it is a **Set A adjective** or a **Set B adjective.** These adjectives are listed with a **hyphen,** indicating that they need a prefix.

(3) -ahyadééna 'wide' (Set A)
-gééda 'heavy' (Set A: *ga-*)
-yóóʔi 'bad' (Set B)
-oodúúhi 'pretty' (Set B)

The inflection of adjectives is distinct from that of verbs. Some verb forms use **final suffixes** to express tense, aspect, and mood; adjectives must use a **helping verb** to indicate these concepts. In (4a) the verb appears in one of five possible stems and is inflected with a final suffix to specify the tense; the adjective in (4b) has neither of these features and needs the helping verb 'be' to express the time frame. It should also be pointed out that whereas both concepts are expressed by an adjective in English, only one is an adjective in Cherokee. The Cherokee language has fewer adjectives than English and often uses verbs to express concepts that English expresses as adjectives.

(4a) ᎠᎵᎢᎵᎡᎢ
aàliiheélîigvv́ʔi
a-aliiheélîig-vv́ʔi
3A-be.happy:INC-EXP
'He was happy.'

(4b) ᎦᎵᏦᎯᏓ ᏥᎨᏒ
galijóóhid jigeesv
ga-alijóóhida ji-gees-v
3A-fat REL-be:INC-EXP
'He was fat.'

Adjectives are like nouns in that they use the **secondary form** of the **distributive prefix** (DST2), while verbs (with a few exceptions) use the basic *dee-* form. (5) exemplifies these two forms.

(5a) ᏚᏍᏆᎵᏐᏅ
duùsgwáàlsohnv
dee-uu-sgwáàls-ohn-v
DST-3B-break(long):CMP-TRM:CMP-EXP
'He broke them.'

(5b) ᏧᎷᏍᏆᎵᏓ ᏥᎨᏒ
juulsgwáàlida jigeesv
di-uu-ali-sgwáàl-da ji-gees-v
DST2-3B-MDL-break(long)-PCP REL-be:INC-EXP
'They were broken.'

Differences in form and function also distinguish adjectives from nouns. Derived nouns typically carry a highfall tone, while many **root nouns** do not. Almost all adjectives, however, do bear this highfall tone. In terms of function, most adjectives take pronominal prefixes, whereas certain nouns do not. Moreover, the inflection patterns of nouns and adjectives are different. These differences are explored in the section below on number inflection.

Adjectives are similar in many ways to adverbs and are often used in similar contexts. Adverbs do not generally inflect, while most adjectives inflect for person and number. Adverbs are discussed at the end of this chapter.

All adjectives are at least two **syllables** long. Many of them carry a highfall tone; if this tone is present, it is on the rightmost long vowel. For several adjectives this rule causes the pronominal prefix to carry the highfall tone, which is indicated as two accents over the first vowel of the adjective. Examples are given in (6) for the adjectives 'big' and 'crooked'. For both examples the **double accent** indicates a **movable tone** that is placed on the rightmost long vowel.

(6a) ᎤᎾᏔᎾ
úúnatana
uunii-ӑ̋tana
3B.NS-big
'big', 'they are big'

(6b) ᎤᎾᏥᏈᏗ
úúnatsgwidi
uunii-ӑ̋tsgwidi
3B.NS-crooked
'crooked', 'they are crooked'

7.1.1. Inflection of Adjectives

7.1.1.1. *Adjective Person Inflection*

All adjectives take either Set A or Set B pronominal prefixes; as with verbs and nouns, which set a given adjective takes is unpredictable and must simply be listed with the adjective's meaning. In (7a) the adjective takes the first person singular Set A prefix, while in (7b) the adjective takes the first person singular Set B prefix. The adjective in these examples is derived from the noun 'dirt' by using the **adjective derivational suffix** (ADJ) *-hááʔi.*

(7a) ᏥᎦᏓᎭᎢ
jigaadaahááʔi
ji-gaadaa-hááʔi
1A-dirt-ADJ
'I am dirty.'

(7b) ᎠᎩᏴᏜ
akiyv́v́dla
agi-hyv́v́dla
1B-cold
'I am cold.'

The pronominal prefixes have been discussed in chapter 3; the Set A and Set B prefixes are repeated in tables 7.1 and 7.2.

Table 7.1. Set A Pronominal Prefixes

Person Reference	*Singular*	*Dual (dl)*	*Plural (pl)*
First Person Inclusive	ji-	iinii-	iidii-
First Person Exclusive (EX)		oosdii-	oojii-
Second Person	hi-	sdii-	iijii-
Third Person	a-, ga-	anii-	

Table 7.2. Set B Pronominal Prefixes

Person reference	*Singular*	*Dual (dl)*	*Plural (pl)*
First Person Inclusive	agi-	ginii-	iigii-
First Person Exclusive (EX)		ooginii-	oogii-
Second Person	ja-	sdii-	iijii-
Third Person	uu-	uunii-	

The Set A adjectives can be further classified into those that take *a-* in the **third person** and those that take *ga-*. The third person *a-* only appears if what is being referred to is **animate,** as demonstrated by the examples in (8).

(8a) ᎦᏓᎭᏤ
gaadaahááʔi
gaadaa-hááʔi
dirt-ADJ
'dirty'

(8b) ᎠᎦᏓᎭᏤ
agaadaahááʔi
a-gaadaa-hááʔi
3A-dirt-ADJ
'He is dirty.'

(8c) ᏗᎦᏓᎭᏤ
digaadaahááʔi
di-gaadaa-hááʔi

DST2-dirt-ADJ
'They (inanimate) are dirty.'

(8d) DhSᏓᏍᏉT
aniigaadaaháá?i
anii-gaadaa-háá?i
3A.NS-dirt-ADJ
'They (animate) are dirty.'

As shown in (9), Set A adjectives that begin with a vowel cause the removal of the Set A third person singular prefix *a-*. Even though it is not pronounced, an **underlying** *a-* is assumed; evidence for this assumption is that the nonsingular form does take a prefix, as seen in (9b). The **inanimate** form has no nonsingular pronominal prefix, as shown in (9c); in this case number is indicated by a distributive prepronominal prefix.

(9a) ᎣᏍᏓ
óósda
a-óósda
3A-good
'good', 'He/she/it is good.'

(9b) DZᏍᏓ
anóósda
anii-óósda
3A.NS-good
'They are good (animate).'

(9c) KᏍᏓ
jóósda
di-óósda
DST2-good
'They are good (inanimate).'

As demonstrated in (10), Set A *ga-* adjectives always carry a prefix regardless of animacy.

(10) SᏊᏓ
gagééda
ga-gééda

3A-heavy
'heavy', 'He/she/it is heavy.'

Similarly, Set B adjectives take Set B pronominal prefixes regardless of animacy, as seen in (11).

(11) ᎤᎯᏴᏓ
uuhyv́v́dla
uu-hyv́v́dla
3B-cold
'cold', 'He/she/it is cold.'

Notice that Set A adjectives distinguish animacy (he/she vs. it) whereas Set B adjectives treat them all the same: all Set B adjectives take pronominal prefixes.

Sample lists of Set A and Set B adjectives are shown in (12) and (13), respectively. Some of these adjectives are marked with a hyphen, indicating that they always have a pronominal prefix. Three kinds of adjectives require pronominal prefixes: inherently animate adjectives (e.g., 'smart'), Set A adjectives that take *ga-*, and all Set B adjectives.

Set A adjectives

(12)

(12)	sakoóníǵééʔi	'blue'
	eehlawééʔi	'quiet'
	giígágééʔi	'red'
	éégwa	'huge'
	-samáádi	'smart'
	-kééwi	'blind'
	-alijóóhida	'fat' (*ga-*)
	-chinóósda	'straight' (*ga-*)
	-vvjahlánv́v́hi	'fried' (*ga-*)

The Set B forms are all preceded by a hyphen, an indication that the actual spoken word must have a pronominal prefix.

Set B adjectives

(13)	-ắtana	'big'
	-eéhnaʔi	'rich'
	-neguújida	'mean'
	-ééti	'old (object)'
	-hyv́v́dla	'cold'
	-asdííʔi	'little'

-sganóóli	‘slow’
-kayóóda	‘dry’
-aleesóóda	‘skinny’
-alsgééda	‘important’, ‘sacred’
-tlóóyi	‘same’
-alsduʔíída	‘open’
-alsuúhwida	‘colored’
-nééga	‘white’

Adjectives derived from verbs with a **frozen** distributive (or any other frozen prepronominal prefix) also bear that prefix, as seen in (14)

(14)

ᏃᏊ	ᏧᏴᏪᏦᏅ	ᎨᏎ	ᏥᏍᏚ
noogw	juuyvwéechonv́	geese	jiisd
noogwu	di-uu-yvwéej-ohn-v́	gees-e	jiisdu
now	DST2-3B-be.tired:CMP-TRM:CMP-DVB	be:INC-NXP	rabbit

‘The rabbit was worn out.’ (The Turtle and the Rabbit, line 37)

7.1.1.2. *Adjective Number Inflection*

Adjectives, unlike nouns, always indicate number. Adjectives modifying non-singular local persons take the appropriate Set A or Set B prefixes. The rules governing the use of third person prefixes are more complex. Adjectives referencing animate beings express nonsingular number with pronominal prefixes, whereas adjectives referencing nonsingular inanimate objects take the distributive (DST2) *di-*. In (15a) the Set A adjective ‘black’ has the nonsingular pronominal prefix because it modifies nonsingular animate ‘horses’; in (15b), however, the Set B adjective ‘thin’ has a default third person singular prefix that does not indicate number for the inanimate noun it is modifying.

(15a)

ᎠᏂᎬᏂᎨ	ᏐᏈᎵ	ᏓᏂᏅᎩ
aniigvv́hnáge	soógwíl	daàniinvv̀g
anii-gvv́hnáge	soógwíli	dee-anii-nvv̀gi
3A.NS-black	horse	DST-3A.NS-fall:IMM

‘The black horses fell.’

(15b)

ᏧᏌᎨ	ᏗᏂᏬᏍᏙᏗ	ᏚᏂᏬᏍᏗ
juuságe	diihnawóosdohdi	duuhnawóosdi
di-uu-ságe	di-a-ahnawoosdohdi	dee-uu-ahnawóosdi
DST2-3B-thin	DST2-3A-cover:INF\INS	DST-3B-cover:PRC

‘He has on thin covers.’ (Feeling 1975a:178)

Two examples with the Set A adjective 'good' are shown in (16). If the adjective modifying an inanimate noun begins with /o/ or /u/, the [*j*] **variant** of the DST2 appears, as in (16b).

(16a) ᎠᏃᏍᏓ ᏐᏉᎵ
anóósd soógwíli
anii-óósda soógwíli
3A.NS-good horse
'good horses'

(16b) ᏦᏍᏓ ᏗᎦᎵᏦᏕ
jóósd digahljoóde
di-óósda di-gahljoóde
DST2-good DST2-house
'good houses'

All nouns uses pronominal prefixes to reference humans, whereas adjectives use pronominal prefixes when modifying nonsingular animate nouns, human or nonhuman. In (17a) both the adjectives and the noun bear the prefix *anii-*, while in (17b) the noun 'chicken' remains uninflected. In (17c) the nonhuman root noun is uninflected for number, but the adjective bears the distributive prefix *di-*, indicating reference to an inanimate noun.

(17a) Ꮎ ᎠᏂᏧᏣ ᎠᏂᎦᏓᎭ
na aniichúúja aniigaadaaha
na anii-chúúja anii-gaadaa-ha
that 3A.NS-boy 3A.NS-dirt-ADJ
'Those are dirty boys.'

(17b) Ꮎ ᏥᏔᎦ ᎠᏂᎦᏓᎭ
na jitaága aniigaadaaha
na jitaága anii-gaadaa-ha
that chicken 3A.NS-dirt-ADJ
'Those are dirty chickens.'

(17c) Ꮎ ᎫᎫ ᏗᎦᏓᎭ
na guùg digaadaaha
na guùgu di-gaadaa-ha
that bottle DST2-dirt-ADJ
'Those are dirty bottles.'

Many adjectives that modify an animate noun are double-marked for nonsingular number, with a pronominal prefix in addition to a distributive prefix. In (18a) the adjective modifying the inanimate noun 'house' receives only a distributive prefix; in (18b) the adjective modifying the animate noun 'horse' has both a nonsingular pronominal prefix and a distributive prepronominal prefix.

(18a) ᏧᏔᎾ ᎦᎵᏦᏕ
júútan gahljoóde
di-uu-ắtana gahljoóde
DST2-3B-big house
'The houses are big.'

(18b) ᏧᎾᏔᎾ ᎠᏂᏐᏈᎵ
júúntana aniisoógwíli
di-uunii-ắtana anii-soógwíli
DST2-3B.NS-big 3A.NS-horse
'The horses are big.'

The ability of adjectives to inflect for number is a phenomenon that varies according to dialect; what is considered animate is also not always straightforward. For example, fruits and vegetables pattern with animate nouns, and adjectives that modify them bear the nonsingular pronominal prefix. In (19) the adjective receives a nonsingular pronominal prefix but not a distributive prefix.

(19) ᏄᎾ ᎠᏂᏅᎯᏓ
nuúna aniinvvhíída
nuúna anii-nvvhíída
potato 3A.NS-long
'sweet potatoes'

The adjective 'rotten' treats the noun it refers to as animate, so it appears with a pronominal prefix, as in (20). The distributive that appears on the verb (the *dee-* form) makes it clear that the object of this sentence is more than one fish.

(20) ᎠᏣᏗ ᏙᎩᏴ ᎤᎾᎪᏏᏓ
ajaʔdi doògiihyv uunagóósida
ajaʔdi dee-oogii-hy-v uunii-agoos-da
fish DST-1B.PL.EX-eat(flexible):CMP-EXP 3B.NS-rot-PCP
'We ate the rotten fish.'

To summarize number inflection, verbs have pronominal prefixes that indicate the number of the subject. Adjectives only inflect for number using pronominal prefixes if they modify animate nouns; if not, then the distributive (DST2) *di-* is used. In (21) the noun is a human noun, so not only the verb takes the *anii-* non-singular pronominal prefix; so do the adjective and the noun itself.

(21)	DhSᏓᏂᎭ	ᏗᏂᏲᎵ	ᏓᎾᏁᎶᎲᏍᎦ
	aniigaadaaha	diiniiyóóhl	daànáàneeloóhv́sga
	anii-gaadaa-ha	di-anii-yóóhli	dee-anii-áàneeloóhv́sga
	3A.NS-dirty-ADJ	DST2-3A.NS-children	DST-3A.NS-play:PRC

'The dirty children are playing.'

7.1.2. Interrogative Adjectives

Interrogative adjectives are used to ask for information about nouns. The interrogative *hila* is used to ask 'which NOUN?'; the interrogative *gaago* is used to ask 'whose NOUN?' An example of each is given in (22).

(22a)	ᎯᎳ	ᎠᏯᏙᎸᎢ	ᎯᎪᎵᏰᎠ
	hila	aàyáàtohlv́v́ʔi	higooliíyéʔa
	hila	aàyáàtohlv́v́ʔi	hi-gooliíyéʔa
	which	chapter	2A-read:PRC

'Which chapter are you reading?' (Feeling 1975a:62)

(22b)	ᎦᎪ	ᎤᏄᏬ	ᎲᎩᎶᎠ
	gaago	uuhnawo	hvhgiilóoʔa
	gaago	uu-ahnawo	hi-vhgiilóoʔa
	who	3B-shirt	2A-wash(flexible):PRC

'Whose shirt are you washing?'

7.2. Demonstratives

Demonstratives are words that appear at the beginning of the noun phrase and help to specify the identity of the noun. They are like adjectives in that they modify nouns; they are distinct from adjectives in that they never take pronominal prefixes. Demonstratives are always part of a noun phrase and do not serve as predicates.

Two examples are shown in (23). The demonstrative *na* can be translated as 'that' or 'the'.

(23a)	ᏃᏊ	ᏭᎪᎮ	ᏩᏟᏍᏛ	Ꮎ	ᏓᎩᏏ
	nogw	wuugoohe	watliisv́	na	daks

noogwu wi-uu-gooh-e wi-a-aditliis-v́ na daksi
now TRN-3B-see:CMP-NXP TRN-3A-run:CMP-DVB the turtle
'He saw the turtle running.' (The Turtle and the Rabbit, line 42)

(23b) ᎠᏂᏩᎶᏏ Ꮎ ᏓᎩᏏ ᎤᎾᎩᏩ
aniiwalóosi na daksi uùnkiʔla
anii-walóosi na daksi uunii-ahkiʔla
3A.NS-frog the turtle 3B.NS-be.sitting.on:PRC
'The frogs are sitting on the turtle.'

Also common is the demonstrative *hiʔa*, typically translated as 'this'. In (24) it modifies a nonsingular noun (indicated on the verb) and is translated as 'these'.

(24) ᏗᎦᏥᏲᏍᏗ ᏂᎨᏒᎾ ᏱᎩ
digajiiyóósdi nigeesv́v́na yigi
di-ga-jii-yóosdi ni-gees-v́v́na yi-gi
DST2-GA-1A.AN-shoot:INF\MOD NI-be:INC-NDV IRR-be:IMM

ᎯᎠ ᏩᏯ Ꮭ ᏱᏗᎦᏥᏛᏓ
hiʔa wahya hla yidigajiitvhda
hiʔa wahya hla yi-di-ga-jii-htvhda
this wolf NEG IRR-DST2-GA-1A.AN-rid:IMM
'If I can't shoot these wolves I can't get rid of them.'

Both of these demonstratives can be used as pronouns, often with the postfix *=na* attached. An example of each is given in (25). In (25b) the postfix attaches to the demonstrative and causes it to lengthen.

(25a) ᎯᎢᎾ ᏦᎩᏍᏗ
hiʔina jóóksdi
hiʔi=na ja-ookisdi
this=FC 2B-smoke:INF\INS
'This is for you to smoke.'

(25b) ᎾᎾ ᎦᏙ ᎤᏍᏗ ᎠᏂᏥᏍᏚ
náana gado úúsd aniijiisdu
na=na gado úúsdi anii-jiisdu
that=FC what thing 3A.NS-rabbit
'What are those?' 'Those are rabbits.'

Less common than the demonstratives mentioned above is *vvsgina,* which refers to nouns further away from the speaker. An example is shown in (26).

(26) ᎦᎪ ᎥᏍᎩᎾ ᎠᎨᏯ
gaag vv̀sgina ageéhya
gaago vv̀sgina a-geéhya
who that 3A-woman
'Who is that woman?' (Feeling 1975a:16)

7.3. Quantifiers

Quantifiers serve as modifiers by specifying the amount or quantity of a noun. There are two classes of quantifiers: those that take inflection and those that do not. The sentence in (27a) has the quantifier 'several' that is uninflected; it is modifying a third person nonsingular noun. In (27b) the quantifier is modifying a dual second person yet remains uninflected.

(27a) ᎯᎸᎥᏍᎩ ᎠᏂᏧᏣ
hilv́v́sgi aniichúúja
hilv́v́sgi anii-chúúja
several 3A.NS-boy
ᏭᎾᏝᎥᏍᏔᏅ ᏗᏍᏓᎦᎸᎢ
wuunatlaʔvvstanv diisdagahlv́v́ʔi
wi-uunii-atlaʔvvstan-v di-asdagahlv́v́ʔi
TRN-3B.NS-run.into:CMP-EXP TOW-cave
'Several boys ran into the cave.'

(27b) ᎢᏧᎳ ᏕᏍᏗᎸᏫᏍᏓᏁᎸ ᏑᎾᎴᎢ
iíjúula deesdiilvv́hwísdaàneélv sunáaléé ʔi
iíjúula dee-sdii-lvv́hwísdaàneél-v sunáaléé ʔi
both DST-2B.DL-work:CMP-FCM tomorrow
'Both of you work tomorrow.' (Feeling 1975a:132)

Several quantifiers do take pronominal prefixes. These are listed in (28); an example sentence is provided in (29).

Inflecting quantifiers

(28) -goòdi 'much', 'a lot of'
-jaáti 'a lot'
-tsgwiísda 'many,' 'a lot'

(29) ᎢᏗᏥᏈᏍᏓ
iidiitsgwiísda

iidii-tsgwiísda
1A.PL-many
'There are many of us.'

The quantifiers that can take pronominal prefixes often don't appear with a third person nonsingular prefix. Such prefixes do appear, however, in a verbless clause as in (30), where the quantifier is the predicate.

(30) ᎠᏂᏥᏉᏍᏓ
aniitsgwiísda
anii-tsgwiísda
3A.NS-a.lot
'There are a lot of them.'

Many of these quantifiers also act like adverbs by modifying verbs. Two examples are shown in (31).

(31a) ᏍᏉᏍᏗ ᎬᏗᏍᎬᎢ ᎠᏎᏃ ᎤᏲᏨᎢ
sgwiísdi gvv̀diísgv́ʔi aaséehno uùyóojvv́ʔi
sgwiísdi ji-vhdiísg-v́ʔi aaséehno uu-yóoj-vv́ʔi
a.lot 1A-use:INC-EXP however 3B-break(I):CMP-EXP
'I used it a lot; however, it broke.'

(31b) ᏥᏉᏍᏗ ᎠᎦᏍᎦ Ꮲ ᎡᏅᏍᏗ ᎪᎯᎢᎦ
tsgwiísdi aàgaasga dlv eenvv̀sdi koohiʔiíga
tsgwiísdi a-gaasga dlv a-eenvv̀sdi koohiʔiíga
a.lot 3A-rain:PRC somewhere 3A-go:INF today
'It's raining too much to go somewhere today.' (Feeling 1975a:15)

As shown in (32), quantifiers may also act as pronouns.

(32) ᎢᎦᏓ ᎤᏂᏍᎦᏃᎵ ᎨᏐ ᎤᎾᏛᏅᎢᏍᏙᏗᎢ
iígáada uuniisganóóli geèso uunadvvnvʔisdóhdííʔi
iígáada uunii-sganóóli geès-o uunii-advvnvʔisdóhdííʔi
some 3B.NS-slow be:INC-HAB 3B.NS-prepare:INF
'Some people are slow to get ready.' (Feeling 1975a:179)

7.4. Numerals

Numerals are similar to demonstratives in that they precede any adjectives; they are similar to adjectives in that they can inflect when modifying nouns referring to humans. This inflection is seen in (33a). Pronominal prefixes on numerals, however, are optional; this is seen in sentences (33b) and (33c), which are from the same speaker.

(33a)	ᎠᏂᏦᎢ	ᎠᏂᏧᏣ	ᎠᏂᏃᎩᎠ
	aniijoʔi	aniijúúja	aàniihnoogíiʔa
	anii-joʔi	anii-júúja	anii-hnoogíiʔa
	3A.NS-three	3A.NS-boy	3A.NS-sing:PRC
	'The three boys are singing.'		

(33b)	Ꮎ	Ꮶ	ᎠᏂᎨᏯ	ᎤᏂᏌᎵᏓᏅ
	naʔ	joʔ	aniigeéyh	uùniisaldaanv
	naʔ	joʔ	anii-geéhya	uunii-saldaan-v
	those	three	3A.NS-woman	3B.NS-lift:CMP-EXP
	'Those three women lifted it.'			

(33c)	Ꮎ	ᎠᏂᏔᎵ	ᎠᏂᏍᎦᏯ	ᎤᏂᏌᎵᏓᏅ
	naʔ	aniitaʔl	aniisgay	uùniisaldaanv
	naʔ	anii-taʔli	anii-sgaya	uunii-saldaan-v
	those	3A.NS-three	3A.NS-man	3B.NS-lift:CMP-EXP
	'Those two men lifted it.'			

Unlike adjectives, numerals do not have prefixes when modifying inanimate objects, as seen in (34).

(34)	ᎯᏍᎩ	ᎾᏕᏘᏯ	ᏃᏥᏁᎶ	ᎫᏐ
	hisgi	nadeetiy	noòjiineélo	guusoo
	hisgi	ni-adeetiya	ni-oojii-neél-o	guusa-ʔi
	five	NI-year	NI-1A.PL.EX-reside:INC-HAB	Muskogee-LOC
	'We have been living in Muskogee for five years.'			

Numerals are able to stand alone and act as nouns, as in (35).

(35)	Ꮶ	ᏱᏣᏂ	ᎨᏎ
	joʔ	yiijani	geèse
	joʔ	yi-iijii-ani	geès-e
	three	IRR-2A.PL-be.there:PRC	be:INC-NXP
	ᎠᏯᏃ	ᎣᏍᏗᏔᎵᏭ	ᏥᎨᏒᎢ
	ayahno	oosdiitaʔliwu	jigeèsvv́ʔi
	aya=hno	oosdii-taʔli=wu	ji-geès-vv́ʔi
	1PRO=CN	1A.DL.EX-two=DT	REL-be:INC-EXP
	'There were three of you and only two of us.'		

The word *iyaníiʔi* 'number of' often appears with *yvvwi* 'person' when a number is specified. An example is given in (36).

(36) ᏍᎪᎯ ᎢᏯᏂᎢ ᏴᏫ ᏚᏬᎥᎢ
sgoóhi iyaníiʔi yvvwi duùwooʔvv́ʔi
sgoóhi iyaníiʔi yvvwi dee-uu-awooʔ-vv́ʔi
ten number.of person DST-3B-bathe:CMP-EXP
'He baptized ten people.' (Feeling 1975a:116)

The **cardinal** numerals 1 to 10 are listed below in (37).

(37) Track 45

ᏌᏊ	saàgwu	'one'
ᏔᎵ	táʔli	'two'
ᏦᎢ	joʔi	'three'
ᏅᎩ	nvhgi	'four'
ᎯᏍᎩ	hisgi	'five'
ᏑᏓᎵ	suúdáli	'six'
ᎦᎵᏉᎩ	gahlgwoógi	'seven'
ᏣᏁᎳ	chaneéla	'eight'
ᏐᏁᎳ	sohneéla	'nine'
ᏍᎪᎯ	sgoóhi	'ten'

The numerals 11–19 are shortened or altered forms of the numerals 1–9 with an additional element added. The numeral 'one' suggests an original element meaning 'one' combined with the **delimiter postfix** *=gwu* 'only'; the original meaning of 'one' was probably 'only one'. Some of the other numerals also undergo changes. These patterns are unpredictable, however, and these numerals should be treated as distinct words rather than derivations of the lower numerals. The numerals 11–19 are listed in (38).

(38) Track 46

ᏌᏚ	sáʔdu	'eleven'
ᏔᎵᏚ	taldu	'twelve'
ᏦᎦᏚ	joogádu	'thirteen'
ᏅᎦᏚ	nvhgádu	'fourteen'
ᎯᏍᎦᏚ	hisgádu	'fifteen'
ᏑᏓᏔᏚ	suudaldu	'sixteen'
ᎦᎵᏆᏚ	gahlgwoodu	'seventeen'
ᏣᏁᎳᏚ	chanelaadu	'eighteen'
ᏐᏁᎳᏚ	sohnelaadu	'nineteen'

The numeral 'twenty' is a **compound** of the numerals 'two' and 'ten'. The numerals above twenty consist of the base ten numeral followed by the single numeral, as seen in (39). In (40) the base numerals up to one hundred are listed (Pulte and Feeling 1975: 228–29).

(39) ᏔᎵᏍᎪᎯᏌᏊ ta?lsgoóhisaàgwu 'twenty-one'

(40) Track 47

ᏔᎵᏍᎪᎯ	talsgoóhi	'twenty'
ᏦᏍᎪᎯ	jo?sgoóhi	'thirty'
ᏅᎩᏍᎪᎯ	nvksgoóhi	'forty'
ᎯᎩᏍᎪᎯ	hiksgoóhi	'fifty'
ᏑᏓᎵᏍᎪᎯ	suudalsgoóhi	'sixty'
ᎦᎵᏆᏍᎪᎯ	gahlgwasgoóhi	'seventy'
ᏁᎵᏍᎪᎯ	nelsgoóhi	'eighty'
ᏐᏁᎵᏍᎪᎯ	sohnelsgoóhi	'ninety'
ᏍᎪᎯᏥᏆ	sgohitsgwa	'one hundred'

Ordinal numerals from 2nd to 10th are formed with the ordinal suffix (ORD) *-iinéé?i*. The ordinal numeral 'first' is irregular and is formed from an unrelated stem. The first five ordinals in their shortened form are found in the sentence in (41).

(41)

ᏃᏭᏃ	ᏔᎵᏁ	ᏭᏂᎷᏣ
noówúhn	ta?liine	wuuníílúhj
noówu=hno	ta?li-iine	wi-uunii-?lúhj-a
now=CN	two-ORD	TRN-3B.NS-arrive:CMP-CVB

ᎤᏠᏱ	ᏅᎾᏛᏁᎴ	ᎠᎴᏍᏊ
uudlóóy	nvvndv́vneele	alesgwu
uu-dlóóyi	ni-ii-uunii-adv́vneel-e	ale=sgwu
3B-same	NI-ITR-3B.NS-do:CMP-NXP	and=DT

ᏦᎢᏁ	ᏅᎩᏁ	ᎯᏍᎩᏁ	ᏑᏓᎵᏁ
jo?iine	nvhgiine	hisgiine	suúdaliine
jo?i-iine	nvhgi-iine	hisgi-iine	suúdali-iine
three-ORD	four-ORD	five-ORD	six-ORD

'And when they arrived at the second, third, fourth, fifth, and sixth [hills] they did the same' (The Wolf and the Crawdad, lines 20–22)

Ordinal numerals above 11th are formed with the suffix *-siinéé?i*. Some examples of ordinal numerals are listed in (42).

(42)

ᏌᏚᏏᏁᎢ	sáduùsiinéé?i	'eleventh'
ᏔᎵᏚᏏᏁᎢ	tálduùsiinéé?i	'twelfth'
ᏦᎠᏚᏏᏁᎢ	jo?áduùsiinéé?i	'thirteenth'

ᏂᎦᏚᏏᏁᎢ	niigáduùsiinéé?i	'fourteenth'
ᏦᏍᎪᎯᏏᏁᎢ	jo?sgoóhisiinéé?i	'thirtieth'
ᏅᎩᏍᎪᎯᏏᏁᎢ	nvksgoóhisiinéé?i	'fortieth'
ᎯᎩᏍᎪᎯᏏᏁᎢ	hiksgoóhisiinéé?i	'fiftieth'
ᏑᏓᎵᏍᎪᎯᏏᏁᎢ	sudalsgoóhisiinéé?i	'sixtieth'
ᎦᎵᏆᏍᎪᎯᏏᏁᎢ	gahlgwasgoóhisiinéé?i	'seventieth'
ᏁᎵᏍᎪᎯᏏᏁᎢ	nelsgoóhisiinéé?i	'eightieth'
ᏐᏁᎵᏍᎪᎯᏏᏁᎢ	sohnelsgoóhisiinéé?i	'ninetieth'

The irregular ordinal form 'first' is shown is (43a). Above twenty-first this numeral has a different form, as in (43b). As seen in this example, only the second part has the ordinal suffix when the numeral has two parts.

(43a) ᏅᏩ ᎠᎬᏱ ᎦᏚᏏ
nvw agv́v́yi gadúus
nvvgwu a-gv́v́yi gadúusi
now 3A-first top

ᏱᎬᎵᏍᎪᎸᏓᏏ ᎠᎬᏱ ᏫᏣᎯᏍᏗ
yigvvlisgohldáàs agv́v́y wijá?lohisdi
yi-gvv-alisgohldáàsi a-gv́v́yi wi-ja-?lohisdi
IRR-1/2-permit:IMM 3A-first TRN-2B-pass:INF
'The first mountain top, I will let you get there first.' (The Turtle and the Rabbit, line 20)

(43b) ᏔᎵᏍᎪ ᏌᏊᏏᏁᎢ
talsgo saàgwusiinéé?i
tal+sgo saàgwu-siinéé?i
two+ten one-ORD
'twenty-first'

(44) is an example of numerals used to indicate dates. The day of the month uses an ordinal numeral, while the cardinal numerals indicate the year.

(44) ᎾᎥᏂᎨᏍᏗ ᏍᎪᎯᏧᏈ ᎢᏯᏂ
na?v́nígeesdi sgoóhítsgwu iiyáni
na?v́nígeesdi sgoóhítsgwu iiyáni
near hundred number.of

ᎠᏂᏣᎳᎩ ᎠᏂᏣᏗ ᎠᏂᏥᎦᏌ
aniijalagi aniijádi aniijiigasa

anii-jalagi	anii-jádi	anii-jiigasa
3A.NS-Cherokee	3A.NS-Choctaw	3A.NS-Chickasaw

ᎠᏂᏏᎻᏃᎵ	ᎠᎴ	ᎠᏂᎫᏌ
aniisiminoli	ale	aniigúúsa
anii-siminoli	ale	anii-gúúsa
3A.NS-Seminole	and	3A.NS-Muskogee

ᎠᏁᎯᏯ	ᏚᎾᏢᏎ	ᎤᏪᏘ
aneehiiya	duùnadloose	uuwééti
anii-eehiiya	dee-uunii-adloos-e	uu-ééti
3A.NS-indigenous	DST-3B.NS-meet:CMP-NXP	3B-old

ᏧᎾᏢᎯᏍᏗ	ᏧᏍᎪᎢ
juunadloohisdi	juúsgóóʔi
di-uunii-adloohisdi	juúsga-ʔi
DST2-3B.NS-meet:INF	oak-LOC

ᏡᎬᎢ	ᎧᏬᏂ	ᎧᎸ
dluhgv́v́ʔi	kawooni	kaʔlv
dluhgv́v́ʔi	kawooni	kaʔlv
tree	April	past.month

ᏔᎵᏍᎪ	ᏑᏓᎵᏁ	ᏔᎵ
talsgo	suúdáliine	taʔli
tali+sgo	suúdáli-iine	taʔli
two+ten	six-ORD	two

ᎢᏯᎦᏴᎵ	ᏑᏓᎵ	ᎤᏕᏘᏴᏌᏗᏒ
iyáqayv́v́li	suúdáli	uudeetiiyvv́sadiisv
iyágayv́v́li	suúdáli	uudeetiiyvv́sadiisv
thousand	six	year.of

ᎠᎾᏅᏓᏗᏍᎨ	ᏍᎪᎯᏧᏆ
aànandadiisge	sgoohítsgwa
anii-ahndadiisg-e	sgoohítsgwa
3A.NS-remember:INC-NXP	hundred

ᎾᏕᏘᏯ	ᎤᏂᎶᎯᏍᏓᏅ
naàdeétîiya	uuniiloohistanv́
ni-aàdeétîiya	uunii-loohistan-v́
NI-year	3B.NS-pass:CMP-DVB

ᏐᏁᎳᏚ ᎢᏍᎪᎯᏧᏈ
sóhneéláàdu iisgoóhítsgwi
sóhneéláàdu ii-sgoóhítsgwi
nineteen NI2-hundred

ᏑᏓᎵ ᏗᎧᏃᏩᏛᏍᏗ ᎤᏂᎶᎯᏍᏔᏅᎢ
suúdáli dikanowdv́vsdi uuniiloòhistanvv́ʔi
suúdáli dikanowdv́vsdi uunii-loòhistan-vv́ʔi
six law 3B.NS-pass:CMP-EXP
'Nearly 100 Cherokee, Choctaw, Chickasaw, Seminole, and Muscogee Creek citizens met at the historic Council Oak tree April 26, 2006, to commemorate the 100th anniversary of the Act of 1906.' (*Cherokee Phoenix,* June 2006)

Numerals can have an **adverbial** function as well. In (45) below, the ordinal form of 'second' conveys the meaning 'again' or 'repeatedly'.

(45) ᏔᎵᏁ ᏫᏣᏚᎦ
taʔlíine wijaduùga
taʔli-íine wi-ja-aduùga
two-ORD TRN-2B-throw:IMM
'Throw it again.'

The **adjective derivation suffix** *-ha* has the meaning 'that number out of the total' when it attaches to numerals, as in (46).

(46a) ᎯᎠ ᎠᏧᏣ ᎯᏍᎩᎭ ᎦᎦᎹ ᏚᏍᏗᎬᎢ
hiʔa achúúja hisgiiha gaágáma duùsdiigvv́ʔi
hiʔa a-chúúja hisgii-ha gaágáma dee-uu-sdiig-vv́ʔi
This 3A-boy five-ADJ cucumber DST-3B-eat(long):CMP-EXP
'This boy ate five of the cucumbers.' (Feeling 1975a:94)

(46b) ᏦᎢᎭ ᏗᎪᏍᏛᏂᏍᏗ
jóʔiiha digoosdv́vniìsdi
jóʔii-ha di-goosdv́vniìsdi
three-ADJ DST2-bat

ᏘᏄᎦ ᎤᎾᎳᏍᎦᎸᏗᎢ
tiinuùga uunlaàsgahldííʔi
di-hi-xxnuùga uunii-alaàsgahldííʔi
DST2-2A-take(long):IMM 3B.NS-play.ball:INF
'Take three bats to the baseball diamond.' (Feeling 1975a:104)

7.5. Adverbs

7.5.1. Adverbs Modifying Verbs

The beginning of this chapter discussed adjectives (words that modify nouns). Adverbs modify verbs by describing the manner in which an action is done, the location where the action occurs, or the time when the action happens. (47a) has an adverb of time, and (47b) and (47c) both have an adverb of place. (47d) has an adverb of manner.

(47a)	ᏙᏓᏩᏓ	ᎠᎩᎾᎸᏨ
	doódáwaad	aàginaálv́v̀jv
	doódáwaada	agi-naálv́v̀j-v
	all.day	1B-angry:CMP-EXP

‘I was angry all day.’

(47b)	Ꮭ	ᎩᎶ	ᎪᏍᏗ	ᏳᎾᏙ	ᎠᎭᏂ
	tla	kilo	góósd	yuuhndo	ahani
	tla	kilo	góósdi	yi-uu-ahnd-o	ahani
	NEG	someone	something	IRR-3B-know:INC-HAB	here

‘No one here ever knows anything.’

(47c)	ᏥᏳ	ᎡᎳ	ᎾᎦᎵᏍᏗ
	jiíyu	eela	nigalsdi
	jiíyu	eela	ni-ga-alisdi
	boat	down	NI-3A-become:PRC

‘The boat is sinking, going down in the water.’

(47d)	ᎴᏍᏗ	Ꮩ	ᏣᏁᎫᏣ
	hléesdi	do	janeégúùja
	hléesdi	do	ja-neégúùja
	NEG.COM	really	2B-be.mean:PRC

‘Quit. You’re being [really] mean.’ (Feeling 1975a:176)

Many adverbs are adjectives that are simply used as adverbs. In (48a) ‘bad’ is used as an adjective and has a nonsingular prefix that agrees with the noun it modifies. This pattern contrasts with (48b), where ‘bad’ carries a singular **dummy prefix** that does not agree with the nonsingular subject.

(48a)	Ꮎ	ᏓᏬᎵ	ᎤᏂᏲᎢ
	na	dawooli	uuniiyóóʔi

na dawooli uunii-yóóʔi
those mushroom 3B.NS-bad
'Those mushrooms are bad.'

(48b) ᎤᏲ ᎠᎾᏓᏅᏖᎮᎭ
uuyo aànadahntehéeha
uu-yo anii-adaa-ahnteh-éeha
3B-bad 3A.NS-MDL-know:CMP-APL:PRC
'They feel bad for him.'

Adverbs such as 'whenever' or 'wherever' can be expressed using a clause with a subordinate helping verb, as in (49).

(49) ᎭᏢᏊ ᎨᏒ ᏱᏥᎸᎾ
haadlvgwuu geesv́ yijiʔlvv́nva
haadlv=gwuu gees-v́ yi-ji-hlvv́na
where=DT be:INC-DVB IRR-1A-go.to.sleep:IMM
'I can go to sleep wherever.'

Many adverbs of place are locations derived with the **locative** (LOC) suffix described in chapter 12. This suffix consists of a **vowel** with a highfall tone followed by *-ʔi* or the less-common form *-hi*. This vowel is usually the same vowel as the **final vowel** of the word, as seen in (50a) and (50b). If the final vowel is /a/, however, there is an unpredictable variation between /o/ and /v/, as seen in (50c) and (50d). Sometimes a word that ends in a vowel besides /a/ takes /v/: these changes probably reflect an older and no longer productive process. An example is shown in (50e).

(50a) ᎣᏏᎢ
óosííʔi
óosi-ʔi
stove-LOC
'into the stove'

(50b) ᏝᏬᏚᎯ
hlawoòtúúhi
hlawootu-hi
mud-LOC
'in the mud' (Feeling 1975a:130)

(50c) ᏅᏙᎯ
nvvdóóhi

nvvda-hi
moon/sun-LOC
'on the moon', 'on the sun'

(50d) ᎠᎼᎯ
amóóhi
ama-hi
water-LOC
'in the water'

(50e) ᎦᏍᎩᎸᎢ
gaasgilv́v́ʔi
gaasgilo-ʔi
table-LOC
'on the table'

7.5.2. Adverbs Modifying Clauses

A few adverbs modify an entire clause. Three examples are shown in (51). In all three examples, the modifier is at the beginning of the phrase. In (51a) the adverb *éélìisdi* says something about the degree of probability of the entire following clause.

(51a)	ᎡᎵᏍᏗ	ᎯᎸᏍᎩ	ᏳᎪᏕ	ᏱᏗᏣᏩᏎᎢ
	éélìisdi	hilv́v́sgi	yuùgóòde	yidichawaséeʔi
	éélìisdi	hilv́v́sgi	yi-uu-góòde	yi-di-ja-hwas-éʔi
	seems	few	IRR-3B-more	IRR-DST2-2B-buy:CMP-NXP

'It seems like you should've bought a few more.'

(51b)	ᎠᏎᏍ	ᏗᎩᏅᏗᏰᏗ	ᏗᏖᎵᏙ
	asées	diginvvdiíyedi	diiteliido
	asée=s	di-ginii-vvdiíyedi	di-ateliido
	must=Q	DST2-1B.DL-wash:INF\MOD	DST2-dish

'Do we have to wash dishes?'

(51c)	ᏙᏳᏃ	ᏍᎩ	ᏄᎾᏛᏁᎴ
	doyúhnóo	sgi	nuùndv́vneele
	doyu=hńoo	sgi	ni-uunii-adv́vneel-e
	really=CN	this	NI-3B.NS-do:CMP-NXP

'Really they did this.' (The Wolf and the Crawdad, line 13)

7.5.3. Negative Adverbs

Two **negative adverbs** modify a verb, adjective, or adverb by negating them. When the **negation adverb** *tla* is used, the irrealis prepronominal prefix *yi-* appears on the verb being negated, as seen in (52).

(52a) <u>Ꮭ</u> ᏯᏆᏅᏔ
<u>tla</u> <u>y</u>agwahnta
tla yi-agi-anvhta
NEG IRR-1B-know:PRC
'I don't know.'

(52b) <u>ᏝᏃ</u> ᏍᏓᏱ <u>Ᏹ</u>ᏗᏥᎸᏫᏍᏓᏁᎰ
<u>tlahno</u> sdááyi <u>yi</u>diìjiilv́hwsdaàneeho
tla=hno sdááyi yi-di-iijii-lv́hwsdaàneeh-o
NEG=CN hard IRR-DST2-2B.PL-work:INC-HAB
'You all don't work very hard.'

The **negative command** adverb *tleesdi* appears with the **command** (COM) *jii-* prepronominal prefix to create a negative command. Two examples are shown in (53).

(53a) ᎴᏍᏗ ᎤᎿ ᏥᎯᏢᏂ
<u>hleesdi</u> uhna jiihihlvv̀ni
hleesdi uhna jii-hi-hlvv̀ni
NEG.COM there COM-2A-sleep:IMM
'Don't go to sleep there!'

(53b) ᎴᏍᏗ ᏥᏍᎩᏅᎯ
<u>hleesdi</u> jiisginv́hi
hleesdi jii-sgi-nv́hi
NEG.COM COM-2/1-call:IMM
'Don't call me!'

Other adverbs acquire a negative meaning when accompanied by the negation adverb, as in (54).

(54) Ꮭ ᎢᎸᏢ ᏱᏓᎨᏏ
hla ilv́vhdlv yidageesi
hla ilv́vhdlv yi-da-ji-ees-i
NEG somewhere IRR-CMF-1A-go:CMP-CMF
'I am going nowhere today.'

7.5.4. Interrogative Adverbs

Interrogative adverbs (question words) are words that ask when, where, or how an event occurs. These sorts of questions are formed by placing the appropriate interrogative adverb at the beginning of the sentence. Two examples of 'where' are shown in (55).

(55a) ᎭᏢ ᏫᎦᏘ
haadlv hwikti
haadlv wi-hi-gahti
where TRN-2A-head.to:PRC
'Where are you headed?'

(55b) ᎭᏢ ᏫᎦᏁᎳ ᎤᏠᎩ
haadlv wiganeéla uuhlogi
haadlv wi-ga-neéla uu-hlogi
where TRN-3A-reside:PRC 3B-aunt
'Where does her aunt live?' (Feeling 1975a:166)

To ask the question 'when?' the interrogative adverb *hiláàyv* is used, as in (56).

(56) ᎯᎳᏴ ᏧᎵᎪᏤ ᎰᎦᏍᎬ
hiláàyv chulgoje hoksgv́
hiláàyv ja-sulgoj-e hi-ogisg-v́
when 2B-quit:CMP-NXP 2A-smoke:INC-DVB
'When did you quit smoking?' (Feeling 1975a:56)

There are several ways to ask a 'why' question. One way is to use the interrogative adverb *gadoohv* as in (57).

(57a) ᎦᏙᎲ ᎤᏤᏩᏍᏗ ᎤᏅᏗ ᏅᎯᏴᏂᏏ
gadoòhv uujeéwáàsdi uunvv́di nvvhiiyv́vnisi
gadoòhv uu-ajeéwáaȁdi uunvv́di ni-ii-hii-v́vnisi
why 3B-spill:INF milk NI-ITR-2A.AN-cause:IMM
'Why did you make him spill his milk?'

(57b) ᎦᏙᎲ ᏙᏣᏲᎯ ᏍᏕᏱᏓ
gadoòhv dojáyohi sdeeyída
gadoòhv dee-ii-ja-yohi sdeeyída
why DST-ITR-2B-release:IMM rope
'Why did you let go of the rope?' (Feeling 1975a:151)

A second way is with *gado* or *gadooke* and the **relativizer prepronominal** (REL) prefix *ji-* attached to the verb. Two examples are given in (58). This prefix is discussed in chapter 10.

(58a) ᎦᏙ ᏧᏞᏰᏗᎭ
gado juùliíyéèdiha
gado ji-uu-liíyéèdiha
why REL-3B-moan:PRC
'Why is he moaning?' (Feeling 1975a:173)

(58b) ᎦᏙᎨ ᏥᏣᎵᏅ
gadoòke jijahlvvnv
gadoòke ji-ja-hlvvn-v
why REL-2B-sleep:CMP-EXP
'Why did you go to sleep?'

As seen in (59), for some speakers the *ji-* prefix is not necessary.

(59) ᎦᏙᎨ ᏂᏚᏳᎪᏛᎾ ᎡᏍᏚᎢᏍᏗᎭ
gadoòke niduuyuukdv́v́na eèsduʔiísdíiha
gadoòke niduuyuukdv́v́na eesdii-uuhiísdíiha
why not.true 2A.DL.AN-accuse:PRC
'Why do you two accuse him wrongly?'

Interrogative adverbs can also question the degree of intensity of an adjective (60a), a verb (60b), or another adverb (60c).

(60a) ᎯᎳ ᏂᎪᏍᏓᏯ ᎯᎠ ᎭᏰᎵᏍᏓ
hila nigoósdaàya hiʔa hayelsda
hila ni-ga-oósdaàya hiʔa hayelsda
how NI-3A-sharp this knife
'How sharp is this knife?'

(60b) ᎦᏙ ᎤᏰᎸᏗ ᎠᎵᎯᎵᎦ
gado uuyééhldi aàliiheélîiga
gado uuyééhldi a-aliiheélîiga
what reason 3A-be.happy
'For what reason is he happy?' (Feeling 1975a:39)

(60c) ᎯᎳ ᎾᎪᎯᎳ ᏂᏥᏁᎶ ᎫᏌ
hila naagoohiíl niìjiineélo guusó
hila naagoohiíla ni-iijii-neél-o guusa-ʔi

how long NI-2A.PL-reside:INC-HAB Muskogee-LOC
'How long have you been living in Muskogee?'

7.6. Modifiers of Adjectives and Adverbs

The adverbs in (61) can also modify adjectives as well as other adverbs.

(61a) Ꮎ ᎦᏓᏘ ᎤᎶᏒᏍᏗ ᎦᏓᎭᎢ ᎦᏛᏗᎢ
na gaadati <u>uulosv́v́sdi</u> gaadaaháá?i gadvv̀díí?i
na gaadati uulosv́v́sdi gaadaa-háá?i ga-advv̀díí?i
that flag too dirt-ADJ 3A-hang(flexible):INF
'That flag is <u>too</u> dirty to hang up.'

(61b) ᏙᏳ ᏍᏓᏯ ᎢᏥᏬᏂᎭ
<u>dooyu</u> sdááya iìjiiwóoniha
dooyu sdááya iijii-wóoniha
very hard 2A.PL-talk:PRC
'You all are talking <u>very</u> loudly.'

(61c) ᎯᎠ ᎠᏍᎦᏯ ᎤᏙᎯᏳ ᎠᎦᏔᎲᎢ
hi?a asgaya <u>uudoohiyúú</u> áktahna?i
hi?a a-sgaya uudoohiyúú a-x́ktahna?i
this 3A-man very 3A-knowledgeable
'This man is <u>very</u> knowledgeable.' (Feeling 1975a:34)

Nonderived adjectives and adverbs can take the **intensifier suffixes** *-géé?í, -iiya,* and *-ka* to express that the quality exists in a greater degree. An example of each is shown in (62).

(62a)	ᎦᎸᏓᏗ	galvv́ládi	'high'
	ᎦᎸᏓᏗᎨᎢ	galvv́ládigéé?i	'higher'
(62b)	ᎠᏌᎹᏗ	asamáádi	'smart'
	ᎠᏌᎹᏗᏯ	asamadiíya	'smarter'
(62c)	ᎤᏍᏗ	uusdíí	'small'
	ᎤᏍᏗᎦ	uusdíika	'smaller' (Pulte and Feeling 1975:337)

Two examples of sentences with these types of adjectives and adverbs are given in (63).

(63a) ᏏᏊ ᏥᏂᎯᏫ ᎤᏍᎦᏃᎵᎨᎢ Track 48
siígwu jiiniihiwi uusganooliigéé?i

siígwu jii-ni-hi-wi uu-sganoolii-géé**ʔ**i
again COM-NI-2A-say:IMM 3B-slow-INT
'Say it again slower.'

(63b) ᎦᎸᎳᏗᎨ ᏫᎶᎦ
galvv́ládige hwiʔloòga
galvv́ládi-ge wi-hi-ʔloòga
higher-INT TRN-2A-climb:IMM
'Climb up higher.' (Feeling 1975a:103)

Although these intensifiers have different forms, they appear to have the same meanings; in other words, which adjective takes which suffix is unpredictable. For this reason, these various intensifier suffixes all take the abbreviation INT. A comprehensive dictionary of Cherokee would need to list these unpredictable forms for each adjective. Two more examples of intensfiers are given in (64).

(64a) ᏍᏓᏲᏒᏛ ᎤᏙᎯᏎ ᏩᏯ
sdaayosv́v́dvv uùtohiise wahya
sdááyi-sv́v́=dvv uu-atohiis-e wahya
hard-INT=EM 3B-whoop:CMP-NXP wolf
'The wolf whooped real loud.' (The Wolf and the Crawdad, line 24)

(64b) ᎤᎿᏅᏍᏊ ᎠᏣᏗ ᏍᏈᏍᏙᏒ
uùhnaanvsgwu ajaʔd sgwiísdosv́
uùhna=na=sgwu ajaʔdi sgwiísdi-sv́
there=FC=DT fish a.lot-INT
'There also was a whole lot of fish.' (The Search Party, line 24)

Adjectives can also be intensified by using the adverbs *uudli* or *uugoodi* 'more'. Three examples are shown in (65).

(65a) ᎤᏝ ᎤᎧᏲᏓ uudli uukayóóda 'more dry'
(65b) ᎤᎪᏗ ᎤᏔᎾ uugóòdi úútana 'bigger' (Feeling 1975a:148)
(65c) ᎤᏝ ᎤᏬᎵᏗ uudli uuwóóhldi 'more funny'

One of the most common ways to form the **superlative** is with the **translocative** (TRN) *wi-* in conjunction with the **deverbalizer** (DVB) that takes the place of the final vowel of the adjective. (66) shows several examples of this construction.

(66a) ᎤᏔᎾ úútana 'big'
ᏭᏔᏅᎢ wuútanv́v́ʔi 'biggest'
(66b) ᎤᎪᏗ úúgodi 'more'
ᏭᎪᏛᎢ wuugoodv́v́ʔi 'most'

(66c) ᎦᎸᎾᏗ galv́v́nadi 'high'
ᏩᎦᎸᎾᏗᏴᎢ wagalvvndiiyv́v́ʔi 'highest'
(66d) ᎪᏍᏓᏱ goòsdaáyi 'sharp'
ᏫᎪᏍᏓᏴᎢ wigoosdayv́v́ʔi 'sharpest'
(66e) ᎤᏍᏗ usdíí 'small'
ᏭᏍᏗᎬᎢ wuúsdíìkv́v́ʔi 'smallest'

Two examples of superlatives in sentences are shown in (67).

(67a) ᏭᎪᏛᎢ ᎠᏕᎳ ᎠᎩᏝ
wuugoodv́v́ʔi adeéla aàgihla
wi-uugoodi-v́v́ʔi adeéla agi-hla
TRN-most-DVB money 1B-have:PRC
'I have the most money.'

(67b) ᎦᏙ ᎤᏍᏗ ᎠᎿᏬ ᏩᎦᏓᎯᏴᎢ
gado úúsd ahnawo wagadahiiyv́v́ʔi
gado úúsdi a-ahnawo wi-a-gadu-hááʔi-iiya-v́v́ʔi
what something 3A-shirt TRN-3A-dirt-ADJ-INT-DVB
'Which shirt is the dirtiest?'

Adjectives formed with the **participle suffix** *-da* take the pronominal prefix but not an intensifier. An example of a participle superlative is given in (68).

(68) ᏪᏌ ᏍᏚᏗ ᏫᏥᎸᏉᏓ ᎠᏣᎳᎩ ᎠᏛᏁᎵᏍᎩ
wes sduudi wijiilvv́gwóòda ajalagi advvneélíísgi
wes sduudi wi-jii-lvv́gwóò-da a-jalagi a-advvneéliísg-i
Wes Studi TRN-1A.AN-like-PCP 3A-Cherokee 3A-act:INC-AGT
'Wes Studi is my favorite Cherokee actor.'

For comparisons between two nouns, the word *sihno* 'than' appears after the adjective, as in (69).

(69a) ᎯᎢᎾ ᎠᎿᏬ ᎤᏟ ᎤᎧᏲᏓ ᏏᏃ Ꮎ ᏗᏑᎶ
hiʔina ahnawo uudli uukayóóda siíhno na diisuulo
hiʔa=na a-ahnawo uudli uu-kayoo-da siíhno na di-a-asuulo
this=FC 3A-shirt more 3B-dry-PCP than that DST2-3A-pants
'This shirt is drier than those pants.'

(69b) ᎢᎦ ᎡᎯ ᏅᏓ ᎤᎪᏗ ᎤᏔᎾ
iiga ééhi nvvda uugóòdi úútana
iiga a-eéh-i nvvda uu-góòdi uu-ű̃tana
day 3A-live:INC-AGT sun/moon more 3B-big

ᏏᏅ   ᏒᏃᏱ   ᎡᎯ   ᏅᏓ   ᎨᏒᎢ
siíhnv   svvnoóyi   ééhi   nvvda   geesvv́ʔi
siíhnv   svvnoóyi   a-eéh-i   nvvda   gees-vv́ʔi
than   at.night   3A-live:INC-AGT   sun/moon   be:INC-EXP
'The sun is bigger than the moon.' (Feeling 1975a:148)

To indicate that a quality exists in a smaller amount, the adverb *gayóóhli* appears before the adjective. If a comparison is being made, the form *gayoóhlígééʔi* appears. Both of these adverbs are exemplified in (70).

(70a)   ᎦᏲᏝᏊ   ᎦᏚᎵᏓ
gayóóhliwu   gaàduulíída
gayóóhli=wu   ga-aàduulíída
little=DT   3A-wet
'It's a little wet.'

(70b)   ᎦᏲᏝᎨᏊ   ᏌᎪᏂᎨ
gayoóhlígééwu   sahkoónínge
gayoóhlígéé=wu   sahkoóníge
less=DT   blue
'It's less blue.'

As demonstrated in (71), adding the prepronominal prefix *ni-* to an adjective or adverb creates the meaning 'so ADJECTIVE/ADVERB.' This prefix is described in chapter 10.

(71)   ᎦᏙᎲ   ᏄᏍᎦᏃᎵ   ᎯᏱᎵ
gadohv   nuusganóóli   hiyili
gadohv   ni-uu-sganóóli   hi-yili
why   NI-3B-slow   2A-drive:PRC
'Why are you driving so slowly?'

Adding the prefix *ni-* and the deverbalizer suffix to an adjective or adverb creates the meaning 'as ADJECTIVE/ADVERB as possible', as in (72).

(72)   ᏄᏝᏍᏛ   ᏤᏒ   ᎯᏲᏎᎸᎢ
nuùhliísdv́   jeesv́   hiiyooseelvvʔi
ni-uùhliísd-v́   di-a-ees-v́   hii-ooseel-vvʔi
NI-quickly-DVB   TOW-3A-walk:CMP-DVB   2A.AN-tell:CMP-FCM
'Tell him to come as quickly as possible.' (Feeling 1975a:148)

7.7. Postpositional Phrases

Postpositions, like English **prepositions,** indicate a noun phrase's relationship to the rest of the clause, typically a relationship of location or time. Like English prepositions, Cherokee postpositions always occur with a noun phrase **complement;** the Cherokee postposition, however, typically follows rather than precedes this noun phrase. The postposition and its noun phrase together constitute a **postpositional phrase.** These phrases serve as modifiers and serve to describe a verb (an adverbial postpositional phrase) or a noun (an **adjectival** postpositional phrase). Some of the common postpositions are listed in (73).

(73)	ᎬᏗ	gv́hdi	'with'
	ᏗᏝ	díidla	'toward'
	ᎭᏫᎾ	hawíína	'under'
	ᎾᎥ	naʔv	'near'
	ᎦᏚ	gadu	'on top of'
	ᎠᏰᏟ	ayééhli	'between,' 'in the middle of'
	ᎢᏳᏍᏗ	iyúúsdi	'like'
	ᎢᎪᎯᏓ	iígóohíída	'during'

A postposition is considered an adverb when it appears without a noun phrase complement. For example, in (74a) the postposition 'near' follows the noun 'bed'; together these two words form the postpositional phrase 'near the bed', which indicates where the action of the verb 'be at' takes place. In (74b), by contrast, 'near' appears as an adverb and directly modifies the verb.

(74a)	ᎦᏂᏟ	ᎾᎥ	ᎠᏁᏙᎲ
	ganiitl	naʔv	aàneéd óòhv́
	ganiitli	naʔv	anii-eédóòh-v́
	bed	near	3A.NS-be.at:INC-DVB

	ᎪᎱᏍᏗ	ᏓᎾᏛᎩ
	goohúúsd	daàntvvgi
	goohúúsdi	dee-anii-ahtvvgi
	something	DST-3A.NS-hear:PRC

'They're hearing something while they're near the bed.'

(74b)	ᎾᎥ	ᎤᏙᎯᏎ	ᏥᏍᏛᎾ
	naʔv	uùtoohiise	jíisdvvna
	naʔv	uu-atohiis-e	jíisdvvna
	near	3B-whoop:CMP-NXP	crawdad

'... right beside him the crawdad whooped.' (The Wolf and the Crawdad, line 19)

Postpositional phrases can be used to indicate information about a noun (serve an adjectival function) or to indicate information about a verb (serve an adverbial function). As seen in (75), the postpositional phrase generally precedes the noun it modifies.

(75)	ᏗᏕᎶᏆᏍᏗ	ᎢᎬᏱᏗᏜ	ᎦᏅᏅ
	diideehlgwasdi	igvv́ydíidla	ganvvhnv
	di-a-adeehlgwasdi	igvv́yi+díidla	ganvvhnv
	DST2-3A-learn:INF	front+toward	road

	ᎤᎾᏒᏍᏗ	ᎢᎩ
	uunasv́v́sdi	iigi
	uu-nasv́v́sdi	ii-gi
	3B-slick	ITR-be:PRC

'The road in front of the school is slick.'

Three examples of adverbial postpositional phrases are shown in (76). In (76a) the underlined postpositional phrase tells how the action was carried out. In (76b) the postpositional phrase tells the amount of time during which the activity took place, and in (76c) it tells where the activity occurs.

(76a)	ᎦᎷᏯᏍᏓ	ᎬᏗ	ᏓᏍᎷᏍᎦ	ᎠᏓ
	galuysda	gv́hdi	daàsluusga	ada
	galuysda	gv́hdi	dee-a-sluusga	ada
	axe	with	DST-3A-split:PRC	wood

'He is splitting wood with an axe.'

(76b)	ᎠᎵᏏᎾᎯᏍᏗᏍᎬ	ᎯᏍᎩ	ᏳᏟᎶᏓ	ᎢᎪᎯᏓ
	aàlsiínáàhisdiisgv	hisgi	yuuhlíilóóda	iígóohíída
	a-alsiínáàhisdiisg-v	hisgi	yuuhlíilóóda	iígóohíída
	3A-exercise:INC-EXP	five	hour	during

'He exercised for five hours.'

(76c)	ᎰᏈ	ᎠᏂᏴᏫᏯ	ᎤᎦᎾᏮ	ᎢᏗᏜ	ᎠᏁᎭ
	hoogwi	aniiyvvwiiya	uúgáanawv	iidíidla	aàneéha
	hoogwi	anii-yvvwiiya	uúgáanawv	iidíidla	anii-eéha
	Hopi	3A.NS-Indian	south	toward	3A.NS-live:PRC

'Hopi Indians live in the South.'

Some postpositions such as 'above' and 'below' frequently appear as part of a compound with 'toward.' Two examples shown are in (77).

(77a)	ᎤᏓᏝ	ᎠᏆᏙᏌᏛ	ᏍᏚᏗ	ᎦᎸᎾᏗᏜ
	uudááhla	aàgwahtóosadv	sduùdi	galv́vndíidla
	uudááhla	agi-ahtóosad-v	sduùdi	galv́vna+díidla
	mistletoe	1B-hang:CMP-EXP	door	above+toward

'I hung up mistletoe above the door.'

(77b) ᏙᏥᏇᏅᏍᎬ
doòjiikweenvvsgv
dee-oojii-kweenvvsg-v
DST-1A.PL.EX-wrap:INC-EXP

ᎢᏡᎬ	ᎭᏫᎾᏗᏜ	ᏦᎩᏗ
ihlgv	hawíindíidla	joogiihdi
ihlgv	hawíina+díidla	di-oogii-hdi
tree	under+toward	DST2-1B.PL.EX-put:INF

'We were wrapping them to put under the tree.'

A frequent difficulty for English speakers learning Cherokee is that the information conveyed by an English preposition is often understood from the verb itself or from the context. This phenomenon is demonstrated in (78).

(78a)	ᎤᏁᎩᎸᏗ	ᎠᏓᏁᎸ	ᎤᏗᏍᎦᏝᏅᎢ
	uunéegihldi	aàdaaneélv	uùdiisgahlánvv́ʔi
	uu-néegihldi	aàdaaneélv	uu-adiisgahlán-vv́ʔi
	3B-ugly	building	3B-hide:INC-EXP

'He was hiding **in** an ugly house.' (Feeling 1975a:176)

(78b)	ᎤᎾᏓᏬᏍᏗ	ᏩᏕᏛᏍᎦ
	uunadawoòsdi	waàdeetv́sga
	uunii-adaa-woòsdi	wi-a-adeetv́sga
	3B.NS-MDL-bathe(T):INF	TRN-3A-dive:PRC

'He is diving **into** the pool.'

(78c)	ᎯᎳ	ᎢᎦ	ᏣᏉᏰᎮ	Ꮎ	ᎠᎵᏍᏇᏚᏬ
	hila	iíga	jakwiyvvhe	na	alsgweètuwo
	hila	iíga	ja-kwiyvvh-e	na	alisgweètuwo
	how	much	2B-pay:CMP-NXP	the	hat

'How much did you pay **for** the hat?' (Feeling 1975a:43)

Cherokee also derives new words indicating location rather than using a post-position. This locative suffix is further described in chapter 12; an example is given in (79).

(79)	ᎠᎦᏓᏢᏓ	ᎦᏑᏴᏍᎪ	ᎧᏫᎢ
	akdadlv́v́da	gaàsuuyv́vsgo	kaáhwííʔi
	akdadlv́v́da	ji-asuuyv́vsg-o	kaáhwi-ʔi
	cream	1A-mix:INC-HAB	coffee-LOC
	'I mix cream in my coffee.'		

7.8. Postfixes

Postfixes are small word-like elements that are only found attached to the end of a word. They are distinct from suffixes in that they can attach to any part of speech but like suffixes in that they are always attached to another word. Some postfixes are like adverbs and adjectives, modifying the element that they are attached to; other postfixes have a function of questioning or emphasizing the word to which they are attached. In many cases their exact meaning is difficult to translate. To maintain the distinction between postfixes and suffixes an **equals sign** (=) is used with the former and a hyphen (-) is used with the latter. The most common postfix is the =*s* that is used to ask 'yes/no' questions. (80a) is an example of this postfix attaching to a noun; (80b), (80c), and (80d) involve an adjective, a verb, and an adverb.

(80a)	ᎩᏟᏍ	ᎯᏩᏎ
	giihlis	hiihwase
	giihli=s	hii-hwas-e
	dog=Q	2A.AN-buy:CMP-NXP
	'Did you buy the dog?'	

(80b)	ᎤᎧᏲᏓᏍ	ᎠᏆᎿᏬ
	uukayóódas	agwáhnawo
	uu-kayoo-da=s	agi-áhnawo
	3B-dry-PCP=Q	1B-shirt
	'Is my shirt dry?'	

(80c)	ᏣᏳᏆᏗᏍᎪᏍ
	chayuukwadiisgos
	ja-ahyuukwadiisg-o=s
	2B-have.toothache:INC-HAB=Q
	'Do you have a toothache?'

(80d) ᏑᎾᎣᏅᏍ ᏓᎦᎷᎯ
sunáales dagáluhji
sunáale=s da-ga-luhj-i
tomorrow=Q CMF-3A-arrive:CMP-CMF
'Will he arrive tomorrow?'

It is possible for more than one postfix to appear. Three examples are shown in (81); (81c) is an instance of three appearing at once.

(81a) ᎯᎠᏊᏛ
hiʔagwúdvv
hiʔa=gwu=dvv
this=DT=EM
'Just this.'

(81b) ᏙᏫᏃ ᏓᎦᎵᏍᏔᏂ ᏄᏍᏫ
doowv́hn dagalstan nv́v́wi
gado=wv=hno da-ga-alistan-i nv́v́wi
what=DT=CN CMF-3A-happen:CMP-CMF now
'Now what is going to happen?'

(81c) ᎤᎿᏩᏛᏃ ᎠᏥᎨᎯᏙᎴ ᏥᏍᏛᎾ
uhnawdvhno ajikehiídóòle jíisdvvn
uhna=wu=dvv=hno aji-hkeh-iídóòl-e jíisdvvna
there=DT=FC=CN 3O-chase:CMP-AMB:CMP-NXP crawdad
'. . . and right then he started chasing him.' (The Wolf and the Crawdad, line 37)

The appearance of a postfix interacts with the final tone of the word to which it attaches. The individual postfixes are explained and exemplified in the following sections. The most common pattern seems to be for the final stress and tone to fall on the final vowel of the word to which the postfix attaches; to indicate the place of this tone and stress, an accent is placed at the end of the word (which is usually unaccented). An example is given in (82). The final vowel for the verb 'feel' would normally be unmarked, as its stress and tone are predictable; as stated in chapter 6, the final vowel of the **full form** of the word is stressed and has a high tone. With the addition of the postfix, however, the accent is added to indicate that the new ending does not receive the normal final stress and tone.

(82) Ꭰ4Ꭹ ᎠᏆᏓᏅᏓᏛ ᏝᎦ
aséégi agwadanhdádvv hléega
a-séégi agi-adanhda=dvv hléega

3A-peculiar 1B-feel:PRC=EM a.while
'I felt peculiar for a while.' (Feeling 1975a:49)

7.8.1. Conducive Question (CQ) Postfix

This common postfix is used to ask questions to which a 'yes' answer is expected. Three examples are shown in (83).

(83a) ᏍᏉ°ᏅᎩᏧ
sgwohlgíju
sgi-ohlgi=ju
2/1-understand:PRC=CQ
'Do you understand me?'

(83b)	ᎦᎯᎪᏩᏘᏧ	Ꮎ	ᎩᏟ
	gaahiigoohwahtíju	na	giihli
	gaa-hii-goohwahti=ju	na	giihli
	ANS-2A.AN-see:PRC=CQ	those	dog
	'Do you see those dogs?'		

(83c) ᏙᎯᏧ
toòhííju
toòhíí=ju
quiet=CQ
'Are you OK?'

The last example is the question that typically follows the standard greeting *osiyo* 'hello.'

7.8.2. 'Or' Question (OQ) Postfix

The postfix =*ke* presents a choice between two alternatives. Two examples are shown in (84). In the second example the **question postfix** =*s* appears on the verb and the alternative question postfix appears on the negative adverb *tla*.

(84a)	ᏲᏁᎦᎸ	ᎠᎴ	ᏣᎳᎩ	ᎦᏬᏂᏍᎪ
	yóoneegáke	ale	jalagi	gawóonisgo
	yóoneega=ke	ale	jalagi	ga-wóonisg-o
	English=OQ	or	Cherokee	3A-speak:INC-HAB
	'Does he speak English or Cherokee?'			

(84b) ᎧᏁᎩᏍ ᏥᏯᎵᏃᎮᏗᏍᎬ ᏝᎨ
kaneègis chiyaliìnohehdiisgv́ hláke
ga-hneègi=s ji-hii-ali-hnohehdiisg-v́ hla=ke
3A-answer:IMM=Q REL-2A.AN-MDL-converse:INC-DVB NEG=OQ
'Did he answer when you were speaking to him or not?' (Feeling 1975a:139)

=ke also appears on question words either to emphasize the question, as in (85a), or to alter the question itself, as in (85b).

(85a) ᎦᎪᎨ ᏗᏓᎾᏫ ᏫᏤᏓᏍᏗ ᏂᏨᏁᎴ
gáàgoke diidaanawv wijeedaàsdi nijv́hneele
gáàgo=ke diidaanawv wi-ja-eedaàsdi ni-ja-v́hneel-e
who=OQ store TRN-2B-be.at:INF NI-2B-cause:CMP-NXP
'Who made you go to the store?'

(85b) ᎯᎳᎨ ᎢᎩᏓ Ꮎ ᏅᏯ
hiláke iíkida na nvv̀ya
hila=ke iíkida na nvv̀ya
how=OQ big that rock
'How big is that rock?'

(85c) ᎦᎪ ᎤᎪᏗ ᎠᏌᎹᏗᏯ ᏂᎯ ᎡᏣᏙᎨ
gáago uugóòdi asamadíiya nihi ejadoke
gáago uu-góòdi a-samáádi-iiya nihi eja-do=ke
who 3B-more 3A-smart-INT 2PRO 2O-sibling=OQ
'Who is smarter, you or your sister?' (Feeling 1975a:46)

7.8.3. Yes/No Question (Q) Postfix

This postfix appears on the word that is being questioned when a 'yes' or 'no' answer is expected. It is the most common postfix. Its full form is *=sgo*, but this form is not common in Oklahoma Cherokee. Five examples are shown in (86).

(86a) ᎠᏯᏢᏗᏍ ᏣᏩᎯᏍᏗ ᏣᏚᎵ
aahyadlv́v́dis chawahisdi jaduuli
aahyadlv́v́di=s ja-hwahisdi ja-aduuli
necktie=Q 2B-buy:INF 2B-want:PRC
'Do you want to buy a necktie?' (Feeling 1975a:27)

(86b) ᏝᏍ ᏰᎵᏍᎪ
tlas hyeèlîisgo
tla=s yi-hi-eèlîisg-o
NEG=Q IRR-2A-think:INC-HAB
'Don't you think so?'

(86c) ᏕᎯᏙᎬᏍ ᏕᏤᏍᏓᏁᎰ
deehídoogvs deejeesdaaneeho
dee-hi-doogv=s dee-ja-eesdaaneeh-o
DST-2A-teeth=Q DST-2B-hurt:INC-HAB
'Do your teeth hurt?'

(86d) ᏍᎪᏂᏱᏍ ᏫᏤᏓᏍᏗ
skoniíyis wijeedaàsdi
skoniíyi=s wi-ja-eedaàsdi
overseas=Q TRN-2B-be.at:INF

ᏄᎵᏍᏔᏁ ᎠᏂᏲᏍᎩ ᏥᏯᎥᎢ
nuùlstane aniiyósgi chiyáʔv́v́ʔi
ni-uu-alistan-e aniiyósgi ji-hi-yáʔ-v́v́ʔi
NI-3B-happen:CMP-NXP military REL-2A-be.in:CMP-DVB
'Did you have to go overseas when you were in the service?' (Feeling 1975a:153)

(86e) ᎡᏣᎪᎵᏰᎦᏍ
eèjagooliyéegas
eeja-gooliy-éega=s
2O-examine:CMP-MOV:PRC=Q
'Are you going to be examined?'

7.8.4. Delimiter (DT) Postfix

This commonly heard postfix often has the meaning 'only' or 'just' and is often emphatic. It also appears as =*sgwu*. Five examples are shown in (87); (87e) has the =*sgwu* form.

(87a) ᎩᎳᏊ ᎠᎩᎲᏏ
kilágwu aàgihvsi
kila=gwu agi-hvsi
just.now=DT 1B-give(solid):IMM
'She (just) gave it to me.'

(87b) ᏦᏊ ᎾᏂᎣ
jógwu naàniiʔo
jo=gwu ni-aniiʔ-o
three=DT NI-3A.NS-HAB
'There are usually only three of them.'

(87c) Ꭼ ᎢᏓᎴᎾᏭ
kv iìdaleénáwu
kv iidii-aleéna=wu
hey 1A.PL-start(I):IMM=DT
'Hey, let's start!'

(87d) ᏫᏄᎷᏨᎾᏊ ᎤᎦᏔᎲᏍᏗ ᎤᏚᎸᎲᎢ
winuuluhjv́v́nagwu uuktahvv̀sdi uuduulvvhvv́ʔi
wi-ni-uu-luhj-v́v́na=gwu uu-agahtahvv̀sdi uu-aduulvvh-vv́ʔi
TRN-NI-3B-arrive:CMP-NDV=DT 3B-turn.back:INF 3B-want:CMP-EXP
'He wanted to turn back before he got there.' (Feeling 1975a:35)

(87e) ᎤᏅ ᎠᎹ ᏭᏂᎷᏤ ᎤᏅᏅᏍᏊ
uùhna áamó wuùniiluhje uùhnanvsg
uùhna áama-hi wi-uunii-luhj-e uùhna=nv=sgwu
there salt-LOC TRN-3B.NS-arrive:CMP-NXP there=FC=DT
'There at "Salt" [Salina] they arrived at that place there.' (The Search Party, line 31)

This postfix is commonly reduced to *=wu,* as in (88a), (88b), and (88c), or to *=wv,* as in (88d). At times it is even shortened to *=w,* as in (88e).

(88a) ᎪᎵᎪᏭ ᎪᎵᏰᏍᎬᎢ
gohlgóowu qooliíyéèsqv́v́ʔi
ga-olihg-óo=wu ga-ooliíyéèsg-v́v́ʔi
3A-understand:INC-HAB=DT 3A-read:INC-DVB
'He understands what he reads.'

(88b) ᎠᏅᏭ ᎨᏙᎮᏍᏗ
áhnawu geédóhéesdi
áhna=wu ji-eédóh-éesdi
here=DT 1A-be.at:INC-PFT
'I'm going to stay here.'

(88c) ᏂᎪᎯᎸᏭ ᎠᏍᎩᏥᏍᎦ Ꮎ ᎠᎨᏳᏣ
niigoóhíilv́wu aàsgiitsga naʔ ageehyúúja

niigoóhíilv́=wu a-asgiitsga naʔ a-geehyúúja
always=DT 3A-dream:PRC that 3A-girl
'He's always dreaming of that girl.'

(88d) ᏍᏉ°ᎵᏓᏏ ᎠᏮᏌᏮ ᏗᎩᏃᎩᏍᏗ
sgwohldaasi awvv́sawv diigihnoogiìsdi
sgi-ohldaasi agi-vv́sa=wv di-agi-hnoogiìsdi
2/1-permit:IMM 1B-EMP.PRO=DT DST2-1B-sing:INF
'Allow me to sing by myself.'

(88e) ᎣᎩᎾᎵᎠᏇ ᏥᎪᏩᏔ
oòginaalíiʔaw jiigoòwaht
ooginii-aalíiʔa=wu jii-gohwahta
1B.DL.EX-friend=DT 1A.AN-see:IMM
'I only saw a friend.'

=*gwu* often combines with the **terminative** derivational suffix to create the meaning 'as soon as', as in (89).

(89) ᏳʷᎵᏍᏓᏴᏃᏁᏊ
yuulsdaayv́v́hnohnagwu
yi-uu-alisdaayvvhn-ohn-a=gwu
IRR-3B-eat:CMP-TRM:CMP-CVB=DT

ᏕᎬᏗᏰᏍᎪ ᏗᏖᎵᏙ
deegv́vdiíyéèsgo diiteeliído
dee-ga-vvdiíyéèsg-o di-ateeliído
DST-3A-wash.dishes:INC-HAB DST2-dish
'She washes the dishes immediately after she finishes eating.' (Feeling 1975a:78)

7.8.5. 'Or' Statement (os) Postfix

This postfix is typically translated as 'or' and attaches to statements. Five examples are shown in (90). In (90e) the postfix attaches to the negative adverb *tla*; the speaker in this instance gave the same translation when the postfix was left off.

(90a) Ꮡ ᏦᏓᎴ ᏱᏭᎷᏣ
sóʔ joodale yiwúúluhj
sóʔ di-ooda=le yi-wi-uu-luhj-a

another TOW-mountain=OS IRR-TRN-3B-arrive:CMP-CVB
'When he got to another mountain . . .' (The Turtle and the Rabbit, line 34)

(90b) ᏌᎻᎴ ᏰᎾ
saámíle yeena
saámi=le yi-a-eena
Sam=OS IRR-3A-go:IMM
'Maybe Sam will go.' (Walker 1975:219)

(90c) ᏧᎵᎢᎴ ᏱᎩ
juulííʔíle yig
di-uu-alííʔi=le yi-gi
DST2-3B-friend=OS IRR-be:IMM
'or friends' (The Turtle and the Rabbit, line 30)

(90d) ᏝᎴ ᏂᎦᏛᏁᎵ
tlale nigadv́vneeli
tla=le ni-ji-adv́vneel-i
NEG=OS NI-1A-do:CMP-CMF
'I'm not going to do it.'

7.8.6. Contrastive (CT) Postfix

Pulte and Feeling (1975: 293) state that the **contrastive** postfix occurs only after the full form of the question postfix =*sgo*, as seen in (91a); but an example without this question postfix is seen in (91b). The postfix appears on *gado* 'what' to form the interrogative adverb *gadohv* 'why' in (91c).

(91a) ᎦᏬᏂᎭᏍᎪᎲ
gawóonihásgoòhv
ga-wóoniha=sgo=hv
3A-speak:PRC=Q=CT
'But is he speaking?' (Pulte and Feeling 1975:293)

(91b) ᎠᎩᏴᎵᎲ
aàgihyvvhlvv́hv
agi-hyvvhl-vv́=hv
1B-enter:CMP-EXP=CT
'But I came in.'

(91c) ᎦᏙᎲ ᏗᏣᎦᏔᎲᏎ
gadoòhv diìjaktahv́vse
gado=hv di-iijii-agahtahv́vs-e
why=CT TOW-2B.PL-turn.back:CMP-NXP
'Why did you turn back?'

7.8.7. Emphatic (EM) Postfix

This common postfix is used to emphasize a word, usually at the beginning of a clause. It is often not translated. Several examples are shown in (92); in all of these examples the postfix appears at the end of the first word in the sentence.

(92a) ᎠᏴᏛ ᏱᏕᏥᏃᎩ
ayv́dvv yideejíʔnoogi
ayv=dvv yi-dee-ji-hnoogi
1PRO=EM IRR-DST-1A-sing:IMM
'**I'm** going to sing it.'

(92b) ᏃᏊᏛ ᏥᏓᏑᎳ
noógwúdvv jidasuúla
noógwu=dvv ji-dee-a-asuúla
now=EM REL-DST-3A-wash.hands:IMM
'He just washed his hands.'

(92c) ᎲᏃᏗᏛ
hvvhnóódídvv
hi-vvhnóódi=dvv
2A-alive=EM
'You're alive!'

(92d) ᏣᎩᎷᏨᏛ
jagilúhjvdvv
ji-agi-lúhj-v=dvv
REL-1B-pick.up:CMP-EXP=EM
'I did come.'

(92e) ᏝᏛ ᎪᎱᏍ ᏱᏂᎦᏛᎦ
tládvv gohúús yinigadvv̀g
tla=dvv gohúús yi-ni-ji-advv̀ga
not=EM something IRR-NI-1A-do:IMM
'I won't do anything.'

(92f) ᏝᏛ ᏱᏓᎨᎦᏈᏴᎡᎵ
tládvv yidageegakwiyvvʔeéli
tla=dvv yi-da-geegii-akwiyvv-eél-i
NEG=EM IRR-CMF-3NS/1PL-pay:CMP-APL:CMP-CMF
'They will not pay us.'

7.8.8. Focus (FC) Postfix

This postfix indicates focus on the word to which it attaches. The difference in meaning from emphatic *=dvv* (EM) is unclear, but it appears less frequently than that postfix does. Its most common occurrence is in the standard response to the question 'How are you?' The response is given in (93a). This same word is shown in (93c) in a declarative sentence; in this instance it seems to be adding emphasis.

(93a) ᎣᏍᏓ ᏂᎯᎾ
óósda nihíina
óósda nihi=na
good 2PRO=FC
'Fine, how about you?'

(93b) ᎾᎾ ᎦᏙ ᎤᏍᏗ
náana gado úúsd
na=na gado úúsdi
those=FC what thing
'What are those?'

(93c) ᏂᎯᎾ ᏍᏗᎨᏳ̈Ꮳ ᏅᏓ
nihíina sdiigeehyúúj nvvda
nihi=na sdii-geehyúúja nvvda
2PRO=FC 2A.DL-girl sun

ᏭᏕᎵᏨ ᎩᎳ ᎢᏍᏗᎷᏤ
wuùdeeliijv́ kila iisdiilúhje
wi-uu-deeliij-v́ kila ii-sdii-lúhj-e
TRN-3B-disappear:CMP-DVB later ITR-2A.DL-arrive:CMP-NXP
'You girls got home after the sun went down.'

In (93b) above the normally short vowel of the demonstrative 'that' is lengthened when the postfix attaches to it. This postfix can be used with the emphatic postfix, as demonstrated in (94).

(94) ᎯᎢᏛᎾ ᎠᏕᎳ ᏥᏕᏨᏁᎸ
hiʔidvvna adeéla jidéejvvneélv
hiʔi=dvv=na adeéla ji-dee-iijvv-hneél-v
this=EM=FC money REL-DST-1/2.PL-give(solid):CMP-EXP
'This is the money I gave you all.'

This postfix is sometimes pronounced as *=nv*; two examples are shown in (95).

(95a) ᏂᎯᏅ ᏣᏯᏄᎵᏧ
nihíinv jayanúúliju
nihi=nv ja-yanúúli=ju
2PRO=FC 2B-fast=CQ
'Are you fast?'

(95b) ᎤᎿᏅ ᏍᏈᏍᏙᏒ ᏚᏂᎪᎮ
uùhnanv sgwisdosv́ duùniigoohe
uùhna=nv sgwíísdi-sv́ dee-uunii-gooh-e
there=FC a.lot-INT DST-3B.NS-see:CMP-NXP
'There they saw a whole lot of them.' (The Search Party, line 20)

7.8.9. Conjunction (CN) Postfix

This postfix serves to link two words together and is often translated as 'and'; another important function is to announce the topic of the sentence.

Several examples are shown in (96). In (96a) and (96b) the postfix is used to announce a new sentence by attaching to the first element of that sentence. In (96c) and (96d) the postfix translates as 'and'. The short forms *=hnoo* and *=hno* are more common than the full form *=heehnoo*; shortened forms appear in all the examples below.

(96a) ᏭᎷᏨᏃ ᎦᎸᎾᏗ ᏗᎨᏒ
wuulúhjv́hno galv́v́nad digeèsv
wi-uu-ʔlúhj-v́=hno galv́v́nadi di-geès-v
TRN-3B-arrive:CMP-DVB=CN on.top.of TOW-be:INC-EXP

ᏩᏯ ᎤᏙᎯᏎ
wahya uùtohise
wahya uu-atohis-e
wolf 3B-whoop:CMP-NXP
'When the wolf got to the top he whooped.' (The Wolf and the Crawdad, lines 17–18)

(96b) ᏥᏍᏛᏅᎾᏃ ᎩᎳᏫᏴ
jíisdvvnahno kilawiyv
jíisdvvna=hno kilawiyv
crawdad=CN at.that.moment

ᏚᎵᏨᏯᏍᏔᏁ ᎤᏅᏙᎩᏯᏍᏗᎢ
duùlchvv́yáàstane uuhntohkiíyáàsdíiʔi
dee-uu-alchvv́yáàstan-e uunii-ahtokiíyáàsdíiʔi
DST-3B-become.brave:CMP-NXP 3B.NS-race:INF
'The crawdad at that moment got brave enough to race (the wolf).'
(The Wolf and the Crawdad, lines 6–7)

(96c) ᎯᎠ ᎠᎨᏳᏣ ᎠᏧᏣᏃ
hiʔa ageehyúúja achúújahno
hiʔa a-geehyúúja a-chúúja=hno
this 3A-girl 3A-boy=CN

ᎤᎾᎵᎪᏗ ᎤᎾᏚᎵᎭ
uunaliìkdi uùnaduulíha
uunii-aliìkdi uunii-aduulíha
3B.NS-go.together:INF 3B.NS-want:PRC
'This boy and girl want to go together.' (Feeling 1975a: 45)

(96d) ᏫᏔᎳᏑᎳᎩ ᏗᎯᏴᎵᏃ
witaláàsuulági diihiyvvhlvhno
wi-di-hi-aláasuulági di-ii-hi-yvvhl-v=hno
TRN-DST2-2A-remove.shoes:IMM TOW-ITR-2A-enter:CMP-FCM=CN
'Take your shoes off and then come back in again.'

This postfix also appears as *-hnv*; three examples are given in (97). In (97b) it is on the question word 'what'; together with the prepronominal prefix *jii-* it expresses a 'why' question. In (97c) it appears on the demonstrative 'that' toward the end of the sentence.

(97a) ᎤᏍᏗ ᎠᏧᏣ ᎧᏁᏌ ᎠᎦᏙᏍᏗ ᏓᎩᏏᏅ
uusdíí ajúúj kaneèsa aàktoósdi daksíhnv
uu-asdíí a-júúja kaneèsa a-agahtoósdi daksi=hnv
3B-little 3A-boy box 3A-look.at:PRC turtle=CN
'The little boy is looking at the box, the turtle also . . .'

(97b) ᎦᏙᏅ ᏥᎩᏙᎵᏨ
gadohnv jiìgiidoólîijv

gado=hnv ji-iigii-doólîij-v
what=CN REL-1B.PL-pity:CMP-EXP
'Why did she forgive us?'

(97c) ᎤᏂᏃᎮᏞ ᏥᏍᏚ ᎾᏅ ᏓᎩᏏ
uuniihnooheéhle jiisd nahn daks
uunii-hnooheéhl-e jiisdu na=hnv daksi
3B.NS-talk:CMP-NXP rabbit the=CN turtle
'The turtle and the rabbit talked about [a race].' (The Turtle and the Rabbit, line 4)

For some speakers, this postfix serves the important function of establishing a reason for an event occurring. In these instances it is often translated as 'because', as in (98).

(98a) ᏥᏯᏓᏱᎭ ᏝᎮᏃ ᏱᏥᏲᎵᎦ
jiiyadaʔyíha hlaheéhnóo yijiiyooliìga
jii-adaʔyíha hla=heéhnóo yi-jii-oolihga
1A.AN-deny:PRC NEG=CN IRR-1A.AN-recognize:PRC
'I am denying him because I don't know him.' (Feeling 1975a:3)

(98b) ᏗᎤᎷᏨᏃ ᏚᏩᏛᎮ
diʔúuluhjv́hnóo duùhwahtvvhe
di-ii-uu-luhj-v́=hnóo dee-uu-hwahtvvh-e
TOW-ITR-3B-arrive:CMP-DVB=CN DST-3B-find:CMP-NXP

ᏔᎵᏁ ᎠᏂᎵᎾᎡᎢ
taliine aànihlinaʔééʔi
tali-iine anii-hlinaʔ-éeʔi
two-ORD 3A.NS-sleep(NS):INC-NXP\SUB

ᏗᏂᎦᏙᎵᏰᏃ ᏗᎦᎨᏗᏳ ᎨᏎᎢ
diiniiktóólihyeéhnóo digageediiyu geeséeʔi
di-anii-gahtóóliyi=heéhnóo di-ga-gééda-iiyu gees-éʔi
DST2-3A.NS-eye=CN DST2-3A-heavy-INT be:INC-NXP
'And when he came back he found them asleep again, for their eyes were heavy.' (*Cherokee New Testament,* Matthew 26:43)

7.8.10. Concessive (cs) Postfix

This postfix is typically translated as 'but'; when attached to a question word, however, it often expresses 'I wonder'. Three examples are shown in (99).

(99a)

ᎭᏢᏍᎩᏂ	ᏚᏩᏍᎪ	ᏧᏑᎶ
haadlv́sginii	duùhwasgo	juusuulo
haadlv=sginii	dee-uu-hwasg-o	di-uu-asuulo
where=CS	DST-3B-buy:INC-HAB	DST2-3B-pants

'I wonder where he buys his pants.' (Feeling 1975a: 180)

(99b)

ᏓᎩᏏᏍᎩᏂ	ᎨᎲᏃ	ᏚᏟᏃᎮᏔᏁ
daksisgin	geèhv́hno	duùhlinohehtane
daksi=sginii	geèh-v́=hnóo	dee-uu-ali-hnohehtan-e
turtle=CS	be:CMP-DVB=CN	DST-3B-MDL-talk:CMP-NXP

'But the turtle talked to his friends and family members living there.' (The Turtle and the Rabbit, line 9)

(99c)

ᎤᏞᏤᏗ	ᎤᏚᎸᎲ
uudleèchéhdi	uùduulvvhv
uu-adleèj-éhdi	uu-aduulvvh-v
3B-take.revenge:CMP-APL:INF	3B-want:CMP-EXP

ᎠᏎᏍᎩᏂ	Ꮭ	ᎥᏍᎩ	ᏱᏄᏛᏁᎴᎢ
aséesginii	hla	vsgi	yinuudv́vneeléʔi
asée=sginii	hla	vsgi	yi-ni-uu-adv́vneel-éʔi
however=CS	NEG	that	IRR-NI-3B-do:CMP-NXP

'He wanted to take revenge against him, but he didn't do it.' (Feeling 1975a:12)

7.8.11. Less Common Postfixes

The less-common postfix =*ka* is discussed by Lindsey (1985:142). He gives only one example of its use, however, as shown below in (100).

(100) ᎩᏟᎧ
giihlíka
giihli=ka
dog=KA
'It's a dog, isn't it?'

King (1975:96) states that this suffix "is only employed when the speaker asks for an affirmative answer." Thus *howa* 'okay' becomes *howaka* 'isn't that right?' So *jadulihaka* would imply 'you (sg) do want it, don't you?'

The postfix *=gi* also is only discussed by Lindsey (1985:142–43); he uses the term 'echo question' but gives only one example of its use, shown in (101).

(101) ᎠᏍᎦᏯᎩ
asgayagi
a-sgaya=gi
3A-man=GI
'(Did you say) a man?'

Feeling (1975a) does not discuss this postfix, but an example of its use in his dictionary is shown in (102).

(102)	ᎦᏙᎩ	ᎭᏗᏍᎨ
	gadogi	hadiisge
	gado=gi	hi-adiisg-e
	what=GI	2A-say:INC-NXP
	'What were you saying?'	

7.9. Interjections

Interjections are short words that express an emotion, a simple response, or a greeting. They do not inflect. Interjections are either used alone or with a clause. Three examples with clauses are given in (103).

(103a)	Ꭵ	ᎾᎯᏳ	ᏓᎦᎷᏥ
	vv	naàhiyu	dagalúhji
	vv	naàhiyu	da-ga-lúhj-i
	yes	then	CMF-3A-arrive:CMP-CMF
	'Yes, at that time he will arrive.'		

(103b)	Ꭷ	ᎢᏓᎴᎾᏭ
	kam	iìdaleénawu
	kam	iidii-aleéna=wu
	hey	1A.PL-start(I):IMM=DT
	'Hey, let's start!	

(103c)	ᏄᎳ	ᏄᎾᏗᏅᏓᏊ	ᎦᏢᏦᏕ
	núúla	nuundiinv̀v́dagwu	gahljoóde

núúla ni-uu-nadiínv̋v̀-da=gwu gahljoóde
hurry NI-3B-sell-PCP=DT house

ᏫᏂᎷᏨᎢ
wiinii?luhjvv?i
wi-iinii-?luhj-vv?i
TRN-1A.DL-arrive:CMP-FCM
'Hurry! Let's get there before he sells the house.' (Feeling 1975a:104)

Most interjections express emotions about a situation, but some serve to confirm or deny a sentence or to question it. Several interjections (e.g., 'yes' and 'no') are the only examples of words in Cherokee that consist of a single syllable. A list of interjections is given in (104).

(104)	Ꭻ	vv	'yes'
	Ꮭ	tla	'no'
	Ꮒ	ni	'Look!'
	ᎣᏏᏲ	osiyo	'Hello'
	ᎠᏲ	ayo	'Ouch!'
	ᏍᎩ	sgi	'Thank you' (used in North Carolina)
	ᏩᏙ	wado	'Thank you' (used in Oklahoma)
	ᏄᎳ	núúla	'Hurry!'
	Ꭷ	kam	'Enough!' 'Now!' 'Come on!' 'Hey!"
	Ꮎ	na	'Here!'
	Ꮟ	si	'Wait!'
	ᎥᏍᎩᎩ	vsgigi	'Isn't it so?' 'Is that a fact?' (Walker 1975:227)

7.10. Sources and Additional Reading

Much of the preceding discussion is based on the description of adjectives from Pulte and Feeling (1975). Holmes (1996) is a useful discussion of comparatives. King (1975:40) refers to adjectives as particles, and Cook (1979:125) describes them as uninflected verbs. Lindsey and Scancarelli (1985:208) claim that Cherokee has a large class of true adjectives that can be divided into a small class of words with adjectival roots and a larger class that is derived. They claim that the adjective in Cherokee is a separate part of speech that can be distinguished from verbs, nouns, and particles by its morphological behavior. According to their findings, although Cherokee does have a small closed class of adjectival roots, most adjectives are derived from verbs or nouns. Haag discusses postfixes (1997, 1999) and their interaction with tone (2001). The description of the intensifier suffixes comes from Pulte and Feeling (1975:336–37).

7.11. Directions for Further Research

The extent to which comparative and superlative constructions are predictable is not well understood. Adjective derivation is also an area in need of further exploration. In this work I have treated the selection of intensifier as idiosyncratic; further research could reveal more predictable patterns.

Studying postfixes systematically would require a large corpus of natural speech; they undoubtedly involve variation among speakers and fine nuances that need to be explored. For example, King (1975:96) calls *=hno* the declarative and says that in the speech of some Qualla, North Carolina, speakers it "is frequently used to indicate the beginning of a new sentence or to designate that the sentence is declarative in nature rather than a command or interrogative." Corpus and archival studies could also help to show the relative distribution of the focus and the emphatic postfixes. Such studies could also reveal previous productive uses for the less-common postfixes.

Part II

EIGHT

How Sounds Change in Different Settings

As seen in earlier chapters, Cherokee words (especially **verbs**) are composed of multiple parts. This chapter describes changes that occur when these parts are combined. Many changes in the pronunciation of the combined parts are triggered by the sound /h/. Chapter 3 discusses how some of the **prefixes** cause this /h/ sound to be removed. The current chapter further explores this phenomenon of **/h/ alternation.** This change causes differences between the **surface form** of a word and its **underlying form.** For example, in (1a) the underlying /h/ causes the **vowel** to its left to be deleted; as a result of this **vowel deletion,** the /h/ is adjacent to /g/. The resulting [k] is the combination of these two sounds. The surface structure differs markedly from its original or underlying structure. In (1b) the **Set A prefix** *ji-* triggers the deletion of the /h/. The **syllabary** spelling of the two words is identical.

(1a) ᏕᎬᎩᎶᎠ
deekgiilóoʔa
dee-ga-vhgiilóoʔa
DST-3A-wash(flexible):PRC
'He is washing them (flexible objects).'

(1b) ᏕᎬᎩᎶᎠ
deegv́v̀giilóoʔa
dee-ji-vhgiilóoʔa
DST-1A-wash(flexible):PRC
'I am washing them (flexible objects).'

The change in (1a) from the underlying to the surface form is triggered by the presence of /h/. This kind of change is discussed in the first section of this chapter. In (1b) this change is prevented from occurring because of the removal of the /h/. The third section describes the order in which these various changes occur. The final section describes changes that occur as a result of everyday **fast speech.**

8.1. Sound Changes Based on Surrounding Sounds

Changes in pronunciation are triggered either by surrounding sounds or by the presence of certain **morphemes.** The first type of change is described in the following section.

8.1.1. Aspiration

Aspiration is an important and pervasive feature of the Cherokee sound system. With the exception of /h/, /s/, /ʔ/, and /m/, all of the **consonants** come in unaspirated and aspirated pairs. For each pair the position of the mouth is the same; the difference in sound is made by the puff of air (aspiration) that follows. These pairs are shown in table 8.1. In the last four pairs, the aspiration is indicated by simply writing ⟨h⟩ with the letter.

Table 8.1. Unaspirated and Aspirated Consonants

Unaspirated consonant	*Aspirated counterpart*
d	t
g	k
gw	kw
j	ch, sometimes ts
dl	tl
l	hl
n	hn
w	hw
y	hy

As noted in chapter 1, the syllabary does not represent the /h/ at the end of a **syllable.** In these cases the /h/ causing the aspiration is referred to as an **intru-**

sive /h/. The 'nonintrusive' /h/ found at the beginning of a syllable is fully represented in the syllabary as Ꭽ ha, Ꭾ he, Ꭿ hi, Ꮀ ho, Ꮁ hu, and Ꮂ hv. The intrusive /h/ can be illustrated with the syllabary character Ꮇ, whose basic sound is /lu/. In (2a), however, a speaker literate in the syllabary would know that the pronunciation in this particular word is /luh/. The intrusive /h/ in this case is at the end of the syllable. In like manner, in (2b) the symbol Ꮿ is **aspiration-neutral.** It represents the sound /ya/, although in this context (as part of a speaker's knowledge of the correct pronunciation of this particular word) it is pronounced as /hya/. In (2b) the intrusive /h/ is at the beginning of the syllable.

(2a) ᎤᏂᎷᏨ uùnilúhjv 'they arrived'
(2b) ᎠᎨᏯ ageéhya 'woman'

The sound /j/ is an unaspirated sound that has two possible aspirated counterparts, /ts/or /ch/, depending on the environment. If it is followed by a vowel, the resulting aspirated sound is /ch/, as shown in (3a); if it is followed by another **obstruent,** the pronunciation for many speakers is /ts/, as in (3b). The first word in (3a) also contains an example of the aspiration of a the initial consonant of the prefix *ga-*.

(3a) ᎧᏁᎩᏍ ᏥᏯᎵᏃᎮᏗᏍᎬ
kaneegis chiiyaliinohehdisgv
ga-hneegi=s ji-hii-ali-hnohehdisg-v
3A-answer:IMM=Q REL-2A.AN-MDL-speak:INC-EXP
'Did he answer when you were speaking to him?' (Feeling 1975a:139)

(3b) ᏣᏢᎦ
tsdlv́vga
ja-hdlv́vga
2B-be.sick:PRC
'You're sick.'

Two processes cause /h/ to be next to a consonant, as discussed in the sections below.

8.1.2. Vowel Deletion

In Cherokee a **short vowel** with a **low tone** undergoes vowel deletion in certain environments, as shown in figure 8.1.

Unaspirated consonant: d, g, j, w, y, n, gw, l	Short vowel ~~a, e, i, o, u, v~~	h	Obstruent or vowel

Figure 8.1. Vowel Deletion

The majority of Cherokee consonants are obstruents: the sounds /d/, /t/, /g/, /k/, /dl/, /tl/, /gw/, /kw/, /j/, /ch/, and /s/. These sounds are characterized by a lot of obstruction of the airflow when they are pronounced. The remaining consonants have less constriction and are known as **sonorants:** the sounds /n/, /hn/, /m/, /l/, /y/, and /hy/. If an obstruent or a vowel is at the end of the sequence described above the vowel is deleted. An immediate consequence of this vowel deletion is the adjacency of the unaspirated consonant with the /h/; in this new environment the sounds /d/ and /g/ are pronounced as aspirated /t/ and /k/. This process is exemplified in table 8.2 with the verb 'be sick'.

Table 8.2. Vowel Deletion for First Person Singular Present Continuous Conjugation of 'Be Sick'

	ᎠᎩᏢᎦ aàkdlv́vga 'I'm sick'
3. [g]+[h] = [k]	aàkdlv́vga
2. vowel deletion	aàg~~i~~hdlv́vga
1. first person Set B + Verb	aàgi + hdlv́vga

The **Set B first person pronominal prefix** attaches to the **stem,** resulting in the combination shown in row 2. The short vowel is deleted in this environment, bringing the unaspirated /g/ and /h/ together, resulting in the **aspirated obstruent** [k].

In the examples in (4), the /h/ precedes a vowel; in (4a), the **completive future prefix** *da-* and the pronominal prefix *hi-* fuse as a result of vowel deletion to form [*ti*]. In (4b) the vowel of the pronominal prefix is lost as well, and the resulting syllable is [*ta*].

(4a)
ᏗᎲᏏ
tihv́vsi
da-hi-hv́vs-i
CMF-2A-set.down:CMP-CMF
'You will set it down.'

(4b) ᏔᏕᏲᎲᏍᎩ
tadeehyóóhvsgi
di-hi-adaa-eehyoóhvsg-i
DST2-2A-MDL-teach:INC-AGT
'Teacher!'

In (5) the Set B **second person** prefix *ja-* undergoes the deletion of its vowel and as a result becomes the aspirated sound [*ch*].

(5) Track 49

ᎦᏙ	ᎤᏍᏗ	ᏨᏏ	Ꮎ	ᎤᏓᎾᏂ
gado	uusdi	chvsi	na	uudaánaʔni
gado	uusdi	ja-h̲vsi	na	uudaánaʔni
what	thing	2B-give(solid):IMM	the	store.owner

'What did the store owner give you?' (Feeling:1975a:158)

It is possible for a single word to delete more than one vowel. In (6a) the /h/ of the second person pronominal prefix attaches to the /w/ of the pronominal prefix after the deletion of the intervening vowel; moreover, the verb stem itself undergoes vowel deletion, resulting in the aspiration of the /g/. Neither of these deletions takes place in (6b). The **first person** pronominal prefix does not contain an /h/; as an **/h/ alternator,** it triggers the replacement of /h/in the verb stem with a **lowfall tone.**

(6a) ᏫᎦᏗ
hwikti
wi-h̲i-gah̲ti
TRN-2A-head.to:PRC
'You're heading there.'

(6b) ᏫᏥᎦᏗ
wijigáàti
wi-ji-gahti
TRN-1A-head.to:PRC
'I'm heading there.'

Deletion does not trigger further deletion. The /h/ of the second person pronominal prefix in (7) aspirates /w/ but does not cause the subsequent deletion of the vowel of the prefix *ni-* and the aspiration of its /n/.

(7) ᏂᏇᏓᏍ
nihweedas

ni-wi-h̲i-eeda=s
NI-TRN-2A-be.at:IMM=Q
'Did you already go?'

When /h/ is adjacent to /l/, the result is the sound /hl/. In (8a) the /h/ is removed through /h/ alternation. The /h/ at the end of the word is not affected, because the vowel that precedes it bears a **high tone.** In (8b), however, the presence of the /h/ does trigger vowel deletion, causing the /h/ to be adjacent to /l/.

(8a) ᎦᎵᎪᏍᏗᎭ
galiì̲kotdíha
ji-alih̲kotdíha
1A-shatter:PRC
'I'm shattering it.'

(8b) ᎠᎵᎪᏍᏗᎭ
aàh̲l̲kotdíha
a-al̲ih̲kotdíha
3A-shatter:PRC
'She's shattering it.'

8.1.3. Exchange

Another common rule also results in the adjacency of an unaspirated consonant and /h/ and the subsequent creation of an aspirated sound. This **exchange** rule occurs in a environment similar to that of the vowel deletion rule. If the second consonant is an **aspirated sonorant** (/hw/, /hy/, /hn/, or /hl/), then the /h/and the vowel switch places and no deletion takes place. This exchange occurs in the environment shown in figure 8.2.

Unaspirated consonant	Short vowel	Aspirated sonorant
d, g, j, w, y, n, gw, l	a, e, i, o, u, v	hw, hy, hn, hl

Figure 8.2. Exchange

For example, the **Immediate** verb stem 'cure' is *-hnv́v́wáàga*; the combination of the stem with the Set B first person prefix *agi-* results in [*aki*]. This example is shown in (9a); the surface form is the result of the /h/ and the vowel changing places. The possible results of exchange include /k/, /t/, or /ch/; these three results are exemplified in (9).

(9a) ᎠᎩᏅᏩᎦ Track 50
aàkinvv́wáàga
agi-hnvv́wáàga
1B-cure:IMM
'He cured me.'

(9b) ᎠᏖᎳᏗᎠ
aàteladíʔa
a-adehladíʔa
3A-join:PRC
'He's joining it.' (Feeling 1975a:59)

(9c) ᏣᎾᎸᏨᎢ Track 51
chanaálv̀v̀jvv́ʔi
ja-hnaálv̀v̀j-vv́ʔi
2B-become.angry:CMP-EXP
'You became angry.'

The underlying stem of a verb that undergoes exchange and deletion is sometimes easier to discern in the third person form. This form is shown in (10a); in (10b) the /h/ has switched places with the vowel and aspirated the /g/ of the prefix.

(10a) uu-hwásga → ᎤᏩᏍᎦ uùhwásga 'she's buying it'
3B-buy:PRC
(10b) agi-hwásga → ᎠᎩᏩᏍᎦ aàkiwásga 'I'm buying it'
1B-buy:PRC

In other cases the second person form best displays the underlying form of the stem. This is demonstrated in (11); in (11a) the /h/ moves in front of the vowel /a/ and aspirates the obstruent, while in (11b) the /h/ is removed due to /h/ alternation. In (11c), however, the /h/ is present.

(11a) ga-hnoohéha → ᎧᏃᎮᏍ kanoohéha 'he's telling it'
3A-tell:PRC
(11b) ji-hnoohéha → ᏥᏃᎮᏍ jiìnoohéha 'I'm telling it'
1A-tell:PRC
(11c) hi-hnoohéha → ᎯᏃᎮᏍ hihnoohéha 'you're telling it'
2A-tell:PRC

This exchange rule is subject to dialectal variation among speakers. Some speakers have the vowel deletion rule but not the exchange rule. Two examples are given in (12); in both examples the stop in the prefix *agi-* remains unaspirated and /h/ is heard at the beginning of the verb stem.

(12a) ᎠᎩᏆᏍᎦ aàgihwasga 'I'm buying it'
(12b) ᏒᎩ ᎠᎩᏘᏒᎢ svv̀gi aàgihwisvv́ʔi 'I planted onions'

In (13) vowel deletion causes the /j/ of the second person plural pronominal prefix *iijii-* 'you all' to aspirate. In this case the **long vowel** /ii/ at the end of the pronominal prefix has already been removed due to **vowel clash** with the vowel-initial stem; the remaining vowel at the beginning of the stem is short and undergoes the vowel deletion rule. The adjacency of this aspirated sound to an obstruent (in this case the /d/ of the verb stem) causes it to be pronounced as /ts/.

(13) ᎠᏕᎳ ᏥᎢᏴ ᎢᏥᏙᏓ
adeéla jiʔiíyv iitsdóhda
adeéla ji-hiíy-v iijii-vhdóhda
money 1A-leave.behind:CMP-EXP 2B.PL-use:INF
'I left money behind for your use.'

In the example above the final vowel of the verb stem is not deleted despite being short and adjacent to /h/. In this case the high tone blocks the deletion.

8.1.4. Shortened Subordination Tone

The **highfall tone** appears on the rightmost long vowel of any word and often appears in a shortened form due to the prevalence of final-vowel dropping in fast speech. When this happens, the new final long vowel frequently has a slightly higher final tone than typically found on a final vowel; this tone is indicated by a high tone accent on the normally unaccented last vowel. For example, in (14) the highfall is inserted on the **experienced past suffix,** indicating its status as a **subordinate verb;** this suffix is subsequently shortened.

(14) ᏥᎪᎥᎢ ᎩᏟ ᏓᏏᏘᏍᎬ Track 52
jiigoʔvv́ʔi giihli dasihwisgv́
jii-gooh-vv́ʔi giihli dee-a-asihwisg-v́vʔi
1A.AN-see:CMP dog DST-3A-bark:INC-EXP\SUB
'I saw the dog that was barking.'

8.2. Sound Changes Based on Surrounding Morphemes

Other changes are triggered by particular morphemes rather than by particular sounds. A morpheme is a meaningful unit such as a prefix, suffix, stem, or even a simple word. The resulting sound changes can affect the conditions causing the changes described in the preceding section.

8.2.1. Pronominal Lengthening

Pronominal prefixes that start with a vowel acquire a lowfall tone when they appear at the beginning of a **main verb** (a verb in an independent clause); if the vowel is originally short, it is also lengthened. An example of this **pronominal lengthening** is shown in (15). In (15a) the third person pronominal prefix has a low tone long vowel at the beginning of the adjective; in (15b) the same prefix at the beginning of a verb has a lowfall tone.

(15a) ᎤᎪᏏᏓ Track 53
uugóósida
uu-agoos-da
3B-rot-PCP
'rotten'

(15b) ᎤᎪᏍᎦ
uùgoosga
uu-agoosga
3B-rot:PRC
'It is rotting'

If the verb appears in its **Infinitive stem**, the pronominal lengthening does not occur. In (16) the main verb 'want' has a lowfall on the prefix, while the **subordinate verb** does not (the **toward prefix** (TOW) *di*-appears as [*j*] before most vowels; this prefix and its forms are discussed in chapter 10). A main verb is a verb in an **independent clause.**

(16)	ᎤᎾᏚᎵ	ᏧᏂᏐᏫᏍᏗ
	uùnaduuli	juuniisóhwiisdi
	uunii-aduuli	di-uunii-sóhwiisdi
	3B.NS-want:PRC	TOW-3B.NS-cross.over:INF

'They want to cross over.'

8.2.2. /h/ Alternation

Stems that contain /h/ replace it with a **glottal stop** or a lowfall tone when certain pronominal prefixes attach to the stem. This process is demonstrated in (17) for a verb stem and in (18) for a noun stem. In (17a) the attachment of the third person pronominal prefix does not change the stem; in (17b), however, the presence of the first person pronominal prefix causes the substitution of /ʔ/ for /h/.

(17a) Stem with /h/
ᎠᏴᎯᎭ
aàyvvh̲íha
a-yvvhíha
3A-enter:PRC
'He's entering.'

(17b) Stem with glottal stop
ᏥᏴᎢᎭ
jiyvʔ̲íha
ji-yvvhíha
1A-enter:PRC
'I'm entering.'

In Oklahoma Cherokee the glottal stop is pronounced as a lowfall tone before a consonant, as seen in (18b). In this example the /h/ alternation occurs on a noun.

(18a) Stem with /h/
ᎯᏴᏐᎵ
hih̲yvvsóóli
hi-hyvvsóóli
2A-nose
'your nose'

(18b) Stem with lowfall tone
ᏥᏴᏐᎵ
jìi̲yvvsóóli
ji-hyvvsóóli
1A-nose
'my nose'

North Carolina Cherokee, unlike Oklahoma Cherokee, retains the glottal stop. In (19) the first person pronominal prefix *ji-* triggers the substitution of /h/ with /ʔ/.

(19) ji + hnéega ᏥᏁᎦ
North Carolina: jiʔnéega
Oklahoma: jiìnéega
'I'm answering.'

The specific prefixes that trigger this alternation—the /h/ alternators—are listed in chapter 9. The interaction of /h/ alternation with vowel deletion and exchange can create the appearance that a verb has distinct stems for different prefixes. For example, on the surface it appears that the verb 'wait for' in (20) has two different stems.

(20a) ᎠᎦᏘᏯ aàktiíya 'he's waiting for it' Track 54
(20b) ᏥᎦᏘᏯ jigaàtiíya 'I'm waiting for it'

These surface differences are caused by /h/ alternation. In (20b) this alternation removes the /h/ and vowel deletion does not take place. Table 8.3 demonstrates how these distinct surface forms both start with the same stem.

Table 8.3. Vowel Deletion for Third and First Person Present Continuous Conjugation of 'Wait'

	ᎠᎦᏘᏯ 'He's waiting for it.' aàktiíya	ᏥᎦᏘᏯ 'I'm waiting for it.' jigaàtiíya
3. Glottal stop realized as lowfall before consonant	NA	jigaàtiíya
2. Vowel deletion	aàghtiíya	NA
1. /h/ replaced by /ʔ/	NA	jigaʔtiíya
	a gahtiíya	ji gahtiíya

In like manner, /h/ alternation and exchange can create what on the surface looks like a different pronominal prefix. In table 8.4 the third person *ga-* is pronounced as [*ka*] after the /h/ changes places with the short vowel and /g/ and /h/ end up next to each other. At the same time, the first person pronominal prefix appears in a slightly different form with lengthening and a lowfall. Again, these differences can be traced back to the effect of /h/ alternation. If the /h/ is removed, it is no longer available to trigger exchange.

Table 8.4. Vowel Deletion for Third and First Person Present Continuous Conjugation of 'Speak', 'Answer'

	ᎧᏁᎦ 'he's speaking' kanéega	ᏥᏁᎦ 'I'm speaking' jiìnéega
3. glottal stop realized as lowfall before consonant	NA	jiìnéega
2. /h/-exchange	ghanéega	NA
1. /h/ replaced by /ʔ/	NA	jiʔnéega
	ga hnéega	ji hnéega

The basic form of the sound /s/ is characterized by a short /h/ sound immediately preceding it. This /h/ is not represented in the writing because it is inherently present. This **inherent /h/** also triggers exchange and vowel deletion. Moreover, /h/ alternation can replace this /h/ with a glottal stop. In table 8.5 the first person Set A pronominal prefix *ji-* (appearing as [*g*] before a vowel) triggers /h/ alternation, thereby removing the inherent /h/. The glottal stop in this first person singular form is pronounced as a lowfall tone in Oklahoma Cherokee.

Table 8.5. Vowel Deletion for First Dual and Singular Conjugation of 'Dance'

	ᎢᎾᎵᏍᎩᎠ 'We two are dancing.'	ᎦᎵᏍᎩᎠ 'I am dancing.'
3. glottal stop realized as lowfall before consonant	NA	galiìsgííʔa
2. vowel deletion	iìnalsgííʔa	NA
1. /h/ replaced by /ʔ/	NA	galiʔsgííʔa
	iinii ali[h]sgííʔa	ji ali[h]sgííʔa

The pronominal prefix *iinii-* 'we two' does not trigger the alternation and the /h/ is therefore available to trigger the vowel deletion. The underlying /l/ is now pronounced as [*hl*] because it is adjacent to the /s/. This sound is not written as the /hl/ because it is always pronounced this way before /s/.

The effects of /h/ alternation are most commonly seen with the unaspirated-aspirated pairs /g/, /k/ and /d/, /t/. This alternation can also create a surface alternation between the sounds /gw/, /kw/ as well as between /j/, /ch/ and /dl/, /tl/. In (21) the unaspirated sound /l/ appears in the first person form of the verb, while the aspirated /hl/ appears in the third person form.

(21a) ᎠᏕᏠᏆᎠ
aàdeehlohgwáʔa
a-adeehlohgwáʔa
3A-learn:PRC
'He's learning it.'

(21b) ᎦᏕᎶᏆᎠ
gadeèlohgwáʔa
ji-adeehlohgwáʔa
1A-learn:PRC
'I'm learning it.'

The unaspirated obstruent /j/ has two different pronunciations when aspirated. If a vowel or sonorant follows it is pronounced /ch/, but if an obstruent follows it is pronounced as /ts/. An example with the second pronunciation is given in (22b); the /h/ that is present with /s/ (but not written) causes vowel deletion and the aspirated /j/ is now adjacent to an obstruent (the /s/ of the stem is indistinguishable when following the /ts/). In (22a) the presence of the *ji-* causes /h/ alternation, resulting in a lengthening of the vowel with a lowfall tone.

(22a) ᎦᏥᏍᎪᎥᏍᎦ
gajiìsgóoʔvsga
ji ajisgóoʔvsga
1A-lie:PRC
'I'm lying.'

(22b) ᎠᏥᏍᎪᎥᏍᎦ
aàtsgóoʔvsga
a-ajisgóoʔvsga
3A-lie:PRC
'He's lying.'

Many speakers of Oklahoma Cherokee pronounce /tl/ as [hl]. As a result, it is difficult to find alternations between /dl/ and /tl/. An example of a /hl/, /tl/ pair is listed in (23). In (23a) the intrusive /h/ occurs before the /tl/; the resulting vowel deletion aspirates the /t/, creating a pair of /tl/ sounds that are pronounced as a single /tl/. In (23b) the /h/ alternation triggered by the prefix causes vowel lengthening with the accompanying lowfall.

(23a) DC Track 55
aàtli
a-adihtli
3A-run:PRC
'He's running.'

(23b) ꮥꭺC
gadiìtli
ji-adihtli
1A-run:PRC
'I'm running.'

It is assumed that the underlying stem is *-adihtli* because the intrusive /h/ would not be evident before an already aspirated /hl/. The underlying sound /hl/ does not participate in /h/ alternation, but the sound /hl/ that represents underlying /tl/ does.

If the vowel bears a high tone, /h/ alternation results in a **falling tone** rather than a lowfall. Two forms of the same verb in (24) illustrate this point. In (24a) the Set A first person singular triggers the alternation and resulting lowfall. In (24b), however, the presence of a **distributive** (DST) prefix alters the tone pattern. A special feature of this prefix (described in chapter 5) is that in its basic form it causes a **high tone** to appear on the syllable immediately following it. As a result, the beginning of the long vowel of the prefix *jii-* receives a high tone, and the lowering of the tone from /h/ alternation results in a falling tone.

(24a) ꮵZꮃD
jii̱nóoyeeʔa
jii-hnóoyeeʔa
1A.AN-fan:PRC
'I'm fanning him.' (Wright 1996:17)

(24b) SꮵZꮃD
deejíi̱nóoyeeʔa
dee-jii-hnóoyeeʔa
DST-1A.AN-fan:PRC
'I'm fanning them.' (Wright 1996:17)

8.2.3. Floating Length and Tone

Certain stems cause a change to the prefixes that attach to them. For example, in the singular person forms of the verb 'sew' the vowel of the second and third person singular forms are lengthened. The abstract feature that triggers these changes is termed **floating tone** or **floating length** because it only occurs when prefixes are attached to the stem; the way it ends up being pronounced depends on the particular prefix. Most verbs do not have this feature, and most singular forms have an inherently short vowel. The lengthening feature is thus considered to be part of the verb. To indicate that the vowel must be lengthened, the letters ⟨xx⟩ are written at the beginning of the verb. These double **dummy vowels** are not pronounced and merely indicate that the vowel attaching to this stem needs to be doubled (lengthened).

Track 56

(25a) ᎯᏰᏩ
hiiyeéwa
hi-xxyeéwa
2A-sew:IMM
'You sewed it.'

(25b) ᏥᏰᏫᏍᎦ
jiiyewiìsga
ji-xxyewisga
1A-sew:PRC
'I am sewing it.'

(25c) ᎦᏰᏫᏍᎦ
gaayewsga
ga-xxyewisga
3A-sew:PRC
'He is sewing it.'

Example (26) shows a contrast between a stem with floating vowel length and a stem without this feature.

(26a) ᏥᏰᏫᏍᎦ
jiiyeewiìsga
ji-xxyewsga
1A-sew:PRC
'I am sewing it.'

(26b) ᏥᏰᎦ
jiyéega
ji-yéega
1A-wake.up:PRC
'I am waking up.'

When the floating length appears before the **animate object prefixes** it appears as the vowel /aa/. In (27a) the vowel-lengthening feature lengthens the vowel of the prefix, while in (27b) the floating length causes the pronominal prefix to appear in its **consonant insertion** form, resulting in the combination [*hiiyaa*]. This combination is aspirated by the preceding prepronominal prefix to form [*tiiyaa*].

(27a) ᎯᏣᎵᎩᏍᎪ
hiijalgíisgo
hi-xxjalgíisg-o
2A-rip:INC-HAB
'You rip it.'

(27b) ᏗᏯᏣᎦᎸ
tiiyaajaagalv
di-hii-xxjaagal-v
DST2-2A.AN-scratch:CMP-FCM
'Scratch him!'

The vowel-lengthening feature is not apparent in the nonsingular forms; all of these prefixes already end in a long vowel. For example, in (28) the **full form** of the pronominal prefix occurs.

(28) ᎢᏂᏰᏪᏍᎦ
iìniiyewsga
iinii-xxyewsga
1A.DL-sew:PRC
'We are sewing it.'

The combination of this vowel-lengthening feature with the third person singular Set B prefix *uu-* results in [*uuwaa*], as in (29).

(29) ᎤᏩᏰᏪᏒᎢ
uùwaayewsvv́ʔi
uu-xxyews-vv́ʔi

3B-sew:CMP-EXP
'He sewed it.'

If the vowel-lengthening feature has a tone associated with it (floating length combined with floating tone), then this tone appears on the lengthened vowel of the pronominal prefix. In the **citation form** the tone is indicated on the dummy vowels ⟨xx⟩; two examples are given in (30).

(30a) ᏥᏟᏏᎭ Track 57
jí̲i̲tliisiíha
ji-x́xtliisiíha
1A-gather:PRC
'You are gathering it.'

(30b) ᎢᏗᏟᏏᎭ
iidí̲i̲tliisiíha
iidii-x́xtliisiíha
1A.PL-gather:PRC
'We are gathering it.'

As discussed in chapter 7, many **adjectives** have a highfall tone. Another special symbol is associated with some adjectives that carry a highfall tone on whatever the rightmost long vowel of the word is. This tone specification is indicated by the symbol ⟨x̋⟩at the beginning of the adjective. An example is given in (31), in which the highfall tone appears on the vowel of the pronominal prefix *uunii-*, which normally has a low tone.

(31a) ᏧᏂᏍᏆᎦᏟ
juuní̲í̲sgwagahl
di-uunii-x̋sgwagahli
DST2-3B.NS-striped
'striped' (The Search Party, line 29)

(31b) ᎠᏂᏔ
aní̲í̲ta
anii-x̋ta
3A.NS-young.woman
'young women'

A vowel bears the **double accent** if the stem starts with a vowel; it should be kept in mind, however, that the highfall may move in order to appear on the rightmost long vowel. In (32a) the final vowel /ii/ of the pronominal prefix *unii-* is removed before the initial /a/ of the stem to which it attaches, while the highfall tone shifts to the rightmost long vowel of the word (in this case the vowel /u/ of the pronominal prefix). In (32b) it is the initial /a/ that is removed, but the highfall still shifts to the rightmost long vowel.

(32a) ᏧᎾᏔᎾ
júúnatana
di-uunii-a̋tana
DST2-3B.NS-big
'big'

(32b) ᎤᏔᎾ
úútana
uu-a̋tana
3B-big
'big'

In (33) the adjective is not vowel-initial so the symbol ⟨x̋⟩ indicates the presence of this highfall.

(33) ᏍᏗᎢᎬᎯᏍᏗ
sdíikvhisdi
sdii-x̋kvhisdi
2B.DL-cute
'You two are cute.'

8.2.4. Preaspiration and Secondary Aspiration

Stops are sounds where the air is stopped in the mouth. In Cherokee the unaspirated stops are /d/, /g/, and /gw/; the corresponding aspirated stops are /t/, /k/, and /kw/. Aspirated stops that have not received their aspiration as part of exchange or vowel deletion also have an automatic initial /h/ referred to as a **preaspiration /h/**. Even though it is predictable, this /h/ is written in order to keep the complex sound changes more apparent. This preaspiration /h/ has already been seen above with 'wait for', 'look at', and 'run'; another example is presented in (34). In (34a) the /h/ does not appear; it cannot cause the preceding vowel to be deleted (because that vowel is long) and a syllable cannot start with/h/ and an aspirated stop. In (34b), however, the short vowel of the prefix is deleted and the unaspirated stop of the prefix aspirates.

(34a) ᎣᎩᎪᏕᏒ
oògiikodéesv
oogii-hkodées-v
1B.PL.EX-shovel:CMP-EXP
'We shoveled it.'

(34b) ᎠᎩᎪᏕᏒ
akkodéesv
agi-hkodées-v
1B-shovel:CMP-EXP
'I shoveled it.'

In (35a) the presence of the /h/ causes the expected vowel deletion of /v/ and subsequent aspiration of the consonant of the pronominal prefix. In (35b) the /h/ is removed because of the presence of the first person singular Set A prefix.

(35a) ᏗᎦᏝᏗᏍᎩ Track 58
diktladiìsgi
di-ga-vhtladiîsg-i
DST2-3A-put.out.fire:INC-AGT
'firefighter'

(35b) ᏗᎬᏝᏗᏍᎩ
digvỳtladiìsgi
di-ji-vhtladiîsg-i
DST2-1A-put.out.fire:INC-AGT
'I am a firefighter.'

In (36a) the preaspiration /h/ does not appear because the pronominal prefix vowel has been lengthened and lowered and /h/ cannot be at the end of this syllable; at the same time, a syllable cannot start with a combination of /h/ and a stop. As a result, the initial /h/ has nowhere to appear and is not pronounced. In (36b) the sound /kw/ loses its aspiration due to /h/ alternation; as a result, the preaspiration is absent as well. In (36c), however, the pronominal prefix neither triggers /h/ alternation nor undergoes pronominal lengthening; as a result, the preaspiration /h/ is pronounced at the end of the syllable.

(36a) ᎠᏈᏱᎭ Track 59
aàkwiyíha
a-ahkwiyíha
3A-pay:PRC
'He's paying it.'

(36b) ᎦᏈᏱᎭ
gagwiyíha
ji-ahkwiyíha
1A-pay:PRC
'I'm paying it.'

(36c) ᎭᏈᏱᎭ
hahkwiyíha
hi-ahkwiyíha
2A-pay:PRC
'You're paying it.'

This phenomenon of preaspiration creates a distinction between two types of aspirated stops: those that have **underlying aspiration** and those that have received aspiration as a result of exchange or deletion, called **secondary aspiration,** which does not exhibit preaspiration. If it did, that would result in a chain reaction of aspiration extending through the word. In (37), for example, the *di-* prefix at the beginning of the word remains unaspirated, even though it is separated by only a short vowel from an aspirated consonant. There is no preaspiration /h/ to trigger vowel deletion. The lack of preaspiration is due to this sound having itself been aspirated as a result of vowel deletion.

(37) ᏗᎦᏝᏗᏍᎩ
diktladiìsg
di-ga-vhtladîìsg-i
DST2-3A-put.out.fire:INC-AGT
'firefighter'

The sounds /ch/ and /ts/ do not have this preaspiration, which is perhaps an indication that they themselves are underlyingly the result of deletion and aspiration. The /l/ in (38) is not aspirated.

(38) ᏚᎵᏨᏯᏍᏔᏁ
duùlchvv́yáàstane
dee-uu-alchvv́yáàstan-e
DST-3B-become.brave:CMP-NXP
'[he] got brave' (The Wolf and the Crawdad, line 7)

The sound /tl/ does seem to have the preaspiration. In (39a) it triggers vowel deletion, while in (39b) it undergoes /h/ alternation.

(39a) VᏍᏍᏓᏜᏟ
doosdattli
dee-oosdii-adihtli
DST-1A.DL.EX-run:PRC
'We're running.'

(39b) ᎦᏗᏟ
gadiìtli
ji-adihtli
1A-run:PRC
'I'm running.'

8.2.5. Postfix Attachment

The attachment of **postfixes** to the end of a word may alter the final tone and **stress** of the word. Postfixes are like suffixes in that they cannot stand alone, while at the same time they are less tightly bound to the word than a suffix. Throughout this grammar the attachment of a prefix or a suffix to a base is indicated by a **hyphen** (-), while the attachment of a postfix is indicated by an **equals sign** (=). Because postfixes are less attached to the word, their effect on the final vowel is less predictable than with suffixes. A suffix is considered part of the word, so the last suffix to attach to a word receives this final stress. For this reason the final vowel of a postfix (and postfixes always appear at the end of the word) is assumed to be a short low tone unless otherwise marked. The final vowel of the word to which the postfix is attaching—normally unmarked—may be marked for tone. An example is in (40); this phenomenon is discussed in chapter 7.

(40) ᎺᎵᏃ ᏚᏓᎾᏅᏁᎵᏙ
meélíhnoo dúudaanv́vneelvv́ʔi
meéli=hnoo dee-ii-uu-adaad-nv́vneel-vv́ʔi
Mary=CN DST-ITR-3B-RFL-give:CMP-EXP
'And Mary gave them right back to him.' (Scancarelli 1987:88)

8.2.6. /h/ Syllabification

Stems that start with an initial /h/ will lose this /h/ to avoid a syllable with a low-fall tone and ending in an /h/. An example of this **/h/ syllabification** is in (41).

(41) ᎤᏢᎦ
uùdlvvga
uu-hdlvvga
3B-be.sick:PRC
'She is sick.'

8.3. Rule Ordering

It is important to bear in mind that the rules described in this chapter occur in a particular order; often the environment that triggers the application of a rule has been altered by the application of an earlier rule. In (42a), it is apparent that the deletion rule applies before the highfall placement, because a high tone blocks the deletion rule. If there is no long vowel for the highfall it appears as a simple high tone on the rightmost short vowel. This vowel would be the vowel of the pronominal prefix *ja-* but the deletion rule applies first and the high tone appears on the next available vowel. In (42b) the highfall placement occurs before /h/ syllabification (the assignment of the preaspiration /h/ to a syllable where it is pronounceable). As is often the case, this /h/ is not pronounced because there is no appropriate syllable where it can appear.

(42a) ᏣᎬᎯᏍᏗ Track 60
tskv̋hisdi
ja-x̋hkvhisdi
2B-cute
'You are cute.'

(42b) ᏍᏗᎬᎯᏍᏗ
sdíikvhisdi
sdii-x̋hkvhisdi
2B.DL-cute
'You two are cute.'

It has already been demonstrated that the /h/ alternation rule applies before the deletion and exchange rules, as this alternation removes the /h/ that triggers these rules. A further example is shown in (43a). This verb starts with a short vowel followed by /h/; in (43b) the /a/ of the pronominal prefix undergoes **vowel removal** when attached to a vowel-initial stem. This removal is followed by the /h/-triggered deletion of the remaining /v/ and the subsequent aspiration of the /g/ of the pronominal prefix. In the third example it appears that the proper environment for vowel deletion exists; the lack of this deletion must mean that this rule applies before the rule that removes the vowel of a pronominal prefix attached to a vowel-initial stem.

(43a) ETPᏅᏍᎦ Track 61
gvʔihlv́sga
ji-vhihlv́sga
1A-link:PRC
'I am linking it.' (Feeling 1975a:144)

(43b) ᎩᏢᏍᎦ
kihlv́sga
ga-vhihlv́sga
3A-link:PRC
'He is linking it.' (Feeling 1975a:144)

(43c) ᎢᏛᏘᏢᏍᎦ
iìdvhitlv́sga
iidii-vhitlv́sga
1A.PL-linki:PRC
'We are linking it.'

The order of the relevant rules is listed in (44).

(44) Order of rules
1. /h/ alternation
2. Exchange/ h-deletion
3. Pronominal vowel deletion
4. Highfall placement
5. Pronominal lengthening
6. /h/ syllabification

8.4. Characteristics of Fast Speech

In everyday spoken Cherokee speakers frequently leave off the final vowel and sometimes simplify a consonant cluster. These processes are further explained below.

8.4.1. /gw/ Reduction

In **fast speech** /gw/ is often reduced to /w/. In (45) the [*agw*] form of the pronominal prefix *agi-* is often pronounced as [*aw*].

(45a) ᎠᏩᏗᏞᎲᏍᎪᎢ
aàwadiihléhv́sgóoʔi
agi-adiihléhv́sg-óoʔi
1B-have.fever:INC-HAB
'I go around with a fever.'

(45b) ᏥᏍᎪᎵ ᎠᏪᏍᏓᏅᎢ
jiìskóól aàwesdáànvv́ʔi
ji-skóóli agi-esdáàn-vv́ʔi
1A-head 1B-hurt:CMP-EXP
'My head hurt.'

The syllabary spelling may or may not reflect the speaker's actual pronunciation of /gw/.

8.4.2. Vowel Merger

Vowel merger occurs when two /a/ vowels of adjacent words are combined. In (46) the vowel of *na* combines with the initial vowel of the following word.

(46) Ꮎ ᎠᏂᏔᎵ ᎠᏂᏍᎦᏯ ᎠᏂᏌᎵᏗᎠ
nv̲ niitaʔl aniisgaya aàniisaldiʔa
na̲ a̲nii-taʔli anii-sgaya anii-saldiʔa
that 3A.NS-two 3A.NS-man 3A.NS-lift:PRC
'Those two men are lifting it.'

8.4.3. Vowel Dropping

In fast speech a stem-initial /a/ may drop when preceded by a pronominal prefix containing the consonant /n/. Two examples are shown in (47a) and (47b). In the second example the short vowel on the noun drops. In both examples the dropped vowels are underlined. This **vowel dropping** may also occur with a singular animate object prefix (i.e. *jii-* or *hii-*) or a **combined prefix**; in the latter case there is no consonant insertion that normally occurs when these prefixes attach to a vowel-initial stem. An example is given in (47c).

(47a) Ꮩ ᎤᎾᏛᏁᎸ
do uùndvvneelv
do uunii-a̲dvvneel-v
what 3B.NS-do:CMP-EXP
'What did they do?'

(47b) ᎣᏳ ᎠᎾᎳᏍᎦᎵᏍᎩ ᎤᎾᏓᏠᏒ
ooyu anlaàsgalíísgi uùnadaátlóòsv
ooyu anii-a̲laàsgaliisg-i uunii-adaátlóòs-v
OU 3A.NS-play.ball:INC-AGT 3B.NS-win:CMP-EXP
'The OU athletes won.'

(47c) ᏱᎬᎵᏍᎪᎵᏓᏏ ᎠᎬᏱ ᏫᏣᎶᎯᏍᏗ
yigvvlisgohldáàs agv́v́y wijáʔlohisdi
yi-gvv-alisgohldáàsi a-gv́v́yi wi-ja-ʔlohisdi
IRR-1/2-permit:IMM 3A-first TRN-2B-pass:INF
'I will let you get there first.' (The Turtle and the Rabbit, line 20)

8.4.4. Final Vowel Dropping

Word-final vowels are often not pronounced in fast speech. These vowels are typically unmarked for tone because they receive the final stress and predictably have a high tone that is slightly higher than a normal high tone. If the underlying final vowel has been dropped, then the new final syllable will receive this final stress; the tone and **nasal** quality, however, will stay the same. Because of this difference, it is necessary to use terms reflecting these two kinds of final vowels. "Word-final vowel" is used to refer to the vowels at the end of the **full form** of the word, whereas "final vowel" simply indicates whatever vowel happens to be at the end of the shortened word. Two examples of this distinction are seen in (48). In the first example the first and third word appear in their full form and have the typical word-final high tone and stress. The final vowel in the second word is stressed, but its tone is that of its underlying vowel, in this case a high tone. The fourth word has a highfall tone on the short form of the word; this slightly higher tone is indicated by the accent on the final vowel. This highfall is also indicated at the end of the shortened word in (48b).

(48a) ᏭᏂᎷᏣ ᎤᏂᎪᎮ ᏐᏈᎵ ᎦᏅ
wúúniiluhja uùniigoohe soógwíli gáʔnv́
wi-uunii-luhj-a uunii-gooh-eʔi soógwíli ga-ʔn-v́v́ʔi

TRN-3B.NS-arrive:CMP-CVB 3B.NS-see:CMP-NXP horse 3A-lie:CMP-DVB
'. . . when they arrived they saw the horse lying' (Pulte and Feeling 1975:354)

(48b) ᏣᎪᏩᏘ
jagoohwtí
ji-a-goohwtííha
REL-3A-see:PRC\SUB
'who he sees'

As seen throughout this grammar, many words receive a highfall tone on the second to last syllable. If the last vowel of the word is dropped, as in the two examples in (48), the **shortened highfall** tone is often heard as a slightly higher than normal high tone. In many cases it is difficult to distinguish the shortened high tone and the normal high tone; for some speakers the final vowel may have a whispered quality. The distinction is made here, because these shortened highfalls almost always indicate a verb subordinated to another verb. Two more examples of the highfall final vowel are shown in (49).

(49a) ᏥᎩᎾᏚᎵᎭ ᎠᏜᏗᏝ
jiginduulííha adladíitla
ji-ginii-aduulííha adladíitla
REL-1B.DL-want:PRC\SUB car
'The car we want.'

(49b) ᎠᏂᎦᏰᎵ ᎨᎬᏕᏦᏅ
aniigayv́v́li geekdéejóhnv́
anii-gayv́v́li geegii-vhdéej-óhn-v́v́ʔi
3A.NS-elder 3NS/1PL-depart.in.death:CMP-TRM:CMP-DVB
'When the elders leave us . . .' (*Cherokee Phoenix*, May 2006)

The dropping of a final vowel can result in a **diphthong,** a combination of a vowel with a /y/ or /w/ that is pronounced as a single unit. In such cases the syllabary character representing the appropriate underlying syllable is used, as exemplified in (50).

(50a) ᎦᎵᏦᏕ ᏙᏱᏗᏜ
gahljoóde doóydidla
gahljoóde doóyi+didla
house outside+toward
'around the outside of the house'

(50b) DᏍᎦᏯ
asgay
a-sgaya
3A-man
'man'

In the example sentence in (51a) both nouns and the verb lose their final vowel; in (51b) *gado* loses its initial syllable. The **distributive prefix** *di-* (DST2) at the beginning of 'brother' changes to [*j*] before most vowels; this important prefix and its different forms are discussed in chapter 6. In this grammar, unlike the examples in (49) and (51), shortened forms are not written in their full form on the **underlying form line** (the third line of the transcription). Obstruents left at the end of a word due to final vowel dropping are often aspirated; many speakers would pronounce the final sound of the last word in (51b) as [t].

(51a)	ᏦᏣᏓᏅᏛᏝ	ᎤᎾᎵ	ᎯᎦᏘᏯ
	joojadaanv́v́tl	uunaalii	hiigaàtiíy
	di-oojii-adaad-nv́v́tla	uunii-aalíiʔi	hii-gahtiíya
	DST2-1A.PL.EX-RFL-brother	3B.NS-friend	2A.AN-wait.for:PRC
	'You are waiting for my brothers' friend.'		

(51b)	ᎯᎾ	Ꮩ	ᎤᏍᏗ
	hin	do	úúsd
	hina	do	úúsdi
	this	what	thing
	'What is this?'		

With verbs the dropping of the final vowels still leaves the first part of the final suffix, so there is no ambiguity concerning the **tense/aspect/mood** of the verb. In (52) examples are given with the **experienced past** (52a), **nonexperienced past** (52b), and **habitual** (52c) final suffixes (these suffixes are explained and exemplified in chapter 5). The sound /h/ is not pronounced in final position, so final-vowel dropping will often result of the elimination of this sound as well, as in (52d).

(52a) ᎤᎪᎲ
uùgoohv
uu-gooh-v
3B-see:CMP-EXP
'He saw it'

(52b) ᎤᎪᎮ
uùgoohe

uu-gooh-e
3B-see:CMP-NXP
'He saw it (I didn't witness it).'

(52c) DAGᏘᎣᏍᎪ
aàgohwtiísgo
a-gowahtiísg-o
3A-see:INC-HAB
'He sees it.'

(52d) ᎤᎾᏚᎵ
uùnaduuli
uunii-aduuli
3B.NS-want:PRC
'They want it.'

Less commonly the verb can be shortened even further as in (53), where the entire final suffix is dropped. The verb stem as well as the prefixes supply the necessary information. In (52) the Completive verb stem *-gooh-* is sufficiently distinct from the Present Continuous, Incompletive, Immediate, and Infinitive stems that the stem itself makes the time frame clear.

(53) ᏓᎩᎪ
daàgigo
dee-agi-gooh-v
DST-1B-see:CMP-EXP
'I saw them.'

Sometimes final vowel dropping can create a verb where most of the word consists of the prefixes. In (54a) the root itself is only evident in the sound /w/. In (54b) the long vowel at the end of the prefix is shortened because its syllable ends in a consonant.

(54a) ᎦᏙ ᏂᎦᏫ
gado nigaw
gado ni-ga-wi
what NI-3A-say:IMM
'What did he say?'

(54b) ᎦᏙ ᎾᏂᏫ
gado naàniw

gado ni-anii-wi
what NI-3A.NS-say:IMM
'What did they say?'

8.5. Sources and Additional Reading

The phenomenon of vowel deletion has been described by King (1975:41–42) and Cook (1979:7–8) and is the topic of articles by Flemming (1996) and Munro (1996a); the description in the current work is heavily indebted to these previous works. In linguistic works exchange is referred to as metathesis. The most in-depth discussion of exchange is found in Flemming (1996). Pronominal lengthening was first described by Lindsey (1985:136). Scancarelli (1987:64) states that this lowfall appears only if no other prefix comes before the pronominal prefix, but there is variation among speakers on this point. Munro (1996a:50) discusses preaspiration; Munro (1996a:59) also suggests the analysis of some /hl/ sounds as underlying /tl/. The most thorough analysis of /h/ alternation comes from Munro (1996a:45–60); the term itself was first used in Lindsey's discussion (1987:4). Scancarelli (1987:55) refers to the two resulting stems as the h-grade and the glottal grade. Wright (1996:17) refers to this deletion of the lowfall as laryngeal delinking.

8.6. Directions for Further Research

Cherokee phonology is still an area where much research is needed. The changes described in this chapter may not occur for all speakers and all dialects, and more research could help delineate the types of variation. Further exploration of the environments that both trigger and block pronominal lengthening is needed.

Fast speech is an unexplored area of Cherokee sociolinguistics, and our knowledge of the language would be greatly expanded by an in-depth study of this phenomenon. It is unclear exactly when it occurs and what it represents. Moreover, there may be other features of fast speech not described in this work.

Much anecdotal evidence suggests that children in the immersion school in Tahlequah are not acquiring the traditional tone patterns. The acquisition of Cherokee phonology by second language learners is an unexplored topic.

NINE

Pronominal Prefixes II

9.1. Overview of Pronominal Prefixes

In Cherokee all **verbs** must have a **prefix** that indicates who or what is involved in the action of the verb. If the verb is **intransitive,** this prefix refers to what is known as a **subject** in English. In (1) below the prefix *agi-* is the equivalent of the English subject 'I'.

(1) ᏓᎩᎸᏫᏍᏓᏁ
daàgilvv́hwsdaane
dee-agi-lvv́hwsdaane
DST-1B-work:PRC
'I'm working.'

A transitive verb has a subject and an **object.** If either the subject or object is **third person singular,** then the appropriate prefix from **Set A** or **Set B** is used. The prefix must refer to the **local person** if a local person is present. Thus in the examples below no part in the Cherokee word explicitly means 'it' or 'him'. Such a participant is an **implied object.** It should be kept in mind, however, that the special lengthened-vowel form of the prefix in (2b) does indicate that the object is animate.

(2a) ᎰᎵᎪ
hoohlgo
hi-oolihg-o
2A-understand:INC-HAB
'You understand it.'

(2b) ᎯᏩᏘᎭ
hiìwahtíha

hii-hwahtíha
2A.AN-find:PRC
'You are finding him.'

In order to produce a **conjugated** verb in Cherokee it is crucial to understand the distinction between local and **nonlocal persons. First person** and **second person** are local, and **third person** is nonlocal. For conjugating verbs two fundamental rules must be borne in mind. First, all verbs must have exactly one **pronominal prefix.** Second, any local person involved in the event described by the verb must be referred to by the prefix. In other words, third person singular subjects and objects are often implied but not expressed. As shown in (3), a third person singular prefix is used if both subject and object are third person singular.

(3) ᏚᏱᎬᎢ
duùhv́vgv̲v̲́ʔi
dee-uu-hv́vg-vv́ʔi
DST-3B-tickle:CMP-EXP
'He tickled him.' (Feeling 1975a:70)

All transitive verbs use Set B prefixes to reference a combination of a nonlocal (third person) singular subject and a local object. In (4a) a first person is acting on a third person and the Set A prefix is used, while in (4b) a third person is acting on a first person, triggering the Set B prefix. The first example has an implied object. The 'it' is implied because the verb is transitive and needs an object. In like manner the example in (4b) has an **implied subject.** In both cases the third person 'it' or 'she' is assumed, while the local person is explicitly referenced by the prefix.

(4a) ᏥᎪᏩᏘᎭ
jigohwtíha
ji-gohwtíha
1A-see:PRC
'I see it.'

(4b) ᎠᎩᎪᏩᏘᎭ
aàgigohwtíha
agi-gohwtíha
1B-see:PRC
'She sees me.'

Chapter 3 describes the forms and functions of the two most common set of prefixes, the Set A and Set B prefixes. This chapter introduces three more sets.

The first two sets are **combined prefixes** that refer to both the subject and the object. The third set is named **object focus** because it refers to only one grammatical **person** where two persons would normally appear. Because the only grammatical person referenced is the object, this set of prefixes creates a result similar to an English passive and is often translated using that construction.

9.2. Combined Nonsingular Subject Pronominal Prefixes

As stated in this chapter's introduction, the pronominal prefix system treats local and nonlocal persons rather differently. A special set of prefixes expresses a combination of a third person nonsingular subject acting on a local person object. In (5) the **animate** subject 'child' is marked with the Set A third person nonsingular prefix; the verb has a prefix indicating that the subject is third person nonsingular and the object is second person singular.

(5) ᏙᏅ ᏗᏂᏲᏟ ᏥᎨᏣᏰᏜᏍᏗᎭ
dohnv diiniiyóóhl jigeejayeétsdiiha
dohnv di-anii-yóóhli ji-<u>geeja</u>-yeéts-sdiiha
why DST2-3A.NS-child REL-<u>3NS/2</u>-laugh-CAU:PRC
'Why were those kids laughing at you?'

These **combined nonsingular subject prefixes** are presented in table 9.1. It is apparent that these prefixes were historically a combination of the Set B prefixes with an initial element. Because it is unclear what the **underlying** form of the initial element is, it is best to treat them as indivisible units. The only member of this set that triggers **/h/ alternation** is *geeji-*; this feature is indicated by an **asterisk.**

Table 9.1. Combined Nonsingular Subject Prefixes

Object Person reference	*Singular*	*Dual (dl)*	*Plural (pl)*
First Person Inclusive	gvvgi- [gvvgw]	geeginii-	geegii-
First Person Exclusive (EX)		googinii-	googii-
Second Person	geeja-	geesdii-	geejii-*

These prefixes are exemplified in (6).

(6a) ᎠᏂᎨᏳᏍᏓ ᎨᎩᏂᎦᏘᏯ
aniigehyúúsda geeginiiktiíya
anii-gehyúúsda geeginii-gahtiíya
3A.NS-girl 3NS/1DL-wait.for:PRC
'The girls are waiting for us'

(6b) Ꮎ ᎠᏂᏴᏫ ᎨᏣᏰᏘᏍᏗᎭ
na aniiyvvwi geèjayeétsdiiha
na anii-yvvwi geeja-yeéts-sdiiha
the 3A.NS-person 3NS/2-laugh:CMP-CAU:PRC
'The people are laughing at you.'

(6c) ᏴᏫ ᏧᎾᏍᏗ ᎨᎦᏜᏩᏍᏗᏕᎪ
yvvwi juunsdi geègadlawsdiídéègo
yvvwi di-uunii-asdi geegii-adlawsdídéèg-o
person DST2-3B.NS-little 3NS/1PL-live.among:INC-HAB
'Little People live among us.'

(6d) ᎨᏍᏗᏍᏕᎸᎲᎢ
geesdiisdeelvvhvv́ʔi
geesdii-sdeelvvh-vv́ʔi
3NS/2DL-help:CMP-EXP
'They helped you.'

(6e) ᎠᎴ ᎤᏲ ᏥᎨᏨᏁᎮᏍᏗ
ale uuyóó jigeejvvnehéesdi
ale uuyóó ji-geejii-vvhneh-éesdi
and evil REL-3NS/2PL-do:INC-PFT
'. . . and when they do evil to you . . .' (*Cherokee New Testament*, Matthew 5:11)

(6f) ᏕᎪᎩᏂᎦᏘᎴᎦ
degooginiiktilega
de-googinii-gahtilega
DST-3NS/1DL.EX-attack:PRC
'They are attacking the two of us.'

(6g) Ꮎ ᎠᏂᏲᏁᎦ ᎪᎩᏁᏄᎵᎭ
na aniiyoneéga goògiineenuúlîiha
na anii-yoneéga googii-neenuúlîiha

the 3A.NS-white 3NS/1DL.EX-threaten:PRC
'Those white people are threatening us.'

Like the Set B prefixes, all combined nonsingular subject prefixes but one undergo **vowel removal** when attaching to a stem starting with a vowel. (7a) is an example of *googinii-* attaching to a consonant-initial stem; in (7b) it attaches to a stem starting with a vowel.

(7a) ᎦᏙ Ꮭ ᎪᏪᎵ ᏱᏓᎪᎩᏂᏅᏍ
gado hla goohweél yidagoòginiinvs
gado hla goohweéli yi-da-googinii-n-v=s
what NEG letter IRR-TOW-3NS/1DL.EX-send:CMP-EXP=Q
'Why didn't they send us a letter?'

(7b) ᏂᎪᎸ ᎪᎩᏅᎨᏫᏍᎪᎢ
nigoólv goòginvvkewsgóoʔi
nigoólv googinii-vvkewsg-óoʔi
always 3NS/1DL.EX-forget:INC-HAB
'They always forget us.'

The first person singular object form *gvvgi-* has the form [*gvvgw*] before a vowel. This prefix is exemplified in (8). In (8c) the initial /h/ of the verb undergoes **exchange** and causes the **aspiration** of the consonant of the pronominal prefix.

(8a) ᎬᎩᎪᎲ
gvvgigoohv
gvvgi-gooh-v
3NS/1-see:CMP-EXP
'They saw me.'

(8b) ᏗᎬᏇᏲᎲᏍᎩ Ꮭ ᏱᎬᎩᎸᏉᏗ
digvvgweehyóóhvsg hla yigvv̀gilvvkwd
di-gvvgi-eehyoóhvsg-i hla yi-gvvgi-lvvgwohdi
DST2-3NS/1-teach:INC-AGT NEG IRR-3NS/1-like:PRC
'My teachers don't like me.'

(8c) ᏕᎬᎩᏴᎩᎠ
deegvv̀kiyv́vgiʔa
dee-gvvgi-hyv́vgiʔa
DST-3NS/1-tickle:PRC

'They're tickling me.'

The prefixes *geeji-* and *geeja-* remove the final vowel when attaching to a vowel initial stem. As a result, verbs with these prefixes may be identical. A pair of such identical forms is shown in (9).

(9a) ᎨᏧᏓᎴᎠ Track 62
geejuudaléeʔa
geeja-uudaléeʔa
3NS/2-unhook:PRC
'They're unhooking you.'

(9b) ᎨᏧᏓᎴᎠ
geejuudaléeʔa
geejii-uudaléeʔa
3NS/2PL-unhook:PRC
'They're unhooking you all.'

The two examples in (10), as in (9), have identical **syllabary** spellings; in (10), however, there is a slight difference in pronunciation; *geeji-* triggers /h/alternation, whereas *geeja-* does not.

(10a) ᎨᏨᏂᎭ
geejvv̀hniha
geeja-vvhniha
3NS/2-hit:PRC
'They hit you.' (Pulte and Feeling 1975:267)

(10b) ᎨᏨᏂᎭ
geejvvniha
geejii-vvhniha
3NS/2PL-hit:PRC
'They hit you all.' (Pulte and Feeling 1975:267)

In the examples in (11) the verb 'help' is shown in its **Present Continuous, Incompletive, Immediate, Completive,** and **Infinitive** stems, respectively. The **inherent /h/** of the /s/ causes the deletion of the **short vowel** of the prefix in (11a) and (11b).

(11a) ᎨᏣᏍᏕᎵᎭᏍ
geetsdeelihas
geeja-sdeeliha=s

3NS/2-help:PRC=Q
'Are they helping you?'

(11b) Ꮭ ᏱᎬᎩᏍᏕᎵᏍᎪ
tla yigvvksdeeliisgo
tla yi-gvvgi-sdeeliisg-o
NEG IRR-3NS/1-help:INC-HAB
'They don't help me.'

(11c) ᎪᎩᏍᏕᎳ
goògiisdeéla
googii-sdeéla
3NS/1DL.EX-help:IMM
'They just helped us.'

(11d) ᏓᎨᎩᏍᏕᎸᎯ
dageegiisdeelvv́hi
da-geegii-sdeelvv́h-i
CMF-3NS/1PL-help:CMP-CMF
'They will help us.'

(11e) ᎬᎩᏍᏕᎵᏗ ᎠᏩᏚᎵ
gvvksdehldi aàwaduuli
gvvgi-sdehldi agi-aduuli
3NS/1-help:INF 1B-help:PRC
'I want them to help me.'

9.3. Combined Local Pronominal Prefixes

Transitive verbs also use **combined local prefixes** to refer to combinations of subject and object where both are local persons. Three examples of their use are shown in (12). In (12a) the combined local prefix *gvv-* indicates that a first person singular is the subject and a second person singular is the object; in (12b) the same prefix appears on the Completive stem, and in (12c) it attaches to the Infinitive stem.

(12a) ᎬᎦᏘᏯ
gvvgaàtiíya
gvv-gahtiíya
1/2-wait.for:PRC
'I am waiting for you.'

(12b) ᎬᏎᏘᏅᎢ
gvvgaàtíidvv́ʔi
gvv-gahtíid-vv́ʔi
1/2-wait.for:CMP-EXP
'I waited for you.'

(12c) ᏣᏚᎵ ᎬᏎᏘᏗᏍᏗ
jaduuli gvvgaàtiídîisdi
ja-aduuli gvv-gahtiídîisdi
2B-want:PRC 1/2-wait.for:INF
'You want me to wait for you.'

These same verb stems are shown in (13) with a combined local prefix indicating a second person subject acting on a first person object. Unlike *gvv-*, the prefix *sgi-* is not an **/h/ alternator.**

(13a) ᏍᎩᏎᏘᏯ
sgiktiíya
sgi-gahtiíya
2/1-wait.for:PRC
'You are waiting for me.'

(13b) ᏍᎩᏎᏘᏅᎢ
sgiktíidvv́ʔi
sgi-gahtíid-vv́ʔi
2/1-wait.for:CMP-EXP
'You waited for me.'

(13c) ᎠᏆᏚᎵ ᏍᎩᏎᏘᏗᏍᏗ
aàgwaduuli sgiktiídîisdi
agi-aduuli sgi-gahtiídîisdi
1B-want:PRC 2/1-wait.for:INF
'I want you to wait for me.'

In (14) the prefix indicates a first person subject and second person object. Either the subject or object (or both) is **dual;** as a result, there are three possible interpretations.

(14) ᎢᏍᏅᏎᏘᏯ
iisdvvgaàtiíya
iisdvv-gahtiíya

1/2.DL-wait.for:PRC
'We two are waiting for you.'
'We two are waiting for you two.'
'I am waiting for you two.'

The complete set of combined local prefixes is presented in table 9.2. The column on the left represents the combination of subject and object; while the top row indicates number. Because these prefixes are combinations of first and second person, there is no **inclusive/exclusive** distinction. Prefixes that trigger /h/ alternation are indicated with an asterisk.

Table 9.2. Combined Local Pronominal Prefixes

Person Reference	*Both subject and object are singular*	*The subject and/or the object is dual (but neither is plural)*	*The subject and/or the object is plural*
2nd Person Subject/ 1st Person Object	sgi- [sgw]	sginii- *	iisgii- [iisgiiy] *
1st Person Subject/ 2nd Person Object	gvv- [gvvy] *	(ii)sdvv- [sdvvy] *	iijvv- [iijvvy] *

The two possible combinations are first person as the subject and second person as the object or second person as the subject and first person as the object. Like the other prefixes, the combined local prefixes have singular, dual, and plural forms. The two factors of number and person combine to create six combined local prefixes. The two prefixes exemplified above in (12) and (13) each have only one possible interpretation: thus *sgi-* in (13) always means that second person singular is the subject and first person singular is the object. In (14) above, and (15) below the conjugated Cherokee verb has three possible English translations.

(15) ᏍᎩᏂᎦᏗᏯ
sginiigaàtiíya
sginii-gahtiíya
2/1.DL-wait.for:PRC
'You are waiting for us two.'
'You two are waiting for us two.'
'You two are waiting for me.'

The plural prefixes in (16) each have five possible meanings. What remains constant in the meaning are the two grammatical persons (first and second person) and the relationship between them—first person acting on second person. The number specification, however, can apply to either or both persons. As in the previous example, this prefix triggers /h/ alternation.

(16a) ᎢᏨᎦᏗᏯ
iìjvvgaàtiíya
iijvv-gahtiíya
1/2.PL-wait.for:PRC
'I am waiting for you all.'
'We two are waiting for you all.'
'We all are waiting for you.'
'We all are waiting for you two.'
'We all are waiting for you all.'

(16b) ᎢᏍᎩᎦᏗᏯ
iisgiigaàtiíya
iisgii-gahtiíya
2/1.PL-wait.for:PRC
'You are waiting for all of us.'
'You all are waiting for all of us.'
'You all are waiting for me.'
'You all are waiting for us two.'
'You two are waiting for all of us.'

As shown in table 9.2, five of the six prefixes have special forms before vowel-initial stems. In (17a) prefix *sgi-* becomes [*sgw*], while in the other examples in (17) **consonant insertion** occurs between the vowel of the prefix and the initial vowel of the stem.

(17a)	ᏓᏍᏆᎵᎮᎵᏤᎵ	ᎯᎠ	ᎠᏕᎳ	ᎬᏁᎸᎢ
	da<u>sgw</u>aliiheélîicheeli	hiʔa	adeéla	gvvneélv́v́ʔi
	da-<u>sgi</u>-aliiheélîich-eel-i	hiʔa	adela	gvv-hneél-v́v́ʔi
	CMF-<u>2/1</u>-be.appreciative:CMP-APL:CMP-CMF	this	money	1/2-give:CMP-DVB

'You are going to thank me when I give you this money.'

(17b) ᎬᏯᎸᎢᎭ
<u>gvvy</u>aʔlv́vʔiha
<u>gvv</u>-ahlv́vʔiha
<u>1/2</u>-tie.up:PRC
'I'm tying you up.' (Pulte and Feeling 1975:257)

(17c) ᏴᏫᏃ ᎢᏍᏗᎦᏯᎷᎥᏍᎩ ᏅᏓᏍᏛᏴᏁᎵ
yvvwihnoo iisdiigayaluʔvsgi nvda<u>sdvvy</u>vvneeli
yvvwi=hnoo iisdii-gayaluʔvsgi ni-da-<u>sdvv</u>-vvhneel-i
person=CN 2A.DL-fisherman NI-CMF-<u>1/2.DL</u>-make:CMP-CMF
'. . . and I will make you fishers of men.' (*Cherokee New Testament,* Matthew 4:19)

(17d) Ꮭ ᏱᏍᎩᏲᎢᏳᎲᏍᎦ
tla yii<u>sgiiy</u>ooʔiyuhvsga
tla yi-<u>isgii</u>-oohiyuhvsga
NEG IRR-<u>2/1.PL</u>-believe:PRC
'You do not believe me.'

(17e) ᎢᏨᏯᎵᏥᏙᏁᎭ
<u>iijvvy</u>aliìjidoóneeha
<u>iijvv-</u>alijidoón-eeha
1/2.PL-preach:CMP-APL:PRC
'We are preaching to you.' (*Cherokee New Testament,* Acts 14:15)

The combined local prefixes are found mainly on verbs, but they do appear on **relationship nouns** that reference two local persons. On relationship nouns one of these is the person(s) to whom the noun refers; the other is the 'possessor' of the relationship. Two examples are shown in (18).

(18a) ᏂᎯ ᎯᏧᏣ ᏍᏇᏥ
nihi hichúúja sgweéji
nihi hi-chúúja sgi-eéji
2PRO 2A-boy 2/1-child
'You, boy, are my son.'

(18b) ᎬᏥ
gvvji
gvv-ji
1/2-mother
'I am your mother.'

The combined local prefix *sgi-* is pronounced as the single sound [k] when attached to a cluster of consonants starting with /s/. The prefix vowel is deleted through the typical process triggered by the inherent /h/ of the stem's /s/. The /s/ of the prefix is deleted in order to avoid an unpronounceable combination of consonants. Two examples are given in (19). Note that the syllabary does indicate the **underlying form.**

(19a) ᏍᎩᏍᏕᎳ 𝄢 Track 63
ksdeéla
sgi-sdeéla
2/1-help:IMM
'Help me!'

(19b) 𝄢 Track 64

ᎡᎵᏊᏍ	ᎦᎶᎯᏍᏗ	ᏱᏍᎩᏍᏚᎢᏏ
eelíigwus	galoohisdi	yiksdúʔiisi
eelíigwu=s	galoohisdi	yi-sgi-sdúʔiis-si
possible=Q	door	2/1-open:CMP-APL:IMM

'Could you open the door for me?'

9.4. Object Focus Pronominal Prefixes

A special set of pronominal prefixes appears on normally transitive verbs to indicate that the subject has been left out because it is unknown or unimportant. These prefixes are shown in table 9.3. Prefixes that trigger /h/ alternation are indicated with an asterisk.

Table 9.3. Object Focus Pronominal Prefixes

Person Reference	*Singular*	*Dual*	*Plural*
First Person	vvgi- [vvgw]	ooginii-	oogii-
Second Person	eeja-	eesdii- *	eejii- *
First and Second Person		eeginii- *	eegii- *
Third Person	aji- [ag] *	geejii- [geeg] *	

Examples of each prefix are shown in (20). (20d) and (20e) demonstrate the expected removal of the final vowel of the prefix before a vowel-initial stem. The abbreviation (O) is used to indicate object focus.

(20a)

ᏗᏜᏍᎦᏟᏗ	ᏛᎩᏕᎸ	ᏓᏂᏍᏓᏲᎯᎲ
diidláásgahldi	dvv̀gideelv	daàniisdayoohihv
di-a-adlaasgahldi	dee-vvgi-deel-v	daàniisdayoohihv
DST2-3A-play.ball:INF\INS	DST-1O-give(long):CMP-EXP	Christmas

'I was given ballsticks for Christmas.'

(20b) ᎨᏥᏍᎦᏡᏨ
geejiisgahljv
geejii-sgahlj-v
3O.PL-bite:CMP-EXP
'They had been bitten.'

(20c) ᎡᏣᎪᎵᏰᎦᏍ
eèjagooliyéegas
eeja-gooliy-éega=s
2O-examine:CMP-MOV:PRC=Q
'Are you going to be examined?'

(20d) ᎡᎩᏅᏂᎭ
eèginvv̀níha
eeginii-vvhníha
2O.DL-hit:PRC
'You and I are being hit.' (Pulte and Feeling 1975:300)

(20e) ᎡᎬᏂᎭ
eègvv̀níha
eegii-vvhníha
2O.PL-hit:PRC
'We are being hit.' (Pulte and Feeling 1975:300)

(20f) ᎤᏬᏢᏗ ᎾᏍᏓᏛᏁᎲ
uwóóhldi nisdadv́vhneehv
uwóóhldi ni-sdii-adv́vhneeh-v
funny NI-2A.DL-do:INC-DVB

ᎡᏍᏗᏰᏣᏍᏙᏗ ᎾᎦᎵᏍᏗᏍᎪ
eèsdiiyeejasdohdi nigalsdiisgo
eesdii-yeejasdohdi ni-ga-alisdiisg-o
2O.DL-laugh.at:INF NI-3A-cause:INC-HAB
'The funny things you do cause you to be laughed at.'

As shown in table 9.3, three of these prefixes have special **variant** forms before vowel-initial stems; these forms are indicated in **square brackets.** Examples of these forms are shown in (21).

(21a) Ꮭ ᏴᏆᏙᎵᏍᏔᏅ
tla yvv̀gwatoolstanv

tla yi-vgi-atool-stan-v
NEG IRR-1O-lend-CAU:CMP-EXP
'It wasn't loaned to me.'

(21b) DSPRPTVᎸ
aàgalii?eélîicheelv
aji-aliiheélîij-eel-v
3O-be.appreciative:CMP-APL:CMP-EXP
'He was thanked.'

(21c) ᎨᎡᏂᏫ
geegvv̀niha
geejii-vhniha
3O.PL-hit:PRC
'They are being hit.' (Pulte and Feeling 1975:300)

9.5. Inverse Use of Set B Prefixes

As seen throughout this chapter, prefixes on Cherokee verbs do not always indicate the subject. The prefix *ja-*, as exemplified in (22a), can indicate second person as the object or the subject; this is an example of a pattern in the language of always indicating local persons involved in the verb. The addition of the noun 'thief' in (22b) makes it clear that the Set B prefix is referring to an object. As discussed, a special form of the Set A prefix *hii-* indicates a second person subject and third person animate object. An example of this form is seen in (22c).

(22a) ᏣᏗᏅᏔᏅ
jadiínv́v̀tanv
ja-adiínv́v̀tan-v
2B-run.over:CMP-EXP
'You ran over it.'
'It ran over you.'

(22b) ᎦᏃᏍᎩᏍᎩ ᏣᏗᏅᏔᏅ
ganoosgiísgi jadiínv́v̀tanv
ga-noosgiisg-i ja-adiínv́v̀tan-v
3A-steal:INC-AGT 2B-run.over:CMP-EXP
'The thief ran you over.'

(22c) ᎦᏃᏍᎩᏍᎩ ᎯᏯᏗᏅᏔᏅ
ganoosgiísgi hiiyadiínv́v̀tanv

ga-noosgiisg-i hii-adiínv̋v̀tan-v
3A-steal:INC-AGT 2A.AN-run.over:CMP-EXP
'You ran over the thief.'

When both subject and object are third person, the animacy of the participants helps to distinguish subject from object. A verb that normally takes the Set A prefix *a-* or *ga-* can take the Set B prefix *uu-* to indicate that the subject is not the subject expected given the specific context of the narrative. The concept **inverse** presupposes an **animacy hierarchy** among participants, with some being more subject-like than others. This ranking is shown in figure 9.1.

1st and 2nd person > 3rd person human > 3rd person nonhuman animate > 3rd person inanimate

Figure 9.1. Cherokee Animacy Hierarchy

If a speaker's variety of Cherokee follows this hierarchy, then there is a preference for assuming that a human participant is the subject when there are two third person participants. For example, (23a) has two nouns. The noun 'woman' is higher than 'horse' on the hierarchy and therefore assumed to be the natural subject. Because this is a Set A verb in the Present Continuous stem, the third person pronominal prefix *a-* is expected to appear. The Set B prefix *uunii-* in (23b) indicates that the assumption of the human as the subject and the nonhuman as the object does not hold. For this speaker, the **animate nonsingular** prefix *gaa-* is the preferred form instead of *dee-* for third person humans as objects; the combination of *gaa-* and *uunii-* creates the form [*gvvwanii*].

(23a) ᎠᏂᎨᏯ ᏐᏈᎵ ᏓᎾᎯᏴᏗᎠ
aniigééhya soogwil daànahyvtéeʔa
anii-gééhya soogwili dee-anii-ahyvtéeʔa
3A.NS-woman horse DST-3A.NS-kick:PRC
'The women are kicking the horses.' (Scancarelli 1987:128)

(23b) ᏐᏈᎵ ᎡᎬᎾᎯᏴᏗᎠ ᎠᏂᎨᏯ
soogwil gvvwanahyvtéeʔa aniigééhya
soogwili gaa-uunii-ahyvtéeʔa anii-gééhya
horse ANS-3B.NS-kick:PRC 3A.NS-woman
'The horses are kicking the women.' (Scancarelli 1987:129)

9.6. Impersonal Pronominal Prefixes

In addition to the Set B prefix *uu-*, there is a less common **impersonal Set B prefix** that has the meaning 'one' (sometimes translated as generic 'you' in English). This form can only appear in a context where a Set B prefix could appear. Three examples are shown in (24); in (24a) and (24b) 'you' has the meaning of an indefinite 'someone' or 'anyone'.

(24a) ᏂᎪᎯᎸ ᎣᏢᎪ
nigohiilv oòdlv́vgo
nigohiilv oo-hdlv́vg-o
always 3B.IP-sick:INC-HAB
'You're always sick.'

(24b) ᏲᏚᎵ ᎣᏰᏥᏍᏗ
yooduuli ooyeetsdi
yi-oo-aduuli oo-yeetsdi
IRR-3B.IP-sick:PRC 3B.IP-laugh:INF
'if you want to laugh' (Scancarelli 1987:85)

(24c) ᎠᎯᏓ ᎣᏩᎨᏫᏍᏗ
ahíída owakeewisdi
a-ahíída oo-vkeewisdi
3A-easy 3B.IP-forget:INF
'It's easy (for anyone) to forget that.'

In (24c) the impersonal Set B prefix *oo-* appears as [*owa*] before a stem-initial /v/, following the pattern of its Set B third person singular counterpart.

This form can appear on nouns as well. Two examples are shown in (25). In (25b) it appears on the **emphatic pronoun** as well as on the Set B verb 'want.'

(25a) ᏦᏕᎪ
joodéego
di-oo-adéeg-o
DST2-3B.IP-throw:INC-HAB
'trash', 'that which you throw away'

(25b) ᏱᏓᏛᎦ ᎣᏩᏌ ᏲᏚᎵ
yidaadvvg owas yooduuli
yi-dee-a-adaad-vvga oo-vv́sa yi-oo-aduuli
IRR-DST-3A-RFL-hit:IMM 3B.IP-EMP.PRO IRR-3B.IP-want:PRC
'You can hit yourself if you want to.'

As shown in (26), Set A verbs do not normally use an impersonal prefix.

(26) ᎤᏪᏘᎢ ᎧᏃᎮᏓ ᎣᏍᏓ ᎠᎪᎵᏰᏗ
uweetííʔi kanooheéda óósda agooliíyéèdi
uu-eetííʔi kanooheéda óósda a-gooliíyéèdi
3B-old gospel good 3A-read:INF
'The Old Testament is good to read.'

However, a **impersonal Set A prefix** does appear when a prepronominal prefix precedes it. The abbreviation for this prefix *-vv-* is 3A.IP. Two examples are given in (27).

(27a) ᏃᏒᎾ ᏴᏓᏅᏖ ᎣᏩᎨᏫᏍᏗ
noosv́v́na yvvdahnte owakééwsdi
noosv́v́na yi-vv-adahnte oo-vkeewsdi
bad.things IRR-3A.IP-think:PRC 3B.IP-forget:INF\MOD
'When you think bad things you need to forget.'

(27b) ᎩᏚᏩ ᏧᏂᏆᎾᏲᏍᏗ Track 65
giduuwá juuniikwanyoosdi
giduuwá di-uunii-kwanyoosdi
Keetoowah DST2-3B.NS-play.cards:INF

ᎠᏕᎳ ᏱᏛᏓᏒᏅ
adeéla yidvvdasvhna
adeéla yi-dee-vv-adasvhna
money IRR-DST-3A.IP-win:IMM
'You can win money at the Keetoowah Casino.'

9.7. Reflexive (RFL) Prefix

The **reflexive prefix** *-adaad-* is one of two prefixes that can appear between the pronominal prefix and the verb stem. It is only used on transitive verbs and indicates that the subject performing the action is the same as the object being affected by the action. As with other prefixes, the environment in which the reflexive appears can alter its form. The form *-adaad-* appears before stems that begin with a vowel other than /a/. The reflexive has the **variant** forms [*ad*] before the vowel /a/ and [*adaa*] before consonants. (28) shows three examples of the full form of the prefix. In (28b) the verb begins with a vowel-lengthening feature that triggers the form [*adaa*]. The long vowel of the prefix also has a **high-**

fall tone; this **modal tone** (MOD) helps to convey the idea of obligation. In (28a) and (28c) the emphatic pronoun *-vvsa* appears to reinforce the idea of reflexivity.

(28a) ᎠᏓᏙᎵᎦ ᎤᏩᏌ
aàdaadohlga uwaása
a-adaad-olihga uu-vv́sa
3A-RFL-recognize:PRC 3B-EMP.PRO
'He recognizes himself.'

(28b) ᎢᏴᏓᎭ ᎤᏓᏀᏓᏗᏍᏙᏗ
iyvdaha uudááhndadisdohdi
iyvdaha uu-adaad-xxnvhdadi-sdohdi
sometimes 3B-RFL-remember(I)-CAU:INF\MOD
'He sometimes has to remind himself.'

(28c) ᎠᏓᏚᎯᏍᏗᎭ ᎤᏩᏌ
aàdaaduuhiísdíha uwaása
a-adaad-uuhiísdíha uu-vv́sa
3A-RFL-accuse:PRC 3B-EMP.PRO
'He is accusing himself.'

The shortened form [*ad*] appears before the vowel /a/. Two examples are shown in (29); the first is commonly heard as a way to say 'good-bye'.

(29a) ᏣᏓᎦᏎᏍᏕᏍᏗ
j<u>ad</u>aksesdéesdi
ja-adaad-agasesd-éesdi
2B-RFL-be.careful:CMP-PFT
'Take care of yourself!'

(29b) ᏕᏓᏓᎦᏙᏍᏗ
déed<u>ad</u>aktoósdi
dee-iidii-adaad-agahtoósdi
DST-1A.PL-look.at:PRC
'We're looking at each other.'

(30) gives two examples with the [*adaa*] form that attaches to consonant initial stems.

(30a) ᎠᏋᏌ ᎠᏆᏓᏃᏎᏗ ᎨᏐ
agwvv́sa agwadaahnóósehdi geeso
agi-vv́sa agi-adaad-hnoosehdi gees-o
1B-EMP.PRO 1B-RFL-tell:INF\MOD be:INC-HAB

ᏲᏁᎦ ᎠᎩᏬᏂᎯᏍᏗᎢ ᏂᎨᏒᎾ
yoneéga agiwoonihisdííʔi nigeesv́v́na
yoneéga agi-woonihisdííʔi ni-gees-v́v́na
English 1B-speak:INF NI-be:INC-NDV
'I have to tell myself not to speak English.'

(30b) ᎠᏆᏓᎪᏩᏘᎭ
aàgwadaagohwtíha
agi-adaad-gohwtíha
1B-RFL-see:PRC
'I see myself.' (Pulte and Feeling 1975:296)

These examples all have a singular subject; when the subject is nonsingular, a distributive prefix is mandatory. This usage is demonstrated in (31). In (31c) the construction can be interpreted as having either a reciprocal or a reflexive function, but the assumption is that the reflexive interpretation refers to a repeated action. If the distributive prefix is not used, the interpretation would be a single act of tying up performed reflexively, with no reciprocal meaning possible.

(31a) ᎠᏩᏓᎦᏙᏍᏔᏅ ᎠᏮᏌ
aàwadaaktoóstánv awvv́sa
agi-adaad-agahtoóstán-v agi-vv́sa
1B-RFL-look.at:CMP-EXP 1B-EMP.PRO
'I looked at myself.'

(31b) ᏙᎩᎾᏓᎦᏙᏍᏔᏅ ᎣᎩᏅᏌ
doògindaaktoóstánv ooginvv́sa
dee-ooginii-adaad-agahtoóstán-v ooginii-vv́sa
DST-1B.DL.EX-RFL-look.at:CMP-EXP 1B.DL.EX-EMP.PRO
'We looked at each other.'

(31c) ᏓᎾᏓᎸᎢᎭ ᎤᏅᏌ
daàndaahlv́vʔíha uunvv́sa
dee-anii-adaad-hlv́vʔíha uunii-vv́sa
DST-3A.NS-RFL-tie.up:PRC 3B.NS-EMP.PRO
'They're tying each other up.'
'They're tying themselves up.' (Scancarelli 1987:67)

An important function of the reflexive prefix is to indicate an unspecified object. Transitive verbs (and nouns derived from them) ordinarily specify an object. Two examples are shown in (32); in (32a) the verb is transitive and is translated into English with an object 'it'. As a derived noun in (32b) with a transitive verb as its base there is no mention of what the 'catcher' catches and the **unspecified object reflexive** *-adaad-* appears. Moreover, the derived **agentive noun** has the distributive prefix to indicate that this is an ongoing or repeated activity.

(32a) ᎦᏂᏰᏍᎪ Track 66
gáʔniiyiísgo
ga-ʔniiyiísg-o
3A-catch:INC-HAB
'He catches it.'

(32b) ᏗᏓᏂᏰᏍᎩ
diidaaniíyiísgi
di-a-adaad-niíyiisg-i
DST2-3A-RFL-catch:INC-AGT
'policeman'

This pattern of deriving agentive nouns is discussed in chapter 12; the unspecified object reflexive is further explained in chapter 14.

9.8. Changes to Pronominal Prefixes

Pronominal prefixes as well as stems undergo the changes described in chapter 8. These changes, however, have a particular importance for the pronominal prefixes because these elements typically may cause the deletion of the /h/ that triggers some of the changes. For this reason they are further exemplified in the following section.

9.8.1. /h/ Alternation

As described in chapter 8, /h/ alternation occurs when certain pronominal prefixes cause an /h/ in the stem to be replaced with a **glottal stop.** This /h/ alternation seems to exist across all dialects for all speakers. The specific person prefixes which trigger the alternation, however, may vary slightly. Lists of the prefixes that trigger the alternation are found in Cook (1979:22–26) and Scancarelli (1987:71, 101–102). If we compare Cook's list of prefixes (which describes North Carolina Cherokee) with those found in Scancarelli, we see very little variation. This comparison is shown in table 9.4.

As shown in (33), the Set A first person singular always triggers /h/ alternation, as does its animate object counterpart.

Table 9.4. Pronominal Prefixes That Trigger /h/ Alternation

Pronominal Prefix		*Scancarelli* (1987:71)	*Cook* (1979:22–26)
Set A			
ji-	1A	Yes	Yes
Animate Object			
jii-	1A.AN	Yes	Yes
hii-	2A.AN	Yes	Yes
eenii-	1A.DL.AN	Yes	Yes
eedii-	1A.PL.AN	Yes	Yes
oosdii-	1A.DL.EX.AN	Yes	No
oojii-	1A.PL.EX.AN	Yes	No
eesdii-	2A.PL.AN	Yes	Yes
eejii-	2A.PL.AN	Yes	Yes
Combined			
gvv-	1/2	Yes	Yes
sdvv-	1/2.DL	Yes	Yes
iijvv-	1/2.PL	Yes	Yes
iisginii-	2/1.DL	Yes	Yes
iisgii-	2/1.PL	Yes	Yes
Object Focus			
aji-	3O	Yes	Yes
geeji-	3O.PL	Yes	Yes
eeginii-	1O.DL	Yes	Yes
eegi-	1O.PL	Yes	Yes
eeji-	2O.PL	Yes	Yes
eesdii-	2O.DL	Yes	Yes
Combined Nonsingular Subject			
geeji-	3NS/2PL	Yes	Yes

(33a) ᎦᏴᏖᏍᎪ
gaàyvhtéesgo
ji-ahyvhtéesg-o
1A-kick:INC-HAB
'I kick it.'

(33b) ᏥᏯᏴᏖᏍᎪ
jiiyaàyvhtéesgo
jii-ahyvhtéesg-o
1A.AN-kick:INC-HAB
'I kick him.'

The examples in (34) demonstrate all of the /h/ alternators; in each case the underlying /h/ is underlined. No Set B prefixes trigger the alternation. It does occur with all of the **animate object prefixes,** most of the combined local prefixes, and most of the object focus prefixes. In each case the /h/ (or aspirated consonant) that is affected is underlined.

(34a) ᎯᎪᎡᏍ
hiigooʔes
hii-gooh-e=s
2A.AN-see:CMP-NXP=Q
'Did you see her?

(34b) ᎠᏎ ᎡᏃᎢᏅᏍᏗ ᎯᎠ ᎠᎦᏴᎵᎨ   Track 67
aase eènooʔiínv́v́sdi hiʔa agayv́v́lige
aase eenii-oohiínvvsdi hiʔa a-gayv́v́lige
must 1A.DL.AN-lead:INF\MOD this 3A-elderly.woman
'We have to lead this elderly woman.'

(34c) ᎡᏓᏈᏴᎮᎸᎢ
eèdagwiyvvh-eel-vv́ʔi
eedii-akwiyvvh-eel-vv́ʔi
1A.PL.AN-pay:CMP-APL:CMP-EXP
'We paid him.'

(34d) ᏧᏠᎦᎴᏓ ᎡᏍᏗᎪᎥ ᎡᏍᏗᏲᎵᎸᎢ   Track 68
juudloogalééda eesdiigooʔv́ eèsdiiyoólîilvvʔi
juudloogaléeda eesdii-gooh-v eesdii-yoólîil-vvʔi
Santa.Claus 2A.DL.AN-see:CMP-DVB 2A.DL.AN-greet:CMP-FCM
'If you two see Santa Claus, greet him.'

(34e) ᎡᏣᏛᏅ ᎠᎴ ᎡᏥᎸ
eèjadvnv ale eèjiilv
eejii-advn-v ale eejii-h̲l-v
2A.PL.AN-crucify:CMP-EXP and 2A.PL.AN-kill:CMP-EXP
'. . . you crucified him and killed him.' (*Cherokee New Testament*, Acts 2:23)

(34f) ᎠᏋᎨᏫᏒ ᎬᏯᎵᎡᎵᏤᏗ
aàgwvvkeewsv gvvyalii?eélîichehdi
agi-vvkeews-v gvv-aliih̲eélîij-ehdi
1B-forget:CMP-EXP 1/2-be.appreciative:CMP-APL:INF

Ꮎ ᏥᏍᏇᎵᏍᏔᏅᎢ
na jisgwelstanv́v́?i
na ji-sgi-elstan-v́v́?i
the REL-2/1-feed:CMP-DVB
'I forget to thank you when you fed me.'

(34g) ᎪᏍᏗᏊ ᎢᏣᏓᏅᏖᏗ ᎢᏨᏁᎭ Track 69
góósdigwu iijadaáhntehdi iìjvvneeha
góósdi=gwu iijii-adahntehdi iijvv-h̲neeha
something=DT 2B.PL-think.about:INF 1/2.PL-give:PRC
'I'm just giving you something to think about.' (Feeling 1975a:6)

(34h) ᎡᏧᎢᏍᏗᎭ
eèju?iísdíha
eejii-uuh̲iísdíha
2O.PL-accuse:PRC
'You all are being accused.'

(34i) ᏍᎩᏂᎦᏘᏯᏍ
sgiiniigaàtiíyas
sgiinii-gah̲tiíya=s
2/1.DL-wait.for:PRC=Q
'Are you two waiting for me?'

(34j) ᎣᏍᏓ ᎠᎦᏈᏴᎡᎰ
óósda aàgagwiiyv́v?eeho
óósda aji-ak̲wiiyv́v?-eeh-o
good 3O-pay:CMP-APL:INC-HAB
'He is paid well.'

(34k) ᎨᏧᎢᏍᏗᎭ
geejuʔiísdíha
geeji-uuhiísdíha
3NS/1PL-accuse:PRC
'They are accusing us.'

(34l)

ᏧᏂᏢᎩ	ᏳᏫᎩᏁᏙᎳ	ᎡᎩᏃᎵᎪ
juuniidlvv̀gi	yuwiginedóóla	eèginoliìgo
juuniidlvv̀gi	yi-wi-ginii-edool-a	eeginii-olihg-o
hospital	IRR-TRN-1B.DL-be.at:CMP-CVB	1O.DL-recognize:INC-HAB

'When we go to the hospital we get recognized.'

(34m) ᎡᎩᏰᎵᏒ
eègiiyeelíisv
eegii-hyeelíis-v
1O.PL-mock:CMP-EXP
'We were made fun of.'

(34n) ᎡᏍᏗᏩᏛᎲ
eesdiìwahtvvhv
eesdii-hwahtvvh-v
2O.DL-find:CMP-EXP
'You two were found.'

The **exclusive** animate object prefixes *oosdii-* and *oojii-* are identical in form to their Set A counterparts used with inanimate objects, but the animate object prefixes may be used in contexts that normally require Set B prefixes. For example, in (35) both verbs are in the Completive, a stem that usually requires the use of a Set B prefix. The Set B Prefix *oogii-* does appear on the verb 'use' (with the inanimate object 'seine') but the animate object prefix *oojii-* appears on the verb 'catch' (with the animate object 'fish').

(35)

ᎠᎦᏯᎷᏗ	ᎣᎬᏔᏅ	ᏙᏥᏂᏴᎲ	ᎠᏣᏗ
agayaludi	oktanv	doojiiniyvhv	ajaʔdi
agayaludi	oogii-vhtan-v	dee-oojii-niyvh-v	ajaʔdi
seine	1B.PL.EX-use:CMP-EXP	DST-1A.PL.EX.AN-catch:CMP-EXP	fish

'We used a seine and caught a fish.'

The exclusive animate objects prefixes also trigger /h/ alternation for some speakers. In (36a) *oojii-* is an animate object prefix and causes the deletion of /h/, while in (36b) *oojii-*does not have an animate object and the /h/ remains.

(36a) Ꮎ ᎠᏧᏣ ᎣᏥᎦᏗᏯ
na achúúja oòjiigaàtiiya
na a-chúúja oojii-gahtiiya
the 3A-boy 1A.PL.EX.AN-wait:PRC
'We are waiting for the boy.'

(36b) ᏗᎦᏚᎴᏂ ᎣᏥᎦᏗᏯ
diiktuuléeni oòjiiktiiya
diiktuuléeni oojii-gahtiiya
car 1A.PL.EX-wait:PRC
'We are waiting for the car.'

In like manner (37a) shows that the animate object prefix *oosdii-* triggers the alternation; in (37b) the non–animate object prefix *oosdii-* does not. These two examples have an identical syllabary spelling.

(37a) ᎣᏍᏙᎵᎦ
oòsdoliìga
oosdii-olihga
1A.PL.EX.AN-recognize:PRC
'We recognize him.'

(37b) ᎣᏍᏙᎵᎦ
oòsdohlga
oosdii-olihga
1A.PL.EX-recognize:PRC
'We recognize it.'

Often /h/ alternation affects the stem, but if the alternation is at the beginning of the stem the pronominal prefix can be lengthened to accommodate the **lowfall** (all tones that rise or fall can only occur on long vowels; see chapter 8). In (38) the stem starts with [s], a sound usually accompanied by an inherent /h/. In (38a) /h/ alternation removes this /h/ and replaces it with the lowfall tone (with accompanying lengthening of the vowel to accommodate the tone). In (38b) the second person prefix does not trigger this alternation and remains a short vowel.

(38a) ᏥᏍᏆᏗ
jiìsgwadi
ji-sgwadi
1A-finish:PRC
'I am finishing it.'

(38b) ᎯᏍᏆᏗ
hisgwadi
hi-sgwadi
2A-finish:PRC
'You are finishing it.'

/h/ alternation also interacts with exchange and **vowel deletion.** The effect of these changes on pronominal prefixes is further explained in the following two sections of this chapter.

9.8.2. Exchange

Exchange and deletion can both affect pronominal prefixes. The third person Set A prefix *ga-* changes to [*ka*] if the stem to which it attaches has /h/ at the beginning or immediately after a short vowel. This sound change is particularly relevant because Cherokee dictionaries and word lists use the third person form of the verb as the main form (for this grammar the citation form is with the pronominal prefix removed). In (39a) one such verb is shown in the third person; its first person counterpart—without the exchange because of /h/ alternation—is shown in (39b).

(39a) ᎧᏃᎮᎭ — Track 70
k̲anoohéha
ga-h̲noohéha
3A-tell:PRC
'He's telling it.'

(39b) ᏥᏃᎮᎭ
jii̲noohéha
ji-h̲noohéha
1A-tell:PRC
'I'm telling it.'

The singular forms commonly undergo exchange because most of them end in short vowels. The example in (40a) shows exchange with the combined local prefix *sgi-* and (40b) shows the same process with the second person Set B prefix *ja-*.

(40a) ᏞᏍᏗ ᏥᏍᎩᏅᎯ
tlesdi jiisk̲invvhi

tlesdi jii-sgi-h̲nvvhi
NEG.COM COM-2/1-call:IMM
'Don't call me.'

(40b) ᎦᎠ ᏣᎾᎸᏍᏔᏁ
gaag c̲h̲anaálv́vstane
gaago ja-h̲naálv́vstan-e
who 2B-make.angry:CMP-NXP
'Who made you mad?'

/h/ alternation can create a contrast for different conjugated forms of Set A verbs that would otherwise sound identical. Recall that some Set A verbs take *ga-* in the third person; if these same verbs are vowel-initial, first and third person might be pronounced alike, as in the pair of examples in (41).

(41a) ᎦᏙᏍᎦ
gadósga
ga-adósga
3A-fall:PRC
'It is falling.'

(41b) ᎦᏙᏍᎦ
gadósga
ji-adósga
1A-fall:PRC
'I am falling.'

Because of /h/ alternation and the related changes of exchange and vowel deletion, there are actually very few instances of such identical-sounding pairs. In (42a) the presence of an underlying /h/ triggers vowel deletion, while in (42b) the pronominal prefix *ji-* (appearing as [*g*] before a vowel) triggers /h/ alternation, thereby removing the /h/ and the environment for vowel deletion to occur. Significantly, the syllabary preserves the underlying form for both conjugations. A detailed description of the changes involved in these two examples is presented in chapter 8.

(42a) ᎪᎵᎦ Track 71
gohlga
ga-olih̲ga
3A-understand:PRC
'He understands it.'

(42b) ᎪᏟᎦ
goliiga
ji-olihga
1A-understand:PRC
'I understand it.'

9.8.3. Vowel Deletion

/h/ alternation can also affect vowel deletion processes, which can in turn change the pronunciation of the pronominal prefix itself. As with exchange, this deletion can cause important changes to the third person citation form. (43) is a comparison of the first and third person forms. Note that the stem begins with a vowel, so there are two different types of vowel loss: first, the stem-initial vowel undergoes **vowel removal,** then the presence of the /h/ on the stem causes the prefix vowel to undergo vowel deletion. Note that the syllabary character beginning this word has a **leftover vowel.**

(43a) ᎬᏗᏍᎪ Track 72
kdiísgo
ga-vhdiísg-o
3A-use:INC-HAB
'He uses it.'

(43b) ᎬᏗᏍᎪ
gvv̀diísgo
ji-vhdiísg-o
1A-use:INC-HAB
'I use it.'

As with exchange, deletion typically happens with the singular forms. In (44a) the Set B form undergoes deletion of its short vowel and aspiration of its consonant as a result of the /h/ (which is unwritten) present before the /s/. In (44b) the second person object focus prefix *eja-* is also aspirated after deletion of its vowel brings the consonant adjacent to /h/. In (44c) the prefix *agi-* is pronounced as [*k*]; both of its vowels have been lost, and the remaining consonant has undergone aspiration.

(44a) ᎠᎩᏍᏗᏍᎬ
akstisgv
agi-stisgv

1B-hair
'my hair'

(44b) ᎦᏙᎲ ᏰᏣᎳᏍᏓᏅᎢ
gadohv yechlasdanvv̋ʔi
gadohv yi-eja-hlasdan-vv̋ʔi
why IRR-2O-invite:CMP-EXP
'Why were you not invited?'

(44c) ᏎᎷ ᏧᏓ ᎠᏰᏟ ᏗᎩᏍᏆᎵᏍᏗ — Track 73
seélu juuda ayééhli dííksgwalsdi
seélu di-uuda ayééhli di-agi-sgwalsdi
corn DST2-cob half DST2-1B-break(long):INF\MOD
'I have to break some corncobs in half.'

The /h/ in the second person may also cause the deletion of a preceding short vowel. In (45) the /h/ causes the deletion of an intervening vowel and the subsequent aspiration of the *ji*-prepronominal prefix. This prepronominal prefix is discussed in chapter 10.

(45a) ᎦᏙ ᏣᎾᎩᎠ — Track 74
gado chanagiiʔa
gado ji-hi-anagiiʔa
why REL-2A-leave:PRC
'Why are you leaving?'

(45b) ᏥᏯᎦᏔᏍᏓᏏ
chiiyagaàtáàsdaàsi
ji-hii-agahtáàsdan-si
REL-2A.AN-wink:CMP-APL:IMM
'You winked at her.'

This /j/ sound found on second person forms changes to [ts] when adjacent to an **obstruent** sound. Two examples are shown in (46).

(46a) ᏚᏳᎪᏛ ᏱᏣᏛᏅᏗ ᎨᏣᏎᎮᏗ — Track 75
duùyuukdv yijadvhndi géétssehehdi
duùyuukdv yi-ja-advhndi geja-asehehdi
correct IRR-2B-do:INF 3NS/2-show:INF\MOD
'They have to show you how to do it right.'

(46b) ᎡᏣᏙᏗ ᏂᎪᎸ ᎭᏚᎢᏍᏗᏍᎪᎢ
eètsdohydi nigoólv hatuʔisdiísgooʔi

eeja-adohydi nigoólv hi-atusdiísg-ooʔi
2O-cut.hair:INF always 2A-promise:INC-HAB
'You always promise to get your hair cut.'

The complexities that exchange and deletion cause can also affect where nouns and adjectives are listed in dictionaries. For example, in the *Cherokee-English Dictionary* (Feeling 1975a) the word 'nose' is listed with the words starting with the letter ⟨k⟩ as in (47). (The dictionary uses superscript numerals to represent tone.)

(47) ka̜^{2}yv^{2}so^{4}li ᎦᏰᏒᎵ 'his nose'

The possession forms for this noun make it clear that its stem is *-hyvvsooli,* as shown in (48). The /h/ is present in the second person form.

(48) ᏥᏰᏒᎵ jìi̥yvvsóóli 'my nose' Track 76
ᏂᏰᏒᎵ hih̲yvvsóóli 'your nose'
ᎦᏰᏒᎵ kayvvsóóli 'his nose'

Cowen (1995: 165) lists this same noun with the words starting with ⟨g⟩ as *gaysoli,* along with the syllabary spelling ᎦᏰᏒᎵ. As seen before, this different pronunciation (and spelling) indicates the absence of the exchange rule. Further complicating matters, some speakers use the Set B prefixes for the same noun, as shown in (49).

(49) ᎠᎩᏰᏒᎵ aàgihyvvsóóli 'my nose'
ᏣᏰᏒᎵ jahyvvsóóli 'your nose'
ᎤᏰᏒᎵ uuhyvvsóóli 'his nose'

For all three possible pronunciations, the underlying stem is *-hyvvsooli.*

9.9. Summary of Transitive Verb Pronominal Prefixes

Because so many possible pronominal prefixes can appear on transitive verbs, it is useful to review the prefixes used with transitive verbs. (50)–(55) give examples of different pronominal prefixes on the transitive verb 'look at'. Like most transitive verbs, this verb uses Set A prefixes. Note the /h/ alternation and subsequent lack of vowel deletion in (51), (53c), (54b), (54c), (55b), and (55c).

-agahtoósdi with Set A pronominal prefixes Track 77

(50a) ᎭᎦᏙᏍᏗ
haktoósdi
hi-agahtoósdi

2A-look.at:PRC
'You are looking at it.'

(50b) ᏍᏓᎦᏙᏍᏗ sdaktoósdi 'you two are looking at it'
(50c) ᎢᏣᎦᏙᏍᏗ iìjaktoósdi 'you all are looking at it'

-agahtoósdi with animate object pronominal prefixes Track 78

(51a) ᎯᏯᎦᏙᏍᏗ
hiiyagaa̱toósdi
hii-agahtoósdi
2A.AN-look.at:PRC
'You are looking at her.'

(51b) ᎡᏍᏓᎦᏙᏍᏗ eèsdagaàtoósdi 'you two are looking at her'
(51c) ᎡᏣᎦᏙᏍᏗ eèjagaàtoósdi 'you all are looking at her'

-agahtoósdi with Set B pronominal prefixes Track 79

(52a) ᏣᎦᏙᏍᏗ
jaktoósdi
ja-agahtoósdi
2B-look.at:PRC
'She is looking at you.'

(52b) ᏍᏓᎦᏙᏍᏗ sdaktoósdi 'she is looking at you two'
(52c) ᎢᏣᎦᏙᏍᏗ iìjaktoósdi 'she is looking at you all'

-agahtoósdi with combined nonsingular subject pronominal prefixes

(53a) ᎨᏣᎦᏙᏍᏗ
geejaktoósdi
geeja-agahtoósdi
3NS/2-look.at:PRC
'They are looking at you.'

(53b) ᎨᏍᏓᎦᏙᏍᏗ geesdaktoósdi 'they are looking at you two'
(53c) ᎨᏣᎦᏙᏍᏗ geejagaàtoósdi 'they are looking at you all'

-agahtoósdi with combined local pronominal prefixes Track 80

(54a) ᏍᏆᎦᏙᏍᏗ
sgwaktoósdi
sgi-agahtoósdi
2/1-look.at:PRC
'You are looking at me.'

(54b) ᎬᏯᎦᏙᏍᏗ gvvyagaàtoósdi 'I am looking at you'
(54c) ᏍᏛᏯᎦᏙᏍᏗ sdvvyagaàtoósdi 'I am looking at you two'
'we two are looking at you two'
'we two are looking at you'

-agahtoósdi with object focus pronominal prefixes

(55a) ᎡᏣᎦᏙᏍᏗ
eèjaktoósdi
eja-agahtoósdi
2O-look.at:PRC
'You are being looked at.'

(55b) ᎡᏍᏓᎦᏙᏍᏗ eèsdagaàtoósdi 'you two are being looked at'
(55c) ᎡᏣᎦᏙᏍᏗ eèjagaàtoósdi 'you all are being looked at'

9.10. Sources and Additional Reading

The most comprehensive source on the use of pronominal prefixes is Scancarelli's dissertation (1987). Scancarelli (1987:162) also provides the first discussion of the inverse use of Set B prefixes. She discusses at length four variables that determine pronominal selection: semantically grounded syntactic relations, lexical specifications, the arguments' inherent referential content (which includes a discussion of the animacy hierarchy), and the syntax of the clause. In her discussion of derivation and inflection, Scancarelli makes reference to the Extended Word and Paradigm theory, the main theory that she uses in her analysis of Cherokee. She concludes the dissertation with an examination of typological and theoretical issues and explores the possibility of Cherokee as a split-intransitive system, including the appropriateness of such terms as passive, ergative, and inverse. Scancarelli concludes by stating her preference for a definition of grammatical relations as defined by Nichols (1986) for the analysis of Cherokee.

Dukes (1996) explores the interaction of this pronominal agreement with the Cherokee animacy hierarchy proposed by Scancarelli and argues that a lexically based analysis that takes into consideration semantic and pragmatic factors is more appropriate for Cherokee than a purely syntactic approach. He supports this claim through a discussion of ditransitive verbs, using a framework from both Relational Grammar and Head-Driven Phrase Structure Grammar. Potter (1996:117) refers to the unspecified object reflexive as the animate covert argument. Many thanks are due to Wyman Kirk for insightful discussions concerning the impersonal prefixes.

9.11. Directions for Further Research

Pulte and Feeling (1975:301) have a different interpretation of the inverse, which they refer to as the second passive; the first passive is their term for what this grammar calls the object focus prefixes. Pulte and Feeling (1975:353) consider Cherokee to have a basic word order of subject-object-verb (SOV); the use of the Set B prefix *uu-* seems to indicate a reordering of what they consider the basic word order and a subsequent focus on the object; hence their use of the English passive. Their interpretation of this special use of *uu-* is markedly different from that of Scancarelli (1987). Scancarelli's characterization of a word order determined by pragmatic factors undermines claims of basic word orders. A thorough study of the use of the inverse therefore requires a comprehensive discourse analysis of a large number of Cherokee texts.

TEN

Prepronominal Prefixes II

10.1. Overview of Prepronominal Prefixes

Chapter 5 discusses six of the **prepronominal prefixes:** the **distributive** (DST) *dee-*, the **irrealis** (IRR) *yi-*, the **translocative** (TRN) *wi-*, the **command** (COM) *jii-*, the **completive future** (CMF) *da-*, and the **animate nonsingular** (ANS) *gaa-*. This chapter describes the other six prefixes out of a total of twelve.

The prepronominal prefixes have a wide range of functions and meanings. Four of the prefixes (*wi-*, *di-*, *ni-*, *ee-*) can indicate position or movement relative to the speaker. Other prefixes have grammatical functions and indicate negation or subordination (*ji-* and *gaa-*). Moreover, some verbs have **frozen prefixes;** in other words, they always appear with these prefixes. The most common frozen prefix is *dee-*; in a few instances *ni-* and *wi-* also appear as frozen prefixes. Some prefixes have two different basic forms. The form that occurs less often—the **secondary prepronominal** form—includes '2' in its **abbreviation.** For example, the form of the distributive prefix that occurs most commonly is *dee-*, which has the abbreviation DST. An alternate form *di-* occurs with the **Infinitive stem, derived nouns** and **adjectives,** and the command form of the **Immediate;** this form has the abbreviation DST2. Both of these basic forms have various predictable **variant forms** based on adjacent sounds.

10.1.1. Relativizer (REL) Prepronominal Prefix

The **relativizer** prefix appears before any other prefixes and cannot appear with the irrealis *yi-* prefix. Although one of its main uses is to indicate that a verb is part of a **relative clause,** it has several other important uses. One of its functions is to indicate a definite past time frame in which the verb took place; in this usage the clause is not subordinate to another clause. Often a verb with this prefix is accompanied by an **adverb** expressing a specific time, as seen in (1). In (1b) the prefix attaches to an Immediate stem and undergoes **aspiration** after **vowel deletion** occurs. The **nonexperienced past** suffix is not used with this prefix.

(1a) Ꮢ ᏥᎨᏒ ᏥᏚᏂᏃᎩᏒ
svv jigeesv́ jiduuniihnoogíisv
svv ji-gees-v́ ji-dee-uunii-hnoogíis-v
yesterday REL-be:CMP-DVB REL-DST-3B.NS-sing:CMP-EXP
'Yesterday they sang it.'

(1b) ᎩᎳᏊ ᏥᎷᎦ
kilagwu chiʔluuga
kila=gwu ji-hi-ʔluuga
just.now=DT REL-2A-climb:IMM
'You climbed it just a moment ago.'

Speakers may also use *ji-* without any specific past reference. In such situations the prefix may be emphasizing that the event took place in the past. Three examples are shown in (2); in (2c) the prefix seems to prevent **pronominal lengthening.**

(2a) ᏣᏩᏦᏔᏅᎢ
jaàwajootanvv́ʔi
ji-agi-ajootan-vv́ʔi
REL-1B-ride:CMP-EXP
'I rode it.'

(2b) ᏦᎳ ᏥᏥᏁᎸᎢ
joola jijiìneélv́vʔi
joola ji-jii-hneél-vv́ʔi
tobacco REL-1A.AN-give:CMP-EXP
'I gave him tobacco.'

(2c) ᏣᎦᎵᏍᎬᎢ
jagáaliisgvv́ʔi
ji-a-gáaliisg-vv́ʔi
REL-3A-be.sunny:INC-EXP
'It was sunny.'

Another important function of this prefix is to create a **relative clause,** a type of **subordinate clause** that modifies a noun. Three examples are given in (3). In

(3c) a **highfall tone** indicating **subordination** (SUB) is inserted on the rightmost **long vowel** of the subordinated verb, with no long vowel.

(3a) ᏥᎩᎾᏚᎵᏍᎬ ᎠᏜᏗᏝᎢ Track 81
jiginaduuliisgv́ adladíitlaʔi
ji-ginii-aduuliisg-v́ adladíitlaʔi
REL-1B.DL-want:INC-DVB car

ᎦᏳᎳ ᎩᎶ ᎤᏩᏎᎢ
gáayuùla kilo uùhwaseʔi
gáayuùla kilo uu-hwas-eʔi
already someone 3B-buy:CMP-NXP
'The car we want has already been bought.'

(3b) ᎠᏏᏬ ᏥᏍᎩᏅᏁᎸ ᏥᏖᏍᎦ
ahnawo jisginv́vneelv́ jiìteesga
a-hnawo ji-sgi-nv́vneel-v́ ji-hteesga
3A-shirt REL-2/1-give(flexible):CMP-DVB 1A-iron:PRC
'I am ironing the shirt that you gave me.'

(3c) ᏱᎦᏪᏍᏗ ᏥᎦᏁᎵᏗᎭ ᏙᏳ ᏍᏓᏱ
yigawéésdi jiganehldíha dooyu sdááyi
yi-ga-weesdi ji-ji-anehldíha dooyu sdááyi
NI2-3A-say:INF\INS REL-1A-translate:PRC\SUB very hard
'The word I'm translating is very hard.'

One way of expressing a 'why' question is by starting a sentence with the question word *gado* and prefixing *ji-* to the verb. Unlike adjectival clauses, these constructions do not have the highfall tone. Three examples are shown in (4); in (4b) and (4c) *gado* appears with a **postfix**.

(4a) ᎦᏙ ᏣᏠᎯᎭ
gado chadloohíha
gado ji-hi-adloohíha
what REL-2A-cry:PRC
'Why are you crying?'

(4b) ᎦᏙᏅ ᏥᎩᏙᎵᏨ
gadohnv jiìgiidoólîîjv
gado=hnv ji-iigii-doólîîj-v
what=CN REL-1B.PL-pity:CMP-EXP
'Why did she forgive us?'

(4c)
ᎦᏙᎨ ᏥᏚᎯᎶᎠ ᏗᎦᏚᎴᏂ
gadoke jììduuhiilóoʔa diiktuuléeni
gado=ke ji-iidii-uuhiilóoʔa diiktuuléeni
why=OQ REL-1A.PL-wash:PRC car
'Why are we washing the car?'

The relativizer *ji-* is distinguished from the command *jii-* prefix (discussed in chapter 5) by **vowel length.** In (5a) the long vowel of the command prefix prevents vowel deletion, while in (5b) the **short vowel** of the relativizer prefix is deleted with the subsequent aspiration of the /j/.

(5a)
ᏞᏍᏗ ᏥᎯᎸᎾ
hlesdi jiihíhlvv́na
hlesdi jii-hi-hlvv́na
NEG.COM COM-2A-sleep:IMM
'Don't go to sleep!'

(5b)
ᎦᏙ ᏥᎸᎾ
gado chihlvv́na
gado ji-hi-hlvv́na
what REL-2A-sleep:IMM
'Why did you go to sleep?'

Also, the command prefix lengthens a following vowel and the relativizer does not. In (6a) the short vowel of *ni-* is deleted, while in (6b) it is lengthened and not deleted.

(6a) Track 82
ᎦᏙ ᎮᎵᏍᎬ ᏥᏂᏫ
gado heelîisgv jihniwi
gado hi-eelîisg-v ji-ni-hi-wi
what 2A-think:INC-EXP REL-NI-2A-say:IMM
'What did you mean when you said that?'

(6b)
ᏏᏊ ᏥᏂᎯᏫ
siígwu jiiniíhiwi
siígwu jii-ni-hi-wi
again COM-NI-2A-say:IMM
'Say it again!'

10.1.2. *ni-* (NI) Prepronominal Prefix

This prefix has several different functions that seem to elude easy generalization; for this reason it is simply referred to as the ***ni-* prefix**. One of its most common functions is to refer to a completed action, in which case it is often translated as 'it'. Two examples with the verb 'do' are shown in (7). While this prefix is not mandatory for this verb, it usually occurs on the verb when referring to a past event.

(7a)
ᎦᏙ ᎤᏍᏗ ᎦᏳᎳ ᏂᏣᏛᏁᎸ ᎪᎯᎦ
gado úúsd gáàyula nijadvv́neelv kohiga
gado úúsdi gáàyula ni-ja-advneel-v kohiga
what thing already NI-2B-do:CMP-EXP today
'What have you already done today?'

(7b)
ᎣᏍᏓ ᏏᏛᎦ
óósda hnadvv̀ga
óósda ni-hi-advv̀ga
good NI-2A-do:IMM
'You did it well.'

In (8a) the *ni-* prefix is used to refer to a specific period that is still continuing into the present; it also appears on the noun meaning 'year'. In (8b) the period finished in the past, so the verb does not take the prefix because it indicates a completed action. The noun 'year' in this second sentence appears with the distributive.

(8a)
ᎯᏍᎩ ᎾᏕᏘᏱ ᏃᏥᏁᎶ ᎫᏐ
hisgi nadeetiy noòjiineélo guusó
hisgi ni-adeetiya ni-oojii-neél-o guusa-ʔi
five NI-year NI-1A.PL.EX-reside:INC-HAB Muskogee-LOC
'We have been living in Muskogee for five years.'

(8b)
ᏍᎪᎯ ᏧᏕᏘᏴᏓ ᎤᏪᎳᏗᏙᎸ ᎦᏘᏲ
sgoóhi juudeetiyv́v́da uùhweldíidoolv gaátíiyo
sgoóhi di-uu-adeetiyv́v́da uu-ehldíidool-v gaátíiyo
ten DST2-3B-year 3B-take.part:CMP-EXP stomp ground
'He took part in the stomp dance activities for ten years.'

The *ni-* prefix also indicates an event that almost took place. To convey this meaning the prefix is used in conjunction with the word *hale*. An example of this construction is given in (9).

(9) ᎭᎴᏊ ᏂᏓᏋᎨᏫᏍᎪ ᏗᏍᏚᎢᏍᏗ
haléegwu nidagwvvgewsgo diisduʔíisdi
hale=gwu ni-dee-agi-vvgewsg-o di-a-sduʔìisdi
almost=DT NI-DST-1B-forget:INC-HAB DST2-1A-open:INF\INS

ᏱᏗᏆᏂᎩᏌ ᏗᏓᏁᎳ
yidiigwahnigíísa dìidaneéla
yi-di-agi-ahnigiis-a di-iidii-aneéla
IRR-DST2-1B-leave:CMP-CVB TOW-1A.PL-reside:PRC
'I almost forget to bring my keys every time I leave the house.'

Pulte and Feeling (1975: 245) report that the *ni-* prefix also indicates "that the person spoken of is in a lateral position to the speaker." In the example in (10) the prefix seems to reinforce the meaning 'aside'.

(10) Ᏼ ᏂᏨᎦ ᎧᎾᎸᏍᏗ
yv́v́ nichvv̀ga kanalvsdi
yv́v́ ni-ja-hvv̀ga kanalvsdi
aside NI-2B-put.down:IMM anger
'Put anger aside.' (Feeling 1975a:139)

This prefix is frozen on several commonly occurring verbs. It always occurs with the important verb *-alisdiha* 'happen', 'become', as illustrated in (11a) and (11b); it also appears on 'make a sound' in (11c), 'seem' in (11d), and 'fix' in (11e). This use of *ni-* does not have any clear purpose; in fact, it seems to have no meaning whatsoever. If it is left out, however, the verb sounds incorrect.

(11a) ᏂᎦᎵᏍᏗᏍᎪ
nigalsdiisgo
ni-ga-alisdiisg-o
NI-3A-happen:INC-HAB
'It happens.'

(11b) ᎦᎾᎦᏘ ᏄᎵᏍᏔᏅᎢ
gáʔnakti nuùlstanv́v́ʔi
gáʔnakti ni-uu-alistan-v́v́ʔi
doctor NI-3B-become:CMP-EXP
'He became a doctor.'

(11c) ᏩᎦ ᏂᎦᏪᎢ
wahga nigawéeʔi

wahga ni-ga-wéeʔi
cow NI-3A-make.sound:PRC
'The cow is mooing.'

(11d) Ꮔ𐒊Ꮿ ᏂᎬᏩᏍᏓ ᎠᎯᏙ
nvv̀ya nigvvwsda aàhiido
nvv̀ya ni-ga-vvwsda a-hiido
rock NI-3A-seem:PRC 3A-carry:PRC
'It seems like he's carrying the rock around.'

(11e) ᎣᏍᏓ ᏄᏩᏁᎶᏅ ᏏᏊ ᎤᏲᏍᏔᏅ
óósda nuuwaneélóhnv́ siigwu uùyóostanv
óósda ni-uu-vvneél-ohn-v́ siigwu uu-yóo-stan-v
good NI-3B-make:CMP-TRM:CMP-DVB again 3B-break(I)-CAU:CMP-EXP
'After fixing it, he broke it again.'

This prefix is used in conjunction with the **negative deverbalizer** (NDV) to create the meaning 'without'; this construction typically translates into English as 'without doing VERB', 'not having done VERB', or 'before doing VERB'. One of the functions of this construction is **adverbial** (to modify another verb). Two examples are shown in (12); in (12b) the *ni-* prefix and negative deverbalizer suffix attach to the verb 'be' that follows the **main verb.**

(12a) ᏄᏲᏏᏍᎬᎾ ᎠᎵᏍᏓᏯᎲᏍᎦ Track 83
nuuyóosiisgv́v́na aàlsdááỳvvhvsga
ni-uu-yóosiisg-v́v́na a-ali-sdááỳvvhvsga
NI-3B-hungry:INC-NDV 3A-MDL-provide.meal:PRC
'He's eating while he's not hungry.'

(12b) ᏗᎦᏥᏲᏍᏗ ᏂᎨᏒᎾ ᏱᎩ
digaajiiyóósdi nigeesv́v́na yígi
di-gaa-jii-yóosdi ni-gees-v́v́na yi-gi
DST2-GA-1A.AN-shoot:INF\MOD NI-be:INC-NDV IRR-be:IMM\SUB

ᎯᎠ ᏩᏯ Ꮭ ᏱᏗᎦᏥᏛᏗ
hiʔa wahya hla yidigááj̀iidvhdi
hiʔa wahya hla yi-di-gaa-jii-dvhdi
these wolf NEG IRR-DST2-GA-1A.AN-rid:INF
'If I can't shoot these wolves, I can't get rid of them.'

The idea of 'before' for an event that may or may not occur is expressed with a combination of the *ni-* prefix and the negative deverbalizer, as is in (13). The main verb in this example, 'take off', always takes the *ni-* prefix; this prefix also appears on the second verb, indicating that the diving occurs afterward. The **subordinating conjunction** *si* 'before' also appears in this example.

(13)	ᏅᏅᏓᎩ	ᏩᏥ	Ꮟ	ᎠᎹᏱ	ᏫᏂᏣᏕᏗᏅᎾ
	hnv́vnhdági	waáji	si	amaáyi	winijadeetinv́v́na
	ni-hi-v́vnhdági	waáji	si	amaáyi	wi-ni-ja-adeetin-v́v́na
	NI-2A-take.off:IMM	watch	still	into.water	TRN-NI-2B-dive:CMP-NDV

'Take your watch off before you dive into the water.' (Feeling 1975a:147)

The *ni-* prefix often appears with the *gaa-* prefix to indicate that something has not happened in a certain amount of time, as in (14).

(14)	ᏔᎵ	ᏳᏟᎶᏓ	ᎤᏩᏌ	ᏂᎬᏩᎵᏍᏓᏴᏅᎢ
	tal	yuutlilood́	uwaás	niigvvwalsdááỳhnv́v́ʔi
	tali	yuutliloóda	uu-vv́sa	ni-gaa-agi-ali-sdááỳhn-v́v́ʔi
	two	hour	3B-EMP.PRO	NI-GA-1B-MDL-provide.meal:CMP-DVB

'It's been two hours since I ate.'

Ni- also appears on adjectives for 'how' questions when the degree to which a quality exists is questioned, as in (15).

(15a)	ᎯᎳ	ᏂᎪᏍᏓᏯ	ᎯᎠ	ᎭᏰᎵᏍᏗ
	hila	nigoósdaàya	hiʔa	hayelsdi
	hila	ni-ga-oósdaàya	hiʔa	hayelsdi
	how	NI-3A-sharp	this	knife

'How sharp is this knife?'

(15b)	ᎯᎳ	ᎾᏯᏄᎳ	Ꮎ	ᏐᏈᎵ
	hila	nayanúúla	na	soógwili
	hila	ni-a-yanúúla	na	soógwili
	how	NI-3A-fast	that	horse

'How fast is that horse?'

To express the idea of 'every time' the *ni-* prefix is used instead of the irrealis *yi-* if an action referred to actually did happen. These two usages are contrasted in (16).

(16a)	ᏄᎦᏁᏂᏒ	ᎦᎷᎪ
	nuugaahnaniisv	gáʔluhgo

ni-uu-gaahnan-iis-v́ ga-ʔluhg-o
NI-3B-rain:CMP-DPL:CMP-DVB 3A-arrive:INC-HAB
'Every time it rained, he arrived.'

(16b) ᏳᎦᎿᎾᏭ ᎦᎷᎪ
yuúgáàhnanawu gáʔluhgo
yi-uu-gaahnan-a=wu ga-ʔluhg-o
IRR-3B-rain:CMP-CVB=DT 3A-arrive:INC-HAB
'Every time it rains, he arrives.'

Ni- also appears in a special construction where it combines with a pronominal prefix and a final suffix; this construction is unusual because it appears not to have any stem. Two examples are shown in (17).

(17a) ᎯᏍᎩ ᏃᏥᎡᏍᏗ
hisgi noòjiiʔéesdi
hisgi ni-oojii-éesdi
five NI-1A.PL-PFT
'There will be five of us.'

(17b) ᏦᏊ ᎾᏂᎣ
jógwu naàniiʔo
jó=gwu ni-anii-o
three=DT NI-3A.NS-HAB
'There are usually only three of them.'

A special usage of the *ni-* prefix is its appearance before the **toward prefix** *da-* on Infinitive stems, as in (18). The distributive appears between these two other prepronominal prefixes here in its variant form [*doo*] because it precedes the toward prefix.

(18) ᎪᏬᏪᎵᏍ ᏂᏙᏓᏥᎾᏫᏗ ᏕᏨᏏᏫᏎ
goohweelis nidoodajiinawiídi déejvvkewse
goohweeli=s ni-dee-da-iijii-nawiídi dee-iijii-vvkews-e
paper=Q NI-DST-TOW-2B.PL-bring:INF DST-2B.PL-forget:CMP-NXP
'Did you forget to bring the paper?'

The *ni-* prefix has the secondary form *ii-* or *yi-* (NI2) used on Infinitive stems and **derived** forms, as in (19). Before a vowel the variant form [*iy*] appears; this is demonstrated in (19b).

(19a) ᎢᏣᏛᏅᏗ ᏣᏁᏟᎳᏁᎢᏍ
iijadvvhndi jaanehltanéʔis

ii-ja-advvhndi   ja-xxnehltan-éʔi=s
NI2-2B-do:INF   2B-try:CMP-NXP=Q
'Did you try to do it?'

(19b) ᏗᏕᏲᎲᏍᎩ   ᎢᏳᎵᏍᏙᏗ   ᎠᏕᏠᏆ
diideehyóóhvsgi   iyulsdohdi   aàdeehlgwa
di-a-adaa-eehyoóhvsg-i   ii-uu-alsdohdi   a-adeehlohgwa
DST2-3A-MDL-teach:INC-AGT   NI2-3B-beome:INF   3A-learn:PRC
'He is studying to become a teacher.'

Ni- is found frozen on many nouns referring to time or quantity. Some of these words are listed in (20). The examples in (20a–e) bear the *ii-* form and are probably derived from verbs.

(20a)	ᎢᏧᏕᏘᏴᏓ	ijuudeetiýv́da	'years (number of)' Track 84
(20b)	ᎢᏯᏔᏬᏍᏔᏅᎢ	iyatahwoòstanv́v́ʔi	'minute'
(20c)	ᎢᏳᏟᎶᏓ	iyuuhliilóóda	'hour'
(20d)	ᎢᏳᏩᎪᏗ	iyuwáákdi	'time(s)'
(20e)	ᎢᏳᎾᏙᏓᏆᏍᏗ	iyuunadoódagwaàsdi	'week'
(20f)	ᏂᎦᏓ	nigááda	'all'
(20g)	ᏂᎪᎯᎸ	nigohiilv	'always'

10.1.3. Toward (TOW) Prepronominal Prefix

The prefix *di-* indicates an action that is facing or approaching the speaker. This prefix can be contrasted with the translocative (TRN) prefix *wi-*, which indicates motion away from the speaker. The *di-* itself undergoes the same changes as the *di-* distributive (DST2), appearing with a long vowel before a deleted /a/ and as [*j*] before the vowels /e/, /o/, and /u/. In (21a) it appears on the verb 'be'. In (21b) the vowel of the prefix is lengthened to indicate a deleted *a-* pronominal prefix, and in (21c) the [*j*] variant appears. Vowel deletion results in aspiration in (21d). In (21a) the perspective is from 'the top of the hill', while in (21b) the prefix indicates that the action taking place is view of the speaker.

(21a) ᏭᎷᏣᏃ   ᎦᎸᎾᏗ   ᏗᎨᏒ
wúúluhjahnóo   galv́v́nad   digeèsv
wi-uu-ʔluhj-a=hnóo   galv́v́nadi   di-geès-v
TRN-3B-arrive:CMP-CVB=CN   on.top.of   TOW-be:INC-EXP

ᏩᏯ   ᎤᏙᎯᏎ
wahya   uùtohise

wahya uu-atohis-e
wolf 3B-whoop:CMP-NXP
'When he got to the top of the hill, the wolf whooped.' (The Wolf and the Crawdad, lines 17–18)

(21b) ᏗᏕᎳ ᏗᎩᎠ
adeel diigíʔa
adeela di-a̧-gíʔ-a
money TOW-3A-pick.up:PRC
'Over that way someone is picking up money.'

(21c) ᎣᏂᏃ ᎣᏓᎸ Ꮎ ᏧᎴᏅ
oohnihno oodalv na juuleenv́
oohni=hno oodalv na di-uu-aleen-v́
last=CN mountain that TOW-3B-start(I):CMP-DVB
'. . . the last mountain where he started.' (The Turtle and the Rabbit, line 51)

(21d) ᏖᎾ
teèna
di-hi-eèna
TOW-2A-go:IMM
'Come here!'

Despite similarities in form, the toward prefix is distinct from the distributive prefix. (22) demonstrates that both prefixes can occur on the same verb. When they do, the distributive prefix appears as [*doo*]. In this example the form [*doo*] causes a **high tone** to appear on the following toward prefix; because this latter prefix is lengthened, it is realized as a **falling tone.**

(22) ᏙᏗᏍᎪᏍᎦ Track 85
doodîisgoosga
dee-di-a-asgoosga
DST-TOW-3A-dig:PRC
'He is digging over there.'

The secondary form of the toward prefix is *da-*, which appears on verbs ending in the **experienced past.** This form of the toward prefix has the abbreviation TOW2; an example is shown in (23c). This form becomes [*day*] before vowels other than /a/ or /i/, as seen in (23a) and (23b). In (23d) the combination of *da-* and the vowel /a/ creates [*dvvgi*].

(23a) ᎣᎩᎾᎵᎢ ᏂᏓᏳᏅᏅ
oogínalííʔi nidayuunv́vnv́
ooginii-alííʔi ni-da-uu-nv́vn-v́
1B.DL.EX-friend NI-TOW2-3B-send:CMP-DVB

ᎪᏪᎵ ᏥᎪᎵᏰᎠ
goohweél jigooliíyéʔa
goohweéli ji-gooliíyéʔa
letter 1A-read:PRC
'I am reading a letter [sent here] from a friend.'

(23b) ᎠᎱᏣᏬᎵᏛ ᏓᏳᎦᏛᎴᏒ ᏧᏠᎦᎴᏓ
ahuujawoóldv dayuuktv́vleesv juudlogaléeda
ahuujawoóldv da-uu-gahtv́vlees-v juudlogaléeda
chimney TOW2-3B-come.through:CMP-EXP Santa.Claus
'Santa Claus came through the chimney.'

(23c) ᏓᎩᎾᏓᎾᏏᏃᎮᎵ
daginadansiinooheéli
da-ginii-adansiinooheéli
MOT-1B.DL-crawl.toward:PRC
'He's crawling to us.'

(23d) ᎢᏢᎬ ᏛᎩᎶᏒᎢ
ihlgv dvvgiloosvv́ʔi
ihlgv da-agi-aloos-vv́ʔi
tree TOW2-1B-fall:CMP-EXP
'I fell from the tree.'

The toward prefix appears on nouns as well as on verbs to indicate a specific place rather than its orientation to the speaker. In (24a) it appears on the verb, while in (24b) it appears on the noun to indicate a specific room. In (24b) the translocative prefix appears on the verb.

(24a) ᎠᎹᏰᏟ ᏗᏇᏁᏅᏒᎢ Track 86
amáyéehli diigweenvvsv́ʔi
ama+ayéehli di-agi-eenvvs-v́v́ʔi
water+center TOW-1B-go:CMP-DVB
'My home is the United States.' (Feeling 1975a:44)

(24b) ᏐᎢ ᏗᎧᏅᏑᎸ ᏩᏴᎭ
sóʔi dikanv́vsuulv waàyvv́ha

sóʔi di-kanv́vsuulv wi-a-yvv́ha
other TOW-room TRN-3A-enter:IMM
'He went in another room.' (Feeling 1975a:154)

Koops (2008a:3) contrasts the toward prefix with the translocative prefix, stating that the translocative assumes "a prior change of location to the current location," whereas the toward prefix merely assumes that the participant has been at the location. Two of his examples are shown in (25).

(25a) ᏚᎵᏏ ᏩᏘᏍᏛ
tulsi waàgwatvsv
tulsa-ʔi wi-agi-atvs-v
Tulsa-LOC TRN-1B-grow(I):CMP-EXP
'I grew up in Tulsa (was born here, then moved there).' (Koops 2008a:3)

(25b) ᏚᎵᏏ ᏗᏘᏍᏛ
tulsi diigwatvsv
tulsa-ʔi di-agi-atvs-v
Tulsa-LOC TOW-1B-grow(I):CMP-EXP
'I grew up in Tulsa (and was born there).' (Koops 2008a:3)

A slightly different prepronominal prefix known as the **motion toward** prefix (MOT) only appears on a few **intransitive** verbs of motion. This prefix is described in the following section.

10.1.4. Motion Toward (MOT) Prepronominal Prefix

The motion toward prefix *da-* is used only on a small set of intransitive verbs of motion when the action is approaching the speaker. This prefix has a similar form and function to the toward prefix but it has a much more limited use; the verbs using this prefix generally end in [*i*] in the **Present Continuous:** *-adanasini* 'crawl', *-nohili* 'fly', *-aʔi* 'walk', *-gahti* 'head toward', and *-adahtli* 'run'. The extent to which this prefix is distinguishable from the toward prefix seems to vary among speakers. Its basic form is exemplified in (26a), while (26b) shows the inserted /y/ that appears before all vowels except /i/ and /a/. In (26c) the combination of *da-* with a following vowel /a/ results in the form [*dvv*].

(26a) ᏓᎦᏃᎯᎵ
daganohili
da-ga-nohili

MOT-3A-fly:PRC
'It's flying (in the direction of the speaker).'

(26b) ᏓᏳᏓᏒᏂᏴᏒ
dayuudansinvsv
da-uu-adanasinvs-v
MOT-3B-crawl:CMP-EXP
'The snake crawled (in the direction of the speaker).'

(26c) Ꮽ̋Ꮯ
dv́v́tli
da-a-adihtli
MOT-3A-run:PRC
'He's running (in the direction of the speaker).' (Pulte and Feeling 1975:251)

The motion toward prefix takes the secondary form *di-* (MOT2) with the **habitual,** nonexperienced past, and **progressive future** suffixes. Three examples are shown in (27); in (27b) the following /a/ is deleted, causing the vowel of the pronominal prefix to be lengthened. Before all other vowels this prefix has the variant form [*j*]; an example is given in (27c).

(27a) ᏗᎦᏃᎯᎵᏐ
diganohiliso
di-ga-nohilis-o
MOT2-3A-fly:INC-HAB
'It flies (in the direction of the speaker).'

(27b) ᏗᏓᏒᏏᏂᏐᎢ
diidánsiiniìsóoʔi
di-a-adánsiiniìs-óoʔi
MOT2-3A-crawl:INC-HAB
'He habitually crawls (in the direction of the speaker).' (Pulte and Feeling 1975:251)

(27c) ᏧᏓᏒᏂᏴᏎᏍ
judansinvses
di-uu-adansinvs-e=s
MOT2-3B-crawl:CMP-NXP=Q
'Did the snake crawl (in the direction of the speaker)?'

The completive future, toward, and motion toward prefixes have similarities in form and meaning and historically were probably a single prefix. But they have developed clear enough distinctions in form and usage to justify their description as three separate prefixes.

An exception to the pattern of forming the future occurs with motion verbs that end in /i/ in the Present Continuous. The completive future suffix is historically related to this ending; this grammar treats it as part of the stem. Because of this historical link, however, these verbs are able to attach the completive future prefix to their Present Continuous stem. An example is shown in (28).

(28) Ꮼ Ꮒ ꮵ ᎦᏯ ꮎ T — ᎣᏂ ᏥᏓᏯᎢ
ohni jidayááʔi
ohni ji-da-a-aaʔi
behind REL-CMF-walk:PRC\SUB
'The one that's coming after me [Jesus referring to John the Baptist].'
(*Cherokee New Testament*, Mathew 3:11)

10.1.5. Iterative (ITR) Prepronominal Prefix

This prefix indicates that an action has been repeated. It has two different forms depending on what kind of stem or final suffix is present, although which stems or final suffixes take which form depends on the speaker. Cook (1979:82) reports that this prefix displays much dialectal variation in North Carolina Cherokee.

Three examples of this prefix are shown in (29). As seen in (29b), some speakers use an initial /h/ with this prefix.

(29a) ᎢᎯᏁᏟᏓ
iiháneehlda
ii-hi-aneehlda
ITR-2A-try:IMM
'Try it again!'

(29b) ᎯᎨᎩᎪᏩᏘ
hiigvvgigohwti
hii-gvvgi-gohwti
ITR-3NS/1-see:PRC
'They're seeing me again.'

(29c) ᎦᏯᎥ ᎢᎲᏅᎬᎪᎦ ᎤᏌᏄᎵᎣ ᎢᎭᏌᏗᎬᎦ
gáayuul iihvnvvgóoga uusanuulííʔo iihasaldv́vga

gáayuula ii-hi-vnvvgóoga uusanuulííʔo ii-hi-asaldv́vga
already ITR-2A-appear:IMM fast ITR-2A-lift:IMM
'You have lifted yourself up very fast.'

This prefix is less common than the other prefixes; moreover, it has some unusual variants depending on the context in which it appears. Three examples are shown in (30). In (30a) the prefix inserts a **glottal stop** before a vowel. For some speakers, however, the iterative merely appears as a high tone on the vowel before the **Set B third person prefix,** as shown in (30b). In (30c) the combination of the distributive and the iterative results in [*doo*].

(30a) Ꮭ ᏱᎤᏬᏂᏎ
hla yiiʔuuwoonise
hla yi-ii-uu-woonis-e
NEG IRR-ITR-3B-speak:CMP-NXP
'He didn't speak again.'

(30b) ᎺᎵᏃ ᏚᏓᏅᏁᎸᎢ
meélíhno dúudaanv́vneelvv́ʔi
meéli=hno dee-ii-uu-adaad-nv́vneel-vv́ʔi
Mary=CN DST-ITR-3B-RFL-give:CMP-EXP
'And Mary gave them right back to him.' (Scancarelli 1987:88)

(30c) ᏅᏆᏞ ᏙᏥᏩᎦᏔ
nvvgwale doojiiwakta
nvvgwale dee-ii-jii-hwakta
again DST-ITR-1A.AN-find:IMM
'I found them again.'

If a vowel precedes this prefix, it becomes [*vv*], as in (31).

(31a) ᎦᏙᎲ ᎤᏤᏩᏍᏗ ᎤᏅᏗ ᏅᎯᏴᏂᏏ
gadoòhv uujeéwáàsdi uunvv́di nvvhiiyv́vnisi
gadoòhv uu-ajeéwáàsdi uunvv́di ni-ii-hii-v́vnisi
why 3B-spill:INF milk NI-ITR-2A.AN-cause:IMM
'Why did you make him spill his milk?'

(31b) Ꮭ ᏴᏆᏚᎵ ᎠᎩᏛᎪᏗ ᏗᎦᏃᎩᏍᏗ
tla yvvgwaduuli aktvgoodi digahnoogíísdi
tla yi-ii-agi-aduuli agi-ahtvgoodi di-ga-hnoogiisdi
NEG IRR-ITR-1B-want:PRC 1B-hear:INF DST2-3A-sing:INF\INS
'I never want to hear that song again.'

(31c) ᎾᏅ ᏧᏲᎱᏒ
naanv juuyoohuusv́
naanv di-uu-yoohuus-v́
where TOW-3B-die:CMP-DVB

ᏨᏚᏙ ᎪᎯ ᏥᎦ
jvvduùdo koohi jig
di-ii-dee-uu-adaa-o koohi ji-ga
TOW-ITR-DST-3B-MDL-name:PRC today REL-be:PRC
'To this day its name is "where one died."' (The Search Party, line 10)

Pulte and Feeling (1975:254) report a secondary form [*vv*] that appears before the prefix *gaa-*; one of their examples is given in (32).

(32) ᎥᎦᏣᏬᏂᏒᎢ
vvgáajawoòniísv́v́ʔi
vv-gaa-ja-woòniís-vv́ʔi
ITR2-GA-2B-speak:CMP-EXP\SUB
'... since you have spoken again.' (Pulte and Feeling 1975:254)

Pulte and Feeling (1975:254) also state that with the Infinitive, nonmotion Present Continuous, and experienced past suffix the form *vv-* (ITR2) is used. An example with the experienced past suffix is shown in (33).

(33) ᎥᏣᏬᏂᏒᎢ
vvjawoòniísvv́ʔi
vv-ja-woòniís-vv́ʔi
ITR2-2B-speak:CMP-EXP
'You spoke again.' (Pulte and Feeling 1975:254)

Other speakers do not make this distinction for the Present Continuous, as seen from the example in (34).

(34) ᎢᎦᏁᏍᎨᎭ
iigáànesgéeha
ii-ji-ahnesgéeha
ITR-1A-build:PRC
'I'm building it again.'

For some speakers the iterative is not used on the Immediate stem and is replaced by the relativizer (REL). In (35), for example, the relativizer forms a 'why' question with the Immediate stem.

(35) ᎦᏙᎲ ᏥᎦᎦᏔᎲᎾ
gadoòhv jiìgagaàtahvv́na
gadoòhv jii-ji-agahtahvv́na
why REL-1A-turn.back:IMM
'Why did I turn back?'

A prepronominal prefix always appears on the Present Continuous form of the irregular verb 'be'; this prefix is usually the iterative. An example is shown in (36a). It appears on other forms of the verb as well; (36b) is an example with the Incompletive stem.

(36a) ᎤᏬᏚᎭ ᎢᎦ ᏣᎳᎩ ᎦᏬᏂᎯᏍᏗ
uwoodúúha iíga jalagi gawooníìhisdi
uu-oodúúha ii-ga jalagi ga-wooniihisdi
3B-beautiful ITR-be:PRC Cherokee 3A-speak:INF\INS
'Cherokee is a beautiful language.'

(36b) ᏗᏍᏚᎢᏓ ᎢᎨᏎᏍᏗ
diisduʔíída iigeeséésdi
di-a-sduʔii-da ii-gees-éesdi
DST2-3A-open-PCP ITR-be:INC-PFT\SUB

ᏗᏦᎳᏂ ᏕᎯᏍᏚᏅᎢ
dijoólaʔni deehisduunvvʔi
di-joólaʔni dee-hi-sduun-vvʔi
DST2-window DST-2A-open:CMP-FCM
'If the windows happen to be open, close them.' (Feeling 1975a:135)

This prefix sometimes appears on a verb in conjunction with the question word to ask a 'why' question, as in (37).

(37a) ᎦᏙᎲ ᎥᎾᏂᎩ
gadoòhv vv̀nahnigi
gadoòhv ii-anii-ahnigi
why ITR-3A.NS-leave:IMM
'Why did they leave?'

(37b) ᎦᏙᎲ ᏣᎳᎩ ᎢᎭᏕᎸᏆ
gadoòhv jalag iihadeehlgwa
gadoòhv jalagi ii-hi-adeehlgwa
why Cherokee ITR-2A-learn:PRC
'Why are you learning Cherokee?'

10.1.6. *gaa-* (GA) Prepronominal Prefix

The most common use of this prefix is to indicate that something has not happened for a certain period. This prefix is one of the least common of all the prepronominal prefixes. Two examples are shown in (38). For some speakers this prefix occurs in conjunction with the *ni-* prefix, as in (38b). As seen in both examples, this 'since' usage puts the verb in a subordinate relationship to another verb; a corresponding highfall tone (indicated by \SUB) appears on the rightmost long vowel.

(38a) ᎦᎩᏂᎪᎲᎢ
gaaginiigoohv̋v́ʔi
gaa-ginii-gooh-vv́ʔi
GA-1B.DL-see:CMP-EXP\SUB
'since you and I saw it' (Pulte and Feeling 1975:255)

(38b)	ᎪᎯᎩ	ᏥᎨᏒ	ᏂᎦᏥᎪᎥ	ᏌᎻ
	kohíigi	jigeèsv	nigaajiigoʔv́	saami
	kohíigi	ji-geès-v	ni-gaa-jii-goh-v	saami
	long.time	REL-be:INC-EXP	NI-GA-1A.AN-see:CMP-EXP\SUB	Sam

'It's a long time since I've seen Sam.' (Walker 1975:218)

This prefix has a variety of different forms depending on the context in which it appears. Two examples are shown in (39). In (39a) it becomes [*gvv*] when followed by /a/. Pulte and Feeling (1975:255) point out that the form [*gvvwa*] results from a combination of the Set B third person prefix *uu-* with *gaa-*; their example is given in (39b).

(39a)	Ꮭ	ᏱᏫᎨᏙ	ᏓᎵᏆ
	tla	yiwigeédo	dalig
	tla	yi-wi-ji-eédo	daligwa
	NEG	IRR-TRN-1A-be.at:PRC	Tahlequah

ᎬᎩᎾᏗᏅᏓ	ᎦᎵᏦᏕ
gvvgindiinvv́d	gahljoóde
gaa-agi-nadiinvv́-da	gahljoóde
GA-1B-sell-PCP	house

'I haven't returned to Tahlequah since my house was sold.'

(39b)	ᏑᏓᎵᏁ	ᏐᎢ	ᏥᎧᎸ	ᎬᏪᏙᎸᎢ
	suudaliiné	sóʔi	jikaʔlv	gvvweedoolv̋v́ʔi
	suudali-iine	sóʔi	ji-kaʔlv	gaa-uu-eedool-vv́ʔi

six-ORD other REL-past.month GA-3B-be.at:CMP-EXP\SUB
'He hasn't been here since the sixth of last month.' (Pulte and Feeling 1975:255)

(40) is an example of the form [*gaay*] that appears before vowels other than /a/ or /u/.

(40) ᏫᎦᏲᎩᏲᎵ
wigaayoògiihyoohlv́
wi-gaa-oogii-hyoohl-v
TRN-GA-1B.PL.EX-bring:CMP-EXP\SUB
'Since we all brought it.' (Scancarelli 2005:367)

As seen in (41), *gaa-* used in conjunction with irrealis *yi-* can result in a more emphatic negative. In both examples this combination occurs on the last word in the sentence; in (41b) the [*gvvwa*] form occurs before /u/.

(41a) ᎾᎩᏍᏕᎵᏍᎬ ᏂᎨᏎᏍᏗ
naksdeeliisgv́ nigeeséesd
ni-agi-sdeeliisg-v́v́na ni-gees-éesdi
NI-1B-help:INC-NDV NI-be:INC-PFT

Ꮭ ᏰᎸ ᏱᎦᏥᏍᏆᏗ
tla yeelv yigaájiìsgwádi
tla yi-eelv yi-gaa-ji-sgwádi
NEG IRR-able IRR-GA-1A-finish:PRC
'Without him helping me I won't be able to finish.'

(41b) ᏧᎵᏨᏯᏍᏗ ᏱᎨᏎ
juulichvv́yaàsdi yigeèsé
di-uu-alichvv́yaàsdi yi-geès-e
DST2-3B-brave IRR-be:INC-NXP\SUB

Ꮭ ᏱᎬᏩᎵᏘᏎ
hla yigvvwahltíise
hla yi-gaa-uu-alihtíis-e
NEG IRR-GA-3B-run:CMP-NXP
'If he were brave he wouldn't have run away.' (Feeling 1975a:137)

Gaa- also appears with a verb in the Infinitive stem and a Set B prefix; this construction indicates an ability to perform an action. As demonstrated in (42), this usage requires a **modal tone** (MOD). The change in tone is indicated by the abbreviation \MOD.

(42) ᎦᏦᏪᎶᏗ ᏱᎩ ᎭᏛᎩᏍᎬ
gaajoohwéélodi yígi háʔtvvgíisgv́
<u>gaa</u>-ja-oohweélodi yi-gi hi-ahtvvgíisg-v́
GA-2B-write:INF\<u>MOD</u> IRR-be:IMM\SUB 2A-hear:INC-DVB

ᏯᏕᏠᏆ ᏣᎳᎩ ᏣᏬᏂᎯᏍᏗᎢ
hyadeehlohgwa jalagi jawooniihisdííʔi
yi-hi-adeehlohgwa jalagi ja-wooniihisdííʔi
IRR-2A-learn:IMM Cherokee 2B-speak:INF
'If you can write down what you hear, you can learn to speak Cherokee.' (*Cherokee Phoenix*, May 2006)

The ability to perform an action is indicated by the *gaa-* prefix attached to an Infinitive stem; this stem also undergoes a modal tone change, as in (43a). By way of contrast the same sentence is shown in (43b) without the prepronominal prefix, resulting in an **obligation Infinitive.**

(43a) Ꮭ ᎪᎱᏍᏗ ᎦᏳᏅᏛᏁᏗ ᏱᎩ
hla gohúúsdi gaayuundv́v́hndi yigi
hla gohúúsdi <u>gaa</u>-uunii-advv̀hndi yi-gi
NEG something GA-3B.NS-do:INF\MOD IRR-be:IMM
'They can't do anything.'

(43b) Ꮭ ᎪᎱᏍᏗ ᏳᏅᏛᏁᏗ ᏱᎩ
hla gohúúsdi yuundv́v́hndi yigi
hla gohúúsdi yi-uunii-advv̀hndi yi-gi
NEG something IRR-3B.NS-do:INF\MOD IRR-be:IMM
'They shouldn't do anything.'

It is also possible to use both *yi-* and *gaa-* together on the Immediate stem to express lack of ability, as is in (44).

(44) Ꮭ ᏱᎦᏥᎷᎦ
hla yigaajiiluùga
hla yi-gaa-jii-luùga
NEG IRR-GA-1A-kill:IMM
'I still can't kill it.'

Pulte and Feeling (1975:255), as well as Cook (1979:83) and King (1975:69), describe a special form [*gee*] that is used with the second person; some speakers, as seen above in (42), prefer *gaa-*. An example with [*gee*] is given in (45).

(45) ᎨᏣᎪᏂᎢ
geejagoohv́v́ʔi
gee-ja-gooh-v́v́ʔi
GA-2B-see:CMP-DVB
'Since you saw it.' (Pulte and Feeling 1975:255)

Cook (1979:75, 84) describes an unusual form of the third person **object focus** prefix that appears when preceded by the *gaa-* prefix. This prefix *aji-*([*ag*] before vowels) becomes [*eji*] ([*eg*] before vowels); furthermore, /y/ is inserted between the *gaa-* and the object focus prefix. An example of this less commonly seen combination is given in (46) below. In this instance the prefix appears on an **agentive** noun.

(46) ᏂᎦᏰᏥᏂᏱᏍᎩ
nigayejiniiyíísg
ni-gaa-aji-niiyiísg-i
NI-GA-3O-catch:INC-AGT
'. . . until he caught him.' (The Wolf and the Crawdad, line 38)

10.1.7. Toward Command (TOC) Prepronominal Prefix

This prefix is similar to the motion toward prefix in that it indicates movement toward the speaker, but it is only used with commands. One of its most common occurrences is in the command in (47a); two other examples are also given.

(47a) ᎡᎯᏴᎭ
eehiyvv́ha
ee-hi-yvv́ha
TOC-2A-enter:IMM
'Come in!'

(47b) ᎡᏍᎩᏍᏕᎳ
eesgiisdeèla
ee-iisgii-sdeèla
TOC-2/1.PL-help:IMM
'Come and help us (you're over there).'

(47c) ᎡᏍᎩᏂᏍᏓᏆᏚᎦ ᏗᏍᏓᏓᏟᎶᏍᏗᏍᎩ
eesginiisdáagwaduùga diisdadaadliiloòsdíísgi
ee-sginii-sdáagwaduùga di-iisdii-adaadliilóosdiisg-i

TOC-2/1.DL-follow:IMM DST2-2A.DL-photgraph:INC-AGT
'You two photographers follow me!'

The toward command prefix is incompatible with the distributive and is replaced by the toward prefix (TOW) when that prefix is present. In (48a), for example, the toward command prefix appears when a **singular object** is indicated, while in (48b) the presence of a **nonsingular** object causes the toward prefix *di-* to appear. In this example the distributive assumes the variant form [*doo*] before the toward prefix.

(48a) RᏍᏋᏏ
eskvsi
ee-sgi-hvsi
TOC-2/1-give:IMM
'Pass me it.'

(48b) ᏙᏗᏍᏋᏏ
doodiskvsi
dee-di-sgi-hvsi
DST-TOW-2/1-give:IMM
'Pass me them.'

10.2. Order of Prepronominal Prefixes

The order of the prefixes varies slightly depending on the speaker, but some general tendencies remain constant. For example, *yi-* and *ji-* always seem to appear in the first position and cannot co-occur. Their usage is demonstrated in (49). In (49a) and (49b) *yi-* and *ji-* appear before the distributive prefix. (49c) demonstrates the incompatibility of irrealis *yi-* and relativizer *ji-*; in this case the irrealis replaces the relativizer. This example also shows that the distributive appears as *di-* when following the irrealis. (49d) demonstrates that the irrealis precedes the iterative. Several of the prefixes undergo further changes when combined with other prefixes; these changes are described in the discussions of the individual prefixes. In (49e) *ji-* comes before *wi-* and *wi-* comes before *dee-*; the combination of *ji-* and *wi-*produces [*ju*] while the vowel of the distributive is deleted before another vowel. In (49f) the command prefix precedes the distributive and the iterative.

First position pronominal prefixes

(49a) Ꮭ ᏱᏗᏨᏁᎴ ᎠᏕᎳ
tla yidiìjvv̀neéle adeéla

tla yi-di-iijvv-hneél-e adeéla
NEG IRR-DST2-1/2.PL-give(solid):CMP-NXP money
'I didn't give you all the money.'

(49b) ᎯᎢᏛᎾ ᎠᏕᎳ ᏥᏕᏨᏁᎸ
hiʔidvvna adeéla jidéejvvneélv
hiʔi=dvv=na adeéla ji-dee-iijvv-hneél-v
this=EM=FC money REL-DST-1/2.PL-give(solid):CMP-EXP
'This is the money I gave you all.'

(49c) ᎯᎢᏛ ᎠᏕᎳ Ꮭ ᏱᏗᏨᏁᎴ
hiʔidvv adeéla hla yidiijv́v̀neéle
hiʔi=dvv adeéla hla yi-di-iijvv-hneél-e
this=EM money NEG IRR-DST2-1/2.PL-give(solid):CMP-NXP
'This is the money that I didn't give you all.'

(49d) Ꮭ ᏱᎤᎷᏤ
hla yiiʔuulúhje
hla yi-ii-uu-lúhj-e
NEG IRR-ITR-3B-arrive:CMP-NXP
'He didn't come back.'

(49e) ᎧᎵᏛ ᏧᏙᎩᏅ
kalídvv judoògiihnv
kali=dvv ji-wi-dee-oogii-hn-v
just.now=EM REL-TRN-DST-1B.PL.EX-send:CMP-EXP
'We already sent them.'

(49f) ᏞᏍᏗ ᏥᏙᏍᎩᏴᎩ ᎦᎵᏍᏓᏴᎲᏍᎬᎢ
hleèsdi jiidóoskiyv́vgi galiìsdayvv́hv́v̀sgv́v́ʔi
hleèsdi jii-dee-ii-sgi-hyv́vgi ji-ali-sdayvv́hv́v̀sg-v́v́ʔi
NEG.COM COM-DST-ITR-2/1-tickle:IMM 1A-MDL-provide.meal:INC-DVB
'Don't tickle me while I am eating.' (Feeling 1975a:70)

(50) shows several more examples indicating the ordering of the other prefixes. In (50a) the translocative *wi-* precedes the distributive. In (50b) the completive future *da-* appears before the iterative *ii-* and the toward prefix *da-* precedes the iterative. (50c) demonstrates that the translocative *wi-* precedes the *ni-* prefix.

(50a) ᏝᏏ ᏫᏙᎩᏅ ᏱᎩ
tlasi widoògiihnv yigi

tlasi wi-dee-oogii-hn-v yi-gi
not.yet TRN-DST-1B.PL.EX-send:CMP-EXP IRR-be:IMM
'We haven't sent them yet.'

(50b) ᏛᏓᏁᏍᎨᎯᏌᏂ ᎤᏃᎴ ᎤᏲᏍᏔᏅ
dvvdahnesgehiísáhni uunoole uùyóostanv́
da-ii-iidii-ahnesgehiísáhn-i uunoole uu-yóo-stan-v́
CMF-ITR-1A.PL-build:CMP-CMF tornado 3B-break(I)-CAU:CMP-DVB
'We will build the house again after the tornado destroyed it.'

(50c) ᎦᏙ ᏫᏂᏣᏪᏎ
gado winijaweese
gado wi-ni-ja-wees-e
what TRN-NI-2B-say:CMP-NXP
'What did you say? (talking to someone on the telephone)'

The final prepronominal position is for *gaa-* and *ee-*; only the pronominal prefixes can come after these two prefixes. In (51) the *gaa-* prefix appears after the irrealis in the second clause.

(51) ᎾᎦᎩᏍᏕᎵᏍᎬᎾ ᏂᎨᏎᏍᏗ
naaksdeeliísgv́v́na nigeeséésd
ni-agi-sdeeliísg-v́v́na ni-gees-éesdi
NI-1B-help:INC-NDV NI-be:INC-PFT\SUB

Ꮭ ᏰᎵ ᏱᎦᏥᏍᏆᏘ
hla yeeli yigáàjiìsgwati
hla yi-eeli yi-gaa-ji-sgwati
NEG IRR-able IRR-GA-1A-finish:IMM
'Without him helping me I won't be able to finish.'

As seen in these examples, the prepronominal prefixes interact in various ways with the pronominal prefixes that follow them. In (52a) the toward prefix *di-* causes the removal of the vowel of the pronominal prefix, but at the same time *di-* undergoes a lengthening of its vowel. In (52b) the *wi-* prefix prevents the expected lengthening of the pronominal prefix. In (52c) the long vowel of the distributive prefix is removed before another vowel.

(52a) ᏗᏂᏔᎴᏍᎦ
diiniitaleesga
di-anii-taleesga

TOW-3A.NS-dig:PRC
'They are digging it in front of us'

(52b) GhWδᏍᏕ
waniitaleesga
wi-anii-taleesga
TRN-3A.NS-dig:PRC
'They are digging it (out of sight).'

(52c) ᏫᏓᎪᏩᏘᎭ
widagoohwtíha
wi-dee-a-goohwtíha
TRN-DST-3A-see:PRC
'He sees them.'

As seen above, some prepronominal prefixes change in unpredictable ways when they are adjacent to certain other prepronominal prefixes. For example, in (53) the irrealis appears as [*yu*] before the translocative *wi-*.

(53)	ᏝᏃ	ᏧᎸᏫᏍᏓᏁᎯᏗ	ᏳᏭᎷᏤ
	hlahno	juulvhwsdaanehdi	yuwuulúhje
	hla=hno	di-uu-lvwhisdanehdi	yi-wi-uu-lúhj-e
	NEG=CN	DST2-3B-work:INF	IRR-TRN-3B-arrive:CMP-NXP

'He did not show up for work.' (*Cherokee Phoenix,* November 2006)

Some of the prefixes change the tone of the stem to which they attach, as already shown with the distributive prefix. In (54) the iterative (ITR) appears as a high tone on the following pronominal prefix.

(54) ᎤᎾᏗᏔᎲᎢ
úunadiitahvv̋ʔi
ii-uunii-adiitah-vv̋ʔi
ITR-3B.NS-drink:CMP-EXP
'They drank it again.'

A special form of the distributive [*doo*] appears before the completive future prefix *da-*, the iterative *ii-*, and the toward prefix *di-*. An example of each is given in (55). In (55a) the irrealis causes a high tone to appear on the **syllable** immediately following the prefix; because the vowel is long, this tone is realized as a falling tone.

(55a)	ᏱᏍᎩᏃᏎᎴᏍ	ᏱᏙᏣᏁᏎ
	yiskinoseelées	yidóòjaneesé

yi-sgi-hnoseel-ée=s yi-dee-ii-ja-nees-e
IRR-2/1-tell:CMP-NXP=Q IRR-DST-ITR-2B-take:CMP-NXP\SUB
'Would you have told me if you had taken them?'

(55b) ᏂᎦᏓᏍ ᏙᏓᏣᏑᎵ
nigáádas doodájasuuli
nigááda=s dee-da-iijii-asuul-i
all=Q DST-CMF-2A.PL-wash.hands:CMP-CMF
'Are you all going to wash your hands?'

(55c) ᏙᎾᏓᎪᎲᎢ
doonadaagoohvvʔi
dee-ii-iinii-adaad-gooh-vvʔi
DST-ITR-1A.DL-RFL-see:CMP-FCM
'Let's see each other again'

(55d) ᏙᏗᏔᎴᏒᎢ
doodiitalesv́v́ʔi
dee-di-a-atales-v́v́ʔi
DST-TOW-3A-make.hole:CMP-DVB
'where the holes are'

10.3. Sources and Additional Reading

Both Cook (1979:55) and King (1975:62) refer to the *ni-* prefix as the partitive. Cook (1979:64) describes the functions as indicating "spatial or temporal parallelism of path or events" and indicates that "partitive" is used for its cognate in the northern Iroquoian languages. Walker (1975:204) translates *ni-* as 'still', 'yet', and 'not yet'. Foley (1980:36) calls this the previative. Cook (1979:55) refers to the relativizer as the positive, while King (1975:61) uses "empirical" and states that "this prefix asserts that the verb should be taken as a matter of fact." Pulte and Feeling (1975:242) use "relative." King (1975:61) says that this prefix is used with past events to indicate that the information has been reliably reported. Cook (1979:57) and King (1975:67) both use "Iterative" for that prepronominal prefix. Pulte and Feeling (1975:253) describe the secondary form of the toward prefix (what they call the cislocative) that appears on verbs ending in the experienced past. Cook (1979:72) states that this change occurs for North Carolina Cherokee with verbs with the experienced past final suffix and agentive nouns as well as verbs in the Immediate and Infinitive stems. King (1975:68) refers to the *gaa-* prefix as the negative and states that it conveys an idea of absolute negation or a negation of some duration. King (1975:62) also describes how it is possible to form "decisively negative verbs" by using three prepronominal prefixes together: the irrealis followed by the iterative then *gaa-*.

10.4. Directions for Further Research

Our understanding of the nuances and ordering of prepronominal prefix usage would be greatly enhanced by corpus studies. Much research remains to be done on the role that dialectal variation plays in the use of these prefixes. Pulte and Feeling (1975:254) state that the completive future, motion toward, and toward prefixes are mutually exclusive but suggest that "further study may indicate that [they] . . . should be analyzed as a single prefix. Such an analysis would require fairly detailed rules to provide the correct form of the prefix in the various contexts." This sort of analysis would be helped by examining large amounts of data.

ELEVEN

Syntax

11.1. Word Order

11.1.1. Grammatical Relations, Animacy, and Word Order

Many languages have what is referred to as a basic word order. English, for example, has an SVO word order: a **subject** followed by a **verb** followed by an **object** ("He reads the book" or "I like Cherokee"). The idea of a basic word order is problematic for Cherokee. While there are word orders that are more common than others, it appears that many different word orders are possible given the right context. This variability is the result of the verb's ability to indicate all the **participants** (the subject and objects) involved with the verb. European languages to varying degrees have **suffixes** on the verb that indicate what the subject of the verb is, while objects are indicated by free-standing **nouns** or **pronouns.** Thus in those languages **transitive** verbs (verbs with subjects and objects) require an independent word (the object) to complete the meaning. In Cherokee such free-standing words are not necessary: the verb supplies enough information to stand on its own as a complete sentence. **Prefixes** indicate the participants involved, while suffixes indicate the **tense, aspect,** and **mood** of the verb. But the prefixes do not always indicate exactly what the subject and the object of the sentence are. For example, in the English sentence 'he saw me' it is readily understood that 'he' is the subject (the one who sees) and 'me' is the object (the person being seen). The Cherokee equivalent of the simple sentence is ambiguous, as seen in (1).

(1) DYAᏲT
aàgigoohv̋ʔi
agi-gooh-v̋ʔi
1B-see:CMP-EXP

'He saw me.'
'I saw it.'

In this example the **stem** (see:CMP) and suffix indicate that an event of seeing took place. The prefix is a **Set B first person singular** prefix (1B) prefix ('I'/'me'). This prefix does not itself indicate if it is a subject or an object. Sentences do not typically exist in isolation, however, and the context helps to determine the meaning. Consider the example in (2).

(2)	Ꮎ	ᎤᎴᏎᏙ	ᎩᏟ	ᎠᎩᎪᎲᎢ
	na	uuleesóód	giihl	aàgigoohvv́ʔi
	na	uu-aleesóóda	giihli	agi-gooh-vv́ʔi
	that	3B-skinny	dog	1B-see:CMP-EXP
	'The skinny dog saw me.'			

In this sentence only one interpretation is possible, and the prefix on the verb only refers to the participant that is being seen: the object. The interpretation is no longer ambiguous because of the importance of **animacy** and the **local person/nonlocal person** distinction in Cherokee grammar. While *agi-* has multiple interpretations, other prefixes have clear meanings that are related to whether one or both of the participants is living. In order to say 'I saw the skinny dog', the prefix *jii-* is required; this single prefix indicates that a first person singular participant is the subject ('I') and a **third person** animate being is the object. This sentence is presented in (3).

(3)	Ꮎ	ᎤᎴᏎᏙ	ᎩᏟ	ᏥᎪᎥᎢ
	na	uuleesóód	giihl	jiigoʔvv́ʔi
	na	uu-aleesóóda	giihli	jii-gooh-vv́ʔi
	that	3B-skinny	dog	1A.AN-see:CMP-EXP
	'I saw that skinny dog.'			

Animacy is often crucial for distinguishing the subjects and objects of a Cherokee sentence. It is important to emphasize that a transitive verb (with a subject and an object) often indicates its participants solely through its prefixes; no other words are necessary to produce a grammatically complete sentence. When a **noun phrase** does appear, the interaction of animacy and the type of **pronominal** prefix on the verb determines whether this noun phrase is the subject or object of the verb.

When two noun phrases are present, animacy plays a role in distinguishing which is the subject and which is the object. If both are of equal animacy, then the **Set A** third person singular prefix or the Set B third person singular prefix appears. In (4a) the verb is in the **Completive** stem and the Set B prefix appears. For this speaker, the position of 'wolf' at the beginning of the **clause** indicates that it is the subject. In (4b) 'crawdad' is the subject and 'tail' (of the wolf) is the object, yet the noun 'crawdad' comes after the verb while the noun 'tail' comes at the beginning of the clause. In this case, however, the two participants are clearly of differing animacy; even though the word order is changed, it is assumed that the most 'natural' situation holds: an animate being is the subject and the inanimate being is the object. The **animacy hierarchy** discussed in chapter 9 determines which participant is the most natural subject. The noun 'tail' occurs at the beginning of the clause because it is new information and therefore the most newsworthy.

(4a) Gꮿ ᎤᏁᏄᏝᏁ
wahya uùneenuuhlane
wahya uu-neenuuhlan-e
wolf 3B-challenge:CMP-NXP

ᏥᏍᏛᎾ ᏧᎾᏙᎩᏯᏍᏗᎢ
jíisdvvna juuhntohgiíyáàsdíiʔi
jíisdvvna di-uunii-ahtohgiíyáàsdíiʔi
crawdad DST2-3B.NS-race:INF
'The wolf challenged the crawdad to race him.' (The Wolf and the Crawdad, line 5)

(4b) ᎦᏂᏓᏛ ᏭᎪᎮ ᏥᏍᏛᎾ
ganíidaʔtv wuùgoohe jíisdvvna
ga-níidaʔtv wi-uu-gooh-e jíisdvvna
3A-tail TRN-3B-see:CMP-NXP crawdad
'The crawdad saw his tail.' (The Wolf and the Crawdad, line 15)

Cherokee word order is highly variable and seems to be governed more by the specific context of the sentence in the larger discourse. Placing the newsworthy elements earlier is a way of emphasizing their importance and relevance to the narrative.

In (5) the verb is preceded by two noun phrases, 'fingers' and 'ears'. The verb is marked for third person singular, with a **distributive** (DST) prefix indicating that the object is **nonsingular.** Both noun phrases are nonsingular; in this case it is probably real-world knowledge that makes clear the relations: it is more common to stick fingers in ears than vice versa, so 'fingers' is the object and 'ears' the location.

(5) ᏕᎦᏰᏌᏛ ᏗᎦᎴᏂ ᏚᏐᏅᏕᎢ
deegáayesádv digaʔlééni duusondéeʔi
dee-ga-x́xyesádv di-ga-ʔlééni dee-uu-sond-eʔi
DST-3A-finger DST2-3A-ear DST-3B-put.in:CMP-NXP
'He put his fingers into his ears.' (*Cherokee New Testament,* Mark 7:33)

Word order in Cherokee is flexible because it is sensitive to contextual factors such as the relative newness, importance, definiteness, or animacy of the participants. This grammar presents many examples taken from larger discourses; the varying word order in any given example should be seen within the larger context. Three sample discourses are provided at the end of this grammar in appendix A; the reader is invited to refer to these texts to understand the context from which the sample sentences are taken. For example, in (4b) the citation indicates that the sentence is from the first text in appendix A and is found on line 15.

11.1.2. Word Order within Phrases

A **phrase** is a group of words centered around a **part of speech** such as a noun or a verb. A noun phrase is thus a noun plus any **demonstratives, quantifiers, adjectives,** or **adjectivals** that add more information about the noun. Word order within phrases, while still variable, is more fixed than in the sentence as a whole. For example, noun modifiers such as demonstratives, quantifiers, and adjectives typically come before the nouns they modify, as seen in (6). In (6a) the demonstrative 'the' precedes the noun that it specifies, while in (6b) the quantifier 'a little' modifies the following noun. In (6c) the underlined adjective precedes the noun. Demonstratives and numerals usually precede the adjectives; more examples of the various ways in which a noun is modified are discussed in chapter 7.

(6a) Ꮎ ᎠᏍᎦᏯ ᎠᏥᎪᏩᏘ
na asgaya aàjigoohwti
na a-sgaya aji-goohwti
the 3A-man 3O-see:PRC
'The man is being seen.'

(6b) ᎦᏲᎵ ᏣᎳᎩ ᏥᏬᏂᏍᎪ Track 87
gaàyóóhli jalagi jiwóoniisgo
gaàyóóhli jalagi ji-wóoniisg-o
a.little Cherokee 1A-speak:INC-HAB
'I speak a little Cherokee.'

(6c) ᏓᎩᏅᏌ ᎤᎵᏍᎨᏓ ᏗᎪᏪᎵ
daàginvvsa uulsgééd digoohweeli
dee-agi-nvvsa uu-alisgééda digoohweeli
DST-1B-give:IMM 3B-sacred book
'She gave me the sacred book.'

In (6c) the verb 'give' has three participants: the subject 'she,' the **primary object** 'me' (the **recipient** of the giving), and the **secondary object** 'sacred book' (the thing being given). Note that in this example the object 'me' is called a primary object because it is referenced on the verb with the pronominal prefix. The terms 'primary object' and 'secondary object' are explained in greater detail in chapter 14.

When a single noun appears as part of a clause it usually comes before the verb. Three examples of a noun before a verb are shown in (7); the first two nouns are objects, while the noun in (7c) is a place.

(7a) ᎦᏓ ᏕᎧᎵᏆᏕᎦ
gaada deekálkwadéega
gaada dee-ga-hlkwadéega
dirt DST-3A-turn.over:PRC
'He's turning dirt over.'

(7b) ᎠᏓᏁᎸ ᎤᏃᏝ
aàdaneélv uùnootla
aàdaneélv uunii-ootla
store 3B.NS-possess:PRC
'They have a store.'

(7c) ᎢᎵᎬ ᏓᏩᏙᏒᎢ
ihlgv daàwadósvv́ʔi
ihlgv da-agi-adós-vv́ʔi
tree TOW-1B-fall:CMP-EXP
'I fell from the tree.'

Objects also appear after their verb, as in (8). The noun phrase 'this box' is the object of the verb 'send', which always has three participants associated with it: the sender, the thing being sent, and the destination to which it is sent. Its subject 'I' is indicated by the pronominal prefix *agi-* and its object by the noun phrase 'this box'; the goal of the sending is indicated by both the **prepronominal prefix** *wi-* and the **interrogative adverb** 'where'. Question words such as 'where' appear at the beginning of the sentence. The verb 'send' is in its **Infinitive stem** (INF) to indicate that it is the object of the main verb 'want'.

(8)

ᎭᏢ	ᏩᎩᏗᏍᏗ	ᏣᏚᎵ	ᎯᎠ	ᎧᏁᏌᎢ
haadlv	wagidiìsdi	jaduuli	hiʔa	kaneèsáʔi
haadlv	wi-agi-diìsdi	ja-aduuli	hiʔa	kaneèsáʔi
where	TRN-1B-send(long):INF	2B-want:PRC	this	box

'Where do you want me to send this box?' (Feeling 1975a:187)

11.1.3. Order of Phrases and Clauses

Adverbials are words or phrases that modify verbs, adjectives, and adverbs as well as clauses. Adverbials often precede what they are modifying; for example, in (9) the **postpositional phrase** 'with a bat' is acting adverbially (by stating how the action was carried out) and is placed before the verb.

(9)

ᎪᏍᏛᏂᏍᏗ	ᎬᏗ	ᎤᏍᏆᎸᏂᏍᏗ
goosdv́vniìsdi (underlined)	gv́hdi (underlined)	uusgwalvv́nîisdi
goosdv́vniìsdi	gv́hdi	uu-sgwalvv́nîisdi
bat	with	3B-hit.on.head:INF

ᎩᏟ	ᎤᏁᎵᏔᏅᎢ
giihli	uùnehltánv́vʔi
giihli	uu-nehltán-v́vʔi
dog	3B-try:CMP-EXP

'He tried to hit the dog on the head with a bat.' (Feeling 1975a:52)

In the example in (9) the verb 'hit on the head' appears in its Infinitive stem form. The object of the verb 'try' is the entire preceding **subordinate clause** 'hit the dog on the head with a bat'. This subordinate clause is a **nominal clause** (a clause functioning like a noun).

Infinitive stems less commonly appear after the **main verb** of which they are the object; typically they precede the verb. (10) is a complex example of verbs acting as objects for other verbs. The **conjugated** verb 'urge' has three participants. The subject is indicated by the pronominal prefix *uu-* (3B), while the primary object 'the listeners' (those who are being urged) is a noun (itself built on the Infinitive stem of the verb 'listen'). The secondary object (that which is being urged) is the nominal clause 'asking to be taught'; the verb 'ask' itself has another verb in the Infinitive form ('teach') as an object. The third line of this sentence is a clause acting as an adverbial (modifying the entire preceding clause by setting a condition for its fulfillment).

(10) ᏚᏂᎳᏕᎸ ᎾᏍᎩ ᎤᎾᏛᏓᏍᏗ
duùniiladeélv nasgi uunatv́dáàsdi
dee-uu-niilad-eél-v nasgi uunii-atv́dáàsdi
DST-3B-urge:CMP-APL:CMP-EXP that 3B.NS-listen:INF

ᎾᏍᎩ ᎤᏂᏔᏲᏍᏗ ᏗᎨᎨᏲᏗ
nasgi uuniitayoosdi digeegeehyohdi
nasgi uunii-htayoosdi di-geejii-eehyohdi
that 3B.NS-ask:INF DST2-3O.PL-teach:INF

Ꮎ ᏳᎾᏚᎵ ᏣᎳᎩ ᎤᎾᏕᎶᏆᏍᏗᎢ
na yuunaduuli jalagi uunadeehlohgwaasdííʔi
na yi-uunii-aduuli jalagi uunii-adehlogwasdííʔi
that IRR-3B.NS-want:PRC Cherokee 3B.NS-learn:INF
'He encouraged the audience to ask for help [to be taught] if they want to learn the language.' (*Cherokee Phoenix,* May 2006)

As stated at the beginning of this section, adverbials typically come before the word or clause that they are modifying. In (11) the first word is a verb functioning as a time adverbial to the **main clause** 'I was trying to work', which displays the typical order of the **Infinitive complement** 'to work' followed by the main verb 'I was trying'.

(11) ᏥᏍᎩᏲᏍᏓᏁᎸ
jisgiyoosdaaneélv́
ji-sgi-yoo-sdaan-eél-v́
REL-2/1-break-CAUS:CMP-APL:CMP-DVB

ᏗᎩᎸᏫᏍᏓᏁᏗ ᎦᏁᎵᏗᏍᎬ
diigilv́hwsdáhndi ganeehldiìsgv
di-agi-lv́hwsdáhndi ji-aneehldiìsg-v
DST2-1B-work:INF 1A-try:INC-EXP
'When you interrupted me I was trying to work.'

11.2. Clauses: An Overview

A minimal Cherokee clause consists of a subject and a **predicate.** The subject is what the clause is about, while the predicate is what is said about that subject. A predicate typically has a verb but can also be verbless, with a noun or an adjective acting as the **subject complement.** Verbs always have a pronominal prefix that indicates what the subject and/or object of the verb is. Many nouns and adjectives can also have pronominal prefixes. If a noun or adjective is unable to have a pronominal prefix, a separate noun may indicate the subject; in many cases a noun is absent and the subject is understood to be third person.

There are two general types of clauses. **Independent clauses** are able to stand on their own (as sentences), while **subordinate clauses** cannot. A subordinate clause can be nominal, adjectival, or adverbial. A nominal clause is a subordinate clause that fills the role of a noun by acting as one of the participants of the main clause. An **adjectival clause** modifies a noun, and an adverbial clause modifies a verb, adjective, adverb, or clause.

Cherokee verbs are able to stand alone as grammatically complete clauses (sentences) because their prefixes and suffixes indicate all participants involved in the verb as well as information about tense, aspect, and mood. A clause consists of at least a verb and may also contain nominals further specifying the identity of its participants as well as adverbials providing more detailed information about the verb (such as time, place, or manner).

If the sentence contains a third person subject and a third person object, the subject generally precedes the object. An example is given in (12); the first underlined portion is the subject, while the second underlined portion is the object

(12)	ᎠᏧᏣ	ᎤᎵᏏ	ᏧᎦᏘᏅᏘᏗ	ᏚᏲᏎᎴ
	<u>achúúja</u>	<u>uuliisi</u>	<u>juuktinv́v́tdi</u>	duùyooséele
	a-chúúja	uu-liisi	di-uu-aktinv́v́tdi	dee-uu-yooséel-e
	3A-boy	3B-grandmother	DST2-3B-glasses	DST-3B-lose:CMP-NXP

'<u>The boy</u> lost <u>his grandmother's glasses.</u>'

If there are multiple nouns, typically the noun expressing place will go after the main object or after the verb. An example is shown in (13); the object 'water' precedes the verb, while the place—in this case 'clothes she is ironing' (the place where the water is sprinkled)—follows the verb. The verb 'iron' is modifying 'clothes' as an **obligation Infinitive;** this idea of obligation is expressed through a **modal tone** (MOD).

(13)	ᎠᎹ	ᏓᏆᏲᎥᏍᎦ	ᏗᎯᎾᏬ	ᏧᏖᏍᏗ
	<u>ama</u>	daàgwayóoʔvsga	<u>diihnawo</u>	<u>juutéésdi</u>
	ama	dee-a-gwayóoʔvsga	di-a-ahnawo	di-uu-teésdi
	water	DST-3A-sprinkle:PRC	DST2-3A-clothes	DST2-3B-iron:INF\MOD

'She is sprinkling <u>water</u> on the <u>clothes she is going to iron.</u>' (Feeling 1975a:72)

A larger clause might include noun phrases further specifying the subject and object of the verb as well as adverbials further specifying how, when, where, or why the verb is carried out. An adjective or a noun can also form a verbless clause. An example of each is shown in (14). In (14b) 'fast' is acting as a subject complement. A clause can be a complete sentence, as in (14a) and (14b), or can be inside of a larger clause. In (14c) the underlined clause is subordinated to the main clause; in this case the act of buying the car is an Infinitive complement of the verb 'want'. In (14d) the underlined subordinate clause is acting as an adjectival by providing more information about the car.

(14a) ᎠᏜᏗᏝ ᎠᏆᏚᎵ
adladíitla agwaduuli
adladíitla agi-aduuli
car 1B-want:PRC
'I want a car.'

(14b) ᎠᏯᏄᎵ Ꮎ ᎠᏜᏗᏝ
aaynúúli na adladíítla
a-xxynúúli na adladíítla
3A-fast that car
'That car is fast.'

(14c) ᎠᏆᏚᎵ ᎠᏜᏗᏝ ᏣᏩᎯᏍᏗ
aàgwaduuli adladíítla jahwáhísdi
agi-aduuli adladíítla ja-hwáhísdi
1B-want:PRC car 2B-buy:INF
'I want you to buy a car.'

(14d) ᎠᏜᏗᏝ ᏣᏆᏚᎵᎭ ᏣᏩᏍᎦ
adladíítla jagwaduulííha chawásga
adladíítla ji-agi-aduuliiha ja-hwásga
car REL-1B-want:PRC:SUB 2B-buy:PRC
'You are buying the car I want.'

11.3. Independent Clauses

Independent clauses can stand alone, but they are often joined together by a **coordinating conjunction.** In (15a) the two clauses are joined by the **conjunction** (=CN) **postfix** 'and'. In Cherokee the verb always has a pronominal prefix referring to its participants. The word order in the first clause in (15b) is the object 'tail' followed by the verb 'see', while in the second clause the subject 'crawdad' is followed by the verb. The sentence in (15c) is a single clause; in this case it is preceded by a postpositional phrase indicating location.

(15a)

ᎠᏂᏍᎦᏯ	ᎠᏂᎾ	ᎠᏂᏧᏣᏃ	ᎠᏂᏙᎾ
aniisgay	aàníina	aniichúújahno	aàniidóòna
anii-sgaya	anii-na	anii-chúúja=hno	anii-dóòna
3A.NS-man	3A.NS-sit(NS):PRC	3A.NS-boy=CN	3A.NS-stand(NS):PRC

'The men are sitting and the boys are standing.'

(15b)

ᎦᏂᏓᏛ	ᏭᎪᎮ
ganíidaʔdv	wuùgoohe
ga-níidaʔdv	wi-uu-gooh-e
3A-tail	TRN-3B-see:CMP-NXP

ᏥᏍᏛᎾ	ᎤᎿᏃ	ᏭᏙᏎᎢ
jíisdvvna	uhnáhno	wuùtoséeʔi
jíisdvvna	uhna=hnóo	wi-uu-ahtos-éʔi
crawdad	there=CN	TRN-3B-latch.onto:CMP-NXP

'The crawdad saw his tail and latched onto it.' (The Wolf and the Crawdad, lines 15–16)

(15c)

ᎣᏏ	ᎾᎥ	ᎤᏬᏝ	ᎤᎦᎾᏬᏍᎦ
óosi	naʔv	uùwoóhla	uùgaanawoosga
óosi	naʔv	uu-oóhla	uu-gaanawoosga
stove	near	3B-sit:PRC	3B-get.warm:PRC

'He's sitting by the stove warming himself.' (Feeling 1975a:167)
('Near the stove he's sitting. He's warming himself.')

The coordinating conjunctions are listed in (16).

(16)

ᏃᏊᎴ	noógwúle	'and then'
ᎾᏊᏃ	naàgwuhnóo	'and then'
ᎠᏎᏃ	aaséehno	'but'
ᎾᎯᏳᎢ	naàhiyúúʔi	'then'
ᎩᎳ	kila	'then'
ᏍᏊ	sgwu	'and'
ᎠᎴ	ale	'and'
ᎾᏍᎩ ᎢᏳᏍᏗ	naasgi iiyúúsdi	'that's why'
ᎢᏳᏍᏗ	iiyúúsdi	'because of'
ᏄᎦᏳᎵᏍᏙᏔᏅ	nugaylsdohtanv́	'because of'
ᎥᏍᎩᏅ ᎢᏳᏍᏗ	vv̀sgihnv iiyúúsdi	'for that reason'

Five examples of these conjunctions are shown in (17).

(17a)	ᏩᏯᏃ	ᎤᏕᎳᎰᏎ	ᎾᏭᏃ	
	wahyáhnóo	uùdelhoose	naàwúhnóo	
	wahya=hnóo	uu-adelhoos-e	naàwuhnóo	
	wolf=CN	3B-notice:CMP-NXP	and.then	
	ᏓᎦᎦᏂᏁ	ᏥᏍᏛᎾ	ᏙᏳᏛ	ᎯᎶᏄᎮ
	daàgagahnane	jíisdvvna	dooyúdvv	hiloonuuhe
	dee-aji-agahnan-e	jíisdvvna	dooyu=dvv	hi-loonuuhe
	DST-3O-look.at:CMP-NXP	crawdad	really=EM	2A-cheat:PRC

‘The wolf noticed and then looked at the crawdad [and said]: “You’re truly cheating.”’ (The Wolf and the Crawdad, lines 33–34)

(17b)	ᏍᎪᎯ	ᏧᏕᏘᏴᏓ	ᎤᏁᎳᏛᎢ	ᏓᎵᏆ
	sgoóhi	juudeetiyv́v́da	uùneéláàdvʔi	daligwa
	sgoóhi	di-uu-adeetiyv́v́da	uu-aneéláàd-vʔi	daligwa
	ten	DST2-3B-year	3B-live:INC-EXP	Tahlequah
	ᎩᎳ	ᎤᏚᎸᎲ	ᎤᏓᏅᏍᏗᎢ	
	kila	uùduulvvhv	uudaʔnvv̀sdííʔi	
	kila	uu-aduulvvh-v	uu-adaʔnvv̀sdííʔi	
	then	3B-want:CMP-EXP	3B-move:INF	

‘He lived in Tahlequah for ten years, then he wanted to move.’ (Feeling 1975a:6)

(17c)	ᏙᏍᏗᎾᏌᏁᎠ	ᎯᎠ	ᎤᏍᏗ	ᏠᎬᎢ
	doòsdiinsanéeʔa	hiʔa	úúsdi	dluhgv́v́ʔi
	dee-oosdii-nsanéeʔa	hiʔa	úúsdi	dluhgv́v́ʔi
	DST-1A.DL.EX-pull:PRC	these	little	tree
	ᎠᏎᏃ	ᎣᎩᏂᏄᎸᎲᏍᎦ	ᎣᎩᏂᏰᎯᏍᏗᎢ	
	aseehnoo	oòginiinuulv́vhvsga	ooginiihyehisdííʔi	
	aseehnoo	ooginii-nuulv́vhvsga	ooginii-hyehisdííʔi	
	but	1B.DL.EX-fail:PRC	1B.DL.EX-pull.out:INF	

‘We are pulling on these little trees but we can't pull them out.’

(17d)	ᏅᎩ	ᎢᏳᏍᎦᏅᏨᎢ	ᎾᏍᎩ	ᎢᏳᏍᏗ	ᎤᏬᏝ
	nvhgi	iyuusgáànvvjv́v́ʔi	naasgi	iyúúsdi	uùwoohla
	nvhgi	ii-uu-sgáànvvj-v́v́ʔi	naasgi	iyúúsdi	uu-oohla
	four	NI2-3B-commit.crime:CMP-DVB	that’s.why		3B-sit:PRC

‘He has four fouls so he is sitting out.’

(17e) ᏗᏂᏲᏟᏛ   ᏓᏂᏢᏍᎬ
diiniiyóóhlidvv   daàniihlvvsgv
di-anii-yóóhli=dvv   dee-anii-hlvvsg-v
DST2-3A.NS-child=EM   DST-3A.NS-be.sleepy:INC-EXP

ᎥᏍᎩᏅ   ᎢᏳᏍᏗ   ᏛᎣᎦᏂᎩᏒᎢ
vvsgihnv   iyúúsdi   dvvʔoogahniigîsvv́ʔi
vvsgihnv   iyúúsdi   di-ii-oogii-ahniigîs-vv́ʔi
that's.why   TOW-ITR-1B.PL.EX-leave:CMP-EXP
'The children were getting sleepy; that's why we came back.' (Feeling 1975a: 96)

As exemplified in (18), *nasgi iyuusdi* 'that's why' may appear with a **relativizer prefix** *ji-* attached to the verb, making it a subordinate clause.

(18) ᏣᎳᎩ   ᏗᏆᏕᏲᏗ   ᎠᏆᏚᎵ
jalagi   diigwadeehyóhdi   aàgwaduuli
jalagi   di-agi-adeehyóhdi   agi-aduuli
Cherokee   DST2-1B-teach:INF   1B-want:PRC

ᎾᏍᎩ   ᎢᏳᏍᏗ   ᏣᎳᎩ   ᏥᎦᏕᎰᏆᎠ
naasgi   iyúúsdi   jalagi   jigadeehlgwaʔa
naasgi   iyúúsdi   jalagi   ji-ji-adeehlgwaʔa
that's.why   Cherokee   REL-1A-learn:PRC
'I want to teach Cherokee, that's why I'm learning Cherokee.'

An independent clause may be also followed by a verb that comments on the preceding clause. Two examples are shown in (19). Note that in the corresponding English translations these elements are at the beginning of the sentence and the following clause is subordinated to it; in Cherokee the two clauses are simply juxtaposed.

(19a) ᎽᏪᎵ   ᎠᏓᏁᎸ   ᏥᎩᎵ   ᎡᎭ   ᎠᎾᏗᏍᎪ
muuweéli   aàdaaneélv   tsgili   eéha   aànadiisgo
muuweéli   aàdaaneélv   tsgili   a-eéha   anii-adiisg-o
Murrell   building   ghost   3A-live:PRC   3A.NS-say:INC-HAB
'They say that a ghost lives in the Murrell Home.'

(19b) ᎡᎵᏊᏍ   ᏣᎳᎩ   ᏕᎭᏕᎰᏆ   ᎮᎵᎠ
eliwus   jalagi   deehádeehlohgwa   heelíʔa
eligwu=s   jalagi   dee-hi-adeehlohgwa   hi-eelíʔa

possible=Q Cherokee DST-2A-learn:IMM 2A-think:PRC
'Do you think you can learn Cherokee?'

The postfix =*s* has a special function of joining two future tense clauses; in this construction it translates as 'or', as in (20).

(20)

ᏞᏍᏗ	ᎥᏍᎩ	ᎢᏍᏓᏱ	ᏗᏣᎸᏫᏍᏓᏁᎮᏍᏗ
hleesdi	vvsgi	isdááyi	dijalvvhwisdaàneehéesdi
hleesdi	vvsgi	isdááyi	di-ja-lvvhwisdaàneeh-éesdi
NEG.COM	SO	hard	DST2-2B-work:INC-PFT

ᏙᏔᏍᏔᏰᏏᏍ
dotastayeesis
dee-da-hi-astayees-i=s
DST-CMF-2A-get.exhausted:CMP-CMF=Q
'Don't work so hard or you'll get exhausted.' (Feeling 1975a:76)

11.4. Subordinate Clauses

A subordinate clause modifies or complements another clause or a phrase. An adverbial clause is a subordinate clause that functions like an adverb by describing how, where, when, or why the action of a verb occurs. Subordinate clauses can also act as a subject or object of a verb; this type of clause is known as a nominal clause. A third type of subordinate clause known as an adjectival clause modifies a noun.

In (21a) the underlined verb is modifying one of the participants (in this case the object 'water') of the main verb. In (21b) the underlined clause is a nominal clause and acts as the object of the main verb; in this case the object is an Infinitive complement. In (21c) the underlined subordinate clause is acting as an adverbial by adding a condition for the main clause.

(21a)

ᎠᎹ	ᎠᏟᏟᏍᎬ	ᎦᎵᏍᏚᏟ
ama	adlidliisgv́	galiìsduudli
ama	a-adlidliisg-v́	ji-ali-sduudli
water	3A-boil:INC-DVB	1A-MDL-splash:IMM

'I splashed boiling water on myself.'

(21b) Track 88

ᎤᎾᏚᎵᏍ	ᏣᎳᎩ	ᎤᏂᏬᏂᎯᏍᏗ
uùnaduulis	jalagi	uuniiwooniíhisdi
uunii-aduuli=s	jalagi	uunii-wooniíhisdi

3B.NS-want:PRC=Q Cherokee 3B.NS-speak:INF
'Do they want to speak Cherokee?'

(21c) DᎣ ᎤᏗᏔᎭ ᎤᏢᏨᏥ 🔊 Track 89
ama uudíítáha uùdlv́vjv?i
ama uu-adiitáh-a uu-hdlv́vj-v?i
water 3B-drink:CMP-CVB 3B-be.sick:CMP-EXP
'He became sick after drinking the water.'

There can be several subordinate clauses inside one another. In (22) the bracketed clause 'the opening door' is a nominal clause and is an object of the verb 'hear'. The larger underlined clause of which it is a part is itself an adverbial clause that is modifying the independent clause 'I knew my father had come home'. In this clause the object of the verb 'know' is the subordinate clause 'my father had come home'. This subordinate relationship is indicated by the **deverbalizer** (DVB) suffix on the subordinate clause's verb. The entire sentence centers on the conjugated verb 'I knew (it)', the subordinate clause at the beginning describes when I knew it ('when the door opened'), and the nominal clause at the end describes what I knew ('That my father had come home').

(22) ᎠᎧᏛᎦᎾ ᏍᏚᏗ ᎠᎵᏍᏚᎢᏍᎬ
aktv́v́gáàna [sduùdi alsdu?iisgv́]
agi-ahtvv́gáàn-a sduùdi a-ali-sdu?iisg-v́
1B-hear:CMP-CVB door 3A-MDL-open:INC-DVB

ᎠᏆᏅᏔ ᎡᏙᏓ ᎤᎷᏨ
aàgwahntv eedooda uùlúhjv́
agi-ahnt-v ee-dooda uu-lúhj-v́
1B-know:CMP-EXP 1B.FAM-father 3B-arrive:CMP-DVB
'When I heard [the door open] I knew my father had come home.'

The three types of subordinate clauses are further explained in the following three sections.

11.4.1. Adjectival Clauses

An adjectival clause is a clause that gives more information about a noun and is thus subordinated to it; in English such clauses are also known as **relative clauses.**

11.4.1.1. *Adjectival Clauses with Noninfinitive Stems*

One of the basic subordination strategies in Cherokee is to use the relativizer prepronominal prefix (REL) *ji-* and a **highfall tone** on the rightmost long vowel, indicating subordination (\SUB). For example, (23a) and (23b) are independent clauses; in (23c) the clause in (23a) is put in a subordinate relationship to the subject of the clause in (23b) by modifying it. The highfall appears on the experienced past (EXP) suffix on the verb 'converse'. Usually the **full form** of this suffix is not pronounced, but the highfall is still apparent in a higher than normal tone at the end, indicated by an accent on the last vowel.

(23a)

Ꮎ	ᎠᏍᎦᏯ	ᏦᏣᏝᏃᎮᏍᎬ
na	asgaya	joojahlnoheesgv
na	a-sgaya	oojii-ali-hnoheesg-v
that	3A-man	1A.PL.EX-MDL-converse:INC-EXP

'I was talking with the man.'

(23b)

ᎠᏍᎦᏯ	ᎠᏂᎩ
asgaya	aàhnigi
a-sgaya	a-aahnigi
3A-man	3A-leave:IMM

'The man left.'

(23c) Track 90

Ꮎ	ᎠᏍᎦᏯ	ᏦᏣᏝᏃᎮᏍᎬ	ᎠᏂᎩ
na	asgaya	joojahlnoheesgv́	aàhnigi
na	a-sgaya	ji-oojii-ali-hnoheesg-v	a-aahnigi
the	3A-man	REL-1A.PL.EX-MDL-converse:INC-EXP\SUB	3A-leave:IMM

'The man that I was talking with left.'

Three more examples are shown in (24). In (24a) the subordinating highfall tone falls on the experienced past suffix (as the rightmost long vowel of the word), while in (24b) it is on the **habitual suffix.** In (24c) the subordinate verb is in the Completive stem to express a future meaning. In (24a) and (24b) the **subordinate tone** appears as a slightly higher tone on the final vowel.

(24a)

ᎠᏏᏬ	ᏥᏍᎩᏁᏅ	ᏥᏖᏍᎦ
ahnawo	jisgihnéehnv́	jiteesga
a-ahnawo	ji-sgi-hneehn-v	ji-teesga
3A-shirt	REL-2/1-give(flexible):CMP-EXP\SUB	1A-iron:PRC

'I am ironing the shirt that you gave me.'

(24b)

ᏥᎩᎾᏚᎵᏍᎪ	ᎠᎵᏗᏝ
jiginduuliisgó	aldíítla
ji-ginii-aduuliisg-o	aldíítla
REL-1B.DL-want:CMP-HAB\SUB	car

ᎦᏳᎳ	ᎩᎶ	ᎤᏩᏎ
gáayuùl	kilo	uùhwase
gáayuùla	kilo	uu-hwas-e
already	someone	3B-buy:CMP-NXP

'The car we want has already been bought.'

(24c)

ᎭᏢ	Ꮎ	ᎠᏧᏣ	ᏥᏛᏑᏫᏏ	ᎠᏐᏴ
haadlv	naʔ	achúúja	jidvvsúúhwisi	aàsoóyv
haadlv	naʔ	a-chúúja	ji-da-a-suúhwis-i	aàsoóyv
where	that	3A-boy	REL-CMF-3A-paint:CMP-CMF\SUB	fence

'Where's that boy who will paint the fence?'

Indefinite relative pronouns such as *nuusdvv* and *iiyuusdi* refer to something inanimate; the pronoun is then followed by an adjectival clause. These constructions do not use the relativizer prefix *ji-*; they are exemplified in (25).

(25a)

ᏄᏍᏛ	ᏚᏚᎪᏔᏅ
nuusdv́v́	duuduuktanv́
nuusdv́v́	dee-uu-ad-uugohtan-v́
that.which	DST-3B-MDL-decide:CMP-DVB

ᏓᎦᏘᎴᎬ	ᏗᏘᏲᎯ
daàktiiléegv	diitiiyóóhi
dee-a-gahtiiléeg-v	di-a-atiiyooh-i
DST-3A-attack:INC-EXP	DST2-3A-argue:INC-AGT

'The lawyer took exception to what was decided.'

(25b)

ᏄᏍᏛ	ᏥᏃᏎᎲ	Ꮭ	ᏱᏓᏓᏂᎸᎦ
nuusdv́v	jiìnooseéhv́	tla	yidadaniilv́vga
nuusdv́v	jii-hnooseéh-v	tla	yi-dee-a-adaniilv́vga
that.which	1A.AN-tell:INC-DVB	NEG	IRR-DST-3A-accept:PRC

'What I'm telling him he doesn't accept.'

(25c) Track 91

ᎭᏑᏯᎩ	ᎢᏳᏍᏗ	ᏣᏚᎵᏍᎬᎢ
hasuuyagi	iiyúúsdi	jaduuliisgv́v́ʔi
hi-asuuyagi	iiyúúsdi	ja-aduuliisg-v́v́ʔi

2A-choose:IMM that.which 2B-want:INC-DVB
'Choose the one that you want.' (Feeling 1975a:56)

When used with the relativizer prefix (REL), *nuusdvv* introduces a subordinate clause describing how something is done, as in (26).

(26) ᏄᏍᏛ ᏨᎴᏂᏙᎵᏒ ᎣᏩᏌ ᏗᎫᎪᏙᏗ
nuusdv jvvléhniidoólîisv́ owaása digukdohdi
nuusdv ji-vv-aléhniidoólîis-v́ oo-vv́sa di-ga-ugohdohdi
that.which REL-3A.IP-live:CMP-DVB 3B.IP-EMP.PRO DST2-3A-decide:INF
'How you live, you decide for yourself.'

11.4.1.2. *Adjectival Clauses with Infinitive Stems*

An **adjectival Infinitive** generally describes the purpose or function of an object. Four examples of the first type are shown in (27). Although speakers sometimes translate these sentences with words like 'have' and 'must', the meaning seems to be not obligation but rather general purpose. This construction may also indicate a general state or quality of the object. A third person prefix is used if no local person is present; this prefix is a Set A prefix for **Set A verbs** and a Set B prefix for **Set B verbs;** in both cases the third person prefix has a **reference function** and refers to the noun being modified.

(27a) Ꮎ ᎤᏲᏨ ᏦᎳᏂ ᎣᏍᏓ ᏱᎬᏅᏗ
na uuyoòjv́ joóla?ni óósda yigv́vhndi
na uu-yoòj-v́ joóla?ni óósda ni-ga-v́vhndi
the 3B-break:CMP-DVB window good NI2-3A-do:INF
'That broken window needs to be fixed.'
('That broken window is to be fixed.')

(27b) ᎤᏅᏗ ᎠᏔᏍᎩᏍᎩ ᏙᏣᏓᎸ ᎦᏅᎵᏰᏗ
uunvv́di atasgíisgi dootsdalv́v ganvvliíyéèdi
uunvv́di atasgíisgi dootsdalv́v ga-nvvliíyéèdi
milk weed sore 3A-rub:INF
'You rub milkweed on sores.'
('Milkweed is to be rubbed on sores.')

(27c) ᏦᎳ ᎢᏳᏍᏗ ᎬᏙᏗ ᎤᎸᏓ ᏳᏓᏝᏣ Track 92
joóla iyúúsdi kdóhdi uulvv́da yuudáátloja
joóla iyúúsdi ga-vhdóhdi uulvv́da yi-uu-adaatloj-a

tobacco like 3A-use:INF poison.ivy IRR-3B-catch:CMP-CVB
'You use tobacco leaves when you catch poison ivy.'
('Tobacco leaves are to be used when one catches poison ivy.')

Two examples of a slightly different adjectival Infinitive construction are shown in (28). In these examples the pronominal prefix on the Infinitive has a **participant function** and refers to the subject that acts on the noun rather than the noun itself. For example, in (28a) the prefix *agi-* refers to the person who will use the object. This type of construction uses Set B prefixes; when appropriate, **animate object** or **combined local** prefixes may appear.

(28a) ᎪᎱᏍᏗ ᎠᎬᏔᏂᏓᏍᏗ ᎦᏙᎵᏍᎨᏍᏗ
goohúúsdi aktaniídáàsdi gaatoolsgéesdi
goohúúsdi agi-vhtaniídáàsdi ji-ahtoolsg-éesdi
something 1B-use:INF 1A-borrow:INC-PFT
'I'll be borrowing something I can use.'
('I'll be borrowing something for me to use.')

(28b) ᏂᎪᎯᎸ ᎤᏅᏗ ᎠᎩᎾᏗᏅᏗ ᎠᎩᏁᎰᎢ
nigoóhíilv uunvv́di aginadiínv́v̀di aàgineehóʔi
nigoóhíilv uunvv́di agi-nadiínv́v̀di agi-neeh-óʔi
always milk 1B-sell:INF 1B-have(liquid):INC-HAB
'I always have milk to sell.' (Feeling 1975a:176)

(28c) ᎦᏍᎩᎸ ᏗᏂᏅᎦᎵᏍᎩ ᎪᎩᎦᏘᏗᏍᏗ
gaasgilv diniinvvgalíísgi goògiiktiídîisdi
gaasgilv di-anii-nvvgaliisg-i googii-gahtiídîisdi
table DST2-3A.NS-clean:INC-AGT 3NS/1PL.EX-wait:INF
'The ones who clean the tables have to wait on us.'
('The ones who clean the tables are to wait on us.')

The adjectival Infinitive may be used with a **modal tone** (MOD) to reflect a sense of obligation or necessity. Two examples are given in (29).

(29a) ᏧᎦᏅᏕᎾ ᎬᏂᏍᏙᏗ ᎯᎬᎭᎷᏯ Track 93
juugahndééna gv́v́hnisdóhdi higvvhaluùya
juugahndééna ga-vvhnisdóhdi hi-gvvhaluùya
cabbage 3A-cook:INF\MOD 2A-chop:IMM
'Chop up some cabbage to cook.' (Feeling 1975a:19)
('Chop it up some cabbage that needs to be cooked.')

(29b)

ᎭᏢ	Ꮎ	ᎠᏧᏣ	ᎤᏑᏫᏍᏗ	ᏥᎩ	ᎠᏐᏴᎢ
haadlv	na	achúúja	uusúúhwisdi	jígi	aàsoóyvvʔi
haadlv	na	a-chúúja	uu-suúhwísdi	ji-gi	aàsoóyvvʔi
where	that	3A-boy	3B-paint:INF\MOD	REL-be:IMM\SUB	fence

Where's that boy who has to paint the fence?'

The obligation Infinitive may be used as the main verb of a sentence and does not always overlap with the adjectival Infinitive. This contrast is illustrated in (30); the verb 'melt' is an obligation Infinitive, and the verb 'prepare a meal' is an adjectival Infinitive.

(30)

ᎪᏢᏅ	ᎤᏩᎾᏬᎯᏍᏗ	ᎩᎳᏃ	ᎠᏓᏍᏓᏱᏙᏗ
gootlvvnv	uwanawóóhisdi	kilahno	adaasdahydohdi
gootlvvnv	uu-vnawoohisdi	kilahno	a-adaad-sdahy-dohdi
butter	3B-melt:INF\MOD	then	3A-RFL-prepare.meal-CAU:INF

'Butter needs to melt before cooking certain things.'
('Butter must be melted and then it is to be used to cook.')

11.4.2. Nominal Clauses

A nominal clause functions as a noun by acting as a subject or object. In (31) the underlined portion is the object of the verb 'hear'.

(31)

ᎠᏧᏣ	ᎤᏪᎷᎬ	ᎠᎦᏛᎦᏅ
achúúja	uùweehlúhgv́	aktvvgaanv
a-chúúja	uu-eehlúhg-v́	agi-ahtvvgaan-v
3A-boy	3B-scream:INC-DVB	1B-hear:CMP-EXP

'I heard the boy screaming.'

A nominal clause can also serve as the subject of the verb, as seen in (32). The underlined verb 'move' is a **topic Infinitive** and serves as the subject.

(32)

ᎠᏓᏅᏍᏗ	ᎠᎯᏗᎨᏍᏙᏗ	ᏃᎦᎵᏍᏔᏁᎸ
adaʔnv́v́sdi	ahiidiigéésdohdi	noogalstahneelv
a-adaʔnvvsdi	ahiidiigéésdohdi	ni-oogii-alistan-eel-v
3A-move:INF\TOP	convenient	NI-1B.PL.EX-become:CMP-APL:CMP-EXP

'Moving became more convenient for us.'

Many nominal clause verbs may appear in either an Infinitive or Noninfinitive stem; what makes the difference is the context. The general principle, illustrated in (33), is that the nominal clause uses the Infinitive stem if the time frame of that clause is understood to be the same as the time frame of the main clause.

(33a) ᏥᏍᎦᎢ ᎠᏩᎦᏙᏍᏗ
jiìsgáàʔi <u>awaktoósdi</u>
ji-sgáàʔi agi-agahtoósdi
1A-be.afraid:PRC 1B-look.at:INF
'I'm afraid <u>to look at it.</u>'

(33b) ᏥᏍᎦᎢ ᏛᎩᏍᎦᏢᏥᏒᎢ
jiìsgáàʔi <u>dvvksgahljiisv́v́ʔi</u>
ji-sgáàʔi da-agi-sgahlj-is-v́v́ʔi
1A-BE.afraid:PRC CMF-1B-bite:CMP-CMF-DVB
'I'm afraid <u>that the dog will bite me.</u>'

Incompletive and Completive nominals follow the same pattern and are discussed in the following section; Infinitive nominals are somewhat different and are discussed in a separate section.

11.4.2.1. *Nominal Clauses with Noninfinitive Stems*
Both the Incompletive and Completive stems can act as the object of a main verb by adding the deverbalizer suffix. This construction is demonstrated in (34). Ongoing actions are in the Incompletive, whereas finished actions are in the Completive. In (34d) the subordination tone falls on the verb 'be' at the end of the sentence.

(34a) ᎤᏕᎶᎰᏒ ᎠᏥᎶᏄᎡᏍᎬᎢ
uùdeelohoosv <u>aàjilonuʔeésgv́v́ʔi</u>
uu-adeelohoos-v aji-lonuheésg-vv́ʔi
3B-find.out:CMP-EXP 3O-cheat:INC-DVB
'He found out <u>he was being cheated.</u>' (Feeling 1975a:9)

(34b) ᎠᏩᏏᏔ ᎤᎷᏨᎢ
aàwahnta <u>uulúhjv́v́ʔi</u>
aki-anvhta uu-lúhj-v́v́ʔi
1B-know:PRC 3B-return:CMP-DVB
'I know <u>that he returned.</u>'

(34c)	ᏒᎦᏔ	ᏕᎦᏃᏍᎩᏍᎬ	ᎫᎯᏍᏗᎭ
	svv̀kta	deegánoosgíisgv́	guuhiísdíha
	svv̀kta	dee-ga-noosgíisg-v́	ga-uuhiísdíha
	apple	DST-3A-steal:INC-DVB	3A-accuse:PRC

‘She's accusing him of stealing apples.’ (Feeling 1975a:125)

(34d)	ᏂᎦᏓᏛ	ᎤᎾᏅᏖ
	nigáádadvv	uùnahnte
	nigááda=dvv	uunii-anvht-e
	all=EM	3B.NS-know:CMP-NXP

ᏥᏍᏚ	ᎣᏍᏓ	ᎠᏟᏙᎯ	ᎨᏒ
jiisd	óósd	atlíidóóhi	geèsv́
jiisdu	óósda	a-aditlíidoóh-i	geès-v́
rabbit	good	3A-run:INC-AGT	be:INC-DVB

‘They all knew that the rabbit was a good runner.’ (The Turtle and the Rabbit, lines 2–3)

Verbs such as ‘know’, ‘appreciate’, and ‘think’ commonly take nominal clauses as their objects; these nominal clauses are usually in the Completive or Incompletive. Three examples are shown in (35). In (35c) the nominal clause verb is in the Infinitive form to express ability; in this instance the conjugated verb ‘be’ is needed to carry the deverbalizer suffix.

(35a)	ᎦᏅᏓᏗᎠ	ᏦᎳᏂ	ᎤᏲᏍᏔᏅᎢ
	ganvv̀dadíʔa	joólani	uuyóostanv́v́ʔi
	ji-anvhdadíʔa	joólani	uu-yóo-stan-v́v́ʔi
	1A-remember:PRC	window	3B-break-CAUS:CMP-DVB

‘I remember him breaking the window.’

(35b)	ᎠᏩᏅᏔ	ᎩᏂᎪᏂᏲᎬᎢ
	aàwahnta	giniigoohniiyoogv́v́ʔi
	agi-anvhta	ginii-goohniiyoog-v́v́ʔi
	1B-know:PRC	1B.DL-be.late:CMP-DVB

‘I know that we were late.’

(35c)	ᎤᏅᏖ	ᎬᏩᏠᎯᏍᏗ	ᎨᎲ
	uuhnte	gvvwtlóóhisd	geehv́
	uu-anvht-e	gaa-uu-atloohisdi	geeh-v́
	3B-know:CMP-NXP	GA-3B-beat:INF\MOD	be:CMP-DVB

‘He knew that he could beat him.’ (The Turtle and the Rabbit, line 5)

Verbs that can take an Incompletive or Completive nominal clause as the object are listed in (36).

(36)	-suuligóoga	'quit'
	-sgwádiʔa	'finish'
	-aleeníha	'start'
	-anvhta	'know'
	-ahtvvgíiʔa	'hear'
	-oohiyuha	'believe'
	-atvvdáàsdi	'listen'
	-x̋xnehldíha	'try'
	-nuulv̋vhvsga	'fail'
	-gahtaha	'know how'

(37) contains three examples of verbs from the list above. The nominal clause acting as the object to each verb is underlined.

(37a)	ᎯᎳᏴ	ᏧᎸᎪᏤ	ᎰᎦᏍᎬ
	hiláàyv	chulgoje	hoksgv̋
	hiláàyv	ja-suligoj-e	hi-ogisg-v̋
	when	2B-quit:CMP-NXP	2A-smoke:INC-DVB

'When did you quit smoking?' (Feeling 1975a:56)

(37b)	ᎣᎩᏍᏆᏛ	ᎣᏣᏁᏍᎨᏍᎬ	ᎦᎸᏦᏕᎢ
	oògiisgwádv	oojáhnesgeesgv̋	gahljoódéʔi
	oogii-sgwád-v	oojii-áhnesgeesg-v̋	gahljoódéʔi
	1B.PL.EX-finish:CMP	1A.PL.EX-build:INC-DVB	house

'We finished building the house.'

(37c)	ᏅᏊ	ᎤᎾᎴᏅ	ᎠᎾᏙᎩᏯᏍᎬ
	nvv̋w	uunaleenv̋	ahntohkiyasgv̋
	nvv̋gwu	uunii-aleenvvh-a	anii-ahtohkiyasg-v̋
	now	3B.NS-start(T):CMP-CVB	3A.NS-race:INC-DVB

'That's when they started racing.' (The Turtle and the Rabbit, line 27)

Relative adverbs are followed by an adjectival clause; the combination of these two elements creates a **nominal**. Two examples are *naahna* 'place where', as in (38a), and *iiyv* 'time when', as in (38b).

(38a)	ᎦᎸᏓᏆᏂᎢ	Ꮭ	ᏯᏆᏅᏔ	ᎾᎿ	ᎨᏒ
	galv̋vdagwaniiʔi	tla	yagwahnta	naàhna	geesv̋

galv́vdagwaniiʔi	tla	yi-agi-anvhta	naàhna	gees-v́
Adilee	NEG	IRR-1B-know:PRC	place.where	be:INC-DVB

'I don't know where Adilee is located.'

(38b) ᎠᏋᎨᏫᏒ ᎢᏴ ᎠᏆᏂᎩᏒ ⦾ Track 94

aàgwvvkewsv	iiyv́	aàgwahnigiisv́
agi-vkews-v	iiyv́	agi-ahnigiis-v́
1B-forget:CMP-EXP	time.when	1B-leave:CMP-DVB

'I forgot when I left.'

11.4.2.2. *Nominal Clauses with Infinitive Stems*

The verb in an object nominal clause is usually in its Infinitive stem when its time frame is understood to be the same as that of the main verb. This kind of Infinitive is known as an Infinitive complement. In (39a) the acts of forgetting and feeding have the same time frame; 'feed' is the Infinitive complement of the main verb 'forget'. In (39b), however, the act of forgetting follows the act of feeding.

(39a) ᎩᏟ ᎯᏰᎵᏍᏗ ᏨᎨᏫᏒ

giihli	hiiyeelsdi	jvvkewsv
giihli	hii-eeslsdi	ja-vkews-v
dog	2A.AN-feed:INF	2B-forget:CMP-EXP

'You forgot to feed the dog.'

(39b) ᎩᏟ ᎯᏰᎶᎸ ᏨᎨᏫᏒ

giihli	hiiyeeloólv́	jvvkewsv
giihli	hii-eeloól-v́	ja-vkews-v
dog	2A.AN-feed:CMP-DVB	2B-forget:CMP-EXP

'You forgot that you had fed the dog.'

It is important to note that Set A prefixes do not appear on Infinitive complement clauses; the stem triggers **prefix shift.** In (40a) the verb 'write' has the Set A prefix, but in (40b) it has a Set B prefix. The distributive prefix appears in the *di-* form (DST2) typical for nouns and adjectives.

(40a) ᏗᏣᎳᎩ ᏕᎪᎣᏪᎵᎠ

dijalagi	deegoohweélíʔa
di-jalagi	dee-ji-oòweélíʔa
DST2-Cherokee	DST-1A-write:PRC

'I am writing Cherokee.'

(40b)	ᎦᏕᎶᏆᎠ	ᏗᏬᏪᎶᏗ	ᏗᏣᎳᎩ	Track 95
	gadehlgwa	diiwoohweélóòdi	dijalagi	
	ji-adeehlohgwa	di-agi-oohweélóòdi	di-jalagi	
	1A-learn:PRC	DST2-1B-write:INF	DST2-Cherokee	
	'I am learning to write Cherokee.'			

Several verbs always cause the nominal clause verb to appear in the Infinitive stem. (41) shows two examples of nominal clauses acting as objects of the verb 'want'; in (41a) the nominal clause has the same subject as the main verb, while in (41b) they are different. In both examples the nominal clause verb is in the Infinitive stem.

(41a)	ᎠᏆᏚᎵ	ᎬᎪᏩᏛᏗ	Track 96
	aag̀waduuli	gvvgoowáhtv́hdi	
	agi-aduuli	gvv-goohwáhtv́hdi	
	1B-want:PRC	1/2-see:INF	
	'I want to see you.'		

(41b)	ᏚᏳᎪᏚᏛᎢ	ᏣᏁᏍᏗ	ᎣᎦᏚᎵ
	duùyuukdúudv́v́ʔi	chanesdi	oògaduuli
	duuyuukdúudv́v́ʔi	ja-hnesdi	oogii-aduuli
	truth	2B-speak:INF	1B.PL.EX-want:PRC
	'We want for you to speak the truth.'		

Verbs like 'want' that can take an Infinitive nominal clause as the object are listed in (42).

(42)	-gahtiíya	'wait'
	-sdeeliha	'help'
	-lv́v́kwohdi	'like'
	-aduuliha	'want'
	-alisgohldáàneha	'permit'
	-yeelvvʔa	'intend', 'mean'
	-x́xnehldíha	'try'
	-gahta	'know how'
	-v́vhneéha	'make'

(43) contains five examples of verbs from the list above. In the last example the Infinitive is in its full form.

(43a)	ᎠᏁᏟᏗ	ᎤᎵᏍᏕᎸᏗ
	áanehldi	uùlsdehldi

a-x́xnehldi uu-ali-sdehldi
3A-try:PRC 3B-MDL-help:INF
'He's trying to help.'

(43b) ᏙᏩᎴᎳ ᎤᏔᎾ ᎤᎾᏦᏗ ᎠᏂᎦᏘᏯ
doowaleel úútan uunajóòdi aàniktiíya
doowaleela uu-ắtana uunii-ajóòdi anii-gahtiíya
car 3B-big 3B.NS-ride:INF 3A.NS-wait:PRC
'They are waiting to ride the bus.'

(43c) ᏴᎩ ᎠᎩᏣᏲᎵ ᎥᎩᏣᏲᏍᏗ ᏂᎦᎵᏍᏙᏓ
yvvgi aàgiijayoohlv vv̀giijayóósdi nigalsdohda
yvvgi agi-xxjayohl-v vgi-xxjayoosdi ni-ga-alisdohda
nail 1B-prick:CMP-EXP 1O-prick:INF\MOD NI-3A-cause:IMM
'A nail stuck me; that caused me to have to get a shot.'

(43d) ᎤᎾᏛᎾᏍᏔᏁᏃ ᏧᎾᏙᎩᏯᏍᏗ
uùndv́vnastanéhnóo juuhntohgiíyáàsdi
uunii-adv́vnastan-e=hnóo di-uunii-ahtohgiíyáàsdi
3B.NS-prepare:CMP-NXP=CN DST2-3B.NS-race:INF
'They got ready to race.' (The Wolf and the Crawdad, line 10)

(43e) ᏍᏆᎵᏍᎪᎵᏓᏏ ᎠᎩᏬᏂᎯᏍᏗᎢ Track 97
sgwalsgohldáàsi agiwoonihisdííʔi
sgi-alisgohldáàsi agi-woonihisdííʔi
2/1-permit:IMM 1B-speak:INF
'Permit me to speak.' (Feeling 1975a: 42)

Relative adverbs such as *uhna* 'there' and *diidla* 'toward', both exemplified in (44), may also be used to introduce an Infinitive complement indicating a place where an event is to take place.

(44a) ᎯᏯᏎᎮᎸ ᎤᎿ ᎤᏗ ᏓᏆᎴᎳ
hiiyaàsehéelv uuhna uuhdi dagwaléela
hii-aàsehéel-v uuhna uu-hdi dagwaléela
2A.AN-show:CMP-FCM there 3B-park:INF car
'Show him where to park the car.'

(44b) ᎤᎴᎾᎵ ᏝᎮᏃ ᏯᎦᏔᎮ
uùleenaáhlv hlahehnoo yaktahe
uu-aleenaáhl-v hla=hehnoo yi-a-gahtah-e
3B-get.lost:CMP-EXP NEG=CN IRR-3A-know.how:INC-EXP

ᎢᏗᏜ ᏭᎶᎯᏍᏗᎢ
idíidla wuuloohisdííʔi
idíidla wi-uu-loohisdííʔi
toward TRN-3B-pass:INF
'He got lost because he didn't know which way to go.' (Feeling 1975a:172)

A topic Infinitive acts as the subject of a clause and typically describes a quality of something or indicates a general state of affairs. For this function a **topic tone** change falls on the rightmost long vowel of the Infinitive. Two examples are shown in (44). The most common pronominal prefix for this construction is a **dummy prefix** that does not undergo prefix shift.

(45a) ᎠᏲᏍᏙᏗ ᎠᏚᏍᏛ Ꮭ ᎣᏏ ᏱᎨᏐ
ayóósdóhdi atusdv tla oosi yigeeso
a-yoòsdóhdi atusdv tla oosi yi-gees-o
3A-break:INF\TOP promise NEG good IRR-be:INC-HAB
'To break a promise is not good.'

(45b) ᏍᏓᏱ ᎠᎪᏩᏛᏗ ᎫᎩ ᎩᎦᎨᎢ
sdááyi agóówahtvhdi guùgi giigagéʔi
sdááyi a-goowahtvhdi guùgi giigagéʔi
hard 3A-see:INF\TOP tick red
'A seed tick is hard to see.'

11.4.3. Adverbial Clauses

Adverbial clauses are subordinate clauses that modify another clause by indicating when, where, why, or how an action occurs. The verb in an adverbial clause may appear in its Incompletive, Completive, or Infinitive stem. Three examples of adverbial clauses with each type of stem are shown in (46). In the first two examples a highfall tone indicating subordination (\SUB) appears on the rightmost long vowel of the subordinate verb. In (46a) the adverbial is expressing a time frame for the main verb. In (46b) the adverbial clause tells the reason for the main verb occurring. The adverbial clause in (46c) uses an Infinitive stem to express the purpose of the main verb. In some cases a **subordinating conjunction** may appear to link the subordinate clause to the main clause; an example with *si* 'before' is given in (46d).

(46a) ᎠᏗᎧᏓ ᎠᏂᎪᎵᏰᏍᎪ
adiikada aàniigooliíyéèsgo
adiikada anii-gooliíyéèsg-o
urine 3A.NS-examine:INC-HAB

ᏓᏄᎪᏗᏍᎬ ᎧᎵᏎᏥ ᏱᏤᎭ
daànúukdiísgv́ kalséèji yijééha
dee-anii-úugohdiísg-v́ kalséèji yi-ji-a-eha
DST-3A.NS-decide:INC-DVB diabetes IRR-REL-3A-live:PRC
'They check your urine when they're deciding if you're diabetic.'

(46b) ᎠᏂᏰᎬᎢ ᎠᎵᏃᎮᏗ ᏳᏃᏴᎵᏌ
aàniiyeegvv́ʔi ahlnoohéhdi yuunoohyv́v́lsa
anii-yeeg-vv́ʔi ahlnoohéhdi yi-uu-noohyv́vls-a
3A.NS-wake.up:INC-EXP phone IRR-3B-make.noise:CMP-CVB
'They were waking up when the phone rang.'

(46c) ᏐᎯ ᏕᎦᏟᏏᎭ ᎦᏅᏥ ᎤᏬᎵᏙᏗ
sohi deegáahliisíha ganvji uwoohlvhdohdi
sohi dee-ga-x́xhlisiha ganvji uu-oohlvh-dohdi
hickory.nut DST-3A-gather:PRC kanuchi 3B-make-CAU:INF
'She's gathering hickory nuts to make kanuchi.' (Feeling 1975a:95)

(46d) ᎭᎵᏍᏚᎳᎩ Ꮟ ᏂᏣᎵᏍᏛᎸᏅᎾ
halsduulagi si nijalsdvvhlunv́v́na
hi-alisduulagi si ni-ja-alisdvvhlun-v́v́na
2A-take.cap.off:IMM before NI-2B-sit.down:CMP-NDV
'Take off your cap before you sit down.'

11.4.3.1. *Adverbial Clauses with Deverbalizer Suffix*

One of the most frequent uses of adverbial clauses is to establish a time frame for the main clause. Time adverbial clauses modify the clause to which they are attached and frequently are placed before the main verb of that clause. In the example in (47a) the adverbial clause is describing an action that takes place before the action of the main verb; the deverbalizer suffix (DVB) indicates that the verb to which it attaches is now acting adverbially. In (47b) the adverbial clause establishes a time frame for the main clause. Time adverbials use either an Incompletive or Completive stem. Set A verbs take the Set B prefix in this construction.

(47a)
ᎤᏬᏂᏐᏅᎢ ᎦᏳᎳ ᎩᎳ ᏩᎩᎷᏨ
uuwóoniisohnv́v́ʔi gáayuul kil waàgiʔlúhjv
uu-wóoniis-ohn-v́v́ʔi gáayuula kila wi-agi-ʔlúhj-v
3B-speak:CMP-TRM:CMP-DVB already just TRN-1B-arrive:CMP-EXP
'When he had completed talking, I arrived.'

(47b)
ᎦᏚ ᏓᏂᏒᎾᏛᏍᎬᎢ
gáadu daniisvvntvsgv́v́ʔi
gáadu dee-anii-svvntvsg-v́v́ʔi
bread DST-3A.NS-fry:INC-DVB

ᎠᎩᎸᏉᏗ ᎦᏥᎦᏙᏍᏙᏗᎢ
aàgilvvkwdi gaajiigaàtosdohdííʔi
agi-lvvgwohdi gaa-jii-gahtosdohdííʔi
1B-like:PRC ANS-1A.AN-watch:INF
'I like to watch them when they're frying bread.'

As seen in (48), these types of adverbials can be translated in English as 'after', 'when', 'until', or 'having done VERB'.

(48a)
ᎤᏗᏔᎲ ᎠᎹ ᎤᏢᏨ
uudiítáhv́ ama uùdlv́vjv
uu-adiítáh-v́ ama uu-hdlv́vj-v
3B-drink:CMP-DVB water 3B-sick:CMP-EXP
'He became sick after drinking the water.'

(48b)
ᏧᎦᎿᏅ ᏣᎩᏍᎪᏒ
juugaahnanv́ jaksgoósv
ji-uu-gaahnan-v́ ji-agi-sgoós-v
REL-3B-rain:CMP-DVB REL-1B-dig:CMP-EXP
'I didn't dig it until it rained.'

(48c)
ᎢᏴᏛᏃ ᏭᏘᏅᏍᏔᏅ
iiyv́v́dvvhnóo wuutinv́vstanv́
iiyv́v́=dvv=hnóo wi-uu-ahtinv́vstan-v́
apart=EM=CN TRN-3B-lead:CMP-DVB

ᎤᏓᏰᎵᎸ ᎤᏂᏣᏘ ᎠᏁᏙᎲᎢ
uùdaayeehlilv uunííjati aàneedoohvv́ʔi
uu-adaayeehlil-v uunii-x̋jati anii-eedooh-vv́ʔi
3B-separate:CMP-EXP 3B.NS-a.lot 3A.NS-be.at:INC-EXP

'After leading him away, he separated him from where the crowd was.' (*Cherokee New Testament*, Mark 7:33)

In (49), the adverbial clause expresses the reason for the action of the main clause; this subordination of the adverbial clause is expressed through the deverbalizer suffix on the verb 'be' toward the end of the sentence.

(49)

ᎤᏅᏖ	ᎬᏩᏢᎯᏍᏗ	ᎨᎲ
uuhnte	gvvwtlóóhisd	geehv́
uu-anvht-e	gaa-uu-atloohisdi	geeh-v́
3B-know:INC-NXP	GA-3B-beat:INF\MOD	be:CMP-DVB

Ꮎ	ᏓᏆᏏ	ᎤᏍᎦᏃᎵ	ᎨᎲ	ᎠᏟᏙᎯ
na	daks	uusganóól	geehv́	atlíidóóhi
na	daksi	uu-sganóóli	geeh-v́	a-aditlíidoóh-i
that	turtle	3B-slow	be:CMP-DVB	3A-run:INC-AGT

'He [Rabbit] knew that he could beat him, because the turtle was a slow runner.' (The Turtle and the Rabbit, lines 5–6)

As seen from these examples, the deverbalizer suffix attaches to either a Completive or Incompletive stem. When it attaches to the Incompletive stem it typically has the meaning 'while'. Two examples shown are in (50a) and (50b). When attached to the Completive, it indicates an action that occurred at a specific time, as in (50c), or the reason why an act occurs, as in (50d).

(50a)

ᎤᎲᏐᎵ	ᎠᏥᏇᏄᎩᏎ	ᎦᏟᏴ
uuhyvvsóól	aàjigwenuugíise	gahliihyv́
uu-hyvvsóóli	aji-gwenuugíis-e	ga-hliihy-v́
3B-nose	3O-scratch:CMP-NXP	3A-sleep:INC-DVB

'His nose got scratched while he slept.'

(50b)

ᏓᎩᎸᏫᏓᏁᎲ	ᎠᎩᏢᏅ
dagilvv́hwsdaaneehv́	aàgitlvvhnv
dee-agi-lvv́hwsdaaneeh-v́	agi-tlvvhn-v
DST-1B-work:INC-DVB	1B-sleep:CMP-EXP

'I fell asleep while working.'

(50c)

ᏥᏍᎩᏲᏍᏓᏁᎸ
jisgiyosdaaneelv́
ji-sgi-yos-sdaan-eel-v́
REL-2/1-break-CAU:CMP-APL:CMP-DVB

ᏗᎩᎸᏫᏍᏓᏂᏗ   ᎦᏁᎵᏗᏍᎬ
digilv́wsdáhndi   ganeehldiìsgv
di-agi-lv́wsdáhndi   ji-aneehldiìsg-v
DST2-1B-work:INF   1A-try:INC-EXP
'When you interrupted, I was trying to work.'

(50d) ᎤᏓᎨᏴᏒ   ᏕᎦᎾᎩᏍᎪ
uùdaageeyv́vsv́   deegáhnoogíisgo
uu-adaad-geeyv́vs-v́   dee-ga-hnoogíisg-o
3B-RFL-love:CMP-DVB   DST-3A-sing:INC-HAB
'He sings because he's in love.'

In the two examples shown in (51) a **terminative derivational suffix** (TRM) appears on the subordinate clause to make clear that one event finished before the other event happened. This suffix is further described in chapter 13.

(51a) ᎩᎵ   ᏥᏥᏰᎶᎶᏅ
giihli   jijiiyeeloólóhnv́
giihli   ji-jii-eeloól-ohn-v́
dog   REL-1A.AN-feed:CMP-TRM:CMP-DVB

ᏗᏇᏅᏒ   ᏣᏆᏂᎩᏒ
diigweenv́vsv́   jaàgwahnigiisv
di-agi-eenv́vs-v́   ji-agi-ahnigiis-v
TOW-1B-go:CMP-DVB   REL-1B-leave:CMP-EXP
'After I fed the dog, I left home.'

(51b) ᎠᏇᏥ   ᎠᏧᏣ   ᏥᏥᏳᏖᏐᏅ
agwééji   achúúja   jijiiyuútéèsohnv́
agi-ééji   a-chúúja   ji-jii-uútéès-ohn-v́
1B-offspring   3A-boy   REL-1A.AN-pick.up:CMP-TRM:CMP-DVB

ᏗᏓᎾᏅ   ᏦᎩᏁᏅᏒ
diidaananv   joògineenv́vsv
di-adaananv   di-ooginii-eenv́vs-v
TOW-store   TOW-1B.DL.EX-go:CMP-EXP
'After I picked up my son, we went to the store.'

The subordinating conjunction *kvvhni* 'until' is followed by a deverbalizer subordinate clause. Set A verbs appear with Set A prefixes in this construction, as in (52).

(52)
ᏞᏍᏗ ᏣᏇᏅᎩᏒᎢ
tleèsdi jaakweenvvgiisvvʔi
tleèsdi ja-xxkweenvvgiis-vvʔi
NEG.COM 2B-unwrap:CMP-FCM

ᎬᏂ ᎡᏥ ᎡᏙᏓᏃ ᏓᏂᏰᏨᎢ
kv́v́hni eeji eedoodahno daaniiyeejv́v́ʔi
kv́v́hni ee-ji ee-dooda=hno dee-anii-yeej-v́v́ʔi
Until 1B.FAM-mother 1B.FAM-father=CN DST-3A.NS-wake.up:CMP-DVB
'Don't unwrap that until Mom and Dad wake up!'

11.4.3.2. *Adverbial Clauses with Converb Suffix*

To express a succession of events, the event that happens first acts as an adverbial establishing a time frame for the second event. One such construction uses the Completive stem with the **converb** (CVB) suffix *-a*. This type of adverbial clause is usually translated into English as 'when' or 'after'. For this construction a subordination highfall tone appears on the rightmost long vowel of the verb. Four examples are given in (53). As with the deverbalizer construction, Set A verbs in these clauses take Set B prefixes.

(53a)
ᏩᏥᏂᏴᏃ ᏩᏥᏯᎣᏁ
wajiniiyv́v́hno waàjiyaʔohne
wi-aji-niiyvvh-a=hno wi-aji-yaʔ-ohn-e
TRN-3O-catch:CMP-CVB=CN TRN-3O-eat-TRM:CMP-NXP
'And when he caught him he ate him up.' (The Wolf and the Crawdad, lines 38–39)

(53b)
ᏑᎨᏓ ᎤᏬᏢᏃᎿ ᏗᎦᏘᏗ ᏭᏝᏅᎢ
suugeéda uuwoohlv́v́hnohna digaàtdi wuùhlanv́vʔi
suugeéda uu-oohlvvhn-ohn-a digaàtdi wi-uu-hlan-vvʔi
dough 3B-make:CMP-TRM:CMP-CVB oven TRN-3B-put.in:CMP-EXP
'After she made the dough, she put it in the oven.' (Feeling 1975a:154)

(53c)
ᏭᎷᏣᏃ ᎦᎸᎾᏗ ᏗᎨᏒ
wúúluhjahnóo galv́v́nad digeèsv
wi-uu-ʔluhj-a=hnóo galv́v́nadi di-geès-v
TRN-3B-arrive:CMP-CVB=CN on.top.of TOW-be:INC-EXP

ᏩᏯ ᎤᏙᎯᏎ
wahya uùtohise

wahya uu-atohis-e
wolf 3B-whoop:CMP-NXP
'When he got to the top of the hill, the wolf whooped.' (The Wolf and the Crawdad, lines 17–18)

(53d) ᎣᏍᏓ ᎠᏍᏙᏍᎪ ᎦᏅᏥ ᏳᏬᎤᏢᏏ   Track 98
óósda aàsdóosgo ganvji yuwoohlv́v́hna
óósda a-sdóosg-o ganvji yi-uu-oohlvvhn-a
good 3A-pound:INC-HAB kanuchi IRR-3B-make:CMP-CVB
'He pounds it out well when he makes kanuchi.'

In (53b) above a terminative derivational suffix (TRM) appears on the subordinate clause to make clear that one event finished before the other event happened.

If the main verb is in the present or future or is a command, the adverbial clause has an element of uncertainty to it; 'when' could be more accurately translated as 'whenever' or 'every time' or even 'if'. This kind of adverbial clause typically carries an **irrealis** (IRR) *yi-* prepronominal prefix in conjunction with the converb suffix. This construction can be used on an Incompletive stem and take a Set A prefix (if it is a Set A verb), as seen in (54a) and (54b). If the Completive stem is used, as in (54c), then the Set B prefix appears; in this example 'wake up' is a Set A verb but appears with the Set B prefix.

(54a) ᎦᎵᏦᏕ ᏱᏫᏥᏴᎭ ᎦᏚ ᎠᎩᏫᏒᎪ
gahljoóde yiwijiyv́v́ha gáádu aàgiwsv́v̀go
gahljoóde yi-wi-ji-yvv́h-a gáádu agi-wsv́v̀g-o
house IRR-TRN-1A-enter:INC-CVB bread 1B-smell:INC-HAB
'Every time I enter the house I smell bread.'

(54b) ᏂᎪᎸ ᎦᎷᎪ ᏲᏣᎵᏍᏓᏴᏂᏍᎦ
nigoolv gáʔluhgo yoòjalsdáàyv́v́hvsga
nigoolv ga-ʔluhg-o yi-oojii-ali-sdáàyvvhvsg-a
always 3A-arrive:INC-HAB IRR-1A.PL.EX-MDL-provide.meal:INC-CVB
'He's always coming over when we're eating.'

(54c) ᏌᎾᎴ ᏱᏣᏰᏣ   Track 99
sanaale yijayééja
sanaale yi-ja-yéej-a
morning IRR-2B-wake(I):CMP-CVB

ᏣᎳᎩ ᎭᏓᏅᏖᏍᎨᏍᏗ
jalagi hadahntesgéesdi

jalagi hi-adanvhtesg-éesdi
Cherokee 2A-think:INC-PFT
'In the morning when you wake up, think Cherokee!' (*Cherokee Phoenix*, May 2006)

(54d) ᏦᏓᎸ ᏱᏭᎷᏨ ᏥᏍᏚ
joodalv yiwúúluhj jiisd
di-oodalv yi-wi-uu-luhj-a jiisdu
TOW-mountain IRR-TRN-3B-arrive:CMP-CVB rabbit
'Whenever the rabbit got to the mountain . . .' (The Wolf and the Crawdad, line 31)

All of these time adverbials carry an element of uncertainty. They indicate events that do or will occur, but it is unclear when exactly they will occur.

11.4.3.3. *Adverbial Clauses with Negative Deverbalizer Suffix*

A ***ni-* prefix** and **negative deverbalizer** (NDV) suffix are also used together to express the idea of 'not having done VERB' or 'without having done VERB'. Three examples are shown in (55); in (55c) the absence of the action is emphasized by the helping verb *yigi*.

(55a) ᏄᏲᏐᏍᎬᎾ ᎠᎵᏍᏓᏰᏫᏍᎦ
nuuyóosiisgv́v́na aàlsdáàyvvhvsg
ni-uu-yóosiisg-v́v́na a-ali-sdáàyvvhvsga
NI-3B-hungry:INC-NDV 3A-MDL-provide.meal:PRC
'He's eating while he's not hungry.'

(55b) ᎠᏍᎦᏯ ᏄᏢᏏᏛᎡᎲᎾ
asgaya nuudlasitvʔeehv́v́na
a-sgaya ni-uu-adlasitvʔeeh-v́v́na
3A-man NI-3B-doubt:INC-NDV

ᏫᏚᎵᏔᏗᏅᎢ
widuùhltadiinvv́ʔi
wi-dee-uu-alihtadiin-vv́ʔi
TRN-DST-3B-jump:CMP-EXP
'Without a care in the world the man jumped.'

(55c) ᏄᎦᏎᏍᏛᎾ ᏱᎩ ᎩᎶ ᎦᎶᎾᏍᏗᏍᎪᎢ
nuuksesdv́v́na yigi kilo galoonáàsdiisgoʔi

ni-uu-agasesd-v́v́na yi-gi kilo ga-loonáàsdiisg-oʔi
NI-3B-be.careful:INC-NDV IRR-be:IMM someone 3A-trick:INC-HAB
'Whenever someone is not alert, he tricks him.' (Feeling 1975a:101)

An adverbial clause expressing the idea of 'before' as an event that may or may not occur uses the *ni-* prepronominal prefix and the negative deverbalizer suffix. This construction is used with an Incompletive stem, as in (56a), or a Completive stem, as in (56b).

(56a) Ꭰ Ꮉ ᎾᏗᏔᏍᎬᎾ ᏣᏔᏕᎪᏗ ᏱᏂᎦᎵᏍᏓ
ama nadiitasgv́v́na jahtadeégóòdi yinigalsda
ama ni-a-adiitasg-v́v́na ja-htadeégóòdi yi-ni-ga-alisda
water NI-3A-drink:INC-NDV 2B-be.thirsty:INF IRR-NI-3A-cause:IMM
'If you don't drink water it causes you to be thirsty.'

(56b) ᏫᏄᎷᏨᎾᏊ ᎤᎦᏔᎲᏍᏗ ᎤᏚᎸᎲᎢ
winuuluhjv́v́nagwu uuktahvv̀sdi uùduulvvhvv́ʔi
wi-ni-uu-luhj-v́v́na=gwu uu-agahtahvv̀sdi uu-aduulvvh-vv́ʔi
TRN-NI-3B-arrive:CMP-NDV=DT 3B-turn.back:INF 3B-want:CMP-EXP
'He wanted to turn back before he got there.' (Feeling 1975a:35)

Sometimes the subordinating conjunction *si* 'before' appears with the negative deverbalizer construction. Two examples are shown in (57).

(57a) Ꮟ ᏫᏄᏑᏅᎾ
si winuusuhnv́v́na
si wi-ni-uu-suhn-v́v́na
before TRN-NI-3B-fish:CMP-NDV

ᏂᎪᎯᎸᎢ ᎤᏥᏈᏍᏗ ᎦᎵᏍᎪᎢ
nigohilv́v́ʔi uutsgwíísdi gahlvvsgóoʔi
nigohilv́v́ʔi uu-tsgwíísdi ga-hlvvsg-óʔi
always 3B-lot 3A-sleep:INC-HAB
'Before he goes fishing he always sleeps a lot.'

(57b) Ꮟ ᎾᏆᏓᏬᎥᎾ ᏕᏥᎾᏙᎬ ᏕᏥᏅᎦᎳ
si nagwadawooʔv́v́na deejinaàdohgv deejínvvgala
si ni-agi-adaa-awooʔ-v́v́na dee-ji-nahdohgv dee-ji-nvvgala
before NI-1B-MDL-bathe:CMP-NDV DST-1A-tooth DST-1A-clean:IMM
'I brushed my teeth before I bathed.'

11.4.3.4. *Adverbial Clauses with Irrealis Prefix*

The irrealis prefix *yi-* creates a subordinate clause describing a condition for the main clause or a contrary to fact situation. In (58a) both events are not real and are marked with the irrealis, while the subordinate clause has the highfall tone. The time frame in this case is the present; in (58b) the unrealized event is in a past time frame.

(58a) Track 100

ᏣᎳᎩ	ᏯᏕᎸᏆᎠ	ᏱᏣᏅᏔ
jalagi	hyadééhlgwaʔa	yijahnta
jalagi	yi-hi-adeehlgwaʔa	yi-ja-anvhta
Cherokee	IRR-2A-learn:PRC\SUB	IRR-2B-know:PRC

'If you were learning Cherokee you would know.'

(58b)

ᏯᎩᎮ	ᎠᏕᎳ
yagihé	adeél
yi-agi-h-e	adeéla
IRR-1B-have:CMP-NXP\SUB	money

ᎦᎵᏦᏕ	ᏯᎩᏩᏎ
gahljoóde	yagihwase
gahljoóde	yi-agi-hwas-e
house	IRR-1B-buy:CMP-NXP

'I would've bought a house if I had the money.'

In (59) the subordinate clause establishes a condition for the fulfillment of the main clause. This example in (59) also has the converb suffix.

(59)

ᏱᏓᎩᎸᏻᏍᏓᏁᎳ	ᎠᏕᎳ	ᏍᎩᏁᏗ
yidagilvv́hwsdanééla	adeéla	sginéhdi
yi-dee-agi-lvv́hwsdaneel-a	adeéla	sgi-nehdi
IRR-DST-1B-work:CMP-CVB	money	2/1-give:INF\MOD

'If I work you have to give me money.'

11.4.3.5. *Adverbial Clauses with Subordination Tone*

An adverbial clause may be created without the use of any special prefixes or suffixes; for these constructions subordination is indicated only by a subordination tone. In these constructions Set A verbs do use their Set A prefixes, a pattern different from the other adverbial clauses described in this chapter. In (60a) the subordinate clause 'When/after the elders leave us' has the deverbalizer suffix;

this subordinate clause is followed by a second subordinate clause using the negative deverbalizer to express 'without anybody knowing our language'. In (60b) the future orientation is expressed by *geeséésdi*; the subordinate status is expressed by the highfall tone, which is also on the **progressive future** suffix, while in (60c) it is on the **nonexperienced past** suffix.

(60a)
ᎠᏂᎦᏴᎵ ᎨᎬᏕᏦᏅ ᎠᎴ
aniigayv́v́li geekdéejohnv́ ale
anii-gayv́v́li geegii-vhdéej-ohn-v́ ale
3A.NS-elder 3NS/1PL-depart.in.death:CMP-TRM:CMP-DVB and

ᎩᎶ ᏄᏓᎴ ᏣᎳᎩ ᎦᏬᏂᎯᏍᏗ
kilo núúdale jalagi gawoòniíhísdi
kilo ni-uu-x̋dale jalagi ga-woòniíhísdi
someone NI-3B-different Cherokee 3A-speak:INF\INS

ᎾᎦᏔᎲᎾ ᎨᏎᏍᏗ
naktahv́v́na geeséésdi
ni-a-gahtah-v́v́na gees-éesdi
NI-3A-know.how:CMP-NDV be:INC-PFT\SUB

ᏂᎦᏓ ᏛᏂᎩᏐᏂ
nigááda dvvhnigîsohni
nigááda da-a-ahnigîs-ohn-i
all CMF-3A-leave:CMP-TRM:CMP-CMF

'When the elders leave us and no one else knows the language, it will be gone.' (*Cherokee Phoenix*, May 2006)

(60b)
ᎤᏅᎸᎲᏍᎨᏍᏗ ᏧᎴᏗ ᏕᎯᏯᎴᏔᏅᎢ
uunv́v́lv̀v̀hvsgéésd juulehdi deehiiyalehtanvvʔi
uu-nv́v́lv̀v̀hvsg-eesdi di-uu-alehdi dee-hii-alehtan-vvʔi
3B-fail:INC-PFT\SUB DST2-3B-stand(I):INF DST-2A.AN-stand(T):CMP-FCM

"If he can't get up, help him.' (Feeling 1975a:73)

(60c)
ᏗᎤᎷᏨᏃ ᏚᏩᏛᎮ
diʔúuluhjv́hnoo duùhwahtvvhe
di-ii-uu-luhj-v=hnoo dee-uu-hwahtvvh-e
TOW-ITR-3B-arrive:CMP-EXP=CN DST-3B-find:CMP-NXP

ᏔᎵᏁ ᎠᏂᏝᎾᎡᎢ
taliine aàniihlinaʔééʔi

tali-iine anii-hlinaʔ-éeʔi
two-ORD 3A.NS-sleep(NS):INC-NXP\SUB
'And when he came back he found them asleep again' (*Cherokee New Testament*, Matthew 26:43)

A subordinating conjunction may be used to emphasize the relationship of the subordinate clause to the main clause. (61a) is an example with *iyuuhno* 'if', and (61b) shows the use of *kv́v́hni* 'until'.

(61a) ᎢᏳᏃ ᎢᎦᏚᎵᏍᎨᏍᏗ
iyúuhnóo iigaduuliisgéésd
iyúuhnóo iigii-aduuliisg-éesdi
if 1B.PL-want:INC-PFT\SUB

ᎢᎦᎵᏏᏅᏙᏗ ᎣᏂ ᏥᏛᎾ
iigalsindohdi oohni jidvvna
iigii-alisindohdi oohni ji-da-anii-áaʔ-i
1B.PL-save:INF behind REL-CMF-3A.NS-walk:INC-AGT
'. . . if we will want to save it [the Cherokee language] for future generations.' (*Cherokee Phoenix*, May 2006)

(61b) ᏞᏍᏗ ᏤᏥᏁᎵ
tleèsdi jeejiineéli
tleèsdi ji-eejii-hneél-i
NEG.COM COM-2A.PL.AN-give:CMP-CMF

ᎬᏂ ᎪᎯᏳᏅᎢ
kv́v́hni goohiiyuunv́v́ʔi
kv́v́hni ga-oohiiyuun-v́v́ʔi
until 3A-believe:CMP-DVB
'Don't give it to him until he believes.'

11.4.3.6. *Adverbial Clauses with Infinitive Stems*

An adverbial clause can be formed with an Infinitive stem to create the meaning 'in order to'. In these constructions the subject of the adverbial clause is the same as the subject of the clause it is modifying. In this construction Set A verbs take Set B prefixes. Three examples of the **adverbial Infinitive** are shown in (62). All three examples appear in the **long form.**

(62a) ᎾᏍᎩᏃ ᎢᏳᏍᏗ ᎢᎦ ᏙᎩᎸᏫᏍᏓᏁᎰ
naàsgíhno iyúúsdi iiga doògiilvv́hwísdaàneeho

naàsgi=hno iyúúsdi ii-ga dee-oogii-lvv́hwísdaàneeh-o
that=CN reason ITR-be:PRC DST-1B.PL.EX-work:INC-HAB

ᎬᏃᏓ ᎢᏳᎵᏍᏙᏗᎢ
gvvhnóóda iyuulsdohdííʔi
ga-vvhnóóda ii-uu-alisdohdííʔi
3A-alive NI2-3B-become:INF
'That's why we struggle to keep it alive.' (*Cherokee Phoenix*, February 2005)

(62b) ᏐᎢ ᎧᎴᏍᏗ ᎠᏆᏜᏅᏓᏕᎮᏍᏗ
sóʔi kaléesdi agwadlanvvdáʔdeehéesdi
sóʔi kal-éesdi agi-adlanvvdáʔdeeh-éesdi
other month-PFT 1B-have.time:INC-PFT

ᏫᎬᏩᏛᎯᏓᏍᏗᎢ
wigvvwahtvvhiídáàsdííʔi
wi-gvv-hwahtvvhiídáàsdííʔi
TRN-1/2-visit:INF
'I'll have time to visit you next month.' (Feeling 1975a:161)

(62c) ᎯᎳ ᏱᎪᎯᏓ ᏓᏟᎵᏙᎰ
hila yigohííd daàhliiliidooho
hila yi-gohíída dee-a-ahliiliidooh-o
how IRR-long DST-3A-take.time:INC-HAB

ᎦᏢᏦᏕ ᎠᏁᎦᏍᏗᎢ
gahljoóde aneksdííʔi
gahljoóde a-aneksdííʔi
house 3A-build:INF
'How much time does it to a house to be built?'

As seen in (63), an adverbial Infinitive may also modify an adjective.

(63) ᏂᎪᎯᎸ ᎠᎦᏟᏱ ᎨᏐ ᎤᏓᏍᏕᏟᏗᎢ
nigoóhíilv agahlííyi geeso uudaasdehldííʔi
nigoóhíilv a-gahlííyi gees-o uu-adaad-sdehldííʔi
always 3A-eager be:INC-HAB 3B-RFL-help:INF
'He's always eager to help.' (Feeling 1975a:14)

11.4.3.7. *Summary of Adverbial Clauses*

Table 11.1 summarizes the different ways of forming adverbials in Cherokee.

Table 11.1. Adverbial Clauses

Function of adverbial clause	*Stem*	*Final suffix*
Establish time frame of main verb 'when he Xed'	Completive	-v̋v́ʔi (DVB)
Establish event previous to main verb 'after having Xed'	Completive (typically with terminative)	-a (CVB)
Establish event in progress when main verb occurs 'while Xing'	Incompletive	-v̋v́ʔi (DVB)
Establish condition that occurs in present or future for main verb to occur 'whenever'	1. Pronominal prefix yi-(IRR) + Completive 2. Pronominal prefix yi-(IRR) + Incompletive	-a (CVB)
Establish reason or cause of main verb	Subordinate tone (SUB) on verb; may have a subordinating conjunction	normal final suffix
Establish purpose: 'in order to'	Infinitive	—

11.5. Helping Verbs

A **helping verb** expresses tense, aspect, and /or negation when the main verb is unable to express these features; it also serves to emphasize these distinctions. The two helping verbs are 'be' and 'become'. In (64a) the negated form of 'be' serves to reinforce the negative sense of the clause. The helping verb in (64b) situates the obligation Infinitive in the past.

(64a) ᎣᏍᏓ ᏂᎦᏛᏁᎲᎾ ᏱᎩ ᎢᏍᎩᏍᎦᏍᏗ
óósda nigadvnehv̋v́na yigi iisgiisgasdi
óósda ni-ji-advneh-v̋v́na yi-gi iisgii-sgasdi
good PRT-1A-do:INC-NDV IRR-be:IMM 2/1.PL-reprimand:INF
'If I'm not doing right you have to reprimand me.'

(64b) ᎦᎸᏅᏗᎠ ᏫᎧᎾᏢᏛ ᎤᏙᎯᏍᏗ ᎨᏒᎢ
galvvndiʔa wikanahltv uutohíísdi geѐsvv́ʔi

galvvndiʔa	wi-kanahltv	uu-atohiisdi	geès-vv́ʔi
on.top	TRN-hill	3B-whoop:INF\MOD	be:INC-EXP

'. . . at the top of the hill [he] was to whoop.' (The Wolf and the Crawdad, line 12)

In (65) the verb *-alisdiha* 'become' accompanies an Infinitive stem in order to situate the obligation in the past.

(65a) ᎬᎩᏁᏄᏝᎾ
gvvgineenúúhlana
gvvgi-neenuuhlan-a
3NS/1-challenge:CMP-CVB

ᏗᎦᏥᏲᏍᏗ	ᏄᎵᏍᏔᏅ
digaajiiyóósdi	nuùlstanv
di-gaa-jii-yoósdi	ni-uu-alistan-v
DST2-ANS-1A.AN-shoot:INF\MOD	NI-3B-happen:CMP-EXP

'When they challenged me I had to shoot them.'

(65b)

ᏣᏁᎫᏨ	ᏂᎦᏳᎵᏍᏙᏔᏅ
janeégúùjv́	nugaylsdohtanv́
ja-neguj-v́	nugaylsdohtanv́
2B-be.mean:INC-DVB	because.of

ᏍᏛᏍᎦᏍᏓᏁᏗ	ᏄᎵᏍᏔᏅ
sdvvsgasdanehdi	nuùlstanv
sdvv-sgasdanehdi	ni-uu-alistan-v
1/2.DL-scare:INF\MOD	NI-3B-happen:CMP-EXP

'Because of your meanness we had to scare you.'

11.6. Sources and Additional Reading

The issue of basic word order has received some attention in the Cherokee literature. King (1975:111) observes that North Carolina Cherokee word order is relatively free except for cases where both subject and object are third person and the same number. He claims that in such situations the subject must precede the object. The concept of newsworthiness is from Mithun (1987:325); elements are newsworthy when they introduce important new information or topics or when they indicate a contrast with other elements in the sentence. Scancarelli (1987:192–93) has applied this concept to Cherokee and states that "the most newsworthy elements come earlier in the sentence." Smythe (1998) takes as a starting point the discussion in Mithun (1987), which suggests that certain languages refer to discourse pragmatics rather than syntax to determine word order. Smythe argues that while this is generally the case for sentential constituents, syntax is still necessary to account for word order within constituents. In the rest of the article she focuses on three specific areas in which the word order is predetermined: demonstratives and numerals precede nouns that they modify, copulas always follow their predicates, and postpositions always come after their complements.

I am grateful to Wyman Kirk for pointing out the use of the adverb *si* with the *ni-* prefix and providing me with examples. He also drew my attention to the tendency of the terminative suffix to appear in subordinate 'after' clauses and provided me with examples of this construction.

11.7. Directions for Further Research

The current literature lacks many details regarding the syntax of the language. Beghelli (1996:105) notes that "Cherokee syntax is largely unexplored territory." Pulte (1972, 1976a) has two papers concerning gapping and the obligatory-optional principle. Williams (1996) describes the interaction of word order and possession: he discusses how word order in Cherokee is free, but discontinuous constituents are no longer allowed when two overt arguments are present and one is possessed.

Very little work has been done on important issues in discourse analysis such as tracking arguments, focus, and topicalization; see Singleton (1979), Scancarelli (1986), and Smythe (1998). Uchihara (2014) has done recent work on noun incorporation.

A thorough understanding of the complex interplay of discourse features with word order and grammatical relations—not to mention the individual and dialectal variations—is a topic deserving of its own study. While this issue is commented on in relevant sections, it is beyond the scope of the present work to offer a comprehensive and unified account of this complex phenomenon. Scancarelli (1987:192) cautions: "It must be borne in mind that sentences with two transitive verbs and two NP arguments [participants], especially sentences in which the two arguments are animate and equally ranked on the animacy hierarchy, are extremely rare in Cherokee." For this reason it is important to base studies of word order on spontaneous and extended discourses.

TWELVE

Creating Nouns and Adjectives

12.1. Noun Derivation

In Cherokee most **nouns** are **derived** from **verb stems.** Three of the five verb stems are used to form nouns: the **Incompletive, Completive,** and **Infinitive.** In (1) two nouns are derived from verbs; the first word is an **agentive noun** derived from an Incompletive stem, and the second word is a **place noun** derived from an Infinitive stem.

(1)

ᏧᎾᏓᏬᏍᎩ	ᏧᏂᎳᏫᏍᏗ	ᎨᎵ
juundaawóósgi	juuniilaàwisdi	géʔli
di-uunii-adaad-awoosg-i	di-uunii-laàwisdi	ji-éhli
DST2-3B.NS-RFL-bathe(T): INC-AGT	DST2-3B.NS-have.church:INF	1A-member

'I'm a Baptist church member.'

The different types of nouns **derivations** are described in the following sections.

12.1.1. Nouns Formed from the Incompletive (INC) Verb Stem

12.1.1.1. *Incompletive Stem with Agentive (AGT) Suffix*
This derivation is very common and creates a noun referring to the person or thing performing the action described by the verb. These nouns are formed from verbs by adding the *-i* suffix (AGT) to the Incompletive stem. Agentive nouns typically have a different tone pattern than the stem from which they derive. These nouns always have **pronominal prefixes.** Five examples of agentive nouns and their verbal counterparts are shown in (2) through (8).

(2a) DᏁᎡᏝᏅᏍᎩ
anééhluhvsgi
anii-eehluhvsg-i
3A.NS-shout:INC-AGT
'cheerleaders'

(2b) DᏁᎡᏝᏅᏍᎪᎢ
aàneehluhvsgóoʔi
anii-eehluhvsg-óoʔi
3A.NS-shout:INC-HAB
'They shout.'

(3a) DᏙᎩᏯᏍᎩ
atohgíiyaasgi
a-ahtohgiíyáàsg-i
3A-run:INC-AGT
'runner'

(3b) DᏙᎩᏯᏍᎪ
aàtohgiíyáàsgo
a-ahtohgiíyáàsg-o
3A-run:INC-HAB
'He runs.'

(4a) ᏗᏓᏬᏍᎩ
diidaawóósgi
di-a-adaad-awoosg-i
DST2-3A-RFL-bathe(T):INC-AGT
'Baptist'

(4b) ᎦᏓᏬᏍᎪᎢ
gadaawóosgóoʔi
ga-adaad-awóosg-óoʔi
3A-RFL-bathe(T):INC-HAB
'She baptizes.'

(5a) ᏧᎸᏫᏍᏓᏁᎯ
juulvv́hwísdaanééhi
di-uu-lvv́hwísdaaneeh-i
DST2-3B-work:INC-AGT
'worker'

(5b) ᏚᎸᏫᏍᏓᏁᎰ
duulvv́hwísdaaneeho
dee-uu-lvv́hwísdaaneeh-o

DST-3B-work:INC-HAB
'He works.'

(6a) ᏗᏕᏠᏝᏍᎩ
diideehlohgwaàsgi
di-a-adeehlohgwáasg-i
DST2-3A-learn:INC-AGT
'student'

(6b) ᎠᏕᏠᏝᏍᎪᎢ
aàdeehlohgwáasgóoʔi
a-adeehlohgwáasg-óoʔi
3A-learn:INC-HAB
'She learns it.'

(7a) ᎠᎳᏍᎦᎵᏍᎩ
alaàsgalíisgi
a-alaàsgaliisg-i
3A-play.ball:INC-AGT
'ballplayer'

(7b) ᎠᎳᏍᎦᎵᏍᎪᎢ
aàlaasgalíisgóoʔi
a-alaasgalíisg-óoʔi
3A-play.ball:INC-HAB
'She plays ball.'

(8a) ᏗᏓᎦᏘᎴᎩ
diidaktiiléég-i
di-a-adaad-gahtiiléèg-i
DST2-3A-RFL-attack:INC-AGT
'attacker'

(8b) ᏓᎦᏘᎴᎪ
daàktiíléègo
dee-a-gahtiíléèg-o
DST-3A-attack:INC-HAB
'He attacks.'

In many of these examples the **distributive prefix** *di-* (DST2) is used on the noun. This pattern of adding this prepronominal prefix to the noun form is not entirely predictable but occurs frequently. Typically the derivation changes the tone pattern of the Incompletive stem.

As seen in (9), it is also possible for agentive nouns to be inanimate.

(9a) DBᏓᏆᏩᏲᎩ
ahyvvdagwaloòsgi
a-hyvvdagwalóòsg-i
3A-thunder:INC-AGT
'thunder'

(9b) DBᏓᏆᏩᏲᎪ
aàhyvvdagwalóòsgo
a-hyvvdagwalóòsg-o
3A-thunder:INC-HAB
'It thunders.'

The agentive noun derivation is very **productive** in Cherokee. Frequently many of these nouns have specialized meanings. The two examples in (10) are Cherokee names for Christian denominations.

(10a) ᏗᎾᏓᏍᏚᏞᏍᎩ
diinadaasdúúdlisgi
di-anii-adaad-sduudlisg-i
DST2-3A.NS-RFL-sprinkle:INC-AGT
'Methodists' ('sprinklers')

(10b) ᏧᎾᎸᏕᎯ
juunalvvdééhi
di-uunii-alvvdeeh-i
DST2-3B.NS-convulse:INC-AGT
'members of the Holiness denomination' ('convulsers')

In (8a) above the **reflexive prefix** *-adaad-* appears on the noun derived from the **transitive** verb, but not on the other nouns derived from **intransitive** verbs. This use of the reflexive is known as the **unspecified object reflexive.** Because the noun derivation frequently refers to an entity that does the action without reference to a specific **object,** this prefix acts as a generic unspecified object. For example, in (11a) the word for 'lender' is shown; it comes from the transitive verb 'lend to' (literally 'cause to borrow'; **causative** constructions are discussed in chapter 14) and ordinarily has an object: the person receiving the loan. Because no object is mentioned, the unspecified object reflexive *-adaad-* appears.

(11a) ᎠᏓᏙᎵᏍᏗᏍᎩ
adaatoolsdíísgi
a-adaad-tool-sdiisg-i

3A-RFL-borrow-CAU:INC-AGT
'lender'

(11b) ᎠᏓᏙᎵᏍᏗᏍᎪ
aàdaatoolsdiísgo
a-adaad-tool-sdiísg-o
3A-RFL-borrow-CAU:INC-HAB
'He lends.'

If the agentive noun is part of a **compound** that mentions the object, the reflexive is no longer used, as seen in (12).

(12) ᎠᏥᎳ ᎠᏁᎮᎶᎯ
ajiíla anééhlohi
ajiíla anii-eehloh-i
fire 3A.NS-feed:INC-AGT
'Catholics' ('fire-feeders')

In like manner, if the agentive noun is used with a **local person** prefix the reflexive does not appear. In (13c) the **Set B prefix** is the object of the healing and the *-adaad-* prefix is absent.

(13a) ᏗᏓᏅᏫᏍᎩ
diidaahnvv́wíisgi
di-a-adaad-hnvv́wîisg-i
DST2-3A-RFL-heal:INC-AGT
'medicine man', 'healer'

(13b) ᎧᏅᏫᏍᎪᎢ
kanvv́wîisgóoʔi
ga-hnvv́wîisg-óʔi
3A-heal:INC-HAB
'He heals him.'

(13c) ᏦᎩᏅᏫᏍᎩ
joogiihnvv́wíisgi
di-oogii-hnvv́wîisg-i
DST2-1B.PL.EX-heal:INC-AGT
'our healer' ('one who cures us')

Note that for agentive nouns the rule of **pronominal lengthening** does not apply. In the noun examples given above the **third person** prefix *a-* remains

short with a **low tone,** while with the verbal counterparts it is lengthened and has a **lowfall tone.**

In the following sentence in (14) three agentive nouns are illustrated. The first form of 'teacher' is **singular** and the second is **nonsingular.** The third derivation comes from the verb 'become' and has the meaning 'they who will become', referring to future teachers.

(14)

ᏗᏕᏲᎲᏍᎩ	ᎾᏍᎩ
diideeyóóhvsgi	nasgi
di-a-adaa-eeyoóhvsg-i	nasgi
DST2-3A-MDL-teach:INC-AGT	that.one

ᏗᎾᏕᏲᎲᏍᎩ	ᏯᎾᎵᏍᏗᏍᎩ
diinadeeyóóhvsgi	yanalsdíísgi
di-anii-adaa-eeyoóhvsg-i	yi-anii-alsdiisg-i
DST2-3A.NS-MDL-teach:INC-AGT	IRR-3A.NS-become:INC-AGT

'instructor for the teacher trainer program'

Two more examples of agentive nouns are shown in (15). In (15a) the tone change is on the stem, while in (15b) it occurs on a derivational suffix (the **applicative**) that attaches to the stem.

(15a) ᎤᏞᎩ
uudléégi
uu-adleeg-i
3B-throw:INC-AGT
'pitcher'

(15b) ᏗᎦᏬᏂᎯᏎᎯ
digawooniihiséého
di-ga-wooniihis-eéh-i
DST2-3A-speak:CMP-APL:INC-AGT
'(radio show) announcer'

Unlike other derived nouns, a pronominal prefix on an agentive noun may have a **reference function:** the prefix indicates the **person** and **number** of the noun itself. An example of this is seen in (16).

(16) ᏦᏣᏕᎶᏆᏍᎩ
joojadeéhlgwaàsgi
di-oojii-adeehlohgwáàsg-i

DST2-1A.PL.EX-learn:INC-AGT

ᏗᎪᏪᎵ ᏙᎦᎬᏎᏍᏗ 🔊 Track 101
digoohweeli doògaksesdi
di-goohweeli dee-oogii-agasesdi
DST2-paper DST-1B.PL.EX-watch:PRC
'We students are studying.'

Some verbs are specified as always having a distributive prefix. Agentive nouns derived from such verbs bear this prepronominal prefix as well, but in its **secondary form** DST2 *di-* instead of the basic *dee-* form that appears on most verb forms. Four examples of agentive nouns with this distributive prefix are shown in (17) through (20); the nouns are listed with their verb counterparts. These examples demonstrate the changes that the DST2 *di-* undergoes in various environments. In (18a) the *di-* form appears in its basic form. In the second example the *di-* appears before the **vowel** /i/. In (19) the pronominal prefix is the **first person dual exclusive** *oosdii-*, which causes the *di-* to appear as [*j*]. In (20a) **vowel deletion** brings the *di-* next to the pronominal prefix *hi-* (shortened to [*h*] before the /v/ that starts the verb stem) to form the single **syllable** [*tv*] in the derived form.

(17a) ᏗᎦᏆᏗᏍᎩ
diktladiìsg
di-ga-vhtladiîsg-i
DST2-3A-put.out.fire:INC-AGT
'firefighter'

(17b) ᏕᎦᏆᏗᏍᎪᎢ
deektladiîsgóoʔi
dee-ga-vhtladiîsg-óoʔi
DST-3A-put.out.fire:INC-HAB
'He puts out fires.'

(18a) ᏗᏂᏆᏗᏍᎩ
diihntladiìsgi
di-iinii-vhtladiîsg-i
DST2-1A.DL-put.out.fire:INC-AGT
'You and I are firefighters.'

(18b) ᏕᏂᏆᏗᏍᎪᎢ
deehntladiîsgóoʔi

dee-iinii-vhtladîisg-óoʔi
DST-1A.DL-put.out.fire:INC-HAB
'You and I put out fires.'

(19a) KᏅᏍᏛᏝᏗᏍᏗᏍᎩ
joosdvhtladiìsgi
di-oosdii-vhtladîisg-i
DST2-1A.DL.EX-put.out.fire:INC-AGT
'He and I are firefighters.'

(19b) VᏅᏍᏛᏝᏗᏍᏗᏍᎪᎢ
doòsdvhtladîisgóoʔi
dee-oosdii-vhtladîisg-óoʔi
DST-1A.DL.EX-put.out.fire:INC-HAB
'He and I put out fires.'

(20a) ᏛᏝᏗᏍᏗᏍᎩ
tvtladiìsgi
di-hi-vhtladîisg-i
DST2-2A-put.out.fire:INC-AGT
'You are a firefighter.'

(20b) ᏕᎲᏝᏗᏍᏗᏍᎪᎢ
deehvtladîisgóoʔi
dee-hi-vhtladîisg-óoʔi
DST-2A-put.out.fire:INC-HAB
'You put out fires.'

In all of these examples the distributive prefixes do not indicate the number of the **subject**; the pronominal prefixes themselves indicate whether the subject is singular or nonsingular. In (21a) the pronominal prefix *a-* indicates a single police officer, while in (21b) the nonsingular form *anii-* indicates two or more police officers. In both cases *di-* probably indicates that the act of catching is performed multiple times and/or distributed over multiple objects. Because this noun is based on a transitive verb, it requires the unspecified object reflexive.

(21a) ᏗᏓᏂᏱᏍᎩ
diidaaniiyíisgi
di-a-adaad-niiyiisg-i
DST2-3A-RFL-catch:INC-AGT
'police officer'

(21b) ᏗᎾᏓᏂᏱᏍᎩ
diinadaaniiyíísgi
di-anii-adaad-niiyiisg-i
DST2-3A.NS-RFL-catch:INC-AGT
'police officers'

Agentive nouns that are derived from transitive verbs can refer to the subject as well as the object. Three examples are shown in (22). (22a) has a **combined local** prefix and translates into English with a possessive pronoun. In (22b) a Set B prefix indicates that a third person is the subject and a local person is the object. (22c) is a compound based on the same verb used to form 'police officer' in the previous examples. Because an object is included, the unspecified object reflexive is not present.

(22a) ᏗᏍᏇᏲᎲᏍᎩ
disgweehyóóhvsgi
di-sgi-eehyoohvsg-i
DST2-2/1-teach:INC-AGT
'You are my teacher.'

(22b) ᎠᎩᏍᏓᏴᎲᏍᎩ
aksdaayv́v́hvsgi
agi-sdaayvv́hvsg-i
1B-provide.meal:INC-AGT
'my wife' ('my cook')

(22c) ᎩᏟ ᏗᏂᏂᏱᏍᎩ
giihli diiniiniiyíísgi
giihli di-anii-ʔniiyiisg-i
dog DST2-3A.NS-catch:INC-AGT
'dog catchers'

Agentive nouns do not always refer to a profession; in some instances they are used much like an *-ing* phrase in English, as in (23).

(23) ᎪᏪᎵ ᏓᎬᎩᏅᏁᎸ
goohweeli dagvvgiinvnelv
goohweeli da-gvvgi-vginvnel-v
letter TOW-3NS/1-send:CMP-EXP

ᎠᎾᏁᎵᏗᏍᎬ ᎠᎩᏃᏎᎯ
ananeldisgv́ akinooséého

anii-aneldisg-v́ agi-hnooseeh-i
3A.NS-get.married:INC-DVB 1B-tell:INC-AGT
'They sent me a letter telling me they were getting married.'

12.1.1.2. *Incompletive Stem with Deverbalizer (DVB) Suffix*

The Incompletive stem and the **deverbalizer** (DVB) **suffix** together create a derived noun. The deverbalizer suffix is similar to the **experienced past** suffix but with a **highfall tone.** Two examples with their verb counterparts are shown in (24) and (25).

(24a) DᏓᎶᏂᏫ
aàdaaleeníha
a-adaa-aleeníha
3A-MDL-begin(I):PRC
'It is beginning.'

(24b) DᏓᎶᏂᏍᎬᎢ
adaleeniisgv́v̀ʔi
a-adaa-aleeniisg-v́v̀ʔi
3A-MDL-begin(I):INC-DVB
'beginning'

(25a) DᏞᏍᏗᎢ
aàdléesgóoʔi
a-adléesg-óoʔi
3A-turn.off:INC-HAB
'He turns off the road.' (Feeling 1975a:12)

(25b) DᏞᏍᎬᎢ
aàdléesgv́v̀ʔi
a-adléesg-v́v̀ʔi
3A-turn.off:INC-DVB
'turn-off' (Feeling 1975a:12)

Some nouns resulting from this process have the characteristics of both nouns and verbs; these derivations are referred to as **verbal nouns.** Pronominal lengthening applies to them as if they were verbs; moreover, the nonsingular is formed with *dee-* rather than with the *di-* form that is usually used on derived nouns. Two examples of this pattern are shown in (26).

(26a) ᏓᏞᏍᎬᎢ
daàdléesgv́v̀ʔi

dee-a-adléesg-v́v́ʔi
DST-3A-turn.off:INC-DVB
'turn-offs' (Feeling 1975a:12)

(26b) ᏚᏭᎬᏛ
duuwuuktv́
dee-uu-uugoht-v́
DST-3B-plan:CMP-DVB
'his plans' (The Turtle and the Rabbit, line 11)

From a function standpoint the word 'turn-off' (on a road) is noun-like in that it can play a typical noun role. In (27) below the derivation 'turn-off' is acting as an object.

(27)	Ꮭ	ᏱᏥᎪᏩᏔ	ᏓᏞᏍᎬᎢ
	hla	yijigohwahta	daàdléesgv́v́ʔi
	hla	yi-ji-gohwahta	dee-a-adléesg-v́v́ʔi
	NEG	IRR-1A-see:IMM	DST-3A-turn.off:INC-DVB
	'I didn't see the turn-off.' (Feeling 1975a:12)		

In (28) 'blooming' is acting like a noun and (together with 'cotton') serves as the object for the verb 'watch'.

(28)	ᎤᏥᎸ	ᎠᏥᎸᏍᎬᎢ	ᎠᎩᎸᏉᏗ	ᎠᏩᎦᏙᏍᏙᏗᎢ
	ujiilv	ajiilvvsgv́v́ʔi	aàgilvvkdi	awaktosdohdííʔi
	ujiilv	a-jiilvvsg-v́v́ʔi	agi-lvvkdi	agi-agahtosdohdííʔi
	cotton	3A-bloom:INC-DVB	1B-like:PRC	1B-watch:INF
	'When the cotton is blooming, I like to watch it.'			

A sample list of these derivations and their verbs of origin is given in (29). The noun in (29b) has the **impersonal Set B prefix** *oo-*.

(29a)	ᎠᏕᏲᎲᎢ	aàdeeyohv́v́ʔi	'curve'
	ᎠᏕᏲᎭ	aàdeyoha	'it's going around'
(29b)	ᎣᏲᏏᏍᎬᎢ	ooyóosiisgv́v́ʔi	'hunger'
	ᎤᏲᏏᏍᎪᎢ	uùyóosiisgóoʔi	'he is hungry'
(29c)	ᎬᏅᎢ	gvvhnv́v́ʔi	'his life'
	ᎬᏏ	gvvhna	'he is alive'
(29d)	ᎠᏫᏒᏅᎢ	aàhwiisvnv́v́ʔi	'garden'
	ᎠᏫᏍᎦ	aàhwisga	'he is planting it'

Many nouns in Cherokee were probably formed this way a long time ago and therefore have stems that are no longer recognizable.

12.1.2. Nouns Formed from the Completive (CMP) Verb Stem

To create a noun that is the result of an action the Completive is used as a stem with the deverbalizer suffix. In (30a) the noun has the meaning 'one who has completely grown up'; the nonsingular form of this noun is shown in (30b). The verb from which this noun derives is given in (30c). The derived form emphasizes that the act of growing has been completed by adding the **terminative** (TRM) derivational suffix to the verb stem. These prefixes are discussed in chapter 13.

(30a) ᎤᏛᏠᏅᎢ
uutvsohnv̋v́ʔi
uu-atvs-ohn-v̋v́ʔi
3B-grow(I):CMP-TRM:CMP-DVB
'old man'

(30b) ᏧᏄᏛᏠᏅᎢ
juuntvsohnv̋v́ʔi
di-uunii-atvs-ohn-v̋v́ʔi
DST2-3B.NS-grow(I):CMP-TRM:CMP-DVB
'old men'

(30c) ᎤᏛᏒᎢ
uùtvsvv́ʔi
uu-atvs-vv́ʔi
3B-grow(I):CMP-EXP
'He grew.'

The noun derivation above follows the more typical derivation pattern of using *di-* (DST2). In (30b) this prefix is before a vowel and appears as [*j*]. As is typical with noun derivations, the pronominal prefix does not undergo pronominal lengthening and remains short. By way of contrast, in (31) the verbal noun derivation has the *dee-* and does undergo the lengthening.

(31) ᏓᏔᎴᏒᎢ
daàtaleesv̋v́ʔi
dee-a-talees-v̋v́ʔi
DST-3A-make.hole:CMP-DVB
'holes' ('that which has been drilled')

Three examples of Completive-based noun derivations are provided in (32). As is common with any derivational process, the new word can have a somewhat different meaning; this new meaning is often more specific than the literal meaning of the derivation. For example, in (32b) the word for 'butter' is simply 'that which is made'; and in (32c) the word for 'my home' is 'where I have gone'.

(32a) ᏗᏓᏟᏝᎼᏔᏅᎢ
diidaahliiloòstanv́v́ʔi
di-a-adaad-ahliiloòstan-v́v́ʔi
DST2-3A-RFL-draw:CMP-DVB
'picture'

(32b) ᎪᏢᏅᎢ
goohlvvnv́v́ʔi
ga-oohlvvn-v́v́ʔi
3A-make:CMP-DVB
'butter'

(32c) ᏗᏇᏅᏒ
diigwéenvvsv́
di-agi-eenvvs-v́
TOW-1B-go:CMP-DVB
'my home'

12.1.3. Nouns Formed from the Infinitive (INF) Verb Stem

The Infinitive stem serves as the base for nouns indicating location and ability as well as nouns referring to objects that are used to perform the action described by the verb. For example, the stem of the verb 'play' can derive two play-related objects, as seen in (33). As is typical for noun derivations, the *di-* form of the distributive also appears on verbs in their Infinitive stem. In (33b) the difference in meaning is expressed through a causative derivational suffix and a tone change.

(33a) ᎠᏁᎵᏗ
aneéhldi
a-neéhldi
3A-play:INF
'doll'

(33b) ᏗᏁᎵᏙᏗ
diinéehldohdi

di-a-neéhl-dohdi
DST2-3A-play-CAU:INF\INS
'toy'

The different kinds of nouns derived from the Infinitive stem are explored below.

12.1.3.1. *Instrumental Noun*

An **instrumental noun** is derived from an Infinitive stem that generally indicates the instrument for performing the verb. Some of these derivations have a tone change to indicate their derivational status and typically use a third person **dummy prefix.** (34) is an example of this derivation along with the **Present Continuous** stem form of the verb.

(34a) ᏗᏎᏍᏗ
diisésdi
di-a-asésdi
DST2-3A-count:INF
'numbers'

(34b) ᏓᏎᎯᎭ
daàsehíha
dee-a-sehíha
DST-3A-count:PRC
'He's counting them.'

This construction is very productive in Cherokee for forming nouns. Four more examples are shown in (35). This nonsingular form is exemplified in (35a) and (35c).

(35a) ᏗᎧᏃᎩᏍᏗ
dikanoogíísdi
di-ga-hnoogiisdi
DST2-3A-sing:INF\INS
'song', 'songbook'

(35b) ᎠᏓᏙᎵᏍᏗ
adaadoólîisdi
a-adaadoólîisdi
3A-pray:INF
'prayer'

(35c) ᏗᏯᏇᏄᎩᏍᏗ
diigweénúùgiisdi
di-a-gweénúùgiisdi
DST2-3A-pinch:INF
'guitar'

(35d) ᎠᏓᏅᏗ
adaáhnedi
a-adaad-hnedi
3A-RFL-give:INF\INS
'gift'

The two examples in (36) have the same basic translation, but with a slightly different emphasis. The highfall tone in (36a) shows that the Infinitive is acting as a noun, while in (36b) the lack of the highfall indicates that it is an **adjectival Infinitive.**

(36a) ᎯᎠᎾ ᏦᎧᏍᏗ Track 102
hiʔina jóóksdi
hiʔi=na ja-ookisdi
this=FC 2B-smoke:INF\INS
'This is for you to smoke.'
('This is your thing for smoking.')

(36b) ᎯᎠᎾ ᏦᎧᏍᏗ
hiʔina jooksdi
hiʔi=na ja-oogisdi
this=FC 2B-smoke:INF
'This is for you to smoke.'
('This is to smoke.')

12.1.3.2. *Place Noun*

A **place noun** indicates where a verb occurs. These forms are typically third person; speakers use either singular or nonsingular pronominal prefixes without a change in meaning. Five examples of this very productive pattern are shown in (37). Many of these derivations bear an unspecified object reflexive prefix to show that the verb from which the noun is derived had no specific object. In this usage the Infinitive can appear in its **long form.** This form is less frequent than the short form; of the five examples below, only the last exemplifies it.

(37a) ᏧᎾᏓᏂᏏᏗ
juunadaaniísóhdi
di-uunii-adaad-niísóhdi
DST2-3B.NS-RFL-bury:INF
'cemetery'

(37b) ᏧᏂᎳᏫᏍᏗ
juuniilaàwisdi
di-uunii-laàwisdi
DST2-3B.NS-have.church:INF
'church'

(37c) ᏧᎾᏗᏔᏍᏗ
juunadiitasdi
di-uunii-adiitasdi
DST2-3B.NS-drink:INF
'bar'

(37d) ᏧᎾᏓᎯᎵᏓᏍᏗ
juundahiʔliídáàsdi
di-uunii-adaad-hiʔliídáàsdi
DST2-3B.NS-RFL-try:INF
'courthouse'

(37e) ᏧᏂᏆᎾᏲᏍᏗᎢ
juuniikwanayosdííʔi
di-uunii-kwanayosdííʔi
DST2-3B.NS-play.cards:INF
'casino'

Place nouns derived from an Infinitive have a prefix with a **participant function;** they often take a default Set B third person nonsingular to create the meaning 'place where they VERB'. In (38a) the usual way of saying 'school' is shown: 'place where they learn'. To create a more specific reference it is possible to change the pronominal prefix. In (38b) the literal meaning is 'place where I learn'. These more specific meanings typically translate into English with a possessive. (38c) demonstrates that the noun remains as a default third person singular regardless of the person marking being singular or nonsingular.

(38a) ᏧᎾᏕᎶᏆᏍᏗ
juundehlohgwaàsdi

di-uunii-adeehlohgwaàsdi
DST2-3B.NS-learn:INF
'school'

(38b) ᏗᎩᏕᎶᏍᏗ
diigwadehlohgwaàsdi
di-agi-adeehlohgwaàsdi
DST2-1B-learn:INF
'my school'

(38c) ᎣᎩᎸᏉᏗ ᏦᎦᏕᎶᏍᏗ
oògiilvv́kwdi joogadeehlgwaàsdi
oogii-lvv́kwdi di-oogii-adeehlohgwaàsdi
1B.PL.EX-like:PRC DST2-1B.PL.EX-learn:INF
'We like our school.'

Many place nouns have the possibility of using the Set A third person singular or the Set B third person nonsingular form of the pronominal prefix. In (39) the two examples were given by two different speakers; both have the meaning 'bank'.

(39a) ᎠᏕᎳᏗᏗ
adeéladiidi
adeéla+di-a-hdi
money+DST2-3A-keep:INF
'bank'

(39b) ᎠᏕᎳᏧᏂᏗ
adeélajuuniidi
adeéla+di-uunii-hdi
money+DST2-3B.NS-keep:INF
'bank'

Sometimes the use of the a third person singular in Set A or a third person nonsingular in Set B represents a slightly different meaning. The addition of the distributive prefix for some speakers further changes the meaning. In (40) the word has different meanings based on the appearance of the distributive as well as the number (singular or nonsingular) of the pronominal prefix.

(40a) ᎠᏗᏔᏍᏗᎢ
adiitasdííʔi

a-adiitasdííʔi
3A-drink:INF
'drinking fountain'

(40b) ᎤᏅᏗᏔᏍᏗᎢ
uunadiitasdííʔi
uunii-adiitasdííʔi
3B.NS-drink:INF
'drinking place (for animals)'

(40c) ᏧᏅᏗᏔᏍᏗᎢ
juunadiitasdííʔi
di-uunii-adiitasdííʔi
DST2-3B.NS-drink:INF
'bar'

12.1.3.3. *Activity Infinitive*

The Infinitive stem can be used as a noun that refers to an activity. An example of this **activity Infinitive** is shown in (41). This use of the Infinitive triggers **prefix shift.**

(41) ᎣᏍᏓ ᏗᏣᏃᎩᏍᏗ
óósda dichanoogiisdi
óósda di-ja-hnoogiisdi
good DST2-2B-sing:INF
'Your singing is good.'

Unlike the **obligation Infinitive,** this derivation does not have a **modal tone** (MOD). These two uses are contrasted in (42).

(42a) ᎣᏍᏓ ᏗᎩᏃᎩᏍᏗᎢ 🔊 Track 103
óósda diikinoogììsdíʔi
óósda di-agi-hnoogììsdíʔi
good DST2-1B-sing:INF
'My singing is good.'

(42b) ᎠᏎ ᎣᏍᏓ ᏗᎩᏃᎩᏍᏗ
ase óósda diikinoogíísdi
ase óósda di-agi-hnoogììsdi
must good DST2-1B-sing:INF\MOD
'I have to sing well.'

12.1.3.4. *Nouns Formed with Causative (CAU) Derivational Suffix*

The Causative suffixes create an object that is used to perform an action. Some of these derivations have an **instrumental tone** (INS) on the rightmost long vowel. Two examples are shown in (43).

(43a) ᏗᏂᏬᏍᏙᏗ
diihnawóósdohd
di-a-ahnawoos-dohdi
DST2-3A-cover-CAU:INF\INS
'bed covers' ('that to cover with')

(43b) ᏗᎵᏌᏆᎴᎵᏙᏗ
diilsagwaleéhlídohdi
di-a-ali-sagwaleéhlí-dohdi
DST2-3A-MDL-roll-CAU:INF
'wheelbarrow'

The **causative base** to which this suffix attaches seems to be either a verb's Infinitive form with the final [*di*] element removed or the Present Continuous stem with the final syllable removed. In (44a) the verb 'be cold' appears in its Infinitive stem; in (44b) the derived noun has added an incompletive causative suffix to form the base for an agentive noun.

(44a)	ᎠᏴᏜᏗᏍᏗ	ᎠᏩᏚᎵ
	ahyvvdladiisdi	aàwaduuli
	a-hyvvdladiis<u>di</u>	agi-aduuli
	3A-get.cold:INF	1B-want:PRC
	'I want it to be cold.'	

(44b) ᎠᏂᏜᏗᏍᏗᏍᎩ
ahyvvdladiisdíísgi
a-hyvvdladiis-dîisg-i
3A-get.cold-CAU:INC-AGT
'refrigerator', 'air conditioner'

(45a)	ᎦᏁᏍᏓᎳᏗᏍᏗ	ᎠᏩᏚᎵ
	ganesdaladiisdi	aàwaduuli
	ga-nesdaladiis<u>di</u>	agi-aduuli
	3A-get.cold:INF	1B-want:PRC
	'I want it to freeze.'	

(45b) ᎦᏁᏍᏓᎳᏗᏍᏗᏍᎩ
ganesdaladiisdíísgi
ga-nesdaladiis-diísg-i
3A-get.cold-CAU:INC-AGT
'ice storm'

If the verb from which the noun is derived is transitive, it is possible for the object of the transitive verb to be part of the noun. An example of this type of compound is shown in (46).

(46)	ᎠᎹ	ᎠᎦᎾᏩᏙᏗ
	ama	agaanahwdóhdi
	ama	a-gaanaw-hdóhdi
	water	3A-get.hot-CAU:INF
	'kettle'	

12.1.3.5. *Infinitive Stem As Nominal Clause*

One of the most frequent uses of the Infinitive is to create a **nominal clause** that is the subject or object of a main verb. The complement Infinitive acts as the object of another verb; this construction is characterized by prefix shift and the ability to appear in the long form. The **topic Infinitive,** by contrast, has a **topic tone** change and therefore does not have a long form; it typically has a dummy prefix that does not undergo prefix shift. Four examples are presented in (47); the first three are complement Infinitives, and the fourth is a topic Infinitive. The long form appears in (47c).

(47a)	ᎨᎦᏟᏃᎮᏙᏗ	ᎤᎾᏚᎵ
	geegahlnoohehdóhdi	uùnaduuli
	geegii-ali-hnoohehdóhdi	uunii-aduuli
	3NS/1PL-MDL-tell:INF	3B.NS-want:PRC
	'They want to talk to us.'	

(47b)	ᎭᏓᎯᏕᏍ	ᏗᏣᎸᏫᏍᏓᏁᏗ
	hadahiides	dijalvv́hwísdaàndi
	hi-adahiide=s	di-ja-lvv́hwísdaàndi
	2A-be.willing:PRC=Q	DST2-2B-work:INF
	'Are you willing to work?'	

(47c)	ᎤᎬᏫᏳᎯ	ᎤᏬᏂᏌ	ᏚᏂᎳᏕᎸ
	uugvvwiyuuhi	uuwóoniísa	duùniíládeélv

uu-gvvwiyuuhi	uu-wóoniis-a	dee-uu-niíládeél-v
3B-chief	3B-speak:CMP-CVB	DST-3B-urge:CMP-EXP

BⲰ	ᏧᎾᎵᏍᏕᎸᏗᎢ
yvvwi	juunalsdehldííʔi
yvvwi	di-uunii-ali-sdehldííʔi
people	DST2-3B.NS-MDL-help:INF

'When the chief spoke, he urged the people to work together.' (Feeling 1975a:109)

(47d)	ᏒᎯᏰᏱ	ᎣᏍᏓ	ᎠᎦᏙᏍᏙᏗ	ᏓᎵᏍᏗᏝᏁᎬ
	svhiyééyi	óósda	aktóósdohdi	dalsdihlaneegv
	svhiyééyi	óósda	a-gahtoósdohdi	dalsdihlaneegv
	at.night	good	3A-watch:INF\TOP	tide

'In the evening it's good to watch the tide.'

12.1.4. Nouns Formed with Participle (PCP) Derivational Suffix

The *-da* **participle suffix** is a productive suffix for creating new nouns, typically denoting an object that is the completed result of the action of a verb. The suffix attaches to the **participle base**, a special shortened form of the Completive stem. Many nouns appear to have a **frozen** *-da* (their original **root** or the process by which they have been derived from their root is unknown). A few of these nouns are shown in (48). Some of the nouns have the ending [*ta*]; this is perhaps an older form of the participle.

(48)	ᏧᏓᎿᏩᏓ	juudáahnawiida	'cross'
	ᎧᏃᎩᏓ	kanoogíída	'song'
	ᎧᏃᎮᏓ	kanooheéda	'news', 'gospel'
	ᎩᏄᏔ	giinúúta	'quarter'
	ᎦᏯᏖᏓ	gayaluúda	'stamp'

Evidence for the status of these words as derived is that they form the non-singular with the distributive (DST2) *di-* used for derived nouns. Two pairs are shown in (49).

(49a)	ᎦᏝᏓ	gáahlida	'arrow'
	ᏗᎦᏝᏓ	digáahlida	'arrows'

(49b)	ᎤᎾᏓᏕᏒᏓ	uunadaadeèsv́v́da	'chain'
	ᏧᎾᏓᏕᏒᏓ	juunadaadeèsv́v́da	'chains'

12.1.5. Nouns Derived from Other Parts of Speech

12.1.5.1. *Nouns Derived from Adjectives*
In Cherokee **adjectives** can be used as nouns. Nouns referring to people that are derived from adjectives receive double marking: their nonsingular status is indicated by both the pronominal prefix as well as the distributive *di-*. Two examples are given in (50) and (51).

(50a)	ᎤᏍᏗᎢ	uusdííʔi	'baby' (from 'small')
(50b)	ᏧᏂᏍᏗᎢ	juunsdííʔi	'babies'
(51a)	ᎠᏲᎵ	ayóóhli	'child' (from 'little')
(51b)	ᏗᏂᏲᎵ	diiniiyóóhli	'children'

12.1.5.2. *Nouns Derived from Other Nouns*
A few suffixes change the meaning of the noun. Location nouns are derived from another noun by adding a suffix that consists of a vowel with a highfall tone followed by *-ʔi*. This **locative** (LOC) suffix creates the meaning 'place of NOUN'. An example of a noun with its derived locative counterpart is shown in (52).

(52a) ᎪᎢ
goʔi
goʔi
'grease', 'oil'

(52b) ᎪᎢᎢ
goʔííʔi
goʔi-ʔi
grease-LOC
'Greasy' (a town in northeastern Oklahoma)

The vowel that has the highfall tone is usually the same vowel that ends the original word. Four examples with words ending in /i/, /u/, and /o/ are shown in (53). The first two are towns in northeastern Oklahoma.

(53a) ᏓᏄᎪ dahnúugo 'gar'
ᏓᏄᎪᎢ dahnúugóóʔi 'Vian' ('place of gar')

(53b) ᎫᎫ guùgu 'bottle'
ᎫᎫᎢ guùgúúʔi 'Bartlesville'

(53c) ᎠᏂᏍᏆᏂ aniisgwaani 'Mexicans'
ᎠᏂᏍᏆᏂᎢ aniisgwaaníiʔi 'Mexico'

If the word ends in /a/, however, the process is unpredictable and the highfall vowel is /o/ or /v/. Because this derivation is unpredictable, a dictionary of Cherokee should list these forms with the original word. Two examples are given in (54).

(54a)	ᏧᏱᎦ	dlaàhyga	'bluejay'
	ᏧᏱᎨᎢ	dlaàhygv́v́ʔi	'Jay' (a town in northeastern Oklahoma)
(54b)	ᎠᎫᏌ	aguúsa	'Creek person'
	ᎫᏐᎢ	guusóóʔi	'Muskogee' (a town in northeastern Oklahoma)

This suffix *-hi* is a less-common variant of the locative and is also used to indicate a location. This suffix is probably no longer **productive,** but it occurs on some high-frequency words. Three examples are shown in (55). (55b) could be literally translated as 'place of rocks'; it most often occurs as an adjective.

(55a) ᏣᎳᎩᎯ ᎠᏰᎵ
jalagííhi ayéehli
jalagi-hi ayéehli
Cherokee-LOC center
'Cherokee Nation'

(55b) ᏅᏲᎯ
nv̀v̀yóóhi
nv̀v̀ya-hi
rock-LOC
'rocky'

(55c) ᎠᎼᎯ
áamóóhi
áama-hi
salt-LOC
'Salina' (a town in northeastern Oklahoma)

The suffix *-yááʔi* is used to indicate 'pure' or 'real'. In (56) the first noun with this suffix is a **root noun;** the last noun meaning 'inhabitant' is itself a derived agentive noun. The highfall tone normally present on the agentive noun is no longer there, as no word can have more than one highfall tone; moreover, this tone is always found on the rightmost long vowel of a word.

(56) ᎠᏂᏴᏫᏯ ᎠᎹᏰᎵ ᎠᏁᎯᏯᎢ 👂 Track 104
aniiyvvwiiya amáyéehli aneéhiyááʔi
anii-yvvwii-ya ama+ayéehli anii-ééh-i-yááʔi

3A.NS-person-real water+center 3A.NS-reside:INC-AGT-real
'Indians are indigenous to America.' (Feeling 1975a:90)

12.1.5.3. *Nouns Derived from Unknown Sources*

Some nouns in Cherokee appear to be derived in that they take the prepronominal prefix *di-* to indicate nonsingular number, but the original roots of these words are unknown. The ability to indicate number is an unpredictable feature of a noun that must simply be learned as a property of the noun. Eight examples are given in (57). With the exception of 'tree', all of these examples have a Set A or Set B prefix. Many body parts fall into this category; the Incompletive object derivation exemplified in (57c) is especially common for this class of nouns.

(57a)	DᏖᏢᏙ	ateeliído	'plate'
	ᏗᏖᏢᏙ	diiteeliído	'plates'
(57b)	ᎤᎩᏙᏓ	uugiìdáhli	'feather'
	ᏧᎩᏙᏓ	juugiìdáhli	'feathers'
(57c)	ᎤᏫᏢᎢ	uùhwídlv́v́ʔi	'his/her wrist'
	ᏚᏫᏢᎢ	duùhwídlv́v́ʔi	'his/her wrists'
(57d)	ᏡᎬᎢ	dluhgv́v́ʔi	'tree'
	ᏕᏡᎬᎢ	deedluhgv́v́ʔi	'trees'
(57e)	ᎠᏆᏍᏙ	akwsdo	'pillow'
	ᏗᏆᏍᏙ	diikwsdo	'pillows'
(57f)	ᎤᏪᎳ	uweela	'liver'
	ᏧᏪᎳ	juweela	'livers'
(57g)	ᎧᏁᏌᎢ	kaneèsáʔi	'box'
	ᏗᎧᏁᏌᎢ	dikaneèsáʔi	'boxes'
(57h)	ᎦᏍᎩᎶ	gaasgilo	'chair', 'table'
	ᏗᎦᏍᎩᎶ	digaasgilo	'chairs', 'tables'

It is possible that over time many such nouns lose the ability to indicate number as their status as derived words is forgotten. Pulte and Feeling (1977:275) address this phenomenon in their study of nineteenth-century descriptions of Cherokee grammars. They point out that Pickering in his 1831 grammar lists several nouns with *di-* that do not take this prefix in their modern form. This ability to indicate number may be subject to individual or dialectal variation. For example, one of the forms that Pulte and Feeling consider unable to indicate number in modern Cherokee is 'knife'; Holmes and Smith (1977:108), however, list a *di-* form of this noun. It is possible that this ability to indicate number is based upon the individual speaker's perception of the noun as being derived or not. For example, Feeling (1975a:189) does not list any nonsingular for *yvvgi* 'fork', 'nail', 'needle'; he also does not refer the reader to a related verb from which this noun could be derived. This noun therefore is a root noun for Feeling and, not surprisingly, has no nonsingular form. Holmes and Smith (1977:108), however, indicate that the literal meaning of *yvvgi* is 'sticks-in', suggesting that they perceive this noun to be derived from a verb meaning 'stick into'. They list the nonsingular form of this noun as *diyvgi.* Likewise *uloogili* 'cloud' has only a singular form for Feeling (1975a:174), while Holmes and Smith (1977:109) list a nonsingular form. Holmes and Smith (1977:109) observe: "In general, words forming plurals with -ni- [the third person nonsingular pronominal prefixes] are thought of as potent, capable of independent movement. Words forming their plurals with *di-* are thought of as a passive, incapable of independent movement."

12.1.6. Compound Nouns

Compound nouns are nouns composed of two or more words. There are many different kinds of compounds. One kind is a **blend compound,** where the two stems have fused somewhat and are no longer pronounced or written as separate words. These compounds are indicated with the plus sign (+) between the parts being joined. Four examples are shown in (58). Most adjectives have a highfall tone; some may lose this tone in a blend compound.

(58a) ᎠᎹᏰᏝ
amáyéehli
ama+ayééhli
water+center
'America'

(58b) ᎪᎶᎮ
goóléého
góóla+a-eéh-i
winter+3A-reside:INC-AGT
'pneumonia' ('it lives in winter') (Feeling 1975a:122)

(58c) ᎠᏕᎳᏧᏢᎢ
adeéljuúhlv̋v̋ʔi
adeéla+di-uu-hl-v̋v̋ʔi
money+DST2-3B-have:INC-DVB
'California' ('where they have money')

(58d) ᏣᎳᎫᏪᏙᏘᎢ
jalaguwéetííʔi
jalagi+uu-éeti-ʔi
Cherokee+3B-old-LOC
'North Carolina' ('place of the old Cherokees')

A typical compound in Cherokee consists of a phrase with two or more separate words. When taken together, these words have a meaning that is more specific than the meaning of their individual parts. These compounds can be further grouped according to their individual elements. One of the most common is a verb-derived noun and its object. Two examples are shown in (59).

(59a) ᏧᏂᏢᎩ ᏗᎦᏘᏯ
juuniidlv́v́gi diiktiíya
di-uunii-hdlv́vg-i di-a-gahtiíya
DST2-3B.NS-be.sick:INC-AGT DST2-3A-wait:PRC
'nurse'

(59b) ᎤᏔᎾ ᎥᏓᎵ ᏍᎪᎯᏗᎯ
úútana vvdali sgohidííhi
uu-ắtana vvdali sgohi+di-a-h-i
3B-big pond ten+DST2-3A-kill:INC-AGT
'Lake Tenkiller'

Compounds can have more than two parts, as in (60).

(60a) ᏙᏓᏩᏍᎬ ᏗᏕᎶᏆᏍᏗ ᏗᏕᏲᎲᏍᎩ
doódáwaàsgv diideehlgwasdi diideehyóóhvsgi
doodawaàsgv di-a-adeehlgwasdi di-a-adaa-eehyoohvsg-i
Sunday DST2-3A-learn:INF DST2-3A-MDL-teach:INC-AGT
'Sunday school teacher'

(60b) ᎣᏩᏌ ᎢᏯᏛᏅᏗ ᎠᏕᎶᏆᏍᏗ
owaásа iyadvhndi adeehlgwaasdi
oo-v́v́sa ii-a-advhndi a-adeehlgwaasdi
3B.IP-EMP.PRO NI2-3A-do:INF 3A-learn:INF
'homework'

Compounds are often descriptive phrases. Some of these phrasal compounds look like a typical sequence of an adjective and a noun. These phrases are identifiable as compounds because their meaning is more specific than can be understood from the individual words. Several examples are given in (61).

(61a) ᏚᏯ ᎠᏂᏤ
duuya aniije
duuya anii-ije
bean 3A.NS-green
'green beans'

(61b) ᎤᏟᏂᎩᏓ ᎠᏗᏔᏍᏗ
uuhliniígid adiitasdi
uu-ahliniígida a-adiitasdi
3B-strong 3A-drink:INF
'whisky'

(61c) ᏌᏊ ᎦᏆᏘ
saagwu gáagwati
saagwu gáagwati
one wheel
'wheelbarrow'

(61d) ᏅᏃᎯ ᏚᎾᏠᏱᎸ
nvvnoóhi duunadloóhyílv́
nvvnoóhi dee-uunii-adloóhyíl-v́
road DST-3B.NS-cry:CMP-DVB
'Trail of Tears'

(61e) ᎤᎾᏓᎶᎯᏍᏗ ᎠᏍᏓᏅᏅ
uundahlohisdi aàsdanvvhnv́
uunii-adahlohisdi a-sdanvvhn-v́
3B.NS-beat.in.a.race:INF 3A-draw:CMP-DVB
'the winning line' (The Turtle and the Rabbit, line 41)

The word *iyúúsdi* 'like' is especially productive for forming compounds. A list of some compounds formed with this word is given in (62).

(62)

ᏘᏁᏆ	ᎢᏳᏍᏗ	tinegwa	iyúúsdi	'shrew' (lit. 'like a mole')
ᎧᏬᏄ	ᎢᏳᏍᏗ	kawonu	iyúúsdi	'mud-hen' (lit. 'like a duck')
ᎢᏤ	ᎢᏳᏍᏗ	ije	iyúúsdi	'green' (lit. 'like new')
ᏃᏥ	ᎢᏳᏍᏗ	nohji	iyúúsdi	'turpentine' (lit. 'like a pine tree')
ᏐᏈᎵ	ᎢᏳᏍᏗ	soógwíli	iyúúsdi	'zebra' (lit. 'like a horse')
ᏓᏬᎵ	ᎢᏳᏍᏗ	dawóoli	iyúúsdi	'cork' (lit. 'like a mushroom')

A common pattern is an instrumental noun preceded by its object; three examples are shown in (63).

(63a) ᏅᏓ ᏗᏎᏍᏗ
nv́v́da diisesdi
nv́v́da di-a-asesdi
sun/moon DST2-3A-count:INF
'calendar' (lit. 'for counting suns and moons')

(63b) ᏗᏂᏲᏟ ᎤᎾᎵᏍᏕᎸᏙᏗ
dii-anii-yóóhli uunii-alsdeehl-dohdi
DST2-3A.NS-child 3B.NS-help-CAU:INF
'alimony'

(63c) ᏍᎩᎾ ᎤᎩᎸᏙᏗ
sgiin uukilv́v́dohd
sgiina uu-kilv́v́dohdi
devil 3B-ride.on:INF
'walking stick (type of insect)'

Another common pattern is an agentive noun preceded by its object, as in (64).

(64a) ᎤᏟ ᏩᏗᏅᏓ ᎠᎯᏙᎢ
udli wadiinv́v́da ahiidóóʔi
udli wi-a-adiinvv́-da a-hiidooʔ-i
away TRN-3A-throw.away-PCP 3A-carry:INC-AGT
'garbage man'

(64b) ᏗᎪᏪᎵ ᏗᎧᏂᏙ
digohweéli dikaniidó
di-gohweéli di-ga-hniidoóh-i
DST2-letter DST2-3A-carry:INC-AGT
'mailman'

(64c) ᎤᏅᏏᏴ ᏗᏂᏝᎲᏍᎩ
uuhnv́vsiiyv diiniítlahv́sgi
uuhnv́vsiiyv di-anii-tlahv́sg-i
cornerstone DST2-3A.NS-set:INC-AGT
'Freemasons'

In summary, derived nouns have the pronominal and prepronominal prefixes of their verbal counterparts. They are distinguished from verbs by different tone patterns and, in most cases, the *di-* (DST2) form of the distributive. Derived nouns are formed from three of the five stems, the Incompletive, Completive, and Infinitive, and can have a number of meanings, including a person or thing that is doing an action, a location where the action is taking place, or an object that is involved with the action or the result of the action. Some of these derivations involve adding a deverbalizer suffix. As described in the following section, deverbalizer suffixes also play an important role in deriving adjectives.

12.2. Adjective Derivation

Adjectives are derived using four derivational suffixes: the deverbalizer suffix *-v́v́ʔi* (DVB), the Participle suffix *-da* (PCP), the **negative deverbalizer** suffix *-v́v́na* (NDV), and the **adjective derivation suffix** *-ha* (ADJ). The new words created by these derivational suffixes also frequently appear as nouns, the only difference being their use in the sentence.

12.2.1. Adjectives Formed with Deverbalizer (DVB) Suffix

Many verbs form adjectives by attaching the deverbalizer to the Completive stem. An example of this process is shown in (65); in (65a) the deverbalized adjective is shown, and in (65b) the Completive stem of the verb with the experienced past suffix is used in a typical past tense verbal construction.

(65a) ᎤᏲᎱᏒ ◉ Track 105
uuyoohuusv́
uu-yoohuus-v́
3B-die:CMP-DVB
'dead'

(65b) ᎤᏲᎱᏒ
uùyoohuusv
uu-yoohuus-v
3B-die:CMP-EXP
'He died.'

Another example of this construction is given in (66). In (66a) the word order object-verb is seen. In (66b) the derived adjective precedes the noun it modifies; moreover, the distributive form *di-* (DST2) typical of adjectives appears.

(66a) ᏅᏯ ᏚᏗᎦᎴᏰᎢ
nvv̀ya duùdiigaléeyvv́ʔi
nvvya dee-uu-adiigaléey-vv́ʔi

rock DST-3B-scatter(T):CMP-EXP
'He scattered the rocks.'

(66b) ᏧᏗᎦᎴᏲᏥ ᏅᏯ
juùdiigaleéyóòjv́ nvv̀ya
di-uu-adiigaleéyóòj-v́ nvv̀ya
DST2-3B-scatter(T):CMP-DVB rock
'scattered rocks'

12.2.2. Adjectives Formed with Participle (PCP) Suffix

Like nouns, the majority of adjectives appear to be derived from verbs. There is a large group of adjectives that end in the participle *-da* suffix. This suffix attaches to the **participle base,** a special shortened form of the Completive stem. Two examples of the participle suffix are shown in (67) and (68); the first example in each pair has a participle adjective, while the second contains the related verb. The participle suffix often causes a highfall tone to appear on the rightmost long vowel of the word.

(67a) ᎤᎧᏲᏓᏍ ᎠᏆᏂᏃ
uukayóódas agwáhnawo
uu-kayoo-da=s agi-áhnawo
3B-dry-PCP=Q 1B-shirt
'Is my shirt dry?'

(67b) ᎠᏆᏂᏃ ᎠᎧᏲᏍᎦ
agwáhnawo aàkayoosga
agi-áhnawo a-kayoosga
1B-shirt 3A-dry:PRC
'My shirt is drying.'

(68a) ᎦᏥᏃᏍᏓ ᎦᏅᏅ ᎠᎩᏑᏰᏒ
gaachinóósd ganvvhnv aksuuyéesv
ga-xxchinóós-da gahnvvnv agi-asuuyées-v
3A-straighten-PCP road 1B-choose:CMP-EXP
'I took the straight road.'

(68b) ᎣᎩᏥᏃᎯᏍᏔᏅ
oògiichinoohistanv
oogii-xxchinoohistan-v

1B.PL.EX-straighten:CMP-EXP
'We straightened it.'

Like derived nouns, derived adjectives bear any pronominal prefixes that their verbal predecessors have. In (69) the adjective takes the distributive prefix that the original verb 'name' always takes; being an adjective, it takes the *di-* form (DST2) instead of the *dee-* form that appears on verbs. In the example, *di-* becomes [*j*] before the vowel /u/.

(69)

ᎠᏍᎦᏯ	ᏑᏓᎵᏗᎯ	ᏧᏙᎢᏓ
asgay	suúdaldííhi	juudóóʔid
a-sgaya	suúdali+di-a-h-i	di-uu-adaa-ooʔi-da
3A-man	six+DST2-3A-kill:INC-AGT	DST2-3B-MDL-name-PCP

'a man named Sixkiller'

12.2.3. Adjectives Formed with Negative Deverbalizer (NDV) Suffix

Some adjectives are formed with the *ni-* prepronominal prefix in combination with the negative deverbalizer (NDV) suffix. The Completive or Incompletive stem is used for this construction. This construction indicates negation or a lack of what is described by the original verb. Three examples are shown in (70).

(70a) ᏄᏬᎯᏳᏒᎾ
nuwoohiyuusv́v́na
ni-uu-oohiyuus-v́v́na
NI-3B-believe:CMP-NDV
'faithless', 'doesn't believe in things'

(70b)

ᏄᎸᏅᎾ	ᎨᏒ	ᎤᏒ
nuhlvvhnv́v́na	geèsv	uusv
ni-uu-hlvvhn-v́v́na	geès-v	uusv
NI-3B-sleep:CMP-NDV	be:INC-EXP	night

'sleepless night'

(70c)

ᎾᎾᎵᎮᎵᎬᎾ	ᏗᏂᏲᏟ
nanaliiheéliìgv́v́na	diiniiyóótli
ni-anii-aliiheéliìg-v́v́na	di-anii-yóótli
NI-3A.NS-be.happy:INC-NDV	DST2-3A.NS-child

'the unhappy children'

12.2.4. Adjectives Formed with Adjective (ADJ) Suffix

Not all adjectives are derived from verbs. Another common suffix that forms adjectives is the **adjective derivation** *-ha* (full form: *-háá?i*). These adjectives are mostly formed from uncountable nouns (e.g., 'dirt', 'blood') and all take Set A prefixes. Two examples are given in (71).

(71a)

ᏞᏍᏗ	ᏍᎩᏅᏁᎸ	ᎠᎵᎭ	ᏣᎿᏬ
tleesdi	sginv́vneélv	aliiha	jahnawo
tleesdi	sgi-nv́vneél-v	alii-ha	ja-ahnawo
NEG.COM	2/1-give(flexible):CMP-FCM	sweat-ADJ	2B-shirt

'Don't give me your sweaty shirt!'

(71b)

ᎤᏅᎦᎸᎲ	ᎪᏍᏚᎭ	ᎪᎰᏪᎵ	ᏗᏢᏗ
uùnvvgalvvhv	kosduuha	goohweel	diitlvv̀di
uu-nvvgalvvh-v	kosduu-ha	goohweeli	di-a-tlvvdi
3B-clean:CMP-EXP	dust-ADJ	book	DST2-3A-put.on:INF\INS

'He cleaned the dusty bookshelf.'

A sample list of these adjectives is given in (72).

(72)

ᎠᏓᎭᎢ	adaháá?i	'woody'
ᎪᏍᏚᎭᎢ	koòsduháá?i	'dusty'
ᏃᏳᎭᎢ	noyuháá?i	'sandy'
ᎦᏓᎭᎢ	gaadaaháá?i	'dirty'
ᎠᎹᏱᎭᎢ	amayiháá?i	'watery'
ᎩᎦᎭᎢ	gigaháá?i	'bloody'
ᎠᎵᎭᎢ	aliháá?i	'sweaty'
ᎣᏝᎭᎢ	ohlaháá?i	'soapy'
ᏝᏬᏚᎭᎢ	hlawoòtuuháá?i	'muddy'
ᎪᎢᎭᎢ	go?iháá?i	'greasy', 'oily'

12.3. Sources and Additional Reading

The discussion in this chapter has benefited from the many wonderful examples in the Feeling dictionary (1975a) as well as the Pulte and Feeling grammar sketch (1975). In his discussion of grammar Walker (1975) emphasizes the preeminent importance of verbs in the language and their usefulness in deriving other parts of speech such as nouns and adjectives.

12.4. Directions for Further Research

As discussed above, over time the third person pronominal prefix tends to drop as the word's derivational ancestry becomes obscured. For example, *atelido* 'plate' has a pronominal prefix for Feeling (1975a) but not for Holmes and Smith (1977), who list it as *telido.* They do, however, list a distributive *di-* to indicate the non-singular form of this noun. An in-depth study of historical materials could expand our knowledge of Cherokee word etymologies and how they are obscured over time.

Some sources treat the locative suffix as inflectional, others as derivational; Mithun (2009) has argued convincingly for the latter. The use of the locative is in need of further study from a diachronic as well as synchronic perspective.

Lindsey and Scancarelli (1985:212) note that there are many adjectives that appear with what looks like a derivational ending yet have no clear source. Further research into archival material could help discover these sources.

Compounds abound in Cherokee and deserve their own in-depth study, as their patterns and constraints have barely been studied at all. Potter (1996:120) does note one type of constraint on agentive nouns forming a compound with an object: if the verb is ditransitive, the noun can only refer to the secondary object.

THIRTEEN

Expanding the Verb's Meaning

13.1. Overview of Verb Derivational Suffixes

In Cherokee **derivational suffixes** attach to verbs to alter the basic meaning. Except for the **causative derivation,** these suffixes are attached to the **Completive stem** of the verb. (1a) is an example of the basic form of the **intransitive** verb 'break' in its Completive stem; in (1b) the same verb has the causative suffix (in its Completive form), indicating that the verb is now transitive. In (1c) a **terminative suffix** (also in its Completive form) appears, indicating that the activity was done thoroughly or to completion.

(1a) ꮜꮵꮸ
uùyóojv
uu-yóoj-v
3B-break(I):CMP-EXP
'It broke.'

(1b) ꮜꮵꮝꮤꮎ
uùyóostanv
uu-yóo-stan-v
3B-break(I)-CAU:CMP-EXP
'He broke it.'

(1c) ꮜꮵꮝꮤꮓꮎ
uùyóostanohnv
uu-yóo-stan-ohn-v
3B-break(I)-CAU:CMP-TRM:CMP-EXP
'He broke it all to pieces.'

Derivational suffixes generally have five forms that correspond to the five types of stems. These suffixes are described below.

13.1.1. Duplicative (DPL) Derivational Suffixes

The **duplicative** suffix indicates that an action is repeated. The five forms of this suffix are indicated in table 13.1; an example of each form is shown in (2). In (2b) and (2c) the **iterative** prepronominal prefix seems to reinforce the repetition of the event.

Table 13.1. The Five Aspect Suffixes of the Duplicative

Present Continuous	-iísíha
Incompletive	-iísíisg-
Immediate	-iísa
Completive	-iisáhn-, -isil-
Infinitive	-iísohdi

(2a) ᎬᎩᎶᎢᏏᎭ
gvv̀giilóoʔiísiha
ji-vhgiilóóʔ-iísiha
1A-wash:CMP-DPL:PRC
'I'm washing it again.'

(2b) ᎢᎯᏍᏓᏲᏟᏏᏍᎪ
iihisdayoohliisiisgo
ii-hi-sdayoohl-iísíisg-o
ITR-2A-shoot:CMP-DPL:INC-HAB
'You re-shoot it.'

(2c) ᏅᎭᏛᏁᎵᏌ
nvvhadv́vneeliísa
ni-ii-hi-adv́vneel-iísa
NI-ITR-2A-do:CMP-DPL:IMM
'You redid it.'

(2d) ᏚᏴᏍᏙᎯᏌᏅ
duùhyvv́sdóòhiisahnv
dee-uu-hyvv́sdóòh-iisahn-v
DST-3B-sneeze:CMP-DPL:CMP-EXP
'He sneezed over and over.'

(2e) ᎢᏳᏛᏁᎵᏐᏗ ᎤᏁᏩᏛᏗ
iyuudv́vneéliísohdi uuneehwahtv́hdi
ii-uu-adv́vneél-iísohdi uu-neehwahtv́hdi
NI2-3B-do:CMP-DPL:INF\MOD 3B-find(liquid):INF
'He has to do it over again to find it.'

The duplicative is **frozen** on certain verbs: these verbs never appear without it. An example is 'gather' in (3). In this example the frozen derivational suffix is underlined.

(3) ᎦᏙ ᎤᏍᏗ ᎯᏟᏏᏍᎨ
gado úúsdi híitliísíisge
gado úúsdi hi-x́xtli<u>ísíisg</u>-e
what thing 2A-gather(T):INC-NXP
'What were you gathering?'

13.1.2. Repetitive (RPT) Derivational Suffixes

The **repetitive** suffix indicates that an action is repeated numerous times. It is often translated as 'repeatedly' or 'over and over'. Table 13.2 shows the five forms, each of which is exemplified in (4).

Table 13.2. The Five Aspect Suffixes of the Repetitive

Present Continuous	-iílóʔa
Incompletive	-iílóòsg-
Immediate	-iiloója
Completive	-iíló-
Infinitive	-iílóòsdi

(4a) Ꮶ ᏳᏩᎧᏘ ᎠᏥᏃᏎᎵᏦᎠ
joʔ yuuwáákti aàjiìnoseel-iílóʔa
joʔ yuuwáákti aji-hnoseel-iílóʔa
three time 3O-tell:CMP-RPT:PRC
'He's being told three times.'

(4b) ᎤᏩᎫᏯᏍᏔᏂᏦᏍᎬᎢ
uuwáakuyáàstaniílóòsgvv́ʔi
uu-x́xkuyáàstan-iílóòsg-vv́ʔi
3B-burp:CMP-RPT:INC-EXP
'He was burping repeatedly.'

(4c) ᏱᏬᏂᏏᎶᏣ
hiwoòniisiiloója
hi-woòniis-iiloója
2A-speak:CMP-RPL:IMM
'Speak repeatedly.' (Pulte and Feeling 1975:284)

(4d) ᎠᏓᏕᏔᏍᏓᏁᎵᎶᎥᎢ
aàdaaktáàsdaneéliíló?vv́?i
a-adaad-gahtáàsdan-eél-iíló?-vv́?i
3A-RFL-wink:CMP-APL:CMP-RPT:CMP-EXP
'He was continually winking at someone.'

(4e) ᎠᏩᏚᎵ ᎠᎩᏁᏥᎶᏍᏗ
aàwaduuli akineejiílóòsdi
agi-aduuli agi-hneej-iílóòsdi
1B-want:PRC 1B-speak:CMP-RPT:INF
'I want to speak over and over.'

13.1.3. Accidental (ACC) Derivational Suffixes

The **accidental** suffix adds the meaning 'do something accidentally'. The forms of this suffix are shown in table 13.3; an example of each form is given in (5). This suffix seems etymologically related to a causative meaning and is used in place of that derivation. For example, the transitive verb 'wake up' is derived from the intransitive verb 'wake up'. In (5d) the transitive verb 'accidentally wake somebody up' derives directly from the intransitive verb. Unlike the causative, however, the accidental attaches to the Completive stem and not a causative base. There is no **Present Continuous** form of this suffix.

Table 13.3. The Four Aspect Suffixes of the Accidental

Incompletive	-dóhdísg-
Immediate	-dóhda
Completive	-dóhtan-
Infinitive	-dóhdi

(5a) ᏊᏇ ᏧᏂᎯᏲ ᎢᏴᏓᎭ Track 106
guhgwe juuníihyóhi iyvv́daaha
guhgwe di-uunii-hyóh-i iyvv́daaha
quail DST2-3B.NS-look.for:INC-AGT sometimes

ᏓᎾᏓᏲᏍᏙᏗᏍᎪᎢ
daànadaayoosdóhdísgóʔi
dee-anii-adaad-yoos-dóhdísg-óʔi
DST-3A.NS-RFL-shoot:CMP-ACC:INC-HAB
'Quail hunters sometimes accidentally shoot one another.'
(Feeling 1975a:124)

(5b)	ᎩᎳᏊ	ᎢᏂᏍᏆᎶᏍᏙᏓ
	kilagwu	ììniisgwaloosdóhda
	kila=gwu	iinii-sgwaloos-dóhda
	just.now=DT	1A.DL-bump.into:CMP-ACC:IMM
	'We just accidentally bumped into it.'	

(5c) ᎬᏰᏥᏙᏔᏅ
gvvyéetsdóhtanv
gvv-yéej-dóhtan-v
1/2-wake:CMP-ACC:CMP-EXP
'I accidentally woke you up.'

(5d)	ᏣᏣᎦᎸᏙᏗ	Ꮭ	ᏲᎩᎾᏚᎸᎲ
	jaajagahldohdi	tla	yoòginaduulvvhv
	ja-xxjagahl-dohdi	tla	yi-ooginii-aduulvvh-v
	2B-rip:CMP-ACC:INF	NEG	IRR-1B.DL.EX-want:CMP-EXP
	'We didn't want you to rip it.'		

13.1.4. Terminative (TRM) Derivational Suffixes

The **terminative** indicates a definitive completion of the action. The five forms of this derivational suffix are listed in table 13.4, with an example of each in (6).

Table 13.4. The Five Aspect Suffixes of the Terminative

Present Continuous	-ohv́sga
Incompletive	-ohv́sg-
Immediate	-ohna
Completive	-ohn-
Infinitive	-ohvsdi

(6a) ᏥᏍᏕᏲᎶᎲᏍᎦ
jiìsdeéyóòlohv́sga
ji-sdeéyóòl-ohv́sga
1A-braid:CMP-TRM:PRC
'I'm about to finish braiding it.'

(6b) ᎣᏍᏓ ᎠᏍᏙᎣᎲᏍᎪ ᎦᏅᏥ ᏳᏬᎵᎿ
óósda aàsdóoʔohv́sgo ganvji yuuwoohlv́v́hna
óósda a-sdóo-ohv́sg-o ganvji yi-uu-oohlvvhn-a
good 3A-pound:CMP-TRM:INC-HAB kanuchi IRR-3B-make:CMP-CVB
'He pounds it out well when he makes kanuchi.'

(6c) ᎦᏬᏂᏏᎿ
gawóoniisóhna
ga-wóoniis-óhna
3A-speak:CMP-TRM:IMM
'He just finished speaking.' (Pulte and Feeling 1975:285)

(6d) ᏂᎦᏓ ᏛᏂᎩᏐᏂ
nigááda dvvhnigîisohni
nigááda da-a-ahnigîis-ohn-i
all CMF-3A-leave:CMP-TRM:CMP-CMF
'It will be all gone.' (*Cherokee Phoenix,* May 2006)

(6e) ᎠᏎ ᎢᏥᏍᏆᏙᎲᏍᏗ
aase iìjíísgwadohv́sdi
aase iijii-sgwad-ohv́sdi
must 2B.PL-finish:CMP-TRM:INF\MOD
'You all have to finish it.'

13.1.5. Ambulative (AMB) Derivational Suffixes

The **ambulative** expresses the idea of repeated movement. The five aspect forms are presented in table 13.5 and shown in (7). Many verbs derived with this suffix have unpredictable meanings; for example, in (7a) this suffix expresses the idea of 'pain all over the body'. In (7c) it indicates a purpose, while in (7d) it appears on the verb 'happen', which is then turned into a noun meaning 'events that happened'. The example in (7e) could also perhaps be translated as 'go around acting up'.

Table 13.5. The Five Aspect Suffixes of the Ambulative

Present Continuous	-iídóòha
Incompletive	-iídóòh-
Immediate	-iída
Completive	-iídóòl-
Infinitive	-iidasdi

(7a) ᏂᎬ ᎤᏪᎯᏍᏓᏁᎵᏙᎭ ᎠᏗᎭ
niikv́ uùweehisdáàneeliídóòha aàdiiha
niikv́ uu-eehisdáàneel-iídóòha a-adiiha
everywhere 3B-ache:CMP-AMB:PRC 3A-say:PRC
'She says she hurts all over.' (Feeling 1975a:147)

(7b) ᏓᏘᏂᏙᎮ ᏓᎿᏩ ᎠᏁᏙ
daàtihniidóohe dahnawa aneedó
dee-a-atihn-iidóoh-e dahnawa anii-eedóóh-i
DST-3A-lead:INC-AMB:INC-NXP war 3A.NS-walk:INC-AGT
'He was leading the war party.' (The Search Party, line 6)

(7c) ᏙᏍᏓᏑᎴᎯᏓ
doòsdasuuleehiída
dee-oosdii-asuuleeh-iída
DST-1A.DL.EX-wash.hands:CMP-AMB:IMM
'We went to wash our hands.'

(7d) ᎤᏲ ᏄᎵᏍᏔᏂᏙᎸ ᏚᏃᏎᎴ
uuyo nuulstaniídóòlv́ duùhnooseéle
uu-yo ni-uu-alistan-iídóòl-v́ dee-uu-hnooseél-e
3B-bad NI-3B-happen:CMP-AMB:CMP-DVB DST-3B-tell:CMP-NXP
'Evil things he told them.'

(7e) ᎨᏍᏓᏛᏁᎸᏂᏓᏍᏗᎢ Ꮭ ᏳᎾᏚᎵᎭ
geesdadv́vneelvvhniidasdííʔi tla yuunaduuliha
gaa-sdii-adv́vneelvvhn-iidasdííʔi tla yi-uunii-aduuliha
GA-2B.DL-act.up:CMP-AMB:INF NEG IRR-3B.NS-want:PRC
'They don't want you to act up.'

An example of the ambulative attaching to a causative base is given in (8).

(8) ᎠᏓᏕᏍᏔᏂᏙᎭ
aàdadéestaniídóòha
a-adadée-stan-iidóòha
3A-bounce(I)-CAU:CMP-AMB:PRC
'She's dribbling it.'

As with the other derivational suffixes, certain verbs have a frozen form of this suffix and do not occur without it. One such verb is 'take time', as seen in (9).

(9) ᎯᎳ ᏱᎪᎯᏓ ᏓᏟᏢᏙᎰ
hila yigohiíd daàhliiliídóòho
hila yi-gohiída dee-a-ahliiliídóòh-o
how NI2-long DST-3A-take.time:INC-HAB

ᎦᏢᏦᏕ ᎠᏁᎬᏍᏗᎢ
gahljoóde ahneksdííʔi
gahljoóde a-ahneksdííʔi
house 3A-build:INF
'How long does it take to build a house?'

13.1.6. Movement (MOV) Derivational Suffixes

The two main purposes of this derivational suffix are to indicate that an action is performed at intervals or that the subject is going somewhere to perform an action. It is etymologically related to the verb of motion 'go'. The six forms of the suffixes are presented in table 13.6 with corresponding examples in (10).

Table 13.6. The Six Aspect Suffixes of the Movement Derivation

Present Continuous	-éega
Incompletive	-éeg-
Immediate Past	-éena
Immediate Command	-úuga
Completive	-v́vs-
Infinitive	-v́vsdi

(10a) ᎡᏣᎪᏢᏰᎦᏍ
eèjagooliyéegas
eja-gooliy-éega=s
2O-examine:CMP-MOV:PRC=Q
'Are you going to go to be examined?'

(10b) ᎪᎦᏍ ᎭᏓᏬᎡᎪ
googas hadaawooʔéego
googa=s hi-adaa-awooʔ-éeg-o
summer=Q 2A-MDL-bathe:CMP-MOV:INC-HAB
'Do you go swimming in the summer?'

(10c) ᎢᎾᎵᏍᏓᏴᏄᎦ
iìnalsdayhnúuga
iinii-ali-sdayhn-úuga
1A.DL-MDL-provide.meal:CMP-MOV:IMM
'Let's go eat!'

(10d) ᎣᎩᎾᎵᏍᏓᏴᏅᏒ
oòginalsdayvhnv́vsv
ooginii-ali-sdayvhn-v́vs-v
1B.DL.EX-MDL-provide.meal:CMP-MOV:CMP-EXP
'We went to eat.'

(10e) ᏣᏑᏅᏍᏗᏍ ᏣᏚᎵ
jasuúhnv́vsdis jaduuli
ja-suúhn-v́vsdi=s ja-aduuli
2B-fish:CMP-MOV:INF=Q 2B-want:PRC
'Do you want to go fishing?'

There are two different forms for the Immediate. In (11a) the form is for a command, while in (11b) it is for a past tense action.

(11a) ᏰᏗᏍᏕᏞᎮᎾ
yeèdiisdeelvvhéena
yi-eedii-sdeelvvh-éena
IRR-1A.PL.AN-help:CMP-MOV:IMM
'When we go to help him.'

(11b) ᎢᏓᎵᏍᏕᏞᎱᎦ
iìdalsdeelvvhúuga
iidii-ali-sdeelvvh-úuga
1A.PL-MDL-help:CMP-MOV:IMM
'Let's all go help!'

13.1.7. Purpose (PRP) Derivational Suffixes

The **purpose suffix** adds the idea 'in order to' to its verb. Feeling (1975a: 287) translates this as 'come to do something'. The five forms of this suffix are presented in table 13.7; examples of each form are given in (12). (12a) bears the causative suffix as well.

Table 13.7. The Five Aspect Suffixes of the Purpose Derivation

Present Continuous	-íiga
Incompletive	-iíhíh-
Immediate	-iiga
Completive	-íihl-
Infinitive	-isdi

(12a) ᏥᏲᏍᏔᏂᎦ
jiyóostaníiga
ji-yóo-stan-íiga
1A-break(I)-CAU:CMP-PRP:PRC
'I came to destroy it.'

(12b) ᎨᎩᎾᎦᏙᏍᏔᏂᎯᎰ
geeginaktoóstaniíhího
geeginii-agahtoóstan-iíhíh-o
3NS/1DL-look.at:CMP-PRP:INC-HAB
'They come to see us.'

(12c) ᏥᏍᏗᏗᎦ
jisdiidíiga
ji-sdii-d-iiga
REL-2A.DL-lay.down (long):CMP-PRP:IMM\SUB
'Where you two came and laid it.' (Scancarelli 2005:355)

(12d) ᎤᎾᏍᎪᏏᎵ
uùnasgoósíihlv
uunii-asgoós-íihl-v
3B.NS-dig:CMP-PRP:CMP-EXP
'They came to dig.'

(12e)

ᎠᏕᎳ	ᎠᏆᏓᏠᎯᏍᏗ	ᏓᎩᎸᏫᏍᏓᏁ
adeéla	awadadlohísdi	daàgilvv́hwsdaane
adeéla	agi-adadloh-ísdi	dee-agi-lvv́hwsdaane
money	1B-earn:CMP-PRP:INF	DST-1B-work:PRC

'I'm working to earn the money.'

13.1.8. Pre-incipient (PRI) Derivational Suffixes

This derivational suffix is attached to the Completive stem and indicates that an action is just about to take place. The four forms of this suffix are listed in table 13.8. The **Immediate stem** use of this suffix indicates that the action is understood as about to happen immediately. This suffix is unusual in that it bears the **highfall** tone typical of derived words. The Present Continuous and Immediate have a similar translation, but speakers indicate that the action is more imminent for verbs in the Immediate stem.

Table 13.8. The Four Aspect Suffixes of the Pre-incipient

Present Continuous	-íídi
Incompletive	-iidíisg-
Immediate	-iidééna
Completive	-iidíis-

(13a) ᎤᏬᏂᏏᏗ
uùwóoniisíídi
uu-wóoniis-íídi
3B-speak:CMP-PRI:PRC
'He is about to speak.' (Pulte and Feeling 1975:289)

(13b) ᎤᏂᏌᎳᏓᏂᏗᏍᎬ
uùniisalaádáàniidíisgv
uunii-salaádáàn-iidíisg-v
3B.NS-lift:CMP-PRI:INC-EXP
'They were about to lift it.'

(13c) ᎤᎪᏏᏕᎾ
uugoosiidééna
uu-goos-iidééna
3B-rot:CMP-PRI:IMM
'It's about to rot.'
'It's destined to rot.'

(13d) ᏙᎦᏍᎦᎴᏍᏔᏂᏗᏒ
doògáasgaléestaniidíisv
dee-oogii-áasgaléestan-iidíis-v
DST-1B.PL.EX-realease:CMP-PRI:CMP-EXP
'We were about to let go of it.'

13.2. Nonproductive Derivation

A few derivational suffixes are no longer **productive**; these patterns of derivation are limited and unpredictable. An example of nonproductive derivation is seen in (14) below. Scancarelli (2005) identifies this as the multiplicative; King (1975:90) calls it the multiple action suffix and states that only a few verbs take it. This suffix does not appear in Pulte and Feeling (1975) or in Cook (1979). An example from Scancarelli is given in (14a); the verb from which it derives is presented in (14b). The derivational element is added to the Completive stem of the verb.

(14a) ТᏊᏉᏚᏩᏥᏒᎤᏏ
ihadeelohoosvvhnv
yi-hi-adeelohoos<u>vvhn</u>-v
IRR-2A-find.out(<u>multiple</u>):CMP-EXP
'If you should see or hear things . . .' (Scancarelli 2005:355)

(14b) ᎤᏚᏩᏥᏒᎢ
uùdeelohoosvv̋ʔi
uu-adeelohoos-vv̋ʔi
3B-find.out:CMP-EXP
'He found it out.' (Feeling 1975a:9)

Pulte and Feeling (1975:282) give a few examples of *-gi-*, a suffix that they call the reversive, which "reverses the basic meaning of the word." An example is given in (15a), followed by its basic form.

(15a) ᎬᏍᎦ
gvv̀sga
ji-vv̀sga
1A-weave:PRC
'I'm weaving it.'

(15b) ᎬᎩᎠ
gvvgíiʔa
ji-vvgíiʔa
1A-unweave:PRC
'I'm unweaving it.'

13.3. Sources and Additional Reading

This discussion of verb derivation is based on the important work by Pulte and Feeling (1975). Both prefixes and suffixes create rich and complex possibilities for verbs; King (1975:34) estimates that "each regular verb stem can have over 21,000 possible forms." Cook (1979:141) calls the duplicative the reiterative and says that it indicates that "the action of the verb is repeated for emphasis or in an improved manner." The terms "ambulative" and "repetitive" are from King (1975:88–92), who calls the movement suffix the andative (1975:91). Scancarelli (2005:373) refers to the purpose suffix as the proximate purposive. She states that Cook first used "purposive"; she adds the modifier "proximate" to distinguish it from what she calls the distant purposive, which is referred to in this grammar as the movement suffix. "Pre-incipient" is from Pulte and Feeling (1975:289); King (1975:88–92) refers to it as the pre-inceptive.

13.4. Directions for Further Research

Much work needs to be done on the functions and meanings of the derivational suffixes and the extent of dialectal variation. The rules for creating the causative base are poorly understood. The causative can also be used with an instrumental meaning; the extent to which this happens warrants further study.

FOURTEEN

Changing Verb Valency

14.1. Overview of Valency

In Cherokee verbs are either **intransitive** or **transitive.** The **subject** of an intransitive verb is its sole **participant,** whereas transitive verbs have a subject and an **object.** The number of participants involved determines the degree of **valency:** an intransitive verb has a valency of one, while a transitive verb has a valency of two. In Cherokee it is possible to change a verb's valency through the use of **derivational suffixes** or a special set of **prefixes.** In (1a) the verb is intransitive: the only participant involved is 'clothes'. In (1b) a formerly intransitive verb has gained one more participant ('you' is now the one who causes the drying) through the addition of a **causative** derivational suffix and now has a valency of two.

(1a) ᏗᏂᏬ ᏓᎧᏲᏍᎦ
diihnawo daàkayoósga
di-a-ahnawo dee-a-kayoósga
DST2-3A-clothes DST-3A-dry:PRC
'The clothes are drying.'

(1b) ᏕᎯᎧᏲᏗᎭᏍ ᏗᏂᏬ
deehíkayoóhdiihas diihnawo
dee-hi-kayoós-sdiiha=s di-a-ahnawo
DST-2A-dry-CAU:PRC=Q DST2-3A-clothes
'Are you drying the clothes?'

A few verbs are **ditransitive** with a subject participant, a **primary object** participant, and a **secondary object** participant; these verbs have a valency of three. Most verbs that involve giving are inherently ditransitive, as they involve a giver (the subject), the person to whom the thing is being given (the primary object), and the thing being given (the secondary object). Three examples are shown in (2). In (2a) the secondary object is an **implied object.** In (2b) the prefix *jii-* refers to the giver and a third person **animate** primary object; the secondary object 'dog' is referred to by the **distributive** prefix (if this were singular, this secondary object would not be referred to on the verb at all). In (2c) the distributive prefix on 'tell' indicates the primary object: the people being told the plans.

(2a) ᏍᎬᏏ
skvsi
sgi-hvsi
2/1-give:IMM
'Give it to me.'

(2b)	ᎠᏍᎦᏯ	ᏕᏥᏯᎧᏁ	ᎩᏟ
	asgaya	deejíiyaàkáàne	giihli
	a-sgaya	dee-jii-aàkáàne	giihli
	3A-man	DST-1A.AN-give(living):PRC	dog

'I'm giving the man dogs.' (Scancarelli 1987:69)

(2c)	ᏄᏍᏛ	ᏚᏭᎫᏛ	ᏚᏃᏎᎴ
	nuusdv	duuwuuktv́	duùhnooseéle
	nuusdv	dee-uu-uugoht-v́	dee-uu-hnooseél-e
	that.which	DST-3B-decide:CMP-DVB	DST-3B-tell:CMP-NXP

'He told them about his plans.' (The Turtle and the Rabbit, line 11)

Through valency-changing processes a transitive verb can be turned into an intransitive verb and vice versa. If a verb that is already transitive has another participant added to it (a primary object) it becomes a ditransitive verb. In (3) a series of valency changes are applied to the same verb. In (3a) the verb is intransitive with only one participant; in (3b) a **causative** suffix has added a person causing the action, creating a transitive verb; in (3c) the **middle voice prefix** has removed the object, creating an intransitive verb. In this third example the middle voice prefix is indistinguishable from the **reflexive** form; the participant in this case is both the causer and the **undergoer** of the noise-making.

(3a)	ᎤᎭᎸᏂ	ᎤᏃᏴᎦ
	uuhalvvni	uùnoohyv́ga
	uuhalvvni	uu-noohyv́ga
	bell	3B-sound(I):PRC

'The bell is sounding.'

(3b) ᎤᎭᎸᏂ ᎯᏃᏴᏟᏍᏗᎭ
uuhalvvni hinoohyvvhlisdiiha
uuhalvvni hi-noohyvvli-sdiiha
bell 2A-sound(I)-CAU:PRC
'You are ringing the bell.'

(3c) ᏐᏈᎵ ᎠᏓᏃᏴᏟᏍᏗᎭ
soógwíli aàdaanoohyvvhlisdiiha
soógwíli a-adaa-noohyvvhli-sdiiha
horse 3A-MDL-sound(I)-CAU:PRC
'The horse is making noise.'

It should be noted that although (3a) and (3c) are both intransitive, they have different meanings. In (3a) the subject is an inanimate object and is itself not controlling or causing the noise to exist but merely undergoing it; in (3c), in contrast, the intransitive subject is purposefully causing noise. If (3a) is 'sounding', then (3b) could be translated as 'causing to sound' and (3c) again as 'sounding'. In other words, the verb in (3c) is built on an intransitive verb (valency: one) that has been transitivized (valency: two) and then turned again into an intransitive. The difference between the basic intransitive in (3a) and the middle voice intransitive in (3c) seems to be one of **animacy.** The middle voice prefix often involves a single participant that is midway between an **agent** (the "doer" of the action) and an undergoer. In the sentence 'the bell is sounding', the bell is **inanimate** and is merely undergoing the action: the bell itself has not decided to start or stop ringing. The sentence 'the horse is making noise' is a different matter. The horse is seen as undergoing the action in the sense that the horse's own body is producing the sound; the horse, as a sentient being, is deciding to start and stop the action. These different processes and their meanings are described in the following section.

A few pairs of intransitive/transitive verbs are very similar in form and meaning but differ in valency. Such pairs are no longer related by any **productive** derivational process; it is possible, however, that such a process existed in the past but has since fallen out of use in the language. An example is seen in (4). In (4a) the verb is transitive, while in (4b) a very similar verb has an intransitive meaning. In (4b) the Completive stem of the verb takes a **deverbalizer** suffix and appears as an adjective.

(4a) ᏅᏯ ᏚᏗᎦᏞᏴᎢ
nvv̀ya duùdiigaléeyvv́ʔi

nvvya dee-uu-adiigaléey-vv́ʔi
rock DST-3B-scatter(T):CMP-EXP
'He scattered the rocks.'

(4b) ᏧᏗᎦᎴᏲᏨ ᏅᏯ
juùdigaleéyóòjv́ nvv̀ya
di-uu-adiigaleéyóòj-v́ nvv̀ya
DST2-3B-scatter(I):CMP-DVB rock
'scattered rocks'

14.2. Valency-Increasing Suffixes

14.2.1. Applicative (APL) Derivational Suffixes

The **applicative** suffix is attached to verbs to indicate the presence of an additional object affected by the verb. In (5a) the verb is in its basic intransitive form, while in (5b) the applicative suffix indicates that the action is being directed at a participant. The addition of the this suffix creates a transitive verb that can now take a **combined local prefix.**

(5a) ᎭᎦᏔᏍᏗᎭ
haktáàsdiiha
hi-agahtáàsdiiha
2A-wink:PRC
'You are winking.'

(5b) ᏍᏆᎦᏔᏍᏓᏁᎭ
sgwaktáàsdaneéha
sgi-agahtáàsdan-eéha
2/1-wink:CMP-APL:PRC
'You are winking at me.'

As demonstrated in this example, the applicative attaches to the **Completive** aspect stem. The applicative has the aspect forms shown in table 14.1; an example of each is given in (6). The **Immediate** form of this suffix causes the preceding /n/ of the Completive stem to delete, as seen in (6c). This example is a command form of the Immediate stem.

Table 14.1. The Six Aspect Suffixes of the Applicative

Present Continuous	-eéha
Incompletive	-eéh-
Immediate Past	-eéli
Immediate Command	-si
Completive	-eél-
Infinitive	-ehdi

(6a) ᎯᎦᏔᏍᏓᏁᎭ
hiigaàtáàsdaàneéha
hii-gahtáàsdaàn-eéha
2A.AN-wink:CMP-APL:PRC
'You are winking at her.'

(6b) ᎯᎦᏔᏍᏓᏁᎰ
hiigaàtáàsdaàneého
hii-gahtáàsdaànà-eéh-o
2A.AN-wink:CMP-APL:INC-HAB
'You wink at her.'

(6c) ᎯᎦᏔᏍᏓᏏ
hiigaàtáàsdaàsi
hii-gahtáàsdaàn-si
2A.AN-wink:CMP-APL:IMM
'Wink at her!'

(6d) ᏥᎦᏔᏍᏓᏁᎸ
hiigaàtasdaàneélv
hii-gahtasdaàn-eél-v
2A.AN-wink:CMP-APL:CMP-EXP
'You winked at her.'

(6e)

ᏣᏚᎵᏍ	ᎯᎦᏔᏍᏓᏁᏗ
jaduulis	hiigaàtáàsdanehdi
ja-aduuli=s	hii-gahtáàsdan-ehdi
2B-want:PRC=Q	2A.AN-wink:CMP-APL:INF

'Do you want to wink at her?'

The Immediate has two forms, a command form seen above in (6c) and a form used to indicate an action that just took place, seen below in (7).

(7) ᏓᎩᎷᏤᎵ
daàgiiluhcheéli
da-iigii-luhj-eéli
TOW-1B.PL-arrive:CMP-APL:IMM
'He came up to us.'

As seen in this example, the applicative suffixes have a special feature that causes stems ending in /j/ to be pronounced as the **aspirated** sound /ch/. Two more examples are shown in (8).

(8a) ᏓᎩᏅᏞᏤᎵ
dagindle<u>che</u>éli
da-ginii-adle<u>j-e</u>él-i
CMF-1B.DL-take.revenge:CMP-APL:CMP-CMF
'He will take revenge on us.'

(8b) ᎣᎩᏂᏲᏤᎸ
oòginiiyóò<u>che</u>élv
ooginii-yóò<u>j-e</u>él-v
1B.DL.EX-break:CMP-APL:CMP-EXP
'It broke down on us.'

If the applicative verb has two objects (a ditransitive verb), any **combined prefixes** that appear on the verb refer to the subject and the primary object. In (9a) the noun 'truth' is not explicitly referenced on the verb with a **pronominal prefix.** In (9b) the combined local prefix refers to the subject 'you' and the primary object 'me'; the **nonsingular** secondary object (that which is peeled) is indicated only by the distributive suffix. The new object that the applicative verb takes is referred to as the primary object (because it can be referenced on the verb through the pronominal prefix), while the other object is known as the secondary object. In (9c) the sentence is an example of three **noun phrases** specifying the three participants involved in the verb. The word order in this example is subject–secondary object–verb–primary object. Factors such as real-world knowledge and animacy (a human is more likely to give a dog than vice versa) as well as nonsingular marking ('child' is marked with the distributive and therefore cannot be the subject, because the verb's pronominal prefix indicates a third person singular subject) help to clarify the meaning.

(9a) ᏚᏳᎪᏛ ᏫᏓᏥᏃᏎᎵ
duùyuukdv widajiìnooseéli

duùyuukdv wi-da-jii-hnoos-eél-i
truth TRN-CMF-1A.AN-tell:CMP-APL:CMP-CMF
'I'm going to tell him the truth.'

(9b) ᏄᎾ ᏗᏍᎩᏁᎬᎸᏏ
nuún disgineegvlv́vsi
nuúna di-sgi-neegvlv́v-si
potato DST2-2/1-peel:CMP-APL:IMM
'Peel those potatoes for me!'

(9c) ᎡᏗ ᎩᏟ ᏕᎦᎧᏁᎠ ᏗᏂᏲᏟ
eédi giihli deegaakáàneeʔa diiniiyóótli
eédi giihli dee-ga-aakáàneeʔa di-anii-yóótli
Ed dog DST-3A-give(living):PRC DST2-3A.NS-child
'Edward is giving the dog to the children.' (Dukes 1996:90)

A common use of the applicative is to refer to an **addressee,** as seen in (10).

(10) ᎦᎪ ᏕᏣᏃᎩᏎᎰ
gáàgo deejáhnoogíiseého
gáàgo dee-ja-hnoogíis-eéh-o
who DST-2B-sing:CMP-APL:INC-HAB
'Who sings it to you?'

The applicative is also used to reference a **beneficiary**—the person who benefits from an action. Two examples are given in (11).

(11a) ᎦᏙ ᎤᏍᏗ ᏍᎩᏟᏌᏁᎮ
gado úúsdi sgíitliísáàneéhe
gado úúsdi sgi-x́xtliísáàn-eéh-e
what thing 2/1-gather:CMP-APL:INC-NXP
'What were you gathering for me?'

(11b) ᏕᏍᎩᏴᏍᏓᏁᎸᎢ
deeskiyvvsdaneelvvʔi
dee-sgi-hyvvsdan-eel-vvʔi
DST-2/1-pick.up:CMP-APL:CMP-FCM
'Pick it up for me.'

Another common use of the applicative is to refer to the **recipient** of the secondary object. Three examples are shown in (12).

(12a) ᎠᎩᏍᏓᏴᎲᏍᎦ ᎠᎩᏩᏎᎸ ᎠᏤ ᎠᏩᏂᏬ
aksdayv́v́hvsg aàkiwáséelv aje awahnawo
agi-sdayv́v́hvsga agi-hwás-eél-v aje agi-ahnawo
1B-wife 1B-buy:CMP-APL:CMP-EXP new 1B-shirt
'My wife bought me a new shirt.'

(12b) ᏫᎦᏥᏗᏁᎸ ᏍᏆᏞᏍᏗ
wigaajiidiineélv sgwahlesdi
wi-gaa-jii-adiin-eél-v sgwahlesdi
TRN-ANS-1A.AN-throw:CMP-APL:CMP-EXP ball
'I threw them the ball.'

(12c) ᏝᏛ ᏱᏓᎨᎦᏈᏴᎡᏟ
tladvv yidageegakwiyvvʔeéli
tla=dvv yi-da-geegii-akwiyvv-eél-i
NEG=DT IRR-CMF-3NS/1PL-pay:CMP-APL:CMP-CMF
'They will not pay us.'

Most verbs that naturally have a recipient are inherently applicative. Verbs of giving have a **frozen** applicative suffix (the stem cannot be separated from the suffix and is meaningless without it). Two examples of giving verbs were presented at the beginning of this section; another example is shown below in (13). The underlined portion is the same as the Immediate form of the applicative.

(13) ᎩᎳᏊ ᎠᎩᎲᏏ
kilágwu aàgiihv<u>si</u>
kila=gwu agi-xxhv<u>si</u>
just=DT 1B-give:IMM
'She just gave it to me.'

The applicative also may reference a **maleficiary**—the person who is adversely affected by the action. Three examples are shown in (14).

(14a) Ꮎ ᏧᎾᏠᎯᏍᏗ ᎬᎩᏁᏟᏴᏏ
na juunadloohisdi gvv̀gineedliiyvv̀si
na di-uunii-adloohisdi gvvgi-needliiyvv̀s-si
the DST2-3B.NS-meet:INF 3NS/1-change:CMP-APL:IMM
'They changed the meeting on me.'

(14b) ᎠᏥᏍᎦᏅᏥᏏ
aàjiìsgánv́v̀chiisi

aji-sgánv́v̀vj-iisi
3O-commit.sin:CMP-APL:IMM
'She fouled her.'

(14c) Ꮜ Ꮩ ᏅᏢᏍᏓᏏ ᏣᏥ — Track 107
gado uùlsdáasi jaji
gado uu-alisdan-si ja-ji
what 3B-happen:CMP-APL:IMM 2B-mother
'What happened to your mother?'

14.2.2. Causative (CAU) Derivational Suffixes

The causative suffix raises the valency of a verb by indicating a participant that causes the action. (15a) is intransitive, while (15b) has the causative suffix and is transitive.

(15a) ᏥᏳ ᏅᏃᏴᏤ
jiíyu uùnoóyv́v̀je
jiíyu uu-noóyv́v̀j-e
boat 3B-sink(I):CMP-NXP
'The boat sank.'

(15b) ᏥᏳ ᎢᏗᏃᏴᏍᏓ
jiíyu iìdiinoóyv́sda
jiíyu iidii-noóyv́-sda
boat 1A.PL-sink(I)-CAU:IMM
'We sank the boat.'

As with the applicative, the causative has five different forms for each of the five verb stems, as listed in table 14.2.

Table 14.2. The Five Aspect Suffixes of the Causative

Present Continuous	-sdiiha/-hdiiha
Incompletive	-sdiisg-/-hdiisg-
Completive	-sdan-/-hdan-
Immediate	-sda/-hda
Infinitive	-sdohdi/-hdohdi

The causative is different from the other derivational suffixes in that it attaches directly to a special form known as the **causative base.** In this grammar verbs are not shown as one of the five stems only for causative bases and **participle bases.** The five forms of the causative suffix are exemplified below in (16). The causative base is either the Infinitive with the [*di*] element removed or the Present Continuous with the final syllable removed.

(16a) ᎠᎩᏴᏍᏕᏍᏗᎭ
aàkiyvsdéesdiiha
agi-hyvsdée-sdiiha
1B-get.drunk-CAU:PRC
'He's getting me drunk.'

(16b) ᎠᎲᏜᏗᏍᏗᏍᎪ
aàhyvvdladiisdiisgo
a-hyvvdladií-sdîisg-o
3A-get.cold-CAU:INC-HAB
'It makes it cold.'

(16c) ᎤᏁᏍᏓᎳᏗᏍᏓᏅ
uùneesdaldiisdanv
uu-neesdaldii-sdan-v
3B-freeze(I)-CAU:CMP-EXP
'He froze it.'

(16d) ᏙᎦᎪᎲᏍᏓᏅ
doògagoohvsdanv
dee-oogii-goohv-sdan-v
DST-1B.PL.EX-burn(I)-CAU:CMP-EXP
'We burned them.'

(16e)

Ꮭ	ᎤᏲᏍᏙᏗ	ᏲᎦᏚᎵ
tla	uuyoosdohdi	yoogaduuli
tla	uu-yoo-sdohdi	yi-oogii-aduuli
NEG	3B-break(I)-CAU:INF	IRR-1B.PL.EX-want:PRC

'We don't want him to break it.'

The Infinitive form of the causative is *-sdohdi*; the lack of **vowel deletion** is unexpected.

The basic forms of the causative suffixes have an initial /s/. If the suffix attaches to a causative base ending in a **sonorant** (a vowel or /w/, /y/, /n/, or /l/), as in the example above, then this is the form that appears. If the suffixes attaches to a base ending in an **obstruent** (/t/, /k/, /tl/, or /j/), then the /s/ of the suffix is replaced by an /h/. This process is seen in (17). The intransitive form is in (17a), while the causative suffix has been added in (17b).

(17a) DᏢCᏐᎣ DᎣᏅ
aàliitlis ama
a-aliitli=s ama
3A-boil(I):PRC=Q water
'Is the water boiling?'

(17b) ᎭᏢCᏓᏐᎣ DᎣᏅ
haliitldas ama
hi-aliitl-sda=s ama
2A-boil(I)-CAU:IMM=Q water
'Did you boil the water?'

The causative is only added to verbs where the original intransitive subject is an undergoer of the action. Intransitive verbs such as 'run' or 'jump' cannot take this suffix because the intransitive subjects for these verbs are agents in control of the action and actively performing it. To express the idea of causing something to happen, these verbs must be used with a separate verb that expresses the idea 'cause' or 'make'. Two examples are given in (18).

(18a) ᏧᏢᏂᏆᏅᏗ ᏂᏴᏂᏏ
juhlniigwanv́vdi hniiyvvniisi
di-uu-alihniigwanv́vdi ni-hii-vvniisi
DST2-3B-kneel(I):INF NI-2A.AN-cause:IMM
'Make your child kneel.'

(18b) ᏗᏕᏲᏅᏍᎩ ᎤᏃᏪᎶᏗ
diideehyóóhvsgi uunoohweélohdi
di-a-adaa-eehyoóhvsg-i uunii-oohweélohdi
DST2-3A-MDL-teach:INC-AGT 3B.NS-write:INF

ᏂᏕᎬᏁ ᏗᏂᏕᎵᏆᏍᎩ
nideegv́vhne diindééhlgwasgi
ni-dee-ga-v́vhne di-anii-adeehlgwasg-i
NI-DST-3A-make:PRC DST2-3A.NS-learn:INC-AGT
'The teacher is making her students write.'

The causative is a derivational suffix, and derived words can acquire specialized meanings, as seen in (19).

(19a) ᎣᏥᏙᎵᎦ
oòjiidoólîiga
oojii-dooliiga
1A.PL.EX.AN-pity:PRC
'We feel sorry for him.'

(19b) ᎣᏣᏓᏙᎵᏍᏗᎭ
oòjadaadoólîisdiiha
oojii-adaad-doólîi-sdiiha
1A.PL.EX-RFL-pity-CAU:PRC
'We are praying.'

(20a) is an example of the intransitive verb 'get drunk'. In (20b) the causative suffix (added to the Completive stem of the verb) creates the meaning 'cause someone to get drunk'; this derivation is then turned into a noun. A causative base of the verb is very productive for forming **agentive** and **instrumental nouns** in Cherokee. (20c) contains an example of a different agentive noun derived from this verb as well as an instrumental noun derived from the verb 'drink alcohol'.

(20a) ᎤᏴᏍᏕᎠ
uùhyvsdéeʔa
uu-hyvsdéeʔa
3B-get.drunk:PRC
'He is getting drunk.'

(20b) ᎠᏓᏴᏍᏕᏍᏗᏍᎩ
adaahyvsdesdíisgi
a-adaad-hyvsde-sdiisg-i
3A-RFL-get.drunk-CAU:INC-AGT
'things that get you drunk'

(20c) ᎤᏴᏍᏕᏍᎩ ᏴᏓᎵᏊ
uuhyvsdéésgi yvvdááligwu
uu-hyvsdéesg-i yvvdááli=gwu
3B-get.drunk:INC-AGT usually=DT

ᏳᏔᏕᎬ ᎠᏚᎩᏍᏗ
yuùtadeegv atuúgíísdi
yi-uu-tadeegv a-atuúgîisdi
IRR-be.thirsty:IMM 3A-drink.alcohol:INF\INS
'A drunkard usually gets thirsty for a drink.'

14.3. Valency-Decreasing Affixes

Cherokee has three types of prefixes that can reduce the valency of a transitive verb. The **unspecified object reflexive** indicates that the object of the normally transitive verb is unknown or unimportant, while the middle voice prefix indicates that the action is somehow affecting the subject of the intransitive verb (the subject is, in a sense, also the object of the verb). **Object focus** prefixes usually result in the agent of the verb being omitted. These three processes are discussed in the section below.

14.3.1. Object Focus (O) Pronominal Prefixes

The object focus pronominal prefixes are discussed in chapter 9; the following section recapitulates their use. These prefixes reduce valency by removing reference to the agent of the action. They only attach to transitive verbs. In (21a) the transitive verb 'see' refers to a subject 'John' and a **first person** singular object; in (21b) the verb only conveys information about the object.

(21a) Gh ᎠᎩᎪᏩᏘᎭ
jaáni aàgigoohwtíiha
jaáni agi-goohwtíiha
John 1B-see:PRC
'John sees me.'

(21b) ᎥᎩᎪᏩᏘᎭ
vv̀gigoohwtíiha
vgi-goohwtíiha
1O-see:PRC
'I feel like I'm being seen.'

Verbs using the object focus prefixes are often translated into English with the **passive** voice or with the subject translated as 'someone' or a vague 'they'. Several examples are shown in (22). In (22a) and (22b) the English passive is used in the translation; in (22c) a vague (nonspecific) 'they' appears in the translation.

(22a) ᎠᏆᏓᏛᏛᏅ ᏚᎪᏗ ᎠᏕᎳ ᏨᎩᏁᏗ
aàgwadaatvvdv́vhnv duugoodi adeéla jvginéhdi
agi-adaad-atvvdv́vhn-v dee-uugoodi adeéla di-vgi-néhdi
1B-RFL-ask:CMP-EXP DST-more money DST2-1O-give:INF
'I asked to be given more money.'

(22b)
ᎭᏓᏛᏛᎭᏍ ᎡᏣᏍᏕᏞᏗ
hadatvvdvvhas etssdehldi
hi-adaad-atvvdvvha=s eja-sdehldi
2A-RFL-ask:IMM=Q 2O-help:INF
'Did you ask to be helped?'

(22c)
ᎠᎫᎢᏍᏗᏍᎬ
aàguʔiisdíisgv
aji-uhiisdíisg-v
3O-accuse:INC-EXP

ᎦᎶᏅᎮᏍᎬ ᏓᏆᎾᏂᏍᎬ
galoonvheésgv́ dakwanyoosgv́
ga-loonvheésg-v́ dee-a-kwanyoosg-v́
3A-cheat:INC-DVB DST-3A-play.cards:INC-DVB
'They accused him of cheating at cards.'

The object focus prefixes also have a function of putting in the background the subject: the identity of the subject is known but is deemphasized. An example is seen in (23). Both participants are known; in fact, the subject is explicitly mentioned. The two noun phrases appear at the very end; the subject 'wolf' is in the final position.

(23)
ᏌᏬᏃ ᎢᏳᏩᎩᏗ ᎠᎦᏚᎵᏍᎬ
saawúhnóo iyúwáákd aàgaduuliísgv
saagwu=hnóo iyúwáákdi aji-aduuliísg-v
one=CN time 3O-want:INC-EXP

ᎠᏥᏰᏍᏗ ᏥᏍᏛᎾ ᏩᏯ
ajiiyeèsdi jíisdvvna wahya
aji-xxhyeèsdi jíisdvvna wahya
3O-eat(living):INF crawdad wolf
'One time wolf wanted to eat the crawdad.' (The Wolf and the Crawdad, lines 3–4)

In the sentence immediately following, shown in (24), the order is subject-verb-object and the **Set B prefix** appears.

(24)
ᏩᏯ ᎤᏁᏄᎴᏁ
wahya uùneenuuhlane
wahya uu-neenuuhlan-e
wolf 3B-challenge:CMP-NXP

ᏥᏍᏛᎾ ᏧᎾᏙᎩᏯᏍᏗᎢ
jíisdvvna juuhntohgiíyáàsdííʔi
jíisdvvna di-uunii-ahtohgiíyáàsdííʔi
crawdad DST2-3B.NS-race:INF
'The wolf challenged the crawdad to race him.' (The Wolf and the Crawdad, line 5)

Often the subject can be deemphasized without using the object focus prefix. One common way is to use the pronominal prefix for 'they', even though no particular group of individuals is referred to, as in (25).

(25) ᎠᏕᎳ ᏓᎩᎲ ᏚᏂᏃᏍᎩᏎ
adeél daàgihv́ duùniinoosgíise
adeéla dee-agi-h-v dee-uunii-noosgíis-e
money DST-1B-have:CMP-EXP\SUB DST-3B.NS-steal:CMP-NXP
'My money got stolen.'

14.3.2. Unspecified Object Reflexive

The object focus prefixes described above allow the speaker not to mention what is causing the action of the normally transitive verb. In like fashion a special use of the reflexive prefix allows the speaker not to mention the object of a normally transitive verb. In (26a) the transitive verb 'help' has a subject and an object, whereas in (26b) there is no mention of an object and the reflexive appears.

(26a) ᎠᎨᏯ ᎠᏍᏕᎵᎭ
ageéhya aàsdeeliha
a-geéhya a-sdeeliha
3A-woman 3A-help:PRC
'He's helping the woman.'

(26b) ᎠᏁᎵᏗ ᎤᏓᏍᏕᎵᏗ
aàneehldi uudaasdehldi
a-aneehldi uu-adaad-sdehldi
3A-try:PRC 3B-RFL-help:INF
'He's trying to help.'

In (27a) the verb 'visit' has an object; in (27b) it no longer has a specific object. In the English translation no object is mentioned.

(27a) ᎠᏆᏛᎯᏙ
aàgwahtvvhiído

agi-ahtvvhiído
1B-visit:PRC
'He is visiting me.'

(27b) ᎭᏓᏩᏛᎯᏙᎭ
hadaahwahtvvhiídóòha
hi-adaad-hwahtvvhiídóòha
2A-RFL-visit:PRC
'You are visiting.'

In (28a) the object is not mentioned, probably because the person who will be voted for is unknown or because the emphasis is on the act of voting itself. In (28b) the unknown identity of the object triggers the unspecified object reflexive. In (28c) the reflexive is used to create a general command without a specific object in mind.

(28a) ᎢᎦᏓᏑᏰᏍᏗᎢ ᎢᏓᏛᏅᏍᏗ
iigadasuyesdííʔi iidadvvnv́sdi
iigii-adaad-asuyesdííʔi iidii-advvnv́sdi
1B.PL-RFL-choose:INF 1A.PL-prepare:PRC
'We are getting ready to vote.'

(28b) ᎭᏓᏙᎵᎦ
hadaadohlga
hi-adaad-oolihga
2A-RFL-recognize:PRC
'You recognize (somebody).'

(28c) ᎤᎵᏍᎨᏗ ᏕᏣᏓᏰᎸᏒᏍᏗ
uulsgéédi déejadaayelvv́séesdi
uu-alsgéédi dee-iijii-adaad-yelvv́s-éesdi
3B-sacred DST-2A.PL-RFL-regard:INC-PFT
'Regard others in a sacred way.'

This reflexive prefix is often used on agentive nouns derived from transitive verbs that normally have an animate object. (29a) has a specific object in mind, while in (29b) no object is mentioned.

(29a) ᏗᎦᏘᎴᎩ
diiktiíléég-i
di-a-gahtiíleeg-i

DST2-3A-attack:INC-AGT
'attacker (of something previously mentioned)'

(29b) ᏗᏓᎦᏘᎴᎩ
diidaktiiléég-i
di-a-adaad-gahtiíleeg-i
DST2-3A-RFL-attack:INC-AGT
'attacker'

The example in (30) is the name of a large lake outside Tahlequah, Oklahoma; this name does not have the unspecified object reflexive prefix because the numeral 'ten' specifies the object.

(30) ᎤᏔᎾ ᎥᏓᎵ ᏍᎪᎯᏗᎯ
úútana vvdali sgohidííhi
uu-ắtana vvdali sgohi+di-a-h-i
3B-big pond ten+DST2-3A-kill:INC-AGT
'Lake Tenkiller'

The reflexive use of the *-adaad-* prefix can be compared to the object focus pronominal prefix. In (31) the first instance of the verb 'bite' is focusing on who was bitten and uses an object focus prefix to deemphasize the biter. In the second instance, the unspecified object reflexive prefix focuses on the biter and deemphasizes what is being bitten. The object focus on the biter in the second instance is reflected in the speaker's translation.

(31) ᎠᏎᏃ ᎠᏥᏍᎦᎳ ᎠᏲᏟᎨ
aaséehno aàjiisgal ayódlige
aaséehno aji-sgala a-yódlige
however 3O-bite:IMM 3A-smaller

ᎤᏔᏂᏗᎨ ᏩᎶᏏ ᎠᏓᏍᎦᎳ
uutaníidige walóos aàdaasgal
uu-ataníidige walóosi a-adaad-sgala
3B-bigger frog 3A-RFL-bite:IMM
'. . . however, the small frog is bitten; the bigger frog did the biting'

Later on in the same story, shown in (33a), *-adaad-* is used on the verb 'tell' because it does not mention who is being told, although within the story the identity of his companions is known. The unspecified object reflexive is therefore not only used when there is no specific object; in larger narratives it serves to put in the background an object that has already been mentioned. Another example is seen in (32b): the identity is established in the first **clause** and backgrounded in the second.

(32a)	ᏅᏅ	ᏓᎩᏏ	ᎠᏓᏃᎯᏎ	ᏄᏛᏁᎸ
	nvvnv	daks	aàdaanohiise	nuudv́vneelv́
	nvvnv	daksi	a-<u>adaad</u>-nohiis-e	ni-uu-adv́vneel-v́
	now	turtle	3A-RFL-tell:CMP-NXP	NI-3B-do:CMP-DVB

'Now the turtle is telling what happened.'

(32b)	ᏣᏂ	ᏚᏅᏁᎴ	ᎺᎵ	ᎠᏂᏥᎸᏍᎩ
	jaán	duùnv́vneele	meéli	aniijilv́v́sgi
	jaáni	dee-uu-nv́vneel-e	meéli	anii-jilv́v́sgi
	John	DST-3B-give:CMP-NXP	Mary	3A.NS-flower

ᎺᎵᏃ	ᏚᏓᏅᏁᎸᎢ
meélíhno	dúudaanv́vneelvv́ʔi
meéli=hno	dee-ii-uu-<u>adaad</u>-nv́vneel-vv́ʔi
Mary=CN	DST-ITR-3B-RFL-give:CMP-EXP

'John gave Mary some flowers, and Mary gave them right back to him.' (Scancarelli 1987:88)

14.3.3. Middle Voice (MDL) Prefixes

A middle voice prefix creates an intransitive verb with a participant that has properties of both subject and object. Two examples of this construction are given in (33); in each example the middle voice prefix attaches to a transitive verb.

(33a) ᎦᎵᏍᏙᏰᎭ
galiìsdooyeéha
ji-ali-sdooyeéha
1A-MDL-trim(T):PRC
'I am cutting my hair.'

(33b) ᎠᏙᎷᏩᏘᎭ
aàdooluhwatiíha
a-adaa-ooluhwatiíha
3A-MDL-develop(T):PRC
'It's in the development stages, it's coming about.'

The middle voice prefix has some similarities in form and meaning to the reflexive and probably developed out of it. This prefix appears the same as the reflexive before **consonants** (other than /h/) and before the vowel /a/; the other forms are distinct.

The middle voice can also be viewed as creating a meaning between an active meaning and a passive meaning. This prefix indicates that the action of the verb is affecting the person or thing that is the subject of that verb. An example of the resulting change in meaning is seen below in (34). The addition of the middle voice prefix makes the verb intransitive and expresses the idea that the bathing is happening to the subject.

(34a) ᎯᏯᏬᎠ
hiiyawóʔa
hii-awóʔa
2A.AN-bathe(T):PRC
'You're bathing him.'

(34b) ᎭᏓᏬᎠ
hadawóʔa
hi-adaa-awóʔa
2A-MDL-bathe(T):PRC
'You're bathing.'

In the previous section on valency-increasing constructions the causative was shown to add a participant that causes the action. One of the functions of the middle voice prefix is to remove the cause of the action. For example, in (35a) the verb 'split something' appears in its basic transitive form; to express the intransitive idea of something splitting by itself, the middle voice prefix is added in (35b).

(35a) ᏓᏍᏢᏳᏍᎦ
daàsdluysga
dee-a-sdluysga
DST-3A-split(T):PRC
'He is splitting it.'

(35b) ᏓᎵᏍᏢᏳᏍᎦ
daàlsdluysga
dee-a-ali-sdluysga
DST-3A-MDL-split(T):PRC
'It is splitting.'

A comparison of the reflexive, unspecified object reflexive, and middle voice prefixes is shown in (36). The first example is the simple transitive form of the verb. Sometimes the addition of the middle voice prefix can alter the meaning; as seen in (36d).

(36a) ᎪᎵᎦ
gohlga
ga-olihga
3A-recognize:PRC
'He recognizes him.'

(36b) ᎠᏓᏙᎵᎦ ᎤᏩᏌ
aàdaadohlga uwaása
a-adaad-olihga uu-vv́sa
3A-RFL-recognize:PRC 3B-EMP.PRO
'He recognizes himself.'

(36c) ᎠᏓᏙᎵᎦ
aàdaadohlga
a-adaad-olihga
3A-RFL-recognize:PRC
'He recognizes (somebody).'

(36d) ᏓᏙᎵᎦ
daàdohlga
dee-a-adaa-olihga
DST-3A-MDL-recognize:PRC
'It fits.'
'It is compatible.'

In (37b) below the middle voice prefix indicates that the food preparation is no longer done for the benefit of someone else but rather for the benefit of the subject. In this case the detransitivized verb means 'eat'.

(37a) ᎯᏍᏓᏯᏫᏍᎦ
hiisdáàyvvhv́sga
hii-sdáàyvvhv́sga
2A.AN-provide.meal:PRC
'You are fixing him a meal.'

(37b) ᎭᎵᏍᏓᏯᏫᏍᎦ
halsdáàyvvhv́sga
hi-ali-sdáàyvvhv́sga

2A-MDL-provide.meal:PRC
'You are eating.'

In (38) the same derived adjective has a slightly different meaning with the middle voice prefix. In the first example the adjective describes a person and implies an object (the thing or things not believed in). In (38b) the adjective refers to a quality of the thing itself.

(38a) ᏄᏬᎯᏳᏒᎾ
nuwoohiyuusv́v́na
ni-uu-oohiyu̥us-v́v́na
NI-3B-believe:CMP-NDV
'faithless', 'doesn't believe in things'

(38b) ᏄᏙᎯᏳᏒᎾ
nuudoohiyuu̥sv́v́na
ni-uu-adaa-oohiyuus-v́v́na
NI-3B-MDL-believe:CMP-NDV
'not real', 'unbelievable'

The middle voice prefix has forms that are distinct from the reflexive. It appears as [*ad*] before vowels, as seen in (39a); *-ali-* before the consonant /h/, as seen with the **inherent /h/** in (39b); and, like the reflexive, as *-adaa-* before all other consonants. This third form is exemplified in (39c).

(39a) ᎠᏚᏓᎴᎠ
aàduudaléeʔḁ
a-adaa-uudaléeʔa
3A-MDL-unhitch(T):PRC
'It is unhitching.'

(39b) ᎠᎾᎵᏌᏆᎴᎵᎭ
aànalsagwaleelíha
anii-ali-sagwaleelíha
3A.NS-MDL-roll(T):PRC
'They are rolling.'

(39c) ᎠᏓᏣᎦᎸᏴᏍᎦ
aàdaajagalvysga
a-adaa-jagalvysga
3A-MDL-rip(T):PRC
'It is ripping.'

The examples in (39) all express an action that happens spontaneously; if an agent is performing this action, the reflexive is used instead. The reflexive has a slight difference in form from the middle voice before vowels other than /a/; this difference can be seen by comparing (39a) above with (40) below.

(40) DᏓᏧᏓᎴᎠ
aàdaaduudaléeʔa
a-adaad-uudaléeʔa
3A-RFL-unhitch(T):PRC
'It is unhitching itself.'

The middle voice prefix appears on some verbs to indicate a reciprocal action. This meaning appears in (41a), while in (41b) the verb is seen in its transitive form. In (41c) the reflexive appears and has the same meaning as in (41a).

(41a) ᏕᏣᎵᏍᏕᎸᏫ
déejalsdeelvvhv
dee-iijii-ali-sdeelvvh-v
DST-2B.PL-MDL-help:CMP-EXP
'You all helped each other.'

(41b) ᏕᏥᏍᏕᎸᏫ
déejiisdeelvvhv
dee-iijii-sdeelvvh-v
DST-2B.PL-help:CMP-EXP
'You all helped them.'

(41c) ᏕᏣᏓᏍᏕᎸᏫ
déejadaasdeelvvhv
dee-iijii-adaad-sdeelvvh-v
DST-2B.PL-RFL-help:CMP-EXP
'You all helped each other.'

Another example of this type of middle voice is 'gather'; the transitive and intransitive forms are contrasted in (42).

(42a) ᏕᏗᏝᏏᎭ
déedíihliisíha
dee-iidii-x́xhliisíha
DST-1A.PL-gather(T):PRC
'We are gathering them up.'

(42b) ꮪꮟꮟꮯꮟꮜ
déedadáahliisíha
dee-iidii-adaa-x̋xhliisíha
DST-1A.PL-MDL-gather(T):PRC
'We are gathering together.'

In a few cases the middle voice prefix is like the unspecified object reflexive in that it simply creates an intransitive verb. For example, in (43a) the usual word for 'teacher' is shown; this form has the middle voice prefix in its [*ad*] form before the vowels (the reflexive form before the vowel /e/ is *-adaad-*). If the sentence indicates the object more specifically this prefix does not appear. In (43b) the first person singular Set B prefix is now the object of the teaching and the middle voice prefix is absent.

(43a) ᏗᏕᎯᏲᏅᏍᎩ
diideehyóóhvsgi
di-a-adaa-eehyoóhvsg-i
DST2-3A-MDL-teach:INC-AGT
'teacher'

(43b) ᎠᏇᎯᏲᏅᏍᎩ
diigweehyóóhvsgi
di-agi-eehyoóhvsg-i
DST2-1B-teach:INC-AGT
'my teacher'

Many verbs appear to have a frozen middle voice prefix. A sample list of these is given in (44).

(44)
alvvdcchíha	'faint'
-alisduhvsga	'bud'
-adeehv́sga	'be born'
-adanasiíni	'crawl'
-adiikáha	'urinate'
-alihiha	'fight'

The verb meaning 'happen' or 'become' appears to consist of a causative suffix and the middle voice prefix, suggesting that the causative prefix was originally a root that over time became a suffix. Two examples of this verb are presented in (45); in (45b) the applicative suffix appears as well.

(45a) ᎦᎵᏦᎫᎯᏓ ᏄᎵᏍᏔᏅ
galjóóhid nuùlstaanv
ga-aljóóhida ni-uu-alistaan-v
3A-fat NI-3B-become:CMP-EXP
'He became fat.'

(45b) ᎦᏙ ᏣᎵᏍᏔᏏ
gado jalstaasi
gado ja-alistaan-si
what 2B-happen:CMP-APL:IMM
'What happened to you?'

Some **adjectives** or nouns that are derived with the *-da* **participle suffix** have a middle voice prefix; such words always take the Set B pronominal prefix. In all three examples in (46) the initial vowel of the form *-ali-* is lost through **vowel clash** with the pronominal prefix, while the final vowel undergoes **vowel deletion** triggered by the inherent /h/ that accompanies the /s/.

(46a) ᎤᎵᏍᏚᎢᏓ uulsduʔíída 'open'
ᎠᏍᏚᎢᎠ aàsdúʔiʔa 'he's opening it'

(46b) ᎤᎵᏍᏆᎵᏓ uulsgwalíída 'broken'
ᎠᏍᏆᎵᏍᎦ aàsgwáalsga 'he's breaking it'

(46c) ᎤᎵᏑᏫᏓ uulsuúhwida 'colored', 'painted'
ᎠᏑᏫᏍᎦ aàsuúhwísga 'he's painting it'

Some noun and adjectives of unknown origin appear to have a frozen middle voice prefix, which suggests their origins as verbs. A few sample adjectives are listed below in (47); in all these examples the initial /a/ of the stem has been deleted by the pronominal prefix.

(47) ᎤᎴᏐᏓ uuleesóóda 'skinny'
ᎠᎳᏂᎩᏓ alahníígida 'strong'
ᎤᎵᏍᎨᏓ uulsgééda 'important', 'sacred'
ᎤᏓᎷᎳ uudaaluúla 'not finished'

The examples in (48) are from the same speaker. At present it is unknown what causes the appearance of the middle voice prefix (in 48b).

(48a) ᎦᎨᏓ
gagééda

ga-gééda
3A-heavy
'He/she/it is heavy.'

(48b) ᎤᏓᎨᏓ
uudagééda
uu-adaa-gééda
3B-MDL-heavy
'He/she/it is heavy.'

The middle voice and the reflexive have similar yet distinctive meanings. The distinction lies in how the event is presented. In a reflexive sentence the subject and the object are the same entity but are presented as distinct, whereas the middle voice is intransitive and more closely identifies the two. In the case of the reflexive, as seen in (49a), the subject is conceived of as performing the action on itself; in (49b) the subject is conceived of as an undergoer of the action or the action is conceived of as happening spontaneously. These examples also have different forms.

(49a) ᎠᏓᏙᏢᏍᎦ
aàdaadoohlvvsga
a-adaad-oohlvvsga
3A-RFL-make:PRC
'It's regenerating itself (e.g., a lizard's tail).'

(49b) ᎠᏙᏢᏍᎦ
aàdoohlvvsga
a-adaa-oohlvvsga
3A-MDL-make:PRC
'It's making itself (e.g., cream).'

The similarity in form and function of the reflexive and middle voice prefixes is a good indication that historically they were the same prefix.

14.4. Sources and Additional Reading

This grammar contains the only systematic exposition of valency-changing operations in Cherokee. "Primary object" and "secondary object" are Dryer's terms (1986). King (1975:89) calls the applicative suffix the benefactive; Cook (1979:139) calls it the dative; and Pulte and Feeling (1975:286) refer to it as the dative-benefactive. "Applicative" is more general in that it encompasses any semantic role that is being brought into the core participant structure of the verb.

Flemming (1996:43) has noted that the lack of vowel deletion for the Infinitive form of causative *-sdohdi* is unexpected; he hypothesizes that this is perhaps a "lexical exception" to this general phonological rule. Scancarelli (1987:84) observes that the use of the unspecified object reflexive is distinct from the use of the indefinite pronoun *kilo* 'someone', which is used "when the identity of the subject is unknown but relevant in context" (the identity of 'someone' will be revealed or will be important).

Most of the discussion of the middle voice prefix has been based on the framework established by Kemmer (1993). The term 'middle' in describing Cherokee is used for the first time in this work, but its use is not unprecedented in Iroquoian linguistics. For Tuscarora, Mithun (1976:68) states that "verb stems may contain a reflexive marker (*-at-*) preceding the verb root." Besides reflexive and reciprocal constructions, she notes that "the reflexive morpheme also appears in middle voice predications, where one's action involves oneself as experiencer." For Mohawk, Bonvillain (1994:87, 95), in addition to describing reflexive *-adaad-*, discusses what she calls a semireflexive prefix *-at-* that "indicates a kind of middle voice." She describes this morpheme as coding subject-affectedness, constructions where an agent is assumed but not mentioned, and spontaneous events. She also describes how some verbs "require *-at-* as part of a frozen verb base."

14.5. Directions for Further Research

Much work remains to be done on the details and nuances of valency-changing operations. The causative alone is complex enough to warrant its own study. King (1975:88) states that this suffix has more allomorphs than any other morpheme in Cherokee and that it is a root for the verbs 'use' and 'happen', which is also includes the middle voice prefix. The discourse function of what Pulte and Feeling (1975) describe as a passive voice (object focus prefixes in the current work) is an area not well understood in Cherokee. They briefly describe three different passive constructions but do not discuss the motivations or contexts for using the different forms. This is an area that merits further examination through the careful study of lengthy discourses. The secondary objects in ditransitives are almost always animate; this is another instance of an animacy preference in the language that could be further investigated. There is also evidence for possessor-raising where the applicative refers to a possessor; Walker (1975:226) has the example *Jisdu udohiyu jalvgwandeha amage'i* 'Rabbit sure likes your hominy'. Speakers liked this example, but I do not have examples of similar spontaneous utterances involving this verb. Corpus studies of older material could perhaps find more examples of this construction.

It would be interesting to study the many verbs in Cherokee that have a frozen middle/reflexive prefix. In her cross-linguistic study, Kemmer (1993:22) refers to frozen middles as deponents and states that their existence is a universal feature of languages with middle voice markers: "verbs in certain MM [middle-marker] classes tend to have unmarked counterparts. The word 'tend' is largely due to a single class of exceptions to this generalization. These exceptions are noticeable because they are quite widespread, in fact, I would venture to suggest, universal in middle-marking languages." She points out that the middle voice form in many languages is quite similar in form or sometimes identical to the reflexive. Kemmer (1993:66) states that the middle voice conceives of the subject and object as being relatively less distinguishable (and thereby less transitive) than the reflexive does: This "relative distinguishability of participants refers to: . . . the degree to which a single physico-mental entity is conceptually distinguished into separate participants, whether body vs. mind, or agent vs. unexpectedly contrasting patient. The fact that the reflexive form appears when the speaker desires to indicate greater conceptual separability of facets of a single referent than the middle would express, suggests that the reflexive marker in general has the function of designating events in which the initiator and endpoint participants are to some extent distinct. . . . The middle marker, on the other hand, has the basic function of indicating that the two semantic roles of Initiator and Endpoint refer to a single holistic entity."

Texts

Excerpts from the following texts are found throughout this grammar as individual words, phrases, or complete sentences. The individual lines are numbered to help the reader find phrases.

A1. The Wolf and the Crawdad

This story is from Marion 'Ed' Jumper. It has a rich variety of postfixes as well as some interesting uses of the object focus (O) prefixes. These types of race stories provide a useful context for studying the interaction of animacy and word order, as they usually contain two animals presumably equal in animacy. Singleton (1979) alludes to a similar story in his brief study of the structure of Cherokee narratives.

(1) ᏩᏯ ᎠᎴ ᏥᏍᏛᎾ
wahya ale jíisdvvna
wahya ale jíistvvna
The Wolf and the Crawdad

(2) ᎪᎯᎬ ᏥᎨᏒ ᎠᏁᎮ ᏩᏯ ᎠᎴ ᏥᏍᏛᎾ
koohigv jigeèsv aàneèhe wahya ale jíisdvvna
koohigv ji-geès-v́ anii-eèh-e wahya ale jíisdvvna
long.ago REL-be:INC-DVB 3A.NS-live:CMP-NXP wolf and crawdad
A long time ago lived a wolf and a crawdad.

(3) ᏌᏬᏃ ᎢᏳᏩᎩᏗ ᎠᎦᏚᎵᏍᎬ
saawúhnóo iyúwáákd aàgaduuliísgv
saagwu=hnóo iyúwáákdi aji-aduuliísg-v
one=CN time 3O-want:INC-EXP
One time wolf wanted

(4)

ᎠᏥᏰᏍᏗ	ᏥᏍᏛᎾ	ᏩᏯ
ajiiyeèsdi	jíisdvvna	wahya
aji-xxhyeèsdi	jíisdvvna	wahya
3O-eat(flexible):INF	crawdad	wolf

to eat the crawdad.

(5)

ᏩᏯ	ᎤᏁᏄᏝᏁ	ᏥᏍᏛᎾ	ᏧᎾᏙᎩᏯᏍᏗᎢ
wahya	uùneenuuhlane	jíisdvvna	juuhntohgiíyáàsdíiʔi
wahya	uu-neenuuhlan-e	jíisdvvna	di-uunii-ahtohgiíyáàsdíiʔi
wolf	3B-challenge:CMP-NXP	crawdad	DST2-3B.NS-race:INF

The wolf challenged the crawdad to race him.

(6)

ᏥᏍᏛᎾᏃ	ᎩᎳᏫᏴ
jíisdvvnáhno	kilawiyv
jíisdvvna=hno	kilawiyv
crawdad=CN	at.that.moment

The crawdad at that moment

(7)

ᏚᎵᏨᏯᏍᏔᏁ	ᎤᎾᏙᎩᏯᏍᏗᎢ
duùlchvv́yáàstane	uuhntohkiíyáàsdíiʔi
dee-uu-alchvv́yáàstan-e	uunii-ahtohkiíyáàsd-íiʔi
DST-3B-become.brave:CMP-NXP	3B.NS-race:INF

got brave enough to race the wolf.

(8)

ᎦᎵᏉᎩᏃ	ᏕᎧᎾᎵᏛ	ᏱᏕᎾᎵᎪᎾ
gahlgwoógíhnóo	deekánahltv	yidéenalgoóna
gahlgwoógi=hnóo	dee-kanahltv	yi-dee-iinii-algoóna
seven=CN	DST-hill	IRR-DST-1A.DL-arrive.first:IMM

"We will see who gets to the seven hills first,"

(9)

ᎤᏛᏁ	ᏩᏯ
uùdvvhne	wahya
uu-advvhn-e	wahya
3B-say:CMP-NXP	wolf

said the wolf.

(10)

ᎤᎾᏛᎾᏍᏔᏁᏃ	ᏧᎾᏙᎩᏯᏍᏗ
uùndvv́nastanéhnóo	juuhntohgiíyáàsdi
uunii-advv́nastan-e=hnóo	di-uunii-ahtohgiíyáàsdi
3B.NS-prepare:CMP-NXP=CN	DST2-3B.NS-race:INF

They got ready to race.

(11) ᎠᎬᏱᏃ ᏭᎷᏨ
agvvyíìhno wuulúhjv́
a-gvvyíí=hnóo wi-uu-ʔlúhj-v́
3A-first=CN TRN-3B-arrive:CMP-DVB
The first one arriving

(12) ᎦᎸᏂᏗᎠ ᏫᎧᎾᏢᏛ ᎤᏙᎯᏍᏗ ᎨᏒᎢ
galvvndiʔa wikanahltv uutohiísdi geèsvv́ʔi
galvvndiʔa wi-kanahltv uu-atohiisdi geès-vv́ʔi
on.top TRN-hill 3B-whoop:INF\MOD be:INC-EXP
at the top of the hill was to whoop.

(13) ᏙᏳᏃ ᏍᎩ ᏄᎾᏛᏁᎴ
doyúhnóo sgi nuùndv́vneele
doyu=hńoo sgi ni-uunii-adv́vneel-e
really=CN this NI-3B.NS-do:CMP-NXP
Really they did this.

(14) ᎠᎬᏱᏛ ᏭᏢᏍᏓᏁ ᏩᏯ
agvvydvv wuùtlvvsdane wahya
a-gvvyíí=dvv wi-uu-atlvvsdan-e wahya
3A-first=EM TRN-3B-take.off:CMP-NXP wolf
The wolf took off first.

(15) ᎦᏂᏓᏛ ᏭᎪᎮ ᏥᏍᏛᎾ
ganíidaʔdv wuùgoohe jíisdvvna
ga-níidaʔdv wi-uu-gooh-e jíisdvvna
3A-tail TRN-3B-see:CMP-NXP crawdad
The crawdad saw his tail

(16) ᎤᏏᏃ ᏭᏙᏎᎢ
uhnáhnóo wuùtoséeʔi
uhna=hnóo wi-uu-ahtos-éʔi
there=CN TRN-3B-latch.onto:CMP-NXP
and latched onto it.

(17) ᏭᎷᏣᏃ ᎦᎸᎾᏗ ᏗᎨᏒ
wúúluhjahnóo galv́vnad digeèsv
wi-uu-ʔluhj-a=hnóo galv́vnadi di-geès-v
TRN-3B-arrive:CMP-CVB=CN on.top.of TOW-be:INC-EXP
When he got to the top of the hill

(18) ᏩᏯ ᎤᏙᎯᏎ
wahya uùtohiise
wahya uu-atohiis-e
wolf 3B-whoop:CMP-NXP
the wolf whooped

(19) ᎥᎾᏫᏛᏍᏊ ᎾᎥ ᎤᏙᎯᏎ ᏥᏍᏛᎾ
vnawdvvsgwu naʔv uùtoohiise jíisdvvna
vnawdvv=sgwu naʔv uu-atohiis-e jíisdvvna
right.then=DT near 3B-whoop:CMP-NXP crawdad
and right then beside him the crawdad whooped.

(20) ᏃᏭᏃ ᏔᎵᏁ ᏭᏂᎷᏣ
noówúhn taʔliiné wuuniílúhj
noówu=hńo taʔli-iiné wi-uunii-ʔlúhj-a
now=CN two-ORD TRN-3B.NS-arrive:CMP-CVB
When they arrived at the second

(21) ᎤᏠᏱ ᏅᎾᏛᏁᎴ ᎠᎴᏍᏊ
uudlóóy nvvndv́vneele alesgwu
uu-dlóóyi ni-ii-uunii-adv́vneel-e ale=sgwu
3B-same NI-ITR-3B.NS-do:CMP-NXP and=DT
they did the same and also

(22) ᏦᎢᏁ ᏅᎩᏁ ᎯᏍᎩᏁ ᏑᏓᎵᏁ
joʔiiné nvhgiiné hisgiiné suúdaliiné
joʔi-iiné nvhgi-iiné hisgi-iiné suúdali-iiné
three-ORD four-ORD five-ORD six-ORD
at the third, fourth, fifth, and sixth [hills]

(23) ᎬᏂᏃ ᎦᎵᏉᎩᏁ ᏭᏂᎷᏨ
kv́v́hnihnóo gahlgwoógiiné wuùniilúhjv́
kv́v́hni=hnóo gahlgwoógi-iiné wi-uunii-ʔlúhj-v́
until=CN seven-ORD TRN-3B.NS-arrive:CMP-DVB
until they got to the seventh one.

(24) ᏍᏓᏲᏒᏛ ᎤᏙᎯᏎ ᏩᏯ
sdaayosv́v́dvv uùtohiise wahya
sdááyi-sv́v́=dvv uu-atohiis-e wahya
hard-INT=EM 3B-whoop:CMP-NXP wolf
The wolf whooped real loud.

(25)

ᏥᏍᏛᎾᏃ	ᎾᏍᏊ	ᎩᎳᏊᏴ	ᎤᏙᎯᏎ
jíisdvvnáhnóo	nasgwu	kilagwuyv	uùtohiise
jíisdvvna=hnóo	na=sgwu	kilagwuyv	uu-ahtohiis-e
crawdad=CN	that=DT	right.away	3B-whoop:CMP-NXP

The crawdad also whooped right away,

(26)

ᎠᏎᏃ	ᏩᏯ	ᎦᏙᎬ
aséehno	wahya	gadokv
aséehno	wahya	gadokv
but	wolf	why

but the wolf said, "How come

(27)

ᎡᎵᏭ	ᏂᏥᏌᏄᎳ	ᎢᏧᎳ
eeliw	nitsanuúla	iíjúula
eeliwu	ni-ji-hi-anuúla	iíjúula
possible	NI-REL-2A-fast	both

if you're so fast how did we both

(28)

ᏥᏂᎷᎩ	ᎠᎭᏂ	ᎧᎾᎵᏛᎢ
diiniílúhg	áhan	kanahltv́v́ʔi
di-iinii-ʔlúhgi	áhani	kanahltv́v́ʔi
TOW-1A.DL-arrive:IMM\SUB	here	hill

get to the hill at the same time?"

(29)

ᏥᏍᏛᎾᏃ	ᏥᏰᏄᎵᏛ	ᎤᏓᏙᏎᎴ
jíisdvvnáhnóo	jiiyenúúlidvv	uùdaadoseéle
jíisdvvna=hnóo	ji-xxyaanúúli=dvv	uu-adaad-oseél-e
crawdad=CN	1A-fast=EM	3B-RFL-tell:CMP-NXP

"I am fast," he told the wolf;

(30)

ᎠᏎᏃ	ᏩᏯ	ᎾᏭ	ᎤᏕᎳᎰᏎ
aséehno	wahya	naàwu	uùdelhoose
aséehno	wahya	na=gwu	uu-adelhoos-e
however	wolf	that=DT	3B-find.out:CMP-NXP

but the wolf found out

(31)

ᎦᏂᏓᏛᏃ	ᎦᏙᏍᎨ	ᏥᏍᏛᎾ	ᎥᏍᎩᏂ	ᏳᏍᏗ
ganiidadv́v́hnóo	gatosge	jíisdvvn	vsgin	yúúsd
ga-niidaʔdv́v́=hnóo	ga-tosg-e	jíisdvvna	vsgini	yúúsdi
3A-tail=CN	3A-latch.onto:INC-NXP	crawdad	that	reason

that he was latching onto his tail, that's why

(32)

ᎢᏧᎳᎭᏬ	ᏩᏂᎷᎩ	ᏕᎧᎾᏢᏛᎢ
iíjúulahaw	waniiluhgi	deekanahltv́v́ʔi
iíjúula-ha=wu	wi-anii-luhgi	dee-kanahltv́v́ʔi
both-only=DT	TRN-3A.NS-arrive:IMM	DST-hill

they got to the hills together.

(33)

ᏩᏯᏃ	ᎤᏕᎳᎰᏎ	ᎾᏭᏃ
wahyáhnóo	uùdelhoose	naàwúhnóo
wahya=hnóo	uu-adelhoos-e	naàwuhnóo
wolf=CN	3B-notice:CMP-NXP	and.then

The wolf noticed and then

(34)

ᏓᎦᎦᏅᏁ	ᏥᏍᏛᎾ	ᏙᏳᏛ	ᎯᎶᏄᎮ
daàgagahnane	jíisdvvna	dooyúdvv	hiloonuuhe
dee-aji-agahnan-e	jíisdvvna	dooyu=dvv	hi-loonuuhe
DST-3O-look.at:CMP-NXP	crawdad	really=EM	2A-cheat:PRC

looked at the crawdad [and said]: “You’re truly cheating.”

(35)

ᏥᏂᏓᏛᏃ	ᏥᏍᎩᎳᏩᏗᏎ
jiniidadv́hnóo	tskilawdiise
ji-niidaʔdv́=hnóo	ji-sgi-hkilawdiis-e
1A-tail=CN	REL-2/1-ride.on:INC-NXP

“You were hanging onto my tail,”

(36)

ᎠᎪᏎᎴ	ᏥᏍᏛᎾ
aàgooseéle	jíisdvvna
aji-ooseél-e	jíisdvvna
3O-tell:CMP-NXP	crawdad

he said to the crawdad

(37)

ᎤᏅᏩᏛᏃ	ᎠᏥᎨᎯᏙᎴ	ᏥᏍᏛᎾ
uhnawdvhno	ajikehiídóòle	jíisdvvn
uhna=wu=dvv=hno	aji-hkeh-iídóòl-e	jíisdvvna
there=DT=FC=CN	3O-chase:CMP-AMB:CMP-NXP	crawdad

and right then he started chasing him

(38)

ᏂᎦᏰᏥᏂᏱᏍᎩ	ᎤᏅᏃ	ᏩᏥᏂᏴᏃ
nigayejiniiyíisg	uhnáhnóo	wajiniiyv́v́hńoo
ni-gaa-aji-niiyiísg-i	uhna=hnóo	wi-aji-niiyvvh-a=hnóo
NI-GA-3O-catch:INC-AGT	there=CN	TRN-3O-catch:CMP-CVB=CN

until he caught him. And when he caught him

(39) ᏩᏥᏯᎣᏁ ᎥᏍᎩᏭᏃ ᏂᎦᎠ
wajiiyaʔohne vv̀sgiwuhnóo nigaáʔa
wi-aji-xxhyaaʔ-ohn-e vv̀sgi=wu=hnóo nigaáʔa
TRN-3O-eat(flexible):CMP-TRM:CMP-NXP that=DT=CN all
he ate him up. And that's the end.

A2. The Search Party

The following story told by Benny Smith involves a search party traveling along the Arkansas River and giving names to several places. This narrative shows an interesting alternation between the transitive verb 'name' and its middle voice counterpart 'be named'. It also contains several examples of the locative suffix that is used on nouns to indicate a place characterized by that noun.

(1) ᏧᎾᎦᏖᏃᎵᏙᎴ
juunaktenoliídóòle
ji-uunii-agahtenol-iídóòl-e
DST2-3B.NS-observe:CMP-AMB:CMP-NXP
The Search Party (literally, 'When They Were Looking Around')

(2) ᎷᎯᏴ ᏥᎨᏒ ᏝᏏ ᎡᏍᎦ ᎤᎾᏕᏅ
luhiyv jigeesv tlasi esgáá uùnadeehnv
luhiyv ji-gees-v tlasi esgáá uunii-adeehn-v
long.ago REL-be:INC-EXP not.yet in.this.vicinity 3B.NS-be.born:CMP-EXP
A long time ago no one yet lived in this area.

(3) ᎤᏂᎷᏨ ᏥᎨᏎ
uùniiʔlúhjv jigeese
uunii-ʔlúhj-v ji-gees-e
3B.NS-arrive:CMP-EXP REL-be:INC-EXP
They arrived,

(4) ᎦᏳᎳ ᎤᏁᏙᎴ ᎤᎾᎦᏖᏃᎵᏙᎴ ᎢᎦᏓ
gáàyul uùneédóòle uùnakteénóòliídóòle iigáád
gáàyula uunii-eédóòl-e uunii-agahteénóòl-iídóòl-e iigááda
already 3B.NS-be.at:CMP-NXP 3B.NS-look.around:CMP-AMB:CMP-NXP few
already a few of them walked around, looked around.

(5) ᎤᎨᎳᏪᏓ ᏥᎨᏒ ᏏᏉᏲ ᏧᎾᏓᏅᏝ
uugeelaweed jigeesv sigwooy juundaanv́v́tl

uugeelaweeda	ji-gees-v	sigwooya	di-uunii-adaad-nv̋tla
Ugelaweda	REL-be:INC-EXP	Sequoyah	DST2-3B.NS-RFL-brother

Ugelawada was Sequoyah's brother.

(6)

ᏓᏗᏂᏙᎮ	ᏓᎿᏩ	ᎠᏁᏙ
daàtihniídóòhe	daahnaw	aneedóó
dee-a-ahtihn-iídóòh-e	daahnawa	anii-eedooh-i
DST-3A-lead:INC-AMB:INC-NXP	war	3A.NS-be.at:INC-AGT

He was leading a war party.

(7)

ᎡᏉᏂ	ᎤᏪᏴ	ᎤᏂᏍᏓᏩᏛᏙᎴ
eegwóón	uùwéeyv	uùniisdáàwadvv̋dóòle
eegwóóni	uùwéeyv	uunii-sdáàwadvv̋s-dóòl-e
Egwoni [Arkansas River]	river	3B.NS-follow:CMP-AMB:CMP-NXP

They followed and stopped along the Arkansas.

(8)

ᎯᎸᏍᎩ	ᎠᏁᎲ	ᎤᏁᏙᎸ
hilv̋vsg	aneehv́	uùneédóòlv
hilv̋vsgi	anii-eeh-v	uunii-eédóòl-v
Several	3A.NS-live:INC-EXP\SUB	3B.NS-be.at:CMP-EXP

Several who were there walked around.

(9)

ᏚᏃᎡ	ᎾᎯᏴ	ᏥᎨᏒ
duùnóoʔe	nahiyv	jigeesv
dee-uunii-óoʔ-e	nahiyv	ji-gees-v
DST-3B.NS-name:CMP-NXP	at.that.time	REL-be:INC-EXP

They named it at that time.

(10)

ᎾᏅ	ᏧᏲᎱᏒ	ᏨᏚᏙ	ᎪᎯ	ᏥᎦ
naanv	juuyoohuusv́	jvvduùdo	koohi	jiga
naanv	di-uu-yoohuus-v́	di-ii-dee-uu-adaa-o	koohi	ji-ga
where	TOW-3B-die:CMP-DVB	TOW-ITR-DST-3B-MDL-name:PRC	today	REL-be:PRC

To this day its name is "where one died."

(11)

ᎤᏁᏙᎴ	ᎤᎿ	ᎤᏂᎪᏩᎲ
uùneédóòle	uùhna	uùniigoowáhv
uunii-eédóòl-e	uùhna	uunii-goowáh-v
3B.NS-be.at:CMP-NXP	there	3B.NS-see:CMP-EXP

They walked around there, they saw

(12)

ᎩᎶ	ᎤᏲᎱᏒ	ᏍᎩᏃᎢᏳᏍᏗ	ᏧᏲᎱᏒ
kilo	uùyoohuusv	sgihnoʔiyúúsd	juuyoohuusv́
kilo	uu-yoohuus-v	sgihnoʔiyúúsdi	di-uu-yoohuus-v́
someone	3B-die:CMP-EXP	that's.why	TOW-3B-die:CMP-DVB

someone had died. That's why "place where one died"

(13)

ᏚᏃᎡ	ᎤᏂᎾ
duùnóoʔe	uùhnáana
dee-uunii-óoʔ-e	uùhna=na
DST-3B.NS-name:CMP-NXP	there=FC

was the name of that place.

(14)

ᏄᎴ	ᏌᎷᏱᏂᎨᏴ	ᏗᏝ	ᎤᏁᏙᎴ	ᎤᏂᎾ
nuule	saluúynigeeyv	diidl	uùneédóòle	uùhnáana
nuu=le	saluúyinigeeyv	diidla	uunii-eédóòl-e	uùhna=na
now=OS	Sallisaw	toward	3B.NS-be.at:CMP-NXP	there=FC

And then they went in the direction of Sallisaw. They walked around there.

(15)

ᎤᏂᎷᏣ	ᏍᏆᏍᏙᏒ	ᏌᎷᏱ	ᎢᏳᏍᏗ
uunííluhj	sgwiisdosv́	salúúy	iyúúsd
uunii-luhj-a	sgwíísdi-sv́	salúúyi	iyúúsdi
3B.NS-arrive:CMP-CVB	a.lot-INT	thicket	like

When they arrived it was very thickety

(16)

ᎤᏩᏂᏕᏍᎩ	ᎢᏳᏍᏗ	ᏌᎷᏱ	ᎨᏎᎢ
uuwandéésg	iyúúsd	saluuy	geese
uuwandéésgi	iyúúsdi	saluuyi	gees-e
flat.long.plain	like	thicket	be:INC-NXP

like a long flat plain of thickets,

(17)

ᎥᏍᎩᏃᏳᏍᏗ	ᏌᎷᏱᏂᎨᏴ	ᏚᏃᎡ
vvsginoyusd	saluúynigeeyv	duùnóoʔe
vvsginoyusdi	saluúynigeeyv	dee-uunii-óoʔe
that's.why	Sallisaw	DST-3B.NS-name:CMP-NXP

that's why they called it Sallisaw.

(18)

ᎤᏂ	ᎤᏪᏴ	ᏄᎴ	ᏓᏄᎪ
uùhna	uùweeyv	nuule	daahnúugó
uùhna	uùweeyv	nuule	daahnúugo=ʔi
there	stream	and.then	gar-LOC

And then there is a stream at Vian,

(19) ᏗᏝ ᎤᏪᏴ ᎤᏂᎷᏤ
didl uùweeyv uùniiluhje
díidla uùweeyv uunii-luhj-e
toward river 3B.NS-arrive:CMP-NXP
they arrived at the river.

(20) ᎤᎿᏅ ᏍᏘᏍᏙᏒ ᏚᏂᎪᎮ
uùhnanv sgwiisdosv́ duùniigoohe
uùhna=nv sgwíísdi-sv́ dee-uunii-gooh-e
there=FC a.lot-INT DST-3B.NS-see:CMP-NXP
There they saw a whole lot of

(21) ᎠᏣᏗ ᏓᏄᎪ ᎢᏳᏍᏗ
ajaʔd daahnúug iyúúsd
ajaʔdi daahnúugo iyúúsdi
fish gar like
fish like gar.

(22) ᎤᏍᎩᏃᏳᏍᏗ ᏥᏚᏙ ᏓᏄᎪ
uusginoyuusd jiduudo dahnugó
uusginoyuusdi ji-dee-uu-adaa-o dahnugo-ʔi
that's.why REL-DST-3B-MDL-name:PRC gar-LOC
That's why it's called 'Gar' [Vian].

(23) ᏄᎴ ᎠᏥᏍᎬᏂᎨᏍᏛ ᎤᏪᏴ ᎤᏂᎷᏤ
nuule ajisgvnigeesdv uùweeyv uùniiluhje
nuule ajisgvnigeesdv uùweeyv uunii-ʔluhj-e
and.then Gore stream 3B.NS-arrive:CMP-NXP
And then at Gore they arrived at the river.

(24) ᎤᎿᏅᏍᏊ ᎠᏣᏗ ᏍᏘᏍᏙᏒ
uùhnaanvsgwu ajaʔd sgwíísdosv́
uùhna=nv=sgwu ajaʔdi sgwíísdi-sv́
there=FC=DT fish a.lot-INT
There also was a whole lot of fish.

(25) ᎠᏂᏥᏍᎬᏂᎨ ᏚᏂᎪᎮ
aniijisgvnige duùniigoohe
anii-jisgvnige dee-uunii-gooh-e
3A.NS-carp DST-3B.NS-see:CMP-NXP
They saw carp.

(26)	ᎤᏍᎩᏃᏳᏍᏗ	ᏥᏚᏙ	ᎠᏥᏍᎬᏂᎨᏍᏛ
	uusginoyúúsd	jiduùdóo	ajisgvnigeesdv
	uusginoyúúsdi	ji-dee-uu-adaa-o	ajisgvnigeesdv
	that's.why	REL-DST-3B-MDL-name:PRC	Gore

That's why it's called Gore.

(27)	ᏄᎴ	ᏧᏍᏆᎦᏟ	ᏥᏚᏙ
	nuule	júúsgwagahli	jiduudóo
	nuule	di-uu-x̃sgwagahli	ji-dee-uu-adaa-óo
	and.then	DST2-3B-striped	REL-DST-3B-MDL-name:PRC

And then at what is called "Striped" [Forth Gibson]

(28)	ᎤᏂᎷᏤ	ᎠᎪᏗ	ᏳᏍᏗ	ᎨᏎ	ᎤᏁᏅ
	uùniiʔluhje	agóódi	yúúsd	geese	uùhnáanv
	uunii-ʔluhj-e	agóódi	yúúsdi	gees-e	uùhna=nv
	3B.NS-arrive:CMP-NXP	prairie	like	be:INC-NXP	there=FC

they arrived, it was like a prairie there.

(29)	ᎠᏂᎠᎭᏫ	ᏧᏂᏍᏆᎦᏟ	ᏍᏈᏍᏙᏒ	ᏚᏂᎪᎮ
	aniiʔahaw	juuníísgwagahl	sgwiisdosv́	duùniigoohe
	anii-ahawi	di-uunii-x̃sgwagahli	sgwíísdi-sv́	dee-uunii-gooh-e
	3A.NS-deer	DST2-3B.NS-striped	a.lot-INT	DST-3B.NS-see:CMP-NXP

There they saw a whole lot of striped deer.

(30)	ᎤᏍᎩᏅ	ᏧᏍᏆᎦᏟ	ᏥᏚᏙᎠ
	uusginv	júúsgwagahli	jiduùdóoʔa
	uusginv	di-uu-x̃sgwagahli	ji-dee-uu-adaa-óoʔa
	that's.why	DST2-3B-striped	REL-DST-3B-MDL-name:PRC

That's why it's called "Striped" [Fort Gibson].

(31)	ᎤᏁ	ᎠᎼ	ᏭᏂᎷᏤ	ᎤᏁᏅᏍᏊ
	uùhna	áamó	wuùniiluhje	uùhnanvsg
	uùhna	áama-hi	wi-uunii-luhj-e	uùhna=nv=sgwu
	there	salt-LOC	TRN-3B.NS-arrive:CMP-NXP	there=FC=DT

There at "Salt" [Salina] they arrived at that place there.

(32)	ᎠᎹ	ᏍᏈᏍᏙᏒ	ᎬᎾᎨᏒ	ᎦᎵᎨᏰ
	áam	sgwiisdosv́	kvnageesv	galgeéye
	áama	sgwíísdo-sv́	kvnageesv	ga-ali-geéy-e
	salt	a.lot-INT	in.the.open	3A-MDL-scatter(T):INC-NXP

A whole lot of salt was scattered about

(33) ᎤᎾᏍᎩᏳ̈ᏍᏗ Ꭰ·Ꮌ ᏥᏚᏙᎡ
uunasgiyúúsd áamó jiduùdóoʔe
uunasginoyúúsdi áama-hi ji-dee-uu-adaa-óoʔ-e
that's.why salt-LOC REL-DST-3B-MDL-name:CMP-NXP
there, that's why it's called "Salt" [Salina].

A3. The Turtle and the Rabbit

The following narrative was told by Rosa M. Carter; a shorter and somewhat different North Carolina version is also found in Speck (1926: 111). This text has a rich variety of adverbials; of particular note is the use of irrealis *yi-* to express subordinate 'if' as well as the 'when(ever)' time adverbial. This prepronominal prefix also is used in this story for negation, conditional, and future meanings. Several Infinitive stems have the *gaa-* prefix and modal tone indicating ability. Unlike the other race narrative in this appendix, this contains no instances of the object focus prefixes; this is notable, because the story centers on two animals of seemingly equal animacy. The less commonly seen Completive form of 'be' also appears several times.

(1) ᏄᎵᏍᏔᏂᏙᎸ ᏓᎦᏏ ᏚᎩᏴ ᏥᏍᏚ
nuulstaniídóòlv daks duukiiyv jiisd
ni-uu-alistan-iídóòl-v daksi dee-uu-kiiy-v jiisdu
NI-3B-happen:CMP-AMB:CMP-EXP turtle DST-3B-beat.in.a.race:CMP-EXP rabbit
How the Turtle Beat the Rabbit

(2) ᏂᎦᏓᏛ ᎤᎾᏅᏖ
nigáádadvv uùnahnte
nigááda=dvv uunii-anvht-e
all=EM 3B.NS-know:CMP-NXP
They all knew that

(3) ᏥᏍᏚ ᎣᏍᏓ ᎠᏟᏙᎯ ᎨᏒ
jiisd óósd atlíidóóhi geèsv́
jiisdu óósda a-aditlíidoóh-i geès-v́
rabbit good 3A-run:INC-AGT be:INC-DVB
the rabbit was a good runner.

(4) ᎤᎾᏙᎩᏯᏍᏗ ᎤᏂᏃᎮᏞ ᏥᏍᏚ ᎾᏅ ᏓᎩᏏ
uuntohgiíyáàsdi uuniihnooheéhle jiisd nahn daks
uunii-ahtohgiíyáàsdi uunii-hnooheéhl-e jiisdu na=hnv daksi

3B.NS-race:INF	3B.NS-talk:CMP-NXP	rabbit	the=CN	turtle

The turtle and the rabbit talked about a race.

(5)	ᎤᏅᏖ	ᎬᏩᏠᎯᏍᏗ	ᎨᎲ
	uuhnte	gvvwtlóóhisd	geehv́
	uu-anvht-e	gaa-uu-atloohisdi	geeh-v́
	3B-know:CMP-NXP	GA-3B-beat:INF\MOD	be:CMP-DVB

He [Rabbit] knew that he could beat him,

(6)	Ꮎ	ᏓᎦᏏ	ᎤᏍᎦᏃᎵ	ᎨᎲ	ᎠᏟᏙᎯ
	na	daks	uusganóól	geehv́	atlíidóóhi
	na	daksi	uu-sganóóli	geeh-v́	a-aditlíidoóh-i
	that	turtle	3B-slow	be:CMP-DVB	3A-run:INC-AGT

because the turtle was a slow runner.

(7)	ᏚᏄᎦᏔᏁ	Ꮎ	Ᏼ	ᎢᎦ
	duùnuktane	na	yv	iig
	dee-uunii-ugahtan-e	na	yv	iiga
	DST-3B.NS-decide:CMP-NXP	that	time.when	day

They decided on what day

(8)	ᎥᏍᎩᎾ	ᏳᎾᏛᏅᏗ
	vv̀sgina	yuundvv̀hndi
	vv̀sgina	yi-uunii-advv̀hndi
	that.way	IRR-3B.NS-do:INF

they would do this.

(9)	ᏓᎩᏏᏍᎩᏂ	ᎨᎲᏃ	ᏚᏟᏃᎮᏔᏁ
	daksisgin	geèhv́hno	duùhlinohehtane
	daksi=sgini	geèh-v́=hno	dee-uu-ali-hnohehtan-e
	turtle=CS	be:CMP-DVB=CN	DST-3B-MDL-talk:CMP-NXP

But the turtle talked to

(10)	ᏧᎵ	ᏃᏬᎴ	ᏏᏓᏁᎸ	ᎠᏂᏁ
	juulíí	noowle	sidaaneelv	aniinéé
	di-uu-alíí	noowle	sidaaneelv	anii-neé
	DST2-3B-friend	and.then	family	3A.NS-live:PRC\SUB

his friends and family members living there.

(11)	ᏄᏍᏛ	ᏚᏭᎬᏛ	ᏚᏃᏎᎴ
	nuusdv	duuwuuktv́	duùhnooseéle

nuusdv dee-uu-uugoht-v́ dee-uu-hnooseél-e
that.which DST-3B-decide:CMP-DVB DST-3B-tell:CMP-NXP
He told them about his plans

(12) ᏂᎬᏩᏛᏗ ᎨᎲ
nigvvwadv́v́hnd geèhv
ni-ga-uu-advvhndi geèh-v́
NI-GA-3B-do:INF\MOD be:CMP-EXP
and what he could do

(13) ᎬᏩᏓᏡᎯᏍᏗ ᎨᎲ
gvvwadaatlóóhisd geèhv́
ga-uu-adaad-atloohisdi geèh-v́
GA-3B-RFL-beat.in.race:INF\MOD be:CMP-DVB
for him to be able to beat him.

(14) ᏃᏭ ᎤᏍᏆᎸᎯᎴ ᎢᎦ
noow uùsgwalvhihle iig
noogwu uu-sgwalvhihl-e iiga
now 3B-come.time:CMP-NXP day
The day came and

(15) ᎠᏁᎿᎢ ᏂᎬ ᎤᎾᏓᏟᏌᏁ
anéehnaʔi nikv́ uundahlisane
anii-éehnaʔi nikv́ uunii-adaa-x́xhlisan-e
3A.NS-animal everywhere 3B.NS-MDL-gather(T):CMP-NXP
all the animals came together

(16) ᎤᎾᎦᏙᏍᏙᏗ ᎠᎾᏙᎩᏯᏍᏗ
uunaktosdohdi ahntohgiíyáàsdi
uunii-agahtosdohdi anii-ahtohgiíyáàsdi
3B.NS-watch:INF 3A.NS-race:INF
to watch the race.

(17) ᏄᎾᏛᏁᎴ ᎠᏂᏐ ᏓᎦᏏ ᏚᏃᏎᎸ
nuùndvvneele aniisoʔ daks duuhnooseelv́
ni-uunii-advvneel-e anii-sóʔ daksi dee-uu-hnooseel-v
NI-3B.NS-do:CMP-NXP 3A.NS-other turtle DST-3B-tell:CMP-EXP\SUB
The others did what the turtle told them,

(18) ᏄᏍᏛᏃ ᏚᏭᎪᏔᏅ
nuusdv́v́hn duuwuuktanv́

nuusdv̋v̋=hnóo	dee-uu-uugohtan-v
that.which=CN	DST-3B-plan:CMP-EXP\SUB

what he had planned.

(19)	ᏅᏊ	ᎠᎬᏱ	ᎦᏚᏏ
	nvw	agv̋v̋yi	gadúus
	nvvgwu	agv̋v̋yi	gadúusi
	now	first	top

“The first mountain top,

(20)	ᏱᎬᎵᏍᎪᎵᏓᏏ	ᎠᎬᏱ	ᏫᏣᎶᎯᏍᏗ
	yigvvlisgohldáàs	agv̋v̋y	wijáʔlohisdi
	yi-gvv-alisgohldáàsi	a-gv̋v̋yi	wi-ja-ʔlohisdi
	IRR-1/2-permit:IMM	3A-first	TRN-2B-pass:INF

“I will let you get there first.

(21)	ᏏᏅ	ᎠᏯ	Ꮶ	ᏯᎩᎷᎳ	ᎣᏂ	ᏱᎦ
	siin	ay	jo	yagiluul	oohni	yigáá
	si=nv	aya	jo	yi-agi-luula	oohni	yi-ji-áa
	still=FC	1PRO	three	IRR-1B-need:IMM	behind	IRR-1A-walk:IMM\SUB

“I will still need three, since I will be behind you,”

(22)	ᎤᏛᏁ	ᏥᏍᏚ
	uudvvne	jiisd
	uu-advvn-e	jiisdu
	3B-say:CMP-NXP	rabbit

the rabbit said.

(23)	ᎥᏍᎩᏂ	ᏄᏍᏛ	ᎤᏂᏃᎮᎵ
	vv̀sgin	nuusdv́	uuniihnooheehlv́
	vv̀sgini	nuusdv́	uunii-hnooheehl-v́
	that.one	that.which	3B.NS-say:CMP-DVB

What they had talked about,

(24)	Ꮎ	ᏄᎾᏛᏁᎴ
	na	nuùndvvneele
	na	ni-uunii-advvneel-e
	that	NI-3B.NS-do:CMP-NXP

they did it.

(25)	ᎤᏂᎩᏎ	ᏓᎦᏏ
	uùhniigiise	daksi

uu-ahniigiis-e	daksi
3B-leave:CMP-NXP	turtle

The turtle left.

(26)	ᎠᎬᏱ	ᏦᏓᎸ	ᏩᏟᏎ	ᏭᎪᎮ	ᏥᏍᏚ
	agv́v́yi	joodalv	watlíísé	wuùgoohe	jiisd
	a-gv́v́yi	di-oodalv	wi-a-adihtlíis-e	wi-uu-gooh-e	jiisdu
	3A-first	TOW-mountain	TRN-3A-run:INC-NXP\SUB	TRN-3B-see:INC-NXP	rabbit

The rabbit saw him running over the first mountain.

(27)	ᏅᏊ	ᎤᎾᎴᏅ	ᎠᎾᏙᎩᏯᏍᎬ
	nv́w	uunaleenv́	ahntohkiyasgv́
	nv́gwu	uunii-aleenvvh-a	anii-ahtohkiyasg-v́
	now	3B.NS-start(T):CMP-CVB	3A.NS-race:INC-DVB

That's when they started racing.

(28)	ᏄᏍᏛ	ᎤᏂᏃᎮᎵ	ᏓᎩᏏᏃ
	nuusdv	uùniihnooheehlv	dakshnóo
	nuusdv	uunii-hnooheehl-v	daksi=hnóo
	that.which	3B.NS-tell:CMP-EXP	turtle=CN

They told how the turtles

(29)	ᎾᏊ	ᎾᎾᏛᏁᎲ	ᏌᏊᎭ
	nagw	nandvvneehv́	saagwuha
	na=gwu	ni-anii-advvneeh-v	saagwu-ha
	that=DT	NI-3A.NS-do:INC-EXP\SUB	one-all

did it one at a time

(30)	ᏏᏓᏁᎸ	ᎠᏁ	ᎤᎿ	ᏧᎵᎢᎴ	ᏱᎩ
	siidanelv́	anéé	uhna	juulííʔíle	yig
	siidanelv́	anii-neé	uhna	di-uu-aliíʔi=le	yi-gi
	family	3A.NS-live:PRC\SUB	there	DST2-3B-friend=OS	IRR-be:IMM

family or friend living there

(31)	ᏦᏓᎸ	ᏱᏭᎷᏣ	ᏥᏍᏚ
	joodalv	yiwúúluhj	jiisd
	di-oodalv	yi-wi-uu-luhj-a	jiisdu
	TOW-mountain	IRR-TRN-3B-arrive:CMP-CVB	rabbit

Whenever the rabbit got to the mountain

(32)	ᎤᏏ	ᏩᎪᏘᏍᎨ	ᏓᎩᏏ	ᏫᎧᎾᎷᏍᎬ
	uhna	wagotisge	daks	wikanaluusgv́
	uhna	wi-a-gotisg-e	daksi	wi-ga-hnaluusg-v́
	there	TRN-3A-see:INC-NXP	turtle	TRN-3A-ascend:INC-DVB

there he saw the turtle going up

(33)	ᏭᏕᎵᎬ	ᏳᏍᏗᎭ
	wuùdéeliigv́	yuusdiiha
	wi-uu-adéeliìg-v́	yuusdiiha
	TRN-3B-go.out.of sight:INC-DVB	every.time

and down every time.

(34)	Ꮠ	ᏦᏓᎴ	ᏱᏭᎷᏣ
	sóʔ	joodale	yiwúúluhj
	sóʔ	di-ooda=le	yi-wi-uu-luhj-a
	another	TOW-mountain=OS	IRR-TRN-3B-arrive:CMP-CVB

When he got to another mountain

(35)	ᎥᏍᎩ	ᎾᎾᏛᏁᎮ	ᎥᏍᎩᏴ	ᎣᏂ	ᏦᏓᎸ
	vv̀sgi	naàndv́vneehe	vvsgiiyv	oohni	joòdalv
	vv̀sgi	ni-anii-adv́vneeh-e	vvsgiiyv	oohni	di-oòdalv
	that	NI-3A.NS-do:INC-NXP	that.far	behind	TOW-mountain

that's how they were doing it. He was that far at the last mountain.

(36)	ᎩᎳ	ᏩᏟᏒ
	kil	waatliisv́
	kila	wi-a-adihtliis-v́
	just.now	TRN-3A-run:INC-DVB

When he was running

(37)	ᏃᏊ	ᏧᏴᏪᏦᏅ	ᎨᏎ	ᏥᏍᏚ
	noogw	juuyvwéechonv́	geese	jiisd
	noogwu	di-uu-yvwéej-ohn-v́	gees-e	jiisdu
	now	DST2-3B-be.tired:CMP-TRM:CMP-DVB	be:INC-NXP	rabbit

the rabbit was worn out.

(38)	ᏃᏊ	ᏭᎷᏣ	ᏭᏏᎷᏒ
	noogw	wúúluhj	wuuhnaluusv́
	noogwu	wi-uu-luhj-a	wi-uu-hnaluus-v́
	now	TRN-3B-arrive:CMP-CVB	TRN-3B-ascend:CMP-DVB

When he got there on the top

(39)

ᎣᏂ	ᏦᏓᎸ	ᏭᎪᎮ
oohni	joodalv	wuùgoohe
oohni	di-oodalv	wi-uu-gooh-e
behind	TOW-mountain	TRN-3B-see:CMP-NXP

of the last mountain that's when he saw

(40)

ᏃᏊ	Ꮎ	ᏓᎩᏍ	ᏚᎩᏯᏍᎬ	ᏫᎦᎶᏍᎬ
noogwu	na	daks	duùkiíyáàsgv́	wigaloosgv́
noogwu	na	daksi	dee-uu-kiíyáàsg-v́	wi-ga-loosg-v́
Now	that	turtle	DST-3B-win:INC-DVB	TRN-3A-pass:INC-DVB

the turtle running ahead of him, crossing

(41)

ᎤᎾᏓᎶᎯᏍᏗ	ᎠᏍᏓᏅᏅ
uundahlohisdi	aàsdanvvhnv́
uunii-adahlohisdi	a-sdanvvhn-v́
3B.NS-beat.in.a.race:INF	3A-draw:CMP-DVB

the winning line.

(42)

ᏃᏊ	ᏭᎪᎮ	ᏩᏟᏒ	Ꮎ	ᏓᎩᏍ
nogw	wuugoohe	watliisv́	na	daks
noogwu	wi-uu-gooh-e	wi-a-aditliis-v́	na	daksi
now	TRN-3B-see:CMP-NXP	TRN-3A-run:CMP-DVB	the	turtle

He saw the turtle running

(43)

ᏥᏍᏚᏅ	ᏧᏯᏪᏦᏅ	ᎨᎮᏃ
jiisduhnv	juuyawéechonv́	geehehno
jiisdu=hnv	di-uu-yawéej-ohn-v́	geeh-e=hno
rabbit=CN	DST2-3B-be.tired:CMP-TRM:CMP-DVB	be:CMP-NXP=CN

and the rabbit was worn out.

(44)

ᏭᏅᏥᏞ	ᎾᎥ
wuúnv́v̀jiitle	naʔv
wi-uu-nvjiitl-e	naʔv
TRN-3B-fall.headfirst:CMP-NXP	near

He fell headfirst near it.

(45)

Ꮭ	ᏳᏅᏖ	ᏥᏍᏚ	ᎨᎮ	ᏄᎾᏛᏁᎸ
tla	yuuhnte	jiisdu	geehe	nuundv́vvneélv́
tla	yi-uu-nvht-e	jiisdu	geeh-e	ni-uunii-adv́vvneél-v
NEG	IRR-3B-know:INC-NXP	rabbit	be:CMP-NXP	NI-3B.NS-do:CMP-EXP\SUB

The rabbit didn't know what they had done.

(46)	ᎠᏎ	ᏂᎦᏓ	ᎤᏂᏠᏱᎭ	ᎨᏎ
	asée	nigáád	uuniitlooyíiha	geese
	asée	nigááda	uunii-tlóóyi-ha	gees-e
	however	all	3B.NS-same-all	be:INC-NXP

However, they all looked the same,

(47)	ᏓᎩᏍ	ᏧᎵ	ᏃᎴ	ᏏᏓᏁᎸ	ᎠᏂᏁ
	daks	juuli	noole	sidaneelv	aniinéé
	daksi	di-uu-ali	noo=le	sidaneelv	anii-neé
	turtle	DST2-3B-friend	now=OS	family	3A.NS-live:PRC\SUB

the turtle's friends and family living there.

(48)	Ꮭ	ᏯᏕᎶᎰᏍᎨ	ᎾᏅᏛᏁᎲ
	tla	yadeelohoosge	nandv́vneéhv́
	tla	yi-a-adeelohoosg-e	ni-anii-adv́vneéh-v́
	NEG	IRR-3A-find.out:INC-NXP	NI-3A.NS-do:INC-DVB

He didn't find out what they were doing.

(49)	Ꮎ	ᏓᎩᏍ	ᏌᏊᎭ	Ꮎ	ᎦᏚᏏ
	na	daks	saagwuha	na	gadúus
	na	daksi	saagwu-ha	na	gadúusi
	that	turtle	one-all	that	top

The turtles one at a time were at the top

(50)	ᎣᏓᎸᎴ	ᏱᎩ	ᎡᏙᎮ	ᎾᏅ
	oodalvle	yig	eèdoohe	nahn
	oodalv=le	yi-gi	a-eèdooh-e	nahnv
	mountain=OS	IRR-be:IMM	3A-be.at:INC-NXP	where

of either the mountain or where he would be

(51)	ᎣᏂᏃ	ᎣᏓᎸ	Ꮎ	ᏧᎴᏅ
	oohnihno	oodalv	na	juuleenv́
	oohni=hno	oodalv	na	di-uu-aleen-v́
	last=CN	mountain	that	TOW-3B-start(I):CMP-DVB

or the last mountain where he started.

(52)	ᏓᎩᏍ	ᎨᏎ	ᏳᏚᎵ	ᎪᏍᏗ	ᎩᎶ
	daks	geese	yuuduulíí	góósd	kilo
	daksi	gees-e	yi-uu-aduuli	góósdi	kilo
	turtle	be:INC-NXP	IRR-3B-want:PRC\SUB	something	someone

As for the turtle, if someone wants

(53) ᎤᏛᏗ ᏄᎵᏍᏔᏂᏙᎸ
uutvdi nuulstaniidoolv́
uu-ahtvdi ni-uu-alistan-iídóòl-v
3B-ask:INF NI-3B-happen:CMP-AMB:CMP-EXP\SUB
to ask him about what happened,

(54) ᏭᏅᏥᏝ Ꮎ ᏥᏍᏗ ᏧᏯᏪᏦᏅ ᎨᏎ
wuúnv́v̀jiíhla na jiisd juuyawéechonv geese
wi-uu-nvvjiihl-a na jiisdu di-uu-yawéej-ohn-v́ gees-e
TRN-3B-fall:CMP-CVB that rabbit DST2-3B-be.tired:CMP-TRM:CMP-DVB be:INC-NXP
when the rabbit fell, he was exhausted

(55) ᎤᏠᏱᏊ ᏥᎾᏛᏁᎰ ᎪᎯᏴ ᏥᎩ
uutlóóyigw jinadv́vneeho kohiyv jíg
uu-tlóóyi=gwu ji-ni-a-adv́vneeh-o kohiyv ji-gi
3B-same=DT REL-NI-3A-do:INC-HAB today REL-be:IMM\SUB
just as he does nowadays;

(56) ᏱᏚᏯᏪᏣ ᏱᎦᏅᎩᏊ
yiduuyawééj yigánv́vgigwu
yi-dee-uu-yawéej-a yi-ga-nv́vgi=gwu
IRR-DST-3B-be.tired:CMP-CVB IRR-3A-fall:IMM=DT
when he gets tired, he'll just fall.

List of Audio Tracks

Disc A. Tracks 1–48

(1)	ᏙᏌ	doosa	'mosquito'
	ᏙᎦ	tohga	'june bug'
	ᎩᏟ	giihli	'dog'
	ᎧᏫ	kaáhwi	'coffee'
	ᏜᎺᎭ	dlaameeha	'bat'
	Ꮭ	tla	'no'
	ᎠᏆᏚᎵ	aàgwaduuli	'I want it'
	ᏆᎾ	kwana	'peach'
	ᏣᎳᎩ	jalagi	'Cherokee'
	ᏧᎦ	chuhga	'flea'
	ᏣᏰᏣ	jayeétsa	'Laugh!'
	ᎶᎶ	loolo	'locust'
	ᎣᏝ	oohla	'soap'
	ᏩᎶᏏ	walóosi	'frog'
	ᎪᏪᎵ	goohweeli	'paper'
	ᏱᏣᏚᎳᏍ	yijaduúlas	'Would you like it?'
	ᏯᏕᏠᏆ	hyadeehlohgwa	'You can learn.'
	ᏃᏥ	nohji	'pine'
	ᏂᏛᎦ	hnadvv̀ga	'You did it.'
	ᎭᏫᏯ	hawiiya	'meat'
	ᏑᏓᎵ	suúdali	'six'
	ᎺᎵ	meéli	'Mary'
	ᎯᎠ	hiʔa	'this'
(2)	ᏦᎢ	joʔi	'three'
	ᎠᎩᎠ	aàgíʔa	'He's eating it.'
	ᎪᎢ	goʔi	'oil'
	ᏔᎵ	taʔli	'two'

(3)	ᎯᏟᎰᎢ	hihlihóoʔi	‘You sleep.’
	ᎦᎵᏉᎩ	gahlgwoógi	‘seven’
	ᎬᏟ	kvv́hli	‘raccoon’
	ᎩᏟ	giihli	‘dog’
(4)	Ꮭ	tla	‘no’
	ᎩᏟ	giitli	‘strand of hair’
	ᎠᏟ	aàtli	‘She’s running.’
	ᏓᎦᏟᎭ	daàktliíha	‘He’s shelling corn.’
(5)	ᎬᏏ	gvvhna	‘He is alive.’
	ᎬᎾ	gv́vna	‘turkey’
	ᎠᏁᎭ	aàneéha	‘They live (there).’
	ᎠᏁᎭ	aàhneha	‘He’s giving it to him.’
	ᎠᏰᎦ	aàhyéega	‘She is taking it (by hand).’
	ᎠᏰᎦ	aàyéega	‘She is waking up.’
(6)	ᎪᏪᎵ	goohweeli	‘paper’
	ᎤᏩᏍᎦ	uùhwasga	‘He’s buying it.’
	ᏣᏩᎯ	jahwahi	‘Buy it!’
(7)	ᏯᏖᎾ	hyahteéna	‘board’
	ᏯᏙᏟ	hyahtóóhli	‘narrow’
	ᏰᎦᎵ	hyehgahli	‘quilt’
(8)	ᎬᏅᎢ	gvvhnv́v́ʔi	‘life’
	ᏅᏅᏓᎩ	hnv́vhndági	‘Take it off.’
	ᏐᏁᎳ	sohneéla	‘nine’
(9)	ᎢᏥᏁᎦ	iìjiihnéega	‘You all are answering.’
	ᎯᏁᎦ	hihnéega	‘You’re answering.’
	ᎧᏁᎦ	kanéega	‘He’s answering.’
(10)	ᏦᎢ	joʔi	‘three’
	ᏣᎳᎩ	jalagi	‘Cherokee’
	ᏦᎯᏳᎭᏍ	joohiyuhas	‘Do you believe it?’
	ᏣᏓᎦᏎᏍᏕᏍᏗ	jadaksesdéesdi	‘Take care of yourself!’
	ᏥᎢᏓ	jiʔiída	‘I just had it (in my hand)’
	ᏣᏚᎵ	jaduuli	‘You want it.’
	ᏣᏲᏏᎭ	jayóosiha	‘You are hungry.’
(11)	ᎠᎹ	ama	‘water’
	ᎠᎹ	áama	‘salt’
	ᎤᎦᎹ	uúgáma	‘soup’
	ᎠᎹᏱ	amaayi	‘near the water’
	ᎠᎺᏉᎢ	améegwóóʔi	‘ocean’

	ᏔᎹᏟ	tamaahli	'tomato'
	ᎧᎹᎹ	kamaama	'elephant', 'butterfly'
	ᏓᎹᎦ	daamága	'horsefly'
	ᎣᎦᎳᎰᎹ	oogalahoóma	'Oklahoma'
	ᎺᎵ	meéli	'Mary'
	ᎨᎻᎵ	keémíli	'camel'
(12)	ᎧᏫ	kaáhwi	'coffee'
	ᏎᏗ	seédi	'walnut'
	ᎢᏌ	iisa	'flour'
	ᎣᏏᏲ	oosíyo	'hello'
	ᏄᎾ	nuúna	'potato'
	ᎤᏅᏗ	uunvv́di	'milk'
(13)	ᏥᎪᏩᏘᎭ	jigoohwtíha	'I see it.'
	ᏥᎪᏩᏘᎭ	jiigoohwtíha	'I see him.'
	ᎠᎹ	ama	'water'
	ᎠᎹ	áama	'salt'
(14)	ᏯᏂᏏ	yansi	'buffalo'
	ᎯᏓ	hida	'Lay it down (something long)!'
	ᎣᏩᏌ	owaása	'oneself'
	ᎠᎬᎭᎵᎭ	aàgvvhaliha	'He's slicing it.'
	ᎩᏟ	giihli	'dog'
	ᎣᏝ	oohla	'soap'
(15)	ᎯᏔᏲᎯᎭ	hihtayoohíha	'You are asking for it.'
	ᎦᎷᎦ	gáʔluhga	'He's arriving.'
	ᎣᏏᏲ	oosíyo	'hello'
	ᎬᎾ	gv́vna	'turkey'
	ᎢᏁᎦ	iìnéega	'We are going.'
	ᎪᎦ	kóoga	'crow'
(16)	ᎦᏓ	gaáda	'dirt', 'land'
	ᏲᎾ	yoóna	'bear'
	ᏩᏥ	waáji	'watch'
	ᎩᎦ	giíga	'blood'
(17)	ᏫᎵ	wiíli	'Will'
	ᎧᏫ	kaáhwi	'coffee'
	ᏩᏥ	waáji	'watch'
	ᏥᏌ	jiísa	'Jesus'
	ᎣᎦᎳᎰᎹ	oogalahoóma	'Oklahoma'
	ᎺᎵ	meéli	'Mary'

	ᎨᎻᎵ	keémíli	‘camel’
	ᎹᎩ	maági	‘Maggie’
(18)	ᏅᏬᏘ	nvvwóòti	‘medicine’
	ᏥᏍᏉᏉ	jiísgwóògwo	‘robin’
	ᎩᏳᎦ	kiyúùga	‘chipmunk’
	ᎤᏄᏩ	uùhnuwa	‘He’s wearing a coat.’
(19)	ᎡᏆ	éégwa	‘large’
	ᎠᎩᎾ	agíína	‘young’
	ᎦᎨᏓ	gaagééda	‘heavy’
	ᎣᏍᏓ	óósda	‘good’
(20)	ᏕᎦᏕᏲᎲᏍᎪᎢ	degadeèyoóhvsgóoʔi	‘I teach.’
	ᏗᎦᏕᏲᎲᏍᎩ	digadeèyóóhvsgi	‘I’m a teacher.’
(21)	ᏅᏯ	nvv̀ya	‘rock’
	ᏒᎩ	svv̀gi	‘onion’
	ᎫᎫ	guùgu	‘tick’
	ᎠᎩᏍᏗ	agiìsdi	‘something to eat’
(22)	ᎨᎢ	geʔi	‘downstream’
	ᎨᎵᎠ	geelíʔa	‘He thinks so.’
	ᏥᏲᏎᎭ	jiiyoòséha	‘I’m saying to her’
	ᎨᎦ	géega	‘I’m going’
	ᎨᎺᎵ	keémíli	‘camel’
	ᎭᎵᏰᏑᏍᏛᏍᎦ	haliyéèsuustv́sga	‘you are putting a ring on’
	ᎮᎾ	heèna	‘go!’
	ᎪᎨᏱ	googééyi	‘spring’
(23)	ᎠᏓ	ada	‘wood’
	ᎠᏓ	áʔda	‘young animal’
(24)	ᏕᏣᏙᎠ	deejadóoʔa	‘your name is . . .’
	ᏣᏰᏣ	jayeétsa	‘laugh!’
	ᏣᏁᎳ	chaneéla	‘eight’
(25)	ᎦᏃᎭᎵᏙᎭ	ganoohaliídóòha	‘he is hunting’
	ᎦᏃᎭᎵᏙᎯ	ganoohaliidóóhi	‘hunter’
(26)	ᎧᏫ ᏍᎩᏁᎲᏏ	kaáhwi sgineehvsi	‘Give me the coffee!’
(27)	ᎯᏍᏚᎲᎦ	hisduùhvv̀ga	‘Close the door!’
	ᎦᎶᎯᏍᏗᎢ	galoohisdííʔi	
(28)	ᏣᎳᎩ ᎬᏗ ᏂᏫ	jalagi gv́hdi hniwi	‘Say it in Cherokee!’
(29)	ᏣᏛᏓᏍᏕᏍᏗ	tstvdasdéesdi	‘Listen!’
	ᏣᏓᎦᏎᏍᏕᏍᏗ	jadaksesdéesdi	‘Take care of yourself!’
(30)	ᏙᎾᏓᎪᎲᎢ	doonadaagoohvvʔi	‘Let’s see each other again!’

(31)	ᎦᏙ ᎤᏍᏗ ᎤᎭ	gado uúsdi uúha	'What does he have?'
(32)	ᎯᎠᎾᏍ ᏚᏳᎪᏛᎢ	hiʔanas duuyuukdv́ʔi	'Is this correct?'
(33)	ᎣᏳ ᎣᏍᏓ ᏗᏕᎰᏆᏍᏗᎢ	ooyu óósda diideehlgwaasdííʔi	'OU is a good school.'
(34)	ᎠᎩᏅᎸᎲᏍᎪ ᏣᎳᎩ ᎠᎩᏬᏂᎯᏍᏗ	aàginvv́lv̀vhvsgo jalagi agiwooniíhísdííʔi	'I can't speak Cherokee.'
(35)	ᏫᎩ	wigi	'Get it!'
	ᏪᎾ	hweèna	'Go!'
(36)	ᏱᏣᏚᎵᎭ	yijaduulííha	'If you want it'
	ᏱᏣᏚᎵᎭ	yiìjaduulííha	'If you all want it'
(37)	ᏏᏊ ᏥᏂᎯᏫ	siígwu jiiniíhiwi	'Say it again!'
(38)	ᏏᏊ ᏥᎭᏗᏔ	siígwu jiihádiita	'Drink it again!'
(39)	ᎦᏙ ᎠᏗ ᏣᎳᎩ ᎬᏗ	gado ad jalagi gv́hdi	'How does one say it in Cherokee?'
(40)	ᎠᏓᏬᏍᎪᎢ	aàdawóosgóoʔi	'She swims.'
	ᎠᏓᏬᏍᎩ	adawóósgi	'She's a swimmer.'
(41)	ᎠᏗᏔᏍᏗ	adiítasdi	'a drink'
	ᏗᏗᏔᏍᏗ	diidiítasdi	'drinks'
(42)	ᎠᏓ	ada	'wood'
	ᎠᎵ	aali	'sweat'
	ᎠᏂ	aʔni	'strawberry'
	ᏓᎩᏏ	daksi	'turtle'
	ᏜᏯᎦ	dlahyga	'blue jay'
	ᏙᏌ	doosa	'mosquito'
	ᏗᎵ	dili	'skunk'
	ᎩᏟ	giihli	'dog'
	ᎩᎦ	giíga	'blood'
	ᎪᎢ	goʔi	'grease'
	ᎫᏇ	guhgwe	'quail'
	ᎫᎫ	guugu	'bottle'
	ᏦᎳ	joóla	'tobacco'
	ᏃᏥ	nohji	'pine'
	ᎣᏝ	oohla	'soap'
	ᏌᏌ	saasa	'goose'
	ᏎᎷ	seélu	'corn'
	ᏘᎾ	tina	'head lice'
	ᏪᏌ	weésa	'cat'

	ᏲᎾ	yoóna	'bear'
(43)	ᎠᏍᎦᏯ	asgaya	'man'
	ᎠᎨᏯ	ageéhya	'woman'
	ᎠᏫᎾ	awíína	'young man'
	ᎠᏔᏄᏣ	atanúúja	'teenage girl'
	ᎠᏧᏣ	achúúja	'boy'
	ᎠᎨᏳᏣ	ageehyúúja	'girl'
	ᎠᎦᏴᎵᎨ	agayvv́lige	'old woman'
(44)	ᎦᏙ ᎤᏍᏗ ᎦᏘᎦ	gado úúsdi gaatihga	'What does this mean?'
(45)	ᏌᏊ	saàgwu	'one'
	ᏔᎵ	táʔli	'two'
	ᏦᎢ	joʔi	'three'
	ᏅᎩ	nvhgi	'four'
	ᎯᏍᎩ	hisgi	'five'
	ᏑᏓᎵ	suúdáli	'six'
	ᎦᎵᏉᎩ	gahlgwoógi	'seven'
	ᏣᏁᎳ	chaneéla	'eight'
	ᏐᏁᎳ	sohneéla	'nine'
	ᏍᎪᎯ	sgoóhi	'ten'
(46)	ᏌᏚ	sáʔdu	'eleven'
	ᏔᎵᏚ	taldu	'twelve'
	ᏦᎦᏚ	joogádu	'thirteen'
	ᏅᎦᏚ	nvhgádu	'fourteen'
	ᎯᏍᎦᏚ	hisgádu	'fifteen'
	ᏑᏓᎳᏚ	suudaldu	'sixteen'
	ᎦᎵᏉᏚ	gahlgwoodu	'seventeen'
	ᏣᏁᎳᏚ	chanelaadu	'eighteen'
	ᏐᏁᎳᏚ	sohnelaadu	'nineteen'
(47)	ᏔᎵᏍᎪᎯ	talsgoóhi	'twenty'
	ᏦᏍᎪᎯ	joʔsgoóhi	'thirty'
	ᏅᎩᏍᎪᎯ	nvksgoóhi	'forty'
	ᎯᎩᏍᎪᎯ	hiksgoóhi	'fifty'
	ᏑᏓᎵᏍᎪᎯ	suudalsgoóhi	'sixty'
	ᎦᎵᏆᏍᎪᎯ	gahlgwasgoóhi	'seventy'
	ᏁᎵᏍᎪᎯ	nelsgoóhi	'eighty'
	ᏐᏁᎵᏍᎪᎯ	sohnelsgoóhi	'ninety'
	ᏍᎪᎯᏥᏆ	sgohitsgwa	'one hundred'
(48)	ᏏᏊ ᏥᏂᎯᏫ ᎤᏍᎦᏃᎵᎨᎢ	siígwu jiiniihiwi uusganooliigééʔi	'Say it again slower.'

Disc B. Tracks 49–107

(49)	ᎦᏙ ᎤᏍᏗ ᏨᏏ Ꮎ ᎤᏓᎾᏂ	gado uusdi chvsi na uudaánaʔni	'What did the store owner give you?'
(50)	ᎠᎩᏅᏩᎦ	aàkinvv́wáàga	'He cured me.'
(51)	ᏣᎾᎸᏨᎢ	chanaálv̀vjvv́ʔi	'You got angry.'
(52)	ᏥᎪᎥᎢ ᎩᏟ ᏓᏏᏫᏍᎬ	jiigoʔvv́ʔi giihli dasihwisgv́	'I saw the dog that was barking.'
(53)	ᎤᎪᏏᏓ	uugóósida	'rotten'
	ᎤᎪᏍᎦ	uùgoosga	'It is rotting.'
(54)	ᎠᎦᏘᏯ	aàktiíya	'He's waiting for it.'
	ᏥᎦᏘᏯ	jigaàtiíya	'I'm waiting for it.'
(55)	ᎠᏟ	aàtli	'He's running.'
	ᎦᏗᏟ	gadiìtli	'I'm running.'
(56)	ᎯᏰᏩ	hiiyeéwa	'You sewed it.'
	ᏥᏰᏫᏍᎦ	jiiyewiisga	'I am sewing it.'
	ᎦᏰᏫᏍᎦ	gaayewsga	'He is sewing it.'
(57)	ᏥᏟᏏᎭ	jíítliisiíha	'You are gathering it.'
	ᎢᏗᏟᏏᎭ	iidíítliisiíha	'We are gathering it.'
(58)	ᏗᎦᏝᏗᏍᎩ	diktladiìsgi	'firefighter'
	ᏗᎬᏝᏗᏍᎩ	digv̀vtladiìsgi	'I am a firefighter.'
(59)	ᎠᏇᏱᎭ	aàkwiyíha	'He's paying it.'
	ᎦᏇᏱᎭ	gagwiyíha	'I'm paying it.'
	ᎭᏇᏱᎭ	hahkwiyíha	'You're paying it.'
(60)	ᏣᎬᎯᏍᏗ	tskv́hisdi	'You are cute.'
	ᏍᏗᎬᎯᏍᏗ	sdííkvhisdi	'You two are cute.'
(61)	ᎬᎢᏢᏍᎦ	gvʔihlv́sga	'I am linking it.'
	ᎩᏢᏍᎦ	kihlv́sga	'He is linking it.'
	ᎢᏛᎯᏢᏍᎦ	iìdvhitlv́sga	'We are linking it.'
(62)	ᎨᏧᏓᎴᎠ	geejuudaléeʔa	'They're unhooking you.'
	ᎨᏧᏓᎴᎠ	geejuudaléeʔa	'They're unhooking you all.'
(63)	ᏍᎩᏍᏕᎳ	ksdeéla	'Help me!'
(64)	ᎡᎵᏊᏍ ᎦᎶᎯᏍᏗ ᏱᏍᎩᏍᏚᎢᏏ	eelíígwus galoohisdi yiksdúʔiisi	'Could you open the door for me?'
(65)	ᎩᏚᏩ ᏧᏂᏆᎾᏲᏍᏗ ᎠᏕᎳ ᏱᏛᏓᏒᏂ	giduuwá juuniikwanyoosdi adeéla yidvvdasvhna	'You can win money at the Keetoowah Casino.'
(66)	ᎦᏂᏱᏍᎪ	gáʔniiyiísgo	'He catches it.'

	ᏗᏓᏂᏱᏍᎩ	diidaaniíyíísgi	‘policeman’
(67)	ᎠᏎ ᎡᏃᎢᏅᏍᏗ ᎯᎠ ᎠᎦᏴᎵᎨ	aase eènoo?iínv́v́sdi hi?a agayv́v́lige	‘We have to lead this elderly woman.’
(68)	ᏧᏠᎦᎴᏓ ᎡᏍᏗᎪᎥ ᎡᏍᏗᏲᎵᎸᎢ	juudloogalééda eesdiigoo?v́ eèsdiiyoólîîlvv?i	‘If you two see Santa Claus, greet him.’
(69)	ᎪᏍᏗᏊ ᎢᏣᏓᏅᏖᏗ ᎢᏨᏁᎭ	góósdigwu iijadaáhntehdi iìjvvneeha	‘I'm just giving you something to think about.’
(70)	ᎧᏃᎮᎭ	kanoohéha	‘He's telling it.’
	ᏥᏃᎮᎭ	jiìnoohéha	‘I'm telling it.’
(71)	ᎪᎵᎦ	gohlga	‘He understands it.’
	ᎪᎵᎦ	goliìga	‘I understand it.’
(72)	ᎬᏗᏍᎪ	kdiísgo	‘He uses it.’
	ᎬᏗᏍᎪ	gvv̀diísgo	‘I use it.’
(73)	ᏎᎷ ᏧᏓ ᎠᏰᏟ ᏗᎩᏍᏆᎵᏍᏗ	seélu juuda ayééhli díiksgwalsdi	‘I have to break some corncobs in half.’
(74)	ᎦᏙ ᏣᎾᎩᎠ	gado chanagii?a	‘Why are you leaving?’
	ᏥᏯᎦᏔᏍᏓᏏ	chiiyagaàtááàsdaàsi	‘You winked at her.’
(75)	ᏚᏳᎪᏛ ᏱᏣᏛᏅᏗ ᎨᏣᏎᎮᏗ	duùyuukdv yijadvhndi géétssehehdi	‘They have to show you how to do it right.’
	ᎡᏣᏙᏗ ᏂᎪᎸ ᎭᏚᎢᏍᏗᏍᎪᎢ	eètsdohydi nigoólv hatu?isdiísgoo?i	‘You always promise to get your hair cut.’
(76)	ᏥᏴᏐᎵ	jiìyvvsóóli	‘my nose’
	ᎯᏴᏐᎵ	hihyvvsóóli	‘your nose’
	ᎧᏴᏐᎵ	kayvvsóóli	‘his nose’
(77)	ᎭᎦᏙᏍᏗ	haktoósdi	‘You are looking at it.’
	ᏍᏓᎦᏙᏍᏗ	sdaktoósdi	‘You two are looking at it.’
	ᎢᏣᎦᏙᏍᏗ	iìjaktoósdi	‘You all are looking at it.’
(78)	ᎯᏯᎦᏙᏍᏗ	hiiyagaàtoósdi	‘You are looking at her.’
	ᎡᏍᏓᎦᏙᏍᏗ	eèsdagaàtoósdi	‘You two are looking at her.’
	ᎡᏣᎦᏙᏍᏗ	eèjagaàtoósdi	‘You all are looking at her.’
(79)	ᏣᎦᏙᏍᏗ	jaktoósdi	‘She is looking at you.’
	ᏍᏓᎦᏙᏍᏗ	sdaktoósdi	‘She is looking at you two.’
	ᎢᏣᎦᏙᏍᏗ	iìjaktoósdi	‘She is looking at you all.’
(80)	ᏍᏆᎦᏙᏍᏗ	sgwaktoósdi	‘You are looking at me.’
	ᎬᏯᎦᏙᏍᏗ	gvvyagaàtoósdi	‘I am looking at you.’

	ᏍᏛᏯᎦᏙᏍᏗ	sdvvyagaàtoósdi	'I am looking at you two.' 'We two are looking at you two.' 'We two are looking at you.'
(81)	ᏥᎩᎾᏚᎵᏍᎬ ᎠᏜᏗᏝᎢ ᎦᏳᎳ ᎩᎶ ᎤᏩᏎᎢ	jiginaduuliisgv́ adladíitlaʔi gáayuùla kilo uùhwaseʔi	'The car we want has already been bought.'
	ᎠᎿᏬ ᏥᏍᎩᏅᏁᎸ ᏥᏖᏍᎦ	ahnawo jisginv́vneelv́ jiìteesga	'I am ironing the shirt that you gave me.'
	ᏱᎦᏪᏍᏗ ᏥᎦᏁᎵᏗᎭ ᏙᏳ ᏍᏓᏱ	yigawéésdi jiganehldíha dooyu sdááyi	'The word I'm translating is very hard.'
(82)	ᎦᏙ ᎮᎵᏍᎬ ᏥᏂᏫ	gado heelîisgv jihniwi	'What did you mean when you said that?'
(83)	ᏄᏲᏏᏍᎬᎾ ᎠᎵᏍᏓᏴᎲᏍᎦ	nuuyóosiisgv́v́na aàlsdááyvvhvsga	'He's eating while he's not hungry.'
(84)	ᎢᏧᏕᏘᏴᏓ	ijuudeetiýv́da	'years (number of)'
	ᎢᏯᏔᏬᏍᏔᏅᎢ	iyatahwoòstanv́v́ʔi	'minute'
	ᎢᏳᏟᎶᏓ	iyuuhliilóóda	'hour'
	ᎢᏳᏩᎪᏗ	iyuwáákdi	'time(s)'
	ᎢᏳᎾᏙᏓᏆᏍᏗ	iyuunadoódagwaàsdi	'week'
	ᏂᎦᏓ	nigááda	'all'
	ᏂᎪᎯᎸ	nigohiilv	'always'
(85)	ᏙᏗᏍᎪᏍᎦ	doodîisgoosga	'He is digging over there.'
(86)	ᎠᎹᏰ ᏗᏇᏅᏒᎢ	amáyéehli diigweenvvsv́ʔi	'My home is the United States.'
	ᏐᎢ ᏗᎧᏅᏑᎸ ᏩᏴᎭ	soʔi dikanvvsuulv waàyvv́ha	'He went in another room.'
(87)	ᎦᏲᏟ ᏣᎳᎩ ᏥᏬᏂᏍᎪ	gaàyóóhli jalagi jiwóoniisgo	'I speak a little Cherokee.'
(88)	ᎤᎾᏚᎵᏍ ᏣᎳᎩ ᎤᏂᏬᏂᎯᏍᏗ	uùnaduulis jalagi uuniiwooniíhisdi	'Do they want to speak Cherokee?'
(89)	ᎠᎹ ᎤᏗᏔᎭ ᎤᏢᏨᎢ	ama uudíitáha uùdlv́vjvʔi	'He became sick after drinking the water.'
(90)	Ꮎ ᎠᏍᎦᏯ ᏦᏣᎵᏃᎮᏍᎬ ᎠᏂᎩ	na asgaya joojahlnoheesgv́ aàhnigi	'The man that I was talking with left.'

(91)	ᎭᏑᏯᎩ ᎢᏳᏍᏗ ᏣᏚᎵᏍᎬᎢ	hasuuyagi iiyúúsdi jaduuliisgv́v́ʔi	'Choose the one that you want.'
(92)	ᏦᎳ ᎢᏳᏍᏗ ᎬᏙᏗ ᎤᎸᏓ ᏳᏓᏠᏣ	joóla iyúúsdi kdóhdi uulvv́da yuudáátloja	'You use tobacco leaves when you catch poison ivy.'
(93)	ᏧᎦᏅᏕᎾ ᎬᏂᏍᏙᏗ ᎯᎬᎭᎷᏯ	juugahndééna gv́v́hnisdóhdi higvvhaluùya	'Chop up some cabbage to cook.'
	ᎭᏢ Ꮎ ᎠᏧᏣ ᎤᏑᏫᏍᏗ ᏥᎩ ᎠᏐᏴᎢ	haadlv na achúúja uusúúhwisdi jígi aàsoóyvvʔi	'Where's that boy who has to paint the fence?'
(94)	ᎠᏋᎨᏫᏒ ᎢᏴ ᎠᏆᏂᎩᏒ	aàgwvvkewsv iiyv́ aàgwahnigiisv	'I forgot when I left.'
(95)	ᎦᏕᎶᏆᎠ ᏗᏬᏪᎶᏗ ᏗᏣᎳᎩ	gadehlgwa diiwoohweélóòdi dijalagi	'I am learning to write Cherokee.'
(96)	ᎠᏆᏚᎵ ᎬᎪᏩᏛᏗ	aaɡ̌waduuli gvvgoowahtv́hdi	'I want to see you.'
(97)	ᏍᏆᎵᏍᎪᎵᏓᏏ ᎠᎩᏬᏂᎯᏍᏗᎢ	sgwalsgohldáàsi agiwoonihisdííʔi	'Permit me to speak.'
(98)	ᎣᏍᏓ ᎠᏍᏙᏍᎪ ᎦᏅᏥ ᏳᏬᏢᎿ	óósda aàsdóosgo ganvji yuwoohlv́v́hna	'He pounds it out well when he makes kanuchi.'
(99)	ᏌᎾᎴ ᏱᏣᏰᏣ ᏣᎳᎩ ᎭᏓᏅᏖᏍᎨᏍᏗ	sanaale yijayééja jalagi hadahntesgéesdi	'In the morning when you wake up, think Cherokee!'
(100)	ᏣᎳᎩ ᏯᏕᏠᏆᎠ ᏱᏣᏅᏔ	jalagi hyadééhlgwaʔa yijahnta	'If you were learning Cherokee you would know.'
(101)	ᏦᏣᏕᏠᏆᏍᎩ ᏗᎪᏪᎵ ᏙᎦᎦᏎᏍᏗ	joojadeéhlgwaàsgi digoohweeli doògaksesdi	'We students are studying.'
(102)	ᎯᎢᎾ ᏦᎩᏍᏗ	hiʔina jóóksdi	'This is for you to smoke.'
	ᎯᎢᎾ ᏦᎩᏍᏗ	hiʔina jooksdi	'This is for you to smoke.'
(103)	ᎣᏍᏓ ᏗᎩᏃᎩᏍᏗᎢ	óósda diikinoogiìsdíʔi	'My singing is good.'
	ᎠᏎ ᎣᏍᏓ ᏗᎩᏃᎩᏍᏗ	ase óósda diikinoogíísdi	'I have to sing well.'

(104)	ᎠᏂᏴᏫᏯ ᎠᎹᏰᏟ ᎠᏁᎯᏯᎢ	aniiyvvwiiya amáyéehli aneéhiyááʔi	'Indians are indigenous to America.'
(105)	ᎤᏲᎱᏒ	uuyoohuusv́	'dead'
	ᎤᏲᎱᏒ	uùyoohuusv	'He died.'
(106)	ᎫᏇ ᏧᏂᏲᎯ ᎢᏴᏓᎭ ᏓᎾᏓᏲᏍᏙᏗᏍᎪᎢ	guhgwe juuníihyóhi iyvv́daaha daànadaayoosdóhdísgóʔi	'Quail hunters sometimes accidentally shoot one another.'
(107)	ᎦᏙ ᎤᎵᏍᏓᏏ ᏣᏥ	gado uùlsdáasi jaji	'What happened to your mother?'

Glossary

All words shown in boldface in this book are listed in this glossary. The following definitions are only meant to apply to the current work. The Cherokee examples in this section are not parsed and are presented in simple phonetics. The relevant sound, morpheme, or word in the example sentences (and corresponding English translation) is in boldface. Words or phrases that are needed to clarify the segment in boldface are underlined.

abbreviation: The label used on the gloss line to describe the function of verb stems, prefixes, suffixes, and postfixes as well as tone changes. An abbreviation is always written in small capital letters. For example, the abbreviation of 'first person Set A dual exclusive prefix' is 1A.DL.EX.

accidental (ACC): The series of derivational suffixes that appear on the Completive stem to derive a verb indicating an event that occurs unintentionally. Example: *Na anagalisi gohweli waginvn**dohtan**v.* 'I **accidentally** sent that email.' See section 13.1.3.

acute accent: The accent used to represent a high tone or highfall tone. To represent a high tone it appears on a short vowel or on the first written vowel of a long vowel. It indicates a rising tone when it appears on the second written vowel of a long vowel. It indicates a falling tone when it appears on the first written vowel of a long vowel and is followed by a vowel with a grave accent. If both vowels have the acute accent it is a highfall. Examples: high tone on short vowel: ⟨é⟩, high tone on long vowel: ⟨ée⟩, rising tone: ⟨eé⟩, falling tone: ⟨éè⟩, highfall tone: ⟨éé⟩. See section 2.1.2.2.

addressee: In a ditransitive verb, the primary object being addressed by the subject. Example: *Esdiyvha **o**ginoselv dagwalela digandegi.* 'The car salesman told **us** to enter.' See section 14.2.1.

adjectival: A postpositional phrase or subordinate clause that functions like an adjective by describing a noun. Example: *Kahwi* ***alihltanv*** *osda aditasdi.* 'Coffee **that is boiled** is good to drink.' See section 12.2.

adjectival clause: A subordinate clause that functions like an adjective by describing a noun. Example: *Tinawida hi'a gwanena* ***jidejahwasv didananv'i.*** 'Take the bananas **you bought at the store.**' See section 11.4.1.

adjectival Infinitive: An Infinitive that acts as an adjective by indicating a general quality, purpose, or function of a noun. This use of the Infinitive often takes a dummy prefix that does not undergo prefix shift. Example: *Sgwatlesdi* ***sdadinvdi*** *dasdvneli.* 'I'm going to give you a ball **to throw.**' See section 11.4.1.2.

adjective: A part of speech that describes a noun. Adjectives are not inflected for tense or aspect but may have pronominal or prepronominal prefixes. Example: *Unalsgisdi gado danedoho* ***jundalenvda*** *aniyvwiya.* '**Different** Indians come to the powwow grounds.' See section 7.1.

adjective derivation (ADJ): The derivational suffix *-ha* (full form *-háá?i*) that attaches to nouns to create an adjective. Example: *Ulosvsdi yugahnana amayiha nigalsdisgo.* 'When it rains it becomes **watery.**' See section 12.2.4.

adjective phrase: A phrase consisting of an adjective and any of its modifiers. *Dosa* ***doyu unistakwisdi.*** 'Mosquitoes are **very bothersome.**' See section 7.6.

adverb: A part of speech that describes how, when, where, or why a verb takes place. It may also be used to modify a sentence. Example: *Hasonvsda* ***ahani.*** 'Click **here.**' See section 7.5.

adverbial: A postpositional phrase, noun phrase, or subordinate clause that functions like an adverb by describing a verb or modifying another clause. Example: *Edudu uhlilv* ***Taline Dahnawa.*** 'My grandfather fought (during) **World War II.**' See sections 7.5 and 7.7.

adverbial clause: A subordinate clause that acts like an adverb by modifying a verb. Example: ***Jisdvna yidigihyalena*** *hilvsgi yigijv idaligohvsgo.* '**When we hunt crawdads** several of us go together.' See section 11.4.3.

adverbial Infinitive: An Infinitive that modifies a verb, adjective, or adverb, typically to indicate a purpose. Example: *Jimi hinvsv'i didananv* ***kahwi wugisdi'i.*** 'Send Jim to the store **to get coffee.**' See section 11.4.3.6.

adverb phrase: A phrase consisting of an adverb and any of its modifiers. Example: ***Doyu usanuli*** *dehaktanawsga.* 'You are blinking **very fast.**' See section 7.6.

affix: A prefix or a suffix.

agent: A verb participant that is in control of the action. For example, in the sentence 'I ran' the subject is an agent, while in the sentence 'I fainted' the subject is not an agent. See section 4.1.3.

agentive (AGT): The suffix *-i* that appears on the Incompletive stem to derive an agentive noun (indicating a person or thing that performs the action). It is often accompanied by a tone change. Example: *Adladitla uhnigisdisgi ulihwojv.* 'The car engine ('car starter') went dead.' See section 12.1.1.1.

agentive noun: A noun derived by attaching an agentive suffix to an Incompletive stem; it indicates a person or thing that performs the action. See section 12.1.1.1.

alphabet: A writing system where the characters represent individual sounds. All European languages use an alphabet.

ambulative (AMB): The series of derivational suffixes that appear on the Completive stem to derive a verb indicating repeated movement, often translated into English as 'go around VERB-ing.' Example: *Hlesdi hyaljikwidohesdi.* 'Don't go around spitting.' See section 13.1.5.

animacy: The state of being alive. In Cherokee grammar different prefixes sometimes are used if an object is animate. It is important to note that Cherokee grammar does not treat all things that are actually alive (e.g., plants or insects) as animate. See section 11.1.

animacy hierarchy: The ranking of animate beings on a scale: the higher on the scale, the more likely they are to be the subject. This ranking is important for the use of inverse pronominal prefixes. When a less animate participant is the subject, the inverse prefix may be used. See section 9.5.

animate: Characterized by animacy (being alive). In Cherokee grammar only certain living entities, mainly higher-order animals and humans, are distinguished as animate.

animate nonsingular (ANS): The prepronominal prefix *gaa-* is used to indicate that the object of a verb is nonsingular and animate. The prefix has the variant form [*gay*] before vowels. Example: ***Ga**hiyatvdasdiha.* 'You are listening to **them**.' See section 5.1.6.

animate object (AN) prefix: A pronominal prefix that indicates a local person subject and a third person animate object. These prefixes are similar in form to the Set A prefixes. Example: *Gohweli dikanidohi jigatiyv'i.* 'I was waiting for the mail carrier.' See section 3.3.4.

applicative (APL): The valency-increasing series of derivational suffixes that appear on the Completive stem to derive a ditransitive verb. Example: *Hila iga hiyagwiyv'ele?* 'How much did you pay him?' See section 14.2.1.

aspect: A property of a verb that indicates the degree of completedness of a state or event. The Present Continuous verb stem indicates aspect (the state or event is in progress) as well as tense (the state or event is happening in the present).

The Incompletive and Completive verb stems are used to indicate that a state or event either is not completed or has been completed, respectively. The habitual final suffix contributes aspectual meaning by indicating that a state or event occurs at frequent intervals. The completive future suffix *-éesdi* indicates tense (the state or event is in the future) as well as aspect (the state or event is ongoing). See sections 4.1–3.

aspirated obstruents: Consonants characterized by an obstruction of the airflow and a puff of air, or /h/, as the obstruction is released. This category includes the sounds /t/, /k/, /kw/, and /tl/. Aspirated obstruents may lose aspiration through /h/ alternation and become /d/, /g/, /gw/, and /dl/. See section 8.1.2.

aspirated sonorants: Consonants characterized by relatively little obstruction of the airflow and a breathy sound, or /h/, as the sound is produced. This category includes the sounds /hn/, /hw/, and /hy/. Aspirated sonorants may lose this aspiration through /h/ alternation and become /n/, /w/, and /y/. See section 8.1.3.

aspirated syllabary character: A syllabary character that is always aspirated. For example, the aspirated character Ꮜ is pronounced as /ka/, while the aspiration-neutral character Ꮝ could be pronounced as /ge/ or /ke/. See section 2.2.

aspiration: The puff of air that accompanies aspirated obstruents or the /h/ quality that accompanies aspirated sonorants. See section 2.1.1.

aspiration-neutral syllabary character: A syllabary character that does not distinguish aspiration. For example, the character Ꭹ could be pronounced as /gi/ or /ki/. See section 2.2.

asterisk: The symbol used to indicate that a prefix is an /h/ alternator.

attributive adjective: An adjective that generally precedes the noun it modifies and does not act as the predicate of the clause. Example: *Hali'idv* <u>*na* ***uweta***</u> <u>*diktulena*</u> *jijaha.* 'Trade your <u>**old** car</u> in.' See section 7.1.

beneficiary: In a ditransitive verb, the primary object that is benefitting from the action. Example: *Na asgaya gadaluganeha* ***na agehya*** *uhwisvdi'i.* 'The man is plowing **the woman's** garden.' See section 14.2.1.

blend compound: A compound where the component words are pronounced and written as a single word. For example, *gola* 'winter' and *ehi* 'resident' combine to create the blend compound *golehi* 'pneumonia.' See section 12.1.6.

cardinal: The basic form of a numeral that is used for counting. Example: ***Sgohi*** *iyunadodawasdi danadehlgwasgo jalagi.* 'They study Cherokee for **ten** weeks.' See section 7.4.

causative (CAU): The valency-changing series of derivational suffixes that appear on a verb to add the meaning that the action is caused by someone else or is done with an instrument. Example: *Desgidloyis**diha** nusdv hihnogisgv.* 'You're **making** us cry with your song.' See section 14.2.2.

causative base: A special form of the verb used when a causative derivational suffix is attached. This base is a shortened Present Continuous stem or an Infinitive stem with the final [*di*] element removed. See section 14.2.2.

citation form: The Present Continuous form of the verb without any prefixes (the dictionary form). See section 4.1.1.

classificatory verb: A transitive verb whose meaning indicates a physical property of its object. There are five types of classificatory verbs: solid/round, living, liquid, long, and flexible. For example, compare *hadv'vsga* 'you're hanging up something flexible' with *hatosadi'a* 'you're hanging up something long.' See section 4.4.

clause: A subject and its predicate. An independent clause is a sentence. See section 11.2.

combined local prefix: A pronominal prefix that expresses both a local subject and a local object. Example: *Sdaya yisdiwoniha yisg**ini**yetsda*. 'If you two talk loud **you** will wake **me** up.' See section 9.3.

combined nonsingular subject prefix: A pronominal prefix that expresses a combination of a third person nonsingular subject and a local person object. Example: ***Ge**jadloysdohas?* 'Are **they** making **you** cry?' See section 9.2.

combined prefix: A pronominal prefix that indicates both the subject and the object (combined local prefixes and combined nonsingular subject prefixes). See sections 9.2 and 9.3.

command (COM): The prepronominal prefix *jii-* used with positive commands with the meaning 'again', as well as with negative commands generally. This prefix has the variant [*j*] before vowels. Example: ***J**ihijislvga na gotv; jikdlosga.* 'Light the fire **again**; it is going out.' See section 5.1.4.

complement: A participant that a verb or postposition needs in order to be complete. A transitive verb needs an object, and a postposition needs a noun phrase complement.

Completive (CMP): A verb stem used to indicate that a state or event has been or will be completed. This stem is the fourth of the five verb stems and always appears with a final suffix. Example: *Galgina Jalagi Julehisanv gohweli dulvhwisdanelv.* 'Elias Boudinot worked on the *Cherokee Phoenix*.' See section 4.2.4.

completive future prefix (CMF): The prepronominal prefix *da-*, used on verbs to indicate that an event or state will take place in the future. This prefix always appears with the completive future suffix *-i*, which has the same abbreviation.

This prefix has the variant forms [*daa*], [*dvv*], and [*day*] based on adjacent sounds or prefixes. Example: *Gagi* ***dvhi'lesi*** *dagwalela?* 'Who is going to drive the car?' See section 5.1.5.

completive future suffix (CMF): The final suffix *-i* used on verbs to indicate that an event or state will take place in the future. This prefix usually appears with the completive future prefix *da-*, which has the same abbreviation. This suffix has /s/ after it if another suffix is attached. Example: *Doyi dagesisv asehnv do uhyvdla.* 'I was going to go outside but it's too cold.' See section 4.3.6.

compound: A word composed of two or more stems or words. In Cherokee most compounds are nouns. Compounds may be written as two words or as a single word in the case of a blend compound. Example: *Dagwalela digandegi* 'car salesman.' See section 12.1.6.

concessive (CS): The postfix *=sginii* is used to express a questioning attitude toward the verb to which it is attached. Example: ***Gadosgini*** *jinusganola jadanv na daks?* 'Why is the turtle moving so slowly?' See section 7.8.10.

conducive question (CQ): The postfix *=ju* is used to form a question to which a 'yes' answer is expected. Example: ***Jalagiju*** *hiwonisgo?* 'Do you speak Cherokee?' See section 7.8.1.

conjugated verb: A verb inflected with all of its necessary prefixes and suffixes. See chapter 4.

conjugation: Adding inflection to a verb (a pronominal prefix and any necessary prepronominal prefixes and final suffixes). See chapter 4.

conjunction (CN): The postfix *=hnoo* is used to link two words, phrases or clauses together and is often translated as 'and', 'so', or 'because'. Its full form is *=hehnoo.* Example: *Uwange gahljode ayesda'a,* ***galasdvsgahno****.* 'The carpet is soft in the house **so I'm stepping on it.**' See section 7.8.9.

consonant: A sound made with some obstruction of the airflow. Cherokee consonants are classified into obstruents and sonorants. All sounds that are not vowels are consonants. See section 2.1.1.

consonant insertion: The insertion of a /y/ or /w/ to avoid vowel clash. For example, when the first person singular animate object prefix *ji-* attaches to the verb *-ehyohvsga* 'teach', it is pronounced as *jiyeyohvsga* 'I am teaching her'. See section 3.3.4.

contour tone: A tone that changes as it is pronounced (rising, falling, highfall, or lowfall). See section 2.1.2.2.

converb (CVB): The final suffix *-a* used on a Completive verb stem to create an adverbial clause. This suffix is accompanied by a highfall tone on the rightmost long vowel of the verb. Adverbial clauses with a converb verb are typically translated as 'when', 'while', or 'because'. Example: *Svhiyeyi ogalsdayvhna tuya dogigv.* 'When we ate in the evening we ate beans.' See section 11.4.3.2.

coordinating conjunction: A word that serves to link two independent clauses. Example: *Dijigatoli daweystane* ***nasgi iyusdi*** *jidegagatinvde'a.* 'My eyes are hurting **and that is why** I'm taking off my glasses.' See section 11.3.

delimiter (DT): The postfix *=gwu* is used to express the meaning 'only' or 'just'. Example: *Gohusdi jiyatvdvha alsguhyagwu.* 'When I asked him something he just nodded.' See section 7.8.4.

demonstrative: A word that signals the beginning of a noun phrase and helps to establish the identity or proximity of the noun. Example: *Aniganvkti anihnvwvga* ***na*** *udlvgi.* 'The doctors cured **the** sick person.' See section 7.2.

derivation: The use of an affix to create a new word. For example, the addition of the agentive suffix *-i* to the Incompletive stem of 'sew' creates the noun *gayewsgi'i* 'sewing machine'. See chapters 12 and 13.

derivational suffix: A suffix added to a word to create a new word. For example, the verb *ahnegesgo'i* 'he builds' becomes the agentive noun *ahnegesgi* 'builder' when the agentive derivational suffix *-i* is added. See chapters 12, 13, and 14.

derived noun: A noun that has been created from another word, typically a verb. Root nouns and derived nouns have different inflection patterns. See section 12.1.

deverbalizer (DVB): The final suffix *-v́* that appears on Incompletive and Completive stems to create an adverbial clause or a nominal clause; it also derives a noun or an adjective from a verb. Its full form is *-v́v́ʔi*. Example: *Dasgwalihelicheli hi'a adela gvnel****v'i***. 'You are going to thank me when I give you this money.' See sections 11.4.3.1 and 12.1.1.2.

diphthong: The combination of a vowel and a following /w/ or /y/. Diphthongs are typically the result of vowel dropping. For example, final vowel dropping in the fast speech pronunciation of *Gado nigawi?* 'What did he say?' results in *Gado nigaw?* See sections 2.1.2 and 8.4.4.

direct addressee: A noun phrase used to address someone directly. Example: ***Tadanahwisgi*** *sgihnvwodi awaduli.* '**Medicine man**, I want you to cure me.' See section 6.1.

distributive (DST): The prepronominal prefix *dee-* is used to indicate nonsingular objects or multiple instances of an action. The prefix has three variant forms based on what sounds or prefixes it appears with: [*d*], [*di*], and [*doo*]. The secondary form of this prefix is the distributive2 *di-*. Example: *Hila iga nuna dehatolsga?* 'How many potatoes are you borrowing?' See section 5.1.3.

distributive2 (DST2): The prepronominal prefix *di-* is the secondary form of the distributive prepronominal prefix. The secondary form appears on adjectives, most nouns, command uses of the Immediate, and all Infinitive stems. This prefix has the variant forms [*dii*], [*j*], and [*ti*] based on adjacent sounds or prefixes. Example: *Jansini-Omali danisdelisgo* ***dinadehlgwasgi.*** 'Johnson-O'Malley assists students.' See section 5.1.3.

ditransitive: A verb that has two objects (primary and secondary), with a valency of three. Verbs with an applicative derivational suffix are usually ditransitive. Example: *Ahwi unodena* ***agikanelv*** *digalogisgi.* 'The farmer gave **me** a sheep.' See section 14.2.1.

double accent: The use of two accents on a single letter to indicate a floating tone.

dual (DL): One of the four categories of grammatical number: exactly two of something. Pronominal prefixes distinguish dual from plural in the first and second person but not in the third person. Example: *Hadlv* ***wisdihvga*** *na ganaji?* 'Where did **you two** send the kanuchi?' See section 3.2.

dummy prefix: A third person singular prefix that does not actually refer to anyone or anything. It appears on nonpossessed body parts and clothing terms as well as in the instrumental derivation. Example: ***u****ska* 'head'. See section 6.2.2.2.

dummy vowel: The letter [x] written at the beginning of a stem to indicate a feature that appears only when a prefix attaches to that stem. For example, the third person pronominal prefix *ga-* on 'sew' is long, so the stem is written as *-xxyewsga* to indicate this lengthening feature. See section 8.2.3.

duplicative (DPL): The series of derivational suffixes that appear on the Completive stem to derive a verb indicating that an event is repeated. Example: *Na uweti adanelv dvdahnesge****sisahni****.* 'We're going to **re**build that old house.' See section 13.1.1.

emphatic (EM): The postfix *=dvv* is used to emphasize or intensify the word to which it is attached. Example: *Dagiyaweg****dv*** *gohusdi agwadvhndi.* 'I am **too** tired to do anything.' See section 7.8.7.

emphatic pronoun (EMP.PRO): The pronoun *-vv́sa* is used to express emphasis, especially for reflexive verbs. It always has a Set B pronominal prefix. Example: *Aditasdi yijaduli* ***jvsa*** *jadlisdohdi.* 'If you want something to drink you have to pour it **yourself**.' See section 6.3.5.

equals sign: The symbol used in this grammar to separate a postfix from its base. A postfix is always written with an equals sign at the beginning to indicate that it must attach to another morpheme. See section 7.8.

exchange: A process in which an /h/ changes places with a short low tone vowel. Exchange occurs when a short low tone vowel is followed by /h/ and a sonorant consonant and preceded by an obstruent. See section 8.1.3.

exclusive (EX): A feature of first person dual and plural pronominal prefixes indicating that the person addressed is not included in the idea of 'we' or 'us'. All four of the exclusive pronominal prefixes start with the sound /o/. Example: ***Og**iji uyohusa, **dog**adlohyilv'i.* 'When **our** mother died, **we** cried.' See section 3.2.

experienced past (EXP): The final suffix *-v* that appears on the Incompletive and Completive verb stems to express an event or state that happened or was happening and that the speaker has personal knowledge of it. Its full form is *-v́v́ʔi.* Example: *Jujayosdi asildv agigalsv.* 'I cut the barbed wire.' See section 4.3.2.

extended phonetics: A writing system based on the Roman alphabet used to represent the Cherokee language. Long vowels are represented by writing the vowel twice, and grave and acute accents are used to represent tone. The glottal stop is represented by the symbol ⟨ʔ⟩. See section 2.1.2.2.

falling tone: A tone that starts as a high tone and falls to a low tone. This tone is always found on a long vowel. It is indicated by a vowel marked with an acute accent followed by a vowel marked with a grave accent. Examples: ⟨éè⟩, ⟨áà⟩. See section 2.1.2.2.

family pronominal prefix (1B.FAM): The prefix *ee-* that is used only on family relationship nouns to express a first person "possessor" of that noun. Example: *eduji* '**my** uncle.' See section 6.2.2.4.

fast speech: The form of everyday spoken Cherokee where syllables are shortened and endings dropped. For example, *Unduli* is the commonly heard way of pronouncing ***Unaduliha***. 'They want it.' See section 8.4.

final suffix: A suffix that appears on the end of the Incompletive and Completive verb stems. Final suffixes are the experienced past (EXP), nonexperienced past (NXP), progressive future (PFT), future command (FCM), converb (CVB), negative deverbalizer (NDV), deverbalizer (DVB), and completive future (CMF). Incompletive and Completive verb stems never appear without a final suffix. See section 4.3.

final vowel: The final vowel in a word as it is actually pronounced. If the word has been shortened, the final vowel may have a shortened highfall tone marked by an acute accent. See section 2.1.2.2.

final vowel dropping: The dropping of a word-final vowel, a common characteristic of fast speech. For example, *gago* 'who' is commonly pronounced as *gag.* See section 8.4.4.

floating length: A feature of certain stems that causes lengthening of the closest vowel of the prefix that attaches to that stem. The floating length is indicated by two dummy vowels [xx]. For example, when the third person Set A prefix *ga-* attaches to *-xxdaluúgíʔa* 'plow', the prefix lengthens to *gaadaluúgíʔa* ('he is plowing it'). See section 8.2.3.

floating tone: A feature of certain stems that causes a tone change on a vowel of the prefix that attaches to that stem. The floating tone is indicated by the appropriate accent above a dummy vowel [x]. For example, when the third person Set A prefix *ga-* attaches to *-x́xdloohíha* 'strap', the prefix lengthens (see floating length above) and acquires a high tone, resulting in *gáadloohíha* ('he is strapping it'). See section 8.2.3.

focus (FC): The postfix *=na* is used to focus attention on the word to which it is attached. Example: *Hi'ina ahyatanalv dikdlohdi dakiwasv digaduhv'i.* 'I bought this to put it on the shelf.' See section 7.8.8.

frozen prefix: A prefix that always appears on a word. Typically a frozen prefix does not seem to contribute to the meaning of the verb and is not translated, but the word seems poorly formed if the prefix is left off. Example: *Unohyvgv ahalugisgi nuwahndosv dagwaleli'i.* 'The muffler came off the car.' See section 5.1.3.

full form: The complete form of a word, stem, or suffix. Full forms typically appear less often than their shorter fast speech counterparts. In this grammar full forms are represented in the underlying form line of a parsed phrase only when a syllabary character representing part of the full form is present. Example: *giihl* 'dog' is represented in the Cherokee syllabary as ᎩᏟ as if it were said in its full form. See section 8.4.

future command (FCM): The final suffix *-vv'i* that appears on Incompletive and Completive stems to create a command. Example: *Atlilosdohdi hidelv'i.* 'Give him a ruler.' See section 4.3.5.

***gaa-* prefix (GA):** The prepronominal prefix *gaa-* is used for a variety of purposes, including to indicate that an event has not taken place in a while or that someone has the ability to do something. This prefix has the variant forms [*gvv*], [*gaay*], [*gee*], and [*gvvwa*] based on adjacent sounds or prefixes. Example: *Akisohdaneha agwadali'i nigvwahnigi'elv'i.* 'I'm lonesome since my wife left me.' See section 10.1.6.

***ga-* verb:** A Set A verb that uses the pronominal prefix *ga-* rather than *a-* in the third person singular. See section 3.3.2.

general present: A time frame referring to events or states that are habitual or ongoing but are not necessarily happening right now. This idea is conveyed by using an Incompletive stem with a habitual final suffix. Example: *Sgwisdi*

***unihna'o** Adahi'i adananv.* '**They have** many things at the Atwoods store.' See section 4.2.2.

gloss: A concise one-word English equivalent of a Cherokee word. Glosses are written on the gloss line. If a single English word is not sufficient to express the Cherokee word, the English words are written together with periods rather than spaces separating them. See section 3.1.

gloss line: The fourth line of the parsed Cherokee phrase where the underlying forms are identified by either an abbreviation or a gloss. See section 3.1.

glottal stop: A consonant pronounced by briefly cutting off the airflow with the glottis, the space between the vocal folds. In English this sound is made in the middle of the word 'uh-oh'. The glottal stop is represented with the symbol ⟨ʔ⟩ in extended phonetics and with an apostrophe in simple phonetics. See section 2.1.1.

grammatical number: See 'number'.

grammatical person: See 'person'.

grave accent: The accent used on the second written vowel of a long vowel to represent a falling tone or a lowfall tone. Examples: falling tone ⟨éè⟩, lowfall tone ⟨eè ⟩. See section 2.1.2.2.

/gw/ reduction: The pronunciation of /gw/ as /w/. For example, *agwaduli* 'I want it' may be pronounced as *awaduli.* This pronunciation is common in fast speech as well as in certain dialects. See section 8.4.1.

habitual (HAB): The final suffix *-o* that appears on the Incompletive and Completive verb stems to express an event or state that is repeated or habitual. Its full form is *-o'i.* Example: *Guso galnvdv Daligwa ayehli <u>galosgo'i</u>*. 'Muskogee Avenue <u>crosses</u> through Tahlequah.' See section 4.3.1.

/h/ alternation: A common process in which certain pronominal prefixes cause a following /h/ to be replaced by a glottal stop or a lowfall tone. See section 8.2.2.

/h/ alternator: A pronominal prefix that triggers /h/ alternation. All of the animate object prefixes and many of the combined local prefixes are /h/ alternators. See section 8.2.2.

helping verb: A verb that is used to expresses the tense, aspect, or negation of another verb when that verb is unable to do so. A helping verb may also serve to reinforce tense, aspect, or negation. The two helping verbs are 'be' and 'become'. Example: *<u>Iyadvnehi nahloyasdvn</u> **<u>yigi</u>** gohwelanv'i hla gohusdi yigadgo.* '<u>Without a verb</u> a sentence really has no meaning.' See section 11.5.

highfall tone: A tone that rises higher than a high tone and then falls a little bit at the end. This tone appears on the rightmost long vowel of a word, often on adjectives and nouns as well as on all subordinated verbs. It never appears on main Noninfinitive verbs. In its basic form this tone is found on a long vowel; but due to the dropping of a word's ending it may appear as a shortened high-fall (written as a high tone) at the end of a word. It is indicated by two vowels marked with an acute accent. Examples: ⟨éé⟩, ⟨áá⟩. See section 2.1.2.2.

high tone: A tone that is higher than the low tone and can be found on a short or a long vowel. It is indicated with an acute accent for a short vowel or with an acute accent on the first written vowel of a long vowel. Examples: high tone on short vowel: ⟨é⟩, high tone on long vowel: ⟨ée⟩. See section 2.1.2.2.

/h/ syllabification: A rule stating that a syllable cannot end in a lowfall tone followed by /h/. When these two elements come together, the /h/ is deleted. See section 8.2.6.

hyphen: The symbol used in this grammar to separate an affix from the rest of the word. A prefix is always written with a hyphen at the end to indicate that another morpheme must follow it; a suffix is always written with a hyphen at the beginning. See section 3.1.

Immediate (IMM): A verb stem used to indicate that a state or event has just happened or to express a command to be performed immediately. This stem is the third of the five verb stems; it does not have a final suffix. Example: *Aksgani didla* ***hideysda***. 'Turn it to the left.' See section 4.2.3.

impersonal Set A prefix (3A.IP): The pronominal prefix *vv-* appears on Set A verbs to indicate that the subject is no one in particular. It only appears after the prepronominal prefixes *yi-*, *dee-*, and *ji-* and often translates into English as 'one' or generic 'you'. Example: *Kahwi yvdlisda akugisdi.* '**You** can put coffee in a cup.' See section 9.6.

impersonal Set B prefix (3B.IP): The pronominal prefix *oo-* appears on Set B verbs to indicate that the subject is no one in particular. This prefix has the variant form [*ow*] before vowels and often translates into English as 'one' or 'you'. Example: *Wadulisi yowejvhya, yowotihisda.* 'When a bumblebee stings **you**, it can make **you** swell.' See section 9.6.

implied object: A third person singular object that is assumed but not indicated by a pronominal prefix. Implied objects are translated as 'him', 'her', or 'it' and occur when a transitive verb has a pronominal prefix referring to a local person subject. Example: *Jigohwtiha.* 'I see **it**.' See section 4.1.3.

implied subject: A third person singular subject that is assumed but not indicated by a pronominal prefix. Implied subjects are translated as 'he', 'she', or 'it' and occur when a transitive verb has a pronominal prefix referring to a local person object. Example: ***Agiyoliha.*** 'He is greeting me.' See section 4.1.3.

inanimate: The characteristic of a noun that does not trigger the appearance of an animate object prefix. What makes a noun inanimate in Cherokee grammar is culturally determined and may vary slightly from speaker to speaker. Humans are always animate and nonliving things are always inanimate.

inclusive: A feature of first person dual and plural pronominal prefixes indicating that the person addressed is included in the idea of 'we' or 'us'. These prefixes are assumed to be inclusive unless their abbreviation identifies them as exclusive (EX). See section 3.2.

Incompletive (INC): A verb stem used to indicate that a state or event is ongoing. This stem is the second of the five verb stems and always appears with a final suffix. Example: *Jalagi Julehisanv* ***jigoliyesgo***. '**I read** the *Cherokee Phoenix*.' See section 4.2.2.

indefinite pronoun: A pronoun used to refer to a person, place, or thing when a more specific identity is unknown or irrelevant. Example: ***Kilo*** *uwohwelanelv ugvwiyu ahljadodhi*. '**Someone** wrote the president's speech.' See section 6.3.3.

indefinite relative pronoun: An indefinite pronoun that combines with an adjectival clause to create a nominal clause. Example: ***Nusdv*** *jitusdanelv Jani gadvnelega*. 'I'm going to do for John **what** I promised.' See section 6.3.4.

independent clause: A clause that is complete and that can stand alone as a sentence. For example, in the following sentence the clause in bold is independent and the preceding and following clauses are subordinate: *Vhnji asgaya yijiyohlvna* ***gvnawosgo*** *si kilo nugohvna*. 'When I build a snowman **it melts** before anyone sees it.' See section 11.3.

Infinitive: A verb stem that does not make reference to the tense or aspect of the verb. This stem is the fifth of the five verb stems and is used to convey obligation and possibility; it also has adverbial, adjectival, and nominal functions. An Infinitive may end in [*di*] or, less commonly, in its long form [*díí?i*]. Example: *Gohusdi ohwasgv alsihntanidasdi*. 'When buying things one must be economical.' See section 4.2.5.

Infinitive complement: An Infinitive that serves as the object of another verb. Example: *Na julasgi anehlda* ***aksgalsdi***. 'That alligator tried **to bite me**.' See section 11.4.2.2.

inflection: The act of adding grammatical information (such as person, number, tense, aspect, or mood) through the use of a prefix or suffix.

inherent /h/: The /h/ sound that accompanies /s/. This /h/ is not written. It can trigger vowel deletion and is subject to /h/ alternation. See section 8.2.2.

instrumental noun: A noun derived from an Infinitive that denotes an object associated with performing the verb; it typically has a third person Set A dummy prefix. This derivation is sometimes accompanied by an instrumental tone change. Example: *ganawohisdi* 'stove'. See section 12.1.3.1.

instrumental tone (INS): The change in tone that occurs on an Infinitive to indicate its derivation into an instrumental (a noun used to perform an action). This tone change is indicated with the abbreviation (INS). For example, the tone change occurs on the underlined vowel in *adahntehdi* 'thought'. See section 12.1.3.1.

intensifier (INT): A cover term for several different derivational suffixes that intensify the meaning of the adjective or adverb to which they attach. Example: *Ahidiya adananesdi Lisasi'i.* 'It's easier to shop at Reasor's.' See section 7.6.

interjection: A word or phrase that is a complete utterance by itself. Interjections are commonly used to express emotion, catch someone's attention, or greet someone. Example: *Wado!* 'Thank you!' See section 7.9.

interrogative adjective: An adjective used to ask about the type or quantity of a noun. Example: ***Hila*** *iyuhliloda dagweli julehwisdi'i?* '**How many** miles is Wagoner?' See section 7.1.2.

interrogative adverb: An adverb used to ask how, when, where, or why a verb takes place. Example: ***Gadoke*** *hisgwohli jijesdasi?* '**Why** did your stomach hurt?' See section 7.5.4.

interrogative pronoun: A pronoun used to ask the identity of a subject or object. Example: ***Gado usdi*** *hadahnteha?* '**What** are you thinking about?' See section 6.3.2.

intransitive verb: A verb that only has a subject and thus has a valency of one. Example: *Na usdi* ***udikada***. 'That baby **has urinated**.' See chapter 4.

intrusive /h/: An /h/ that is not represented by the Cherokee syllabary. Example: the basic pronunciation of the syllabary character V is/do/, but in the word ᏗᏕᎶᏆᏍᏙᏗ *didehlohgwas**doh**di* 'dictionary' the actual syllable is /doh/. See section 2.2.

inverse: Using a Set B prefix where a Set A prefix is expected. Inverse marking occurs when both participants are third person and the subject is lower on the animacy hierarchy than the object. See section 9.5.

irrealis (IRR): The prepronominal prefix *yi-* is used to indicate that a state or event is hypothetical; it is also used to negate verbs. This prefix has the variant form [y] before vowels. Example: *Wisgi denatugisgv eliwu* ***yi****deginiyvsdesda.* 'Drinking whisky will probably get us drunk.' See section 5.1.2.

iterative (ITR): The prepronominal prefix *ii-* is used to indicate that an action is repeated. The secondary form of this prefix is *vv-*. Example: *Sigwu ta'li digagwati* ***i****gakilvdiha*. 'I'm riding the bike **again**.' See section 10.1.5.

iterative (ITR2): The prepronominal prefix *vv-* is the secondary form of the Iterative prepronominal prefix. The appearance of this secondary form varies among speakers; for some it is used with Infinitive stems, nonmotion Present Continuous, and the experienced past suffix. Example: *Inage wv'ulosv hlvdaji ulitisa.* 'The lion went **back** into the wilderness when it escaped.' See section 10.1.5.

leftover vowel: A vowel that is part of the syllabary representation of a word but is not actually pronounced. For example, *daksi* 'turtle' is written in the syllabary as ᏓᏅᏏ; the middle syllabary character has a leftover vowel. See section 2.2.

level tone: A tone that does not rise or fall. The two level tones are the low tone and the high tone. See section 2.1.2.2.

local person: A cover term for first and second person; third person is nonlocal. This is an important distinction in Cherokee; for example, combined local prefixes are combinations of local persons. See section 4.1.3.

locative (LOC): The derivational suffix *-íiʔi* appears on nouns and adjectives to indicate a location characterized by the adjective or noun. It also is a common way of creating a Cherokee word from an English word indicating a place. Example: *Uhlisdi alsdahydi yvgi Megvdanvl**i'i***. 'You can get fast food **at** McDonald's.' See section 12.1.3.2.

long form: A form of the Infinitive that may appear for emphasis, typically when the Infinitive is at the end of a sentence. An Infinitive with the long form ends in [*díiʔi*]; the more common short form ends in [*di*]. Complement Infinitives, adverbial Infinitives, and place nouns may appear in the long form.

long vowel: A vowel that takes approximately twice as long to pronounce as a short vowel. It is represented in extended phonetics by writing the same vowel twice. The syllabary does not distinguish long and short vowels. See section 2.1.2.2.

lowfall tone: A tone that starts as a low tone and falls a little bit lower. This tone is always found on a long vowel. It is indicated by an unaccented vowel followed by a vowel marked with a grave accent. Examples: ⟨eè⟩, ⟨aà⟩. See section 2.1.2.2.

low tone: The basic or default tone. This tone can be found on a short or a long vowel. It is not marked with any accent. Examples: low tone on short vowel: ⟨e⟩, low tone on long vowel: ⟨ee⟩. See section 2.1.2.2.

main verb: A verb that is itself modified by an adverbial clause or whose clause is modified by an adverbial clause. Example: *Judalehna yidawaliyo unalikdi **sginvneho***. 'When I have different socks on **you give me** the matching one.' See section 11.2.

maleficiary: In a ditransitive verb, the primary object that is adversely affected by the action. Example: *Ayilidasdi gohweli **vgina'elv'i***. 'My driver's license was taken **from me**.' See section 14.2.1.

middle voice (MDL) prefix: The prefixes *-adaa-* or *-ali-* appear after the pronominal prefix and before the stem, indicating that the action is happening spontaneously, by itself, or for its own benefit. For example, compare *jisdoyeha* 'I am shaving him' with ***galisdoyeha*** 'I am shaving'. See section 14.3.3.

modal (MOD) tone: The change in tone that occurs on an Infinitive to indicate the ability or obligation to perform an action. This tone (generally a highfall) is indicated with the abbreviation MOD. For example, the highfall tone appears on the underlined vowel in *Asedv jugohahldi gvgisdi nogwu yidiga.* 'He has to cut the watermelon, then we will eat it.' See section 11.4.1.2.

modality: A property of a verb that indicates the speaker's attitude toward the event in terms of probability, possibility, ability, or obligation. For example, the irrealis prepronominal prefix is used to indicate ability and possibility, and the modal tone change on the Infinitive is used to expresses ability and obligation. In the sentence *Uwodige usgasehdi kananesgi* ***yadaluga*** *anadisgo.* 'They say a brown recluse spider **can** kill you.' the irrealis prefix indicates the possibility of the event occurring. See section 4.6.

mood: A property of a verb that indicates whether it is a statement, a question, or a command. See section 4.6.

morpheme: The smallest unit of meaning or grammatical function. A morpheme may be a prefix, a suffix, a stem, or a word. In the parsed examples in this grammar morpheme breaks are indicated by hyphens.

motion toward (MOT): The prepronominal prefix *da-* is used on intransitive verbs of motion to indicate that the motion is approaching the speaker. This prefix has the variant forms [*d*], [*day*], and [d*vv*]. The secondary form of this prefix is *di-*. Example: ***Dandansini.*** 'They are crawling (**in the direction of the speaker**).' See section 10.1.4.

motion toward2 (MOT2): The prepronominal prefix *di-*, the secondary form of the motion toward prepronominal prefix. The secondary form appears with the habitual, nonexperienced past, and progressive future final suffixes. This prefix has the variant form [*dii*] and [*j*] before vowels. Example: ***Ditliso.*** 'He runs (**in the direction of the speaker**).' See section 10.1.4.

movement (MOV): The series of derivational suffixes that appear on the Completive stem to derive a verb indicating movement to a place to perform an action. Example: *Talasuhlvga Jimi ale tadehlagwa'**uga***. 'Put your shoes on, Jim, and **go** to school.' See section 13.1.6.

nasal: The quality of a consonant or vowel when it is pronounced with air going through the nose. The consonants /m/ and /n/ and the vowel /v/ are nasal; final vowels also typically have a nasal quality. See section 2.1.1.

negation adverb (NEG): The adverb *tla* is used in conjunction with the irrealis prefix *yi-* to negate a verb. It may also appear alone as an answer to a yes/no question. Example: ***Tla*** *ahani yalehwisdisgo na digajanuli.* 'The train doesn't stop here.' See section 7.5.3.

negative adverb: A cover term for the negation adverb *tla* and the negative command adverb *tleesdi.* See section 7.5.3.

negative command (NEG.COM): The adverb *tlesdi* is used with the prepronominal prefix *ji-* or *yi-* to create a negative command. Example: ***Hlesdi*** *jijayoseli ulani adawosdi.* '**Don't** lose your sweater.' See section 7.5.3.

negative deverbalizer (NDV): The final suffix *-v́v́na* that appears on the Incompletive and Completive stems to create an adverbial clause or to derive a noun or adjective. This suffix always appears with the prefix *ni-*. Example: *Ejanosgisdi nijadulisg**vna** yigi, jvsgahldi.* 'If you don't want it stolen, you hide it.' See section 11.4.3.3.

***ni-* prefix (NI):** The prepronominal prefix *ni-* is used for a variety of purposes, including to indicate the meanings 'it', 'already', and 'almost' and, together with the negative deverbalizer, to create a subordinate verb or create an adjective out of a verb. It also appears as a frozen prefix on some common verbs and nouns. This prefix has the variant form [*n*] before vowels. The secondary form of this prefix is *ii-/yi-*. Example: *Uhwedadv diktuleni agwajeli uhwedadv nigvndosga.* 'The fender on my car is coming off.' See section 10.1.2.

***ni-* prefix 2 (NI2):** The prepronominal prefix *ii-/yi-*, the secondary form of the *ni-* prepronominal prefix, appears on Infinitive stems and derived forms. This prefix has the variant form [*iy*] before vowels. Example: *Adasehehi ahtvdasdanehdi ohnosehv iyadvhndi.* 'You listen to the director when he's telling you what to do.' See section 10.1.2.

nominal: A word, phrase, or clause that acts like a noun by functioning as the subject or object of a verb. Example: ***Dikgilo'v*** *dejile'a dikgilosdohdi'i.* '**What I've washed** I'm taking out of the washer.' See section 12.1.

nominal clause: A subordinate clause that acts like a noun by functioning as the subject or object of a verb. Example: *Tsgili danisdayohihv ulosohnv uwohihydanelv ugeyuhna **nugeyuhnavna yulsdohdi**.* 'The Ghost of Christmas Past convinced Scrooge **to be generous**.' See section 11.4.2.

nonexperienced past (NXP): The final suffix *-e* that appears on the Incompletive and Completive verb stems to express a past event or state that the speaker has not personally experienced. Its full form is *-e'i.* Example: *Ije Ijoda Dadlohisdv uwohwelane Ganvdahlagi.* 'Major Ridge signed the Treaty of New Echota.' See section 4.3.3.

Noninfinitive: The four verb stems that are not the Infinitive: the Present Continuous, Incompletive, Immediate, and Completive. See section 4.2.

nonlocal person: A term for third person to distinguish it from first and second person, which are referred to as local person. See section 4.1.3.

nonsingular (NS): One of the four categories of grammatical number: more than one.

nonsingular verb: A verb that is only used with nonsingular, dual, or plural pronominal prefixes, indicated by (NS) after its gloss. See section 4.1.1.

noun: A part of speech that may act as the subject or object of a sentence. Nouns are not inflected for tense or aspect but may have pronominal or prepronominal prefixes. See chapter 6.

noun phrase: A phrase consisting of a noun and any of its modifiers. A noun phrase may function as a subject, object, or object of a postposition. Example: ***Na aja'di*** *jinolasda* ***ditlilostanv ujiya*** *gvhdi.* 'I tricked **that fish** with **a fake worm**.' See section 6.4.

number: A grammatical category that refers to the number of people or objects. Number may be singular, nonsingular, dual, or plural. This grammatical category is expressed with pronominal prefixes as well as the distributive and animate nonsingular prepronominal prefixes.

object: In a transitive verb clause, the participant that is undergoing the action and/or in less control of the action. Example: *Sigwoya* ***alsgwanosdi*** *ulsdulv.* 'Sequoyah wore a **turban**.'

object focus prefixes: A set of prefixes that reference the object and not the subject. These prefixes are often translated into English with a passive. Example: *Dinilawigi anohihdisgi adahyahndohdi* ***wajinvnelv.*** '**He** was sent a summons to be a juror.' See section 9.4.

obligation Infinitive: An Infinitive that expresses an obligation or necessity to perform that action. This function is usually indicated with a modal tone (MOD). Example: *Yawaduli awadatlohisdi nihi* ***gvyasuyesdi***. 'If I want to win **I have to choose you**.' See section 4.6.7.

obstruent: A sound where the airflow is stopped or significantly obstructed. In Cherokee the obstruents are /d/, /t/, /g/, /k/, /dl/, /tl/, /gw/, /kw/, /j/, /ch/, /h/, and /s/. Sounds that are not obstruents are sonorants. See section 8.1.1.

ordinal (ORD): The derivational suffix *-ine* (full form *-inéé?i*) is attached to a cardinal numeral to indicate that it is part of a series. Example: *Mary Fallin nasgi* ***talsgogahlgwogine*** *nugvwiyusv Ogalahoma.* 'Mary Fallin is the twenty-seventh governor of Oklahoma.' See section 7.4.

'or' question (OQ): The postfix *=ke* is used to express an either-or choice. Example: *Hadawoja, tlake yudihlehga.* 'Swim!; isn't it hot?' See section 7.8.2.

'or' statement postfix (OS): The postfix =*le* is typically used to express doubt or an either-or choice. Example: *Tla yogahnte yojisganvche tlale yigi.* 'We didn't know if we were committing a crime against him or not.' See section 7.8.5.

paradigm: A table that depicts forms of a word in a systematic way. For example, a verb paradigm shows the forms of a verb based on the features of person and number.

parse: To break a word down into its underlying parts (morphemes) and label and gloss each morpheme. See section 3.1.

participant: The cover term for the roles of subject and object. An intransitive verb has one participant, a transitive verb has two participants, and a ditransitive verb has three participants. A participant may be singular, nonsingular, dual, or plural as well as first, second, or third person.

participant function: The function of a pronominal prefix on a derived noun when it refers to the participant of the activity indicated by the noun rather than to the noun itself or to a possessor of the noun. For example, the prefix on the noun *junalsdahydi* 'restaurant' ('place where they eat') refers to the participants of the intransitive verb from which it derives. It does not have a possession function (it does not mean 'their restaurant') or a reference function (it does not mean 'they are a restaurant'). See section 12.1.3.2.

participle (PCP): The derivational suffix *-da* attaches to the participle base of verbs to create an adjective or a noun. Example: *Jola agisdoda gahlv aljikwsdi.* 'There was chewed tobacco in the spittoon.' See section 12.2.2.

participle base: A special shortened form of the Completive stem used when the participle derivational suffix *-da* is attached. See section 12.2.2.

part of speech: A category of words with common characteristics. The four major parts of speech in Cherokee are nouns, verbs, adjectives, and adverbs.

passive: An English construction that makes the object of a transitive verb the subject. For example, the passive of 'the boy chased the skunk' is 'the skunk was chased'. Cherokee often conveys a passive-type meaning with an object focus prefix. Example: *Degadoga wagalvndiyv ayosgi yagvnelv gese.* 'Stand Watie was made a high-ranking officer.' See section 14.3.1.

person: A grammatical category that refers to the speaker(s) (first person), the person(s) spoken to (second person), or the person or thing spoken about (third person). This grammatical category is expressed with pronominal prefixes.

personal pronoun (PRO): The pronoun *aya* that expresses first person (1PRO) or the pronoun *nihi* that expresses second person (2PRO). These two pronouns are used for emphasis or to answer a question. Example: ***Nihisgwu** hega!* '**You also** are going!' See section 6.3.1.

phrase: A unit that centers around a major part of speech. In addition to the main word (a noun, verb, adjective, adverb, or postposition), a phrase may also contain complements or modifiers. A noun phrase, for example, consists of a noun and any determiners, adjectives, or adjectivals that modify it.

place noun: A noun derived from an Infinitive to indicate a place where the verb takes place. The prefix on this noun is typically third person Set B. A place noun ends in [*di*] or, less commonly, in the long form [*dííʔi*]. Example: *Junigvwahldohdi unohlv Kadusa gaduhv.* 'They have a casino ('where they play cards') in the town of Catoosa.' See section 12.1.3.2.

plural: One of the four categories of grammatical number; it indicates three or more of something. Plurality is expressed by first and second person pronominal prefixes. Example: *Sgohidihihi vdalv* ***ogasuhnv.*** '**We fished** in Lake Tenkiller.'

possession function: The function of a pronominal prefix that indicates the possessor of the noun to which it is attached rather than the noun itself. For example, the prefix in *Jijalagi* 'I am a Cherokee' indicates the identity of the noun 'Cherokee', while in ***g****alisgwtuwo* '**my** hat' the prefix refers to the possessor of the hat and does not mean 'I am a hat.' See section 6.2.

possession pronoun (POS.PRO): The pronoun *-ajeéli* (full form *-ajeélííʔi*) is used to indicate possession of a noun that cannot itself express possession. This pronoun always appears with a Set B pronominal prefix. Example: *Na ayohli gakwehnvgi'a* ***ujeli*** *adahnehdi.* 'The child is unwrapping **his** present.' See section 6.3.6.

postfix: A suffix-like morpheme that attaches to the end of a word. Unlike suffixes, postfixes can attach to the end of any part of speech as well as to each other. An example is the postfix =*s* that creates a 'yes/no' question. Example: *Desdoksgas?* 'Are you two smoking?' See section 7.8.

postposition: A part of speech that comes after a noun phrase and indicates its relationship to the rest of the clause. Examples: *Gado usdi hiluysga galuysgidi* ***gvhdi?*** 'What are you cutting **with** the axe?' See section 7.7.

postpositional phrase: A phrase consisting of a postposition and its noun phrase. Postpositional phrases are either adverbial or adjectival. Example: ***Ahwi uniyvsdi na'v*** *dodayojihnogisi.* 'We are going to sing **near Park Hill**.' See section 7.7.

preaspiration /h/: An inherent /h/that precedes an aspirated stop that has not received its aspiration as part of exchange or vowel deletion. See section 8.2.4.

predicate: The part of a clause that describes the subject or what the subject is doing. The predicate is usually a verb but may also be a noun phrase or an adjective phrase. Example: *Nanvyehi* ***ajigeyu'i agehya gese'i.*** 'Nancy Ward **was a beloved woman**.' See section 11.2.

predicate adjective: An adjective that serves as a subject complement. Example: ***Ehlawe nisdalsda,*** *disdhlvna.* '**You two be quiet**, go to sleep.' See section 7.1.

prefix: A morpheme that cannot stand alone and attaches to the beginning of a stem. The two main kinds of prefixes are pronominal and prepronominal. See chapters 3, 5, 9, and 10.

prefix shift: The use of a Set B prefix on a Set A verb triggered by the past use of the Completive stem as well as most uses of the Infinitive stem. For example, *Jiwoniha.* '**I** am talking.' becomes ***Agi****wonisv.* '**I** talked.'

pre-incipient (PRI): The series of derivational suffixes that appear on the Completive stem to derive a verb with the meaning 'about to VERB'. Example: *Unisaladani****disgv.*** 'They were **about to** lift it.' See section 13.1.8.

preposition: An English part of speech that relates a noun phrase to the rest of the clause (e.g., 'during', 'at', 'from'). Prepositions precede their noun phrases. The Cherokee equivalent of a preposition is a postposition.

prepronominal prefix: A prefix that precedes a pronominal prefix. Example: *Hila iga'i svkta* ***de****sdihwahi?* 'How many apples did you buy?' See chapters 5 and 10.

Present Continuous (PRC): A verb stem used to indicate that a state or event is taking place in the present. This stem is the first of the five verb stems; it does not have a final suffix. Example: *Na wesa galvndiya ihlgv gale****ga****.* 'The cat **is climbing** to the top of the tree.' See section 4.2.1.

primary object: The object that the pronominal prefix alludes to in a ditransitive verb. For example, the animate object prefix in *uwohwelodi yijaduli digohwelodi* ***hi****dehdi* 'if you want someone to write, **you give him** a pencil' is animate because of the primary object (the recipient of the giving). In this example 'pencil' is the secondary object. See section 14.2.1.

productive: A term used to describe a derivational suffix that is currently used to create new words. Nonproductive suffixes created words in the past but are no longer able to perform this function (they are frozen on their base). See sections 12.1.5.3 and 13.2.

progressive future (PFT): The final suffix *-éesdi* appears on the Incompletive and Completive stems to express that an action will be ongoing in the future. Example: *So'i walenvhv na'v iyogadali anadanvsg****esdi****.* 'Next week our neighbors **will be** moving.' See section 4.3.4.

pronominal lengthening: A process whereby a pronominal prefix on a verb is lengthened and a lowfall tone is inserted. This process does not happen when certain prepronominal prefixes are present or if the verb is subordinate. See section 8.2.1.

pronominal prefix: A prefix that indicates person and number. All verbs must have a pronominal prefix; some adjectives and nouns also may have them. The six different sets of pronominal prefixes are Set A, Set B, Set A animate object, combined local, combined nonsingular subject, and object focus. Example: *Nawaho* ***aniyvwiya*** *Ewasona* ***aneha***. 'Navajo Indians live in Arizona.' See chapters 3 and 9.

pronoun: A word that replaces a more specific nominal. Example: ***Kilo*** *watlisv wajiyolv.* '**Someone** got shot while on the run.' See section 6.3.

purpose (PRP): The series of derivational suffixes that appear on the Completive stem to derive a verb indicating the idea 'in order to'. Example: *Igvyi Uniluhjv Duyadatv unanehl****dihle***. 'The Old Settlers **came to live** in Arkansas.' See section 13.1.7.

quantifier: A word that modifies a noun by indicating the amount of something. Example: ***Tsgwiya*** *dihnawo yidigala dikgilosdi, tla yanadigwalvdeyoho.* 'If there are **too many** clothes in the washer they do not spin.' See section 7.3.

question (Q): The postfix *=s* is used to form a 'yes/no' question. Example: *Hijalagis?* 'Are you Cherokee?' See section 7.8.3.

recipient: In a ditransitive verb, the primary object that is receiving the secondary object. Example: *Gago utolstane'i na dagwalela?* 'Who loaned **him** the car?' See section 14.2.1.

reciprocal relationship noun: Relationship words like 'sibling' or 'friend' that typically refer to both people in the relationship and thus usually take a nonsingular, dual, or plural pronoun. For example, *oginali* 'my friend' uses the Set B dual exclusive prefix *ogini-*. See section 6.2.2.4.

reference function: The function of a pronominal prefix on a noun to indicate that the participant represented by the prefix is the same as the noun itself. A nonreference function does not equate the participant and the noun. For example, the prefix in ***jo****gadana'ni* '**we** are store owners' has a reference function and equates 'we' and 'store owners', while in ***jo****galiyesulo* '**our** mittens' the prefix refers to the possessor of the mittens and does not mean 'we are mittens'. See section 6.2.

reflexive (RFL) prefix: The prefix *-adaad-* appearing after the pronominal prefix indicates that the object of the action is the same as the subject of the action. Example: *Ganyegiyo owasa* ***ada****saldodi*. 'It is dangerous to exalt oneself.' See section 9.7.

relationship noun: A noun that indicates a relationship between two or more people. These nouns have pronominal prefixes with a combined reference and possession function. Example: *Sgi****doda***. 'You are my **father**.' See section 6.2.2.4.

relative adverb: An adverb that combines with an adjectival clause to create a nominal clause. Example: *Unatlilo'v* ***vhna ahneksdi'i.*** 'They measured **where they were going to build.**' See section 11.4.2.1.

relative clause: A subordinate clause that modifies a noun. In this grammar this type of clause is referred to as an adjectival clause. Example: *Hlahno digvwanahwtvhdi yigese digohweli* ***jidejayosehv'i.*** 'He could not find the papers **that you were looking for.**' See section 11.4.1.

relativizer (REL): The main use of the prepronominal prefix *ji-* on a verb is to indicate that it is part of a relative (adjectival) clause. It is also used on main clause verbs to indicate an action that took place at some definite point in the past. This prefix has the variant form [*j*] before vowels. Example: *Kilo jasganvgo digahnawadvsdi ayosdisgi anoseho.* 'Someone who does wrong they call a rule breaker.'

repetitive (RPT): The series of derivational suffixes that appear on the Completive stem to derive a verb indicating that an event is repeated numerous times. Example: *Awaduli akineej**ilosdi***. 'I want to speak **over and over**.' See section 13.1.2.

rising tone: A tone that starts as a low tone and rises to a high tone. This tone is always found on a long vowel. It is indicated by an unaccented vowel followed by a vowel marked with an acute accent. Examples: ⟨eé⟩, ⟨aá⟩. See section 2.1.2.2.

Roman alphabet: The alphabet used to write English and many of the languages of Europe. This alphabet is named for the Romans, who used it to write Latin. See section 2.1.

Roman characters: The characters of the Roman alphabet. Both the simple and extended phonetic writing systems use these characters. See section 2.1.

romanized writing: A writing system that uses Roman characters. See section 2.1.

root: The morpheme that represents the core meaning of a word. In this grammar verbs are not usually presented in root form but rather in one of the five stem forms.

root noun: A noun that is not derived from another word. Root nouns and derived nouns have distinct inflection patterns. See section 6.2.

secondary aspiration: Aspiration that is the result of vowel deletion or exchange. It is important to distinguish secondary aspiration from underlying aspiration, which triggers the sound changes of vowel deletion and exchange; secondary aspiration does not. See section 8.2.4.

secondary form: The less common form of a prepronominal prefix; its use is based on the type of stem it attaches to. Secondary forms have a '2' after their name. This term should not be confused with 'variant' (the manner in which a prefix is pronounced based on certain adjacent sounds or prefixes). For example, the *ni-* prepronominal prefix has the secondary form *ii-* on an Infinitive stem; the variant form of this prefix before a vowel is [*iy*]: *Dadahnechelv gohwelv nasgi* ***iy****advhndi.* 'What's written in a contract is what you do.' See section 5.1.

secondary object: In a ditransitive verb, the object that is not referred to by the pronominal prefix on the verb. For example, the prefix *gv-* in ***Ganulv agalsdi*** *gvyatolsdiha* 'I am loaning you a **lawn mower**' refers to the subject 'I' and the primary object 'you' but not to the secondary object 'lawn mower'. See section 14.1.

second person: A grammatical category that indicates the person spoken to. A second person pronominal prefix translates into English as 'you' or 'your'. See section 3.2.

Set A adjective: An adjective that can use Set A pronominal prefixes. See section 7.1.1.1.

Set A noun: A noun that can use Set A pronominal prefixes. See section 6.2.2.

Set A prefixes: One of the two main sets of pronominal prefixes. On verbs it indicates either the subject (for an intransitive verb) or the combination of a subject and a third-person inanimate object (for a transitive verb). See section 3.3.

Set A verb: A verb that can use Set A pronominal prefixes in the Present Continuous, Incompletive, and Immediate stems. See section 4.1.1.

Set B adjective: An adjective that uses pronominal prefixes but cannot use Set A pronominal prefixes. See section 7.1.1.1.

Set B noun: A noun that uses pronominal prefixes but cannot use Set A pronominal prefixes. See section 6.2.2.

Set B prefixes: One of the two main sets of pronominal prefixes. See section 3.4.

Set B verb: A verb that cannot use Set A pronominal prefixes. See section 4.1.1.

shortened highfall tone: A highfall tone that is not at the end of a the full form of a verb but appears as a high tone at the end of a word due to final syllable dropping. It may also appear on a nonfinal vowel when a highfall tone is forced onto a short vowel. Like the high tone, it is indicated by a vowel marked with an acute accent. See section 8.4.4.

short vowel: A vowel that takes approximately half as long to pronounce as a long vowel. It is represented in extended phonetics by writing the same vowel once, whereas a long vowel is represented by writing the same vowel twice. The syllabary does not distinguish long and short vowels. See section 2.1.2.2.

simple phonetics: A writing system based on the Roman alphabet to represent the Cherokee language. Long vowels and tone are not represented, and the glottal stop is written as an apostrophe. Simple phonetics may be used to transcribe written Cherokee where the tone and vowel length cannot be determined; it is also frequently used in beginning Cherokee language classes. See section 2.1.2.2.

singular: One of the four categories of grammatical number, indicating exactly one of something. This number is expressed through pronominal prefixes.

sonorant: A sound that is made without a significant restriction of the airflow. In Cherokee the vowels are all sonorants as well as the consonants [m], [n], [hn] [l], [y], [hy], [w], and [hw]. See section 8.1.2.

square brackets: The symbols used to set off the variant forms of morphemes. Square brackets are used to distinguish the variant forms from the underlying forms, which are never in square brackets. For example, [*agw*] is a variant form of the prefix *agi-* that appears when the prefix attaches to a vowel-initial stem. See section 3.1.

stem: The base to which prefixes and suffixes attach. See section 3.1.

stop: A sound where the airflow is stopped. In Cherokee the stops are /d/, /t/, /g/, /k/, /gw/, and /kw/. See section 8.2.4.

subject: The participant of an intransitive verb or the more active participant of a transitive verb. In a verbless clause the subject is what the clause is about. Example: ***Galgina*** *Jalagi Julehisanv gohweli dulvhwisdanelv.* '**Elias Boudinot** worked on the *Cherokee Phoenix*.'

subject complement: A noun phrase, adjective phrase, or Infinitive that complements the subject in an intransitive verb clause or a verbless clause. Example: *Wili Loji* ***jalagi advnelisgi*** *gesv'i.* 'Will Rogers was **a Cherokee actor.**' See section 6.1.

subordinate clause: A clause that cannot stand alone and that modifies a word or another clause. Subordinate clauses are nominal, adjectival, or adverbial. Example: ***Yijaduli isginihydi,*** *sgisonvsdi.* '**If you want to catch me**, you have to wound me.' See section 11.4.

subordinate tone (SUB): A highfall tone inserted on a verb to indicate that it is a part of a subordinate clause. For example, the highfall tone appears on the underlined vowel in *Tlesdi digoksdi ilvhlv yidijvyesdi* ***nahiyu edolv'i.*** 'Don't have any cigarettes in the house **when he visits**.' See section 11.4.

subordinate verb: A verb that is part of a subordinate clause. Example: *Asgwadawu ahtvdvhvsgi jahniga.* '**When he finished** the test he left.' See section 11.4.

subordinating conjunction: A conjunction that joins a subordinate clause to an independent clause. Example: *Hlesdi judalesv asgwangodisg* ***kvhni** na gohweli asgwangohtanv'i*. 'Don't turn off the computer **until** it has saved your document.' See section 11.4.3.

suffix: A morpheme that cannot stand alone and attaches to the end of a stem. See chapters 3, 5, 9, and 10.

superlative form: The form of an adjective that expresses the highest possible degree of that quality; it is expressed with the prefix *wi-* and the deverbalizer suffix. Example: *Kolana wagvhnage'iyv jisgwa*. 'The raven is the blackest bird.' See section 7.6.

surface form: The manner in which a morpheme is actually pronounced depending on the surrounding sounds and morphemes. In this grammar the second line of parsed examples indicates the surface form in extended phonetics. When a surface form is discussed in the text, it is italicized and in square brackets. See the beginning of chapter 8.

syllabary: A writing system with characters that represent syllables. Cherokee, Japanese, and some dialects of Ojibwe are written with a syllabary. See section 2.1.

syllable: A sequence of sounds centered on a vowel. In Cherokee a syllable may consist of a single vowel, a vowel preceded by a consonant, or a vowel both preceded and followed by a consonant; syllables may also start with /s/ and a consonant. The Cherokee syllabary uses characters that represent syllables consisting of a single vowel or a vowel and a consonant. See section 2.1.

tense: The property of a verb that indicates the time frame of that verb. For example, the Present Continuous verb stem indicates present tense. See sections 4.1–3.

terminative (TRM): The series of derivational suffixes that appear on the Completive stem to derive a verb indicating that an event has been or will be definitively completed. Example: *Dusgwalso**hnv** nigad digvnosasdi*. 'He **completely** broke all the brooms.' See section 13.1.4.

third person: A grammatical category that indicates something or someone spoken about. A third person pronominal prefix translates into English as 'he', 'she', 'his', 'her', 'him', 'it', 'its', 'they', 'them', or 'their'. Third person is either singular or nonsingular; there is no dual/plural number distinction. See, section 3.2.

tone: The relative pitch of certain vowels. Unlike English, changes in tone in Cherokee change the meaning of the word. Cherokee has six tones: low, high, rising, falling, lowfall, and highfall. These tones are represented by unmarked vowels as well as by vowels marked with acute or grave accents. Examples: low tone on short vowel: ⟨e⟩, low tone on long vowel: ⟨ee⟩, high tone on short vowel: ⟨é⟩, high tone on long vowel: ⟨ée⟩, rising tone: ⟨eé⟩, falling tone: ⟨éè⟩, lowfall tone: ⟨eè⟩, highfall tone: ⟨éé⟩. See section 2.1.2.2.

topic Infinitive: An Infinitive stem used as the subject of a clause. This use of the Infinitive often takes a dummy prefix that does not undergo prefix shift. A topic tone (TOP) appears on this Infinitive. Example: ***Atayosdi*** *gesv udehohisdiyu.* 'To **demand** is embarrassing.' See section 11.4.2.2.

topic tone (TOP): A highfall tone inserted on an Infinitive to indicate that it is the subject of a clause. For example, the highfall tone appears on the underlined vowel in *Osi* ***diktosdohdi*** *anadvnelisgi kamama.* 'It's good **to watch** circus elephants.' See section 11.4.2.2.

toward (TOW): The prepronominal prefix *di-* is used to indicate that an action or state is taking place facing the speaker; when used on nonmotion verbs it indicates that the action is approaching the speaker. This prefix has the variant forms [*dii*], [*j*] and [*ti*] based on adjacent sounds or prefixes. The secondary form of this prefix is *da-*. Example: *Ihlgv dodihltadega*. 'He is jumping from the tree.' See section 10.1.3.

toward command (TOC): The prepronominal prefix *ee-* is used on commands when the motion is toward the speaker. Example: *Uhlisdi digakahvsdohdi esgidisi*. 'Hand me the remote control.' See section 10.1.7.

toward2 (TOW2): The prepronominal prefix *da-*, the secondary form of the *di-* prepronominal prefix, appears on verbs ending in the experienced past final suffix. This prefix has the variant forms [*dvv*] and [*day*] based on adjacent sounds or prefixes. Example: *Daluga* ***dayunugojv*** *taldu uhlilohla.* 'The cuckoo came out at 12 o'clock.' See section 10.1.3.

transitive verb: A verb with two participants (a subject and an object). A transitive verb has a valency of two. See section 4.1.1

transitivity: The state of a verb being intransitive, transitive, or ditransitive. See sections 4.1.1 and 14.1.

translocative (TRN): The prepronominal prefix *wi-* is used to indicate that an event or state is taking place at a distance from the speaker or moving away from the speaker. This prefix has the variant form [*w*] before vowels. Example: *Wudeligv gayaleni wagalvndiyv jundehlgwasdi* ***widagedoli***. 'I am going to go to Western Carolina University.' See section 5.1.1.

unaspirated consonant: A consonant that lacks the /h/ sound characteristic of aspirated consonants. The consonants [d], [g], [j], [w], [y], [n], [gw], [m], and [l] are all unaspirated. See section 8.1.1.

undergoer: A verb participant that is not doing the action but rather undergoing the action. The opposite of undergoer is agent. Example: ***Akdlvga.*** 'I am sick.' See section 14.1.

underlying aspiration: Aspiration that is not the result of vowel deletion or exchange. It is important to distinguish secondary aspiration from underlying aspiration, which triggers the sound changes of vowel deletion and exchange; secondary aspiration does not. See section 8.1.1.

underlying form: A morpheme's form before it undergoes changes. In this grammar the third line of parsed examples indicates underlying forms in extended phonetics. When these forms are discussed in the text they are italicized. See section 3.1.

underlying form line: The third line of the parsed Cherokee phrase where the underlying forms are represented. See section 3.1.

unspecified object reflexive: The use of the reflexive prefix on a transitive verb to indicate that the verb has no specific object. This unspecified object may be translated into English as 'one' or 'you'. Example: *Guwisguwi junadanisohdi yadasgasdasi usv'i yigi.* 'The Ross Cemetery will scare **you** at night.' See section 14.3.2.

valency: The number of participants that a verb has. An intransitive verb has a subject and a valency of one, while a transitive verb has a subject and object and a valency of two. The verb in the following example is ditransitive and has a valency of three: *Hiyakasi Susi na unega wesa.* 'Give Susie that white cat.' See section 14.1.

variant form: The form that a prefix takes based on certain adjacent sounds or prefixes. This should not be confused with secondary form (the less common form of a prepronominal prefix). In isolation a variant form is always written between square brackets to distinguish it from its underlying form. For example, the first person Set A prefix *ji-* appears as [g] before a vowel, as in *Dikanesdi gadgv'i nigolv gvdisgo'i.* 'I use a dictionary always.' See section 5.1.

verb: A part of speech that expresses an action, event, or state. All verbs must have exactly one pronominal prefix, and all Noninfinitive verbs express tense and aspect. See chapter 4.

verbal noun: A derived noun that maintains the verb-like properties of pronominal lengthening and use of DST rather than DST2. See section 12.1.1.2.

vowel: A sound made with no obstruction of the airflow. The six Cherokee vowels are /a/, /e/, /i/, /o/, /u/, and /v/. The vowel /v/ sounds like a more nasal version of the vowel at the end of the English word 'drama'. These vowels are either short or long and have tone. All sounds that are not vowels are consonants. See section 2.1.1.

vowel clash: The rule that two vowels cannot be together. The result will be vowel removal to avoid the clash or consonant insertion to keep them apart. See sections 3.3.3 and 3.4.2.

vowel deletion: A process in which a short low tone vowel is deleted when followed by /h/ and a vowel or obstruent and preceded by an obstruent. In the following example the /i/ of *sgi-* is deleted, causing the /g/ to be aspirated and pronounced as /k/: *Gohlvhnv eksdela*. 'Pass me some butter.' See section 8.1.2.

vowel dropping: A characteristic of fast speech in which the initial /a/ of a stem is dropped when preceded by a pronominal prefix with an /n/ sound, an animate object prefix, or a combined local prefix. For example, *anadisgahlvsga* 'they are hiding' is often pronounced as *andisgahlvsga*. See section 8.4.3.

vowel length: The duration of a vowel. In extended phonetics a long vowel is represented by writing the same vowel twice, while a short vowel is represented by writing the vowel only once. The syllabary does not distinguish long and short vowels. See section 2.1.2.2.

vowel merger: A characteristic of fast speech in which two adjacent /a/ sounds of two separate words form a single sound /v/. This merger occurs when a word ending in /a/ is followed by a word beginning with /a/. See section 8.4.2.

vowel removal: The removal of one of the vowels as a result of vowel clash. For example, the combination of the vowels /i/ and /a/ when *hi-* attaches to *-ahnigi'a* results in the removal of the /i/; the conjugated verb is ***hahnigi'a*** 'you are leaving'. See sections 3.3.3 and 3.4.2.

word-final vowel: The vowel that occurs at the end of the full form of the word. The word-final vowel typically has a high tone and carries the main stress of the word; it may also have a nasal quality. See section 2.3.

Bibliography

Alexander, J. T. 1971. *A Dictionary of the Cherokee Indian Language.* Sperry, Okla.: J.T. Alexander.

Arrington, Ruth. 1971. Speech Activities in Tahlequah, Cherokee Nation, during the Seventies. Ph.D. dissertation. Baton Rouge, Louisiana State University.

Beghelli, Filippo. 1996. Cherokee Clause Structure. In *Cherokee Papers from UCLA: UCLA Occasional Papers in Linguistics 16,* ed. Pamela Munro, 105–14. Los Angeles: University of California.

Bender, Ernest. 1949. Cherokee II. *International Journal of American Linguistics* 15.4: 223–28.

Bender, Ernest, and Zellig Harris. 1946. The Phonemes of North Carolina Cherokee. *International Journal of American Linguistics* 12.1: 14–21.

Bender, Margaret. 2002a. From "Easy Phonetics" to the Syllabary: An Orthographic Division of Labor in Cherokee Language Education. *Anthropology and Education Quarterly* 33: 90–117.

———. 2002b. The Gendering of Langue and Parole: Literacy in Cherokee. In *Southern Indians and Anthropologists: Culture, Politics, and Identity,* ed. Lisa Lefler and Frederic Gleach, 77–88. Southern Anthropological Society Proceedings 35. Athens: University of Georgia Press.

———. 2002c. *Signs of Cherokee Culture: Sequoyah's Syllabary in Eastern Cherokee Life.* Chapel Hill: University of North Carolina Press.

Bentley, Mayrene. 2005. *Cherokee and Conformity to General Principles of Animacy Marking.* Paper presented at the annual meeting of the Society for the Study of the Indigenous Languages of the Americas, Oakland, Calif.

Berdan, Robert, Alvin So, and Angel Sanchez. 1982. *Language among the Cherokee: Patterns of Language Use in Northeastern Oklahoma, Part 1.* Los Alamitos, Calif.: National Center for Bilingual Research.

Berge, Anna. 1998. Language Reacquisition in a Cherokee Semi-Speaker: Evidence from Clause Construction. In *Proceedings from the First Workshop on American Indigenous Languages* 8: 30–41.

Blankenship, Barbara. 1996. Classificatory Verbs in Cherokee. In *Cherokee Papers from UCLA: UCLA Occasional Papers in Linguistics 16,* ed. Pamela Munro, 61–74. Los Angeles: University of California.

Bonvillain, Nancy. 1994. Reflexives in Mohawk. *Kansas Working Papers in Linguistics* 19.2: 87–114.

Brooks, Barbara. 1992. Language Maintenance and Language Renewal among Cherokee People in Oklahoma. *Kansas Working Papers in Linguistics* 17.2: 109–24.

———. 1996. Language and Cultural Identity: A Sociolinguistic Analysis of the Symbolic Value of Literacy in Oklahoma Cherokee. Ph.D. dissertation. Chicago, Northwestern University.

Chafe, Wallace. 1964. Another Look at Siouan and Iroquoian. *American Anthropologist* 66: 852–62.

Chafe, Wallace, and Jack Frederick Kilpatrick. 1963. Inconsistencies in Cherokee Spelling. *AES Symposium on Language and Culture,* ed. Viola Garfield, 60–63. Seattle: University of Washington.

Charles, Julian. 2010. A History of the Iroquoian Languages. Ph.D. dissertation. Winnipeg, University of Manitoba.

Cherokee Nation. 2003. *Ga-Du-Gi: A Vision for Working Together to Revitalize the Cherokee Language.* Tahlequah, Okla.: Cherokee Nation.

Cherokee New Testament. 1995. Tulsa, Okla.: Cherokee Language and Culture.

Cherokee Phoenix. 2005. Cherokee Translation: Rocky Ford Man Keeps Tradition Alive. February.

———. 2006a. Cherokee Translation: Cherokee Speakers Discuss Language Revitalization Efforts. May.

———. 2006b. Cherokee Translation: Five Tribes Meet to Commemorate Historic Act. June.

———. 2006c. Cherokee Translation: Texas Group Searches Tenkiller for Missing Cherokee. November.

Comrie, Bernard. 1977. *Aspect: An Introduction to the Study of Verbal Aspect and Related Problems.* Cambridge: Cambridge University Press.

Conley, Robert. 2005. *The Cherokee Nation: A History.* Albuquerque: University of New Mexico Press.

———. 2007. *Cherokee Encyclopedia.* Albuquerque: University of New Mexico Press.

Cook, William. 1979. A Grammar of North Carolina Cherokee. Ph.D. dissertation. New Haven, Yale University.

Cowen, Agnes. 1995. *Cherokee-English Language Reference Book.* Tahlequah, Okla.: Heritage Printing.

Cushman, Ellen. 2010. The Cherokee Syllabary from Script to Print. *Ethnohistory.* 57.4: 625–49.

———. 2011a. The Cherokee Syllabary: A Writing System in Its Own Right. *Written Communication.* 28.3: 255–81.

———. 2011b. *The Cherokee Syllabary: Writing the People's Perseverance.* Norman: University of Oklahoma Press.

———. 2011c. "We're Taking the Genius of Sequoyah into This Century": The Cherokee Syllabary, Peoplehood, and Perseverance. *Wicazo Sa Review Journal* 26.2: 67–83.

———. 2012. Learning from the Cherokee Syllabary: A Rhetorical Approach to Media Research and Teaching. *JAC: A Journal of Rhetoric, Culture, and Politics* 32.3–4: 541–65.

Dryer, Matthew. 1986. Primary Objects, Secondary Objects, and Antidative. *Language* 62: 808–45.

Dukes, Michael. 1996. Animacy and Agreement in Cherokee. In *Cherokee Papers from UCLA: UCLA Occasional Papers in Linguistics 16,* ed. Pamela Munro, 75–96. Los Angeles: University of California.

Eastern Band of Cherokee Indians. 2005. Comprehensive Cherokee Language Survey EBCI Dept. of Cultural Resources. Cherokee, N.C.: Eastern Band of Cherokee Indians.

Ethnologue. 2008. http://www.ethnologue.com/show_language.asp?abbreviation=chr.

Feeling, Durbin. 1975a. *Cherokee-English Dictionary.* Tahlequah: Cherokee Nation of Oklahoma.

———. 1975b. A Structured Approach to Learning the Basic Inflections of the Cherokee Verb. MS.

Flemming, Edward. 1996. Laryngeal Exchange and Vowel Deletion in Cherokee. In *Cherokee Papers from UCLA: UCLA Occasional Papers in Linguistics 16,* ed. Pamela Munro, 23–44. Los Angeles: University of California.

Foley, Lawrence. 1980. *Phonological Variation in Western Cherokee.* New York: Garland Publishing.

Foreman, Grant. 2012. *Sequoyah.* Norman: University of Oklahoma Press.

Frey, Benjamin E. 2013. Toward a General Theory of Language Shift: A Case Study in Wisconsin German and North Carolina Cherokee. Ph.D. dissertation. Ann Arbor, University of Michigan.

Gillespie, John Douglas. ca. 1954. A Grammar of the Western Dialect of the Cherokee Language of the Iroquoian Family. Unpublished notes based upon fieldwork in Oklahoma and North Carolina.

Guyette, Suzanne. 1975. Sociolinguistic Determinants of Native Language Vitality: A Comparative Study of Two Oklahoma Cherokee Communities. Ph.D. dissertation, Dallas, Southern Methodist University.

———. 1981. An Examination of Cherokee Language Vitality. *Anthropological Linguistics* 23.5: 215–26.

Haag, Marcia. 1997. Cherokee Evidence for Separation of the Morphological and Prosodic Word. In *Papers from the 1997 Mid-America Linguistics Conference,* 343–49. Columbia: University of Missouri, Columbia.

———. 1999. Cherokee Clitics: The Word Boundary Problem. *Kansas Working Papers in Linguistics* 24: 33–44.

———. 2001. Cherokee Tone Associations with Overt Morphology. *Chicago Linguistics Society* 37.2: 413–25.

Haas, Mary. 1948. Classificatory Verbs in Muskogee. *International Journal of American Linguistics* 14: 244–46.

———. 1961. Comment on Floyd G. Lounsbury's "Iroquois-Cherokee Linguistic Relations." *Bulletin of the Bureau of American Ethnology* 180: 9–17.

Hickerson, Harold, Glen Turner, and Nancy Hickerson. 1952. Testing Procedures for Estimating Transfer of Information among Iroquois Dialects and Languages. *International Journal of American Linguistics* 118: 1–8.

Hill, Archibald. 1952. A Note on Primitive Languages. *International Journal of American Linguistics* 18: 122–77.

Hinkle, Lawrence. 1935. The Cherokee Language. *Bulletin of the Archaeological Society of North Carolina* 2: 1–9.

Hirata-Edds, Tracy. 2007. Influence of Second Language Immersion in Cherokee on Children's Development of Past Tense in Their First Language. Ph.D. dissertation, Lawrence, University of Kansas.

Hirata-Edds, Tracy, Mary Linn, Lizette Peter, and Akira Yamamoto. 2003. Indigenous Language Teacher Training Seminars in Oklahoma and Florida. *Cultural Survival Quarterly* 27: 48–52.

Holmes, Ruth Bradley. 1996. Comparative Adjectives in Cherokee. In *Papers from the 1994 Mid-America Linguistics Conference,* ed. Frances Ingemann, 561–75. Lawrence, University of Kansas.

Holmes, Ruth Bradley, and Betty Sharp Smith. 1977. *Beginning Cherokee.* Norman: University of Oklahoma Press.

Jelinek, Eloise. 1984. Empty Categories, Case, and Configurationality. *Natural Language and Linguistic Theory* 2: 39–76.

Johnson, Keith. 2005. Tone and Pitch Accent in Cherokee Nouns. Berkeley, University of California, MS.

Kemmer, Suzanne. 1993. *The Middle Voice.* Amsterdam: John Benjamins.

King, Duane. 1975. A Grammar and Dictionary of the Cherokee Language. Ph.D. dissertation. Athens, University of Georgia.

———. 1978. Cherokee Classificatory Verbs. *Journal of Cherokee Studies* 3: 40–48.

Koops, Chris. 2008a. Frames of Reference, Verticality and the 'On/Off-Ground' Distinction. Paper presented at the annual meeting of the Linguistic Society of America, Chicago.

———. 2008b. Semantic Extensions of Cherokee Locative Prefixes: Location, Orientation, and Visibility. Paper presented at the annual meeting of the Society for the Study of the Indigenous Languages of the Americas, Chicago.

Krueger, John (ed.) 1993. Two Early Grammars of Cherokee. *Anthropological Linguistics* 35: 291–358.

Lance, Kathleen M. 1977. Pitch Accent in Cherokee. Master's thesis, Lawrence, University of Kansas.

Lindsey, Geoffrey. 1985. Intonation and Interrogation: Tonal Structure and the Expression of a Pragmatic Function in English and Other Languages. Ph.D. dissertation, Los Angeles, UCLA.

———. 1987. Cherokee Pitch Phonology. London, University College, MS.

Lindsey, Geoffrey, and Janine Scancarelli. 1985. Where Have All the Adjectives Come From? The Case of Cherokee. In *Proceedings of the Eleventh Annual Meeting of the Berkeley Linguistics Society,* ed. by Mary Niepokuj et al., 11:207–15. Berkeley: University of California.

Lounsbury, Floyd G. 1953. *Oneida Verb Morphology.* New Haven, Conn.: Yale University Press.

———. 1961. Iroquois-Cherokee Linguistic Relations. In *Symposium on Cherokee and Iroquois Culture,* 7–11. Smithsonian Institution Bureau of American Ethnology. Washington, D.C.: U.S. Government Printing Office.

———. 1978. Iroquoian Languages. In *Handbook of North American Indians, Vol. 15: Northeast,* ed. Bruce Trigger, 334–43. Washington, D.C.: Smithsonian Institution.

Mankiller, Wilma. 1993. *A Chief and Her People.* New York: St. Martin's Press.

Mithun, Marianne. 1976. *A Grammar of Tuscarora.* New York: Garland Publishing.

———. 1979. Iroquoian. In *The Languages of Native America: Historical and Comparative Assessments,* ed. Lyle Campbell and Marianne Mithun, 133–212. Austin: University of Texas Press.

———. 1987. Pragmatic Word Order. In *Coherence and Grounding in Discourse,* ed. Russell S. Tomlin, 281–328. Amsterdam: Benjamins.

———. 1999. *The Languages of Native North America.* Cambridge: Cambridge University Press.

———. 2009. Location, Location, Location. Presented at the Oklahoma Workshop on Native American Languages. Northeastern State University, Tahlequah, Oklahoma.

Monteith, Carmelita. 1984. Literacy among the Cherokee in the Early Nineteenth Century. *Journal of Cherokee Studies* 9.2: 56–75.

Montgomery-Anderson, Brad. 2008. Citing Verbs in Polysynthetic Languages: The Case of the Cherokee-English Dictionary. *Southwest Journal of Linguistics* 27.1: 53–73.

———. 2010. Creating Partnerships between the Indigenous Language Community and the University: The Cherokee Education Degree Program. In *Building Communities and Making Connections,* ed. Susana Rivera-Mills and Juan Trujillo, 83–99. Newcastle Upon Tyne: Cambridge Scholarly Press.

———. 2011. Teaching Underlying Forms: Examples of Cherokee Verb Games. In *Indigenous Languages across the Generations: Strengthening Families and Communities,* ed. Mary Eunice Romero-Little, Simon J. Ortiz, and Teresa L. McCarty, with Ran Chen, 180–93. Tempe: Arizona State University Center for Indian Education.

———. 2013. Macro-Scale Features of School-Based Language Revitalization Programs. *Journal of American Indian Education* 52.3: 41–64.

Mooney, James. 1995. *Myths of the Cherokee.* Mineola, N.Y.: Dover Press.

Munro, Pamela. 1996a. The Cherokee /h/ Alternation Rule. In *Cherokee Papers from UCLA: UCLA Occasional Papers in Linguistics* 16, ed. Pamela Munro, 45–60. Los Angeles: University of California.

———. 1996b. Cherokee Papers from UCLA: An Introduction. In *Cherokee Papers from UCLA: UCLA Occasional Papers in Linguistics* 16, ed. Pamela Munro, 3–9. Los Angeles: University of California.

——— (ed.). 1996c. *Cherokee Papers from UCLA: UCLA Occasional Papers in Linguistics* 16. Los Angeles: University of California.

———. 2002. Entries for Verbs in Native American Language Dictionaries. In *Making Dictionaries: Preserving Indigenous Languages of the Americas,* ed. William Frawley, Kenneth C. Hill, and Pamela Munro, 86–107. Berkeley: University of California Press.

Nichols, Johanna. 1986. Head-Marking and Dependent-Marking Grammar. *Language* 62.1: 56–119.

Olbrechts, Frans M. 1931. Two Cherokee Texts. *International Journal of American Linguistics* 6: 179–84.

Oosahwee, Harry. 2008. Language Immersion: An Effective Initiative for Teaching the Cherokee Language. Master's thesis, Tahlequah, Northeastern State University.

Parins, James. 2013. *Literacy and Intellectual Life in the Cherokee Nation, 1820–1906.* Norman: University of Oklahoma Press.

Payne, Thomas E. 1997. *Describing Morphosyntax: A Guide for Field Linguists.* Cambridge: Cambridge University Press.

Peter, Lizette. 2003. A Naturalistic Study of the Cherokee Language Immersion Preschool Project. Ph.D. dissertation, Lawrence, University of Kansas.

———. 2007. "Our Beloved Cherokee": A Naturalistic Study of Cherokee Preschool Language Immersion. *Anthropology and Education Quarterly* 38: 323–42.

Peter, Lizette, with Ella Christie, Marilyn Cochran, Dora Dunn, Lula Elk, Ed Fields, JoAnn Fields, Tracy Hirata-Edds, Anna Huckaby, Margaret Raymond, Deputy Chief Hastings Shade, Gloria Sly, George Wickliffe, and Akira Yamamoto. 2003. Assessing the Impact of Total Immersion on Cherokee Language Revitalization: A Culturally Responsive, Participatory Approach. In *Nurturing Native Languages,* ed. Jon Reyhner, Octaviana V. Trujillo, Roberto Luis Carrasco, and Louise Lockard, 7–23. Flagstaff: Center for Excellence in Education, Northern Arizona University.

Peter, Lizette, and Tracy Hirata-Edds. 2006. Using Assessment to Inform Instruction in Cherokee Language Revitalization. *International Journal of Bilingual Education and Bilingualism* 9.5: 643–58.

Peter, Lizette, Tracy Hirata-Edds, and Brad Montgomery-Anderson. 2008. Acquiring Cherokee as a Second Language through Kindergarten Immersion: Issues for Consideration. *International Journal of Applied Linguistics* 18.2: 166–87.

Potter, Brian. 1996. Cherokee Agentive Nominalizations. In *Cherokee Papers from UCLA: UCLA Occasional Papers in Linguistics* 16, ed. Pamela Munro, 115–31. Los Angeles: University of California.

Pulte, William. 1972. Some Claims Regarding Gapping: The Evidence from Cherokee. In *Mid-America Linguistics Conference Papers,* ed. by John Battle, 255–60. Stillwater: Oklahoma State University Press.

——— 1976a. The Obligatory-Optional Principle: A Counterexample from Cherokee. In *The Third LACUS Forum 1976,* ed. Robert J. DiPietro and Edward L. Blansitt, Jr., 77–79. Columbia, S.C.: Hornbeam Press.

——— 1976b. Writing Systems and Underlying Representation: The Case of the Cherokee Syllabary. In *1975 Mid-America Linguistic Conference Papers,* ed. Frances Ingemann, 388–93. Lawrence: University of Kansas Linguistics Department.

———. 1979. Cherokee: A Flourishing or Obsolescing Language? In *Language and Society,* ed. William C. McCormack and Sol Wurm, 423–32. The Hague: Mouton Publishers.

———. 1985. The Experienced and Nonexperienced Past in Cherokee. *International Journal of American Linguistics* 51.4: 543–44.

———. 1986. Cherokee Syllabary Charts and Cherokee Literacy. In *Proceedings of the Sixth Annual International Language Issues Institute,* ed. Suzanne Weryackwe, 70–73. Norman, Okla.

Pulte, William, and Durbin Feeling. 1975. *Outline of Cherokee Grammar with Cherokee-English Dictionary.* Tahlequah: Cherokee Nation of Oklahoma.

———. 1977. The Nineteenth Century Cherokee Grammars. *Anthropological Linguistics* 19.6: 274–79.

———. 1987. The Use of Cherokee in Religious Services. In *Proceedings of the Seventh Annual International Institute on Native American Language Issues.* Calgary, Canada.

———. 2002. Morphology in Cherokee Lexicography: The Cherokee-English Dictionary. In *Making Dictionaries: Preserving Indigenous Languages of the Americas,* ed. William Frawley, Kenneth C. Hill, and Pamela Munro, 60–69. Berkeley: University of California Press.

Reyburn, William D. 1953a. Cherokee Verb Morphology, Part I. *International Journal of American Linguistics* 19: 172–80.

———. 1953b. Cherokee Verb Morphology, Part II. *International Journal of American Linguistics* 19: 259–73.

———. 1954. Cherokee Verb Morphology, Part III. *International Journal of American Linguistics* 20: 44–64.

Robinson, Prentice. 2002. *Workbook of Intermediate Cherokee Language.* Tulsa: Cherokee Language and Culture.

Scancarelli, Janine. 1986. Pragmatic Roles in Cherokee Grammar. *Berkeley Linguistics Society* 12: 224–34.

———. 1987. Grammatical Relations and Verb Agreement in Cherokee. Ph.D. dissertation, Los Angeles, UCLA.

———. 1988. Variation and Change in Cherokee: Evidence from the Pronominal Prefixes. In *In Honor of Mary Haas,* ed. William Shipley, 675–92. Berlin: Mouton de Gruyter.

———. 1992. Aspiration and Cherokee Orthographies. In *The Linguistics of Literacy,* ed. Pamela A. Downing, Susan D. Lima, and Michael Noonan, 135–52. Amsterdam: Benjamins.

———. 1994. Another Look at a "Primitive Language." *International Journal of American Linguistics* 60: 149–60.

———. 1996a. Cherokee Stories of the Supernatural. *Kansas Working Papers in Linguistics* 21: 143–58.

———. 1996b. Cherokee Writing. In *The World's Writing Systems,* ed. Peter Daniels and William Bright, 587–92. Oxford: Oxford University Press.

———. 1996c. Learning to Write in the Cherokee Syllabary. In *Papers from the 1994 Mid-America Linguistics Conference,* ed. Frances Ingemann, 644–56. Lawrence: University of Kansas.

———. 2005. Cherokee. In *Native Languages of the Southeastern United States,* ed. Janine Scancarelli and Heather K. Hardy, 351–84. Lincoln: University of Nebraska Press.

Sequoyah Lady Indians Basketball Championship. DVD of March 11, 2006, game with Cherokee play-by-play by David Scott and Dennis Sixkiller. Tahlequah, Okla.: Sequoyah High School.

Silver, Shirley, and Wick R. Miller. 2000. *American Indian Languages: Cultural and Social Contexts.* Tucson: University of Arizona Press.

Singleton, Gary. 1979. Cherokee Narrative Discourse: A Preliminary View. In *Papers of the 1978 Mid-America Linguistics Conference,* ed. by Ralph. E. Cooley et al., 102–11. Norman: University of Oklahoma.

Smith, Adalene. 1975. *Cherokee Literacy Handbook.* Tahlequah, Okla.: Cherokee Bilingual Education Center.

Smythe, Susan. 1997. Laryngeal Exchange in North Carolina Cherokee. Austin, University of Texas, MS.

———. 1998. Syntactic Versus Pragmatic Word Order in Cherokee. Master's thesis, Austin, University of Texas.

———. 2003. Accounting for Verbal Argument Indexing in Cherokee. In *SCIL 11: Proceedings of the 11th Student Conference in Linguistics, MIT Working Papers in Linguistics 45,* ed. Susan Smythe, Steve McCartney, and Gail Coelho, 217–31. Working Papers in Linguistics. Cambridge, Mass.: MIT.

Speck, Frank G. 1926. Some Eastern Cherokee Texts. *International Journal of American Linguistics* 4: 111–13.

Strickland, Rennard. 1980. *Indians in Oklahoma.* Norman: University of Oklahoma Press.

Uchihara, Hiroto. 2007a. Cherokee Phonology and Verb Morphology. Master's thesis, University of Tokyo.

———. 2007b. Laryngeal Alternation, Laryngeal Exchange and Aspirated Consonants in Oklahoma Cherokee. *Tokyo University Linguistic Papers* 26: 49–72.

———. 2009. High Tone in Oklahoma Cherokee. *International Journal of American Linguistics,* 75.3: 317–36.

———. 2014. Noun Incorporation in Cherokee Revisited. *International Journal of American Linguistics* 80.1: 5–38.

UNESCO. 2003. Language Vitality and Endangerment. Retrieved March 27, 2014. http://www.unesco.org/culture/ich/doc/src/00120-EN.pdf.

Vance, Victor, and Durbin Feeling. 2001. *See, Say, Write Method of Teaching the Cherokee Language.* Tahlequah: Cherokee Nation.

Van Tuyl, Charles. 1994. *An Outline of Basic Inflections of Oklahoma Cherokee.* Muskogee, Okla.: Bacone College.

Walker, Willard. 1975. Cherokee. In Studies in Southeastern Indian Languages, ed. James M. Crawford, 189–236. Athens: University of Georgia Press.

———. 1984. The Design of Native Literacy Programs and How Literacy Came to the Cherokees. *Anthropological Linguistics* 26.2: 161–69.

———. 1985. The Roles of Samuel A. Worcester and Elias Boudinot in the Emergence of a Printed Cherokee Syllabic Literature. *International Journal of American Linguistics* 51: 610–12.

Walker, Willard, and James Sarbaugh. 1993. The Early History of the Cherokee Syllabary. *Ethnohistory* 40: 70–94.

White, John. 1962. On the Revival of Printing in the Cherokee Language. *Current Anthropology* 3: 511–14.

Williams, Robert S. 1996. Cherokee Possession and the Status of *-jeeli.* In *Cherokee Papers from UCLA: UCLA Occasional Papers in Linguistics 16,* ed. Pamela Munro, 97–104. Los Angeles: University of California.

Woodward, Grace Steele. 1963. *The Cherokees.* Norman: University of Oklahoma Press.

Wright, Richard. 1996. Tone and Accent in Oklahoma Cherokee. In *Cherokee Papers from UCLA: UCLA Occasional Papers in Linguistics 16,* ed. Pamela Munro, 11–22. Los Angeles: University of California.

Index

Colophon

Many people are involved in taking an author's manuscript to a published book. While some of the work is routine, it is never mindless. Occasionally, as with the *Cherokee Reference Grammar*, the work is neither mindless nor routine. When a book is as complex as the *Grammar*, yet looks and reads like a straightforward text, we can be assured that work was done with care and skill.

Stephanie Attia Evans and Emmy Ezzell shepherded the project from manuscript to bound books. Copyediting was done by Kathleen Lewis. The original files were converted to Unicode by Shannon Gering, Emmy Ezzell, and Larry Tseng. Indexing was by Linda M. Gregonis. Charles Ellertson designed the book; composition was by Tseng Information Systems, Inc. The books were printed and bound by Edwards Brothers Malloy, Inc. Ross Mills provided Huronia in bold italic when the need for it was occasioned by the glossary.

A note on the type

The type used for the text of this book is Huronia, designed by Ross Mills of Tiro Typeworks. An open source font named Merope was used for some of the display setting. One reason for selecting Huronia was it includes the characters of the Cherokee syllabary, properly encoded in Unicode. In passing, it also includes the Canadian syllabics used by several tribes.

The syllabary, however, is only part of the story.

The availability of the syllabary does not remove the need to set Cherokee using the Latin alphabet. Even with the syllabary, Cherokee is sometimes presented in a romanized form—in this book, the first line of each example is set using the syllabary, the second and third lines are set in romanized Cherokee. And therein lies the rub: for a book like the *Grammar*, there is no compelling reason why the text set with the syllabary needs to be in the same font as the text that uses the Latin alphabet. What would be anathema would be to use different fonts within a word set using the Latin script, simply because the chosen font lacked the necessary diacriticals and phonetic characters.

A brief aside: the written forms of Native American languages were often developed by anthropologists, some with a missionary background, some without. They created written forms of the languages using the Latin alphabet; of course, their problem, their task, was to represent the *sounds* of the spoken language. Working in the field, especially before typewriters were commonplace, the pen allowed using either diacriticals or phonetic characters to represent the sounds. Later, the convenience of the typewriter favored certain constructions—for example, doubling a vowel rather than putting a macron over it. When using a typewriter, any needed accents were easily added with a pen; adding phonetic characters was more difficult. Still, the precision of phonetic characters was occasionally desired. As one might expect with such quandaries, one result was that there was no single, dominant orthography for many of the languages. This is still true—there are today over ten orthographies for Lakota alone.

Even today, most contemporary OpenType fonts lack the common accents—the combining diacriticals—in their proper Unicode positions. That most lack phonetic characters is less surprising. However, the specialized fonts developed for Native American languages usually lack the craft found in commercial fonts. As a result, there are very, very few fonts that have both the needed characters and the needed excellence. Huronia is one.

˺ ˺ ˺

Perhaps because of its association with Native American languages, Huronia has been called a storyteller's font—Indians, campfires, storytelling. But stories have also been told in Manhattan speakeasies, Southern roadhouses, and Georgian drawing rooms. Dashiel Hammett wrote his early stories in a cheap San Francisco hotel. Earlier, Jane Austen and the Brontë sisters wrote in somewhat more refined accommodations. Nor are stories always fiction—there are "news stories," "magazine stories." With that thought, it's not too great a stretch to follow Jacques Barzun, to call history, even in an academic context, "a story."

A book designer has any number of reasons for selecting a particular typeface for a text. Sometimes there is a historical allusion. Other times, a font is chosen because in some unfathomable way, it can help present an earlier time to a new, younger audience. Fonts are also tools; a font may be chosen because it will set a large number of characters on a page while remaining quite readable. Allowing there are numerous reasons for setting a book in any particular font, I would have no qualms about selecting Huronia for an edition of *The Glass Key*, or *Jane Eyre*, or *Northanger Abbey*. Or, for that matter, works in history and the social sciences other than Native American studies.

Charles M. Ellertson